The Working Men's College Journal: Conducted By Members Of The Working Men's College, London, Volume 10, Issues 167-188...

Working Men's College (London, England)

The Working Men's College Journal

sub: M

The Working Men's College. CROWNDALE ROAD St PANCRAS · LONDON · N·W· FOUNDED IN 1854 BY THE LATE Frederick Denison Maurice ·

Contents for
JANUARY, 1907

College Supper

Old Students' Club

College Notes

Correspondence

Society and
        Club News

THE Working Men's College Journal.

Conducted by Members of the Working Men's College, Crowndale Road, London, N.W.

Vol. X.—No. 167.   JANUARY, 1907.   Price Twopence.

OLD STUDENTS' CLUB SUPPER.

THE thirtieth annual Supper of the Old Students' Club, commonly known as The College Supper, was held in the Maurice Hall on Saturday, 15th December. Mr. R. H. MARKS, the President of the Old Students' Club, took the chair as usual, and although there were present about twenty less than last year, the Hall was comfortably filled. The portrait of Maurice, by Mr. Lowes Dickinson, was mounted on an easel on the platform, and of the other Founders, Dr. Furnivall and Mr. Westlake were present. The guests also included the Principal and Vice-Principal, Major General Sir Frederick Maurice, Messrs. Arthur and Goldsworthy Lowes Dickinson, Mr. G. P. Gooch, M.P., Mr. Caröe, the architect, and Mr. Douglas Forster, the clerk of the works of the new building, Mr. Cornford, Dr. C. W. Kimmins, Mr. P. J. Hartog, Mr. C. T. Millis, and Mr. A. A. Jack. The letters of regret from absent friends referred to by Mr. Marks as chairman included those from the Rev. J. Llewelyn Davies, Rev. B. H. Alford, Sir R. Mowbray, M.P., the Hon. Alfred Lyttelton. K.C., M.P., Dr. W. Garnett, L.C.C., Prof. Osler, Prof. M. E. Sadler, and Messrs. C. E. Maurice, George A. Macmillan, Arthur B. Shaw, Harold Spender, R. W. R. Stokes, Sidney Webb, and Richard Whiteing. The supper was well served, and the punch excellent, as usual, although Jones had not this year the customary assistance of Castell in the making thereof. The speeches were characterized by the usual freedom of thought and expression, and absence of any kind of restraint. We like to think that in probably no other place could such contrary opinions be stated and listened to with such good humour as those which were expressed by Professor Dicey and Dr. Furnivall respectively on the subject of our hereditary Upper Chamber.

There were 179 present at the Supper, namely, Messrs. G. M. Atkins, E. C. Atkinson, F. Atterbury, Thomas Austin, T. M. Balson, George Beavis, James Benny, W. H. Berry, B. Black, S. Bradgate, H. de Brent, E. A. Brett, A. J. Bride, J. Bromhall, J. Bromhall, junr., F. E. Brooks, G. Buckland, S. W. Burns, G. T. Butler, Auguste Canivet, W. D. Caröe, C. G. Cash, J. R. Chandler, Tom Coan, E. R. Cole, A. Coleman, E. T. Colesby, William might appoint, it was evident that the members present had their backs up, and that they keenly resented the manner in which the proposed rules were formulated.

After Mr. Randall's remarks, the chairman suggested that it should first be settled whether the rules should be taken and discussed separately or as a whole. Mr. W. C. Jones proposed that the principle of the rules should first be discussed. Mr. J. J. Munro (C. R. C.) moved, and Mr. A. Hepburn (C. R. C.) seconded, that they be discussed in sections, rule I. first, then rules II. and III., then IV. to VII., and so on. Mr. T. Barnard asked whether the Shakespeare readers came within the rules; and Mr. Randall replied that they would not, until they levied a subscription. Mr. Castell said the real gist of the matter lay in rules VIII. and IX., as to custody of club funds and assets. He objected to the Common Room Committee, however, being the body appointed to carry out any such rules. The secretary or one other member of each club should form a committee to carry them out. Mr. A. E. Homewood, rising to move an amendment, described the Common Room Committee as an "egregious gang of outrageous swankers," at which there was much laughter and loud cries of "withdraw." He protested against the proceedings as a whole. The Committee were a parcel of students, more or less irresponsible, and he objected to their having the control of the clubs. He proposed that the Executive be asked to furnish a statement of the existing rules of the clubs, and moved that the proposed rules be rejected by the meeting. This motion was not accepted in that form, and was altered to an amendment that the rules be discussed *en bloc*. Mr. Jones seconded the amendment, and referred to the previous attempts made, under his guidance, to introduce fundamental rules for the College clubs, not many years ago. A set of rules was then agreed to by the secretaries of the clubs, and approved by the Executive, but when referred to the club members for their acceptance, they threw them out and declined to be governed by them. He now urged that the proposed rules were unnecessary, and that they would fail in their object to protect club funds. He considered them tactless, and thought each club must be left to legislate for itself. The amendment was put, and carried by a large majority.

Mr. J. C. Castell then moved, and Mr. W. C. Jones seconded, that the rules be rejected *en bloc* as unnecessary. Mr. Munro, amidst much interruption, endeavoured to meet Mr. Jones's statements. Mr. Munro referred to an application made by the Club and Institute Union for the club rules, and thought this was a reason for codifying them. Mr. Dent explained that the Union did not want the rules of the College clubs, but those of the Common Room, which was affiliated to the Union, whilst the College clubs were not. Mr. Hepburn quaintly suggested the Committee should wear badges. Mr. Torrington (C. R. C.) protested against the affair being treated as a huge joke; he thought the rules necessary, and that they should be referred to some persons whom we could trust, for consideration. Mr. Hayward thought the question should be adequately discussed, and the rules amended. Mr. Reglar said club affairs should be left to the club members themselves. Mr. Starling spoke in support of the rules, and Messrs. Wildey, Melzer, and Crawley against them. Mr. Randall having also spoken again in reply, the motion that the rules be rejected *en bloc* as being unnecessary was put, and carried by 46 votes to 10 amidst great cheering.

THE SHAKESPEARE READINGS.

ANOTHER "LADIES" NIGHT.

FEBRUARY 3rd.—"The Taming of the Shrew." There were eighteen of us and we spent a very pleasant evening. The play, in reading, didn't cause so much fun as we anticipated. A good deal of the humour is due to actor's "business" and stage "properties." These, of course, were missing. Some of the descriptive lines made amends for this—the pictures of Petruchio, his horse, and his servant Grumio, for instance.

Gates Fowler read the part of Petruchio with the requisite boldness, and Paterson expressed the Shrew's moods with much skill. The note of submission in Kate's final speech was touching. It contrasted strangely with recent utterances on the woman-question. M. K. Field spoke well as Baptista.

New readers continue to join us. Among recent additions we welcome Messrs. Buckland, Brett, Manton, E. W. Davis, and Eyres.

February 17th.—"Richard III." A very large audience assembled, attracted mainly, I think, by a powerful cast. The attendance, numbering nearly fifty, exceeded any in my recollection.

Our good friend Mrs. Tansley was present, together with Mrs. and Miss Peck, Miss Steptoe, and Miss L. Walford. Prominent among the visitors were Mr. and Mrs. Holroyd-Chaplin, introduced by Mr. Peck, who came with a lengthy experience of Shakespeare Readings in a kindred Society. Mrs. Holroyd-Chaplin added to our enjoyment by kindly reading Duchess of York.

Peck, in the title-part, succeeded well in bringing out Richard's wonderful character—his hypocricies, his ruthfulness, his grim humour. We were singularly fortunate in our lady readers. All the parts were in good hands. Mrs. Tansley read Queen Elizabeth; Miss Walford, Queen Margaret; Miss Steptoe, Lady Anne. The scene with the young princes, undertaken by Miss Peck and Miss Forsythe, was very pleasing. For Clarence we were indebted to Paterson, and for the two murderers to A. E. Homewood and Gates Fowler. Fenton was a vigorous Richmond; Barnett, Hastings; and Barnard, Buckingham. The rest of a long cast had little to say. Indeed some had nothing at all, as big cuts became imperative near the close of the meeting.

March 3rd.—"As You Like It." A capital attendance, including one or two readers likely to prove great acquisitions, notably Mayhew, who read the part of the banished Duke. Paterson was Rosalind; Gates Fowler, Orlando; and Barnard, Jaques. Hayward, as usual, amused us very much as Touchstone, which he read at very short notice. To Barnett, Paterson, and Homewood, we were indebted for songs and music.

Paterson very kindly undertakes the arrangements for the first meeting of the Shakespeare Readings next season as Barnard is giving up the Presidency, owing to increased pressure of private work.

For the final College Reading this season, on April 28th, ladies are invited. In accordance with custom, on this occasion, we forsake Shakespeare for Sheridan. The play selected is "The School for Scandal." T. B.

W.M.C. CONVALESCENT HOME SOCIETY.

ON Monday, March 4th, the annual meeting of this Society was held in the Coffee Room, Mr. J. J. Dent, President, in the chair. The hon. secretary, Mr. E. S. Landells, read the report, from which we make the following extracts :—"Last year there were 3 donations and 58 members' subscriptions, amounting to £4 3s.; but this year (1906—7) there have been 4 donations and 106 subscriptions, realising £6 9s. The society has increased its contribution to the Club Union Home from one to two guineas. The only member of the College who has yet taken advantage of the benefits of the Society says—'I am writing to thank the Society for the three weeks' change I was enabled to have at Pegwell Bay. I should also like to say a word or two in appreciation of the Home, especially as to the freedom granted to the convalescents. One might almost imagine oneself in a big hotel or boarding house, there is so little sense of restriction. The bedrooms are comfortable, with good beds, and the food plentiful and good. The superintendent and his wife I found to be kindness itself.'

"As in the case of Friendly Societies and Insurance Companies, so with our Convalescent Home. It is only by large numbers contributing regularly a small subscription to the Home that it can be maintained for the benefit of those of us who may unfortunately fall ill and need a few weeks' residence in the sea air and pleasant surroundings of Pegwell Bay. The average cost to the Home, per resident, is nearly £3 10s. for three weeks' stay ; and as this benefit can be obtained, when necessary, by an annual subscription of one shilling per annum, it is, we venture to say, one of the best investments a College man can make. Up to the end of last year, the clubs and the College subscribing to the Home were entitled to nominate a resident for each guinea subscribed by them to the Home, the resident paying—or having paid for him by his club—an additional 5s. per week and 5s. for a return railway ticket. It has been found that it is not possible to efficiently maintain the Home upon this basis ; and with the beginning of this year, a new method has been adopted, which, while relieving the resident from the necessity of making any payment whatever beyond his one shilling a year, will increase the funds annually available for maintenance, and put the home upon a self-supporting basis. The new plan is that the local clubs and societies shall send to the Central Fund the whole of their annual subscriptions of one shilling a year per member ; and in return the Home Committee will admit residents without any additional payment, and will supply free the return railway ticket from London. It will keep a ledger account for each society or club, crediting it with the shillings sent in annually, and debiting the account with 15s. per week for each member using the Home. The balance between the 45s. so debited and the 66s., which is about the average cost of a three weeks' residence, will be met by the surplus contributions of those clubs whose members are fortunate enough not to require to use the Home up to the full value of their contributions. By this system of co-operation, a splendid Home will be at the service, without any charge, of all members who may need to recuperate after illness, and most of us know how helpful a three weeks' stay, with good food and pleasant surroundings, at the seaside, is at such a time. We shall in addition have the great satisfaction of knowing that, even if we do not need ourselves to take advantage of it, we are helping many others less fortunate than ourselves, and this without any resort to charity. The Home is a co-operative institution, managed upon democratic principles and business lines, by the men who contribute to its support. No one is asked for financial help outside the members of the clubs, to whom the Home belongs and who are entitled to its advantages. It is an institution of which club men are rightly proud, and the more so in that they themselves provide all the money and management necessary for its successful maintenance. We hope that every student in the College will avail himself of the privilege of joining the society and contributing 1s. a year to this good work."

Several questions were asked, and Mr. Dent, who wrote the greater part of the report, addressed the meeting in reply. The following officers were elected :—President, Mr. J. J. Dent ; Auditor, Mr. R. II. Marks ; Secretary, Mr. M. Staal ; Committee, Messrs. Balson, Butler, Hepburn, Landells, and Murphy.

On the following day, the sum of £6 6s., being practically the whole of the subscriptions collected for the past year, was handed in to the Central Fund through the hands of Mr. W. H. Berry, in accordance with the new plan above referred to.

ACCOUNT FOR THE YEAR 1906-7.

Receipts.	£	s.	d.	*Payments.*	£	s.	d.
Balance forward ...	3	o	9	Subscription to Club			
Donation, Mr. Dent ...	o	5	o	Union Convalescent			
,, Mr. Marks ...	o	5	o	Home	2	2	o
,, Cycling Club	o	9	o	Maintenance of member			
,, Mr. Read ...	o	3	o	at Home for 3 weeks	o	15	o
105 Subscriptions ...	5	5	o	Receipt book, etc. ...	o	o	9
1 do. at 2s.	o	2	o	Balance	6	12	o
	£9	9	o		£9	9	o

ERNEST S. LANDELLS, *Hon. Secretary.*

Audited and found correct, R. H. MARKS.   February 25th, 1907.

————— ✦•✦•✦ —————

THE LEICESTER WORKING MEN'S COLLEGE.

WE are glad to learn that this College, founded by the Rev. Canon Vaughan, D.D., a friend of the Rev. J. Llewelyn Davies, in 1862, is still flourishing and doing good work. For the first six years of its existence, it was known as the "Working Men's Institute," but in 1868, when there were 400 students, the title was changed to "The Leicester Working Men's College." It consists of men, women, and youths, and has a total membership of about 2000. The Committee is going to put up a building suitable for its new home. "Until this is done," the report says, "the Working Men's College cannot take its place among the institutions of the town in a manner commensurate with its tried value."

Tenders for the new College have already been invited, and it is hoped that building operations will commence early in March. The College will require about £8000, of which it has already about £6000. The students themselves are anxious to do their full share of work in the raising of this amount. Mrs. Vaughan, the widow of Canon Vaughan, has taken her husband's place in devoting herself to the interests of the College. Two members of our own College, who were on a flying visit to Leicester on February 15th, called on Mrs. Vaughan, and she was pleased to see the representatives of the London College. She said she had written to the Vice-Principal, Mr. Lionel Jacob, for information and advice, and had a most kind letter in reply. She was pleased that the new building would soon be begun, and said that the aim of the Committee would be to maintain instruction in the humanities, rather than on the technical side, and they would endeavour to secure the support and sympathy of the educational authority for the county. The prospectus concludes by saying that—"The Committee will be glad to have its purely education work co-ordinated with that of the local educational authority, but there will then remain a field for the College's humanizing influence. In the view of the Committee, the College has yet a career before it for the intellectual and moral uplifting of the citizens of Leicester. They feel that the *spirit of brotherhood*, which is a mark of its vigorous life, is yet capable of unmeasured blessings to this and future generations of our good old town." The Leicester Working Men's College has the cordial good wishes of the London Working Men's College in its good work.

OBITUARY.

HODGSON PRATT.

ONE of the great workers of the world for the benefit of humanity, Mr. Hodgson Pratt, passed away on February 26th, at Le Pecq, in France, at the age of 83. From the time of his retirement from the service of the East India Company, shortly after the Mutiny, he devoted his life to at least three great causes—education, co-operation, and international peace. He was one of the foremost men in the great co-operative movement, and the founder of the Working Men's Club and Institute Union. He took a leading part in the foundation of the International Arbitration and Peace Association, the furtherance of the objects of which more especially occupied the later years of his long and active life. He was one of the most conscientious of men, full of noble thoughts and ideals. His utterances were remarkable for liberality of view and fairmindedness. He strove rather to lead men to think for themselves, than to persuade them by other means, and the chief object which he kept in view throughout his many humanitarian efforts was how to make men better and nobler citizens. Of course, such a man was attached to, and interested in, this College. He was one of our Saturday evening lecturers some twenty years ago, and he attended one or two of the course of lectures in the College on " Co-operative Life," taking the chair for Mr. M. E. Sadler, and speaking on another occasion when Mr. Cunningham lectured and Mr. G. J. Holyoake was chairman. We have also heard him speak at one of the Old Students' Suppers. Mr. Hodgson Pratt was of an extremely lovable disposition, possessed of great kindliness of heart and simplicity of manner. His great courtesy and manliness, and his true nobility of character, impressed those who came into contact with him. There was an old-time charm about him, and a certain grandeur of presence too, that were very pleasing. So far, one of the old school ; yet how marvellously fresh and new, and before their time, were his ideas and views ! His influence for good must have been widespread indeed.

Mr. Pratt was buried at Highgate Cemetery on March 5th, the College being represented at the funeral by Messrs. C. Edmund Maurice, J. J. Dent, T. F. Hobson, R. H. Marks, and L. Pocock. About sixty delegates from Working Men's Clubs throughout England attended, and about that number of floral tokens from the clubs were laid around his grave.

LUBBOCK FIELD CLUB.

FEBRUARY 10th was a dull and misty day, and although at times the sun seemed likely to clear the air, the conditions were not such as to tempt out any but the stalwarts. At starting the ground was frozen slightly, but speedily became particularly soft, except on the roads. We reached Denham by G.W.R. at 10 o'clock, and striking northward, made our way to Ditton Marsh Farm. The lanes we traversed were very picturesque, but the melting hoar frost on the trees interfered sadly with our comfort. After crossing Oakend Wood, we found ourselves in Chalfont Park, and the opinion was general that the manner in which we emerged was not a usual one. Crossing the railway, we reached Gerrard's Cross Common, and then entered upon a series of pretty paths leading across Bulstrode Park to Hedgerley. Here we halted for lunch and fared very well, the apples provided by our host being particularly appreciated. We continued our route westward across the fields, and emerged on the road just to the north of Collum Green. Turning south, we followed one of the beautiful roads just within the border of Burnham Beeches, and on reaching East Burnham

Common turned our faces homeward. The route followed was across and round Brockhurst Wood, across Stoke Common, and through the pretty village of Fulmer. We reached the Uxbridge and Beaconsfield Road at the 18th milestone, and after a detour by Denham Mount, regained our starting place in ample time for the 5.39 train.

Hazel catkins were the chief indications that the winter was wearing on, but primrose leaves were breaking through in all directions. A remarkable tree in Bulstrode Park attracted our attention. It had evidently fallen at some time, after which the trunk had again sought the vertical, while the prostrate portion had been fortified with masonry. Two large bunches of mistletoe adorned it, but opinion was divided as to its nature. Curious ice formations appeared on several ponds, the investigation of which involved wet feet to one member of the party.

Next walk, April 14th, to Great and Little Hampden, and Whiteleaf Cross. Take excursion ticket to Great Missenden (Great Central Railway), 2s. 6d. Train leaves Marylebone at 9.30. Provide lunch.

J. HOLLOWAY, *Hon. Secretary.*

FURNIVALL CYCLING CLUB.

AT this club's annual meeting held on February 23rd, the hon. secretary, Mr. W. Melzer, read the committee's 12th report, some extracts from which follow:—The club has 35 ordinary and 12 honorary members. The average attendance at runs was about 12, and all the 27 runs on the fixture card were carried out. Miss M. Grellier won the ladies' attendance prize with the large total of 134 points. The previous best was 76 points, obtained by Miss K. Adams two years ago. The captain, Mr. W. C. Jones, who has been in the club since its foundation, secured the men's attendance prize with 140 points, whilst both Messrs. Lewis and Melzer scored well over 100. The report referred to the Easter and Whitsun tours, the entertainment provided by the president of the club, Dr. Furnivall, at Canbury Island on July 22nd, and the kind hospitality of Mr. and Mrs. Denmead on the visit to their house at South Mimms, on June 16th.

A supper, admirably prepared by Mrs. Robbie, preceded the meeting, 23 members attending. Dr. Furnivall took the chair, and cigars and cigarettes having been handed round by Mr. Julius Jacob, the meeting passed off very pleasantly. After the report and balance sheet had been presented, Dr. Furnivall was elected president; Messrs. Julius Jacob and W. C. Jones, vice-presidents; Mr. A. J. Wildey, captain; Mr. C. T. Young, vice-captain; Mr. A. Haynes, committee-man; and Mr. W. Melzer, hon. secretary. The latter will he glad to hear of any new members. Subscription, 1s. per ann.

At Easter, the club again tours to Brighton. First Sunday run, April 7th, to Hedgerley; meet at Swiss Cottage. A social run to Pinner will be held on Saturday, April 13th; meet at Swiss Cottage or Shepherds Bush Empire at 4.30 p.m. Friends are cordially invited. Other runs are:— Saturday, April 20th, Sunbury; Sunday, April 28th, Wheathampstead.

W. MELZER, *Hon. Secretary.*

BALANCE SHEET, 1906—7.

Receipts.	£	s.	d.	*Payments.*	£	s.	d.
Balance forward ...	2	7	10	Printing	0	15	0
Balance from Supper ...	0	6	0	Locker rent	0	2	6
Donation, Dr. Furnivall	0	10	0	Runs expenses	0	3	2
Members' subscriptions	1	15	0	"Cycling"	0	4	2
Honorary do. do. ...	0	12	0	Attendance prizes ...	1	0	0
Sale of 9 badges ...	0	18	0	12 badges	1	4	0
				Postage	0	8	6
				Convalescent Home ...	0	9	0
				Coffee Room Fund ...	0	10	0
				Balance	1	12	6
	£6	8	10		£6	8	10

COLLEGE NOTES.

AT the Council Meeting held on February 26th, the Vice-Principal moved that an expression of condolence upon the death of Sir Godfrey Lushington be sent to Lady Lushington, and in so doing stated that Mr. Lowes Dickinson wished to be associated with this vote. Dr. Oswald having seconded, and Messrs. Forster and Marks having supported the motion, it was put, and carried unanimously.

The report of the Executive Committee was read. This document, of which our Superintendent is as usual the author, makes such excellent reading, that we may perhaps, with propriety, here give the subjoined extracts from it :—

Student and Class Entries.—This time last year the College had emerged almost entirely from the chaos in which the building remained during the October term of 1905. The passages were floored, the windows glazed, the apparatus for heating and lighting was at work, and the science laboratories were, if not quite complete, available for two-thirds of their present accommodation. The result was that a large number of new members joined in that term, and made the total as large for the second as it had often been for the first term of former sessions. Before dealing further with the comparative entries for the present term, it may be of interest to notice the student entries for the October term of this session. The number of individual entries for the first term amounted to 948, or within fifty of the total for the whole of the preceding year; of these no less than 556 were new students, leaving 392 as the number of those who had renewed their membership. This works out as an eleven per cent. increase on the average of old students who have rejoined during the past five years in the October term. Returning to the figures for the present term, as available up to a week ago, we find that 654 students have joined, as against 527 at this time last year. Of these 161 are new students, who last year numbered 183. It therefore follows that the percentage of old students, which was a feature of the October term, has so far risen considerably; the exact figures being 493 for this term, as against 344 last year. For as large a number of old students in the January term we have to go back to 1899, and there the figures relate to the entry for the whole term, whereas this term has yet another month to run. Upon analysing the comparative class entries, it appears that of the thirty-one subjects which are common to the two terms, no fewer than 21 have improved as compared with last year. Art, French, German, Greek, Building Construction, Electricity, Shorthand, Singing, Chemistry, and that most inspiring and admirable class known as Mr. Scott's class, all show most substantial increases. At the end of last session some fear was expressed that the competition provided by the London County Council Evening Schools might adversely affect our College classes in Modern Languages. Some thought it would be wise to lower the fees for these classes, and this suggestion was debated at length both by the Studies Committee and the Executive Committee. Finally, it was resolved that no such reduction should be made, but that students should be given the option of a sessional fee of 10s. 6d. or of paying the usual term fee of 5s. The faith of those who deemed it unnecessary to lower our fees has been justified by the event, the two languages, French and German, in which competition was most feared, both show a substantial increase, French of 78, and German of 55 per cent.

At this time last year, the drop in the class entries for French and German coincided with a marked increase in Italian and Spanish. It is curious to note that the position this year is entirely reversed, Italian and Spanish both having suffered a decrease, the former more severely, however, than the latter. For a long time it has seemed impossible to attract to the study of Economics any but the smallest number of students, and therefore the fact that Mr. Morison has in his second term no fewer than sixteen students deserves more than the passing notice this class would receive when the comparative entries are read. A course of five lectures on Economics is also being given on Thursday evenings by Professor A. W. Kirkaldy. These, up to the present, have been attended by an average of forty students, so that Economics during this session has been a distinct success.

The comparative figures are as follows :—

	1906.	1907.		1906.	1907.
Preparatory	32	36	Astronomy	0	10
Algebra	28	26	Botany	15	9
Ambulance	17	9	Building Construction	20	51
Arithmetic	30	36	Electricity	47	75
Art	49	86	Geology	6	11
Book-keeping	61	67	Geometry	1	0
Composition	23	17	Mechanics	8	0
Economics	0	16	Physiology	8	11
English Literature	18	31	Singing	10	58
Euclid	11	5	Spanish	30	23
English for Foreigners	18	19	Shorthand	73	104
French	91	170	Violin	12	15
Geography	5	6	History	9	7
German	43	67	Italian	25	14
Grammar	38	39	Mr. Scott's Class	9	21
Greek	5	18	Chemistry	16	45
Latin	43	26	Zoology	10	7
Law	38	51			
			Totals	849	1176
			Student Entries	527	654

Classes and Teachers.—Two new subjects, Astronomy and Esperanto, have been added to the programme this term, both at the request of the students themselves.

Mr. Henkel, who was for four years in charge of Mackree Observatory, in the North of Ireland, has undertaken to teach the former, and Mr. G. L. Browne, the latter; both as unpaid teachers. The singing class, which last term proved so great a success, again attracted a number of beginners, for whom it was thought advisable to provide a special class. For this beginners' class the College has been fortunate in obtaining as teacher Mr. Mason Tarr, whose brother has been so well known for years in connection with the musical life of the College, and under him the class has proved a great success.

.The Classical side this term has been a great trouble to its director, Mr. Lupton. Having obtained with considerable difficulty Mr. R. N. M. Bailey as teacher for the Beginners' Greek, and having failed to secure a teacher for the corresponding class in Latin, Mr. Lupton himself undertook the Latin Class temporarily, and then, after three weeks, found himself left with the Beginners' Class in Greek, owing to its new teacher falling ill with scarlet fever. In these circumstances, temporary assistance was found for the Latin, and Mr. Lupton added to his other duties that of teaching the Beginners' Greek. Thanks to Mr. Dent, the College has found a most valuable recruit in Mr. Strauss, who has put at the College's disposal his one free evening, and has undertaken a literature and conversation class for the help of our advanced students in French—a class which he hopes to run on the same lines as those taken in the old College with such success by Mr. Jastrzebski. A practice class for French beginners too being wanted, D. Bardin, a student of some years' standing, has undertaken the work. In Shorthand, Mr. Hill and Mr. D. Robson have been obliged to give up their classes, the former through press of other claims, the latter through ill-health. Messrs. Randall and Alaway have kindly filled these vacancies.

Lectures.—The lecture lists for this session are most attractive ones, yet the attendances have not been on the average at all good. It seems as if the earlier hour of commencement does not suit the audience as well as the later. Certainly many more come in late than when the lectures commenced at 8.30, and the numbers attending are not as large as in the broken session of last year. Both Thursday and Saturday lectures have been affected, though the former have certainly suffered the more. Classes as a rule commence at 7.30, and many end at 8.30, so that an 8 o'clock lecture fails to get men who would otherwise come, if their classes were not thus interrupted. The two University Extension series have not proved equally attractive. The course on "Architecture" has secured an entry of 44, but that on "Europe after Napoleon" has attracted only thirteen. A third course on "The Literature of the reign of Queen Anne," given by Mr. Guthkelch, and arranged by the London County Council, has not proved so attractive as had been hoped ; probably had it been arranged early enough to have appeared in our term programme, the entry would have been much larger.

Besides giving the results of examinations, and setting out the recent gifts to the Library, the Committee's report contained lengthy references to the social life of the College, passing in review the Sketching Club Supper, Old Students' Club Supper, Furnivall Children's Treat, Joint Clubs' Supper, Collegians' Dance, Chess match with Trinity men, Musical Society's Concert and Supper, Student and Teachers' Meeting, the new Literary Society, and the Linguists.

Dr. Furnivall moved the adoption of the report, with thanks to the Executive and the Superintendent. Dr. Oswald seconded, and the motion was carried unanimously.

The Vice-Principal moved, "That the Executive Committee be empowered to elect honorary members of the College, such Members not to exceed ten in number at any one time, and honorary membership not to continue for a longer term than one year except in case of re-election." The Vice-Principal explained that the object of his motion was to allow a few members to be elected who might be useful to the College, though they were not prepared either to teach or to study. Mr. Marks seconded this motion, which was carried *nem. con.*

Mr. F. M. Kingdon has examined the Algebra class, in the first stage, with the result that out of eight who sat, three passed, namely H. C. Webb (exc.), C. E. Horsman (exc.), and D. R. Newlands.

At the St. John's Ambulance Association's examination on December 14th, Dr. G. Clark examined Dr. Forbes's class of 13 men, of whom two passed and gained medallions, P. A. Gannaway and David Robson ; ten passed in First Aid, W. J. Fender, Jesse James, T. A. Paterson, W. J. Slade, A. J. Sweetman, T. J. Hemming, W. A. Jermey, James Scott, James M. Stears, and Charles H. Welti ; and only one failed.

In the Preparatory examination, 5 sat for Grammar, and 4 passed, E. Tilli (exc.), F. J. Crome (exc.), John Hagerty, and J. T. Hutchings ; 6 sat for Arithmetic, and 5 passed, A. E. Hogh (exc.), E. Tilli (exc.), C. W. Tuck, A. Fuller, and A. R. Dixon ; 8 sat for Dictation, and 6 passed, A. Fuller (exc.), F. T. Blake (exc.), A. E. Hogh (exc.), J. Hagerty, E. W. Townsend, and H. Jones.

At the next meeting of the Old Students' Club, to be held on Saturday, April 6th, at 7.45, it is intended to do honour to Mr. R. H. Marks, President of the Club, by making him a presentation, in recognition of his long and faithful services to the College, which he joined about fifty years ago Members of the club will have received notification that they are welcome to bring their lady friends with them to this meeting.

———

We have been asked to make special mention of the fact— and we do it with a great deal of pleasure—that the next Musical Society's evening will be Saturday, the 20th April, when a concert will be given by the "Glowworms' Glee Club," conducted by Mr. J. F. Budge. The programme will consist of male voice glees, part songs, etc., and an excellent concert is promised, so we hope the audience will be large, and come early —at 8 o'clock.

———

On March 9th, Mr. A. J. Ashton, K.C., gave an interesting lecture on "Dr. Johnson." Mr. Ashton, who taught for some time in the College, and is known to many of the older students, said that he always had a warm corner in his heart for the place. Mr. Bros, the Clerkenwell Police Court magistrate, who was chairman, also said it was a pleasure to him to come again to the College.

———

Under date of February 14th, Rev. T. E. S. Catterns, who is still recuperating at Mentone, writes to the Secretary of the Old Students' Club—" You have had severe weather in England, and it has been severe here. Strong winds, heavy seas, and above all, ice for days in succession. There was a profusion of flowers up to Christmas, but there are very few now. On February 5th, the *première bataille des fleurs* took place, and was the poorest known. There were only a dozen carriages, fully decorated as you see them in the illustrations ; the three best with white lilac, red roses, and mimosa bloom. The last probably would not have been placed but for the occupants—six young and fairly good-looking English girls, with cream-coloured dresses. The Carnival procession was on the 7th, and was pretty good. There was a run on the gigantic,—the king on an enormous goose and his spouse on a swing. The mounted men were arrayed in gorgeous Spanish costume, and looked very handsome There were twelve old maids seven feet high or more ; the girls inside were twelve to fourteen, and in a strong wind found it difficult to progress. The crowd were largely arrayed in costumes, masks, and dominos. Plenty of fun, and very little vulgarity ; the rough element is at night, and I did not go out. The procession was repeated on Sunday, and again on Tuesday, Mardi Gras, and the figures were burned that night."

Mr. F. W. Finn, old student, reports from Calcutta, February 28th, that the hot season has started about a month earlier than usual. He longs for some of our cold weather.

We congratulate our friend G. A. Hurcomb and his wife on their escape with their lives from the Jamaica earthquake; but we are exceedingly sorry to learn, from the contents of the following letter addressed to the Secretary of the Old Students' Club, on February 10th, that he has suffered such a severe loss of property, and we hope that the insurance companies may yet make some satisfactory arrangement:—

Both my wife and myself escaped the terrible earthquake of the 14th. I only got a few bruises—just missing a few tons of falling bricks by an inch or so,—for I ran out in the street. In less time than it takes to tell, the air became so full of dust from the falling walls that you could see absolutely nothing. I was in our store at the time, and after groping about trying to find some others, got into the street, to find the pavement rocking like the deck of a ship in a heavy sea. When the dust cleared off, the sight was too awful for words; everywhere men, women, children, horses, and mules covered with blood, some dead, others with parts of their bodies crushed to pulp, but still alive, groaning and shrieking. How many were buried under falling bricks, etc., nobody will ever know. For the past four weeks—to-morrow will make exactly four weeks—the bodies have been dug out and burnt or buried. Out of the staff of fifteen in our store, the only one injured was a man that ran out and got buried. We pulled him out, and he is now recovering. All the rest stayed in, and luckily the first floor of our building stood well, and protected those below from that portion of the upper part of our walls that fell inside. Our stock, too, was intact and undamaged—some of it only covered with dust. Immediately after the earthquake, most of our staff pulled themselves together in a wonderful way. One little girl in particular played an heroic part; alert and active, pulling people from under bricks, or rather showing the way and getting others to help her take the bricks off people, bathing and binding up wounds. It is not true, as I have seen stated, that the earthquake destroyed the water mains, for immediately after we got plenty out of our pipe, and the pressure was good. I drank some, for I had a horrible dry choky feeling in the throat. I stayed in the store for about forty-five minutes after. We put all books in the safe, and closed and locked all doors before leaving. Misfortunes never come singly. Fire started some blocks distant, and reached our store some hours afterwards, completely burning up everything. We are insured in leading English Companies, but they disclaim liability, although they paid in San Francisco in an exactly similar case. It is said, however, that their reason for paying in San Francisco was that they knew that the decision of the United States Courts would be against them. It was a case of either pay, or clear out of the United States. But Jamaica is only a small British Colony. I see that the German Courts have just ordered German Insurance Companies to pay San Francisco Fire Claims, in spite of the earthquake clause in their policies. I cannot believe that British justice is inferior to German. If it is, then I say, so much the worse for the British Empire. One of these same British Companies, just prior to this fire, was advertising in the Kingston papers that their "losses in San Francisco, amounting to one million pounds or so sterling, were promptly paid without touching their capital!" All the policies bristle with conditions which, if enforced, would enable the Companies to avoid payment of nearly every claim. And when you questioned the agents about these conditions they said, "Oh! that's only a matter of form—to protect the Companies against fraud. It is never enforced in *bona fide* cases." I must beg your pardon. I did not start with the intention of writing you this; but the fact is every business man here will be ruined if fire losses are not settled on an equitable basis—I say fire losses, not earthquake losses. As for myself, all I possessed is burnt to ashes, and I now have to start life over again.

THE COFFEE ROOM FUND.

THE fund for the decoration of the Coffee Room has already been more than half collected, and if to the money now in the treasurers' hands be added the amounts promised, the total is about £65. Another £35 is therefore required to be subscribed before the order can be given for the work. At present all that has been done of a special nature towards raising the fund has been the holding of the meeting of February 11th and the issue of a circular to the members. The Decoration Committee have not found it necessary to work very hard at collecting, as yet. The chief labour has fallen upon the hon. secretary, Mr. H. K. Randall, in making out receipts, acknowledging contributions, and keeping account of the same. The last £20 will, we suspect, be the hardest to get; but the Committee is a strong one, and the issue is not to be doubted If the Common Room Committee come along with the pecuniary assistance they are able to offer, the contract for the decoration work may probably be entered into before the end of the current session.

The following further sums have been received :—

	£	s.	d.		£	s.	d.
C. F. Marshall	0	2	6	W. J. Spray	0	10	0
H. J. Johns	0	10	0	L. E. Knifton	0	2	6
P. J. Brett	0	2	0	Dr. F. J. Furnivall	0	10	0
H. Gallaher	0	5	0	R. W. Wilkinson	0	5	0
The Linguists	0	10	0	Mr. Wilkinson's class	0	2	0
A. Wilshaw	0	2	6	Prof. A. V. Dicey, K.C	1	0	0
C. Holloway	0	1	0	F. E. Liddlelow	0	3	0
F. Atha	0	0	6	H. Sumner	0	1	0
J. Rigby Smith	0	5	0	R. Freeman	0	5	0
Rev. J. Llewelyn Davies	0	10	0	F. Fenton	0	2	6
Musical Society	2	2	0	F. E. Laurerce	0	1	0
M. W. Starling	0	6	0	W. C. Riddle	0	2	6
C. G. Cash	0	4	0	Joint Clubs' Supper	0	15	0
F. Hughes	0	1	0	J. Dale	0	5	0
Tom Martin	0	2	6	Mrs. T. Hopkins	0	2	6
F. Wildman	0	2	6	Miss Steptoe	0	2	6
Sidney Stagg	0	10	0	J. Hopkins	0	2	0
Lord Avebury	2	2	0	W. R. J. Hickman	0	10	6
C. H. Perry	0	10	0	H. Spencer	0	2	0
Mr. A. J. Bride's class	1	17	0	L. Page	0	0	6
A. E. Hughes	0	1	0	E. A. Harrison	0	5	0
C. P. Lucas	1	0	0	Karl Brückner	0	1	6
R. J. Mure	2	0	0	Gates Fowler	0	1	0
F. J. Hytch	0	10	6	Herbert Wilcockson	1	0	0
R. W. Everard	0	2	6	J. McWilliams	0	1	0
Frank Samuel	0	10	0	J. Day	0	1	0
N. Atha	0	0	6				
C. H. Cooper	0	1	0		£21	5	0

TANSLEY SWIMMING CLUB.

THE Club meets every Tuesday evening at 7.30, at Whitfield Street, Tottenham Court Road, Baths. The Committee earnestly ask all old members to keep the Club going by turning up as often as they can. Any College student desiring to learn to swim will find it beneficial to join the Club. Some attractive races will shortly be announced. During the summer, if members so desire, open air swimming will be started. Subscription, 1s. per annum.   W. H. BARNETT, *Hon. Secretary.*

CORRESPONDENCE.

[Under this heading the Editor will be glad to publish letters of interest to past and present members, but he declines all responsibility for the views therein expressed.]

COFFEE ROOM DECORATION FUND.

To the Editor of the WORKING MEN'S COLLEGE JOURNAL.

DEAR SIR,—Anon.'s complaint in last month's JOURNAL is, I presume' unique in the annals of our College, and I trust that the cause of a gentle grumble I intend to indulge in, Mr. Editor, can also be included in that category, and that I may enter my earnest protest at the publication of the amount each individual subscribed towards the redecoration of the Coffee Room. I do so on the grounds that such a publication defeats the object the promoters have in view—one that every student must desire—the most success-ful consummation. It is difficult to write with a due sense of responsibility, as the whole thing is so obviously insincere. There can be no defence, and as I trust it will not recur, perhaps I may be forgiven if I attempt to anticipate the only half-hearted defence which in my opinion may be raised. Can it be intended to stimulate those who have not subscribed? If so, why not place the names of those who subscribed the largest amount first. It must be carelessness, it cannot be design, that some are more prominent than others. The work at the College of the men that head the list is sufficient refutation for that suggestion. I firmly believe, Sir, that a great deal of harm has been done to the fund, and feeling raised, by this ridiculous publication ; and as a humble student who would do anything for the common weal of the College, I trust you will allow this letter to be published, and that it will not be taken in the spirit of carping criticism. but in that of a broad-minded interest in a matter of College history, and a sincere desire for the success of the project.—Yours faithfully, EDWARD HAYWARD.

[The publication of the amounts subscribed is not unique in our annals. It has been the custom, hitherto, to publish such details. One object of giving the list is, of course, to draw the attention of those likely to contribute, to the fact that the fund is being raised, *pour encourager les autres,* as the saying is. The JOURNAL circulates amongst a number of members who are likely to give upon seeing such a list, and during the fortnight following upon the appearance of last month's number, we find that both the number of receipts issued and the sum collected were more than doubled. Another reason for printing the sums in the JOURNAL is the ordinary one which actuates the publication of any accounts of this kind—so that the donors may have not only the due acknowledgment of their individual donations, but may see, as a matter of account, how the fund is being raised. The names are given in the order in which they come in. This must necessarily be the case until the fund has been closed. To deal with the principle under-lying Mr. Hayward's criticism, I hope he will believe that no reader of the COLLEGE JOURNAL thinks ill, or thinks otherwise than well, of a man who gives a small subscription. Here, so far as our experience goes, every true College man gives freely of his time and money, to the best of his ability, for the benefit of his fellow members and of the College, without thought either of reward or of what other men may think. It is well known, and often said, in the College, that the gift of a shilling from some men may be more worthy than the gift of a pound from others. What need then is there for a man to be ashamed to give a shilling, or even less? None whatever. So far from it being a "ridiculous publication" to give the donations of those who can least afford them, we count it as an honourable record.—ED.]

Matter held over for want of space :—Debating Society and Field Club Notices. Report of gifts to the Library. Article on Solitary Chess. Letters from Abroad.

MRS. TANSLEY'S CONCERT.

IT has been remarked before in these pages, in regard to a Concert given by Mrs. Tansley, that it was one of the best ever heard in the College. The Concert of Saturday, March 2nd, however, eclipsed any of its predecessors, and was on all hands declared to be the best we have ever had. In the Maurice Hall, we have more space for the Orchestra, and the platform provides a good vantage ground for the Choir. Both Orchestra and Choir were most ably conducted by Mrs. Julian Marshall, they performed well together, and the result was excellent. Soloists—vocal and instrumental— also played well their part, including Mrs. Eugene Oswald at the piano. The first part of the programme consisted of a pastoral, entitled "The May-Queen," written by Henry F. Chorley, and composed by Sir W. Sterndale Bennett. The soloists who contributed to this piece were Miss Hettie Stammer, one of the most pleasing sopranos we have ever listened to, who took the part of the May-Queen ; Mr. Stanley Ridout, a capital tenor, as the Lover ; Miss Clutterbuck, who very kindly, in the absence of Mrs. Teasdale through indisposition, filled and filled well the rôle of Queen ; and Mr. W. Savage Cooper, as Robin Hood, Captain of the Foresters, whose deep bass voice suited the part admirably. Where all worked so excellently together, we need say little more, but we think that, by common consent, Miss Hettie Stammer won the most delighted applause from the audience. The hardest worker for our pleasure was Mrs. Julian Marshall. It was marvellous to watch her conducting both the large choir, who filled the platform, and the orchestra at the same time. She evidently took a keen pleasure in doing it ; her heart was in her work ; and consequently the best effect was produced. Both choir and orchestra contained many of our old friends. Mrs. Tansley herself was in the former, along with Mr. and Mrs. William Tarr, Mr. and Mrs. Mason Tarr, Mr. and Mrs Perry, Miss Hutchings, and others whom we had heard before. We understand that for more than three weeks constant rehearsals had been going on, which must have meant a great deal of labour for Mrs. Tansley and her helpers. She and they were accorded a very hearty vote of thanks, upon the motion of Mr. Lionel Jacob, our Vice-Principal, when the interval came ; and advantage was also taken of the occasion to recognize both the marriage of Mr. William Tarr and his long, zealous, and self-sacrificing devotion to College musical work and entertainments, by presenting him with a choice set of volumes, subscribed for by his many friends in the College. He was heartily cheered, and made a neat little speech in acknowledging the gift, which came to him and his wife as a complete surprise.

The second part of the concert comprised :—Trio and Chorus, "The Chough and Crow" (Bishop), Miss Edith Nettleship, Miss Amy Gardner, and Mr. H. K. Gardner ; Violin solo, Swedish Dances (Max Bruch), Miss Oonah Sumner ; Song, "Who is Sylvia?" (Schubert), Miss Clutterbuck ; Three Madrigals by the Choir ; "Kathleen Mavourneen," and encore, "Chloe," Mr. W. Savage Cooper ; Song, "Once" (Hervey), and encore, "Ever so long ago," Miss Hettie Stammer ; Valse (Tschaikowsky), the Orchestra ; Song, "Take a pair of sparkling eyes" (Sullivan), Mr. Ridout ; duet, "Spring will bring" (Caryll), Miss Hettie Stammer and Mr. Ridout ; two Irish songs, "I remember meeting you" (Hermann Löhr), and "You'd better ask me," Mr. C. H. Perry ; and Chorus, "Carnovale" (Rossini).

THE WORKING MEN'S COLLEGE JOURNAL *is supported partly by Annual Subscribers living in different parts of the World, and partly by circulation among the Students and Members. Its success depends upon a regular demand, and to ensure this, the Editor would be glad if as many readers as can will become Subscribers. Subscription 2s. 6d. per annum, post free.*

LONDON : Printed by W. HUDSON & Co., Red Lion Street, High Holborn, and published at THE WORKING MEN'S COLLEGE, Crowndale Road, London, N.W.—April 1st, 1907.

Educ T245.4

Gratis

The Working Men's College Journal

Sub: M

The Working Men's College,
CROWNDALE ROAD
ST PANCRAS
LONDON·N·W·
FOUNDED
IN 1854
BY THE LATE

Frederick Denison Maurice.

Contents for MAY, 1907.

Marks Presentation Meeting

College Notes

Glowworms Concert

Solitary Chess

Correspondence

Club News

THE

Working Men's College Journal.

Conducted by Members of the Working Men's College,
Crowndale Road, London, N.W.

Vol. X.—No. 172.   JUNE, 1907.   Price Twopence.

SHORT STUDIES IN SHAKESPEARE.

I.—The Invisible Supernatural, and the relation of "Ariel" to the Same.

THE element of the supernatural in Shakespeare's plays furnishes an interesting subject of study. It is a feature frequently met with, and is used for the purpose of furnishing a plot or of giving life or colour to the same; of creating an atmosphere, or as a means of diversion; of marking a situation, or giving prevalence to an idea. We find it in its grosser or material aspects in witches and hags, and other abortions of the flesh or something worse; in unsubstantial forms as ghosts or apparitions; as airy shapes and elemental forces, with but shadowy personifications; or as an influence working secretly but effectually in the minds of men.

In this paper we are concerned only with what has been called the "Invisible Supernatural." But, although the range of our inquiry is necessarily narrowed, there is yet ample scope for the exercise of bent and skill, for the idea itself opens out a splendid field for study and speculation. It has been pointed out that in the play of *Richard II.*, there is an undercurrent of the Invisible Supernatural. Thus, at some time previous to the actual period of the play, the Duke of Gloster, an uncle of the King, had been murdered. As the Duke had been prominent among a party which had for some time thwarted Richard in his vicious pursuits, there were many who thought that the murder was an act of vengeance on his part. This unnatural act was, then, the origin of the "Invisible Supernatural" element referred to. Mowbray, Duke of Norfolk, was supposed to have been Richard's tool in getting rid of Gloster, and at the opening of the play we see Bolingbroke charging Norfolk with having plotted the crime. This is our first acquaintance with the prevalent feeling of repulsion thus engendered; and all through the play we find it welling up, now here and now there, resulting in that general falling away from allegiance to the King which led to his rapid downfall.

19, LOWER MALL, HAMMERSMITH.

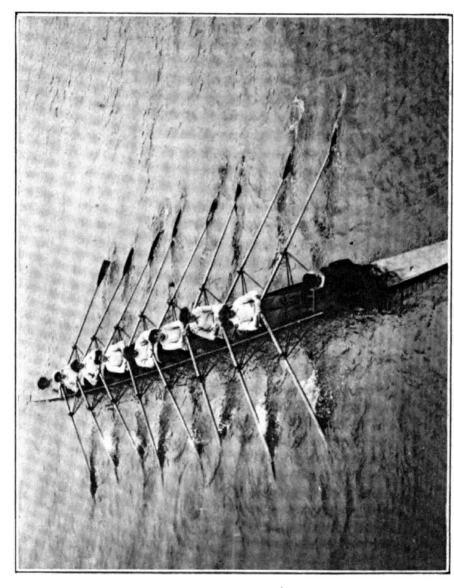

The girls out for their second paddle in their racing Clasper eight, on 15th June, 1907. Photo (1) taken from Hammersmith Bridge. Photo (2) from the Club Raft, the stern of the boat being held there.

Crew: Misses KATE LOCK, *Stroke*; NELLIE LANSDELL, 7; ETHEL ALLEN, 6; EMMIE SEWELL, 5; LIZZIE SKINNER, 4; ALICE

Crew: Misses Kate Lock, *Stroke*; Nellie Lansdell, 7; Ethel Allen, 6; Emmie Sewell, 5; Lizzie Skinner, 4; Alice Dewar, 3; Maud Allen, 2; Gwen Jarvis, *Bow*. *Cox*, Dr. F. J. Furnivall, Trin. Hall, Cambs., Founder of the Club, 1896.

THE

Working Men's College Journal.

Conducted by Members of the Working Men's College,
Crowndale Road, London, N.W.

Vol. X.—No. 173.   JULY, 1907.   Price Twopence.

SHORT STUDIES IN SHAKESPEARE.

II.—The Basic Element in Hamlet's Character.

ACCORDING to the general verdict concerning the characters delineated by Shakespeare, that of Hamlet stands unique, and, in some respects, without an equal. This pre-eminence has been fitly emphasized in the idea that in Hamlet there is a basic element of character, in which the mind of Shakespeare is revealed as it is revealed nowhere else. Further, it is suggested that the particular qualities forming this basic element may be traced in certain other characters in the plays, there being presented in each case a more or less modified reflex of the character of Hamlet, or of such features in it as we are now concerned with.

In this and the following paper our attention will be given to two characters, Hamlet and Prince Henry of Monmouth, afterwards Henry V.

Undoubtedly it is mainly as a study in psychology that the story of Hamlet holds the field. For while the situations and incidents of the play are full of interest and pathos, it is the mental attitude of the introspective, irresolute Hamlet, and his pregnant utterances on the philosophy of life and the ironies of time and fate, that remain with us after the glamour and excitement of the action have passed away. It is, then, with the inner life of Hamlet that we are mainly concerned. At the same time there is so much of interest in the contrast between his inner and his outer life, that it will be well to take note of the salient features in the latter.

When we first see Hamlet, he is brooding over the recent loss of his father, the late King of Denmark, to whom he had been greatly attached. He is suspicious at the circumstance that his less-than-two months widowed mother has married his uncle, who has usurped the crown. He is, too, in love—with Ophelia. Following on this, the revelation made to him by his father's ghost confirms his worst fears as to the manner of his parent's death, and his mental perturbation is intensified. But the injunction he has received to avenge the unnatural crime committed by his uncle, gives him an object in life, which in his own characteristic way, he pursues.   Thus, instead of an upheaval of the State, which might be expected to mark the situation here, we find Hamlet still at the Court, but feigning madness in order to secure his own safety while he matures his plans, and so that he may speak out his mind without fear of consequence.   Soon after, he arranges a play at the royal palace, in order to satisfy himself that the ghost scene was a reality, and that his uncle is the murderer he believes him to be; and in this way gets convincing proof of his guilt.   But this fails to bring him up to the sticking point, otherwise than in resolve.   Thus, when presently the looked-for opportunity comes, he fails to take advantage of it.   For at the time Claudius was at his prayers, and lest his death while engaged in so holy an exercise should gain for him a too easy access into heaven, Hamlet decides to hold his hand and await a more suitable occasion for sending the miscreant whither he will get his deserts.

Along with Hamlet, Ophelia shares our deepest sympathy with an untoward fate.   Hamlet's love for her had been a true love, "more than that of forty thousand brothers," as he told Laertes ; but the distractions of the time rudely shattered it, and on one occasion, at least, he was not kind to her.   This and the fact that her lover had, although unwittingly, killed her father, drove the poor damsel really mad ; and the loss of her reason cost her her dear life.   It is in the churchyard where she was laid to rest that we get a notable view of Hamlet.

That random but deadly spear-thrust through the arras, by which Hamlet struck down the eaves-dropping Polonius, instead of the murderous Claudius, marks a turning-point in the play. For Hamlet, now more than ever in his uncle's power, is hurriedly sent off out of harm's way—but really to his intended death—to England.   During the voyage thither there is a crisis in his fate, in which he shows an unwonted promptitude of decision as well as of action.   For he finds documentary proof of what the journey is intended to mean for him, and he turns the tables on his two guardians—"engineers hoist with their own petard"—and sends them on to their death ; on, be it noted, for it was only by written word and the pressure of a seal that he took this drastic step.   But it was by actual promptitude of action that he effected his own escape, and again reaching the shores of Denmark, is found in the graveyard with Horatio and the grave-diggers.   After the exciting burial scene, we rapidly approach the close of the play.   We see Hamlet in confidential talk with Horatio repeating his old resolve to right the wrong; and we also get to know that the King is plotting more than one means of getting rid of Hamlet.   In the concluding catastrophe, we have another case of the engineer being hoist with his own petard.   For while Laertes meets with a too honest death for his deserving, at the hands of Hamlet (albeit he would rather have taken him to his arms as a friend and brother), the

Queen dies from poison intended for Hamlet, and the King is prevented from doing further mischief by the same poisoned dagger that, along with the poisoned cup, silences the ringing yet pathetic words of Hamlet. After this it only remains for the good Horatio to cherish and vindicate the memory of his lost friend, and immediately to have the *débris* of human carcases cleared away to make room for the coming of young Fortinbras to reach the crown that Hamlet, by his taint of inaction, had failed to take hold upon.

Now, for our purpose, the complement of the foregoing narrative of action associated with Hamlet's career is the element of individual characteristics embodied in his personality. Of the three distinctive features comprising this personality— the will, the spirit, and the mind—the first was maimed by an extreme sensibility, and overborne by the fecundity of his mental powers ; the second was generous to a degree, but was up in arms against treachery, could not brook blatant commonplace, and was distraught by the outrageous fortune that marked his career ; the third was virtually the all, for it was supreme in his life and dominated his very being. Devoid of "this noble and most sovereign reason," Hamlet would make no great appeal to us ; but with it, and with the power to mould it into form and give it due expression, there are few acquaintances in our intellectual life we would not sooner part with.

There is perhaps no more distinctive feature in the mental constitution of Hamlet than the quality of detachment. Possessing this, even when his life is most on the rack, he is able to elude the pricks and thorns of his environment, and being transported into another sphere, finds fitting and more congenial employment for his lofty spirit. But in this transition he does not elude his readers, but draws them with him into his new world. Here they have the satisfaction, or something more, of seeing a master mind, in a transport of wrought-up feeling, working with the tools of a fine imagination and deep penetrating thought, a wonderful power of manipulation and an unlooked-for sanity, delving into the cracks and crevices of human nature, or ranging forth, grappling with the mysteries of man's existence here and hereafter.

Does not this quality of detachment form one of the basic elements we are in search of? It appears to be so ; and in it, too, we get a reflex of a marked feature in the character of Shakespeare. For undoubtedly it was by his freedom as a poet from the particular movements and tendencies of his time—full of throbbing life and national import as they were—that, with a full knowledge of all that was passing around him, he was able to give such splendid effect to his genius for the universal and elemental in man and his surroundings.

Continuing our search, we find that Hamlet had a vocation to think, and think supremely. For he takes us as it were to the springs of thought, so that truly his ideas are creations. Now, a vocation such as this surely constitutes a basic element of character in the individual possessing it, for it marks him off as an original, and not a mere copy of something that may be met with elsewhere. In somewhat the same way, although to a lesser degree, the perfect sanity of his mind, together with his faculty for so marvellously crystallizing his ideas and making them into perfect images that we can recognize and remember, have a claim to be admitted into this category. For if not original in kind, they are original in degree, and in that respect stand apart, at any rate in the ante-chamber to the elemental. And here again our thoughts revert to Shakespeare, and we see his mind in the working, and his works in the making, so great is the similitude of cause and effect in his case to that we have here dwelt upon.

But there is one other aspect of this matter to which we must give brief attention. Regarding Hamlet as an individual, and not as a mere compound of feelings and faculties, we find him from the beginning to the ending of the play, in every scene and situation, to be a person of distinction. His very presence creates an atmosphere which cannot be misunderstood or withstood, either by those who actually come into contact with him, or even those who are mere onlookers. In this atmosphere he always appears to advantage in spite of disadvantage; and however much he may be hated or feared by those who have cause to hate or fear him, he is never held in contempt or even subject to disparagement. (If the latter conclusion is liable to qualification, the fact of it being so is only a reminder of the danger involved in the assumption of a part—insanity—so merging into the reality as to be mistaken for it.) This is due to the essential qualities in the man, which cannot be dissected or explained; we can only accept it as a fact which adds to the perplexity and also the interest of the play.

And now, in concluding this study, we would note the fact that a basic element can be traced in the very plot of the play. In our study of *The Tempest*, we saw the benefit accruing from character dominating intellect, a disciplined will holding the intellect in check, albeit it be fit and available for service. In *Hamlet*, the conditions are reversed, and the course of events is perfectly consistent with the same; the intellect is dominant, and the effect of this is disastrous to all concerned.

Thus we get further testimony to the innate sanity of Shakespeare, in so shaping the course of events in his dramas as to be in the result true to life.   G. S.

"FREDERICK DENISON MAURICE."—The Vice-Principal has presented to the Library a copy of Mr. C. F. G. Masterman's Book under this title. It is an excellent work, and will doubtless be widely read by College men, when they find it may be borrowed. The volume forms one of the series, "Leaders of the Church, 1800—1900," edited by G. W. E. Russell, and published by Mowbray & Co.

HODGSON PRATT.

ON Thursday, May 30th, a meeting convened by the Working Men's Club and Institute Union was held in the Union Hall, in commemoration of the life work of the late Hodgson Pratt. The chair was taken by Mr. Stephen Seaward Tayler, president of the Union, a friend and colleague of Mr. Pratt for more than forty years ; and the following resolution was passed, upon the motion of Mr. William Minet, J.P., seconded by Lord Weardale : —"That this meeting is of opinion that the life work of the late Hodgson Pratt is deserving of a permanent memorial, and pledges itself to assist in any efforts that may be made for this purpose by the organizations of working men's clubs, of co-operative societies, and of peace associations." This College was represented on the platform by the Vice-Principal, Mr. C. Edmund Maurice, Mr. J. J. Dent, Mr. T. F. Hobson, and Mr. Leonard Pocock, and amongst the letters referred to were those from Mr. C. P. Lucas, Mr. J. M. Ludlow, Dr. Oswald, and Mr. Thomas Burt, M.P. The motion was supported by Mr. R. Cremer, M.P., Mrs. Holyoake Marsh, Mr. James Rowlands, M.P., the Rev. Canon Barnett (Toynbee Hall), Miss Tourhier, Mr. J. J. Dent, Lord Brassey, and the Rev. Page Hopps ; and Mr. Warren Hastings Sands moved and Mr. T. F. Hobson seconded a vote of thanks to the chairman. All the speakers were unanimous in testifying to Mr. Pratt's remarkable devotion to public service, to his unwearying energy, to his great and inspiring belief in the value of the principle of association, to his great love of humanity, and to his wonderful self-sacrifice and self-effacement.

A joint committee, representing the Co-operative Union, the Working Men's Club and Institute Union, and the International Arbitration Association, has been formed to consider the most suitable form of memorial. Any friends who desire to join in the effort to establish some permanent memorial to one who for many years rendered splendid service to the co-operative movement should communicate with Mr. B. T. Hall, Club Union Buildings, Clerkenwell Road, London, E.C., who is acting as hon. secretary *pro tem.*

The following extracts from letters written by Mr. Hodgson Pratt contain references to the Working Men's College.

Extract from letter from Mr. Hodgson Pratt, December 12th, 1904 :—

" I have received from my friend, Mr. J. J. Dent, a copy of the History of the College. Few things could have given me more pleasure and more hope for the future of England than the perusal of this book. If I desired to give 'an intelligent foreigner' the most favourable possible impression of our people, I should put that volume in his hands. I am not too fond of eulogizing my country, but in that narrative there is ground for pride and satisfaction beyond measure."

Extract from letter from Mr. Hodgson Pratt, December 17th, 1904 :—

" Your letter of the 13th instant has given me much pleasure, and I thank you heartily for it. Nevertheless, I feel, when reading your remarks as to my own efforts, that you give me more praise than I deserve—an uncomfortable feeling too often experienced when old friends and fellow-workers write to me. After all, those who snatch a few hours from daily toil for bare life, for the service of their fellows, such as . . . and . . . and many others whom I have known, are those for whom praise should be reserved. And, with or without praise, they have their reward in the consciousness that they are doing something to lessen the vast sum of human ignorance and suffering. No country owes so much to these real workers as England, and I do not know in what a sad plight she would now find herself, but for the faithful efforts of working men 'leaders' in the Trades' Union, Co-operative, and other movements.

"An enormous responsibility rests on those who have ample leisure, some knowledge, and more than their share of this world's goods, which, indeed, they have *not earned.* . . . . Anyone who has taken a part in the admirable and delightful organization of the Working Men's College has served his comrades and the cause of social progress generally. I can well understand how great a blessing to your own life, and to that of many hundreds of other toilers, that College has brought. What an immense service it is given to such men as Frederick Denison Maurice to accomplish! These are the true 'saviours of Society,' and, though I am not given to excessive 'patriotism,' I believe we have more of such men in England than elsewhere. I hope that the growth of the love of money and of self-enjoyment may not diminish the number of those who seek, above all things, to serve their fellow-men. Perhaps—*perhaps*—there would be more growth in all that is truly good and noble, in justice and philanthropy, if we had a different sort of Commonwealth, one relieved from the moral, social, and political drawbacks which come from an hereditary aristocracy, monopolizing the ownership of land, and setting a perpetual example of folly, and waste and luxury.

"But I am wandering—I rejoice to learn how much the College has been to you, and I doubt not that many, many others owe a brightness in their lives to this source, such as you have."

SATURDAY AFTERNOON CONDUCTED OUTINGS.

ON June 1st, the first conducted outing of the year took place, and under the guidance of Mr. Lionel Jacob, our Vice-Principal, we visited the Charter House and the Priory Church of St. Bartholomew the Great. The party was limited to 30, and I was much surprised to find all but two at the appointed spot promptly to time—a most unusual feat for College men. We were received at the Charter House by the Rev. Mr. Le Bas, the chaplain, who made us feel quite at home by telling us that he counted our Founder, Maurice, among his friends, and that he had also had the pleasure of speaking to Kingsley upon one occasion.   Thus we all settled down comfortably to a most interesting and chatty lecture upon the famous old buildings and their former inhabitants, during which it became an easy task to conjure up a picture of the Charterhouse monks entertaining their guests in the fine old oak dining hall in which we were seated, and to realize in succession the different occupants the old place had seen down to the present day.   Mr. Le Bas then took us into the chapel and other interesting parts ; and as one gazed down upon the quiet green playing field of the Merchant Taylors' boys, it was difficult to imagine that without was the noise and bustle of Smithfield Market.   After a casual inspection of the quarters of the Charterhouse pensioners, we visited the fine old Norman Priory Church, and Mr. Jacob gave us a sketch of its history.   After about half-an-hour's stay in the church, we made our way to the College, where Mrs. Robbie had prepared tea for the party, to which we all did ample justice. Then we repaired to the Coffee Room, and were again much interested in a discourse by Mr. Jacob upon what we had seen and upon old London History ; the quietness of the party told its own tale of the interest taken in his chat, and the many questions asked showed how keenly he had been followed.   An enthusiastic vote of thanks was given Mr. Jacob, and then the evening was devoted to the Musical Society's concert, everybody feeling perfectly satisfied with the outing, which had proved such a great success.

On June 15th, a party of fifty members visited St. Paul's Cathedral, when the Bishop of Stepney kindly conducted us over Wren's famous building. Commencing with a most interesting talk upon St. Paul's No. 1, he next passed to what is historically known as Old St. Paul's, and so on to the present edifice. He then, in his kind and courteous manner, ordered us forward at "quick march," stopping at the most interesting spots only. The development of empire was indicated by the chapel of the Order of St. Michael and St. George, recently inaugurated by the King, thus linking up the religious traditions of the past—over a few hundred years —with the present time, in the history and expansion of England and her colonies. Wellington's monument was referred to as being one of the few specimens of pure English monumental art in Great Britain. The wood carving of Grinling Gibbons and its excellent craftsmanship, the details of the reredos, the paintings under the dome, the design and complete symbolical composition of the present decorations, were all dilated upon; and it was explained that the new encaustic work alone had been the means of founding a small school of artists in England, so that we are no longer under the necessity of commissioning foreign artists for English work. Richmond's scheme of mosaic decoration of the small domes, ceilings, and panels was much admired by all, notwithstanding that the light was none too bright. We also visited the crypt and inspected the tombs of the great men who are buried there, including those of Nelson and Wellington. We next ascended to the whispering gallery, and when we were all quietly seated the attendant gave us his well-known weird little lecture, whilst we listened attentively with our ears held closely against the wall; more steps were then mounted to the Stone Gallery outside the dome, but the outlook was far too misty to permit of an extensive view being obtained. By this time the bell was ringing, calling us to the evening service, so we hurried downstairs to attend evensong, after which we repaired to the Chapter House for tea. Here the Bishop again joined us, and said a few kindly words about our College and its Founders—mentioning that "he himself had been brought up under the traditions of Maurice, Kingsley, aud Hughes "—to which Mr. Levinsohn appropriately replied, thanking him for his kindness in showing us round the Cathedral. Tea was then served, and after a visit to the chapter-room to inspect the pictures, we dispersed, all feeling we had spent a most happy afternoon together.

I conclude with a recommendation to our members who have recently written letters to the JOURNAL complaining of the difficulty experienced in making friends in the Common Room. These conducted outings are widely advertised in the College, and every member has an equal chance to join in them. If malcontents will accompany us, they will find plenty of men willing to talk to them; in any event they must do their part, whether they are sitting in quiet corners or out with a party. Let everyone come to the Garden Party on July 13th next, and join in the fun. All will be welcome.   H. K. RANDALL, *Hon. Secretary, G.R.C.*

FURNIVALL SCULLING CLUB.

THE Club's Annual Regatta was held on June 8th, and was favoured by a fine afternoon, and a large number of members were present. Results:— Men's Doubles—Richardson, Hoad, (Ingram, cox) beat Munro, Fisher, (Mowberry, cox). "Barker Cup," Mixed Doubles—F. Sammons, Miss E. Sewell, (C. Clarke, cox) beat W. Allen, Miss L. Skinner, (J. Sewell, cox). Rum-tums—J. Munro beat A. G. Fisher (2), and H. Mowberry (3). Girls' Fours—Miss R. Lock (stroke), N. Lansdell, E. Allen, E. Sewell, (W. Pettle, cox) beat Miss L. Skinner (stroke), A. Dewar, R. Skinner, M. Allen, (L. Ingram, cox). Men's Fours—Hoad (stroke) Allen, Sammons, Mowberry, (Pettle, cox) beat Munro (stroke), Owen, Mead, Fisher, (Ingram, cox) (2), and Williams (stroke), Thirkell, Howard, Richardson, (Sewell, cox) (3).

On June 15th, we pulled our annual race with the Polytechnic R. C. Our previous efforts in the "eight" having been unsuccessful, we this year reverted to the old conditions—sculling and rowing in "fours." Our men, Munro (stroke), Hoad, Fisher, Richardson, (Ingram, cox) won the race in fine style, and quite surprised even the ever sanguine Doctor.

H. S. HOWARD, *Hon. Secretary.*

COLLEGE NOTES.

THE Council held its usual meeting on May 28th, when the Report of the Executive Committee was received, containing the undermentioned records of College progress and work :—

Student and Class Entries.—Student and class entries this term are curiously parallel to those reported in the corresponding term of last year. In some repects that report could almost apply verbatim to the one now presented. Student entries, now, as then, have been so good that although the term has run only half its course, they are already greater than for the whole of the corresponding term last year, and again, the total entry shows an increase of ten per cent. There is, however, one very important difference. Last year the improvement was due solely to the large number of new students who joined in April: this year the total of new students is less by one-third than at this time last year, but the loss in new has been more than made up for by the larger number of old students who have re-joined. The latter is a more satisfactory result, as it shows that a larger proportion of the students are completing their full three terms' course.

The comparative entries are as follows :—

	1906.	1907.		1906.	1907.
Preparatory	27	12	Italian	8	16
Algebra	18	17	Latin	17	22
Ambulance	12	14	Law	18	10
Arithmetic	28	37	Astronomy	0	12
Art	50	86	Botany	15	10
Book-keeping	28	33	Building Construction	20	33
Economics	0	12	Electricity	49	75
English Composition	19	8	Geology	6	12
English Literature	13	14	Machine Drawing	0	26
Euclid	2	4	Physiology	8	12
English for Foreigners	13	7	Singing	10	54
French	81	114	Spanish	22	15
Geography	3	4	Esperanto	0	8
German	42	41	Shorthand	69	86
Grammar	11	15	Violin	14	14
Greek	6	13	Chemistry	15	45
History	0	5			
			Totals	622	886
			Student Entries	370	407

Classes and Teachers.—This term there have been rather more changes in the teaching staff than is usual. The Rev. B. H. Alford's Sunday class ceased at Easter, according to custom; Mr. Scott's class ended with the completion of its second term, as also did Mr. Iselin's and Mr. McGillivray's Law classes, Mr. Jones's Algebra, Mr. Slater's Arithmetic, Mr. Hilton Young's Grammar, Mr. Thompson's Practical Mathematics, and

Mr. Torrington's German. The Arithmetic class has been undertaken by Mr. J. R. Jones, the son of a former student of the College, and the German by Mr. J. B. West. In addition to these, the College welcomes new teachers in the persons of Mr. R. N. Bailey, who has undertaken a Latin Class, and Messrs. Trott and Martin, who teach Shorthand.

The two courses of London University Extension lectures, held here under the auspices of the London County Council, have been completed since the last report. The course on Architecture, for which Mr. Banister Fletcher was the teacher, proved the more attractive of the two. This secured an entry of 44, and an average attendance of 31. The History course, the first ten lectures of which were taken by Mr. G. M. Trevelyan, and the subsequent 15 by Mr. H. Travis Mills, only obtained an entry of 31, and an average attendance of 14. The London County Council have decided to try the College again as a centre next session for two more courses, and with the longer notice and ampler opportunity for advertisement, it is hoped that of these greater advantage may be taken.

Very little use indeed has been made of the College in the day time. In the second week of March last, the London County Council Education Committee inspected the College with a view to its being used for the purpose of a Secondary Day School for Girls. The arrangements of the College having been found suitable, the County Council asked upon what terms and conditions the accommodation required by them would be granted. The Executive Committee, having taken into consideration the fact that the London County Council have made the College an annual maintenance grant of £500, suggested certain terms and conditions, upon which negotiations are now taking place, and they hope to be able to report at the next Council meeting that an agreement has been arrived at.

Various social functions were noticed in the Report, which referred to our recent dramatic performance thus :— On Wednesday evening, May 1st, a most delightful performance of W. S. Gilbert's fantastic comedy *Engaged* was given by Miss Lowes Dickinson and a party of her friends. The scenery was designed and painted by some members of the College Art Class under the superintendence of their teacher, Mr. R. W. Wilkinson, and of Mr. Silk, the senior art student; the lighting was arranged by Messrs. Denton and Beach, the teacher and demonstrator respectively of the Electricity class; and College men acted as stewards, whilst Mr. Marks sold programmes. The performance attracted a large audience, who much enjoyed the excellent acting. Everybody seemed delighted—the audience with the actors; the actors with the audience and with the manner in which the scenery had been painted and the stage arranged.   After paying all expenses, a sum of £44 6s. 1d. remained, which, with Miss Dickinson's approval, has been handed to the Building Committee towards decorating some part of the College.   The Executive Committee have expressed by a formal vote of thanks their deep gratitude to Miss Lowes Dickinson, for the large amount of thought and trouble in which this entertainment must have involved her, and for the substantial and useful addition which the proceeds have made to the Building Fund.

Honorary Members.—Acting with the power conferred by the resolution passed at the Council Meeting of February 26th last, the Executive Committee have elected the Rev. H. S. Beard and Messrs. W. Pett Ridge and W. E. Church as Honorary Members of the College.

Mr. Reginald J. Mure moved, and Dr. Furnivall seconded, the following resolution, which was carried unanimously :— " That the Council desire to express to Mr. W. D. Caröe, the architect of the College, their high appreciation of the attention and skill which he has devoted to the design and construction of the new building, and of the remarkable success which, notwithstanding the restrictions unavoidably imposed by the financial position of the College, he has achieved in the work, whether regarded from an artistic or a practical point of view "— and it was also resolved to communicate the resolution to Mr. Caröe.

A recommendation, made by the Executive Committee, that the Thursday and Saturday evening lectures should in future begin at 8.30 p.m., was adopted.

We are delighted to hear that our Principal, Professor A. V. Dicey, K.C., has received the honorary degree of D.C.L. This honour was formally conferred upon him at a big meeting in the Sheldonian Theatre, Oxford, on the 26th ult., when a number of learned and distinguished men were present, and Mr. Sidney Lee was among those on whom degrees were conferred.   This College delegated Duchesne, Marks, and Torrington to represent it at the meeting.

The Board to promote the extension of University Teaching have issued their report upon the subject of "The History of Architecture," as taught at the Working Men's College centre, in the session for 1906—1907.   The lecturer, Mr. Banister Fletcher, stated that the weekly work was of a very high order, and that many of the students were architects' assistants and school teachers.   The examiner reported that there was a considerable knowledge of detail shown, combined with a clear grasp of principles; great pains had evidently been taken to master the subject thoroughly; the drawings showed spirit, and the style was vigorous, though somewhat crude. Six certificates were granted—four of merit, and two of special distinction. The latter were gained by Albert Lakeman and Henry G. Warren; the former by Benjamin C. Eastwell, Charles Morley, James A. G. Reeve, and Herbert A. Welch.

A College Teacher, reporting to the Director of his section, makes the following remarks on the subject of examinations, which are applicable to many of the classes :—

The only available method of measuring the success of an educational class such as ours is by examination results, and to get good results of such a kind you must have men working earnestly for the examination as an immediate end. Men will not do this unless they are compelled. I am sorry to say I have in my mind cases where students could have, perhaps, contributed to the ostensible success of the class by passing the examination, had they exerted the effort that remained dormant in them. In these cases, where internal compulsion, in the form of ambition, emulation, or love of work, is absent, it seems hard that time and material should be spent by the College without apparent return. If it could be managed without offence to the ideals of the College I am of opinion that a little external compulsion exam.-wards is desirable, as it undoubtedly is necessary.

Professor John Westlake, K.C., one of our founders, has presented to the College a portrait of himself, in response to an intimation made to the effect that the College would like to possess one, and Mrs. J. A. Forster has also sent one of her husband.

Our old friends, Messrs. R. H. Marks and Herbert Wilcockson have, between them, given two hat and coat stands to the Common and Coffee Rooms; and Dr. Furnivall has given three Indian cloths for decorating the Maurice Hall on festive occasions.

A capital portrait of Dr. Furnivall appeared in the May issue of *The World To-day* (Chicago), together with an appreciative article on the Doctor by F. M. Padelford, being the first of a series under the title of "Patriots who are not soldiers." Several other notices and pictorial representations of the Doctor and his Sculling Club girls have recently appeared in the papers. On one day, June 17th, the *Tribune, Daily News*, and *Daily Mirror* all published photographic illustrations of the lady crew of the sculling eight, in two of which they are depicted "manning" the boat, with sculls in hand, at the easy, and with Dr. Furnivall as cox. The Doctor has had blocks prepared of two of the photos taken by the Sports and General Co., and is sending us copies to enclose for the readers of the JOURNAL.

Under the heading "Thoughts on the Irish Council Bill," a letter of nearly a column in length appeared in the *Times* of June 8th, from the pen of the Principal.

In recognition of the benefits derived by her late son Frank Maslen Colton from the College, Mrs. Colton has given Five guineas to the Coffee Room Decoration Fund and Five guineas to the Building and Maintenance Fund, and has promised a guinea a year to the latter.

———

Writing from Foochow, China, on May 6th, H. J. Sceats says :—"The JOURNAL reaches me regularly, and I am always very interested in reading its contents. It is now only three years since I left London, but already I notice that several names which previously used to be continually mentioned have almost entirely disappeared. Please remember me very kindly to Torrington when you see him next, and tell him I shall never forget the way he helped me, when I had the distinction of being Secretary of the Debating Society, by opening debates when I had been disappointed by others. . . . I hope you will not fail to remember me very kindly to the Doctor when you see him next, also to Hopkins, Nye, Castell, Reglar, Harley, Aldridge, and any others who might remember me."

———

Thanks to Hayward, the *Citizens'* monthly dining parties have materialized. At the first meeting, on June 6th, seventeen College men sat down to their mid-day meal, and had the pleasure of meeting their friends and enjoying a chat, in the third floor front room at "Read's," in Cheapside (opposite Bennett's). The next meeting will be on Thursday, July 4th, at the same place, at 1.30 p.m., and all College members are invited to join the party.

———

Mr. Dent has secured a promise from Mr. W. T. Wilson, M.P., for West Houghton, to address a Trades' Union Conference on July 20th, and accordingly a Conference will be held at the College on that date. The arrangements are left in the hands of Mr. Dent and the Superintendent, and the delegates will be invited to take tea in the College.

———◆•◆———

GARDEN PARTY AND FIELD SPORTS.

THE Common Room Committee have arranged for a Garden Party and Field Sports to take place on Saturday, July 13th, at Wembley Park, to which all members of the College are invited to come and bring their lady friends. The Sports, which will begin at 3.30, will be held in front of the Polo Ground, and entries of both ladies and gentlemen for the various competitions will be taken on the spot. Prizes will be given to winners at the close of the Sports. Tea at 5 p.m. And to finish the day, a Concert will be held at 8 o'clock in the Pavilion, in the rear of the Grand Stand. Tickets, including tea and return railway fare from Baker Street, may be obtained (price 2s. each), in the Office, and from Balson, Flint, Hopkins, Melzer, Moore, Munro, Nye, Staal, Torrington, and

H. K. RANDALL, *Hon. Secretary.*

TANSLEY SWIMMING CLUB.

A TWO lengths' handicap took place at the Baths on April 30th, when 13 entered, Chappell, Gay, W. Hagerty, J. Hagerty, Barnett, Read, Fisher, R. Hagerty, Hurt, Seeley, Thomas, E. Hagerty and Wedderburn.

Results:—1st Heat—J. Hagerty (1 sec.) 1 ; Gay (2 secs.) 2 ; Chappell (26 secs.) 3 ; Time, 1 min. 14 secs.

2nd Heat—Fisher (13 secs.) 1 ; R. Hagerty (scratch) 2 ; Barnett (24 secs.) 3 ; Time 1 min. 12 secs.

3rd Heat—E. Hagerty (6 secs.) 1 ; Wedderburn (6 secs.) 2 ; Seeley (21 secs.) 3 ; Time 1 min. 13 secs.

The first two in each heat qualified for the final, which was held on May 28th, with this result : Fisher (13 secs.) 1 ; Wedderburn (6 secs.) 2 ; E. Haggerty (6 secs.) 3 ; Gay (2 secs.) 4 ; R. Hagerty (scr.) 5 ; Winner's time, 58¼ secs. The first two in the final receive medals. The handicaps worked out very well, considering the committee were not in a position to judge the members' qualifications, and the races resulted in some splendid swimming. The final was very exciting, and resulted in an extremely close finish, all the men finishing within two seconds of one another.

W. H. BARNETT, *Hon. Secretary.*

COFFEE ROOM DECORATION.

AT a Meeting of the Coffee Room Decoration Fund Committee held 10th June, 1907, it was reported that the fund stood at £100 0s. 9d.; and it was resolved that the Treasurers be authorized to hand the fund to the Superintendent, for the Executive Committee. The following recommendations were made to the Executive Committee :—(a) That the old lockers in the Coffee Room be cleared away. (b) That suitable cupboards be provided in the recess between the fireplace and the windows. (c) That the Executive Committee should form a Committee to carry out the decoration of the Room, and that Balson, Randall and Silk, members of the Decoration Committee, should serve thereon. (d) That, under the advice of Mr. Caröe, the architect, a competitive tender be invited for the work ; and (e) That the balance of the fund be handed to the Common Room Committee for furnishing the Room.

These recommendations have been adopted by the Executive Committee, who have formed a Committee to carry out the decorations, consisting of Marks, Dent, Bradgate, Pocock, and the members above mentioned.

The following further donations to the Fund, making up the £100 0s. 9d., have to be reported :—

	£	s.	d.		£	s.	d.
Tom Barnard	0	1	0	J. W. Roberts	0	2	6
J. W. McCauley	0	1	6	H. Sumner	0	2	0
H. C. Dumbrill	0	2	0	S. A. Sweetman	0	2	6
A. Lewis	0	10	0	A. W. Matthews	0	4	0
Miss Estall	0	2	6	Art Class and Sketching			
E. W. Jones	0	3	0	Club	0	19	6
J. G. Offer	0	1	0	Thos. Austin	1	0	0
A. Osborne	0	2	6	R. J. Poultney	0	1	0
Debating Society	1	1	0	O. Ray	0	10	0
H. W. Windsor	0	2	0	Mrs. Colton	5	5	0
H. V. Birrell				H. D. Marks	1	0	0
(Johannesburg)	0	5	0	Realized by Musical			
S. G. Pearce				Society's Concert on			
(Johannesburg)	0	5	0	June 1st	12	13	2
Miss Bertha Pocock	0	10	0	Collected in Box, etc., at			
J. P. Jones	0	5	0	that Concert	0	15	0
W. E. Miller	0	5	0	Mrs. George Tansley	0	5	0

MUSICAL SOCIETY'S CONCERT IN AID OF THE COFFEE ROOM DECORATION FUND.

THE Working Men's College Musical Society fully maintained its reputation at the Concert given on Saturday, June 1st, in aid of the above Fund. Its active members may well be proud of the achievements of that evening. The chair was taken by Ernest Reglar, who discharged his arduous duties with the necessary firmness, for encores were frequently demanded, but owing to the great length of the programme, could not be permitted until after all the scheduled items had been gone through. It should be specially mentioned that the stage of the Maurice Hall was greatly improved for concert purposes by the stage scenery, erected by the Art Class for the recent dramatic performance. It formed an appropriate setting for such songs as Jones's "Glorious Devon," and for A. E. Green's capital representation of "The Village Constable." At the piano, of course, was William Tarr ; and C. H. Perry acted as musical director, as well as in divers other capacities. We were indebted to the Misses M. Allen, A. Dewar, E. Lidington, and N. Moulden, for selling the programmes, whilst Nye, W. Hudson, Randall, and various other College men officiated as stewards. We were all sorry to learn that indisposition prevented our old friend Jastrzebski from coming to give us his inimitable "Rumpsey Bumpsey Bay," and that for a like reason Hammant was absent, so that his "So ho, Jolly Jenkin" had to be deleted. There were left, however, a score of other items, besides the chairman's speech, and the interval for refreshments, and all these served to carry us from 8 to 11 o'clock without a dull moment. Then came the encores, and Brodie accepted the invitation to give us a piano solo not on the programme. It speaks well of the Society that its whole strength was not exhausted, although twenty items were allotted to twenty different performers. In part I., we had the pleasure of hearing—song, "Land of Hope and Glory" (Elgar), F. E. Lawrence ; song, "Bust the Bugle," M. K. Field ; song, "The Old Green Isle" (Gordon Temple), E. W. Davis ; song, "Vanity Fair" (Clutsam), Miss Phœbe Craib ; trio. "I am so proud," from the *Mikado* (Sullivan), W. C. Jones, T. A. Paterson, and C. H. Perry ; recitations, "The uninvited guest" and "Liberty Jack," Miss Bessie Bromhall (Miss Reglar accompanying) ; song, "The fleeting years" (Edwin Green), Frank R. Webb ; song, "Glorious Devon" (German), W. C. Jones ; and song, "Dear Heart," Mrs. Mason Tarr.

The chairman's speech was short and to the point. He hoped £8 would be realized by the concert, and that would leave £12 more wanted. He proposed we should thank the Society and the artists performing, for the concert, and this we all did, right heartily.

Part II.— Monologue, "The Village Constable" (Chevalier), A. E. Green ; song, "A Corporal's Ditty," R. E. Tyler ; song, "April morn" (R. Batten), Miss Evelyne King, L.R.A.M. ; song, "Our Resterong" (Chevalier), F. J. Nield ; recitation, "Absolution," T. Barnard ; song, "On the rocky road to Dublin," H. C. Dumbrill ; song, "The Veteran's Song" (Stephen Adams), J. Pendle ; song, "When the heart is young" (Dudley Buck), Mrs. H. C. Dumbrill ; song, "The Witch behind the moon" (Weslyn and Albert), T. A. Paterson ; song, "What never?" from *H.M.S. Pinafore* (Sullivan), C. H. Perry.

The writer of this report is not a musical reporter or critic of any pretensions whatever, and what is printed below must be taken with all reserve accordingly, and allowance made for mistakes due to ignorance. Dumbrill, on his rocky road to Dublin, was simply splendid. How much better we like him in that piece than in any of the gory, bloodthirsty ballads of Kipling. We were very pleased to see Mrs. Dumbrill, introduced by the chairman as "an old friend under a new name," once more on the College platform. Miss King, with her trained voice and wide compass, was rightly one of those allowed an encore, "Annie Laurie," after the end of the second part. For perfection in the art of recitation, we should give the palm to Miss Bromhall and to Tom Barnard. The College is indeed fortunate to command the unstinted services of such accomplished artists as these,

Miss Bromhall successfully appeals to our emotions and quickly moves those feelings which are near the surface ; Barnard stirs us to the very depths. In coupling their names apart from that of A. E. Green, we in no way detract, nor wish to do so, from the praise due to him. His " get-up " as the Village Constable, and his acting and rendering of that worthy's part, were extremely fine. Both Green and Barnard gave encores by desire, the former, " Old Memories " and " Jimmy Law " ; the latter, " Rubinstein's piano." Why is it that Nield and Perry are both such favorites? We feel that they are deservedly so, and are inclined to think it is chiefly because they are men of character. Perry's look of contempt for the audience, because they failed to respond in the chorus to *Pinafore,* was delightfully killing. The many pieces demanded of him by way of encore would have provided a great part of an evening's entertainment, and in giving us a chorus verse, " An Englishman " he fooled us well again. In the matter of choruses, the audience had not got the hang of Field's " Bust the Bugle," nor of Tyler's " Corporal's Ditty " ; but they delighted to essay Nield's emphasized words " resterong," " garcon," " John," " on," etc. His final verse we may here repeat :—

> I'll sing you a verse on the Coffee Room,
>   And the things we hope to do ;
> For I think I'm right, when I say we might
>   Start the work in a month or two.
>   But we want a trifle more,
>   Say of five pounds—just four ;
> So remember in your will—we are wanting money still
>   For our Coffee Room.

> For our Coffee Room !—Won't it be grand
> To come and take stock—of a practical clock,
> Not like the one the students mock ;
>   And when matters are in hand
>   We want a *decent* stand,
> Not the feet and head—of a folding bed—
>   In our Coffee Room.

SECRETARIES' REPORT.

IN presenting our report of the results of the above Concert, we have to sincerely thank all those ladies and gentlemen who so kindly contributed their aid and support to our efforts. It is impossible for us to thank them individually, owing to numbers, but we feel greatly indebted to those College men who undertook the sale of the tickets, to those members and their lady friends who gave us such an excellent entertainment, and to the ladies of the Furnivall Sculling Club and their College Colleagues who helped in the capacity of stewards and programme sellers. All worked in such an unselfish and enthusiastic manner that it became impossible for the Concert to be otherwise than a great social and financial success. The sale of tickets provided £11 10s. 6d., programmes, £1 13s. 8d., and a sum of 10s. was given anonymously to Randall to partly recompense us for unsold tickets, which, by the way, were few. The total expenditure was £1 1s. for printing, thus leaving a balance of £12 13s. 2d., which has been handed over to Randall for the benefit of the Fund. The happy thought which induced Pocock to send round the collecting box realized 14s.

C. H. PERRY, } *Hon. Secretaries.*
H. E. NYE. }

The following announcement of the marriage of a grandson of our Founder, appeared in the papers last month :—

MAURICE—HOARE.—On May 30th, at the Parish Church, Hampstead, by the Rev. Canon Holmes, assisted by the Rev. J. V. Macmillan, Lawrence Colley Maurice, Royal Engineers, son of Major-Gen. Sir Frederick Maurice, K.C.B., R.A , to Kathleen Elsie Sophia, daughter of the late Rev. J. N. Hoare and Mrs. Hoare,

THE VAUGHAN LEICESTER WORKING MEN'S COLLEGE.

THE ceremony of laying the foundation stone of the new buildings to be erected in Great Central Street, Leicester, took place on Saturday, June 15th. The inscription on the stone, which was laid by the Mayor of Leicester, Sir Edward Wood, recorded the fact that it was a memorial to Canon David James Vaughan, who founded the College in 1862. The proceedings were opened by singing a hymn written by Tom Hughes ("O God of Truth"), followed by an address to the Mayor and various speeches, and concluding with three short prayers—the last one for the prosperity of the College, being the one composed for our own College by the Rev. J. Llewellyn Davies, one of our founders, for the like ceremony in July, 1905. To be able to maintain without official control the personal element and the spirit of brotherhood, which has always been the distinguishing feature of the College, the governors hope to increase their annual subscription list from £50 to £100. Mrs. David Vaughan takes the greatest interest in the College which her husband founded with so much success, and is always working for its benefit. The best thing we can wish for the Leicester Working Men's College is that the new buildings may prove as useful and look as handsome as our own buildings in the Crowndale Road, and that, as in our own case, their sphere of usefulness may be extended.

CORRESPONDENCE.

[Under this heading the Editor will be glad to publish letters of interest to past and present members, but he declines all responsibility for the views therein expressed.]

ANON.'S GRIEVANCE.

To the Editor of the WORKING MEN'S COLLEGE JOURNAL.

DEAR SIR,—It seems desirable that new men should have it forcibly brought to their notice, that they are expected to take part in the general life of the College, and not merely to come to the classes. Unless this is done, it may never strike them that this is the case. A paragraph to this effect might be inserted in all prospectuses in future.

DEBATES AND NON-SMOKERS.

I see from the report of the Debating Society that the members of that Society not only have free tobacco, but that they nearly smoked the said Society into a state of bankruptcy. I suppose the tobacco is issued to sooth the savage breast under fire from the opponent's battery. Now, as a non-smoker, I rise to ask what kind of soother is offered to non-smokers? I pause for a reply.—Yours truly,   SELIM.

THE WORKING MEN'S COLLEGE JOURNAL *is supported partly by Annual Subscribers living in different parts of the World, and partly by circulation among the Students and Members. Its success depends upon a regular demand, and to ensure this, the Editor would be glad if as many readers as can will become Subscribers. Subscription 2s. 6d. per annum, post free.*

LONDON: Printed by W. HUDSON & Co., Red Lion Street, High Holborn, and published at THE WORKING MEN'S COLLEGE, Crowndale Road, London, N.W.—July 1st, 1907.

The Working Men's · College Journal ·

sub: M

The Working Men's College · Crowndale Road · St Pancras · London · N·W· Founded in 1854 by the late Frederick Denison Maurice ·

Contents for

AUG.-SEP., 1907.

Shakespeare Studies
Oxford
    Commemoration
Mr. Scott's Class
Field Sports
College Notes
"Little Italy"
Club Notices

THE

𝔚orking 𝔐en's 𝔠ollege 𝔍ournal.

Conducted by Members of the Working Men's College, Crowndale Road, London, N.W.

Vol. X.—No. 174.   AUG.—SEPT., 1907.   PRICE TWOPENCE.

SHORT STUDIES IN SHAKESPEARE.

III.—THE BASIC ELEMENT OF CHARACTER.

N this paper we continue our study of the basic element of character, as found in Hamlet and in Prince Henry of Monmouth.

In the former of these two, we have an individual the underlying forces in whose career may be fitly likened to a subterranean fire, burning in a region of domestic disturbance ; burning fiercely, yet silently and ineffectually, until an accretion of fiery particles causes a deadly outburst, shattering the central fire with the little world around it, and leaving at the finish a dreary waste of dust and ashes.   The life-failure thus symbolized was due, primarily, to an unwonted sensibility of spirit, and an obsession of introspective and speculative thought ; the two together paralyzing Hamlet's power of action, and making him practically devoid of enterprise and resource.

It is this combination in his personality, of unique and lofty traits of character with inherent defects which, while not at all debasing, were fatal to success, that makes Hamlet a world's spectacle.   It is, too, this same paradoxical combination of characteristics that forms the main feature in the basic element of character we are concerned with ; and from it we get a clue as to the trail we are to follow, in our further pursuit of the subject.

In Henry of Monmouth, we undoubtedly have another and very different "mixture of earth's mould" from that we have just been considering.   The two characters are similar in one respect, and one respect only—that is, in the possession of an essentially distinguished personality ; but in active qualities and mental constitution, what a gulf divides them !   Hamlet's defects of character are paradoxical, innate, and in a sense, venial ; while Henry's are anomalous and foreign to his nature, involving such defects of conduct as to be not easily condoned.   Thus, in the play of *Henry IV.*, we see a solicitous parent suffering distraction through the wantonness of his son, in whom he discerns princely qualities, but whom he deems to be his "nearest and dearest enemy." So that he thinks that it had been better for his peace of mind to have had a changeling, upon whom to centre his affections, rather than such a son. [By the bye, is it not true, that in the almost-wished-for changeling, Hotspur, we have a character who runs Henry very close for supremacy in our regard?] Far from moving " about in worlds not realized," or "sitting in the clouds with the wise," Henry lives in a too literal association with flesh and blood—the former exhibited in the questionable companionships of his vagabond life, and the latter, happily, marked by deeds worthy of a valorous prince.

The character of Henry cannot be regarded as an original creation, nor is there anything connected with it to move our wonder ; except it be that such a high-souled prince could have descended so low as to frequent the notorious " Boar's Head," and find recreation there in the company of such a set of reprobates. Yet another cause for wonder is, that he could wallow in such filth and not be contaminated by it ; this of course being a testimony to the strength and purity of his character. In regard to the ugly feature in his life just referred to, it is difficult to form a precise opinion as to its meaning. Nor does the manner in which Henry himself refers to it help us at all. At a time when he was in the midst of the stew, he tells his confidant, Poins, that he is intentionally indulging in such loose behaviour in order that, when he does become King, the contrast between the life he has been leading and the life he will then lead, will heighten the glory of his reign. At another time and under similar circumstances, he again unbosoms his mind to Poins, and speaking in a different strain, tells him that he could be sad, and " sad indeed," at causing so much pain to his sick father. But later still, when he has reached the mark of his ambition, he refers to his old life as a bad dream which he now despises, and would have the " tutor and feeder " of his riots banished and not come near him on pain of death.

From the foregoing testimony, we are led to conclude that the vices Henry besmirched himself with did not really appeal to him, and that he may have had an ulterior motive in thus committing himself. At the same time, is it not difficult to believe that he was so mean and callous as intentionally to dull his reputation as a prince and a son, in order to satisfy a morbid craving after an ill-gotten glory? For indeed, from the evidence of his valour and generosity we get in the course of the play, and especially from the sincere contrition expressed by him to his dying father, and his noble bearing towards those who had reason to fear his displeasure when he gained untrammeled power, we are bound to recognize his worth, and to read his true disposition in the memorable request made by him to his brothers, " Let me but bear your love, I'll bear your cares."

And now, coming to the point as to whether there is a basic element of character in Prince Henry, as presented by Shakespeare, we would remark that such an element may be, in its nature, either subjective or objective. In Hamlet it is the former; but in the case of Henry it must, if it exist at all, be objective. For we do not attach any importance to Prince Henry's thoughts as such, but only as they express his life, or elucidate for us his aims and motives. The basic element must, therefore, be sought for in his objective existence—in his personal life and achievements.

In our previous study of this subject, we arrived at the conclusion that, given an individual with a vocation, such individual must necessarily possess a basic element of character. It is therefore relevant to our purpose to ask the question— Did Prince Henry have a vocation? Well, the answer to this query must be in the affirmative; for he had a vocation to be a right royal King, just as much as Hamlet had to think supremely, or Prospero to right the wrong : and he realized it. At any rate Shakespeare makes it appear that he did; and for a man to have had such a vocation and to have realized it, he must have been a genius—with aberrations such as are not infrequently met with. Thus, we have reason to believe that in actual life, men of genius, when under the spell of inspiration, are carried out of themselves whither they wot not, and thus get into situations and achieve or perpetrate things otherwise quite unaccountable. Now, may not this example of cause and effect, working under strange conditions, explain—to some extent at least—the enigma of Henry's course of life, in which he again and again touched a debasing depth of English society, pursuing the uneven tenor of his way, without coming to any permanent harm?

It must be admitted that this conclusion, valid though it may be, was really not looked for at the outset of our inquiry. If it be objected that it does not stand on all fours with the facts and ethics of the case, it may at any rate be urged that it errs on the side of charity towards one who, as we have seen, came to repent of his misdoings, and did his best to atone for them.

We have thus cursorily examined two quite diverse aspects of this basic element of character, and have specially dwelt upon the bearing of the same on the lives of two contrasted individuals. We have found the theory of its existence valuable, in enabling us to arrive at certain conclusions respecting the relations of cause and effect in their careers, which otherwise we might have entirely failed to reach.

In concluding this paper, we purpose touching upon the subject of the character of Falstaff, especially as it is related to that of Hamlet. Falstaff is undoubtedly one of Shakespeare's original creations, and is in that respect equal in degree, although not in kind, with Hamlet. The particular thing that Falstaff stands for—that is, the supreme embodiment of jest—is so powerfully and effectively expressed, that there is nothing elsewhere to compete with it. Undoubtedly Falstaff has a vocation to be the world's jester, and thus he must be said to possess a basic element of character. It seems almost absurd to class Falstaff with Hamlet as an intellectual ; but there is that quality of elemental power in his wit and humour which compels us to do so. For it is innate, spontaneous, pregnant, and irresistible ; in a word, it may be said that, in a suitable environment, it creates an atmosphere so charged with jest that nothing incompatible with it can survive its presence. This mention of suitable environment suggests the query, as to whether there are any limitations to his capacity for jesting— that is, in regard to place or company ; and the correct answer would appear to be,—No. For, from what we see of him in diverse situations in the play with which we are concerned, it must be concluded that, in season and out of season, he could be no other than a jester ; that he could not even by accident stumble into sober sense ; but that such sanity and wisdom as he possessed had to be expressed in a characteristic jest. It is a moot point as to how far he was dependent upon the inevitable " sack " for the essence of his humour. No doubt a plenitude of that beverage bedewed the soil in which the contagion grew ; it tended to intensify the flow of wit, if it did not clarify it.

In exhibiting Henry in a penitent mood, Shakespeare hit Falstaff very hard. It is strange that the shock of rude surprise the discredited knight met with at the hands of Henry should have had the effect of putting an end to his existence. He must, in spite of his coarseness, have been extremely sensitive of his reputation ; at any rate, it was chagrin at the loss either of his prestige or his friend that broke his heart. But Shakespeare could not forget him even amid more stirring scenes, and the last view he gives us of the dying jester softens our heart towards him, and we are glad to know that towards the last the innocent days of his childhood came back to him, and that " 'a babbled of green fields." G. S.

MR. SCOTT'S CLASS.

Mr. John Scott is perhaps the most extraordinary—using the word literally, as meaning beyond the ordinary—teacher in the College. The diversity of his subjects is magnificent. He is equally at home with physiography, chemistry, or geology, and with literature ; with grammar or composition, and with art. He is a teacher of teachers—his methods are refreshing, and calculated to widen the mind. His reports on his work are also refreshing. From that on his last series of class lectures on Greek Sculpture, English and Foreign Painting, and Engraving, we take the following excerpts :—

AIMS.—(After setting out the syllabus) I hoped to get men desiring an intelligent knowledge of *elementary* art, and to help them somewhat in making use of and finding joy in the art collections at hand, and especially in the minor (?) arts of etching, mezzotint, wood and steel engraving, and modern methods of illustration and reproduction, because of their value as art and their commonness and cheapness. I was anxious to do something to encourage an *every-day* appreciation of beauty and art—at home, in magazines and periodicals, in shop-windows, streets, sky, walks, in their own collections, *e.g.*, wood engraving, and in short frequent leisurely visits to galleries, that they might "live" with masterpieces.

METHOD.—To take a typical example of the artist, have a cast or repro: duction large enough to be seen by all from blackboard, or smaller ones to each member of the class, and to *exhaust* it, get *from it* the whole of its art ; and making it the basis or centre for all comments on the artist's characteristics and power, to get at his point of view.

Then to draw attention to, comment upon, exhibit, and talk about other works ; particularly those selected for special study at the British Museum, National Gallery, or South Kensington Museum ; examples, text books passed round. At end of lesson, informal talks, discussions, having-it-out.

THE CLASS.—Some of the best and longest standing men of the College— doubtless their presence was largely loyalty to me, and the attempt at higher work—a beautiful though pathetic thing. Many others new to the College, but of the kind the College wants—several, all I think, distinct acquisitions.

All were keen, well, often curiously, read. Many for years reading best works on Art, and showing a familiarity with such, and works of art and *minutiæ* of technical processes, quite appalling, and to a teacher unacquainted with Working Men's College classes most disturbing ; they had also attended many courses on art, or were members of the University Extension class on Architecture, and even artists (*e.g.*, Mr. Hertford). They were exceedingly kind, friendly, loyal, and took with delightful good humour my many obvious amateurish flounderings. I frequently said, with patent sincerity, though only to their frank amusement and kindly dissent, the class was of all my College frauds the biggest, and I should end a sadder *and* wiser man. Their knowledge of art, or at least of many sections, was so intimate, first-hand, and of long standing, that we ought to have changed places. My consolation is that I solemnly warned them at the outset that the class was only for elementary beginners, and at the end of first term that it was a manifest delusion. But they elected to start, and afterwards to continue. So I have an "absolution" for the Vice-Principal and the Recording Angel. And the title "Literature and Art," was a stroke of genius. When the art was bad, I said I was dealing with the literary side, and *vice versa*, though sometimes both were bad.

SUCCESS.—Being at least for me a pioneer course, and one I had not dabbled in before to any extent, it meant enormous preparation. I think worthy and useful work was done in Botticelli, Rembrandt, M. Angelo, Raphael, Perugino, Velasquez, Fra Angelico, Correggio, Da Vinci, F. Hals, V. Dyck, Holbein, Reynolds, Gainsborough, Parthenon frieze pediments, Phigaleian frieze, Frieze of Temple of Nike Apteros, Laocoon, Praxiteles, Demeter and Persephone, Venus, Archaic Greek School, M. Angelo, Wood Engraving, Etching and Mezzotint and Line, Process line and half tone, Colour Printing, Japanese Colour Blocks, Impressionism.

LESSONS LEARNED.—1. Such a class a most desirable one for the College.

2. The best work was done when the lesson was the *most concrete*, that is when no statement was made unless there and then clearly illustrated by the picture or cast exhibited, or it arose out of the exhibit ; and when we had good material and enough for individual examination, to test and see the truth or falsity of every comment of the lecturer.

3. With such material, the method of exhaustive treatment, and centring the artist and his work in a masterpiece, is I think the best.

4. A possible method containing the gain of a *lantern* lecture, without its objections, (to me) so serious as to make most of them almost valueless.

OXFORD COMMEMORATION,
JUNE 26th, 1907.

AMONGST the many distinguished men whom the University of Oxford delighted to honour, and had chosen as worthy of the high distinction of a doctor's degree, were our Principal, Professor Dicey, and two old friends of the College —Mr. Sidney Lee, also a great friend of our Vice-Principal, and Canon Scott Holland. In order to mark the satisfaction and the interest of the College in the event, the Executive Committee sent the Superintendent and two of its members as delegates to represent the College at the Commemoration. Tickets of admission to the function having been duly applied for and secured, the three representatives, who rightly regarded themselves as much honoured and favoured by being entrusted with such a duty, presented themselves at the south-door of the Sheldonian Theatre at 10.45, to find it packed with ladies, University graduates and undergraduates ; but they were fortunate enough to get inside the door, from whence they were able to see the whole of the procession as it entered and left, and also to enjoy the fresh air from the outside. The Chancellor, Lord Curzon, did his part well, with dignity and ease, his face frequently relaxing into a smile at some telling interjections from the undergraduates in the gallery. Among those on whom degrees were conferred besides the Principal, Mr. Sidney Lee, and Canon Scott Holland, were the Duke of Connaught, the Prime Minister, the Lord Chief Justice, the Speaker, Sir Edward Grey, Sir Evelyn Wood, Dr. Butler, of Trinity, Cambridge, General Booth, S. L. Clemens (Mark Twain), Rudyard Kipling, and others. The Chancellor, in the case of the Principal, asked :
" Placetne Venerabili Convocationi ut in Virum Illustrissimum,
" Albertum Venn Dicey, Artium Magister, Baccalaureum Civilis
" Legis, Collegii Omnium Animarum Socium, Juris Anglici
" Professorem Vinerianum, gradus Doctoris in Jure Civili con-
" feratur honoris causa ? Placetne vobis, Domini Doctores ?
" Placetne vobis, Magistri ? " To which question the Venerable Convocation in this case and in all the others gave an affirmative answer by acclamation, and the degrees were conferred. After the presentation of the Principal by Dr. Goudy, Regius Professor of Civil Law, the Chancellor addressed the following words to him :
" Vir eloquentissime, in forma et consuetudine nostræ civitatis
" versate, nec non Hiberniæ domi retinendæ acerrime adsertor,
" ego auctoritate mea et totius Universitatis admitto te ad gradum
" Doctoris in Jure Civili honoris causa." After the ceremony, which lasted for three hours, the College representatives proceeded to Balliol College, where they found Mr. Louis Dyer, a friend and contemporary of Lucas, waiting at the gate to receive them. Mr. Dyer introduced them to Mr. Urquhart, a don and tutor of the College, and an American Professor from

Philadelphia. Immediately after getting to Mr. Urquhart's rooms at Balliol, the Principal, clothed in all the glory of his Doctor's robes and wearing the quaint beef-eater hat, came smiling radiantly to bid them welcome to Oxford, and to tell them how pleased he was to see them. They saw many things of interest in Mr. Urquhart's rooms, where they discussed a good luncheon, cigarettes, and various subjects, English and American. Mr. Dyer, who all through showed them the greatest attention and kindness, conducted them over Balliol and Trinity. They were much struck by the portrait of Jowett to be seen in the Fellows' Common Room at Balliol. Naturally Balliol has a special interest for Working Men's College men, as being the Principal's, Lucas's, and Moore's College. Trinity is the College that attracts them most at Cambridge, Balliol at Oxford. After a call on a former secretary, Mr. C. C. Ord, and a tea at Miss Arnatt's in the " High," they returned to London, feeling they had been highly honoured, and as proud of it as any of those on whom degrees had been conferred.

◆•◆•◆

LUBBOCK FIELD CLUB.

On June 9th the club started from Hatfield, and wandered north by Woodhall Farm and Attamore Hall to Tewin. Here a series of halts took place, first to avoid a heavy shower, secondly to examine the ruins of Lady Grimston's tomb, and thirdly to partake of lunch in one of the Herts Public House Trust's establishments. The line of route then lay across the common, through several woods, to Bulls Green and Woolmer Green, where the main road was crossed. Mardley Heath was examined in spite of threatening notice boards, and then the expedition turned south through Danesbury to Welwyn. A heavy shower broke over us while we were at tea, but cleared off before we started our homeward journey. After a spell of road work, we turned off by Brocket Park to Lemsford Mill, where we encountered more rain, which continued to fall at intervals until we were safe in Hatfield Station. The country visited was very pretty, but too highly cultivated to produce much of exceptional interest. A big show of wood pimpernels was seen, a lot of Bear's Garlic in fruit, one or two spotted orchids in bud, and a few Algæ.

On June 22nd, a joint trip to the Chislehurst Caves was arranged with the Common Room Committee, and a party of thirty-three turned up, six of whom were ladies. We reached Chislehurst at 3 o'clock, and, after a couple of hours on the Common, had tea before commencing on the great object of the expedition. The "Caves" are long galleries driven through the chalk, a few feet below the overlying Sands and Gravel, but sometimes as much as 130 feet below the ground above. They communicate with the surface now and again by "Dene Holes." Of these, two were open, but we were unable to inspect them owing to recent rain and consequent mud. The distance covered in the round to the inner workings is stated to be four to five miles, and in our case the journey occupied two hours. The galleries seem to ramify in all directions, and in most cases were sufficiently lofty to enable us to stand upright. Here and there we encountered heaps of broken flints, and our guide told of stone weapons and gun flints found from time to time. At one spot we were shown a well about 50 feet deep in the floor of the passage, while recesses were described as Druid's altars, treasure chambers, priests' rooms, and so forth. The guide displayed with great pride a fossil sea urchin and the vertebrum of an

Icthyosaurus, also the scratches left by some imprisoned animal. He stated that the passages were supposed to extend to Eltham, but exploration had been stopped by a fall of the roof. Apart from the open Dene Holes, we only encountered water in two places, and the air was everywhere fresh and pure. The temperature was about 50°, which seemed decidedly cool in contrast with the air outside. The galleries near the entrance are lighted by electric lamps, and at one point a small stage had been erected; but further in, the lamps we carried were very necessary. The floors of the passages were mostly covered by sand, but here and there were very rough with great blocks of chalk lying about. The caves extend under the greater part of the Common and the grounds of Camden House. On leaving the workings the party divided, some returning at once to town, while the others waited for the 10.9 train.

The following morning two of the explorers, together with Britton and Turner, reached Amberley at 10.50. It was a beautiful day, bright, with a strong breeze from the sea. Towards the evening the sky became overclouded, and finally a sharp shower fell, but as it was accompanied by a beautiful rainbow we were not upset thereby. On leaving the station, we skirted the big chalk pit and climbed Amberley Mount, where we were rewarded by a magnificent view, including the Isle of Wight, Chichester Spire, Littlehampton, Selsey Bill, Hascombe Hill, Leith Hill, and the chalk pits at Betchworth, Reigate, and Oxted. After comparing notes with a local worthy, we proceeded along the ridge to Rackham Hill, and descended the steep north slope to the wood above Springhead, where we lunched. The climb back was a stiff job, and we reached the summit near some big earthworks not marked on the map. At Kilhurst Hill we turned south west, and skirted Perry Hill to Burphan, passing more ancient terraces on the way. At Burphan the chalk cliff forms a curious promontory, the village end of which is strongly fortified by an ancient mound. While waiting for tea, we inspected the church, in one of the transepts of which is a beautiful Norman arch. Tea disposed of, we walked by road and path, following the river and the striking chalk cliffs, back to Amberley, where we caught the 7.14 train.

We found eight species of orchid in various stages of growth, and were all of opinion that a finer display of the Fragrant Orchis could not be imagined.

Next outing—August 11th, Excursion to the Buntingford country. Take excursion ticket to Rye House, 1s. 9d. Train leaves Liverpool Street at 9.56. Provide lunch.　　　　　　　　　　　　　J. HOLLOWAY, *Hon. Secretary.*

W.M.C. DEBATING SOCIETY.

THE Annual General Meeting of this Society was held in the Common Room on Tuesday, the 23rd of April, and a well-filled room marked the occasion of the final meeting of the season. Our President, Mr. Lupton, took the chair. The minutes of the previous annual meeting having been read and confirmed, the Secretary proceeded to read the Report, which was adopted as drawn. The funds of the Society were considered, and Mr. Randall's motion that £1 1s. should be voted to the Coffee Room Decoration Fund was carried. A donation of 10s. was also voted to Mrs. Robbie.

Mr. B. P. MOORE introduced the motion standing in his name: "That it would be to the interest of the College for the society to hold occasional public debates, similar to those held at the Passmore Edwards' Settlement." This suggestion, however, did not meet with approval, and it was rejected by 21 votes to 10.

The election of officers then took place for the following year. Mr. A. E. Homewood was elected to fill the office of President; Mr. C. F. W. Mead, Vice-President; and Mr. A. J. White, Secretary. The following were elected to serve as committee-men: Messrs. Cash, Hayward, Howard, Munro, Staal, and Sweeting.

Mr. B. P. MOORE proposed a warm vote of thanks to Mr. Lupton and Mr. Mead, which was carried by the meeting with much heartiness, and to which those gentlemen briefly responded.

In accordance with time-honoured custom, the surplus tobacco of the Society was put up for auction, and, as auctioneer, our President was seen to much advantage. Flourishing a one-time jam jar before him, he enlarged upon and extolled the qualities of the contents thereof with great effect. He called to mind the fact that he was fortunate enough to secure the surplus stock of last year's sale, and as—with the judicious application of a small piece of potato—he still had some left, he could personally testify to the wonderful lasting powers of the brand in question. The booty was eventually carried off by Messrs. Hepburn and Nye for 5½d. and 6½d. respectively. At this the meeting closed. C. F. W. MEAD, *Hon. Secretary.*

FINANCIAL STATEMENT, 1906—1907.

Receipts.	£	s.	d.	*Payments.*	£	s.	d.
Balance forward	2	6	2	Stamps on 96 Circular Post			
26 Subscriptions	1	6	0	Cards (October) ...	0	4	0
Sale of surplus tobacco ...	0	1	0	Pipe and cigarette tobacco	0	3	11
				Stationery	0	1	10
				Locker rent	0	2	6
				Postages	0	7	5
				Donation, Mrs. Robbie ...	0	10	0
				Donation, Coffee Room			
				Decoration Fund ...	1	1	0
				Balance	1	2	6
	£3	13	2		£3	13	2

Audited and found correct.—LEONARD POCOCK, July 8th, 1907.

—◆•◆•◆—

TRADE UNIONISTS AND EDUCATION.

A CONFERENCE was held at the College on Saturday, July 20th, by delegates of Trade Unions and others, to discuss the above subject, when our Vice-Principal, Mr. Lionel Jacob, presided; and among those who took part were Mr. T. W. Wilson, M.P. (West Houghton), Mr G. P. Gooch, M.P. (Bath), Mr. J. J. Dent, Mr. T. F. Hobson, and Mr. A. S. Lupton.

In welcoming the delegates, Mr. JACOB said that the average Englishman filled up his life, when not earning his living, with sport. Delightful though it was to watch the young people enjoying their cricket, watching sport took up too much of an old man's time. The study of history, economics, and law, as pursued at this College, would enable a man to become a better and wiser citizen.

Mr. GOOCH said that the study of economics was essential to a proper understanding of home politics and of colonial questions as well. Without it, a man could not intellectually utilize his vote at the General Election. To-day, the working-man had control of the destinies of England, as was evidenced by the Colne Valley election; and it was his duty to make himself worthy of his powers, accompanied as they were by the new and sacred responsibility of enlarging his intellectual horizon so as to understand fully the economical, social, and financial problems of the government of great cities, and of a still greater country and empire.

Mr. WILSON thought present-day literature did not imbue the young man with a desire to develop his education. The College should take into consideration the adverse circumstances in which working-men were sometimes situated, and be careful not to aim over their heads.

At the close of the Conference, tea was provided by the College, after which the delegates were shown over the building by some of our members.

COLLEGE NOTES.

THE College vacation, which began on June 30th, continues until September 23rd, on which day the October term will commence. It is proposed to inaugurate the session by a concert and social meeting in the Common Room, on Saturday, September 21st.

At the Council Meeting on July 16th, a letter was read from Mr. Caröe, acknowledging the resolution passed at the previous meeting, which he said gave him much pleasure. He hoped that his connection with the College would not terminate with the completion of the building.

The Report of the Executive Committee was presented as usual, and from it we make the following extracts:—

Examinations.—College examinations this year have been somehow very difficult to arrange, and have, on the whole, taken place somewhat later than usual, so that fewer results are to hand. The entries have been fair, but, with the exception of the Ambulance Class, no set of students showed any great enthusiasm to submit themselves for examination. A large number of students did, it is true, enter for the various examinations conducted by the Board of Education, but of these a considerable number did not sit. As for certain of these Government examinations there is an entrance fee, which the College has hitherto paid, your Committee have drawn the attention of these students to that fact, and have taken steps to prevent the occurrence of this laxity in the future. For the Chamber of Commerce and Society of Arts examinations, for both of which this College is a centre, the entries were very small. (The examination results will be given in our next issue.)

October Programme.—The arrangements for next session are in a very forward state. The term programme is almost complete, and every lecture Saturday but one in the first term has been filled up. Promises to give Saturday evening lectures have been made by Sir Charles Bruce; Drs. Flett, Parkyn and Saleeby; Miss Spurgeon, and Messrs. Kirkman and Mackail. The Principal, Professor Kirkaldy, and Messrs. Rait and Rowntree have promised to lecture on Thursdays; whilst in the London University Extension series, Mr. Dudley Heath will lecture on Tuesdays and Dr. J. W. Slaughter on Fridays. The list of classes will remain much as before, with the important additions of classes in Plane and Practical Geometry, Sound, Light, and Heat, and an additional class in Chemistry. The opening meeting next session will be of a more domestic character than heretofore. Instead of a public concert in the Maurice Hall, it has been decided to try a smoking concert and social gathering in the Coffee and Common Rooms. The

Vice-Principal and Mr. Lucas have promised to speak, and to give a special welcome to those new students who will have joined during the preceding enrolment week. To each of these, as he joins, a printed invitation card will be given. One other new feature will appear on the term programme in the shape of the announcement of an annual "Marks" Prize, which will be awarded to the writer of the best essay on some subject to be formally announced at the beginning of the session.

Library.—The following books have been presented to the Library :—

By Mrs. Colton, various books belonging to her late son—by E. J. Turner, "Modern Buildings, their planning, construction and equipment"—by Messrs. Jordan & Sons, Ltd., Gore Browne and Jordan's "Handy Book on the formation, management, and winding-up of Joint Stock Companies" and three other works, all published by them—by Mrs. Winkworth, "Cobden as a Citizen"—by the author, "The Licensed Trades," E. A. Pratt—by T. F. Hobson, "Survey of London" (2 vols.), Stowe—by the Vice-Principal, "F. D. Maurice," Masterman—by Miss Cooper, Three Historical Works.

Other gifts to the College have been—two hat and coat stands from Messrs. Marks and Wilcockson ; a portrait of Mr. J. A. Forster from Mrs. Forster, a portrait of Professor Westlake from his wife, an engraving from Mr. F. J. Nield, and a collection of butterflies made by the late J. T. Stephen from his sister Mrs. Bell. The Coffee Room Decoration Committee have succeeded in collecting £100 towards the cost of carrying out the proposed scheme, whereby the Coffee Room will be decorated and panelled in the same manner as the Common Room. Mr. Caröe is now engaged in obtaining estimates for carrying out the work, with a view to its being completed before the beginning of next term.

Social Functions.—The Saturday afternoon excursions referred to in the last report have been a great success. That on June 1st, conducted by the Vice-Principal, to the Charter House and St. Bartholomew's Church, attracted its full complement of thirty, whilst a party of fifty visited St. Paul's a fortnight later. To the Rev. Le Bas and the Bishop of Stepney, respectively, hearty thanks are due for the trouble they took to make these outings so instructive and pleasurable.

On June 26th, the Principal received from the University of Oxford, the Honorary Degree of D.C.L. The Executive Committee, on the suggestion of Mr. Lucas, sent Messrs. Marks and Torrington and the Superintendent, as a deputation to attend the Encaenia at which the degree was conferred. After the ceremony these delegates were entertained by Mr. Louis Dyer to lunch at Balliol College, the Principal in his new robes looking in to greet them, whilst on his way to other celebrations connected with the festival.

The Sketching Club were entertained by Mr. Pocock at his house on Saturday, June 28th.   The party arrived some three hours late in a rather moist condition, after having been caught in one of the heavy rain storms which have not been infrequent of late.   The Cycling Club were more fortunate on Saturday, July 6th, as the weather allowed them to accept the hospitality of Mr. Denmead at South Myms without any such unpleasant experience to mar their enjoyment.   The Cycling Club, at the invitation of Mr. John Fotheringham, had a most enjoyable outing at Fawkham on Sunday, July 7th.

Dr. Furnivall asked if the Oxford Dictionary, of which a considerable portion is already in the Library, could not be completed so far as published.   It was agreed that the work was one which ought to be there, if possible, and the Vice-Principal undertook that the matter should be brought before the Librarian.

The report of the chairman of the Appeal Committee was read by him and adopted.

Mr. Caröe, being engaged on the work of renewing the sculpture and facing of the Bell Tower, Canterbury Cathedral, has very kindly invited a party of College members down to see the work, whilst the scaffolding is still up.   The visit will probably be arranged for a Saturday afternoon early in September, and the necessary arrangements are in the hands of Mr. H. K. Randall, the secretary of the Common Room Committee, of whom enquiries should be made.   Mr. Caröe will bear all expenses, except the railway fare.

The Working Men's College Choir, represented by 32 members of the Singing classes, formed one of the thirty-six London and Provincial Adult Choirs who took part in the Jubilee Festival of the Tonic Sol-fa Association, at the Crystal Palace, on June 29th last.   There were upwards of 5000 certificated children's voices at the afternoon concert; and at the evening adult concert, with full orchestral accompaniment, Mr. Leonard C. Venables conducted for the 21st year.   About 30 singers who took part in the first concert held fifty years ago (in 1857), came up to the platform to receive the Jubilee medal presented by Miss Susan Lushington, daughter of Mr. Vernon Lushington, K.C., a former teacher in the College.   The Jubilee singers were most enthusiastically cheered by the large choir and audience; and the men in the choir, together with the veterans, joined heartily in the singing of the part-song, "My Old Friend John."   Five choirs contested in the Choral and Sight-singing Competition, and the following prizes were awarded—"The Curwen" silver Challenge Shield, and two silver cups and a gold-mounted baton from the Tonic Sol-fa College.

The Committee formed to carry out the decoration of the Coffee Room have accepted the lowest tender obtained by Mr. Caröe, our architect, for the work, amounting to £114; and inasmuch as only £100 has been collected (that being thought ample for the purpose), it has been decided to re-open the list of contributors for the purpose of getting in the additional £14. Several of those members who have already given having expressed their desire to contribute further to the Decoration Fund, if necessary, we need only make it known that Mr. Randall will be pleased to receive further donations either from them or from those who have not already subscribed. In the meantime, in order that the order may be given for the work forthwith, Mr. Lionel Jacob has kindly guaranteed the whole £114 required. We feel sure, however, that none of our readers would wish him to lose over his generosity, and we hope that a hundred half-crowns will speedily roll into Randall's coffers.

The fund raised by the dramatic performance recently given by Miss Lowes Dickinson and her friends at the College is to be devoted to the decoration of the entrance hall, vestibule, corridor, the office, the superintendent's room, and possibly another room.

Miss Savage, daughter of an old College student, has very generously forwarded 10s. for the Maintenance Fund. This money, coming from the source from which it is sent, possesses for this College, in one sense, a manifold value. R. H. Marks has also contributed £5 to the fund.

The London County Council have made a grant of £600 towards the expenses of equipment of the College.

By the invitation of Mr. J. C. Bailey, who set the paper for the recently held English Composition examination, the candidates assembled at his house, 20, Egerton Gardens, to discuss certain points raised in the course of dealing with the questions on the paper. He expressed himself highly pleased with the intelligence and promise shown by the students, and advised them to continue the study they had taken up. After the more serious business of the evening had been disposed of, Mr. Bailey took his guests into the library, and showed them his fine collection of literary treasures. Much interest was taken in quite a number of old prints, and the rare editions were much admired. Light refreshments followed, and it was late when our men bade their genial host " Good-night."

All letters to the Editor after August 17th should be addressed :—" Leonard Pocock, ' Prestwood,' 91, Humber Road, Blackheath, S.E." whither he is about to remove.

A few evenings ago, a parcel addressed to Mr. W. J. Homewood was left in the office, the bearer saying that the senders desired to remain unknown. Mr. Homewood was apprised of the fact, and proceeded to attempt to unravel the mystery by opening the parcel. To his great surprise and delight, it was found to contain a beautiful bust of Molière. "From whom could it have come?" quoth he. After pondering awhile, he remembered having had a chat about holidays in Paris with two of the members of his French practice class; and this, coupled with the fact that the bust was undoubtedly of French workmanship, led him to conclude—(1) that the bust was a present, (2) that the method of presentation, though eccentric, was distinctly "College," and (3) that the "College spirit," though old-fashioned, was as lively as ever.

———

Mr. Cuthbert Mead, teacher of Shorthand in the College, and well known as secretary of the Debating Society and in other capacities, was the best candidate out of two-hundred who recently applied for a clerkship in the Law and Parliamentary Department of the Metropolitan Water Board. His many College friends will congratulate him on his success, and wish him a successful career in the Department, which has secured a good man.

———

Herr Karl Brückner, of Dresden, writing from there to the Secretary of the Old Students' Club on June 10th, says:—

"Neulich habe ich auf hiesigem Bahnhofe Ihre Landsleute, die Englischen Journalisten, mit empfangen. Es war aber eine Hetztour, sie haben alles nur im Fluge gesehen. Wenn nur den schönen Worten, die ausgetaucht wurden, auch die Taten folgten; denn nach meiner Aussicht, und der allgemeinen Aussicht aller vernünftigen Menschen, ist diese Hetzerei auf beiden Seiten frevelhaft und schuftig. Kein Mensch in Deutschland denkt an einen Krieg mit England. Es wäre für die Welt von grossem Werte wenn Deutschland und England sich gegenseitig die Hände reichten um den Frieden zu erhalten, und die andere Mächte zur Ruhe zu zwingen. Nach dem jetzigen Konstellationen ist aber genug Zündstoff vorhanden um einmal über Nacht mit Frankreich—oder durch die Revolution im Osten mit Russland—Krieg zu bekommen. Was konnte Deutschland und England gemeinschaftlich Gutes wirken, wenn nicht die Presse, mit französischem Gelde gespickt, alles verdürbe! Ihre Landsleute, deren es hier in Dresden sehr viel gibt, fühlen sich hier ausserordentlich wohl."

———

Mr. Thomas Denham, writing to the Secretary of the Old Students' Club, from Kotageri and the Nilgeris, South India, on May 18th last, says: "I have had five delightful weeks on the Nilgeri Hills, and another two weeks will see me back in harness at Mysore. What we poor Anglo-Indians would do without these charming hill stations, I don't know. Here I am nearly 7000 feet above the sea, in the midst of the most delightful surroundings, and breathing an atmosphere like that of a warm English spring. Nor are social activities wanting—in fact they are almost too much in evidence—tournaments of all kinds, badmington, tennis, billiards, and bridge. I came out easily top in the men's single at tennis, which is not bad for an old stager of fifty-one; and I took the leading part in some theatricals, and looked on the stage as I feel, somewhere about thirty, so you see India is not doing me any harm. The unrest in the country makes one a little anxious now and then, but I think we shall tide over the crisis. I am glad John Morley is supporting the executive, and at the same time is not being frightened out of the path of reform and progress. At all costs disloyalty and sedition out here ought to be ruthlessly crushed. It would never do for the people to get the idea that we are afraid of them. They will never love us, but we ought to make them respect us—as in fact they did until recently."

Mr. John Levack, one of Monsieur Petré's old students, recently visited the College on his return to London, after an absence of six years in Bagdad, Turkish Arabia, whither he intends to return on the expiration of his leave of absence in December next. In returning to England, Mr. Levack journeyed overland, and visited many interesting places on the way, such as Nineveh and Beppo, besides experiencing all the excitement and novelty of travelling through the desert in a caravan.

OUR LADY OF MOUNT CARMEL.

TRAVEL or books are the ordinary means by which one may study foreign nationalities; but a dweller in this great London of ours may find, almost at his very door, great colonies of people of different races, customs, and speech. Within a radius of about half a mile of our old College one may hear many foreign tongues, the chief of which are the "Amurrican" of Bloomsbury, the French of Soho, and the Italian round about Saffron Hill. Of these three districts the least known to the ordinary Londoner is "Little Italy." It is not an inviting quarter, for its streets are mean and narrow, and its people too often are squalid also. Probably they are not really dirtier than our own poor of the same class, and they are handicapped by the natural swarthiness of their skins. Their natural vivacity, like their inborn love of the picturesque, struggles bravely against the drab surroundings, and on one day a year at least they make a brave show. It is the day on which Our Lady of Mount Carmel is borne round the quarter.

It is a hot Sunday in mid-July, Hatton Garden is blank and empty; Clerkenwell Road, sordid and desolate, seems to sweat in the sun. But Back Hill is bravely festooned with flags, and here and there at the windows are little shrines with plaster images and coloured lamps; bright kerchiefs and aprons splash the scene with vivid colour, and the streets are full of expectant people.

Boom! Boom! goes the great bell from the flat-roofed, round-arched church, and a few policemen come to clear the way for the procession. The crowd is orderly enough, though scattered here and there are men with green caps and scarves and big blackthorns. They are the Knights of St. Patrick. They are no use here, but in their own distressful country it sometimes happens that Orangemen interfere with the processions. Then there is trouble.

There is a sound of distant music—a slow and solemn chant, and a glimpse of fluttering banners. Then comes a band and some robed priests, and after them scores of little boys, bareheaded and carrying flowers. Little girls follow, and they are the prettiest part of all. They are all in white, with pale blue sashes and long white veils; each wears a garland of flowers, and many bear big Annunciation lilies. There are raven-haired Italians and fresh-faced English, and the red hair and gray eyes of Ireland. Many of them are beautiful, and all are proud and happy, and their pretty childish voices ring sweetly :—

Ave, ave, ave, Maria !

Next come the women, with long hoods as blue as the sky above them—long ranks of turquoise and sapphire; and their banner is blue, with blue streamers, blue as a vein of the Madonna's breast. Then follow more bands and banners, choristers in scarlet cassocks and priests in glowing vestments; candles shining faintly in the sun, and glittering crucifixes and golden symbols. Censers sway and swing, and the strange strong smell of the incense smoke conjures up a thousand memories. In the midst of all, on a flower-bedecked litter, are the Mother and Child. Her robes are white with stars of gold, and her eyes are solemn and loving beneath the golden crown. Deep and rich the chant swells up, deep and solemn the great bell tolls; till they reach the church, and in one gorgeous un-English blaze of colour, hood and cope, stole and banner, pass in, and the procession ends. Perhaps its effects do not. Beside me, in the crowd was a big coarse man with a hard, sullen face. As the procession passed a softer look came into his eyes, and at last, half-shyly, he took off his cap. When all was done, he passed away thoughtful, with an afterglow of something upon him which seemed to make him a better man. It may be that he was. It is good for us to realize sometimes, however dimly, that our little lives and surroundings are not all; to listen, even for a little, to the music of the great ocean that rolls around us—the ocean of Eternity.

A. E. HOMEWOOD.

FURNIVALL SCULLING CLUB.

THE first week in July opened with characteristic 1907 weather, but our camping party at Henley survived.

The Club were entertained on June 23rd, as in previous years, by Mr. Radford, in his garden at Surbiton, and by Mr. Munday at Putney on July 21st, while we, in our turn, have entertained two large parties of poor children from London schools at the Club House.

A large number of our members attended the College Sports on July 13th. They tell us that they lifted the cup in the Tug o' War competition, open to all the College clubs. This should be an instruction to non-sculling College men.

GARDEN PARTY AND FIELD SPORTS.

THE Common Room Committee are to be congratulated upon the success of this event, arranged by them for Saturday, July 13th, at Wembley Park, and especially are we indebted to H. K. Randall, hon. secretary of the committee, H. E. Nye, T. M. Balson, and a few other men, for the unselfish work done by them, so that their friends might have an enjoyable afternoon and evening. The number present, 251, exceeded all previous records; the price of the tickets, including railway fare from Baker Street, entrance to the Park, and an excellent tea with strawberries and cream, was only two shillings; there was no hitch in the proceedings from start to finish, and in spite of a shower in the early part of the afternoon, all seemed to enjoy themselves. The prizes, of which no competitor was allowed to receive more than two, consisted of books selected by J. J Munro.

Officials :—Judges, S. Bradgate, H. R. Levinsohn, L. Pocock, and R. H. Marks. Referee, Lionel Jacob, Vice-Principal. Starter, C. F. W. Mead. Clerks of the Course, H. E. Nye and M. W. Starling. Stewards, T. M. Balson, T. Hopkins, W. Melzer, B. P. Moore, J. J. Munro, M. Staal, and W. J. Torrington.

RESULTS OF EVENTS.

SPRINT RACE, at 3.30 p.m., about 80 yards, for men only, 2 prizes, 20 entered. Entries taken by H. E. Nye.—First heat, Balson (1), Duchesne (2). Second heat, Sumner (1), Bartlett (2). Third heat, Williams (1), Driver (2). Final, Driver and Sumner tied and then ran off the tie, with the result that Driver won the first prize and Sumner the second. The other entries were Barnett, Young, Wade, Staal, Cannif, C. Ball, W. A. Ball, Goodwin, Moxey, Jennings, Howard, Dawson, Melzer, and Tyler.

THROWING THE CRICKET BALL, ladies only, 2 prizes, 23 entries taken by C. F. W. Mead.—Miss Engelhart (1), Dolly Duchesne (2), Miss Cawthorn (3), Mrs. Nield and Miss Bromhall (4), Misses Toyé, W. Toyé, Miles, Klemm, Elsie Marks, Halpin, Hamilton, Sewell, Mason, Maggie Jacob, Mead, Smith, Allen, Holmyard, Mrs. Bartlett, Mrs. Pocock, Mrs. Chaplin, and Mrs. Sumner.

THREE-LEGGED RACE, 4 prizes, 24 entries taken by T. M. Balson.— First heat, Duchesne and McWilliams (1), J. G. Williams and J. P. Pert (2), Avery and Gant, Young and Barnett. Second heat, Driver and Dawson (1), Bartlett and Sumner (2), W. A. Ball and Goodwin, Jennings and Moxey, Howard and Staal. Third heat, Lawrence and Roberts (1), Mead and Munro (2), Harrison and Sweetman, Owen and Wade. First and second pairs ran in final:—Duchesne and McWilliams (1), Lawrence and Roberts (2), Driver and Dawson (3).

NEEDLE AND THREAD RACE, for ladies and gentlemen. Gentleman runs to lady at half-way mark, and threads a needle which she holds. Couples then finish the course together. 4 prizes. 50 entries taken by T. Hopkins.— First heat, Mr. and Mrs. J. C. Denmead (1), S. Wade and Miss Dolly Smith (2), Moxey and Miss Fletcher, Barnett and Miss Fletcher, E. A. Harrison and Mrs. Pocock, Lawrence and Miss Hamilton, Young and Miss Sewell, Sweetman and lady. Second heat, Duchesne and daughter Dolly (1), Roberts and Miss Halpin (2), Cowling and Miss Klemm, Jennings and Miss Moxey, Ball and Miss Bromhall, Howard and Miss W. Toyé, Goodwin and lady, Driver and lady. Third heat, C. F. W. Mead and Miss Allen (1), Sumner and Mrs. Sumner (2), L. Barnard and Miss Moulden (3), and Staal, Tyler, Bartlett, Hopkins, Moore, and Owen, with their respective partners, whose names are not recorded. The first two pairs in each heat ran in the final:—Wade and Miss Smith (1), Mead and Miss Allen (2), Mr. and Mrs. Sumner (3).

VICTORIA CROSS RACE, 4 prizes. 12 pairs of competitors, entries taken by W. Melzer.—Driver and McWilliams (1), Howard and Gant (2), Munro and Mead (3), Wade and Melzer, Balson and Hopkins, Bartlett and Young, Staal and Barnett, Jennings and Moxey, Bonner and Osborne, Owen and Reglar, W. Dean and C. Dean, Sumner and Williams.

SLOW BICYCLE RACE, for ladies, 2 prizes, 6 entries taken by W. Melzer. —Miss Shearman (1), Miss Maggie Jacob (2), Misses Ford, English, Duchesne, and Tyler.

SLOW BICYCLE RACE, for gentlemen, 2 prizes, 19 entries taken by Melzer. –First heat, S. Wade (1), Nye, Hopkins, Lawrence, and Upton. Second heat, Balson (1), Gant, Avery, Barnett and Melzer. Third heat, Cowling (1), Young, Howard, Haggerty, and Tyler. Fourth heat, McLatter (1), Randall, Driver, and Murphy. Final, Cowling (1), Wade (2).

DONKEY RACE, for ladies, 2 prizes, 45 entries taken by M. Staal.—First heat, Dolly Duchesne (1), Miss Moulden (2), Misses M. Jacob, Francis, Klemm, Halpin, and 2 others. Second heat, Miss Windsor (1), Mrs. Martin, Mrs. Sumner, Misses Saunders, Holmyard, Dixon, Hughes, and Mason. Third heat, Miss Bird (1), Miss Lily Barnett (2), Misses Deane, V. Deane, Toyé, Jarvis, and Hyde. Fourth heat, Miss Annie Rogers (1), Mrs. Robbie, Misses Laura Rogers, Lidington, Sutton, Hemmerde, Hyde, and English. Fifth heat, Miss Lilian Tyler (1), Misses Tyler, Harley, Dockling, Miles, Taffe, Engelhart, and another. Sixth heat, Miss Allen (1), Misses Steptoe, Ford, Shearman, and Fletcher. Final, Miss Annie Rogers (1), Miss Lilian Tyler (2).

DONKEY RACE, for men, 2 prizes, 48 entries taken by M. Staal.—1st heat, won by W. Reed ; second, by C. F. W. Mead ; third, by Goodwin ; fourth, by Windley; fifth, by A. Osborne ; and sixth, by W. F. Jennings. Final, Mead (1), Osborne and Goodwin, dead heat (2). The latter rode off the dead heat and Osborne won the second prize.

CIGARETTE RACE, for ladies and gentlemen, 4 prizes, about 24 entries taken by T. Hopkins.—Gentlemen started from one end of the course, each picking up a cigarette at half the distance, and running to his lady partner, she applied a match. The two then ran back to the starting place. Prizes were awarded to the first two couples arriving with cigarettes alight.—First heat, won by Charles Ball and Miss Ball ; second, by Mr. and Mrs. Sumner ; third, by E. W. Davis and Miss Barth. Final, Charles Ball and Miss Ball (1), E. W. Davis and Miss Barth (2).

TUG OF WAR, College Clubs, three a side, three prizes, 24 entries taken by W. J. Torrington.—The Gymnastic Society, Bonner, Sumner and Ewings, won against the Swimming Club, W. Haggerty, Wedderburn, and Driver. The Furnivall Sculling Club, Howard, Owen, and Williams, pulled over the Debating Society, A. E. Homewood, Starling, and Staal. The Musical Society, Martin, Tyler, and Balson, won against the Literary Society, Mead, Munro, and Duchesne. The Cricket Club, Bartlett, Reglar, and Roberts, pulled the Cycling Club, Gant, Cowley, and Young. In the semi-finals, the Musical Society team beat the Gymnastic Society, and the Sculling Club pulled over the Cricket Club. In the final, the Sculling Club wrested the prize from the Musical Society.

LADIES' TUG OF WAR. 4 prizes, 24 entries taken by H. E. Nye.— First Heat, Misses N. Toyé, W. Toyé, Mason, and Halpin, beat Misses Ball, Laura Rogers, Annie Rogers, and Mrs. Perry. Second Heat, Misses C. Greenaway, G. E. Greenaway, Engelhart, and Mrs. Pocock, beat Misses Lidington, Read, Vinters, and Sutton. Third heat, Misses Steptoe, Francis, Quar, and Mrs. Martin, beat Misses E. Sewell, D. Smith, N. Moulden, and Mrs. Robbie. Semi-finals, Miss Steptoe's team beat Miss Toyé's, but was beaten by Miss Greenaway's team, who won.

Whilst the concluding events were being contested, Munro was seeing that the winners selected their prizes, and Randall was busy writing the labels for them. The distribution then took place in the Pavilion, the successful candidates receiving the books at the hands of our Vice-Principal, Mr. Lionel Jacob, who said he was determined not to mar the proceedings by inflicting on us a speech. Dances and songs brought the evening to a close. Various College members and their friends contributed the following programme :—Madam Kate Peake and Mr. Ells, duet, "When you come down the Vale," and "Anchored," as an encore ; Miss L. Steptoe, "Coming through the Rye"; Miss Bromhall, recitations, "Joe and I at the theatre," a humorous description of Shakespeare's Hamlet, and

"A legal Smack"; F. J. Nield, "Our Resterong"; Davis, "The Carnival"; Perry, "The Judge's Song" and "The First Lord's Song" (*Pinafore*). Miss Frances Reglar, who is ever ready to assist the College men in their efforts at entertaining, kindly officiated at the piano, and received the support of Messrs. Brodie and Howard. Our thanks are due to all of these ladies and gentlemen for supplying a pleasant finish to a most enjoyable day.

PRIZE SUMMARY.

Events.		Winners.	Titles of Prizes.
Sprint race.	(1)	H. O. Driver.	Beaconsfield's Novels.
	(2)	H. Sumner.	"By-paths of Nature."
Throwing cricket ball.	(1)	Miss Engelhart.	R. L. Stevenson's "Kronstadt."
	(2)	Miss Dolly Duchesne.	Golden Book of Coleridge. "Last of the Barons."
Three-legged race.	(1)	E. C. Duchesne.	"Rise and Growth of Japan."
		J. McWilliams.	Autocrat Series (3 vols.)
	(2)	F. E. Lawrence.	"Voyage of the Beagle." "A Tale of Two Cities."
		J. W. Roberts.	Browning's Poems (2 vols.)
Needle and thread race.	(1)	S. Wade.	McCarthy's Life of Gladstone.
		Miss D. Smith.	"Peg Woffington."
	(2)	C. F. W. Mead.	"Pickwick" and "Hard Times."
		Miss Maud Allen.	Shakespeare Anthology.
Victoria Cross race.	(1)	H. O. Driver.	Sheridan's Plays, Leigh Hunt's Essays, and "Henry Esmond."
		J. McWilliams.	Emerson's Essays and Cook's Voyages.
	(2)	H. S. Howard.	"Riches of Chaucer."
		W. B. Gant.	Travels of Harry de Windt.
Slow cycle race. (ladies)	(1)	Miss Shearman.	"Adam Bede."
	(2)	Miss M. Jacob.	"Famous Books."
Slow cycle race. (men)	(1)	P. Cowling.	Borrow's "Lavengro," and "Bible in Spain."
	(2)	S. Wade.	Two vols. of Dumas.
Donkey race. (ladies)	(1)	Miss Annie Rogers.	Wordsworth's Poems.
	(2)	Miss Lilian Tyler.	Tales from Shakespeare. "Harold" (Lytton.)
Donkey race. (men)	(1)	C. F. W. Mead.	"The Newcomes."
	(2)	A. Osborne.	Burnet's Reformation.
Cigarette race.	(1)	Charles Ball.	"Japhet in search of a Father."
		Miss Ball.	"Hajji Baba."
	(2)	E. W. Davis.	Novel by Jokai.
		Miss Barth.	"Master of Ballantrae" (Stevenson)
Tugs of war. (Winning teams)—		Miss C. Greenaway.	"Jocelin of Brakelonde."
		Miss G. E. Greenaway.	"Barbara Fleming" (Meredith).
Ladies.		Miss Engelhart.	Benjamin Franklin's Autobiography and Carlyle's "Cromwell."
		Mrs. Pocock.	Poe's Works.
Furnivall Sculling Club.		H. S. Howard.	"The English Gardener."
		A. Owen.	Marmontel's Tales.
		J. Williams.	Prescot's "Mexico."

SUMMER FESTIVAL AT THE COLLEGE FOR WORKING WOMEN.

THE above Festival, which included addresses, distribution of prizes, and the presentation of bouquets to the students present, took place in the Maurice Hall of the College, at 7, Fitzroy Street, W., on July 4th last. The Rev. J. LLEWELYN DAVIES, one of the Founders of our own College, and Chairman of Council of the College for Working Women, presided over the gathering, and said that the College was a kind of monument to Frederick Denison Maurice, founder of the Working Men's College. It was founded on the lofty principles enunciated by Matthew Arnold,—the principles of universal knowledge. He thought all the students recognized the efforts of the teachers and members of the Council in that direction. There was a peculiar grandeur and loftiness about the aims of Mr. Maurice, and at the same time he was simple and humble. That which Mr. Maurice had done for working men, Miss Martin was doing for working women in that College. They were inspired by the lofty sentiments of the great writers and thinkers who had preceded them.

Mrs. NATHANIEL E. COHEN compared the educational opportunities for women of to-day with those of sixty years ago. Mr. Maurice sought the means of providing better opportunities to men and women to acquire knowledge ; and the fundamental principle on which he founded the colleges for working men and women was universal learning, apart from competitive examinations,—that was the basis on which both Queen's College and the Working Men's College were founded.

Mr. C. P. LUCAS, C.B., referred to the work Miss Martin had done for that college for working women. One of the greatest things she had done was the gathering round her of such a band of workers. After referring to the educational value of such an institution as the College for Working Women, Mr. LUCAS said that among the great advantages of belonging to classes of that kind was companionship. No man or woman could stand quite alone. It was instinctive with humans to belong to something. They wanted a standard to live up to. That College not only gave them knowledge, but it gave them personal guidance and strength to live up to a high standard. Another advantage of such a college was that it afforded the working woman a chance of acquiring special knowledge. Let them learn more than others knew of some subject. Let them make it a hobby to get possession of some kind of knowledge, to know a little more about something than other people knew, and then they would be in the happy position of being able to impart that special knowledge to others.

Among those present were Miss Frances Martin, Principal ; Lady Otteline Morrell, who distributed medals, certificates and prizes to the students ; Mrs. Du Maurier, Member of Council ; Miss Francis, Hon. Secretary ; Miss Marie Arnold, Superintendent ; Dr. James Cantlie, Ambulance Examiner, and Mr. Francis Morris, Treasurer.

THE WORKING MEN'S COLLEGE JOURNAL *is supported partly by Annual Subscribers living in different parts of the World, and partly by circulation among the Students and Members. Its success depends upon a regular demand, and to ensure this, the Editor would be glad if as many readers as can will become Subscribers. Subscription 2s. 6d. per annum, post free.*

LONDON : Printed by W. HUDSON & Co., Red Lion Street, High Holborn, and published at THE WORKING MEN'S COLLEGE, Crowndale Road, London, N.W.—August 9th, 1907.

The Working Men's College Journal

sub.A

The
Working
Men's
College.
CROWNDALE
ROAD.
ST PANCRAS.
LONDON NW
FOUNDED
IN 1854
BY THE LATE
Frederick
Denison
Maurice

Contents for OCTOBER, 1907.

The Working
 Men's College—
Four articles
 by Students
College Notes
Lubbock Field Club

a history of uplifting, of the giving of the franchise, of the attention of parliaments to domestic legislation. The passage of British vessels through every sea, the domination of many races by the British race, and our immense progress in commerce, had broadened men's ideas and weakened old prejudices. Once the old prejudices began to go, the mind was free to attack unmolested the infinity of problems which surround our human life ; and the amazing mass of new and undreamt-of facts which came rushing like a motley crowd into human ken, and which are still coming every day, have still further weakened prejudice and shaken old theories and beliefs. Old methods were superseded by new ; machinery, even yet, as things are, a somewhat mixed blessing, replaced hand labour ; and more important still, perfected transit gave more facilities for intercourse, and linked together the remotest parts ; newspapers brought home to men's doors the facts of the great world around them ; the old scholastic metaphysical philosophy, with its habit of commencing at the supernatural and descending thence to the concrete, had to compete with a new empiricism in which theories were permitted only on the elaborate sifting of masses of accumulated data. This was the method in all things ; and this was fatal to old ideas and theories. The very principles of ethics and of human nature came to be called into question, as by Schopenhauer and Nietzsche : politics changed considerably ; revolution broke out and sometimes triumphed ; and poverty boldly asked riches the justification for its plenty. The idea of the equality of men, really implied in the ethics of Jesus, but never tacitly admitted except as a fine theory throughout the ages, now had philosophical and poetic utterance ; Carlyle thundered it with his tremendous voice ; Henry George founded his school of socialism ; Burns in his northern home had told in his immortal lines that,

> The rank is but a guinea's stamp ;
> The Man's the gowd for a' that ;

and Dickens was to picture the sorrow and misery of poverty ; the Chartist movement was started ; clubs for working men began to spring up ; and the political importance of the artisan class was to increase a thousandfold on the exercise of the franchise. Education began to receive attention ; it was a commercial, a political, and an ethical necessity. How greatly social ideas were in the atmosphere is shown by many small particulars : when Pitman and Ellis were conducting their spelling-reform campaign about 1850, one of their great arguments was the inability of an enormous number of people to read and write, and they demonstrated how important their movement was politically. Even Disraeli was affected : when Dr. Furnivall and others tried to help the ballast-heavers of the Thames-side, a deputation of Furnivall and several heavers waited on Dizzy in his drawing-room overlooking Hyde Park in Park Lane ; and there sat these rough heavers, but fellow-men, on the minister's white and gilt chairs—looking uncomfortable. Dizzy helped them.

There are two systems of education, the system which aims at commercial ends and the system which aims at æsthetic ends. The education of the Mid-Victorian era and after, such as was obtainable by poorer people, was strictly practical and exceedingly scanty. It taught a man to read and to reckon, and no more. It aimed at getting food for the body only ; it thought little of food for the mind. But the best educational institution can only be that, wherein, as in the Universities, the two systems of education are combined, wherein a man is taught not only that which will enable him to earn bread, but that also which will enable him to enjoy the beauties of art and of literature, and interest himself in philosophy and politics ; where he learns also that which will develop his resource and independence, and train his manhood to indulge in pure thoughts and noble actions. The best institution is where there are fellowship and esteem, where there are always friends and welcome, help and sympathy, where there is occasion for talk and laughter and the exchange of ideas on subjects of moment. With such a conception of education as this, with a stirring manhood and a love for his fellow men, Frederick Denison Maurice started the Working Men's College. His idea was to give to working men the benefits such as university men enjoy. A band of young and ardent university men, Furnivall, Ludlow, Westlake, Lowes Dickinson, and others, had gathered round him. Their beginning was unpretentious enough, but by the nobility of their efforts and their self-sacrifice their school grew more and more, until it became the Working Men's College that we knew in Great Ormond Street, and the College now situated by Oakley Square. To the College they gave their learning, their time, and their money ; more still, they imbued it with their personality, and gave it the birthright of good-fellowship that they brought with them from their Colleges at Oxford and Cambridge.

And what makes the traditions of great institutions? Is it not surely the characters and deeds of the men who have formerly formed part of them? The things which endure are not material things, bricks and mortar, stone and iron ; immortality is not, certainly, a property of rooms and houses ; the things which last are thoughts which evince themselves in actions, and love and sympathy which create our attitude to fellow-men. And thus the characters of the founders of our , so rich in these things, are influences which are among us, are ever leading men to develop natures and do the deeds of love and service which m. The history of our College in the past is self-sacrifice of a number of gifted men ; the e in the present is still a similar history of Here men meet men *as men*, and know obler title. Here one meets all kinds of character; all sorts of opinions are advanced and discussed. A number of vigorous societies, each with its object—intercourse, study, or sport—are in existence. Students of all kinds, young and old, fortunate and less fortunate in this world's goods, meet for mutual help and enjoyment. There is access everywhere, and freedom for everybody. We of to-day, with some of our Founders yet with us, carry on with some ease the life of our institution, such as they conceived it; and it is for us to hand it on. Generations of scholars will come after us when we have gone : may they take up the story and carry it onward, adding to its glory and feeling in it pride ; and may we too continue to honour it also, and leave it the greater and the better for our lives !   J. J. M.

THE WORKING MEN'S COLLEGE AS IT IS TO-DAY.

Do we not all truly believe the days of our childhood to have been our happiest ? And what untold pleasure do we not know when we recall a holiday of a decade or less back? Only the brightest and most pleasant incidents stand out in our memories, and we grow enthusiastic and live them over again, as we recount them to a younger friend who perhaps has a mind to make the same trips as we ourselves have made. But in childhood, as in our later holiday, there were times when the waters were often troubled for us, and life was not always free from cloud. Yet our misfortunes soon sink into oblivion and are forgotten, and only the best of thoughts remain. It is well so.

As with individuals so with institutions, and this is why we look back on the beginnings of an institution with which we are closely and dearly associated with feelings of pride and joy. The romance and the picturesqueness of the early days, when great and illustrious men walked the same ground that we now walk, and looked round on the same surroundings as we see now, hold us with a strange fascination.

Few institutions are more resplendent in their old associations and traditions than our College, and we of to-day are apt to wander back into the past, and to momentarily forget the glories of the present. Well, let us be forgiven for this not unnatural hero-worship of those who have shaken off life's mortal coil.

Let me say at once that my aim is to write on the College as it is to-day, and to try to give new men who are joining us some idea of the place they are coming to, to tell how it differs from other educational institutions, and what are the characteristics of the good fellows they will meet.

In this age a liberal education is within the reach of the children of even the very poorest classes, but provision for the enlightenment of working men undoubtedly might be made far more extensive than it is.   Frederick Denison Maurice ardently believed that there were men who, although engaged in arduous manual labour, nevertheless in their leisure moments desired the acquisition of knowledge for its own sake, quite apart from considerations of trade or professional advancement.   To these men, who have perhaps forgotten their. early learning, the College affords opportunities of a sound academic —one might almost say a University—education.   Many men, of course, join the College for the purpose of making themselves more efficient in their trades, and improving their position by the acquisition of knowledge which will help them in their business life, and care has been taken to provide for such as these.

There exists, however, in our College, an education which no amount of book-learning can give, and this perhaps makes it quite unique, and distinguishes it from almost all educational institutions, both past and present.   In this education is embodied the spirit of mutual help, the intermingling of minds, and the clashing of ideas between fellow-men.   Here we find students fresh from a University, and young fellows who have not had that advantage, but who are just as keen on the acquisition of knowledge, all rubbing shoulders together; whether as teacher or as student, all are united in friendship. Many a College student in his turn teaches in the College the subject which has most appealed to him and in which he has specialized.   How well he knows and feels the difficulties experienced by his students; his enthusiasm, and his youthful hope and energy help him to succeed where many would fail. Here you feel that your teacher is your friend, possessed with an ardent zeal to impart to you that which he himself has gained much happiness in learning.

This learning is carried into the social life of the College. There is the Old Students' Club, the chief object of which is to foster friendly feelings amongst past and present students of the College, and every December, since 1876, the year of its foundation, "past and present" have gathered round the festive board at the Old Students' Club Supper, and listened to the impressive speeches of some of our Founders—who are happily still with us—and of others who have followed in their steps and in the steps of those who have passed away.   Another feature is the Debating Society, where, whatever a man's political persuasion may be, he always secures a patient hearing, and the maiden effort of the young and budding orator is received with as much good feeling as the more brilliant rhetoric of an old stager.   The members of the Field Club, too, headed by James Holloway, who teaches Zoology in the College, are always on the look out for natural history specimens on their Sunday wanderings into the country.   So with R. R. Flint, our genial and popular Assistant Superintendent, who emulates Tom Hughes in teaching a select little circle the art of fisticuffs on Saturday afternoons. Of course, like his great and distinguished predecessor, when a man gets too warm for him and therefore a nuisance—well—he makes a deputy of him, and why not? Ah me, how proud I should be to have been the recipient of a good punch from Tom Hughes's fine muscular arm!

Collegiate friendships are carried far beyond the confines of the College walls, for we find students taking their summer holidays together and arranging walking and cycling tours both in this country and on the Continent. Saturday afternoon and Sunday walking is much indulged in, too, and many College men take an active part in the Furnivall Sculling Club, founded by Dr. Furnivall and lighted by the flame of his grand personality. He himself rarely misses a pull from the Club-house at Hammersmith to Richmond and back every winter Sunday in a racing eight or four, and College men are invariably to be found in his crew or in one of the crews which accompany him.

By the way, a recent instance of Collegiate friendship strikes me. One of our students, a sort of walking French dictionary, recently returned from Paris, where he had been holiday-making with a number of French College students gone back to France. These fellows, whom he met in business, he used to trot along to the College and introduce to us, so as to help them with their English and at the same time improve our own acquaintance with the French language. Well, they say they will never forget his kindness, and they are for ever inviting him over to France. Such a condition of things can only tend to strengthen the ties of national affection.

Recently a very happy thought struck one of our well-known and esteemed members. It was that the students should raise a fund for the purpose of decorating and furnishing the Coffee Room, so as to make it harmonize with the Common Room, which adjoins it, and which was lately magnificently decorated at the expense of a member and student of the old days. £120 was wanted, it is being raised, and the work is now proceeding merrily. Some of the class-rooms have been decorated during the vacation and the College looks more cosy than ever. The new term bids fair to be a great success New students are joining in goodly numbers and there is every indication that the College continues to extend its sphere of usefulness.

When we think of the old days when the College first took definite form in Little Ormond Yard, a place where a policeman durst not venture alone at night—and then look on our magnificent edifice in Crowndale Road, we recognize that it is a real and lasting monument to the memory of those who created it and to those who have worked so nobly in its development.

C. F. W. M.

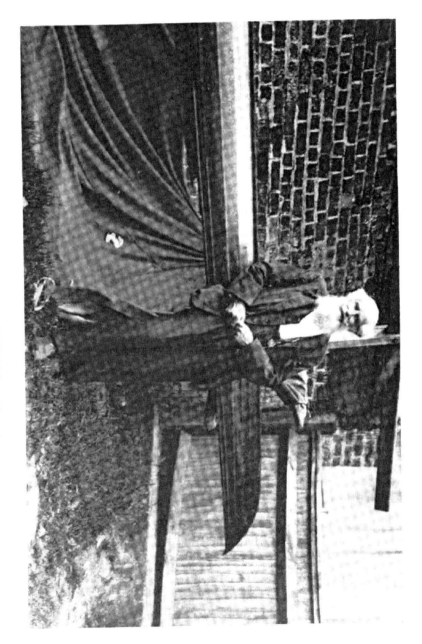

Dr. F. J. FURNIVALL, (82-3),

M.A., TRINITY HALL, CAMBRIDGE; D.LITT., OXFORD; PH.D., BERLIN;
President of the Furnivall Sculling Club; and one of the Founders and
Member of Council, Working Men's College.

In the Forecourt of the Furnivall Sculling Club, Lower Mall, Hammersmith,
Saturday, 20th July, 1907.

A FIRST IMPRESSION.

I CAN quite understand the complaint against the College which came from a girl after visiting the newly decorated Common Room : "You make the men too comfortable here," she said, "I wonder they ever want to go home."

I was dragged into the College one night to attend a Smoking Concert. The time for starting arrived punctually as usual, but the College men with laudable politeness arrived later. During this interval I was taken into the Common Room.

My first experience was pleasant. I called for refreshments, and then found it was against the rules for me to pay. The Licensing Act has its compensations. My friend pointed out the pictures on the walls, told me of the illustrious names associated with the portraits, and gave me a brief account of the old-fashioned house in which we stood. There was something about a stolen seal and a strange kitchen, but I remember nothing clearly, as the narrative was interrupted by frequent salutations. Either my friend knew everybody, or else everybody was " beastly" sociable. However, the Common Room seemed a jolly sort of meeting-house. There was a scarcity of newspapers, it is true, but then no one appeared inclined to read the news. They were telling it to each other, in revised versions. You could, it turned out, get everything here except peace and quietness, which were kept upstairs in the Library. Teas and suppers were provided, and—to my surprise—even beer. I was astonished too, at discovering that boxing was taught on the premises. Remember please, that I had graduated in a provincial Y.M.C.A., and came here straight from a suburban Polytechnic.

The men interested me most. I had never found such variety in so small a space. One or two were speaking French or German almost like natives. I observed so to my friend. "Don't be funny," said he, " of course they *are* natives. We have a big foreign section, awfully good fellows, always ready to help you with 'conversation' and all that."

Then again, the men were of no particular class -I mean, no special social standing. The only qualification apparently was to have the appearance of being a man. They seemed to embrace every rank and profession. Seeking further information, I found among those present, an engraver, a Somerset House clerk, a barrister, an old-print dealer, a compositor, and a book-binder. I was staggered! If I was good I was promised the sight of a grocer's assistant and a big government official.

Opinions? Well, they all had them. And above all, they weren't afraid to voice them. I began to breathe more freely. Here at all events a man could express doubts on social and theological questions, without fear of ostracism. In one night I met a Roman Catholic and a Protestant, a High Churchman and an Agnostic. Later, when my nerves were steadier, I ran up against an Anarchist! What then was the common ground upon which these diverse elements met ; met, mind you, to mingle in social pleasure as well as to increase knowledge? As far as I could make out, the idea was to educate men in the real sense of the word. The classes were novel, inasmuch as they cost little, and the students were often much older in years than the teachers. They were unique in one way. 'Varsity men came to teach and working men to learn. The funny result was that often the positions were reversed. Anyhow, the traditions of having had such teachers in the past as Ruskin, Rossetti, Burne Jones, Asquith, Lyttelton, and others. induced clever young fellows to come on here from the Universities to complete their education. They brought with them all that was new and best in thought. Their inexperience in teaching was made up by youth and enthusiasm. The benefit they gained perhaps was contact with learners older in years, more used to practical affairs, and thus able to bother them with criticism derived from the stern facts of existence.

The spirit animating the College seemed to me to be that of gentle manliness. We were there to learn things not for the purpose of "getting on" or making money, but in order to appreciate blessings already within our reach. I mean, of course, the beauties of Nature and Art

Thus, instead of loafing about and becoming a nuisance to ourselves and others, our eyes were to be opened to see what was before us, free to all: Picture galleries, music, rambles made interesting by a knowledge of botany, geology, architecture, and the like. Books too, naturally enough; but I was amused to learn that shop-windows and even the play of light and shade in a lady's hair were convenient means for the study of art. All this suggested, "What a slack time for the music halls when all London attends the College!"

I discovered that nearly every learner was also a teacher, especially in sports and games. No sooner did a man get a grip of some game, than he started out to make me lend a hand. I found that I must learn chess, scull, join the Debating Society, play draughts, etc., etc. This "lend a hand" craze extended to heavy articles like pianos, to light ones like addressing College JOURNALS, to taking charge of a class for one night only, and to romping with, and even kissing, a delightful crowd of kiddies brought into the Hall to remind us that Christmas is the children's festival.

Well, I come back to the portraits on the walls, and the thought of those men passing away without seeing these results made me sad. Their names were so familiar. I was, so to speak, brought up on memoirs of Maurice, Kingsley, and Tom Hughes. Now at last I had stumbled across the very place embodying their spirits. I felt no greater joy could come to me. My youthful dreams were about to be realized. I left the College that night, resolved at all costs to become a member. There was one difficulty. I should have to join a class. I made a wild selection, but anything would do rather than I should be shut out of my heaven. And that is why I attended a class on "Partnerships," or was it "Torts"?   C. H. A.

ANOTHER EXPERIENCE.

DEAR MR. EDITOR,—I understand you wish me to confess how the College and I found each other. Well, looking back, it appears to have happened somehow this way. When I left school it seemed unto me that my education was still incomplete, so I looked for a place to improve the same. First I tried a big Institute. It was a fine Institute, got up regardless of expense; it had gorgeous Social Rooms, with lovely ottomans and things, and a fine Swimming Bath and Gymnasium. It was an every-prospect-pleases-and-only-man-is -vile place. For though I splashed in the Bath and nearly broke my neck in the Gym., the *soi-disant* social rooms choked me off.

They were in the possession of frigid little cliques of pompous nonentities, among which I wandered lonely as a lop-eared leper on a desert island, barking my moral shins against their scarcely-veiled hostility. So I gave it up, and went to the old College.

At first I was shy of the dear old Common Room, though it was easy to see what a different atmosphere prevailed. I studied German with a jolly white-haired old boy in a queer little underground room, till, a term or so after I came, he came to a tragic end. I thought of the quality of my German, and missed divers terms, conscience-stricken. Subsequently I rejoined, and began to mix with the real College life—the social life.

Now the worst things I have heard about the College have the slenderest foundation in fact, like the definition of the child who said a demagogue was a " vessel for containing beer and other drinks." Of such are the statements that the Superintendent is an avowed poacher ; that the office is tenanted by a bruiser, who with heart of flint and hand of iron, overawes the riotous ; that fustian and corduroy are *de rigueur* ; and that the " Old Students " are a disguised revolutionary conclave of Marxists. Dear old College ! What men one meets ! Men of broad minds and sympathies ; men from the Universities, with all the learning they have to offer, mixing with us in good-natured, unpretentious equality ; quiet, clever students who are such good fellows that it is hard to realize that they are so brilliant at Natural History, and Music, and Art, and so on.

For this is the result of the College spirit, that all who come within its influence are good fellows ; they discuss and compare all things, but treat each other's opinions with respect and forbearance. It gives an atmosphere of a pleasant sort, of a search for genuine culture, and it breeds strong and lasting friendships.

What becomes of the bounders—there is usually a proportion in all communities? Well, they disappear. Generally, they reform. It is impossible to " swank " long when surrounded by men who are modest, but nevertheless obviously superior to oneself. Or—I have another theory. Hush ! speak low. Next to the old College was a hospital, where an occasional corpse would be useful for dissection, and there was communication between the buildings . . . .

Well, we ought to get a lot of freshmen in the new term. May they make free use of the Common Room ! We, the older members, only desire to make them welcome.

Vale,

A. E. HOMEWOOD.

COFFEE ROOM DECORATION FUND.

IN response to the appeal for the further £14 required, in addition to the £100 already collected, to make up the £114, contract price for the work of decorating the Coffee Room, the following donations have been received : —

	£	s.	d.		£	s.	d.
W. J. Gray	0	10	0	J. J. Munro	0	10	0
Miss Beatrice Pocock				G. Elton Mayo (Adelaide)	0	10	0
(Brisbane)	0	10	0	G. A. Taylor	0	5	0
Leonard Pocock ...	0	5	0	W. R. Emslie ...	1	0	0

Any further donations will be thankfully received and duly acknowledged.

COLLEGE NOTES.

THE first, or October, term of the fifty-fourth year of the College begins on September 23rd and ends on December 21st. There is every prospect of its being one of the most successful terms in the College history; the class and lecture lists are very attractive, and a spirit of activity and effectiveness is in evidence. It is, however, necessary now, as at all other times, to spread a knowledge of the College and its work amongst those to whom it is likely to be of use. Every reader of the JOURNAL is therefore invited to do his or her best to introduce at least one new member this session, and to hand a copy of the term programme to some young man who may desire, or be induced, to join. No better service could be rendered to a man, no better turn could be done to a friend, than to put him in the way of becoming a working member of the Working Men's College

The new session will be inaugurated by a social meeting and smoking concert, to be held in the Common and Coffee Rooms on Saturday, September 21st. on which evening the Vice-Principal and Mr. Lucas will address the students, and the musical arrangements will be in the hands of Mr. Perry. The previous week is to be specially devoted to the enrolment of new members, and some of the Studies Committee will be in attendance each evening to answer questions and give advice as to the classes.

The articles with which this number begins are written by four well-known members of the College, of not many years' acquaintance. The experiences which they narrate and the views which they express are a fair sample of those which many a man has had upon getting to know the College. We need add little more.

The chief object of the College is to unite men in the common work of teaching and learning. Its main purpose is educational—using the word in its highest and widest sense; and it is mainly through the teaching in the classes that effect is given to this aim.

We have not space; nor is it necessary here to mention all the classes in the list, but we observe that the Rev. B. H. Alford resumes his Old Testament class on Sundays at 6 p.m., commencing on October 13th, with "The End of the Hebrew Monarchy and the Captivity." This class is free to all members and to ladies accompanying them, and those who have attended in previous years testify to the interesting way in which Mr. Alford treats his subject.

Mr. G. M. Trevelyan begins on October 8th, a Shakespeare Literature class, "Macbeth" and "As you like it" being the plays selected for discussion.

———

Under the head of "Law and Economics," we find four classes, all of which ought to draw well at the present time— "Criminal Law," by Mr. J. F. Iselin; "Insurance Law," by Mr. H. C. Gutteridge; "The Law of Master and Servant," by Mr. H. Freeman; and "Elementary Economics," by Mr. T. Morison.

———

Our old and valued friend Mons. Lazare is taking a rest from teaching French here in the evenings, and the French classes will be taught by Mons. Canivet, whom we already know, and Mons. E. Pointin (Diplomé), with their assistants in the practice classes. In German, Mr. A. Hargreaves, Ph.D., succeeds Mr. Farndell. Spanish finds Mr. Juan Victoria at his post as usual. Mr. Carlo Gatti is taking a Beginners class in Portuguese, in addition to his Italian classes, in the Advanced of which he deals with "The Love-poets to Petrarch and the XIV. Century."

———

The Ancient Languages, Mathematics, Science, Art, and Music are all well staffed in the Higher Division. The Lower Division has its usual complement, in Arithmetic, History, Geography, and Grammar, and its Foreigners' Section. The Preparatory is being run by Student Teachers, and in the Special Division, amongst Shorthand, Book-keeping, Esperanto, Ambulance, and Gymnastics—(a somewhat curious *Olla podrida*, this) is to be found a new class in Commercial Arithmetic taken by Mr. A. J. Bride.

———

The name of Mr. John Scott does not appear on the list this term. He is to give a course of lectures on "Browning" or "Tennyson" *after* Christmas, in the Literature section. We cannot afford to lose him, and this will tell those who are loyal to him that he has not forsaken the College.

———

The Principal will deliver a course of lectures this session on "The Fundamental Principles of the Law of the Constitution," the first two of which will be given on Thursdays, November 7th and December 5th, at 8.30 p.m. The Law of the Constitution is a favourite subject with Professor Dicey, and he contrives to make it interesting to all who hear him discourse upon it.

———

The following are the other Thursday evening lectures which have been arranged :—

Oct. 10 and 24.—E. W. Rowntree, B.A. "Measurement."
  „ 17 and 31.—R. Rait, M.A. "History of London."
Nov. 14 and 28. – R. Rait, M.A. "History of London."
Dec. 12 and 19.—Prof. A. W. Kirkaldy, M.A., B.Litt. "History of Writing."

Courses of twenty-five lectures, under the auspices of the London County Council, have also been arranged, as follows:— On Monday evenings, at 7.30, "The romantic revival in English Poetry," by A. C. L. Guthkelch, B.A. On Tuesday evenings, at 8 o'clock, a London University Extension course on "The Italian Painters," by Dudley Heath. And on Friday evenings, at 8 o'clock, another London University Extension course on "Child Study," by J. W. Slaughter, Ph.D. Details of all the above courses and of many of the classes may be obtained free, on application to the Assistant Superintendent in the Office.

The following free Saturday evening lectures and other fixtures have been arranged, to be delivered at 8.30 p.m.

Sept. 28.—Sir Charles Bruce, G.C.M.G. "Life and Labour in the Tropics." (Illustrated).

Oct.   5.—J. F. Crace, M.A. "Sparta and Athens." (Illustrated).

„   12.—Musical Society's Concert.

„   19.—H. Beaumont. "Chartres Cathedral." (Illustrated).

„   26.—Maj.-Gen. Sir F. Maurice, K.C.B. Distribution of Certificates, and Lecture on "Sir John Moore."

The following examination results are to hand:—

English Composition.—Examiner, Mr. J. C. Bailey. Ten sat and six passed, J. W. Roberts and A. U. Penny, both "excellent," and C. H. R. St. John, H. O. Driver, G. W. A. Coleman, and John Wonfer.

Economics.—Examiner, Mr. H. J. Tozer. Seven sat and four passed, E. J. H. Reglar, H. W. Stevenson, H. K. Randall, and A. H. B. Stock.

Law of Landlord and Tenant.—Examiner, Mr. J. H. Redman. Three sat and two passed, both "excellent," R. W. Everard and E. W. Theodore Brumby.

Commercial Law.—Examiner, Mr. H. C. Gutteridge. Four sat, three passed, Fredk. W. Unwin, Claude Fairbairn, and R. H. Hewson. Reginald Samuel Hitchcock passed in the Society of Arts examination in this subject, stage III.

Latin, Intermediate.—Examiner, Mr. W. R. H. Merriman. Four sat; two passed, A. C. Martin (excellent), and J. McWilliams.— Advanced stage: Examiner, Mr. C. D. Robertson. One sat and passed, C. F. Endersby.

French.—Examiner, Mr. B. Dumville. Advanced stage: six sat, three passed, W. L. E. Cooper (excellent), R. W. Alaway, and H. C. Hunter. Elementary stage: eight sat and all passed, J. J. Bush, R. M. Emslie, and H. Stock (all three "excellent"), and O. Ricks, D. Seath, H. Crawford, R. Wedderburn, and W. Walker. Arthur Harry Casey passed the Society of Arts French examination, in stage III., and Harry C. Hunter and W. L. E. Cooper in stage II.

German, Advanced stage.—Examiner, Mr. H. R. Levinsohn. Three sat, and two passed, J. Parsons and A. Leakey.

Spanish.—Examiner, Mr. D. Bowman. Advanced: one sat and passed, A. Urry.—Intermediate: four sat, three passed, R. J. Davies, H. S. Parr, and H. W. Windsor.—Elementary, five sat, all passed, V. Hereck, J. J. Jamieson, H. Mortilan, E. Morris, and J. Maccaine. R. J. Davies also took the Society of Arts second grade certificate in Spanish.

Euclid.—Examiner, Mr. P. Thompson. J. W. Roberts sat for the first stage, and obtained an "excellent." One sat for advanced, and failed.

Board of Education, South Kensington, Science Examinations.—Machine Construction and Drawing, seven sat, six passed. In the first stage, first class, George T. Benjamin, Samuel Hughes, Reginald Atkinson, Russell E. Connold, and William J. E. Brown; second class, Arthur A. Simmons.—Magnetism and Electricity, eleven sat, four passed. First stage, first class, Frederick S. Baxter; second class, John S. Rowe and Russell E. Connold. Second stage, first class, Arthur C. G. Beach.—Geology, one sat and passed, John W. Bagshaw, first stage, first class.—Theoretical Inorganic Chemistry, Stage I., five sat and all passed, Henry S. Yates, Thomas M. Balson, and Alfred Quick, first class; and Frank Lakeman and Benjamin Wathen, second class.—Practical Inorganic Chemistry, Stage I., five sat and four passed, Henry S. Yates and Thomas M. Balson, first class; and Benjamn Wathen and Alfred Quick, second class.—Human Physiology, four sat and one passed, Frederick E. Windley, second stage, second class.—Building Construction and Drawing, eleven sat, eight passed; in the first stage, first class, John F. Reeve, Robert C. Biles, Edward G. Knowles; second class, Charles W. Deuchar, Edward Hayward, Charles E. Smethers, and James Price; and in the second stage, second class, William Stallard.—Zoology, two sat, one passed, Wilfrid J. Homewood, first stage, first class.—Botany, five sat, three passed, George T. Butler, first stage, second class; Charles T. Buckhurst and Henry T. Wilkin, second stage, second class.

Board of Education, South Kensington, Art Examinations.—Painting Ornament, Ebenezer W. Silk, second class.—Drawing in Light and Shade, ten sat, six passed. First class, Richard E. Tyler; second class, William A. Ball, Robert C. Biles, Alfred T. Hurt, William M. Routh, and Edgar C. Seeley.—Model Drawing, five sat, four passed. First class, Richard E. Tyler; second class, Alfred T. Hurt, William A. Ball, and Edgar C. Seeley.—Freehand Drawing in Outline, William A. Ball and Edgar C. Seeley, first class.—Design, Stage I., Richard E. Tyler, second class.—Memory Drawing of Plant Form, Alfred T. Hurt, second class. Five students submitted works for the Art Class Teacher's Certificate, and that of William A. Ball was accepted.

Senior Studentship Examination. Five sat and one passed, A. C. Martin.

Arithmetic, First stage.—Examiner, Mr. F. M. Kingdon. Eight sat, four passed, A. H. B. Stock and H. W. Le Dieu (both excellent), and W. H. Johnson and H. Spencer.

English Grammar.—Examiner, Mr. H. R. Ladell. First stage, five sat, three passed, all "excellent," C. W. Horsman, H. O. Driver, and E. C. Cuming. Advanced stage: five sat, all passed, one "excellent," H. Brunnert (excellent), W. H. Watson, Frank Lakeman, J. Foley, and H. O. Driver.

Book-keeping.—Examiner, Mr. A. C. Turberville. Four sat and passed, S. Goddard and J. S. Williams, "both excellent," and J. H. Pert and F. A. Taylor. Pert also passed the Chamber of Commerce Senior Examination in this subject, and Charles G. Ball gained the Society of Arts second grade certificate therein.

Music.—Mrs. Julian Marshall examined in the old notation. Six sat and all passed, P. Cowling (excellent), Miss D. Klemm, A. F. Gough, Miss A. Quar, Miss B. Francis, and Miss S. Hughes.

Violin.—Eight sat and five passed, L. Read and J. D. Challen, both "excellent," Miss M. Scott, W. Stangham, and A. Reuben.

Ambulance.—Examiner, Dr. Tunstall, for the St. John's Ambulance Association. Eleven sat and all passed. First aid, H. E. Winkworth, G. E. Buckland, G. C. Lang, P. V. Wareham, W. G. Medhurst, H. R. Densham, and E. H. Chappell; passed for vouchers, W. A. G. Jones and A. H. Casey; passed for medallions, J. R. Evans and C. T. Young.

Shorthand.—Examiner, Mr. E. H. Carter, H.M.I.; Theory, seven sat, two passed, H. H. Hughes and W. Lloyd. Reporting, four sat and three passed, R. W. Alaway, "excellent," at 120 words per minute, A. H. B. Stock pass at 120 words, and C. F. Rogers, "excellent," at 100 words per minute.

In the Preparatory Division, in Dictation, G. Thompson, "excellent," and W. Slater passed; in Arithmetic, A. E. Hogh, "excellent," and G. Thompson passed; and in Grammar, W. Windley was awarded "excellent."

Amongst the many clubs connected with the College, a list of which is given in the Term Programme, one of the largest and most important is the Old Students' Club, which serves the purpose of bringing together four or five times during the year those old students who are unable to keep up constant attendance at the College, and of enabling them to meet one another and some of the newer men. At its meetings, held on Saturday evenings, various subjects of general interest are discussed.

The Debating Society, now perhaps equally as large and important in its way as the older club, meets more frequently—every Tuesday during the winter—to hold debates. Conducted on orderly and systematic lines, and attended by speakers of some considerable practice and talent, this society provides a very useful channel for the public expression of members' opinions.

Shakespeare Readings are held on alternate Sundays at the College during the winter; the "Linguists" are formed, in club fashion, to promote conversation in foreign languages; the Maurice Chess and Draughts Club affords practice in the games indicated, besides matches and tournaments; the Musical Society and Glee Club, a large and particularly useful and talented organization, gives us our concerts and musical entertainments; whilst the Sketching Club and Field Club meet and make excursions according to their programmes. Clubs for Swimming, Cycling, and Sculling also exist.

Dr. F. J. Furnivall, the President of the last mentioned—the Furnivall Sculling Club, is one of the Founders of the College, and we are proud and happy at having him still working, aye, and playing too, with us. One of the best known literary men of our day, he is happiest when with his young friends, sculling with them, in a boat, or joining in their talk and amusements. Although he has been very much photographed and so published abroad lately, we may be allowed the pleasure of circulating with this number (at his expense) the accompanying full length portrait of him, taken at Hammersmith.

In Mr. A. C. Martin we welcome a new Fellow of the College, and a good fellow to boot. The honours records show that he passed three examinations in Law, in 1899, 1900, and 1901, in the first of which he took an "excellent" certificate. In 1906 he took a first stage in Euclid, and this year an intermediate stage "excellent" in Latin. Having also passed the Senior Student Examination he becomes an Associate, and having taught in the College for upwards of six consecutive terms he is entitled to the College honour of Fellow, and to all the privileges of the College, including the classes, free, for life. We heartily congratulate him.

One of the hardest working and most popular members of the College, Mr. T. M. Balson, has been posted as an Associate. He joined in October 3rd, 1898. His record of examination passes is:—Arithmetic and Grammar, 1st stage, 1899; Advanced, 1900 (his Arithmetic certificate being "excellent"); Senior Student, 1900; Physiology, Stage I., class II., 1905; Tansley Prizeman, 1905; French, advanced, 1906; Theoretical and Practical Chemistry, 1907. Mr. Balson is teaching in the Preparatory Division, so we hope soon to greet him as a Fellow.

The "Marks" Prize may be competed for this year for the first time. It will be awarded for the best Essay upon a subject to be announced in October.

Portraits of two of the earliest students, Mr. Alfred Grugeon and the late Mr. William Thrower, have been added to the pictures of College celebrities which adorn our walls. The Executive Committee had these two enlarged from photographs obtained for the purpose.

One of the oldest of the student teachers, Mr. E. R. Cole, whose pet subject was Geography, has had to retire from the Post Office on account of the age limit in the service, and has removed from London to Chester. We therefore, with great regret, lose him as a College teacher and frequenter of the Common Room, in which for many years he was one of our best exponents of chess.

Mr. R. M. Emslie is giving up his practice class in German, after several years' good work, and Mr. Macgillivray finds himself obliged, owing to some special work on which he is engaged, to relinquish teaching in the Law classes, in which he earned the grateful thanks of his students and of the Executive.

All who know them in the College heard with great pleasure of the marriage of four more or less prominent student teachers. William Charles Jones, Fellow of the College, was married on August 17th to Miss Grellier, an honorary member of the Furnivall Cycling Club. James Holloway was married on the same day to Miss Milly Read. E. T. Colesby was married six days later to Miss Edith Read, sister of Mrs. Holloway, and of Mrs. Wiedhofft, the wife of another well-known College man. And W. F. Jennings was married on July 25th to Miss Agnes M. Fletcher. We wish them all—husbands and wives—every joy and happiness and long and contented lives.

———

The decoration of the Coffee Room has been proceeded with during the vacation, and is expected to be completed by the beginning of the new term. So far as can be judged, it will be very satisfactory. The design of the ceiling consists of square panels or plaques, and the ornamentation of the plaques nearer the walls includes separate representations of the English rose, the Scotch thistle and the harps of Ireland and Wales. Towards the centre of the room these emblems commingle and unite. The panelling around the room and the colouring of the walls agree with the adjoining Common Room. The fund for the purpose of meeting the expense of this work is still open, and contributions thereto may be sent to the hon. secretary, Mr. H. K. Randall, at the College.

———

The proceeds of the dramatic entertainment organized by Miss Lowes Dickinson have been expended on the decoration of the entrance hall and stairs, the main corridor and the one above it, the rooms of the Superintendent and his assistant, and class rooms No. 21 (the Tansley Room) and No. 22. The tint of green selected for the corridors harmonizes well with the colour of the paint on the room doors and the general effect is very homely and pleasing.

———

Arrangements have been concluded for the letting of the College in the day-time to the London County Council, for use as a secondary school. It was opened on September 17th as the St. Pancras Secondary School for Girls, under the government of the Higher Education Sub-Committee of the Education Committee of the Council, and the Head Mistress is Miss H. Bartram, M.A., lately Mathematical Mistress at the North London Collegiate School. The object of the school is to provide a sound, liberal, and useful education for girls, and the course will lead up to the "school leaving examination" of the University of London, a form in which the matriculation examination may now be taken.

———

It is hoped that the letting may result in an addition to the College income, but inasmuch as there are many expenses attaching to it, we must await the appearance of the next year's accounts before being too sanguine on that score.

G. Elton Mayo, writing from Adelaide with subscriptions to the JOURNAL and other College objects, expresses a very kindly feeling for the College, which marks, he says, quite one of the brightest periods of his career. He asks to be remembered to his old chums in the College.

The " Citizens"—that is to say, any College men who care to meet and lunch or dine once a month in the City—will hold their next gathering as usual on the first Thursday in October at 1.30 p.m., at Read's Restaurant, 94, Cheapside, in the front room on the third floor.

In the early part of August, Mrs. Robbie unfortunately met with an accident, from the effects of which she is still suffering. She was on a visit to Porchester, and whilst climbing Porchester Hill, slipped and fell, straining her hip severely. She has experienced considerable pain, the doctors have had difficulty in diagnosing the extent of her injuries, and she has been making but slow progress towards recovery. After having spent six weeks in bed she was removed to University College Hospital on Wednesday last. We all hope that our excellent caretaker and cateress will now soon regain her strength and wonted activity.

Mr. George Allen, the well-known publisher, who died at his residence, "Sunnyside," Orpington, on September 5th, aged 76, was in his youth a member of this College. Dr. Furnivall has kindly sent us a cutting from the *Daily Chronicle* of the 7th, containing an obituary notice, from which we quote the following :—

Mr. Allen's honourable and successful carreer is one of the romances of literary and industrial history. He was in early youth a skilled joiner, He became engaged to the maid of Ruskin's mother, and "for love of her," as Ruskin wrote, he attended the drawing classes which were conducted by Ruskin and Rossetti at the Working Men's College, then in Red Lion Square. There his artistic gifts, no less than his sterling qualities of character, soon attracted Ruskin's particular attention. He was an admirable draughtsman, and as an etcher and engraver he achieved wonderful delicacy and skill. He was one of two or three pupils and assistants who have had the experience of being shown their own handiwork as examples of Ruskin's beautiful drawing. Most of the plates in Ruskin's later books, and some in " Modern Painters," were engraved by Mr. Allen. Ruskin, shortly after making his acquaintance at the Working Men's College, had taken Mr. Allen into his service as an assistant, and, indeed, factotum, in his art work. He sent Mr. Allen on sketching tours, persuaded distinguished engravers to give him lessons, and in other ways directed his artistic educa- tion. Ruskin soon came to trust Mr. Allen more and more, and to treat him as a valued friend and companion. It was Mr. Allen, among others, who assisted Ruskin, in his laborious sorting of the Turner water-colour sketches at the National Gallery, and Mr. Allen was often his companion in the Alps. Like his master, Mr. Allen was much interested in geology and mineralogy, and he was as fond and proud as Ruskin himself, of the beautiful specimens which he had collected.

The College has from time to time received from Mr. Allen gifts of Ruskin's books, which have a resting place in a corner of the Library, and recently, through Dr. Furnivall, he sent us eighty drawings and engravings by or after Ruskin. Mr. Allen was one of the first subscribers to this JOURNAL, which he continued to support till the end of his life.

From advices received from Johannesburg, South Africa, we much regret to learn that Mr. J. B. Upperton, an old member of the College and of the Old Students' Club, died in that town on the 7th of July last, after a short illness. Mr. Upperton, who was about fifty years of age, went to South Africa for the benefit of his health some twenty years ago, and there settled down, but he always maintained his interest in the College.

WHAT THE COLONIAL SECRETARY SAID IN THE HOUSE OF LORDS.

IN reply to a question from the Earl of Jersey, in the House of Lords on August 22nd last, as to the better ordering of the business of the self-governing Colonies, and of the Imperial Conference, the Earl of Elgin, the Colonial Secretary, said it was proposed to divide the office into Three Departments instead of Four, *i.e.*, the Dominion Department, the Colonial Department, and the General Department, and he added that he proposed to put at the head of the Dominion Department the Senior Assistant Under-Secretary of State. Mr. Lucas was a gentlemen of very high academical and literary distinction, who had managed, even amongst the pre-occupations of his official duties, to find time for works of merit on Colonial and especially on Canadian History. He had had a long experience in Colonial administration, and his attractive and sympathetic personality had made him friends in every quarter. It was certain that the task of recommending this new department to our brethren beyond the seas could be safely entrusted to him.

The Colonial Secretary then referred to another College friend and a friend of Mr. Lucas as follows :—"The second appointment was the nomination of the Secretary of the Conference. The promise made was to select from the Colonial Office staff a gentleman for the special duties arising out of the work of the Conference, acquainted with its past as well as with what was contemplated in the future. This post ought to be filled up by a man of proved ability, and of a standing which would justify his access whenever necessary to the Secretary of State. He was glad to say he could secure at once continuity from Conference to Conference ; for he felt able to promote to this new post the gentleman who occupied the position of joint secretary to the late Conference. Mr. Just had an experience of Colonial affairs second to none, and had a special knowledge of South African business, having visited that country with a former Secretary of State. He held the rank of an assistant-secretary, and he claimed that he was appointing to this post a man of experience, merit, and position."—[Extracted from *The Times* of August 23rd.]

LUBBOCK FIELD CLUB.

JULY 7TH.—The report of our enjoyable visit to Mr. Fotheringham's on this date is held over, for want of space.

July 21st.—Only four turned out, and reaching Chesham at eleven o'clock, started across the fields to Leyhill Common, by Cowcroft. We then struck north by Jason's Hill and Moor's Farm across a wood to Whelpley Hill, where we found a path leading to Ashley Green. Here we halted for lunch. That over, we turned north through a big wood, and on reaching the road made our way to Marlin Chapel Farm. A series of paths commenced here, ending on Hawridge Common, near the Church. We walked the whole length of the Common, and visited Cholesbury Church, and Camp. From here another path connected with the Asheridge Road, by which we returned to Chesham. Here we had tea, and returned by the 6.48 train, just escaping a big thunderstorm, which had been gathering all day. The day was dull and oppressive, and the country, though very picturesque, was productive of little of interest. Monotropa was observed in a wood, and Lemna Minor in flower. The distance walked was about sixteen miles. Several sand-pits were visited, showing the junction with the chalk.

On July 23rd, a general meeting of the Club was held at the College to consider several points of importance in connection with the future of the Club. The chair was taken by Mr. Alfred Grugeon, president, and over two dozen members were present. Mr. Holloway, hon. secretary, brought before the meeting four matters requiring attention. For the information of those who had only known the Club during the past few years, he mentioned that the idea of Sunday rambles was well to the front in 1857—1862, under Furnivall and Fotheringham. The present club was, he said, the successor to one started in 1873, with the late Professor Flower as president ; Mr. Litchfield, vice-president ; Messrs. Ebenezer Cooke and Alfred Grugeon, committee ; Mr. Fleming, curator ; and Mr. Fotheringham, secretary and treasurer, succeeded by Mr. Cooke in 1875. This club lasted only a few years. It held weekly meeting and outings, the latter attended by ladies. In 1890, the botanical walks, under Mr. Grugeon, aroused much enthusiasm, and at the end of the course the Lubbock Field Club was formed, in March, 1893. Formal meetings were held, a president, vice-president, secretary and committee of four were elected, and rules were made, providing for annual general meetings, indoor meetings weekly from June to September, and fortnightly the rest of the year, with outdoor meetings on Saturdays and Sundays as arranged. There was an annual subscription of 1s. 6d., membership was confined to past or present members of the College, and on Mr. Grugeon's suggestion the permission of Sir John Lubbock was obtained to call the club by his name. Throughout that summer the programme was carried out completely and papers were read fortnightly, alternating with exhibition meetings. As the winter came on, however, it was decided to limit the meetings to one indoor and one outdoor monthly, and by the beginning of 1894 it had become increasingly difficult to get members to attend meetings or read papers. In 1895, the Saturday meetings were revived, and Mr. Shurlock, the secretary, had programmes printed and circularized. Notwithstanding this, by the end of the year he was seriously discussing the question of winding up the club. Then came the lamented death of Mr. Shurlock, whereupon all his friends decided that an object he had so much at heart should not be allowed to disappear. At a meeting on June 10th, 1896, the club was re-constituted, with the speaker (Mr. Holloway) as secretary. The second Sunday in each month was fixed upon for the monthly excursion, and a monthly paper and exhibition meeting was arranged for. After several attempts to carry them on, the indoor meetings were dropped, or were only held at long intervals. The club is now practically an outdoor club. No regular subscription is levied, but those members desiring notices of meetings are expected to defray postage. The outings are better attended now than in former years, averaging last year 9 or 10, the figures being lower in summer. The distance covered averaged 14 miles. The record attendance of 19 was beaten on June 22nd, when a party of 33, including 6 ladies, visited the Chislehurst Caves.

Mr. HOLLOWAY then referred to the first subject for discussion, namely, as to whether members of the club, being past but not present members of the College, should be allowed to participate in or should be excluded from certain advantages of membership, *e.g.*, invitations to the club. In his view, the success of the club was due almost entirely to the outsiders. The most successful College clubs were those not absolutely restricted to College men, as the Cycling, Shakespeare, Field, and Furnivall Sculling Clubs.

Mr. GRUGEON supported the inclusion of all club members in invitations. Messrs. C. F. Marshall, Castell, Randall, Warren, Cambridge, Pocock, and the Vice-Principal spoke. Mr. CASTELL moved and Mr. RANDALL seconded a motion that honorary members be admitted. Mersrs. Melzer, Pocock, Holloway, Hayward, Grugeon, Marshall, and Smart having debated this, Mr. Castell withdrew his motion, and it was agreed without dissent that the rules of the club should be left as they stood, so that invitations to the club should extend to all members, whether past or present members of the College.

The second question had been revived, said the hon. secretary, by our old friend Newey, who considered the club had degenerated, from a scientific point of view, and that it got over too much country to do proper collecting. On the whole, he (Holloway) did not think we did much more than we had always done, except in winter, when there was little temptation to linger and little to collect. We might arrange two walks monthly, one of the botanical, and one of the athletic type. Wildey had suggested joint trips with the Cycling Club, which would be very pleasant. Messrs. Grugeon, Pocock, Marshall, Levinsohn, the Vice-Principal, and another having spoken, and various suggestions having been made, including one that on each walk the party should divide itself into slow and fast ramblers and arrange meeting places for meals, the matter was allowed to rest.

In connection with the third point—indoor meetings—Holloway alluded to Mr. Matthews' letter to the JOURNAL suggesting a College Scientific Society, also to Mr. Levinsohn's suggestion that the new Laboratory should form a centre for practical biological work, and to the scope offered for the energies of willing members in the museum collections, other than the geological specimens, which were so well looked after by Mr. Warren. Ultimately Mr. Grugeon offered a paper at a meeting to be arranged, on "Shelling Peas."

The fourth matter to which attention was drawn was the good work done by the Northern Footpaths Association, as to which a letter was read from Mr. Marks.

The next excursion takes place on October 13th, and will be to the wooded country lying between Hatfield and the Lea. Take return ticket to Potters Bar, 1s. 9d. Train leaves King's Cross at 9 o'clock. Provide lunch.

J. HOLLOWAY, *Hon. Secretary.*

THE WORKING MEN'S COLLEGE JOURNAL *is supported partly by Annual Subscribers living in different parts of the World, and partly by circulation among the Students and Members. Its success depends upon a regular demand, and to ensure this, the Editor would be glad if as many readers as can will become Subscribers. Subscription* 2s. 6d. *per annum, post free.*

LONDON: Printed by W. HUDSON & Co., Red Lion Street, High Holborn, and published at THE WORKING MEN'S COLLEGE, Crowndale Road, London, N.W.—Sept. 21st, 1907.

The Working Men's College Journal

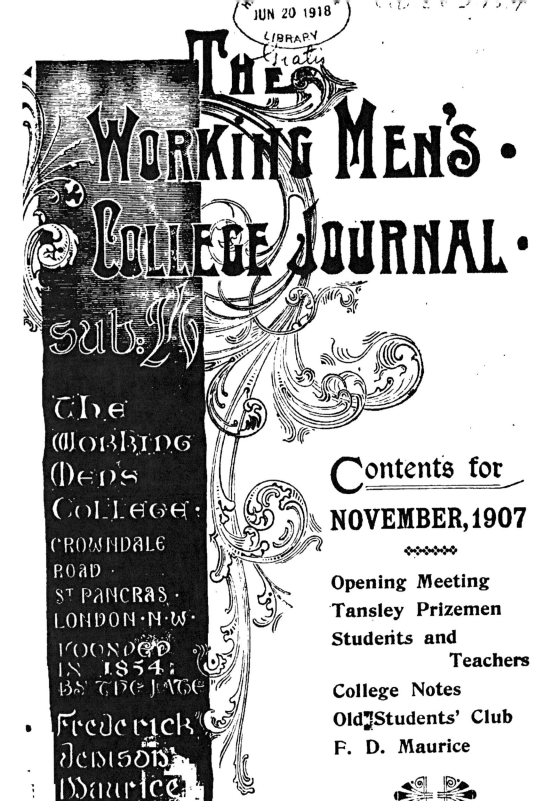

sub: 2

The Working Men's College:
CROWNDALE ROAD
ST PANCRAS
LONDON·N·W·
FOUNDED IN 1854;
BY THE LATE

Frederick Denison Maurice

Contents for

NOVEMBER, 1907

Opening Meeting
Tansley Prizemen
Students and Teachers
College Notes
Old Students' Club
F. D. Maurice

Working Men's College Journal.

Conducted by Members of the Working Men's College, Crowndale Road, London, N.W.

Vol. X.—No. 176.   NOVEMBER, 1907.   PRICE TWOPENCE.

INAUGURAL MEETING.

ADDRESS BY MR. LUCAS.

HE October term of the 54th year of the College was opened by a Smoking Concert in the Common and Coffee Rooms, presided over by Mr. Lionel Jacob, Vice-Principal, on Saturday, September 21st, and in the interval between the first and second parts, Mr. Jacob and Mr. Lucas addressed the students.

Mr. JACOB said he would like to bid the new students a very hearty welcome on behalf of the College, and he read to them a few words of welcome contained in a letter received from a dear old friend, Mr. Lowes Dickinson (cheers), who was too advanced in years to be there, but who wrote to wish us well, and who had been one of the best and most closely attached friends the College had had, since he helped Maurice to found it fifty-three years ago. The fine collection of portraits on the Common Room walls were painted by Mr. Lowes Dickinson with love and affection, as indeed were all his pictures.

The old students, continued Mr. JACOB, like the birds migrating, were coming back to their old home, after the fleeting and often disappointing flights of the summer—getting back to the solid comforts of winter, which never disappointed us. The old students were new not so very long ago, and he expressed the hope that the new students he was addressing might soon feel as much attached to the College as the older men. We had generally had more of a public meeting at the beginning of a new session, but had changed the arrangements for two reasons. One of them was the decoration of the Coffee Room, which, two months ago, had bare walls and ceiling, bearing witness to the poor state of the College finances, and which owed its present state of embellishment to the students of the College, and was now worthy of its fellow Common Room, whose grandeur was due to our old and faithful friend, Mr. Forster. We now saw the Coffee Room completed, and adorned by pictures of old friends, and especially our dear friend we all missed that evening, Mr. Marks (cheers). It was no light cause which kept Marks away that night—it was the great anxiety he had for his son who was lying ill.* All our hearts went out to

---

* We much regret to say that Mr. Marks's son, Harry, died early the following morning, September 22nd.

him in his trouble, and we all felt extremely friendly towards him.   Another portrait was that of Grugeon (cheers), an old student, if one could think of him as old, to whom we owed a great deal for his teaching of botany, and for the passion for it shown by successive generations of students.   A working man himself, he had left us his work and shown us what was the value of real education.   For the Coffee Room as it now was, we were specially grateful to Randall for his work for the fund, early and late, also to Balson and Nye, and others known to them.   He welcomed the new men to those rooms, the centre of the best part of our College life.   There was nothing like doing something in common with others, whether it was cycling, singing, or above all, studying, and in these rooms men met to do these things and others in common.   The life of the Common Room could be read about in the JOURNAL, in the four articles written by men who knew the place.   Mr. JACOB then dwelt upon the importance and the advantages of study, which enabled us to master the facts and principles of some branch of knowledge.   George Tansley, the man to whom the College owed most, for his work in it, whose portrait was at the end of the room, always put study in the first place, and then next to it, the comradeship which came from studying *together.*   It was necessary to put forth effort to learn ; teachers could help, but students must make the effort, and they could then master a subject and make it their own.   The teachers, many of them from the Universities, did not wish merely to address their students in class ; they wanted men to ask them questions, to consult them, to help with the work.   Students should go to them frankly with their difficulties—they asked for nothing better.   Some of the studies were simply in " bread and butter " subjects, needed to help a man to earn his living, and it was quite right to want to be more competent in one's work.   But there was another thing besides earning a living—one needed to learn something that would be a possession for life and a part of one's life.   Special knowledge acquired in this way, whether of foreign languages, science, or literature, was of great value, enabling us to know something of the wider world beyond the little world in which we lived—to know and also to admire the greatness of other men, and find our own level (cheers).

Mr. LUCAS :—Mr. Vice-Principal and gentlemen, I have so often in this College said all I have to say, and more also, that I propose to-night to say to you a few words about Nothing at all.   I read that in the political history of the United States there came a party called the " Know Nothings."   The nothing that they knew seemed to have been something, for they played a considerable part for a few years ; but in the end they died of inanition, which is a pretty way of saying that they came to nothing at all.   I want to say a few words, first, about men who come to nothing at all, and secondly about men who rise from nothing—a few words for new students in this College, which is able to prevent men from coming to nothing at all, and which enables them to rise from little or nothing.   Of the men who are said to come to nothing at all some are unfairly charged. They begin as nobodies and they end as nobodies, but they are no worse than their neighbours. In early life fond mothers sometimes say their children are going to do wonders; but the wonders do not happen, and people ask, Will it come to anything after all? It is a bad thing to over-praise young people, but it is worse, I think, to snub them. Dr. Ridding, my old master at Winchester, said he would have praised his boys more, if he had known how they were going to turn out. Some men come to nothing, because the sins of their fathers are visited on the children. Sometimes the sins come out in after life. Some men come to nothing, because of simple ill-health. I warn you, if you are going to do good work, to take care of your health. It is of great importance to you, and as a rule, good health is necessary, for good work to be done. But there are exceptions to this rule. Some of you may know what it is to be bad sleepers. I read that Prince Bismarck and Charles Darwin were bad sleepers; and I was comforted, because I thought, being a bad sleeper myself, I might become a Bismarck or a Darwin, but it has not come off yet. (Laughter.) I have taken down this from the *Spectator*:—" It is worth recording that, in the opinion of a very great physician, the true remedy for the sleeplessness which is the most distressing symptom of overwork, is not opium, but Bass's beer drunk at bedtime, instead of dinner." Some men suffer from their eyes. I know that. You have the example of Fawcett, the great Postmaster-General, before you, to show you that even blindness is not a bar to good work; and I can give you another example of the American historian, Parkman, whose story of Canada, from the days of Cabot to those of Wolfe and Montcalm, is one of the most delightful books you can read, and yet his eyes were so bad, he could only use them five minutes at a time. These, however, are the exceptions which prove the rule of *mens sana in corpore sano*. If you want to do good work, take care of your health. Then there are the cases of those over-pressed when young. I have known head-masters who have used their all, by getting scholarships. In the race of life, as on the river, when you are rounding the corner, and coming into the straight, you must have something in hand, or you will lose. I come next to the men who are clever, healthy, not over-pressed, and yet who come to nothing. Why? I find the answer in the fact that they do not take pains—they do not concentrate their minds on single objects. You know the phrase, " Know something of everything and everything of something." Those men are content to know something of everything, but they need to go on, to know everything of something. They forget, as someone—Fox, I think—has reminded us, that " Genius consists in an infinite capacity for taking pains." Emerson says, " The one prudence in life is concentration ; the one evil is dissipation." He does not mean taking to drink, but exhausting your powers on too many objects. You must have known this class of men. I have known them. They seem to be more clever than you are in all sorts of things, and yet they come to nothing. I find the reason is that they do not concentrate on one object. That means accuracy, and accuracy makes the difference between an effective and an ineffective man. Men who do not concentrate are shallow, and become relatively shallower as time goes on, because the less gifted men have concentrated and forged ahead. Our Founders concentrated their minds on definite objects, and carried them through ; and you who knew the man of whom our Vice-Principal has spoken, my great friend George

Tansley, will remember the determination with which, day by day,
week by week, he fixed his eyes on the object he had in view, and
was thorough and steadfast from beginning to end, and carried it
through absolutely, strictly, and with perfection, never wavering, never
faltering, but with restless energy labouring until no single bond was
left untied. I ask you young men to be true to our traditions. Do
not spend your energy on too many things, and think, because you
can talk about a lot of things, that you have knowledge, because
you have not. You are here to make your way in the world, and
you are here to make the College a little better for having you in it.
Do not take too many classes, and do not make the mistake of
thinking that hearing lectures will give you the whole of knowledge.
You must work yourselves. You must have few objects. You must
master those objects. And if you do this, *you must come to something*.
Take the converse, men who rise from nothing. Benjamin Franklin
has told us that when he was a boy, he used to walk to Philadelphia
with a twopenny roll in his pocket. There does not seem to be much
in that. Mark Twain said, " I would undertake to do the same."
It is all very well to joke about it, but these are the men who rise
from nothing. But what is it in them that makes them rise? They
have something in them that *creates*, that enables them to make
something out of nothing. Froude takes two classes of men, " Men
who do great things, and men who talk and make speeches about
them " ; and he gives the palm to the first. I like to think that doing
things is characteristic of the English race. Some of you will
remember the time when there was a strong feeling against England,
and she had but few friends abroad. One of them, David Wells, an
American political economist, said of us, however, " Where England
has gone, two blades of grass have grown where one grew before."
That is a very noble estimate of our people, and I like to think and
believe it is true. Thomas Carlyle says, " The English are a dumb
people ; they can do great acts, but not describe them." Doing,
making, is characteristic of our College. Maurice and those who
worked with him made, created, brought something out of nothing.
You have heard the Vice-Principal tell of these two rooms, one made
by yourselves, the other by his and my great friend, J. A. Forster,
who started life as a working lapidary, and who has made his
position, made himself and his surroundings prosperous and happy,
as we know well, and who has remained true to this College all his
life. I like to think of this Common Room thus—Here is something
made by our friend Mr. Forster. I echo what our Vice-Principal said
with regard to what you have done in making the Coffee Room
what it is. It is a practical illustration of what I am saying. You
have made something. You can say, Here we have done this.
Depend upon it, the great thing is, not to write a smart article or to
make a clever speech, but to do or make something. Two sayings I
am very fond of. One is the text, " Whatsoever thy hand *findeth*
to do, do it with thy might." The point lies in the " findeth." The
other maxim I like is, " Men who never make mistakes never make
anything." Go away and make something—a good chair or table—
make a good mistake. Thomas Cromwell said, " Make or mar."
Construct, do not destroy. Do not merely talk and criticize. Listen
to Carlyle again,—" To make some nook of God's creation a little
fruitfuler, better, more worthy of God ; to make some human hearts
a little wiser, manfuler, happier, more blessed, less accursed,—it is
work for a god." That is the message I want to give you to-night.
We are here to breed good citizens. Resolve, as students of this
College, to create something. (Cheers.)

In the smoking concert which formed the setting of this address, the following students performed :—M. K. Field, "Bust the Bugle" ; R. E. Tyler, "The Bandolero" and "The Bugler" ; W. J. Davis, recitations, "Uncle Podger" and "The run for the Coach" ; T. A. Paterson, "Meg of Margate" and "The Longshoreman" ; C. H. Perry, "The Nightmare," "John Wellington Wells," and "The Judge's song " ; H. C. Dumbrill, "Screw Guns," and "The Gallants of England" ; W. Hagerty, "Nita Gitana" ; Moxey, "Hearts of Oak" ; Gallaher, recitation, "Barker's Picture" ; and F. J. Nield, "When I was a boy at school."

LUBBOCK FIELD CLUB.

JULY 7TH.—On this day the Club enjoyed a visit to Mr. Fotheringham's at Kingsdown. There were eleven of us at the outset, namely, Field, Peckham, Penny, Staal, Holloway, Cambridge, Knight, Warren, Smart, Wildey and Schwyn, and Marks joined us late in the afternoon. We reached Eynsford at 9.45, and were met by Mr. Fotheringham on the station. We took the path just beyond the church, and followed it down to Maplescombe, when we struck the road. Just opposite the ruined chapel, we took the road up the hill to a cave that had been inhabited by tramps for some years until the local authorities interfered. After some frantic attempts to keep off the Maidstone Road, we reached Kingsdown, and again visited the gravel pit near the top of the hill, where is to be seen a fine chalk boulder surrounded by gravel. We then walked smartly back to Barnshatch, where we were received by Mrs. and Miss Fotheringham, and regaled with a sumptuous lunch. That disposed of, the majority of us settled down to smoke and talk, while the more active inspected the gold-fish pond, the orchard, the model pigstye, the beehives, the fern-house, the wood, and the neighbouring chalk-pit. We also had the opportunity of overhauling our host's mineral treasures. Tea was served on the verandah in picnic fashion, accompanied by heaps of strawberries. All too soon, it became necessary to move homewards, and we struck north-west, across the fields, to the paper mills at Eynsford. The train was only a quarter-of-an-hour late, and left Eynsford at nine o'clock. The day was dull and cool, and a few spots of rain fell in the evening, but the country was in grand condition. The distance walked was about thirteen miles. Botanical captures were not numerous, but included the Bee and Pyramidal Orchids and Spurge Laurel. In the geological way many fossils were seen, although none were of sufficient value to keep. We spent some time in hunting for eoliths and the green-coated flints that indicate the old level of the Chalk Plateau. We wish to record our grateful thanks to Mr. and Mrs. Fotheringham for their kind hospitality, which made the day extremely enjoyable.

On August 11th, the Club had a most enjoyable outing, striking country that was new to most of the members. A start was made from the Rye House, and a number of paths followed in a northerly direction until Standon was reached, the road being carefully avoided until the claims of tea made themselves felt in the afternoon. The route followed was across Rye Meads to Stansted Abbotts, thence east of Easneye Park and across the Ash at Mardocks. Lunch was partaken of at Wareside, and after a pretty stroll through woods and cornfields, a road was reached at Burleigh Common. Thence the course of the river Rib was closely followed to Great Barwick, and, as mentioned above, a couple of miles along a road ended at Standon. After tea, there was time for a short stroll before catching the 6.49 train home. Among the many items of interest observed was a big block of conglomerate erected as a Jubilee monument at Standon. It bore a curious resemblance to a human figure. Crayfish were found in the Rib, and the Fœtid Hellebore was noticed at Sawtrees.

Next outing, November 10th.—Excursion to Burnham Beeches and neighbourhood. Take walking tour ticket, No. 1, out to Gerrard's Cross, back from Slough, 1s. 11d. Train leaves Paddington, 9.23. Provide lunch.

J. HOLLOWAY, *Hon. Secretary.*

THE TANSLEY PRIZEMEN OF 1907.

THE Tansley Memorial Prizes, which, we may be pardoned for reminding our readers, are awarded to the three most meritorious students during the College year, have been awarded this year to Messrs. E. J. H. Reglar, J. W. Roberts, and E. W. Silk. It may be also noted that the Prize Committee, in examining the credentials of the different candidates, consider amongst other things regular attendance at classes and results of examinations. The wisdom of the Committee is shown in their selection, and the result of their labours this year will be deservedly popular.

Ernest James Henley Reglar joined the College rather more than thirteen years ago, taking as his study English Grammar, with the result that he obtained a first stage certificate in this subject. This small success, coupled with the fact that he readily fell into the social life of the place, encouraged Mr. Reglar to further effort, and he obtained in 1906 certificates in Grammar (Advanced Stage) and History. The next six years of his College life was devoted to desultory reading and study, and in taking part in the voluntary work, for which all good College men are noted. The records of the College show no success until June, 1902, when we find Mr. Reglar gazetted Senior Student. Teaching in the Preparatory Division followed as a natural consequence, and in this as in other work he found himself quite at home, making many friends. His inclination next took him to the Higher Division, and in June, 1905, he gained a certificate of proficiency in the Law of Contract. During the past year he has studied Political Economy under Mr. Theodore Morison, and at the end of a course of brilliant lectures and useful discussions an examination was held, and we find Mr. Reglar's name amongst those of the successful candidates.

Mr. Reglar has been in turn Secretary of the Common Room Committee, Maurice Cricket Club, Athletic Sports, and Children's Tea. He is an enthusiastic cricketer, is fond of cycling, sculling, and yachting on the Broads, and he enjoys a dance as well as anything. He is now a member of the Executive Committee and Director of the Preparatory Division. He is a clerk by profession.

Mr. John Walter Roberts joined the College in 1904, when he took up the study of French under Mons. J. Lazare, gaining a first stage certificate in June, 1906. He then seems to have become desirous of matriculating, and with this object in view, he began to study those of the necessary subjects for which he could find time. French, Euclid, and English, he took at one time. That he is making satisfactory progress is shown by the fact that his name appears on this year's Honours List for certificates in Euclid and English Literature. Yielding to the persuasion of his friends, he, without preparation, essayed the Senior Student Examination, and only just missed success by three marks in one of the required subjects, passing very high in the other two. His tutors regard Mr. Roberts as a most promising student, and being still quite young we may reasonably expect great things of him. Mr. Roberts is a nephew of the famous billiard champion of that name, a fact which may account in some measure for his aptitude and inclination for Euclid. His favourite sports are cricket, football, chess, and swimming, while he has gained some proficiency in boxing and never enjoys himself more than when he is having a "good hard mill" in the Gymnasium with "Old Flint." Mr. Roberts speaks at our debates, sings at our "smokers," and is quite a good social unit. He is a clerk by profession.

Quite a rare example of concentration and assiduity is Mr. Ebenezer William Silk. Becoming one of us as far back as 1895, being a signwriter at the time, he took up Art as a study, and sought no other during his long connection with the College. No fewer than seventeen certificates have fallen to his lot during the past twelve years. In almost every department of Art has Mr. Silk succeeded. Finding himself so gifted, he has set himself to work to assist and to encourage those desirous of "learning to draw." He is and has been of great assistance to his tutor, Mr. R. W. Wilkinson, and that gentleman is justly proud of such a pupil. Nor has his phenomenal success robbed Mr. Silk of his own natural modesty, so rarely found in clever young artists nowadays, for he thinks nothing of his own achievements, being ever ready to praise the work of others to the belittlement of his own. This is particularly true in the case of new young students.

Mr. Silk's hobby is Art, strange as it may seem. He is devoted to it, but he contrives to steal from his exacting mistress sufficient time to ably manage the affairs of the Working Men's College Sketching Club. R. R. F.

LITERARY SOCIETY.

THE first meeting of the Literary Society this season will take place on Thursday, 7th November, at 9.30, when Mr. A. S. Lupton will read a paper, entitled "A plea for wider Reading."

The society meets every alternate Thursday, and Mr. E. M. Forster has kindly arranged to read a paper on "Dante," on 21st November.

All members are cordially invited to attend.

C. F. W. MEAD, *Hon. Secretary.*

TANSLEY SWIMMING CLUB.

MEMBERS are informed that the Club will meet during the winter season on Tuesdays, at 7.30 p.m., at King Street Baths, two minutes from the College.

The Team race and 100 yards Championship race are postponed owing to insufficient entries, but the secretary will arrange them when at least eight competitors enter. Names are required for those wishing to enter for a life-saving class.

W. H. BARNETT, *Hon. Secretary.*

STUDENTS AND TEACHERS' MEETING.

MR. JASTRZEBSKI ON THE COLLEGE.

ON Monday, October 21st, at 9.30 p.m., a well attended meeting of students and teachers, convened by the Common Room Committee, took place in the Common and Coffee Rooms, with Tom Barnard in the chair, and T. T. S. de Jastrzebski gave one of the finest addresses on the subject of the College, its work and traditions, that it has been our good fortune to hear.

The CHAIRMAN heartily welcomed to the social rooms of the College all new men who might be there, and announced some of the coming events of interest to the students. He then introduced "Shemski" as one of the most versatile and brilliant of our members, director of studies of the language section, teacher of German, able to speak nearly every European language (including English), as an excellent singer, and as possessing one quality in particular—a wonderful sense of humour. (Cheers.)

Having, by some of his brilliant sallies of wit, put himself on good terms with his audience, JASTRZEBSKI narrated one of his teaching experiences. Nothing, he said, could be more absolutely inspiring than to have taken the Foreigners' class at the old College.   One term I began with ten students, every one of whom represented a different nationality, and spoke a different language.   One was an Armenian, and his vocabulary was confined to Armenian, of which I knew not a word, in spite of what Barnard has said about me.   I was reduced to the elementary language of signs.   Some people say it is easy to make yourself understood by signs.   Let them try it. I tried, and made a most hideous hash of it.   Another in the class was a Levantine Jew.   I got on a little better with him, because he spoke Spanish, and although my "Spanish" was not very "juicy"—(laughter), I could get along in it.   I set him an exercise, and he brought it duly written in Spanish —at least, he said it was—but it was in Hebrew characters (laughter), so that it was a bit of a failure from the point of view of my trying to correct it.   My good friend Dr. Oswald examined the class, and gave a dictation exercise under the title of "The widow and the hen."   My Armenian wrote: "A window kept an enn wich laid an age every mornings." (Laughter.)   Dr. Oswald asked me what he meant.   I said I thought he was trying to account for the flight of time.   As I am to talk about the students and teachers of this College, I might recall some of the earlier days, when some of the older men were not the staid and respectable parties they have since become—when Marks was a teetotaller, for instance—or when our friend Forster was a revolutionary, and led the revolt for beer and other liberties.   But after all, they are still with us, and I do not want to make them different in your eyes, from what they seem.   It would be interesting to trace the influence of the College on men who never have been students—Dent, for example.   They say you would have to stew Dent, before you could make a stu-dent of him—that when he came to the College, he could not smoke, but now you never see him without a pipe.   It is also recorded of him that he never knew what a "bug in the blanket" was, until he came to the College.   Every man who comes here, becomes something other than he was before.   I turn to that most extraordinary and brilliant bye-product of the College, the student teacher.   My schoolmaster was fond of letting off a few tags at us when I was at school.   He used to say that the difference between a practical man and a theoretical man was this—that a practical man could do a thing, but did not know how he did it ; whereas a theoretical man thought he could do a thing, but could not ; while the practical-theoretical man thought he could do it, but couldn't, and believed he knew how to do it, but didn't !   Do not imagine that I wish you to infer that a student teacher is one who has been a failure as a student and is not a success as a teacher.   On the contrary, he is of the salt of the earth. Student teachers are absolutely our own product, and we are extremely proud of them. I am one of them myself. (Laughter.) I will invoke the aid of the muse upon the subject—

> The gentle student who is filled
> With yearning deep and true for knowledge,
> He comes and finds that teachers skilled
> Are found in plenty at our College.
>
> And if his heart collegiate burns,
> He soon becomes a different creature,
> For in the course of time he turns
> Into the noble student-teacher !

There is an admirable story told of St. John the Divine. One day, when playing leap-frog with the disciples, and having a very good time, he called out suddenly, "Stop, we must be serious, there is a fool coming." I hope you will appreciate the moral. Now, I am not going to be serious because we have a fool coming—he never does come. By some selective process we never get them within these walls ; or if they do come, they soon leave us. I have been told that there is a certain tendency, on occasions of formal meetings, to bring out a formidable sort of ghost—"the College Tradition," which I am given to understand weighs very heavily on the minds of some of the younger students. Some of us are getting older—I am in the half-way stage myself—and we do not always see things from the point of view of the next generation. Herrick has said, "That age is best which comes the first, When youth and blood are warmer" ; and most of us who have passed the meridian know that Herrick was right. We here have also a tendency to look back fondly to those times when youth and blood were warmer. And this College Tradition—is it such a dreadful incubus? It seems to me to amount to this, that the men who founded this institution had the extraordinary courage and insight to grasp the idea, that a *College* was possible among working-men and among all the different classes of our social organization. They saw that there could be an association for a common aim, where all united to give the best within them for the common service ; and although it may seem to us something of a commonplace that this College should exist, it was really only by a sublime act of faith on the part of Maurice and his helpers that this College was brought into being. We are their spiritual successors. In ourselves their ideal lives, moves, and has its being ; and our tradition is that we associate one with another to give what we can to help on the common weal There can be nothing more stimulating and elevating than our College tradition. The Founders of this College were not of a solemn, severe, and gloomy frame of mind. They were the most sanguine, the most hopeful of men, or they never could have got through the work they did. Not only were they, amongst themselves, of this cheerful faith, they were able to inspire the new generation to be of the same way of thinking. When the first flush of enthusiasm in such a movement has passed away, it is in the second stage that the difficulties come. Happily with us these have been long surmounted. Some of the Founders are still with us—we reverence them every one ; and they were able to inspire the next generation with their ideas, and those who have followed them have inspired another and yet another generation. You are co-heirs and co-partakers in one of the noblest works which ever man put his hand to in this country. (Cheers.) A good friend of mine and an enthusiastic teacher has come to me with long lists of the successes of his class, and said to me, "I don't see any of your fellows down—aren't you disappointed?" I said, "No, not a bit. I know I have stimulated men to do the work I have been doing. Through me they have been inspired to do their part. This to me is more encouraging than any mere examination results can ever be." We are carrying the torch we have had handed on to us ; and when our steps begin to falter and breath is scant, we shall pass it on to others whom we have stimulated in the same way as we ourselves have been ; so that the soul of this College, like that of John Brown, goes marching on for ever. The College tradition, the College spirit, is a real, active, and living principle. I look on the face of that old friend whose portrait hangs behind me, and remember that I never come to the College and try to teach without thinking of the stimulus Tansley was to me. You had only got to have five minutes' talk with Tansley, and you felt rejuvenated and reinvigorated. As long as I live, the presence of that man will ever be with me. Those other men, whose faces look down on you from the walls in this room—some of them great and famous men, others known to yourselves only—they are still the living College, they being dead yet speak, and they will be with, and of this College till the end of time. Their very names may be forgotten ; it does not matter—their work, their noble enthusiasm and their spirit live, and will go on after we too have gone to join the great majority. It is the finest and most stimulating and most invigorating thought to me, that I, too, have had a share in this work. Every brick is as essential to the building as the foundation stone you have put there. The College is not made by the teachers or the governing body alone. It is as much formed by the students as by the teachers. Reverting to my own personal experience, whatever I may have taught here, I have learnt far more. This College has enabled me to realize what seems to me to be the ultimate truth in human philosophy— What a man gives, he gets. It is what you give away, not what you keep, that is of value. It comes back to you a thousand-fold. There is hardly a man here I cannot call my friend, because we have worked here together for a common object. I have only to say this, for you to realize that the debt I owe to the Working Men's College is incalculable. Another thing that has always struck me as being one of the finest features, in connection with the men who have done the main work of this College, is this—their extraordinary appreciation of everybody's work but their own. One of the most marked characteristics of the men who do the most work here is the way in which they appreciate other men's work, and minimize their own. Tansley's enthusiasm in the work of others, and depreciation of his own, are well known to those of you who remember him ; and those who know our present Vice-Principal are well aware that he is afflicted with the same failing. (Hear, hear.) I hope I have not been too serious. May I repeat what our friend in the chair has said, and as an older member of the College, and as a portion of the government, welcome you most sincerely and most heartily into our midst ? We want you to be of us and among us. The best this College has to give is yours, and it is to be found in the College itself, and not merely in the classes. Here ·in these rooms is the rallying ground, where meet all sorts and conditions of men, and where they meet on absolutely equal terms. It lies with you whether this College shall maintain the great and glorious tradition I have spoken of, and go on from strength to strength. Mere numbers we do not care about ; so long as we can get the College reasonably filled with men who will use it in the right spirit, we shall not have failed in our endeavour to hand on to you that which we have received from those who have founded the College and who have kept it going ever since. (Applause.)

The chairman having called upon speakers, MARKS endorsed Jastrzebski's welcome, spoke of the many years he had been in the College himself and the great pleasure and many friends he had gained in it. CRAWLEY spoke of the extent to which the College had become part of his life—so much so that, when away for years in South Africa, there was no other magazine he looked for so eagerly as the COLLEGE JOURNAL. POCOCK suggested, as a ready means for new men to get to know their fellow-members, the joining of one of the numerous clubs in the College. LANDELLS instanced the attachment of a French student he had met in Paris, and from whom he received great kindness. REGLAR amused us by describing one of the Cricket Clubs of the past ; reminded us of the peculiarity that no one was ever heard to swear in the College, although College men could do so outside, as for instance on the Broads, after continually knocking their heads in the same place coming up the hatchway—all except Tarr. (Laughter.) HOMEWOOD gave some holiday experiences at Felday. And the VICE-PRINCIPAL, referring to Jastrzebski and his charming address, reminded us of an old saying, " No one is quite wise, unless he has a spice of folly in him." Jastrzebski had the requisite amount, and he had also that wisdom which justified the folly. He had summed up what we meant by the College, as well as he (Mr. Jacob) had ever heard it summed up. If men helped each other in their class work, they would derive great benefit. If they came to the College intending to make the most of it, to make friendships, to learn and help others to learn, it would be one of the greatest and best influences of their lives ; and in a few years those who were new now would be speaking of the College with the same words of love and attachment they had just heard. (Cheers, and a vote of thanks to Barnard, with gusto.)

THE STUDENTS' CALENDAR FOR NOVEMBER.

Fri., 1st.—Lecture, "Child Study," Dr. Slaughter, 8 p.m.

Sat., 2nd.—Lecture, "The Future Evolution of Man," Dr. Saleeby, 8.30.

Sun., 3rd.—Lecture, "The Hebrew Monarchy," Rev. B. H. Alford, 6 p.m.

Mon., 4th.—Lecture, "The Romantic Revival in English Poetry," Mr. Guthkelch, 7.30.

Tues., 5th.—Executive Committee, 8 p.m. Lecture, "Italian Painters," Mr. Dudley Heath, 8 p.m. Swimming Club practice, King Street Baths, 7.30. Debating Society meeting, 9.30.

Thurs., 7th.—Lecture, "The Fundamental Principles of the Law of the Constitution," The Principal, 8.30. Literary Society meeting, Mr. A. S. Lupton's paper, "A plea for wider Reading," 9.30. Citizens' lunch, 1.30.

Fri., 8th.—Lecture, "Child Study," Dr. Slaughter, 8 p.m.

Sat., 9th.—Lecture, "Earthquakes, great and small," illustrated, Dr. Flett, 8.30. Smoking Concert, 9.30.

Sun., 10th.—Field Club Walk to Burnham Beeches ; train leaves Paddington, 9.23 a.m. Lecture, "Hebrew Monarchy," Rev. B. H. Alford, 6 p.m. Shakespeare Reading, "Macbeth," 7.30 p.m.

Mon., 11th.—Latest day for nomination of student members of the Council. Lecture, "English Poetry," Mr. Guthkelch, 7.30.

Tues., 12th.—Executive Committee, 8 p.m. Lecture, "Italian Painters," Mr. Dudley Heath, 8 p.m. Swimming Club practice, 7.30. Chess match, Whitfield Institute, 8 p.m. Debating Society meeting, 9.30.

Thurs., 14th.—Lecture, "History of London," Mr. R. Rait, M.A., 8.30.

Fri., 15th.—Lecture, "Child Study," Dr. Slaughter, 8 p.m.

Sat., 16th.—Lecture, "John Ruskin," Miss Spurgeon, 8.30. Old Students' Club meeting, 7.45, to discuss "Has Party Government worked well, and can it be improved ?" Mr. C. E. Maurice.

Sun., 17th.—Lecture, "Hebrew Monarchy," Rev. B. H. Alford, 6 p.m.

Mon., 18th.—Election of three student members of Council begins. Lecture, "English Poetry," Mr. Guthkelch, 7.30.

Tues., 19th.—Executive Committee, 8 p.m. Lecture, "Italian Painters," Mr. Dudley Heath, 8 p.m. Swimming Club practice, 7.30. Debating Society meeting, 9.30.

Thurs., 21st.—Literary Society meeting, 9.30. Mr. E. M. Forster's paper on "Dante."

Fri., 22nd.—Lecture, "Child Study," Dr. Slaughter, 8 p.m.

Sat., 23rd.—Lecture, "Art and Puritanism," Mr. J. W. Mackail, M.A., LL.D.

Sun., 24th.—Lecture, "Hebrew Monarchy," Rev. B. H. Alford, 6 p.m. Shakespeare Reading, "King John" (ladies' night), 7.30 p.m.

Mon., 25th.—Lecture, "English Poetry," Mr. Guthkelch, 7.30. Common Room general meeting and Election, 9.30.

Tues., 26th.—Council Meeting, 8 p.m. Lecture, "Italian Painters," Mr. Dudley Heath, 7.30. Debating Society meeting, 9.30.

Wed., 27th—Lubbock Field Club Exhibition meeting, 8 p.m.

Thurs., 28th.—Lecture, "History of London," Mr. R. Rait, 8.30. Chess match, "Chess Bohemians," 136, Cheapside, 8 p.m.

Fri., 29th.—Lecture, "Child Study," Dr. Slaughter, 8 p.m.

Sat., 30th.—Lecture, "Sir Robin Redbreast and his family," Mr. F. B. Kirkman, B.A., 8.30.

COLLEGE NOTES.

THE opening of the winter session of the fifty-fourth year of the College was marked by two excellent addresses to the students, one by Mr. Lucas on September 21st, and the other by Mr. Jastrzebski on October 21st. In both cases the speakers, whose wit and humour are so well known, gave us messages of weight and earnestness, and we are fortunate to be able to present reports of both their speeches.

On October 26th, Sir Frederick Maurice, K.C.B., distributed the College honours gained during the past year, and afterwards gave a lecture on "Sir John Moore." There was a good attendance of students, and each of the successful ones was cheered as he went up to the platform to receive his certificate. Those to whom the largest share of applause fell were the winners of the highest honours, but they were applauded no less for their success than for their being well known in the College as good fellows in every respect. These were E. J. H. Reglar, Tansley Scholar; J. W. Roberts, Tansley Prizeman; A. C. Martin, Senior Student Scholar, Associate, and Fellow; and T. M. Balson, Associate. E. W. Silk, strange to say, declined to take his Tansley Prize.

Immediately before the distribution meeting, an exhibition of sketches and other works of art was held in the Ruskin Art Room. These were well arranged by Mr. Wilkinson, Silk, and others, and formed a very creditable collection. Mr. Lowes Dickinson, hearing of the proposed exhibition, showed his interest in it by coming to the College in the afternoon. He was very pleased with it, and praised especially the works of S. J. Hertford. He would much like to have stayed to the evening meeting, but the cold and dampness of the season would not allow this. His two daughters, however, were present, as also were Lady Maurice, the Vice-Principal (in the chair), Mrs. Jacob, and two of her daughters.

Two College elections take place this month. One is the election of three student members of the Council, by and from among the fellows, student teachers, associates, senior students, and students of one year's standing. The last day for nominations of candidates for this election is November 11th, and the following names are already posted in the Common Room :—

Candidate.	Proposer.	Seconder.
R. M. Emslie.	E. S. Landells.	G. T. Butler.
J. J. Munro.	C. F. W. Mead.	Leonard Pocock.
H. N. Gill.	T. M. Balson.	P. J. Brett.
J. Crawley.	P. J. Brett.	T. M. Balson.
H. K. Randall.	M. Staal.	W. Melzer.

The retiring student members of Council are J. Crawley, H. N. Gill, W. J. Gray, F. J. Nield, and C. H. Perry, three of whom were elected members and two co-opted. All are eligible for re-election.

The other election is that of the Common Room Committee, in whose hands is the management of the Common and Coffee Rooms. This committee consists of seven members, elected annually by and from among the members of the Common Room; and the election this year will take place during the week following the annual general meeting of the members, to be held on November 25th, at 9.30 p.m. Any person who has been a member of the College for the six months immediately preceding the day of election, is eligible for election, and the names of candidates already posted are given below:—

Candidate.	Proposer.	Seconder.
H. K. Randall.	T. M. Balson.	J. Crawley.
E. Hayward.	E. S. Landells.	W. Melzer.
M. Staal.	W. Melzer.	H. E. Nye.
A. Owen.	J. B. West.	W. Melzer.
W. Melzer.	J. Hagerty.	J. B. West.
B. P. Moore.	A. Owen.	H. K. Randall.
C. F. W. Mead.	H. K. Randall.	H. E. Nye.

There were about thirty present on October 13th, at the first Shakespeare Reading of the session, held in the Common Room, and the readers had an intellectual treat, for "The Merchant of Venice" was the play, and H. F. A. Peck took the part of Shylock. This is one of Peck's favourite impersonations. He must have devoted much time and thought to it, and he reads it well. He was well supported by W. P. Harley as Antonio; T. Barnard, Bassanio; Miss Steptoe, Portia; Miss Walford, Nerissa; Miss Forsythe as Jessica; and others taking minor characters. For October 27th, "Much ado about Nothing" was the play selected.

Mr. J. B. West has been presented by his fellow-clubmates of the Furnivall Sculling Club with a Gladstone bag and a kit bag, in testimony of his valuable services as secretary of that Club, which position he had held for the two years previous to his resignation in April last. Doctor Furnivall, in making the presentation, referred to the good work he is now doing at the College in teaching English to our foreign friends, and also made a passing reference to his private duties. Mr. West is the only member of the College who has been secretary of the Furnivall Sculling Club.

The next *Citizens'* lunch will be eaten on the first Thursday in the month as usual, November 7th, at 1.30, in the third floor front room at Read's, in Cheapside.

We regret to announce the death of two old members of the College and of the Old Students' Club.   Mr. Henry Thomas Lewin died at the age of 72 on September 29th, and Mr. James Clayton, at about the same age, on September 22nd.   Mr. Lewin joined the College with Mr. C. Castle in 1862, and was well-known as a member of Dr. Oswald's class and as a practice class teacher in French.   In later years Mr. Lewin, who always kept up his connection with the College, delighted to take part in its social gatherings in company with his wife and daughter. Mr. Clayton, who joined the College at the end of the fifties, was a competent linguist, knowing French, German, Italian, and Spanish.   He was a member of the French class under M. Geney, M. Duhart-Fauvet, and lastly under Dr. Oswald, for whom he always had the greatest respect and esteem.   On account of his knowledge of French, he was chosen by the Government to represent the Post Office in the Exhibition held in Paris in 1867. Francis Lynch, also a distinguished linguist and a teacher of Grammar in the College, and Jim Donovan, of Corps and boxing fame, were Clayton's special friends, the tie which bound them together being one of country and religion; they were all Roman Catholics, and the best of good fellows, with a strong attachment to the College.   Mr. Clayton began his career as a carpenter, and retired from the service of the Post Office a few years ago when Postmaster at Lombard Street, one of the most important offices in the City, where his knowledge of languages often enabled him to render useful service to foreigners.

A penny series of "Pioneer Biographies of Social Reformers" is being issued, the first three of which, on G. J. Holyoake, Charles Kingsley, and Joseph Mazzini, are written by Mr. W. Henry Brown.   Others embody the lives of Robert Owen, Arnold Toynbee, and John Ruskin.   In his Kingsley biography, Mr Brown mentions the Working Men's College, and the attempts at forming co-operative workshops which led up to its foundation; and he extracts from the College History a reminiscence of an early Field Club ramble illustrative of Kingsley's love of sport and Nature.

We have received a prospectus of Classes of the Vaughan Working Men's College, Leicester, for the session 1907—8, being its 45th year.   The prospectus shows that between 25 and 30 subjects are taught, including Ambulance, Arithmetic, Book-keeping, Composition, Electricity, Elocution, English Literature, French, German, Greek, Latin, Music, Shorthand, besides such subjects as Cutting-out, Dressmaking, Home Nursing, Horti-culture, Millinery, Needlework, Photography, and Wood Carving. The College is indeed comprehensive in its operations, and caters alike for women and youths as well as for men.   It also has a Library, a Reading Room, a Debating Class, a St. John's Ambulance Brigade, a Sick Benefit Society, College Ramblers,

Cyclists' Association, Photographic Association, Provident Society, Book Club, Christmas Club, and a Magazine Department. The entries for last session comprised 998 men, 679 women, and 253 youths, making a total of 1930. The usual fee for a class is one shilling on entrance, and a penny for each attendance. The Educational Committee had hoped to welcome the students of 1907—8 in the new College, now in course of erection, but it was found impossible to get the building ready in time. It is expected however that the formal opening of the new College will take place early next year.

Referring to the report, in our Aug.-Sept. issue (page 164), of the Summer Festival at the College for Working Women at 7, Fitzroy Street, W., on July 4th last, Miss Frances Martin writes:—

"I have read the report of our July meeting, in the WORKING MEN'S COLLEGE JOURNAL, with great interest. There is one little error in speaking of Miss Francis as Secretary. I am the Hon. Secretary, and there is no other, nor ever has been—and we have no Principal. Under our deed of Incorporation, we have a Chairman and a Council of 12 Members, so that Mr. Llewelyn Davies is really the head and chief of our College." The First Term of the 34th Session of this College began on October 7th.

From the *Tribune* of October 12th:—

OUR NOTEBOOK.—The billposter is responsible for a startling announcement in Oxford Street. By accident or design the Drury Lane play-bill has been placed immediately above a placard issued by the Working Men's College. The following is the shocking result:—
SINS OF SOCIETY
EVENING CLASSES FOR BEGINNERS.
Whatever will Father Vaughan say now!

FURNIVALL SCULLING CLUB.

THE Club held its half-yearly general meeting on Sunday, 6th October A record number of members turned out in the morning for the opening of the winter sculling season, all the light boats being out. The stimulating effect of the pull was very evident in the evening, nearly everybody having something to say. Business done—W. Allen elected boat captain in place of A. G. Fisher, resigned ; and Misses A. Sutton and M. Coleman elected to the two vacant places on the committee, caused by the retirement of Misses K. Lock and V. Deane.

The Doctor read the annual report—drafted by C. F. W. Mead in his best literary form—and it was passed in its entirety. A number of propositions were also passed or negatived, which the secretary is still trying to remember.   H. S. HOWARD, *Hon. Secretary.*

THE LIBRARY.

THE following books have been added recently:—Presented by Dr. Furnivall, "Phases of Faith," by F. W. Newman ; "Pioneer Humanists," by J. M. Robertson ; "Rise of Christianity," by A. Kalthoff ; "The Bible in School," by J. A. Picton ; and a volume of Sir A. Lyall's "Asiatic Studies." Presented by Mr. Carlo Gatti, "Lydia," and some Sociological Papers ; presented by Rev. B. H. Alford, Driver's "Jeremiah," also Huxley and Martin's "Practical Biology."

One or two more helpers are required for odd jobs in the Library, and any students desirous of assisting the College in this way are invited to apply to the Librarian.   E. J. TURNER.

OLD STUDENTS' CLUB.

INEQUALITIES AND TAXATION.

THE first meeting of this Club for the present session was held in the Common Room on Saturday, October 19th, at 7.45 p.m., when 70 members were present, namely, Messrs. T. Austin, Tom Barnard, T. M. Balson, B. Black, Sydney Bradgate, E. J. Brennan, E. A. Brett, P. J. Brett, F. E. Brooks, G. Buckland, C. G. Cash, C. Castle, J. R. Chandler, J. W. Chapman, A. W. Coombs, S. J. Coombs, W. C. Cutts, John Dale, J. J. Dent, W. Duke, R. M. Emslie, Harold Eyers, M. K. Field, E. M. Forster, W. J. Gates Fowler, R. Freeman, S. B. W. Gay, Alfred Grugeon, C. G. Gümpel, S. Hamilton, W. Hart, E. Hayward, A. Hepburn, S. J. Hertford, William Hudson, Julius Jacob, Lionel Jacob, C. T. Jeffery, C. P. King, H. R. Levinsohn, A. Lewis, R. H. Marks, A. W. Matthews, C. E. Maurice, C. F. W. Mead, H. W. Miles, Charles Monteath, E. Murphy, G. S. Offer, Dr. E. Oswald, — Phelps, Leonard Pocock, S. Presburg, C. W. Rapley, R. A. Reed, E. J. H. Reglar, J. W. Roberts, F. C. Roper, E. W. Silk, W. J. Spray, M. Staal, M. W. Starling, S. A. Sweetman, W. Tirrell, W. J. Torrington, G. Wanklin, C. R. Williams, A. Wilshaw, Charles Wright, and Harold Wright.

The chairman and president of the club, Mr. R. H. MARKS, referred to the losses which the club had sustained by the death of four of its members, Messrs. Frank Colton, J. B. Upperton, Henry T. Lewin, and James Clayton, and to the fact that another old member, Mr. E. R. Cole, had retired and gone to live at Chester. The balance sheet was then read and adopted, with the usual joking about the auditor, the secretary remarking that on the last occasion the club had expressed some doubts as to the fitness of the auditor, so the committee, after mature consideration, had decided to revert to the old practice, and leave the balance sheet unaudited. This appeared quite satisfactory, and upon the motion of the VICE-PRINCIPAL the whole of the officers of the club were re-elected, Marks as president, secretary, committee, and auditor; and Grugeon and Pocock as vice-presidents. The balance sheet, as passed, is appended :—

BALANCE SHEET, 1906—7.

Receipts.	£	s.	d.	*Expenditure.*	£	s.	d.
Balance forward	4	12	6	Printing, stationery, and			
218 subscriptions at 1s. ...	10	18	0	stamps	5	18	3
Received from College for				Rent of locker	0	2	6
Supper printing ...	0	11	6	Gratuity to Mrs. Robbie ...	0	7	6
				Donation to Coffee Room			
				Decoration Fund ...	1	1	0
				Donation to Maintenance			
				Fund	5	0	0
				Donation to Children's			
				Christmas Fund ...	0	10	0
				Balance forward	3	2	9
	£16	2	0		£16	2	0

The President then expressed his pleasure in calling upon Mr. Charles Wright to open the subject for discussion. Mr. Wright had joined the College thirty-six years ago, on the evening on which Frederick Denison Maurice, our Founder, gave his last address to us, and was a pupil and friend of a man always to be revered in this College, Charles Crawley. (Cheers).

Mr. WRIGHT then put his question, "How far is it reasonable and practicable to mitigate inequalities by Taxation?" I am putting a question, he said, and not making an assertion, because on this important matter, although my mind is turned in one direction, I resemble a certain statesman in that I have not yet attained to settled convictions. I seize the opportunity to ask the question in this club, because my desire is not so much to administer guidance as to receive it, and I do not know where to find a body of men better able to help one in questions of this character than here in the Old Students' Club. Now, if it is suggested that inequalities require mitigation, we must ask whether the inequalities that exist are gross and intolerable. I am indebted for the statistics I shall place before you to Mr. Chiozza Money's book on " Poverty and Riches " ; and, to begin with, let me say that the conditions in this country have been far worse than they are to-day, and might conceivably be far worse again. Therefore we must take care that in any changes we attempt to bring about, we shall not lose ground. Mr. Money has presented the following figures, which I will use in support of my contention, showing our material progress between the years 1867 and 1903, the figures for the former year being given first :—Population, 30 millions, 42 millions ; average earnings, £30, £45 ; consumption of wheat, 140 lbs., 232 lbs.; sugar, 44 lbs., 82 lbs.; tea, 3¾ lbs., 6 lbs.; beer (1881) 28 gals., (1903) 30 gals. ; deaths, 634,000, 667,000, (i.e., mortality almost stationary, though population increased about 40 per cent.) ; criminals convicted, 19,450, 13,162 ; savings banks deposits 46 millions. 200 millions ; price of 4 lb. loaf, 8d., 5d. and 5½d. The price of 45 commodities, according to Board of Trade statistics, in 1871, bore the proportion to the price of 1903, of 100 to 78.5. Probably the most beneficent national movement we have seen commenced in 1870, and now our system of national free education has reached a high degree of development. In interfering with the conditions that have brought these improvements into existence, we must take care that we do not make a movement to the rear. The guiding principle should be this—that nothing in the way of division should be done so as to diminish the totality of the wealth to be divided. Let us now consider the nature of the inequality which exists. Chiozza Money estimates the income of the United Kingdom at £1,710,000,000—that 5 million people receive 830 millions, 38 million receive 880 millions, 1,250,000 receive 585 millions, and 3,750,000 receive 245 millions, so that one third of the total income is taken by one-thirtieth of the people. Passing to the values of estates left on deaths, the averages from 1899 to 1904 show that 27,500 people leave £257,500,000, and 686,541 people, £29,600,000, i.e., nearly 90 per cent. of the property is owned by 4 per cent. of the persons dying. By elaborate calculations, Mr. Money estimates the total private property in the Kingdom at £9,142,000,000 owned by persons here, and they have also about £2,000,000,000 abroad. He shows that 4,400,000 people own £7,974,000,000 ; that 38,600,000 own £639,000,000 ; and 600,000 own £5,916,000,000—i.e., one-seventieth of the population hold a great deal more than half the total property. Moreover, 240 families, representing 1100 persons, own £642,000,000. Hence 1100 persons own more than 38 million persons I pass to the ownership of land. Out of the total area of 77 millions of acres, more than half, or 40 millions, are owned by 2500 persons. With regard to housing accommodation, in one room each lived families forming 507,763 people ; two rooms, 2,158,644 ; three rooms, 3,186,640 ; four rooms, 7,130,062. I venture to describe those conditions as intolerable, and I wish to inquire to-night—it would be grossly venturesome to suppose that one could come to a definite conclusion—but I want to ask, Whether these conditions can be improved by altering the incidence of, and otherwise dealing with, taxation ? During the lifetimes of many of us, a very great deal has been done—many things—to ameliorate conditions, to the expense of which the whole of the property-owners have had to contribute, notwithstanding that many of them have not directly benefited by the outlay. I refer to schools, tramways, municipal control of water and gas, public libraries, baths, picture galleries, parks and open spaces, and many more improvements. The question is, Whether more can be done and ought to be done ? I do not suppose that anyone had until recently a correct idea of the extent of the inequalities to which I have referred ; but still, the fact that they did exist to a gross extent has weighed upon the consciences of the possessors of property, and large sums have been expended by them in charity. This is far better than nothing, and I do not wish to say a word, except in honour, of those who have so generously given their money, still more of those who have contributed their work as well, to charitable objects. But there are many objections to charities. They are haphazard and partial in operation, frequently overlapping, give rise to pauperism to an extent that State action would hardly cause, and many of them are governed by the pernicious system of voting (hear, hear). Yet, except for State action, I do not see how the voting system can be improved upon, because I do not see how the money would be forthcoming but for that system. At all events, we have the fact that the duty lying upon the community is recognized by the best people in the community. Something ought to be done, and done thoroughly, and the powers of the State should, if necessary, be invoked. I do not think, however, that many economists of standing have had the idea of mitigating the inequalities by taxation ; and in bringing forward such a more or less revolutionary proposal as this is, I should like to quote John Stuart Mill for a guiding principle. I take an isolated sentence, but I do not think I misrepresent the author by taking it from the context. He says, "The object to be aimed at in the present stage of human improvement is not the subversion of the system of individual property, but the improvement of it, and the full participation of every member of the community in its benefits." In order that we may attain this object, I throw out one or two suggestions—first, the abolition of food taxes, which are contributed to by every class, but which press more heavily upon the poorer than upon any other class ; and secondly, that some means should be taken to reduce the burden upon the rates. It has been too much the custom of the legislature, when anything in the way of social improvement has had to be done, to place a greater share of the burden upon the rates. If we were to attempt any development in the direction I have indicated at the expense of the ratepayer, the effect would be to depress into the class of the poor numbers of persons just struggling upon the verge of poverty. I hold that some alteration in the incidence of rates is imperative. But, if you wish to reduce the burden, without reducing the expenditure, you must seek compensation in other directions. I suggest these alterations—(*a*) further graduation of the income tax, (*b*) further graduation of the death duties, (*c*) the imposition of an additional local income tax, and (*d*) an extension of the principle of escheat. With regard to the graduation of the income tax, I think that it was a mistake to allow the remission of 25 per cent. upon earned incomes in the case of such high incomes as £2000. In my opinion £1000 is the very highest income that should enjoy such a remission. In saying that, I recognize that the Chancellor of the Exchequer must go by steps, and must also consider what opposition he is likely to encounter. Then death duties I have always thought offer a wonderful field for the Chancellor of the Exchequer. Before Sir William Harcourt introduced his great scheme, I remember coming across the opinions of Bentham on this subject, and being struck with the validity of his arguments. In 1795, Bentham proposed an extension of the existing law of escheat, a law coeval with the very first elements of the constitution, and a corresponding limitation of the power of bequest. The effect intended was to be the appropriating to the use of the public all vacant successions, property of every denomination included, on the failure of near relations, will or no will, subject only to the power of bequest as hereinafter limited. By near relations, he means "such relations as stand within the degrees prohibited with reference to marriage." Further, in the case of such relations within the pale as are childless and without prospect of children, they should take a life annuity. He permits the bequest of only half the property. He says, "Hardship depends on disappointment, disappointment on expectation, and expectation on the *known* dispensations of the law." If you have nothing to expect, you are not disappointed ; and if you are not disappointed, there is no hardship. (Laughter.) These are not cut and dried proposals, but merely suggestions. They will be enough to horrify a great many worthy persons. For my part, I read with much astonishment the language used by Lord Balfour of Burleigh in his encyclical to the newspapers the other day, not because of the object he had in view, but because of the phrases he used in support of his object. He contends, for instance, for "a strict application of the principle that the earnings of each individual shall be securely preserved to him." One might imagine he was a red hot Socialist. He is not content with "application"—he must have "a *strict* application of the principle." Well now, in a village, it is possible for two babes to be born at the same moment, one heir to large estates, and the other a labourer's child. Now, are we to say that the earnings of each of those two individuals shall be securely preserved to him? Is it not obvious that the one is predestined to *receive*, and the other is predestined to *pay*? Take the case of the heir to a business. It is his lot in life to *receive*. What becomes of the principle for which Lord Balfour requires "strict application"? Later on in his letter, he says—"The evil to the community is as great, whether the plunderer be merely an individual member of society, or society itself. In either case the citizen is deprived of the fruit of his labours, and the result to him is the same." That is to say, if one individual takes the property of another, and applies it to his own selfish purposes, the result is the same as if that property had been applied to corporate purposes. I cannot imagine a proposition more absurd or immoral. We need to cultivate a sense of duty to the State. We have been accustomed, in our education, too much to urge the importance of "getting on" in the world; and too little have we inculcated the idea that a young man's aim in life should be to be of service to the community. Now, Mr. Wells in his book on "America," speaking of the American nation, but not differentiating in his remarks between that nation and the English, says of a commercial man, "He has no perception that his business activities, his private employments, are constituents in a large collective process; that they affect other people and the world for ever, and cannot, as he imagines, begin and end with him." We want to cultivate the sense that we are citizens of a State, and that our business is to render service to that State. Whether we are members of the House of Peers or of the Old Students' Club, we cannot do better than foster the belief in solidarity, the sense of service to the community, and the desire to live not entirely for ourselves. I have been very much puzzled by the attitude of the *Spectator* with regard to Old Age Pensions. The *Spectator* is a paper which professes, and generally promotes, high ideals. It is ostensibly, and I think to a great extent in practice, a Christian paper, and therefore it is that its attitude on this question is a puzzle to me. It is not so much that the *Spectator* objects to the proposal of Old Age Pensions; it is that in doing so, it acquiesces in the present condition of things, and it does appear to me that the present condition of things is absolutely intolerable—on *Spectator* and "Christian" principles. I cannot comprehend the justification of the present state of society. On Christian principles, if I understand them correctly, I would ask whether any one really owns property at all? Are they not all trustees, and if so, are they not very often fraudulent trustees? We are told that if you grant to a poor old soldier of labour a pension of 5s. a week at the age of 65, you are pauperizing him. But the same people do not tell us that you pauperize a young man, if you leave him a hundred thousand pounds. What is pauperizing? Is it the receiving of an income which is not earned? I presume so. The moral effect on the young man is as disastrous as it can possibly be. But one would not imagine that the moral effect on a man of 65, of his receiving five shillings a week, would be particularly overwhelming. (Laughter.) Another noble lord, for whom we have the greatest respect in this College, of which he was formerly Principal, writing to the *Times* on October 8th, says—"The rich do not advocate the practice of thrift because they are well off; they are well off because they or their parents practised thrift." Now, in saying that, Lord Avebury is inculcating upon men receiving £1 a week that they should put by a certain portion for Old Age Pensions. If you consider the qualities that would enable a man to do that—to save 2s. a week out of £1—consider the qualities of self-restraint, self-control, absolute iron strength of will and firmness of character, and sum these all up in one word "thrift," I would ask if you have not to find another word to describe the action of the man with £10,000 a year, who saves ten per cent. of his income. I don't think the same word "thrift" would do, possibly "avarice" might. Having had experience of various incomes myself, I have come to the conclusion that if a man had practically a certainty, at the age of 65, of getting a pension of 5s. a week, it would probably be the greatest incentive to him to save another 5s. a week. I don't think we need fear demoralization of character as the outcome of giving 5s. a week to a man of 65. We are told this is dreadful, because it is Socialism. I do not appear before you this evening as a Socialist, and my attitude to any proposal is not affected by whether it is Socialism or any other 'ism, but by whether it is sound. [Mr. Wright here caused considerable amusement by reading a remarkable recent utterance by Mr. Rutherford, advocating amongst other things, Army reform, with promotion from the ranks, nationalization of the railways, payment of members, reform of the House of Lords, adult franchise, etc., and urging that these reforms might form a platform for Conservatives and Liberals to join together. Unfortunately, in conclusion, Mr. Rutherford destroyed the good impression produced by his proposals by stating that the Tory Democratic plan for providing the necessary revenue was "Tariff Reform."] The present conditions seem so deplorable and so indefensible, that I would rather acquiesce in some risky experiments than fold hands in the presence of boundless wealth and grinding poverty. One stands astounded at the depth of self-deception which can be persuaded that these monstrous inequalities have their basis in sound reason and justice. And this too in a nation possessing the inestimable advantage of a state-established religion, whose professors believe that an ancient writer was inspired by God when he declared that—"The whole law is fulfilled in one word, even in this, Thou shalt love thy neighbour as thyself. But if ye bite and devour one another, take heed that ye be not consumed one of another." The concentration of enormous wealth in a few hands brings corruption to the accumulators and danger to the State. Would not some reasonable re-adjustment prove a blessing to rich and poor alike? Is the very rich man, especially the newly rich man, an enviable person? As he grows richer, he is in danger of eating and drinking too much; he buys astounding machines for transporting him from one place where he doesn't wish to be, to another place where he doesn't wish to be; in transit he makes life intolerable to his fellow-citizens by dust and stench, although he sometimes, perhaps mercifully, ends their existence. Already possessing too much, he works patiently for more. His mind is devoted to thwarting competitors, and becomes useless for any other purpose. Being constantly carted about in weird conveyances, his legs become atrophied, his liver congested, so that his existence can only be prolonged by periodical washings out at German Spas. He feels himself the victim of intolerable oppression in that after all too few years, he has got to die like other people and go to his own place. What a benefit to such a one, if a benevolent legislature could relieve him of some of these encumbering possessions, and could devote some portion of the wealth which demoralizes him to brightening the lives of his fellow citizens! (Cheers.)

Mr. S. J. COOMBS opened the debate, after eulogizing Mr. Wright's paper, by deprecating the increase of the cost of administration which Old Age Pensions and similar reforms would entail. He was in general agreement as to abolishing food taxes, and as to the burden of the rates. He thought Mr. Asquith's action in taking off 3d. from the income tax on earned incomes would be justified by the result, and would lead to more accurate disclosures of incomes, and no net decrease in revenue. With regard to the criticism of Lord Balfour of Burleigh, a man might have a wasteful son or daughter, but still he ought to give each a fair portion of his property; it was his duty to the State to do so. As to Wells and the Americans, here in England it was a case of give a man a title and ruin him; but in America men had no titles to seek, and it must not be forgotten that there the great desire of a rich man was to have his name connected with some beneficent object, such as a university.

Mr. GUMPEL supported Mr. Wright, and was followed by the VICE-PRINCIPAL, who added a word of tribute to Mr. Wright for his clearly reasoned speech on rather a difficult subject. There was one person he had not done justice to—himself, in saying that he had no fixed opinion. Evidently, he had one, and it went very far. There was another person he had not quite done justice to—the rich man, at the end. He (Mr. Jacob) knew several rich men, and, on the whole, he thought them the hardest working men he had come across. As leaders of industry they had to work hard. With regard to leaving money to their heirs, and leaving them nothing to do but to step in and take an income, he fancied they did not do that now-a-days. This might be done if the money were in other property, but if it were in a big business, the heir would soon find his income disappear if he did not look after the business. Changes happened very quickly at the present time, and it needed a capable man to manage a large concern. In many companies, the capital was held by a large number of people, and those at the head did not get enormous incomes. It was a mistake to suppose that all the very rich were idle, and all the very poor, industrious. The great bulk of the people too, were neither very rich nor very poor. And speaking critically of Mr. Wright's suggestion to take off the taxes on food, it should be remembered that England was a democracy, whose principle was that those who paid the taxes should have the control. It would be a dangerous thing to allow any large section of the people to have votes and no taxes to pay. It was so easy to deal with other people's money. If he had the disposition of a millionaire's wealth, he could distribute it very generously, but if it were only his own that he had to deal with, he would be less generous and more just. It was not possible to remedy the evils of society merely by shifting the incidence of taxation on the wealthy [Mr. Wright : Hear, hear.] We here ought to guard against thinking that. We believed that you could not take properly unless you gave. Every man must take his share in the State, as men did in this College, if the State was to be a living and a healthy thing. What did we do for the State? Some of us served on juries, and in some cases that was the only active service. We voted, or were dragged out to vote, and we paid taxes. A great number of people who were not on the jury lists only paid taxes, and there their service to the State ended. He would like to see the way clear in this matter. No great change should be brought about unless it would improve both the division of wealth and the whole State. We must require this to be proved, and especially because, as Mr. Wright had pointed out, the rich were not getting richer, nor the poor, poorer. This was not entirely an economic question ; it was also partly a moral one. (Cheers.)

Mr. C. E. MAURICE had somewhat the same feeling, expressed by Mr. Jacob, that we might think a great deal too much of the result of taxation. The sufferings of the poor were caused by a great many other things, and would continue to be affected by them, even if the incidence of taxation were altered. Taxation would not settle the question of the better adjustment of wages, the better use of the land, the question of sanitary and other reforms. If we were to hand over to the State a number of things now left to private people, we might develop a bureaucracy instead of a democracy. There was also the danger of raising false expectations. With regard to Old Age Pensions, why was it that the demand for help from the State was not satisfied by the present poor law? There seemed to be two reasons, the restraint on liberty, and the publicity attending the arrangements. He could not understand how any system of Old Age Pensions could work which did not present those two evils, without an amount of jobbery which would be ruinous. You would need strict enquiry into people's special conditions and very strict oversight of the way in which they spent their money. You would then have the same outcry that you now had against the workhouse and out-door relief. He quite agreed there was a good deal of exaggeration in the talk about the evils of Socialism—if you had a State in its first form, you committed yourself to a certain amount of Socialism—and we had committed ourselves to a great deal, in the Post Office, Factory Acts, etc. ; but the question remained how far we could trust officials to do things, and how far it was best to leave them to natural development. Whenever a body acquired enormous irresponsible power—the railways, for instance—the State should step in, to secure free conditions. But the danger of officialism must be reckoned with. Two great State institutions were now on trial—the police, and the poor law guardians. Before extending existing State power, we should see that we are likely to get a better organization in the place of the powers that be. (Cheers.)

Mr. GAY thought the matter could only be finally settled in one way—by *love*, and the millennium. Every working man should get a fair wage, 25s. a week, a decent house, and work assured him.

Mr. PRESBURG pointed out that the opener merely argued, that the existing conditions of individualism were unsound. By the present-day organization of finances, a small man's efforts were stultified. The big monopolist cared nothing about the moral trend of his actions. No industry or invention could flourish now, without corruption. The reason why such writers as Money and Webb urged re-arrangement of taxation was, not that they necessarily fell back on collectivism, but that through taxation the path of least resistance to economic improvement might be attained.

Mr. HEPBURN asserted that no man could by his own earnings acquire a competence. He could only acquire a competence when he commanded the labour of another. The other essential was that the other man needed the sovereign. He could imagine many capitalists believing in Old Age Pensions, that would provide for those who could no longer work—" They come between the wind and their nobility." But that was not the real point. The beauty of the French law of inheritance was that by many subdivisions, the wealth at last came to the people it belonged to.

Mr. LEVINSOHN thought a double income tax, suggested by Mr. Wright, would have no advantage, and would be attended by more expense in collection. Increase in death duties might result in less revenue, because testators would give their property away in their lifetime. There was a point beyond which, too, it would be inexpedient to raise the income tax. Too high a tax would drive the rich abroad, and wealth would leave the country. We should avoid a single tax, and should broaden, and not narrow, the basis of taxation.

Mr. TIRRELL said we must remember that labour, in whatever form, owed in some way for what had been done in the past for the country. Also we must not neglect to recognize the value of the brain that organized and financed. Mr. Hepburn had said no man could earn a competence by himself. But he knew a man who had done so, a joiner, who rose to be the manager of a shop at Cubitt's, and bought a small house—[Mr. Hepburn: Then he began to live on someone else]. Mr. Tirrell objected to the interruption of his remarks. His friend got no pension from his firm, and lived comfortably on what he had earned.

Mr. HEPBURN said his point was that a man might save sufficient to finish his life in comfort, but no man by his own earnings could save a fortune without compelling others to work for him.

Mr. WRIGHT replied. He had not heard his two points disputed—that gross inequalities did exist, or that it was right to attempt to rectify those inequalities by taxation. As to a local income tax, he suggested it because he knew that the present basis of the rates—the value of a man's house—was frequently quite out of proportion to the extent to which he ought to contribute to the burdens now laid upon the ratepayer (hear, hear). In reply to the Vice-Principal's remarks about heirs to business, he knew of a case where, of two sons who had succeeded to a large business, one had drunk himself to death, and the other was doing the same thing. Yet under a manager, who took nothing approaching their share, the business was as flourishing as ever. He recognized the vital importance, however, of Mr. Jacob's criticism upon his suggested removal of food taxes. But the inequalities disclosed seemed to justify the proposal. The worker, whether he paid taxes or not, would always have a great interest in the apportionment of taxation. He agreed, and had himself urged, that there must be great caution used in passing any reforming measures. Replying to Mr. Maurice, as to Old Age Pensions, he would not propose to discriminate and enquire into people's means, but to pay the pension to every man over 65, within certain specified limits. If raising death duties induced men to part with wealth during their lives, so much the better. In graduating income tax higher, caution must be used,. of course ; but he was very sceptical whether the rich man would at any time find, on this planet, a place where his property was as secure as it was in old England. (Cheers.)

A hearty vote of thanks, by acclamation, was accorded Mr. Wright ; and the. chairman then announced that the next meeting would be held on November 16th, when Mr. C. E. Maurice would open on "Has Party Government worked well, and can it be improved ?"

EMPLOYMENT BUREAU FOR VOLUNTARY WORKERS.

THE British Institute of Social Service, 11, Southampton Row, W.C., has just opened a Register of Voluntary Social Workers, to be conducted on the same lines as Labour or Employment Bureaux for those who are seeking paid positions.

It has been found that there are in London a considerable number of persons who would be willing to give a part of their time and energy to such work as helping with clubs, visiting, conducting investigations, clerical or secretarial work for social organizations, if they could readily find an opening. Owing sometimes to the segregation of classes or other geographical conditions in London, and to the fact that those willing to work are not in touch with various existing organizations in their own neighbourhood, or to their lack of initiative or experience, they do not know where to apply and their services go unused.

On the other hand, there is an almost insatiable demand for workers by Settlements and the numerous other bodies organized for ameliorative social effort.

The Register is now open for the names of those willing to give their services, and for the applications of those who need voluntary workers. Correspondence will receive prompt attention, and applicants who prefer to call are requested to do so between 11 a.m. and 1 p.m. on Wednesdays, or by appointment. There is no charge for the use of the Register, the present policy of the Institute being to give its services freely in all departments.

FURNIVALL CYCLING CLUB.

THE final run to "Ye Cocoa Tree," at Pinner, on Saturday, October 5th last, concluded another very successful season. The day was dull, and did not look at all promising for the ride. However, 26 members cycled and 16 members went by train,—a very good number, considering the bad weather. After tea, we all went for a walk in the lanes, but were driven back to the "Cocoa Tree" by the drizzling rain. The rest of the evening was spent in dancing and singing. The thanks of the Club are due to the Misses F. and R. Reglar, S. Dockery, N. Moulden, and C. Read, and Messrs. Howard, Hagerty, and others who helped to make the social evening an extremely enjoyable one.

The return journey was a most eventful one, punctures and side-slips being very numerous. Fortunately no one was seriously hurt, and eventually all the members of the party reached their respective homes in the early hours of Sunday morning.   W. MELZER, *Hon. Secretary.*

FREDERICK DENISON MAURICE.

THE following article appeared in the *Manchester Guardian* for August 5th. My hope in writing it was that I might be able to give some help towards the right understanding of Maurice, the Prophet and Reformer. I have been assured by some of my friends that my revered Master is not so forgotten in the world "that counts" of to-day as I had assumed. In the Working Men's College, his name, at least, is a sacred one; and I am grateful to the conductors of the JOURNAL for bringing under the eyes of their readers what Mr. Masterman's interesting book suggested to me to say, by way of explanation and correction, about the Founder of the College.

J. LL. D.

F. D. MAURICE.*

THE name of Maurice, which was regarded with a good deal of interest fifty years ago by certain classes of our countrymen, is now almost forgotten, even in the religious world, and amongst the more thoughtful of the working people. There is hardly a living reporter who, if he heard the name pronounced, would not write it down Morris. This oblivion is partly due to something incomprehensible in Maurice's nature and action. Literary critics in particular were provoked by him. Mr. C. F. G. Masterman begins his book on Maurice as one of the "Leaders of the Church" in the last century, by astonishing his readers with contradictory estimates of the subject of his sketch. He quotes a letter of Froude's, in which he says: "As thinkers, Maurice and, still more, the Mauricians, appear to me the most hideously imbecile that any section of the world have been driven to believe in." He might have added a similarly contemptuous opinion expressed by Leslie Stephen in a letter published in his recent biography. Writers of letters do not weigh their words. I remember a fairly respectful article on Maurice by Leslie Stephen, in one of our monthly journals. I had just seen it advertised when I met Stephen in Oxford Street, and I referred to it, adding, "I thought there was no one more completely out of sympathy with Maurice than you." He replied, in his half-hesitating way, "Yes, but I thought it might be interesting to show how he looks to one quite on the outside." Those to whom Maurice's faith was an impossible one, and who smiled at his ardour, were irritated by its being demanded of them that they should take account of him as a man of undeniable intellectual powers. So they expressed their irritation with freedom in private intercourse. Against their estimates Mr. Masterman sets others. He begins—"'The greatest mind since Plato,' was Archdeacon Hare's deliberate verdict upon his brother-in-law." It may be acceptable to some readers if I mention that it was to me, and in private conversation, that this remarkable opinion was expressed. I only saw Archdeacon Hare once or twice; and it excited him a little, perhaps, to know that he was speaking of one whom the world did not appreciate to a young disciple upon whose unlimited sympathy he could count. Whether he used the words "the greatest mind," or some more discriminating phrase, I am not sure. The words that struck me, and lived in my memory, as they well might, were "since Plato." At all events, there was something in Maurice that reminded a man of fine mind and rare learning, who knew him intimately, of Plato.

It was not the temperament of Maurice that anyone could liken to Plato's. I have a letter from Thomas Carlyle about the "Republic" of Plato, in which he speaks of the philosopher with interest and admiration. He was "a lofty Athenian gentleman," but he was "terribly 'at ease in Zion.'" Maurice was at the opposite pole to this ease. It is perhaps the

---

* "Leaders of the Church, 1800—1900." Edited by George W. E. Russell.—Frederick Denison Maurice. By C. F. G. Masterman.—London: A. R. Mowbray and Co. Pp. xi. 240. 3s. 6d. net.

chief merit of Mr. Masterman's account of Maurice, that he does justice to the depth and ardour of his emotions and to the intensely "prophetical" spirit of his denunciations. More than any other thinking man not only of his own generation but of many generations, Maurice lived in an unseen world, and his unseen world was that of the Kingdom of Heaven proclaimed by the Gospel. It was the world of truth and righteousness and love, of a living Father who was leading mankind onwards and revealing Himself to men, and calling and drawing them to Himself. If this world is imaginary, Maurice was a deluded fanatic, entitled to the pity of the literary critics, for he was quite sure that it was real. With peculiar thoroughness and simplicity, Maurice saw everything in the light of this unseen world, and referred all human and personal history to it ; and his faith in it was not weakened, but made more vehement, by the mysteries of evil and of a non-moral Nature which seem to throw darkness over it.

Mr. Masterman, a sympathetic describer but not a "hideously imbecile Maurician," is much impressed by Maurice's controversialist manner, which he has excuse for calling "savage." The explanation of it is that Maurice was not wrestling with flesh and blood, but with the world-rulers of this darkness ; and he felt specially called to unmask and assail any worldly principle which asserted itself in the guise of religion or respectability. He seems sometimes possessed with a kind of fury against competition, for example, and against the religious press. In actual life he could be quite tolerant of various forms of competition and friendly with persons who wrote for the religious newspapers. But the competition which he denounced was the assumption, that men were sent into the world to fight each for himself and against his neighbour, and the religious newspaper represented party spirit and persecution speaking in the name of God. Mr. Masterman is quite right in calling attention to Maurice's vehemence, and he does not omit to dwell on the very remarkable humility and gentleness with which the vehemence was compatible ; but his readers might hardly be aware how sociable and kindly Maurice was with his neighbours. I remember his coming to give a lecture to my Whitechapel parishioners, on the day that he was expelled from King's College for throwing doubt on the doctrine of endless torment. He loved to do anything that he was asked to do. I do not know whether he ever distributed prizes to competitors, but he might easily have been persuaded to do so ; he consented to be a competitor himself for public appointments. Whilst in the main, and increasingly as life advanced, he acted with Liberals in State and Church, he used very strong language against Liberalism, meaning by it, chiefly, a complacent satisfaction in *not* believing this or that. So, when he defended anything, he looked through the thing itself to the motive or principle of the attack, and it was not difficult to him to change or modify his opinion about measures. This might be illustrated by what he has written about the Athanasian Creed, subscription to the Thirty-nine Articles, national education, democracy, and Broad Churchism. He was moved to attack, or to defend, as the high interests of supreme righteousness and love seemed to him to demand.

Something of the hastiness of journalism may be detected on many of Mr. Masterman's pages, and I venture to express the hope that an essay which is on the whole so just as well as so readable an appreciation of so remarkable a man may be amended into a still better book. For instance, we are told that—"His exegesis remains to-day in part as a monument of the failure of a man, supreme in one field of knowledge, to enter into the inheritance of another" (p. 5). I remember the Master of Trinity College, Cambridge, Dr. Butler, observing to me many years ago, "Whatever else may be said of Maurice, he has certainly thrown a flood of light on the New Testament." I know that some questionable interpretations may be found in his commentaries. Jowett once complained to me that Maurice had somewhere understood "Cursed is the ground for thy sake," as if "for thy sake" meant "for thy benefit." My impression is that Maurice saw that the curse was really in the Divine purpose a blessing, and that his rapid expression of this view was open to the sense which Jowett put upon it. So he says of the warning, "Woe unto you that laugh now, for ye shall mourn and weep,"—"He promises that those who are indulging that sort of laughter shall weep. I use the word *promise* advisedly. It is a promise, not a threatening; or, if you please, a threat which contains a promise." Those who wish to understand Maurice must always be ready to look with him through what is on the surface to what is spiritual or eternal. But he has one title to the gratitude and respect of English readers of the Bible which can easily be set forth. He was the first divine who recognised the Kingdom of Heaven as the subject of the New Testament. This received title, "The New Testament," may indeed be translated "The Kingdom of Heaven." But this was not perceived. Maurice read the sacred volume from beginning to end in the light of this its subject. And he went on to see the same Kingdom in all human history. In this view of history, Maurice may be said still to stand almost alone. But all divines of any insight can now see that the New Testament is a collection of writings which illustrate the Kingdom of Heaven. So far from Maurice failing in "exegesis," it is his glory to be the father, for Englishmen at least, of all the more illuminating exegesis of to-day.

On the same page we read: "His influence has been almost entirely in the strengthening of a movement in the Church whose leaders he fought unwearyingly for nearly half a century; and, as Mark Pattison said of T. H. Green at Oxford, the bulk of his 'honey' passed into the 'Ritualistic hive.'" What is true in this is that the form which the mediævalizing or "Ritualistic" movement now exhibits, under the leadership of Bishop Gore, is largely due to Maurice's influence. There is not an essay in the volume entitled "Lux Mundi" that does not show traces of his teaching. But there is no mention of Maurice in the volume. The writers knew and know that the belief to which they cling—that "the Church," if it and its voice could be identified, is commissioned to speak with Divine authority on the earth—was to him a sort of idolatry. That Mr. Masterman should say of him, "He was a dogmatist to the backbone," is only another argument for the expulsion of the word "dogma" from our common speech; for Maurice was always denouncing "propositions" and "opinions," to the great perplexity of many of his hearers and readers, as putting themselves in the way of the living spiritual realities in which or in whom he believed.

So when Mr. Masterman describes his knowledge as "encyclopædic" (p. 19), he is speaking loosely. Maurice had a profound knowledge of history and philosophy, he was a fair classical scholar, and he was familiar with Shakspere and the best English literature; but he had no pretension to the universal acquaintance with books and things which is commonly meant by encyclopædic knowledge. On the other hand, Mr. Masterman's unfavourable opinion of Maurice's writings surprises me. "Here is little grace or beauty of style . . . Much of his work is dictated matter, and bears all the evidences of dictated matter. . . . It repeats itself. It sprawls over chapters and pages. It is often extraordinarily tangled and obscure" (p. 219). I should like to challenge proof of this criticism. My opinion is not an unprejudiced one, for I looked over the proofs of most of Maurice's volumes and was encouraged to point out doubtful expressions, as well as to correct simple misprints; but my own belief is—and I think I am not insensitive to what is slipshod and sprawling and obscure in literature—that Maurice's thought cannot be surpassed for order and directness, that his English is singularly pure and forcible, and that his sentences often have a solemn charm. We that were about him often wondered at his power of speaking on any question with an order and precision that seemed to imply preparation. I long to quote passages from his writings, which I am sure would commend themselves to the ears of my readers as they do to mine. [Such passages may be found in abundance in "Lessons of Hope: Readings from the Works of F. D. Maurice."] But I must refrain; and I part from Mr. Masterman with grateful acknowledgment of what he has done to make known to readers of this time one whom he pronounces to be "the greatest thinker of the English Church in the nineteenth century" (p. 6).

J. LLEWELYN DAVIES.

W.M.C. DEBATING SOCIETY.

THE Debating Society, which this year is fully maintaining its presidential prestige in the person of Mr. A. E. Homewood, who combines with a charming personality the gift of effective and witty speech, held its inaugural meeting in the Common Room on Tuesday, October 8th, when the excellent attendance showed how strong is the hold of this popular institution upon all sections in the College.

The subject chosen on this occasion by Mr. G. M. Trevelyan, M.A., whose re-appearance was very welcome, was the one of the moment— The House of Lords ; and in moving, "That the plan suggested by the Government for dealing with this august body is the best which is practicable," he rendered a distinct service to us by his lucid explanation of what would be the effect of such action upon that fearsome object, the British constitution. In the course of his remarks, he referred to the need of the times necessitating a large legislative output each session, and claimed that no matter what the complexion of the Government of the day might be, they ought to be assured of a comparatively free hand, and this Liberalism intended to bring about. An opposer was forthcoming in Mr. Bertrand Breakspear, a visitor who, although handicapped by what must on occasions appear to be a somewhat severe time limit, succeeded in the course of an eloquent speech, not only in giving a short historical retrospect of the House of Lords and in dealing in some detail with the recent rejected measures upon which the present campaign is principally based, but also in devoting some time to questioning the *bonâ fides* of Liberals in the matter, and their legislative tendency generally. The result of the voting, 30 for, and 12 against, in no way represents the extent of the gathering, as the opinion generally expressed by subsequent speakers - among whom were Messrs. Hepburn, O'Keeffe, Munro, Klinger, and Bradgate—was in favour of a single chamber, to which creed a large number of the members would appear to incline.

The second meeting, on October 15th, was devoted to a consideration of the question "Is Esperanto capable of literature?" Although the opener, Mr. Brown, organizing secretary of the Esperanto League, did not arrive until the evening was well advanced, the president and Mr. Stagg, the opposer, provided excellent material in their interesting speeches for a debate, which was well carried on by Messrs. Jacqermann, Driver, and O'Keeffe. After a vigorous effort by Mr. Brown, in the course of which he illustrated the elocutionary powers of the language, the motion was carried by 11 votes to 8.

At the moment of going to press a resumé of the refreshing speech of Mr. Lupton, who, on October 22nd, advocated the abolition of the Lower Chamber, and the neat reply of Mr. Halford, a visitor, is in preparation. It will also be of interest to state that Mr. Morison, M.A, intends on the 29th October, to propose a resolution insisting that the individual must contribute towards any provision made for old age, and he will be opposed by Mr. Driver. The dates and subjects for November are not yet complete, but the excellent beginning we have made will more than be sustained. In conclusion it may be said that opportunities will gladly be afforded for members to deal with subjects which may be of general interest. If they are not prepared to go so far as to open a debate, will they come forward as opposers, and render a service not only to the Society, but to the—at times— worried secretary ?   F. E. LIDDELOW.

COLLEGIANS' DANCE.

THE 23rd Collegians' Dance—the first of the 1907-8 season—will take place in the Maurice Hall, on Saturday, 7th December next. Dancing will start at 6.45 p.m. Tickets can be had of Hitchcock, Hogh, Owen, Reglar, and West. Only a limited number will be issued, and to prevent disappointment early application should be made.

MAURICE CHESS CLUB.

THE Maurice Chess Club held their annual general meeting on 9th October, when the committee and officers for the ensuing season were elected; and, after effecting one or two minor alterations in the rules, the meeting adjourned to allow time for a statement of the accounts in respect of the past season to be prepared. Mr. Fred. Smith, the late secretary, was unanimously elected a vice-president, the members present heartily thanking him for his past services.

Messrs. Nield, Crawley, V. Ray, O. Henke, and Thomas, constitute the committee, Mr. S. R. Briggs is match captain, and Mr. J. F. Halford, secretary and treasurer.

A good list of about twenty-four matches is being arranged for the season, and as usual a championship and handicap tournaments will be held amongst the members of the club. The entrance list for these tournaments closes early in November. Members who intend entering should lose no time in doing so.

The match captain will give a series of lectures during the season for beginners, and later on lectures for advanced players will also be given. For further information hereon as to dates and time, etc., apply to the captain or any of the committee.

The winner of the championship tournament of 1906-7 will be either Hammant or Henke, who will play for first place shortly; and the prizes for best averages in match play were won by Hammant for league matches, Halford for friendlies, and Briggs for all matches.

The club night is fixed for Mondays.   J. F. HALFORD, *Hon. Sec.*

COFEEE ROOM DECORATION FUND.

Further donations to this fund have been received as under :—

	£	s.	d		£	s.	d.
Sydney Bradgate	0	5	0	G. Hagerty	0	1	0
E. Murphy	0	5	0	W. G. Chadwin	0	1	0
J. C. Castell	0	2	6	E. J. H. Reglar	0	5	0
Herbert Wilcockson	0	10	0	F. J. Nield	0	2	6
Richard C. Taylor	0	15	6	F. Hitchman	0	5	0
Mrs. Frances Herbert	0	10	0	R. Robson	0	2	0
C. T. Young	0	1	0	R. H. Marks	1	0	0
A. J. Wildey	0	1	0	W. Fulton	0	2	6
W. Melzer	0	1	0	A. C. Martin	0	2	0
R. S. Hitchcock	0	1	0	Dr. F. J. Furnivall	0	5	0
F. E. Lawrence	0	1	0	F. Wright	0	2	6
Anon.	0	1	0	Charles Wright	1	0	0
M. Wilson	0	2	6	Charles Monteath	0	1	0

About £10 is still required to complete the fund and pay the necessary architect's fees.

THE WORKING MEN'S COLLEGE JOURNAL *is supported partly by Annual Subscribers living in different parts of the World, and partly by circulation among the Students and Members. Its success depends upon a regular demand, and to ensure this, the Editor would be glad if as many readers as can will become Subscribers. Subscription 2s. 6d. per annum, post free.*

LONDON: Printed by W. HUDSON & Co., Red Lion Street, High Holborn, and published at THE WORKING MEN'S COLLEGE, Crowndale Road, London, N.W.—November 1st, 1907.

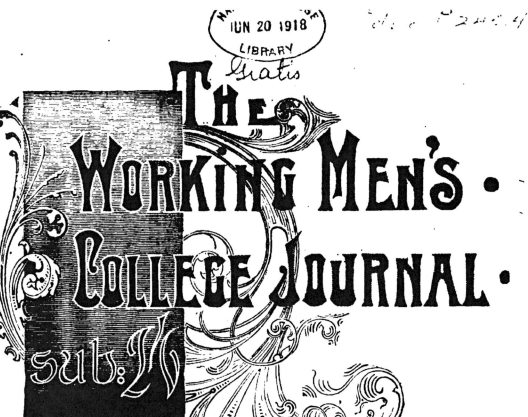

The Working Men's College Journal

sub: 2d

The Working Men's College, CROWNDALE ROAD, ST PANCRAS, LONDON N.W. FOUNDED IN 1854 BY THE LATE Frederick Denison Maurice

Contents for

DECEMBER, 1907

Sir C. P. Lucas,
    C.B., K.C.M.G.
Shelling Peas
Literary Society
Debating Society
College Notes
Old Students' Club
Saturday Lectures

Working Men's College Journal.

Conducted by Members of the Working Men's College,
Crowndale Road, London, N.W..

Vol. X.—No. 177.   DECEMBER, 1907.   Price Twopence.

SIR C. P. LUCAS, C.B., K.C.M.G.

IT was with feelings of keen delight and great satisfaction that all Mr. Lucas's many friends in the College learnt that his name was down in the list of Birthday Honours, on November 9th, as a Knight Commander of St. Michael and St. George, the motto of which order is the same as that of the College, "Auspicium Melioris Ævi." All felt that the honour was well deserved and well

SIR C. P. LUCAS, C.B., K.C.M.G.*

bestowed. There was also the feeling that we in the College were honoured along with him; there was a sense of greater importance, and of wholesome pride at being associated here with a man of his character and distinction, upon this recognition of his merits, as though we too were all thereby raised in the social scale with him.

Sir Charles Prestwood Lucas became connected with this

* Photo by Vandyk, reproduced by kind permission of the proprietors of the *Graphic*, from the picture in their issue of November 16th.

College about twenty-six years ago, and during that time has served it in various capacities.   He taught Geography in the Preparatory Division, under his and our great friend, George Tansley, to whom he always refers with so much love and admiration.   He was Vice-Principal of the College from 1897, when he succeeded Mr. Mure, to 1904, when Mr. Lionel Jacob was elected to that office.   As a member of Council throughout his connection, and as one of the Corporation or Trustees, he has taken a prominent and an able part in the government of the institution.   But it is for his kindness of heart, his sterling character, and his high principles that we love and respect him most; whilst his wit and humour, his judgment and sympathy, as a speaker, have always captivated us.

Sir Charles was educated at Winchester College, where he was head boy for three years.   He left there, as an open exhibitioner, for Balliol College, Oxford, where he took a first class in moderates and also in final classical schools, and in 1877, the Chancellor's medal for Latin essay.   He was called to the bar at Lincoln's Inn, in 1885.   After passing the competitive clerkship examination, he entered the Colonial Office in 1877, and was private secretary to Sir R. Herbert in 1881, to Earl Granville in February, 1886, and again to Sir R. Herbert in that year.   He acted as Chairman of the Committee of the Emigrants' Information Office for ten years, till the end of 1896. He became a first-class clerk in 1892, principal clerk in 1896, and in June, 1897, was appointed Assistant Under-Secretary of State for the Colonies.   He was made a C.B. in the New Year's honours of 1901.   Upon the re-organization of the Colonial Office this year, he, being then Senior Assistant Under-Secretary, was placed at the head of the new Dominions Department.

Sir C. P. Lucas is a well-known authority on Colonial History, amongst his works being "An Historical Geography of the British Colonies" (six vols.), and "The Canadian War of 1812," copies of which he has presented to our Library.

From the *Times* of November 21st, we take the following report of a dinner in his honour :—

The West Indian Club entertained at dinner last night, at the Grand Hotel, Sir Charles Prestwood Lucas, on his retirement from the West Indian Department of the Colonial Office to take up his position as chief of the Dominions Department.   SIR NEVILE LUBBOCK, chairman of the club, occupied the chair ; and among those present were Lord Strathcona, the Hon A. C. Ponsonby, Sir H. Jerningham, Sir W. R. Buckle, Sir R. Solomon, Sir R. Llewelyn, Sir H. Davson, Sir J. Roper Parkington, Captain R. Muirhead Collins, the Hon. W. Pember Reeves, Mr. R. L. Antrobus, C.B., Mr. H. W. Just, C.B., Admiral Stewart, Mr. Owen Philipps, M.P., Mr. G. Martineau, C.B., Mr. Walsh Wrightson, Mr. C. Czarnikow, Mr. Robert Donald, his Honour E. J. Cameron. Administrator of St. Vincent, and Mr. W. A. M. Goode, hon. secretary.

After dinner, the toast of "The King" having been honoured,

The HON. SECRETARY read a number of letters and telegrams apologizing for absence, and among them one from Mr. Chamberlain, in which he said :—"I am very glad to find from your letter of November 5th, that Sir Charles Prestwood Lucas is about to receive the hospitable welcome of the West Indian Club, and that his long service in the Colonial Office is to be recognized by you. No public servant deserves this appreciation more thoroughly than does Sir Charles Lucas ; and my experience enables me with some confidence to join in your welcome and to confirm the estimate you have formed of the value of his services. In fact, I think that the public has hardly yet appreciated what it owes to the splendid permanent Civil Service which, in every department of the State, secures for it the position which it has attained in all quarters. Those who, like myself, have served only in a political capacity, know how much they owe to those who quietly and unostentatiously give their life's best labour to the public service, and often deserve the credit which is assumed by their temp rary chiefs. Sir Charles Lucas is the best type of these men, and in gratitude for the help and co-operation which I have received from him, as for the aid he has given to others, I rejoice that you should think well at this time to recognize his unselfish labour. I hope that I may have other opportunities of recognizing his service, and nothing but the state of my health would prevent me from asking to make one of those who have decided to recognize it upon the present occasion."

The CHAIRMAN proposed the health of the guest of the evening. Having offered to Sir Charles Lucas his hearty congratulations on the well-deserved honour which the King had recently bestowed upon him, he said he first made his acquaintance on the Emigration Information Committee, of which Sir Charles was chairman, and he was very much impressed by the painstaking way in which he conducted the work of that committee. When Sir Charles took charge of the West Indian department of the Colonial Office, he showed great sympathy with those colonies, and no one could have discussed the questions that affected them more courteously or more sympathetically. Naturally there were many questions on which he did not agree with the view Sir Charles took, but he even found it more pleasant to disagree with him than to agree with him. (Laughter.) Sir Charles had been placed at the head of the Dominions department ; and he ventured to think that before 20 years were out, that department would become one of enormous importance—in fact, one of the most important departments of the State. (Cheers.) He congratulated the self-governing Colonies on having obtained Sir Charles's services. (Cheers.)

SIR C. LUCAS, who was very warmly received on rising to reply, said he accepted the invitation for that evening for two reasons. The first was, of course, a personal one. The British public did not lavish so many marks of affection on gentlemen in public offices that they could afford to refuse a compliment when it came their way. The West Indies, in dispensing with his services, had given him a character (laughter) ; and he, in dissolving the partnership, entirely declined to part with the goodwill. (Laughter.) His second reason was that he wished to take the opportunity of speaking of the great services rendered by Sir Nevile Lubbock to the West Indies. It was a great advantage to those Colonies, in the troublous times through which they had passed, to have as their spokesman in this country a man whose character was as high as his courage, and who had been always above and beyond the slightest suspicion of self-seeking. (Cheers.) During the last ten years he had been connected with the West Indies. He had served under three Secretaries of State. Mr. Chamberlain was Secretary of State in 1897, and whatever Mr. Chamberlain touched, he made live and grow. (Cheers.) When he lost Mr. Chamberlain, he was delighted to find that his new master was his old friend, whom to know was to love, Mr. Alfred Lyttelton ; and after him, he again fell into the hands of another old friend, the present Secretary of State to whom he owed so much. During the years he was connected with the West Indies, he was brought face to face with men who were fighting a life and death battle against adverse conditions, and it went into his soul how easy it was for a man sitting in an office and drawing a fixed salary to write well-turned homilies to men whose livelihood and fortunes were at stake ; and he learnt then that the more humane a Government office was, the more it would win and keep the confidence of those outside. (Cheers.) Another impression he gained was how much the West Indies had lost by not being one. They all wished the West Indies were one, but they all knew how great were the difficulties. The 19th century had been a time of distress. The 20th century, he firmly believed, would be a time of West Indian regeneration. There were many signs that made them hopeful. Whatever might be the outcome of the sugar negotiations, he would never believe that a system radically vicious and hopelessly wrong, when it had once been rudely shaken, would ever recover its former strength. Looking back on the past and looking forward to the future, he would be a fool who would attempt to set limits to the productiveness of Nature and the ingenuity of man. Who could doubt, for instance, that when the Panama Canal was completed, it would bring added wealth and importance to the West Indies? Whatever the future might have in store, good fortune was the due of the West Indies; indeed, it was long overdue. (Cheers.)

Subsequently Mr. OWEN PHILIPPS, M.P., proposed "The Self-Governing Colonies," to which LORD STRATHCONA, CAPTAIN MUIRHEAD COLLINS, Mr. PEMBER REEVES, and SIR RICHARD SOLOMON responded.

LUBBOCK FIELD CLUB.

ON September 8th, the club turned its attention to Kent. Starting from Sevenoaks, Knole park was entered by the postern gate in Seal Hollow. We emerged near Godden Green, and after some hesitation, continued through the woods to Bitchett Green and by road towards Stone Street. Before long we were attracted by a path leading through orchards, woods, cornfields, and hopfields, and entering the road nearly opposite the Mote House at Igtham. As our path went through the grounds, we took the opportunity to closely examine the grand old place before halting for lunch in an adjacent field. We again struck a road at Fairlawns, and continued along it, through Plaxtol, over the stream, and up the hill into Hurst Wood. Turning north we followed paths through the woods for a couple of miles, and in due course reached Plant. From here to Boro' Green we had a stretch of motor-frequented road. We had time for a comfortable tea before making for the station and the 5.49 train. In the woods we noticed a glow-worm, and we spent some time watching a hawk hovering. The blackberries were very backward, and little of botanic interest was observed. On the other hand, the country traversed was of the most delightful description, and the views, although slightly obscured by the heat mist, were extensive and beautiful. The soil throughout was sandy, but in places the presence of clay in the subsoil was made evident by the mud. At the start the weather was dull, but speedily cleared up and was most brilliant, with, however, a pleasant breeze.

October 13th.—Ten members walked from Potter's Bar by paths to South Mimms and thence by the old road to Mimmshall Wood. We took the path through the wood and across North Mimms Park and Water End to Welham Green. We intended to lunch at Bell Bar, but found to our disgust that the inn there had only a six-day license, so we had to walk four miles further to Tyler's Causeway, where we refreshed. On our way back to Potter's Bar we crossed Northaw Great Wood. Distance, just over 18 miles. The country was in grand condition, the green lit up here and there by the early autumn tints; the weather, delightfully bright and clear. Riccia and other liverworts were collected, a large number of crabapples were gathered by the secretary, and one or two blackberries were seen. A bat was observed entomologizing in brilliant sunlight.

October 30th.—Our president, Mr. Alfred Grugeon, read an interesting paper, entitled "Shelling Peas," in the Club Room at the College.

November 10th.—Fourteen members walked from Gerrard's Cross to Burnham Beeches, and back to Slough. The woods were in all the glory of their autumn foliage, and fungi were numerous and varied. Blackberries and crabapples occurred in fair quantity, and one member gathered about a dozen spring flowers. Another reported a fox, and the microscopist captured a hydra.

Next walk, December 8th.—Excursion to Norbury Park, Fetsham Downs, and Leith Hill. Take excursion ticket to Leatherhead, 2s. Train leaves Waterloo, South station, 10.5. Provide lunch.   J. HOLLOWAY, *Hon. Sec.*

W.M.C. MUSICAL SOCIETY.

CONCERT AND GENERAL MEETING.

THIS society gave an exceedingly good concert at the College on October 12th, when Dr. Furnivall took the chair, C. H. Perry being musical director, and William Tarr accompanist. This was the 114th concert of the society, and a ladies' night. We had many of our old College friends both as performers and in the audience. Items—H. C. Dumbrill, " Mandalay " and " The Gallants of England "; Miss S. Dockery, " Bid me discourse " and Tosti's " Good-bye "; C. F. Marshall, 'cello solos, " Träumerei " and " Danse Rustique "; S. de Jastrzebski, " 'Tis all that I can say," encore, " Rumpsey, Bumpsey, Bay "—" I'm not myself at all," and encore, " Philliloo "; recitations by W. J. Davis, " Catching the coach," " Hanging the picture," and encore, " The owl critic "; songs, Miss Steptoe, " All Souls' Day," " Resolution," and " A Japanese love song "; song, Miss Cook, " A may morning," and encore; songs, F. C. Hammant, " Give a man a horse he can ride," " Ho, Jolly Jenkin," and encore " Glorious Devon "; and F. J. Nield, " When father laid the carpet," encore, " Darling Sue," and " The Burglar's serenade."

Jastrzebski was simply perfect in his singing. He was accompanied by his wife and daughter Nora at the piano, Miss F. Reglar accompanying Miss Steptoe. Davis has made a name and fame in the College by his droll recitations. F. C. Hammant, with his splendid voice, is a welcome addition to the society's talent, as also is Miss Dockery, with her delicate notes. Miss Cook, the youngest of the singers, astonished us by her knowledge of the art, and by the ease with which she rendered difficult pieces. The other old friends we have mentioned played well their parts as usual; and the efforts of all were duly recognized by the audience, and also by the Doctor, who made a very neat speech at the interval.

At the general meeting of the society on October 19th, G. S. Offer and F. E. Lawrence were elected joint secretaries, and the president and vice-presidents were re-elected. Perry presented the eleventh report and balance sheet. The former set forth that twelve concerts had been held during the year, five ladies' and seven smoking. The June concert resulted in £12 19s. being handed to the Coffee Room Decoration Fund. The financial outlook of the society was gloomy, as they had had to draw on their reserve to pay current expenses. This was owing to the membership falling off, there being only 104 members this year.

INCOME AND EXPENDITURE ACCOUNT.

	£	s.	d.		£	s.	d.
Balance	1	8	11	Decoration Fund	2	2	0
Sales	2	2	6	Broadwood	1	1	0
Interest	0	6	0	Printing and stationery ...	5	13	0
Subscriptions ...	8	0	0	Postages	1	11	11
				Refreshments ...	1	4	0
				Overpaid into bank ...	0	1	0
				Balance	0	4	6
	£11	17	5		£11	17	5

BALANCE SHEET.

Assets.	£	s.	d.	*Liabilities.*	£	s.	d.
Balance	31	11	7½	Property account ...	38	1	10
Piano Fund ...	21	0	0	Cash at bank ...	14	14	4
Income balance ...	0	4	6½				
	£52	16	2		£52	16	2

Audited and found correct.—E. C. DUCHESNE, October 19th, 1907.

SHELLING PEAS.*

SUGGESTION FOR A KINDERGARTEN LESSON.

Is shelling peas a pastime, or is it an occupation? I think it may be either. If we regard it as a means towards an end, and that end is sustenance and nutrition, we may consider it a very useful occupation. On the other hand, if it is taken up just to pass an hour away indoors, instead of going out, it is a pastime; and the pastime may be more beneficial to the individual than the occupation would have been. For he may question himself, whether the human race has the special privilege or ability to perform the work?—or if it seems natural to use our fingers and thumb in the desired manner?—or if we would act in the same uniform manner, if we had not been taught? Do other creatures do the same thing in the same way? You may have observed monkeys engaged in feeding themselves on similar products, but there is no process like shelling. They extract the seeds from the pods with their teeth, beginning at the centre; and some birds, thrushes, blackbirds, and others, have acquired the art of getting at the contents in a somewhat similar manner, with their bills.

While you are shelling, it may occur to you that for some purposes some kinds of peas need no preparation of any kind, as for instance split peas, for soups or puddings, and you may endeavour to solve the mystery that surrounds them. What peas are they? and why are they left to mature, instead of being sold in the earlier stage as green peas? I have never seen a mill or other apparatus for the splitting of peas, nor have I seen the profession noticed in any trade directory, yet the peas themselves and the hulls which are sold as pea-chaff attest the fact that a process goes on of which I assume we know nothing. We do not have to shell these, and so we do not look them in the face and all round them.

In shelling peas, we have to do with various sorts, as they are called by our greengrocers, and the practice becomes interesting as we note their differences, which increase every season as new forms are brought under our notice. My earlier recollection only embraces two kinds, the earliest of which is still on the market, and is known among growers as Daniel A. Rooke, and Sangster's number one. This is a small, poor thing, with little flavour and a poor yield, about four in a pod, but they are eagerly bought when there are no others. They will vary in a fortnight from two shillings and sixpence a peck to threepence. The other pea that I knew, but know now no longer, was the Prussian Blue. This was a larger pea, better flavoured, better filled, a good, honest, reliable sort. They commanded a slightly higher price, but were the cheapest, because the yield was larger. The shells had a bluish tint, and so had

---

* Summary of a paper read by Mr. Grugeon to the Lubbock Field Club, October 30th, 1907.

the coats of the seeds. They were called Prussian Blues, in compliment to Marshal Blucher, while the memory of Waterloo was fresh in the minds of the people, and Blucher was as high in the esteem of the English people as was Lord Wellington. Then Germany and England were friends with common interests, a state of things which has gradually changed; we have become keen rivals, both in commerce and manufactures, causing mutual jealousies, which are easily fed by interested and unscrupulous pressmen, and the disappearance of the Prussian Blue pea from our markets and our tables has rather favoured this estrangement.

There is another pea I wish to say something about, and that is the Grey Pea, or Field Pea. This has a speckled brownish seed coat and is not gathered till the seeds are mature. They were until very recently boiled and eaten with bacon, and associated with Ash Wednesday. It could not have been a Church festival, as the day commences a long fast. But the curious custom of having pancakes on the previous day, Shrove Tuesday, wants explaining. This is not a fast day. It has seemed to me that the days have been inverted. How far Grey Peas and bacon is a British festival, I cannot ascertain. One thing is certain, that stomachs of mowers were essential for the proper enjoyment of such food. I believe that it must be conceded now that we do not, perhaps cannot, take such food, —certainly no town stomach could do it. Another festival has become fashionable, which seems limited to towns, being exclusively indulged in by workers in factories or workshops. I mean the beanfeast, though the beans are quite accidental, and not at all essential.

We will dismiss the Grey or Field Pea, as it has achieved its purpose, in introducing the Green Pea—the pea in which we take a much larger interest, a pea differing in the colour of its flower, in the colour of the seed coat, and the increased vigour of its growth. We must consider the latter as the outcome of the Field Pea, having first made its appearance in the same limited geographical area occupied by its progenitor, and having no area of its own, apart from cultivation. The forms and varieties now in cultivation are most numerous, but for our purpose we must limit them to a few,—the dwarf, the long-podded, the sugar pea, which is cooked shells and all, and the quadrangular, or four-sided pod. The dwarf pea, exemplified by Maclean's Little Gem, growing only a foot in height, requiring no sticks, and, owing to its limited size, not a heavy cropper, was useless for market purposes, but was a favourite among private growers, or amateurs, because it entailed no trouble, made a neat appearance in the garden, and a very creditable one on the table.

There are two of the long-podded kinds that I should like to mention—the Marrowfat and the Scimitar, the latter so called from the shape of the pod, which is somewhat sickle-shaped, having a gentle curve from the ventral to the dorsal sides of the pod, which makes it one of the most pleasant kinds to shell, as it also is to eat. While this kind is in season, it is wise to have them, because you ensure tranquility in the kitchen, in the nursery, and it follows as a matter of course, in the dining room.

To know the best peas you must grow them, and of course take trouble with them, and treat them like children that you love. Your first trouble will be when they are germinating and emerge above the soil. They then afford a most tempting morsel for the ubiquitous sparrow, who seems to mow them down as an occupation. This can be got over easily now, by the employment of wire netting; but as you save your plants that way, you must be careful and not be too lavish with your seed, or you will be as badly off, or perhaps worse off, than if the sparrows had been allowed to take toll. Then comes the process of training. Having ascertained from your seedsman the height of the different sorts you are trying, you will judge the distance apart that the rows should be; the height of the pea should represent the space between the rows. After having inserted your sticks for climbing, you must hoe the ground between the rows about twice, and then you are in a fair way of getting satisfaction, if you have not got any choice kinds. But if you should have choice kinds, as you ought, then the vexation of spirit begins. Your most costly crop, both in time and money, is promising well, and you walk down the rows, dwelling on them with pride and beaming with satisfaction, thinking which day will be the most appropriate for the gathering of the harvest, when, to your amazement, on the very morning you meant to come to a decision, the matter is decided for you. The peas have gone, and you are astonished by the appearance of the empty shells, hanging just as they did previously, but now to no purpose whatever, and you are a disappointed man, perhaps a wiser one. If you have been bragging among your friends about what you were growing (and a man is very apt to do that, especially when he is inexperienced), your humiliation is great. The picture is too sad. We will look at the obverse, and assume that the thrushes and blackbirds have not visited you and taken toll, that you have raised a crop of wrinkled Marrowfats, have gathered them yourself, with none the less enjoyment that you had no occasion to stoop, but could stand upright, as the pods were really above the level of your shoulders. You place them in a basket or tray, with admiration, and wish you had bought a new one, they would have looked so much nicer. With what pride you take them indoors to show the family! You do, perhaps, what you have never done before, take part in the shelling, with the most pleasant feelings of freshness and fragrance that belongs exclusively to fresh vegetables. You feel sorry when the job is finished, but find consolation in the thought that dinner will not be long. You even postpone your cigar, so that nothing shall interfere with the culmination of your patience and efforts. And that dinner—

will it ever be forgotten ?   Food for the gods—shoulder of lamb and Knight's wrinkled Marrowfat Peas, fresh from the garden ! Now, can, or does the Carlton, the Cecil, or any high class club or restaurant have anything to equal what you have attained ? The verdict is, " I'll have another go next year," and all the household agrees that you ought.   You are resolved that next summer will be the one to be remembered, and are thinking of replacing the shoulder of lamb with a pair of Aylesbury ducks, and of inviting Bobby Marks and some other College fellow, who is an expert in garden work, to dinner and talk.   You may depend upon it that spades will be trumps on that occasion.   ALFRED GRUGEON.

SHAKESPEARE READINGS.

ON October 27th, a successful reading of " Much Ado about Nothing " was given in the Common Room.   It was noticed that the reading went more briskly than usual, the cues being taken up with exemplary rapidity. The principal parts were sustained by Messrs. Wallace Davis and Gates Fowler (Beatrice and Benedict) neither of whom seemed quite comfortable in his rôle, while Tom Barnard gave the lines of Don Pedro with his usual faultless diction.   The Dogberry of Ted Hayward was splendid ; he seems to have caught the spirit of Elizabethan humour.   Several new men were present and appeared to take considerable pleasure in the reading.   On this occasion a casting committee of four was elected, Davis, Barnard, Gates Fowler, and Paterson (president).

" Macbeth " was read on November 10th, when the audience was larger. Wallace Davis read the lines of the cowardly remorse-ridden king to Tom Barnard's splendid interpretation of Lady Macbeth.   He seemed to be the very incarnation of ruthless purpose in the first act, screwing up the courage of the half-hearted murdering conspirator.   For the rest, Peck gave distinction to the Witches' lines, Starling read Banquo, while Mead and Gates Fowler had a good time in the last act as Malcolm and Macduff.   After the reading, Barnard rose to take the sense of the meeting upon a proposition to invite ladies to *all* the readings.   In a persuasive speech, in which he wished the ladies a more eloquent champion, he took as much wind out of the sails of the opposition as possible by detailing all the objections that he had heard urged against the proposition.   He was closely followed by Peck, who implored the opposition to come out in the open and fight—not to be mute, but to state their reasons for the faith that was in them.   Gates Fowler opposed, and pointed out disadvantages.   He seemed to fear that the Society would degenerate into a clique, into which nothing would be able to enter except under the aegis of the eternal feminine, a thing intolerable in a Men's College.   Hayward followed, and demonstrated other disadvantages, *e.g.*, stupid cuts and the prohibition of tobacco.   He implored Barnard to withdraw his motion.   Barnard however preferred to go forward.   Mead and Buckland also spoke strongly against the resolution, and Starling made a speech which was claimed as support.   At the suggestion of Gates Fowler, the vote was by ballot instead of show of hands, and the motion was decisively defeated by 14 votes to 9.   Barnard then brought forward another resolution to the effect that ladies be invited every second reading.   Gates Fowler moved an amendment that they be invited once every twelve years. This was lost, there being several abstentions, and the resolution was carried by 14 to 7—the total attendance being twenty-five.   Hayward then gave notice that he would appeal to the Executive against the resolution.

It is desirable, in the interests of the Society, that all students who admire Shakespeare and care for reading his plays should attend, either to read or to listen.   There is a voluntary subscription of 1s. to defray postages, etc.

LITERARY SOCIETY.

THE first meeting of the Literary Society this season was held on Thursday, November 7th, when Mr. A. S. LUPTON, M.A., spoke on "A Plea for Wider Reading." Mr. Lupton is a favourite speaker at the College, and a large audience was in attendance to hear him on this important subject.

Dr. FURNIVALL, the President of the Society, took the chair, and, in a few preliminary remarks, said he quite agreed with the opener's plea for wider reading, but he should like him to tell us how we were to find the necessary time in which to do it.

Mr. LUPTON, who, on rising, was received with enthusiasm, said that Dr. Furnivall had raised the point of how to find the time, and it was an important point; but he thought that in these days, there was a good deal read which was not worth reading. He urged that too much time was spent on reading the Newspapers, a large part of which was taken up with the chronicles of the Old Bailey, the Police Court, and the Divorce Court; and the remainder to setting the special class of readers of the particular paper against all other classes in the country, and their own particular country against all the other countries in the world. Their use was merely to acquaint one with what was going on, and one should not spend too much time over them. He was reminded of Austin Dobson's Wordsworthian sonnet:—

> "The Presse is too much with us; small and great,
> We are undone of chatter and *on dit*,
> Report, Retort, Rejoinder, Repartee,
> Mole-hill, and Mare's Nest, fiction up-to-date,
> Babble of booklets, bicker of debate,
> Aspect of A and attitude of B—
> A waste of words that drive us like a Sea,
> Mere derelict of ourselves, and helpless freight.
> Oh, for a lodge in some vast wilderness,
> Some refuge unapproachable of Print,
> Where never cablegram could gain access
> And Telephones were not, nor any hint ·
> Of tidings new or old, but man might pipe
> His Soul to nature,—careless of the Type."

And he would like to put into less polished Anglo-Saxon a protest against too much reading of Newspapers. Furthermore, on the question of time, it had often been suggested that we were apt to over-sleep, and somewhat drastic measures of reform had, from time to time, been proposed. With many of these he was not in accord, and he could not agree with a sixteenth century writer who recommended the alarum, or at any rate, a firm resolution not to slumber after a certain hour. He called to mind the words of Erasmus, which conveyed exceedingly good advice as to how to utilize time: "Don't suffer what you hear to slip out of your memory, but recite it over to yourself or to other persons. Nor let this suffice you, but set apart some certain time for meditation, which one thing, as St. Aurelius writes, does most conduce to assist both wit and memory. If you are in doubt of anything, do not be ashamed to ask; or if you have committed an error, to be corrected. Avoid late and unseasonable studies, for they murder wit, and are very prejudicial to health. The Muses love the morning, and that is a fit time for study. . . . A little before you go to sleep, read something that is exquisite, and worth remembering; and contemplate upon it before you fall asleep; and when you awake in the morning, call yourself to an account for it." In enlarging upon this passage of Erasmus, Mr. Lupton recommended that a certain portion of the time we allowed for reading should be set aside for reading what interested us, and interested us without effort. For his own part, he thought the Novel was a type of literature which could be read without a deal of effort. To be in the swim, one must read George Meredith and Thomas Hardy. He confessed he had not a great liking for either, because he did not think they were artists; but of actual very recent writers, Stevenson, who wrote in perfectly lucid English, and took us apart from our own country, gave him most pleasure. When one lived and worked in London, it was a great delight to be wafted away for half-an-hour among the Pacific Islands. On the whole he preferred to read novelists who had lived some considerable time before him, whose characters were unlike the people of our own time, because it was interesting to trace our progress from other days. Jane Austen always took such uninteresting people to describe, but her way of description was delightful. Fielding's "Tom Jones" was one of the best novels ever written. Its vividness and life made it stand out above all the other novels of the same date. Every Englishman should know the "Pickwick Papers" by heart; "David Copperfield" and "A Tale of Two Cities" he was never tired of reading. Many people had a preference for Thackeray over Dickens, but Becky Sharp was the only female character of Thackeray that he could read and really enjoy. Charles Reade's "Cloister and the Hearth" was quite a perfect novel.

Another point he wished to make was that there were great areas of literature in our country and others, that were never touched upon. Dr. Furnivall and the Early English Text Society had done much to open up these untrodden paths, but still there was a great lack of width. This was largely attributable to our examination system, the tendency of which was to create a state of things in which everyone read the same books, within certain areas. He admitted that these areas were enough for one man; but the point was that every man confined himself to the same areas. He therefore urged it to be a good thing that people should spend some time in reading, not in the furrows which had been ploughed over and over again, but off the beaten tracks; which would impart more life and interest to subjects generally, and enable them to be approached from many very different points of view.

He thought, too, that a certain time each day should be devoted to reading something which required the exercise of some mental strain— something which would become more interesting to us as we became more developed, and in this connection it would be better that we should be guided in the direction of our own tastes. One might take a certain period of a country's history, and read everything in it worth reading; or one who knew his own language pretty well would find a vast field of pleasure in Chaucer. A wide study of the Drama would also be delightfully interesting, and in this connection the College Shakspere Readings did good work. Dealing with History proper, he thought that people who studied it merely with a text-book made a very dull work of it. In his view, the proper way to treat a text-book was to regard it as a sort of map to help one in one's travels; and one should read the actual writings of any period, fill in the gaps from the text-book, and then get the opinions of the great historians who had read and written on the same periods. One who knew a foreign language would also find much interest in studying other countries as well as other times. The reading of books of travel was an excellent means of getting to know the dispositions of the people without very much effort. In this way one could regard one's own times by the light of other times and other peoples. Differences were found from the present day, and resemblances to them, too, and this was a great guide in working out what tendencies of our own times were good and what were bad.

Dr. FURNIVALL, in an interesting and characteristic speech, urged strongly the need for a study of man and nature.

Mr. LIONEL JACOB pointed out that the great advantage of books was that they threw the world of man open to us. One should read as good writers as possible, before reading the small, and thus acquire the standard by which to judge great writing and to understand it. That was the first thing in reading, and that wanted aim and effort.

Messrs. A. E. HOMEWOOD, J. J. MUNRO, and JAMES PERRY contributed their views in speeches full of interest, which brought to a close a most enjoyable and instructive evening. C. F. W. MEAD, *Hon. Secretary.*

DEBATING SOCIETY.

JUST a word by way of preface to the monthly chronicle with regard to the well-being of the Society. Whilst the average attendance is fairly satisfactory, one cannot help feeling that from so large an organization as the College, there should be no difficulty in filling the Common Room ; and a careful analysis of those usually present at our gatherings shows that the new students do not so readily avail themselves of this excellent means of becoming conversant with the trend of thought in the College, with regard to those interesting social and political conditions which face us at the present day, as might be expected in an educational assembly. Whilst readily agreeing that, in the main, membership of the College implies the pursuit of a definite branch of learning, let us not forget the broadening effects of contact with the minds of our fellow members. In no way can men more readily avail themselves of this than in the meetings of this Society. The subjects dealt with are always alive and interesting, the principal speakers excellent, inasmuch as they are usually experts in the matters upon which they debate ; and above all, there is the opportunity of training oneself in the art of thinking aloud—one of the most necessary adjuncts of an educated man. Remember, therefore, ye who wildly career down the main staircase to the front door, that there is an equally efficient means of reaching the ground floor by a smaller staircase which leads into the Common Room ; and on Tuesday evenings, at 9.30, always use this means of egress.

Since writing my previous notice, many events of moment have engaged our attention. On October 22nd, Mr. Lupton devoted some time to our edification with a motion to abolish the Lower Chamber, in the proposing of which he gave vent to some scathing criticisms. So low has the popular assembly fallen in his estimation, that it not only fails to represent, as we fondly imagined, all that is best in public life, but it could not even supply him with the names of five members worthy of classification in his high standard of public servants. Frankly he considered it as merely a political assembly, constantly engaged in tactics necessary to keeping office or turning one's opponents out ; with the deplorable result that matters of urgent social import had been, and were still, and had every prospect of being, to the end of our time, beyond the region of their legislative efforts. Whilst not disclosing any alternative plan, by which he showed himself to be a true politician, Mr. Lupton's subtle references to the lethal chamber for Cabinet Ministers after one turn of office, pointed to the remedy being as complete as it was drastic. An opposer was forthcoming in Mr. James Halford, not unknown as a speaker in Hornsey, who, although a sturdy Liberal, still had faith in one part at least of the British Constitution. Whilst admitting the House of Commons had many defects, he felt they were blemishes of degree and not of principle, and argued that the institution of proportional representation or the second ballot would give us a more truly representative chamber, so much so, that even Mr. Lupton's views might find expression. He saw nothing abnormal in the section or sections, which contributed most to the creation of the Government of the day, figuring more largely in its councils, and merely regarded this as the spoils of war. Finally, he thought he knew his fellow-cititzen sufficiently to believe that when the necessity arose, he could rise above political feeling ; and contended that the Lower Chamber had usually risen to the occasion, when national necessities demanded it. The debate was warmly entered into, excellent contributions being made by Messrs. Peck, Perry, and the President ; and on the motion being put, it was lost by 16 votes to 7.

The following Tuesday, October 29th, was devoted to a consideration of Old Age Pensions, Mr. T. Morison, M.A., moving the following resolution, "That in every scheme for the payment of Old Age Pensions, the obligation of the individual to contribute towards a provision for his old age should be enforced." In the course of a thoughtful speech, he laid stress upon inculcating self-reliance in the individual ; and whilst admitting the inequalities which unfortunately existed, thought that as far as possible the pauperizing element of State aid in its entirety should be absent from our national life.

He believed the average man was able and willing to contribute to a scheme in which also his employer and the State had their part. The opposer, Mr. Perry, in a trenchant but good-humoured criticism, referred particularly to the baneful influences exercised by the economic conditions existing in this country, and submitted that if public servants like Lord Cromer, Lord Kitchener, and others were not pauperized by receiving grants for services rendered, surely no such stigma could rest upon the ordinary citizen who also, in a humble way, contributed to the well-being of the State. The subsequent speakers, among whom were Messrs. Randall, Lupton, Hayward, Torrington, E. E. Homewood, Klinger, and Bradgate, principally inclined to this aspect of the case, and the motion was consequently lost by 11 votes to 15.

On November 5th, a return was made to the Tariff question, which can always be trusted to provide new material, and on this occasion Mr. Frank Beard, a visitor, invited the House to acquiesce in the following motion touching the colonial aspect of the case—"That this House regrets the attitude taken up by the Government at the Colonial Conference on the question of Preferential Trade, and expresses the belief that the adoption of such a policy would increase considerably the trade between the Mother Country and the British Dominions beyond the sea." In the course of his advocacy, which revealed an intimate acquaintance with the subject, he referred to the unfortunate position in which the Government found themselves, owing to the pledges they had given before properly considering the matter, and felt that an opportunity, which was not likely to present itself again, had been lost, of not only binding the component parts of the Empire together, but of extending and consolidating the markets of the new world, so essential to a manufacturing community such as ours. In a reference to the taxation of food, he ridiculed the present system of raising revenue upon articles which we could not produce, thus necessitating the whole tax falling upon the consumer, and suggested the removal of sugar, tea, and other like commodities from the Exchequer's grasp, and their replacement by articles in which there was a home, colonial, and foreign supply, maintaining that the stress of competition would absolve the consumer from the imposition levied. Mr. W. J. Torrington, in combating these principles, sought to show that harm would thereby be done to our large foreign trade, which must be preserved at all costs ; and remarking upon the danger of this country being dependent upon any circumscribed area for its food supply, he drew attention to the liability of the Australian to drought and other evils which at times resulted in a short harvest.

The debate, which was one of the best this session, drew remarks from Messrs. Offer, Dingwall, E. E. Homewood, Bradgate, Lupton, and Mead ; and although the opener dealt most fully, and as some think completely, with the queries raised, the motion was rejected by 20 votes to 12.

Tuesday, November 12th, brought forth the following motion, "That this House welcomed the passing of the Advertisements Regulation Act, and desires the better protection of the public from modern advertising developments on the roads and railways," which was moved by Mr. John C. Bailey, M.A., in a most scholarly speech, the opposition being voiced by Mr. C. F. W. Mead in a very creditable manner. After a good debate, however, the motion was carried by 26 votes to 2.

Tuesday, November 19th, produced a debate as to whether "A useful and practical education was a real education," the negative view being put forth by Mr. H. G. A. Baker, and the affirmative by Mr. O'Keeffe, a promising young recruit to the Society. That a somewhat humorous discussion ensued will be gathered from the fact that Messrs. Starling, Lupton, and Moore were the principal participants. The fixtures to the end of the half session are as follows :—

December 3rd.—"Nationalization of Railways." Opener, Mr. W. R. J. Hickman ; opposer, Mr. Smith, of University College.

December 10th.—"Is Germany a danger to Great Britain?" Opener, Dr. Emil Reich.

December 17th.—Subject to be arranged. Mr. E. J. Turner, the Librarian, will essay a bout with Mr. B. P. Moore.

F. E. LIDDELOW, *Hon. Secretary.*

COLLEGE NOTES.

THE thirty-first annual Supper of the Old Students' Club will take place in the Maurice Hall, on Saturday, December 14th, at 7 p.m. Guests will assemble at 6.30. This supper is the chief College social gathering of the year, and all members are heartily welcome. The chair will be taken by Mr. R. H. Marks, president of the club, and there are expected to be present the Principal, Professor A. V. Dicey; the Vice-Principal, Mr. Lionel Jacob; the Rev. B. H. Alford, Professor J. Westlake, K.C., Dr. F. J. Furnivall, Sir Charles Lucas, K.C.M.G., Gen. Sir Frederick Maurice, K.C.B., Dr. Eugène Oswald, Mr. G. P. Gooch, M.P., and Messrs. Richard Whiteing, W. Pett Ridge, Sydney Bradgate, A. J. Bride, F. M. Cornford, J. J. Dent, J. A. Forster, T. F. Hobson, A. E. Homewood, Julius Jacob, T. T. S. de Jastrzebski, Jules Lazare, H R. Levinsohn, A. S. Lupton, B. P. Moore, Theodore Morison, R. J. Mure, C. H. Perry, B. J. Rose, A. B. Shaw, W. J. Torrington, G. M. Trevelyan, E. J. Turner, Juan Victoria, R. W. Wilkinson, and many other teachers, students, and friends. Tickets, price 3s. each, may be obtained of Mr. Marks or in the office.

Those members to whom tickets have been sent, and who find themselves unable to attend, are particularly requested to return their tickets by Tuesday, December 10th, otherwise seats will be reserved for them. It will also assist the hon. secretary in seating the guests, if ticket holders will signify the names of those with whom they would like to sit.

The Marks Prize, 1908, open to all students, will be awarded to the writer of the best essay on either of the following subjects: —(a) Discuss Shakespeare's view of Democracy, especially as exemplified by the plays of "Julius Cæsar" and "Coriolanus"; (b) Criticize the view that the characters of Dickens are caricatures. Essays are to be sent in by April 30th.

A remarkably brilliant lecture, showing a great amount of learning, research, and thought, and affording food for much reflection, was that given by Mr. J. W. Mackail on November 23rd, on "Art and Puritanism." A somewhat smaller audience than usual was deeply interested in the lecture, at the close of which, after the customary vote of thanks, the Rev. B. H. Alford expressed the hope that we might at some future time be able to see it in print. The view that Mr. Mackail wished to place before us was that Art must be the proper vocation of a perfect life, and that in this imperfect world we must see that we neither ignore the claims of Art to a place in our imperfect life, nor yet give Art a place which, by interfering with other things equally important, would not only vitiate life, but would vitiate and corrupt Art itself.

Now that the College Library is provided with so well equipped and suitable a resting-place, the Executive Committee has decided to open a subscription list, with the object of raising £100, in order to supply the many deficiencies in the books, and to furnish the blanks upon the shelves. Donations may be sent to Mr. E. C. Duchesne, Superintendent of the College.

Those students who have in past years attended some of Mr. John Scott's special courses of class lectures will be glad to know that he is to give a series next term, devoted to Studies in the Mind and Art of Robert Browning, as illustrated in the Poems, 1844 to 1864, viz., "Dramatic Romances and Lyrics," "Christmas Eve and Easter Day," "Men and Women," and "Dramatis Personæ." The lectures will be given on Wednesdays at 7.45, commencing on January 15th. Special attention will be paid to the poet's treatment of Nature, Art, Religion, Love, Immortality; to his theory of Human Life, Optimism, and his solution of the problem of Evil. Mr. Scott recommends each member of the class to use Vol. II. of the Poems and Plays of Robert Browning, 1844—1864 (No. 42 of Everyman's Library.)

An interesting reference to the Founder of this College is to be found in Volume II. of "The Letters of Queen Victoria" (A. C. Benson and Viscount Esher), recently published, at page 54. Writing on 15th September, 1845, Sir Robert Peel informed the late Queen that there was a vacancy in the Deanery of Lincoln, and recommended that an offer of this preferment should be made to Mr. Ward, the then rector of St. James's. Sir Robert Peel's letter to Her Majesty continued thus :—

Should Mr. Ward decline, there is a clergyman of the name of Maurice, of whom the Archbishop says, "Of unbeneficed London Clergy, there is no one, I believe, who is so much distinguished by his learning and literary talent as the Rev. Frederick Maurice, Chaplain of Guy's Hospital. His private character is equally estimable." Should Mr. Ward decline the Deanery it might, should your Majesty approve of it, be offered to Mr. Maurice. The Archbishop says that the appointment of Mr. Maurice would be very gratifying to the King of Prussia.

Mr. Ward accepted the Deanery, otherwise perhaps this College would not have existed.

Since the last notice on the subject, Mr. Randall, hon. secretary of the Coffee Room Decoration Fund, has received £1 1s. from Mr. W. E. G. Read, and 2s. 6d. from Mr. H. W. Miles. This left £5 2s. 6d. required to complete the fund, and Mr. Randall announced at the Common Room meeting on November 25th that that sum would be provided by the Common Room Committee. He is to be heartily congratulated on the successful results of his work in this connection—one of many branches of his activities in the College.

The election, held last month, of Student members of Council, resulted in the choice of C. H. Perry, F. J. Nield, and H. K. Randall, who secured 32, 30, and 29 votes respectively. Only 57 members voted. The unsuccessful candidates were J. Crawley, H. N. Gill, R. M. Emslie, and F. E. Liddelow.

Randall again asks for help from readers of the JOURNAL, in connection with the Furnivall Children's Treat, to be given on December 21st. We feel sure he will not ask in vain, and that with the assistance of Nye and Offer, the usual contributions, and the willing hands and hearts of our young lady friends, the children may count upon having a happy time. See Randall's letter, on another page.

The Joint Clubs' Supper is being looked after this year by Perry, Reglar, Jones, and Castell. It will take place on December 28th, at 7 p.m., when the chair will be taken by W. J. Torrington, a deservedly popular favourite amongst College Clubites. It will facilitate the arrangements, if early application is made for tickets, 2s. 6d. each.

All tickets for the dance on December 7th have of course been taken long ago. The next dance will be held in the Maurice Hall, on January 4th. Early application for tickets should be made, as they are very speedily sold.

Miss Helen Fotheringham, eldest daughter of John Fotheringham, of Fawkham, an old member of the College, lately completed a reredos for the Church of St. Edmund the King, at Kingsdown, near Sevenoaks. The reredos is of oak, and will occupy the whole width of the chancel. Miss Fotheringham, who recently successfully executed a reredos for St. Margaret's, Rochester, designed the reredos, and practically carved the whole herself. The reredos was consecrated at a service at which there was a full congregation, on November 19th, when the Dean of Rochester officiated, assisted by the Rev. F. W. Warland, Rector of Kingsdown, the Rector of Stanstead, and the Rector of Meopham

We regret to announce the death of Mr. E. Bown, in September last, at the age of 77. Mr. Bown was an old member of the College and of the Old Students' Club, and for many years he filled the office of custodian of the Common Room. Although unable to get far away from his home in Chelsea during recent years, he always maintained his connection with the College, and supported the JOURNAL up to the time of his death.

At the annual general meeting of the members of the Common Room held on Monday, November 25th, Mr. Sydney

Bradgate took the chair, and Mr. H. K. Randall, the hon. secretary of the Common Room Committee, read a very well written and comprehensive report on the Common Room and social life of the College for the year ending 31st October, and also presented the balance sheet of the Committee to that date. We hope to reproduce these documents in the JOURNAL in due course. The report and accounts were adopted, and the usual heckling of the candidates for the new committee for the ensuing year followed, the chief subjects of the questions asked being the proposed club rules, the price and quality of the beer, and the willingness of candidates to fill the offices of secretary and custodian, if called upon to do so.

The summary of the proceedings at the November Council meeting is held over until our next issue.

THE STUDENTS' CALENDAR FOR DECEMBER.

Sun., 1st.—Lecture, "The Hebrew Monarchy," Rev. B. H. Alford, 6 p.m.

Mon., 2nd.—Lecture, "The Romantic Revival in English Poetry," Dr. R. G. Watkin, 7.30. Election of Common Room Committee, Polling begins.

Tues., 3rd.—Executive Committee, 8 p.m. Lecture, "Italian Painters," Mr. Dudley Heath, 8 p.m. Tansley Swimming Club practice, King Street Baths, 7.30. Maurice Chess Club match v. Claremont, home, 8 p.m. Debating Society meeting, Mr. W. R. J. Hickman opens, 9.30.

Wed., 4th.—Musical Society's Smoking Concert, 9.30.

Thurs. 5th.—Lecture, "The Fundamental Principles of the Law of the Constitution," The Principal, 8.30. Literary Society meeting, Mr. J. J. Munro's paper "The Origin and Development of Romeo and Juliet," 9.30. Life-saving class, 9.30. Citizens' Lunch, 1.30.

Fri., 6th.—Lecture, "Child Study," Dr. Slaughter, 8 p.m.

Sat., 7th.—Collegians' 23rd Dance, Maurice Hall, 7 p.m.

Sun., 8th.—Lubbock Field Club Walk to Surrey Hills; train leaves Waterloo South Station, 10.5 a.m. Lecture, "The Hebrew Monarchy," Rev. B. H. Alford, 6 p.m. Shakespeare Reading, "Cymbeline," 7.30.

Mon., 9th.—Lecture, "English Poetry." Dr. Watkin, 7.30.

Tues., 10th.—Executive Committee, 8 p.m. Swimming Club practice, King Street Baths, 7.30. Debating Society meeting, Dr. Emil Reich opens, 9.30.

Wed., 11th.—Chess Match, Wheatsheaf v. Maurice, 10 boards, 79, Farringdon Street, 8 p.m.

Thurs., 12th.—Life-saving class, 9.30.

Sat., 14th.—Old Students' Club Supper, 7 p.m., assemble 6.30.

Sun., 15th.—Lecture, "The Hebrew Monarchy," Rev. B. H. Alford, 6 p.m.

Mon., 16th.—Lecture, "English Poetry," Dr. Watkin, 7.30. Maurice Chess Club match v. Wood Green, home, 8 p.m.

Tues., 17th.—Executive Committee, 8 p.m. Swimming Club practice, King Street Baths, 7.30. Debating Society meeting, Mr. E. J. Turner opens, 9.30.

Thurs., 19th.—Chess Match, St. Martin's v. Maurice, 10 boards, 122, Newgate Street, 8 p.m. Life-saving class, 9.30.

Fri., 20th.—Shorthand Examination at 7.30.

Sat., 21st.—First term ends. Furnivall Children's Treat.

Sun., 22nd.—Shakespeare Reading, 7.30.

Wed., 25th.—Christmas Day. } College closed.
Thurs., 26th.—Boxing Day. }

Sat., 28th.—Joint Clubs' Supper, 7 p.m., assemble 6.30.

OLD STUDENTS' CLUB.

PARTY GOVERNMENT AND PROPORTIONAL REPRESENTATION.

THE second meeting of the club for the present session was held on Saturday, November 16th, at 7.45, when Mr. C. Edmund Maurice, son of our Founder, opened the subject for discussion: "Has Party Government worked well, and can it be improved?"—Proportional Representation was also dealt with. There were over 60 members present, including Messrs. J. T. Baker, T. M. Balson, W. H. Barnett, George Beavis, James Benny, Sydney Bradgate, G. T. Butler, C. Castle, J. R. Chandler, J. W. Chapman, A. W. Coombs, A. E. Coombs, S. J. Coombs, W. J. Davis, H. C. Dumbrill, Harold Eyers, J. W. Gates Fowler, R. Freeman, G. C. Gümpel, S. Hamilton, W. Hart, E. Hayward, T. Hopkins, Wm. Hudson, A. Levett, Julius Jacob, J. W. Jenkins, C. P. King, James Kirk, H. R. Levinsohn, J. D. Macnair, R. H. Marks, A. W. Matthews, C. E Maurice, J. McWilliam, H. W. Miles, Charles Monteath, E. D. A. Morshead, J. J. Munro, G. S. Offer, H. Osborn, Leonard Pocock, Sydney Presburg, C. W. Rapley, E. J. H. Reglar, J. W Roberts, F. C. Roper, J. Rigby Smith, W. J. Spray, M. Staal, M. W. Starling, F. G. Sweeting, W. Tirrell, H. Trott, G. Wanklin, Herbert Wilcockson, C. R. Williams, A. Wilshaw, and Charles Wright.

Before Mr. MARKS called upon Mr. Maurice, he proposed the following resolution, which was seconded by Mr. A. W. COOMBS, and carried by acclamation: "That this meeting of the Old Students' Club offers its hearty congratulations, in the name of the Club, to Sir Charles Lucas, C.B., K.C.M.G., on the honour bestowed on him, and desires to record the fact that the bestowal of the distinction has given great pleasure to all his friends in the College."

Mr. MAURICE, who was received with cheers, said:—There are few subjects that have been more confused, partly by honest misapprehension, partly by dishonest cant, than the question of Party Government. Vices which are inherent in certain kinds of human nature are supposed to owe their origin, or at least their chief opportunity of development, to this institution; and, on the other hand, certain clap-trap phrases have enabled rather second-rate orators to claim for themselves some mysterious virtue, when they are really only gratifying personal vanity, or in many cases indulging in the very vice of which they accuse their opponents. All such mistakes arise, in the main, from not considering the real meaning of the words used. I should like, therefore, to open this account of Party Government by quoting the words in which Macaulay describes the introduction in 1693 of the first clear attempt at the establishment of a ministry responsible to the House of Commons, and dependent on a majority of that body: "The Ministry," he says, "is, in fact, a committee of leading members of the two Houses. It is nominated by the Crown, but it consists exclusively of statesmen whose opinions on the pressing questions of the time agree, in the main, with the opinions of the majority of the House of Commons. Among the members of the committee are distributed the great departments of the administration. Each Minister conducts the ordinary business of his own office, without reference to his colleagues. But the most important business of every office, and especially such business as is likely to be the subject of discussion in Parliament, is brought under the consideration of the whole Ministry. In Parliament the Ministers are bound to act as one man, on all questions relating to the Executive Government. If one of them dissents from the rest on a question too important to admit of a compromise, it is his duty to retire. While the Ministers retain the confidence of the parliamentary majority, that majority supports them against opposition, and rejects every motion which reflects on them or is likely to embarrass them. If they forfeit that confidence, if the parliamentary majority is dissatisfied with the way in which patronage is distributed, with the way in which the prerogative of mercy is used, with the conduct of foreign affairs, with the conduct of a war, the remedy is simple. It is not necessary that the Commons should take on themselves the business of administration, that they should request the Crown to make this man a bishop and that man a judge, to pardon this criminal and to execute another, to negotiate a treaty on a particular basis, or to send an expedition to a particular place. They have merely to declare that they have ceased to trust the Ministry, and to ask for a Ministry which they can trust."—There is more than one detail in this passage to which I shall have to call your attention later on. But my reason for quoting the passage at such full length is that you may see the reasonableness, and I may add, the peaceableness, of this method of securing popular Government. If you compare it with the method of the old Greek Democracy, of banishing from the State the representative of the minority ; with the early method of the Roman Plebeians, of retiring from the State altogether to a neighbouring hill ; or with the riots and bloodshed which hindered the working of the more perfect constitution of the Florentine Democracy,—you will see what a great stride the introduction of Party Government made towards the peaceable methods of securing popular Government. Still more vividly and impressively does this appear, when you compare the effort which the parliaments of the early part of the seventeenth century had hitherto made towards securing their liberty. Even when not engaged in civil war and rebellion, their chief idea of securing justice was to demand the impeachment of some leading minister, to be followed by his imprisonment, if not by his death When, therefore, we hear people talking of Party Government, as if it were something that introduced an element of unnatural bitterness and antagonism, we should remember that, on the contrary, it is the substitute for far bitterer forms of division. Then again, there is the delusion that in some way or other Party Government has a narrowing and degrading influence ; and people are very fond of calling on their opponents to rise above party, or to place country before party. Now, I would point out with regard to this second claim, that, if logically analysed, it implies that the person who uses it must have chosen his party with an eye to something else than the service of his country. The whole assumption of the principle of Party Government is, that men consider the party which they have joined the best organization for securing good service to the country ; in other words, that serving one's party is the most immediately practical way of serving the country. At the same time, we ought to admit that there is a very natural confusion in this phrase, arising partly from the double character of party allegiance. A man will vote for a party, because it has advocated and continues to advocate certain measures which its supporters believe to be the most important then required by the country ; or he may vote for it, because it is led by men in whose character and general tendencies he has confidence. Now, the opponents of such leaders probably distrust both them and their measures ; and, as nothing is more difficult to realize than the causes of an admiration which one does not share, it is quite natural that when such opponents see the followers of the leaders of whom I have spoken, subordinating their known desires for particular measures to their desire to keep a special Minister in power, such subordination is set down to self-seeking servility, or to want of independent judgment. [Mr. MAURICE illustrated his meaning by several concrete instances.] But in order to secure the effective working of our present system of Party Government, it is necessary that there should be a clear issue of principles between the two parties which are at present supposed to divide the country. When, as Macaulay has shown, this system was first established in 1693, the struggle was still going on between the champions of William III.'s Government and the supporters of the Stuart dynasty. This division coloured all the views of the contending parties about the wars with France, and the alliance with the Dutch ; and in a less direct but very perceptible manner, their feelings to Scotland and Ireland, to the Church of England, even in some measure to questions of trade, and most of all to the arrangements to be thereafter made for the succession to the English throne. But when the Hanoverian dynasty was firmly seated on the throne of England, and the Jacobites had become a mere set of discredited rebels, it seemed, for a time, as if the clear divisions of Party had been obliterated. Then followed a time in which personal factions took the place of parties divided by political principles—a time in which the different sections of the Whigs were wrangling for place, and when, by a natural consequence, corrupt motives took the place of public spirit. And this process has been repeated in our own time, both in Italy and France. In Italy, the completion of national unity in 1870, by the securing of Rome as the national capital, was followed by a decree of the Pope's, forbidding the faithful Catholics to take any part in the political life in Italy. Thus there remained in power a number of men all calling themselves Liberals, all pledged, more or less, to certain reforms, for ever squabbling among each other as to who should carry out those reforms. When I was in Italy in 1885, this state of things had facilitated the rise to power of a very unscrupulous man named Depretis, who seemed to have no political principles, except the determination to keep himself in power, by all possible means. So again, after the fall of MacMahon in France, the conclusion of the struggle between Republicans and Royalists made way for a similar period of corruption and self-seeking. I have mentioned these three instances together, to show you that this is a phenomenon for which we must always be prepared in Party Government. England, France, and Italy, all struggled out of this degrading condition, and were helped out of it by the rise of important questions which produced new divisions of principle   How this danger may, in some measure, be guarded against, I hope to show later on.   Now I merely want to remark that corruption and self-seeking are not the necessary outcome of Party Government, nor can they be destroyed by returning to any condition which existed previously to the creation of Party Government.   That such a return to the past would be fraught with danger, is perhaps most strikingly proved by a passing attempt to set aside Party Government, which was made by George III. and the elder Pitt, soon after the great struggle about the Stamp Act had shown the reviving vigour of parliamentary government, and the consequent weakening of the royal power   William Pitt, though in many ways a great statesman, was overwhelmingly conscious of his own importance ; and when he found that the fall of the Grenville ministry was not followed by his own return to office, he treated the Rockingham ministry in a cold and distrustful way.   This conduct, considering that the new ministry were trying to carry out, in the main, the principles for which he was contending, must be accepted as a proof at once of arrogance and want of magnanimity.   George III. noted this weakness in the statesman, who had hitherto opposed his policy, and realizing that Pitt could be neither intimidated, corrupted, nor successfully defied, resolved to win him by flattery. Pitt was to be recognized as the one trusty minister, who could rise above party. The Rockingham Ministry were driven from office, and Pitt was empowered to form a ministry, out of the very inferior materials that were left him. The Nemesis soon followed : the excitement brought on by these proceedings eventually drove the gout into Pitt's head, and incapacitated him from any useful action.   The ministry, freed from his direction, returned to the very policy which he had condemned ; and, by their renewed attempts at taxation, drove the American colonies into revolt. The failure of the efforts to coerce them into obedience discredited the attempt of George III. to secure exceptional power for himself and his ministers, and prepared the way for a return to parliamentary government.

I have thus endeavoured to show you, both the weakness and the strength of Party Government. I now wish to point out in what respect the conditions of this arrangement have changed, since the times which I have been describing ; and what improvements may now be possible, which would hardly have been thought necessary in the eighteenth century. First of all then, as the most essential point, you should note that the system I have been describing is a purely *two* party Government. Now, *that* condition worked well enough up to the close of the Peninsular war in 1815. In the early stage of Party Government, the issue, as I have shown you, was mainly between the champions of the Revolution of 1688, and the supporters of the Stuart Dynasty. After the close of that dreary period of selfish faction, which marked the reign of the two first Georges, the issue became, in the main, a struggle to assert Parliamentary independence against the power which George III. was trying to gather into his hands. This struggle was often connected with foreign and colonial wars, and at the close of the eighteenth and beginning of the nineteenth centuries, it concentrated itself in the opposition to the methods by which the younger Pitt and his successors were endeavouring to carry on the war against France. But, after that war was over, the needs and sufferings of the poor began gradually to attract attention. At first, indeed, the desperate struggle for freedom of speech in its various forms, of free trial, free meeting, and free printing, prevented any definite or hopeful attempt to put into parliamentary shape the redress of other grievances. But, after the Reform Bill of 1832 had struck a blow at the old monarchical and aristocratic system, the demand that Parliament should deal with certain questions which it had hitherto ignored, became more persistent ; and, with each extension of the suffrage, the demands increased in variety, and their champions in hopefulness. The consequence has been that people had become less and less contented with the settlement by the leaders of any one Party of the order of precedence to be given to special reforms ; and, while an Irish Party and a Labour Party have formed themselves in distinction alike from Liberals and Conservatives, there is every indication that other parliamentary sections are resolved to press forward the special reforms in which they are interested, without too much consideration for the leaders of Liberalism or Conservatism.

I have dwelt on these changes in the conditions of Party Government, in order to show you that, however well it has worked in the past, important changes may now be needed. But, before describing the reforms which have been proposed, I should like to point out two great defects, which have arisen from the ordinary working of this form of Government, and which may, in some measure, be modified by the proposed reform.

In the first place, the idea of voting for a Party involves the imposition on the electors of an office which the main body of them are utterly unfitted to fulfil ; while it deprives them of the very privilege which representative Government was intended to secure them. They are expected to decide on all the most complicated questions of Home and Foreign Policy, which are legally supposed to be decided after careful debate in Parliament ; and at the same time the actual choice of the men whom they are to send to Parliament is practically taken out of their hands by obscure committees, sometimes even committees of a distant London club, aided in their arrangements by a class of very second-rate lawyers. Thus, representative Government is destroyed ; and I noted that in a translation of an Essay of the great philosopher Kant, he is shewn to have condemned as utterly bad, representative democracy. Two of the objects, therefore, of any reform in Party Government should be to secure to the electors, as far as possible, the right of choosing the men whom they think really the most fit to represent them ; and at the same time to protect the important questions of Home and Foreign policy from the confusion and hurry produced by the immediate influence of popular election. And this latter part of the change may, to some extent, help in lessening another of the incidental evils of Party Government. From time to time a government is tempted to stake its existence on some important measure of Home policy, and in appealing to the electors, the champions of such a reform seem compelled to paint the coming change as likely to produce results which no material reform could possibly effect. Hence there follows, on the disappointment caused, either outbursts of violence, showing a general distrust of all peaceable government ; or else that violent swing of the pendulum, which arises from the belief that, since the change which was effected had not produced all the results expected of it, the whole plan of reform must have been misleading, and the only chance of improvement must lie in the return to an exactly opposite policy. A notable instance of each of these forms of reaction may be found in the history of the nineteenth century. The Reform Bill of 1830 was expected to produce a new era in politics, and to secure the satisfaction of the needs of all the most suffering classes. When the great bulk of the people found their expectations unsatisfied, there followed the fierce outbreak of the Chartist movement, and all that bitter era of class distrust and antagonism, which the Christian Socialists undertook to meet by milder and less sensational methods. On the other hand the great measure of the Repeal of the Corn Laws, and the general policy of Free Trade which followed that measure, were found, to the surprise of a large section of the community, not to have removed all the evils from which the Working Classes suffered ; and hence arose, as a reaction against that policy, an excessive demand for government interference, and a desire (on the part of a large number of politicians) to return to the old protective system. If, therefore, we are to secure a better system of representative government, we must find some means of fixing the minds of the electors rather on the choosing of men than on the deciding of large questions of policy ; and, at the same time, we should secure to Parliament a greater power of deliberation, less hampered on the one hand by the violent pressure of popular cries, or, on the other, by the arbitrary decision of certain leading administrators, as to the comparative usefulness and necessity of certain measures presented to Parliament.

During the many efforts that were made to deal with the question of parliamentary reform in the latter half of the nineteenth century, it was natural that the attention of the reformers should be called to the incompleteness of the ordinary devices for securing real representation. But, at first, the ideas of reformers did not go beyond an attempt to balance more justly the representation of the respective parties ; and the first proposal made in this direction was, that in the cities and boroughs returning three members, no elector should vote for more than two candidates. This proposal, first made in 1854, and finally adopted in 1867, could obviously affect only a small number of constituencies, and those constituencies were still limited as much as possible, to the ordinary candidates of the Party. But, in 1866 John Stuart Mill placed before Parliament a reform which went much further than this, and aimed at introducing a more personal ideal of representation. This was the scheme which was first propounded by Mr. Thomas Hare, the father-in-law of one of the founders of the Working Men's College. The object which he had in view may be gathered from a few sentences in Mr. Hare's book : "In the state of Society at which we have arrived," he says, "the vesting in every elector of a power to act, if such be his will, without any trammel created by the particular section of voters to which he is nominally annexed, is the key-stone of parliamentary reform." In another sentence he says, "By making elections nothing but a question of adhesion to one or two or three parties, the standard of merit and qualification in the candidate is lowered to a bare question of Party tests." To secure, then, the advantages of greater freedom of choice to each elector, and the chance, at least, of a higher stamp of candidate, Mr. Hare proposed that, instead of limiting the choice of the electors to the candidates before their special constituency, each elector should be allowed to give his vote for any candidate in any part of the kingdom ; that any candidate who obtained a certain definite quota of votes should be thereby returned to Parliament, from wheresoever the votes should be obtained ; that, if any candidate should obtain more than this quota, the votes, which in such a scheme would be wasted on him, might be passed on to other candidates ; and that, in order to insure that such an arrangement would secure the representation desired, every elector should send in to the Registrar a complete list of the candidates for whom he wished to vote, marking them with numbers, in the order in which he wished his votes to be given. In order to secure that every elector should know his possibilities of choice, a list of the candidates standing for all the constituencies in the Kingdom was to be sent by a central Registrar to the local authorities, and by them transmitted to each elector.

I have endeavoured to explain, in my previous remarks, the chief advantages to be obtained by this scheme. But there are two criticisms

HODGSON PRATT.

ON November 12th, in the hall of the Club and Institute Union, Lord Brassey presided over a meeting to consider in what way to preserve the memory of Mr. Hodgson Pratt. After opening the proceedings, Lord Brassey was succeeded in the chair by Mr. J. J. Dent, who called upon Mr. J. C. Gray to move :—That this meeting, representing the Peace and Arbitration, Co-operative, and Working Men's organizations of England, is of opinion that a committee should be appointed to enlist subscriptions for the purpose of promoting a memorial of the life-work of Hodgson Pratt upon all or any of the following forms: (1) A portrait in the National Portrait Gallery ; (2) a tablet in Westminster Abbey ; (3) the founding of travelling scholarships at Ruskin College, or the Working Men's College ; and (4) a prize essay—to be competed for annually—on " The Principles of Fraternity and Association."

This resolution was seconded by Miss Macdonogh, on behalf of Mr. J. M. Ludlow, and supported by Mr. F. Maddison, M.P., Mr. H. Burrows, and Mr. C. E. Maurice, and was carried unanimously. Mr. T. F. Hobson, Mr. J. F. Green, and Mr. C. T. Millis were also amongst the speakers. Lord Brassey was elected chairman of the memorial committee, with Lord Avebury as treasurer, and Messrs. J. C. Gray (Co-operative Union), J. F. Green (Peace and Arbitration Society), and B. T. Hall (Club and Institute Union), joint secretaries. The committee included the Marquis of Ripon, the Rt. Hon. Thomas Burt, M.P., Sir H. J. Vansittart Neale, Mr. H. Vivian, M.P., Mr. F. Maddison, M.P., Canon Barnett, and other well-known persons.

MAURICE CHESS CLUB.

THE Maurice Chess Club played the first match of this season with the Tottenham and West Green Chess Club on the 26th October, and won by two games.

The Tournament lists are now up on the club board. Members are requested to play their tournament games at an early opportunity. A third prize, Blackburn's book on Chess, will be given in the Handicap Tournament by Mr. V. Ray, but players in Sections IV., V., and VI., only are eligible for this. Mr. Nield is presenting a handsome framed engraving to the club, to be awarded to the member gaining the highest percentage of points in match play.

The Club paid its annual visit to Trinity College, Cambridge, on Saturday, November 23rd, and, as on former occasions, our team was royally entertained, from start to finish, by their opponents, dined and slept in College, and had a splendid time. It is pleasant also to report that for the first time the Maurice were victorious, by 5½ to 3½, a result arrived at after several tough struggles, particularly between the players at the first board, Mr. H. A. Webb (Cambridge), and Mr. F. J. Nield, their game being drawn after very fine play on both sides. On Sunday we had tea with Mr. Cornford, in whose genial company a very enjoyable evening was spent.

The following are the results of matches played :—

Oct. 26th, v. Tottenham and West Green.—Maurice won by 5 games to 3.
  ,, 30th, v. Metropolitan II.—Maurice lost by 2 games to 5.
Nov. 12th, v. Whitfield's.—Maurice lost by 3 games to 5.
  ,, 23rd, v. Trinity College.—Maurice won by 5½ games to 3½.

The return Match with Trinity College will be played at the College on Saturday, January 11th, 1908. Fixtures for the coming month :—

Dec. 3rd, Claremont, at Home, 10 boards.
  ,, 11th, Wheatsheaf, at 79, Farringdon Street, E.C., 10 boards.
  ,, 16th, Wood Green, at Home, 8 boards.
  ,, 19th, St. Martin's, at 122, Newgate Street, E.C., 10 boards.

J. F. HALFORD, *Hon. Secretary.*

SATURDAY NIGHT LECTURES.

SPARTA AND ATHENS.*

THE lecturer claimed that the subject of "Sparta and Athens" was one of permanent interest, because it was a fragment in the history of social life and citizenship, even though the two towns were small in size and remote in date. "Spartan" and "Laconic" were words in our language which reflected a definite ideal of conduct, while the name of Athens was familiar at least as the mother-city of literature and art. The small size of the cities of ancient times, and some of the chief differences made by this fact in the details of every-day life, were alluded to; and the ideals represented by the two towns were summarized in contrast,—the exacting discipline of Sparta, where individuality was lost in subservience to the State, and the independence and self-development which were the cherished ideals of the Athenians, an independence, however, not incompatible with intense patriotism. The rigorous training through which the Spartan boy was prepared for the chief object of a Spartan life, to fight for his country, was described—the discipline and exercises which made it possible for Spartans to boast, " Our lads are our walls." All Spartans had much that corresponded to our modern physical drill, with music and dancing, but very little purely intellectual training. And the severity and simplicity of their life were maintained rigorously among the grown men, the whole state being organized as a standing camp of soldier-citizens. Herodotus wrote in praise of their wonderful discipline: "There is one master whom they obey, and that is Law; whatever that master commands, they do; and his command is always the same, he bids them never flee in battle whatever the number of their foes, but stand firm, and either conquer or die." After describing the social penalties of cowardice, the lecturer spoke of the limitations of the Spartan ideal, its one-sidedness, its intense conservatism, and the failure of Spartans to adapt themselves to changing circumstances or to rise worthily to positions of independent responsibility.

Turning to Athens, the lecturer quoted the following from Sir George Trevelyan, showing his appreciation of Athenian life:—" Had I the choice of time and place wherein to spend the term of existence, considerations of religion and morality apart, I would without hesitation prefer to be an Athenian in the age of Pericles; for such a man led a life the plan of which was exquisitely tempered with good sense, refinement, and simplicity. He knew nothing of the passions which agitate a modern votary of fashion, who is for ever jostling amidst an endless throng of competitors towards a common centre. . . . Society then had a less constrained and artificial aspect than it has ever worn in any famous and highly-civilized community. Men talked for amusement and instruction, rather than for display. They lived with those whom they liked, not with those whom they feared. Their festivities and social gatherings were not special and extraordinary occasions, but formed an integral part of their every-day existence. They did not dine an hour and a half later than was pleasant, nor sit up five hours later than was wholesome. They did not suffer themselves to be hustled upstairs by the ladies of their family, a little before midnight, to dress for a ball where they would have no space to dance. They did not get together to settle the affairs of the nation in a badly-ventilated senate-house at an hour when all honest men should be in bed—at an hour when, if we are to believe certain cynics, all honest men *are* in bed." The Constitution of Athens was democratic, and the spirit of its citizens characteristically enterprising and restless. They, too, were soldiers, but they fought to live, and did not live to fight, like the Spartans. It was not merely the case that among them great artists were common, the whole standard of popular taste and intelligence was wonderfully high; the art and literature which were popularly approved then are the models from which modern criticism seeks to instruct the popular taste of to-day. Nor did the lively intellectual activity of the Athenians

---

.* Lecture delivered at the College on October 5th, by J. F. Crace, M.A.

preclude that bodily training to which the Spartan sacrificed so much : it was the Athenians' boast that they left no gift of human nature undeveloped, and they made the proud claim, not without good reason, that they could cultivate taste without effeminacy. Sir George Trevelyan's description of the bearing of the Athenians at the battle of Marathon may well find a place here. He says, " In the year 490 before Christ, an innumerable host of Persians landed on Athenian soil—Persians who had found nothing that could resist the terror of their name from the Indus to the Ægean Sea. The crisis was awful. The States of Greece stood aloft in fear and amazement. . . . . But the threatened city was true to herself. Her able-bodied sons turned out to a man, and marched forth to make appeal to the God of battles. Shopkeepers and mechanics, artists, merchants, and farmers—they took down their spears and shields, pocketed their biscuit and salt fish, kissed their children, and walked through their doors without any notion that they were going to take part in an affair which all coming generations would remember with gratitude and admiration. And when they came to the sacred plain of Marathon, they did not stop to count the odds ; but went at a run straight into the midst of the twenty myriads of Medes and Phœnicians, out of breath, but not of heart, with such line as they could keep, and with so much martial science as a city militia might recall in the heat of contest ; they fought foot to foot and beard to beard, until the conquerors of the world broke and fled. And that very night they marched home to their supper ; all save 192, who were lying, with clenched teeth and knit brows and wounds all in front, on the threshhold of their dear country, where it becomes brave men to lie."

Slides were shown of Sparta, of an early statue of Apollo, the characteristic god of order and self-control, and of the principal buildings remaining in Athens, especially those upon the Acropolis, together with some details of their sculpture.

THE FUTURE EVOLUTION OF MAN

was the subject of a very interesting lecture delivered by Dr. Saleeby, on Saturday, November 2nd, in the Maurice Hall.

The lecturer opened his discourse by remarking that, in forecasting the future evolution of man, one ought to endeavour by looking into the past to observe the direction in which human evolution is moving, and thereby to forecast, not perhaps so much what we would desire to see, as that which seems likely to happen. If we discover in any species those characters which seem to have survival value, we are on the way to discover changes which are likely to occur in that species. There are two definite characters—the psychical and physical ; and, owing to the superiority of the psychical, we find the earth in the possession of a creature which is very feeble in terms of the physical. The history of animal life upon the earth is the history of the vertebrate. We find the first vertebrate in the very primitive fish, which is essentially a horizontal creature, and in the course of time we have the emergence of limbs as suggested by fins. In the lower animals all the limbs are used for locomotion, and it is only man who has been able to liberate his fore limbs entirely from locomotive purposes A line dropped from the centre of gravity of the body of an adult man or even of a child falls behind the hip joints, whereas in the most erect ape the line falls in front, and such a creature can only stand erect with difficulty. The worm has been raised until it has become, not a creepy thing, but an erect thing ; and it is difficult to imagine what changes of a positive kind can be effected in the body of man. The changes which will occur will be mainly negative in respect of getting rid of superfluities, and will be on the whole for the convenience and advantage of everyone, except the surgeons. Survival of the fittest—that which has survival value—amounts to natural selection ; and natural selection in the past has been chiefly on physical grounds, but natural selection to-day is acting more and more upon psychical factors, and it would be disastrous were it otherwise. The great reptiles of antiquity ceased to exist because they became so big that they were unable to get about. There are inherent limits to physical development, but there are no limits to psychical developments. Men are chosen for their mental capabilities, and such characters are transmitted in no small degree. Man is at least 500,000 years old, but considering the millions of years that are before him, he is still an infant having only just discovered himself. What is there in the human capacity? We know that certain human beings have achieved most amazing, splendid, and sublime things already; and, as Herbert Spencer says, what is in the capacity of one man, such as Shakespeare, Beethoven, or Newton, is within the capacity of whatever forces make for humanity, and it is conceivable that the level which has been reached by a single man or woman here may be in the future reached by mankind and womankind at large. Man, however, may interfere with the natural course of selection; and it is conceivable that in a civilization there may from one cause or another come a spirit which will exalt the *physical*, and then the course of upward evolution will be first arrested and then reversed. The lecturer thought that those things had happened to former civilizations, such as that of Babylon, which remained dominant for 4,000 years—twice the duration of the Christian era; and that they were the cause of their being overthrown by later civilizations which had exalted the psychical.

CORRESPONDENCE.

[Under this heading the Editor will be glad to publish letters of interest to past and present members, but he declines all responsibility for the views therein expressed.]

DR. FURNIVALL'S CHILDRENS' PARTY, DECEMBER 21ST.
To the Editor of the WORKING MEN'S COLLEGE JOURNAL.

DEAR MR. EDITOR,—Will you allow me once more to appeal to our members and friends, through the medium of the JOURNAL, to help us give the little ones a few hours' pleasure? Last year we were very successful in our appeal for cast-off clothing, and we were able to give nearly every girl a garment of some kind. Our Ladies' Committee worked very hard in sorting the parcels, and in picking out from our guests deserving cases of want of clothing.

We found, however, that the quantity of boys' clothes was in very small proportion to that sent for the girls; and I ask our friends not to be shy in sending along old jackets and knickers, for however old the clothes may be, we can accommodate some of the boys, whose clothes are much worse.

Any parcel sent to the College will be gratefully received and acknowledged. I was unable to do this in several instances last year, as some of the parcels bore no name.

Subscriptions to the fund will also be welcome, and can be handed either to H. E. Nye, Geo. S. Offer, or myself. A list of subscribers is now on the notice board in the Common Room.—Believe me, yours faithfully,

H. K. RANDALL.

THE WORKING MEN'S COLLEGE JOURNAL *is supported partly by Annual Subscribers living in different parts of the World, and partly by circulation among the Students and Members. Its success depends upon a regular demand, and to ensure this, the Editor would be glad if as many readers as can will become Subscribers. Subscription 2s. 6d. per annum, post free.*

LONDON: Printed by W. HUDSON & Co., Red Lion Street, High Holborn, and published at THE WORKING MEN'S COLLEGE, Crowndale Road, London, N.W.—December 1st, 1907.

THE WORKING MEN'S · COLLEGE JOURNAL ·

sub: N

The
Working
Men's
College·
CROWNDALE
ROAD·
St. PANCRAS
LONDON·N·W·
FOUNDED
IN 1854
BY THE LATE

Frederick
Denison
Maurice·

Contents for
JANUARY, 1908.

Old Students' Supper

Common Room Meet-
ing and Election

College Notes

Debating Society

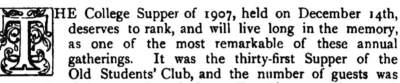

THE

Working Men's College Journal.

Conducted by Members of the Working Men's College
Crowndale Road, London, N.W.

VOL. X.—No. 178.	JANUARY, 1908.	PRICE TWOPENCE.

OLD STUDENTS' SUPPER, 1907.

THE College Supper of 1907, held on December 14th, deserves to rank, and will live long in the memory, as one of the most remarkable of these annual gatherings. It was the thirty-first Supper of the Old Students' Club, and the number of guests was greater than it had ever been before. For this reason the caterer deemed it advisable to provide tables and seats for forty members in Room 19, over whom Mr. Julius Jacob was good enough to preside, until they joined the larger crowd in the Maurice Hall, after the eatables had been disposed of. Mr. R. H. MARKS, President of the Club, took the chair, and many distinguished members and friends of the College were present, including the Principal, Professor A. V. Dicey, the Vice Principal, Mr. Lionel Jacob; two founders, Professor Westlake and Dr. Furnivall; Sir Charles Lucas, C.B., K.C.M.G., Sir Frederick Pollock, the Right Hon. Alfred Lyttelton, M.P., Mr. G. P. Gooch, M.P., Mr. C. P. Trevelyan, M.P., the Rev. B. H. Alford, Mr. W. D. Caröe, Mr. Robert Chalmers, C.B., Mr. J. M. Dodds, C.B., Mr. G. Lowes Dickinson, Dr. Sidney Lee, Mr. Pett Ridge, Mr. G. M. Trevelyan, and Mr. Richard Whiteing. The speeches were of more than usual excellence. and provided a very varied and enjoyable feast for the mind, whilst the body was well catered for, so far as the supper was concerned, to say nothing of the punch, concocted by W. C. Jones. Amongst the many incidents of the evening, it was delightful to witness the Principal's enjoyment of Mr. Pett Ridge's anecdotes, whilst Sir Charles Lucas showed us that his title has made no difference to his wit. Dr. Furnivall was as youthful and aggressive as ever; and he did not forget his young friends the poor children, for whom a collection, made in tumblers during Sir Frederick Pollock's speech, realized the handsome sum of £8 10s.

After the supper, grace having been said by the Rev. B. H. Alford, the first toast "The Memory of Frederick Denison Maurice, Founder of the College, and of George Tansley, Founder and First President of the Old Students' Club," was honoured, upstanding, and in silence. Smoking was then permitted.

Before continuing the toast list, the Chairman announced that Mr. Lowes Dickinson, now in his 89th year, had sent a message by his son, Mr. G. Lowes Dickinson, to say how sorry he was not to be able to be present; that General Sir Frederick Maurice was unable to be with us on account of illness, for which we were very sorry; and that the Bursar, Mr. Mure, much regretted his inability to attend through being confined to the house with a cold. The Bursar had not been absent from the dinner for many years.

Mr. MARKS, President of the Club, who on rising was greeted with loud cheers, said,—Mr. Principal and Gentlemen, I am pleased to be able to say that the College is still progressing and developing satisfactorily on all sides. Our members are a few less than last year, but they still nearly reach 900. In looking at the class-list for the past term, it will be seen that we have again had the advantage of Mr. Trevelyan's teaching in the First Section under Mr. Lupton's charge; that Mr. Morison's Economics class has been well supported, and Greek and Latin have held their own, but Law has not done so well. In the Second Section, under Mr. Jastrzebski, the modern language classes have been doing good work; of the thirteen teachers in that section, eight are student-teachers. In the Third and Fourth Sections, under the care of Mr. Julius Jacob and Mr. Rose, are included our Science and Art Departments, both of which do much good work. So far as the Art Department is concerned, it is very active at least three nights a week; and Mr. Wilkinson, the art master, is always able to produce an exhibition of his students' work, as he did on October 26th last, when Mr. Lowes Dickinson came to see it and criticize the exhibits. One of our art students, Mr. J. S. Hertford, had a picture in this year's Academy, upon which he is to be congratulated. (Hear, hear.) The Sixth Section is devoted to music, under Mr. Perry's charge; all the classes are doing well. The Monday night class has a membership of ninety men and women's voices, which it is hoped will some day develop into a Working Men's College choir. Since the beginning of the present year, much has been done in the way of decorating the building. In February last a fund was started by the Common Room Committee for the purpose of decorating the Coffee Room to match the Common Room. In the course of a few months, the necessary amount, £114, was raised; and under the superintendence of our architect, Mr. Caröe, to whom we are greatly indebted for his help, the Coffee Room has been handsomely decorated to harmonize with the Common Room. The College has now two rooms for its social side of which it may well be proud—rooms that are not to be found in any similar institution in London. In addition to the Coffee Room, the Tansley Room, the Superintendent's Room, the office, and the ground-floor corridors have been tastily coloured. Much yet remains to be done, and we are prepared to entertain offers from millionaires and others to decorate the Hall, the Library, the Museum, or the remaining class-rooms and corridors. Our finances are so far satisfactory that we are nearly able to balance income and expenditure. Since our removal into this building, we have developed a remarkable capacity for spending money. Our total expenditure for 1904—5 was roughly £1300; and for the year 1906—7 up to the end of July last, it amounted to over £2000, showing an increase in expenditure of £700. Arrangements have been made with the County Council by which the building is let in the day time as a Secondary School for girls, and it is hoped the result will show a profit to the College in the next financial year. The school has been carried on since last October, and everything has worked well and satisfactorily. Our maintenance or endowment fund now stands at a little over £3000 [£3125]. It ought to be ten times that amount. This fund is of importance to the College, as it would do much to secure its independence. To both the Board of Education and to the County Council we have to express our thanks for their help and for their liberality towards us. At the present time we are making a special appeal to the City Companies for the sum of £100 to improve our Library ; and we shall also be grateful for any help from our friends in raising this sum. There has been no lack of social events during the year. In December last, the Furnivall Children's Party was held, and 280 poor children were entertained at a cost of £18 18s. 7d. In addition to being entertained, each child carried away some gift, in many a case garments provided by our friends. In consequence of the regretted illness of Mr. Cornford in May, the excursion to Cambridge in that month did not take place. On May 4th, Miss Dickinson and her friends, to whom our thanks are due, gave a dramatic entertainment in the hall, the proceeds of which, amounting to about £45, were devoted to decorating the walls of the College, as already mentioned. The Garden Party and Sports, held on July 13th, at Wembley Park, organized and carried through by the Common Room Committee, was attended by 251 members and friends, and proved a most successful outing. Before referring to the honours bestowed by the College, mention should be made of honours bestowed from without on our College friends. At Oxford Commemoration on June 26th, in company with a large number of other distinguished men, our Principal had the honorary degree of D.C.L. conferred upon him, (cheers), and three members of the College were sent to represent it on that occasion. On November 9th, the King's birthday, to our great satisfaction, our old friend Lucas was made a K.C.M.G. (cheers), and he is now known to us as " Sir Charles." To both we offer our hearty congratulations. Among the recipients of College honours, we welcome a new fellow in Mr. A. C. Martin, who has done good work in the College, like our new associate and old friend, Mr. T. M. Balson. The Tansley scholar and prizeman for the year is Mr. E. J. H. Reglar, and Mr. J. W. Roberts is the Tansley prizeman. Mr. Reglar has long been known among us as a diligent student and an indefatigable worker, always ready to help, when help is needed. Mr. J. W. Roberts is also a diligent student, and he has already shown his readiness to serve the College. Referring to the Clubs, the indoor ones appear to have been more active than the outdoor ones, although the Sketching Club has been very industrious this season. It has one advantage over the other outdoor clubs, in having something to show as the result of its outings. At the art exhibitions in the College, the sketches made by the members find a prominent place. The Field Club, which seeks to explore the country around London and to dodge the motors, and occasionally makes some captures of botanical and biological interest, was entertained by Mr. Fotheringham, at Fawkham, in June last ; and the Cycling Club was also entertained on the previous day by Mr. Denmead, at South Mimms. The Furnivall Sculling Club, of which many of our men are members, continues to wax strong and to flourish ; the Tansley Swimming Club was recently in low water, but was revived by the fostering care of Barnett, who started a life saving class in connection with it, but this has failed to resuscitate the club, which is now reported to be *in extremis*. Of the indoor Clubs, the Chess Club is a very popular and busy one. During the past season it played 41 matches, and won 22. On November 23rd, it again played Trinity College, Cambridge, and for the first time won by 5½ to 3½. It is reported that our Mr. Nield and Mr. Webb of Trinity had a draw, after a five hours' struggle. Needless to say, our team were royally entertained by their hosts, and had a splendid time, thanks to Messrs. Cornford and Webb. We look forward with pleasure to the return match in the College, in January. During the present term the Linguists have been dumb in all languages; even the advent of Esperanto has failed to quicken them into life. On the other hand, the Literary Society has been highly articulate, and has produced some excellent papers. The Debating Society, which meets every Tuesday at 9.30, continues to discuss and to settle the most momentous questions of the day. It has already granted female suffrage, nationalized the land, and formed a scheme for the federation of the empire. The Musical Society, in the period under review, has shown much activity, having given several good concerts in the hall, and well-attended smokers in the Coffee Room. The concerts are most useful in fostering the social life, and helping us to introduce our women-folk into the College. The Old Students' Club is still to the fore, and has a roll of some 250 members. During the past term, we have been fortunate in securing some excellent lectures. On Thursday evenings, we had the Principal and Mr. Rait, of Oxford, whom the Principal introduced to us. Mr. Rait's lectures were much appreciated, and his subject—"The History of London" —was an attractive one to most of us here. The Saturday evening lecturers were well attended; among the lecturers were Sir Frederick Maurice, Sir Charles Bruce, Miss Spurgeon, and Mr. Mackail, the subjects ranging from Sir Robin Redbreast to Earthquakes. The Italian class is reading a book entitled "Il dolce far Niente," and we are glad to know that neither our Superintendent, our Vice-Principal, nor our Principal is in that class, for fear that they might be led away from their present strenuous life. The Superintendent is always resourceful, courteous, and ready to help; the Vice-Principal is ever thinking and working for the College—his heart is in it, and he never spares himself; the Principal, as always, delights to serve the College, and he is ever ready to do so by writing a begging letter for our benefit, or by journeying from Oxford to London in any weather, either to lecture or to attend a function. Gentlemen, I give you the toast of the College, coupled with the name of the Principal. (Hearty cheering.)

Professor DICEY, who was received with cheers, after complimenting the Chairman upon his speech, said there were two points on which he would like to dwell. The first was the extraordinary good work done by those who founded the College. It had been a success of a kind which one could hardly, fifty years or more ago, have expected. The very modest hopes of that time had been more than met. There was a curious contrast between the great hopes of every great undertaking, even if successfully achieved, and the greatness of the persons who founded it, and of the designs for which it was founded. There was always a sense that the second temple was not like the first. We hoped and trusted that we were to some extent carrying on the work the Founders had so nobly begun. He ventured to give a reason which satisfied him that this College was progressing in a right way. There were various tests one might apply to see whether an institution was prospering or not. At one time he was in the habit of asking, in order to test the prosperity of an institution, the question, Was it a democratic institution? In those days he believed that every democratic institution was certain to be flourishing, because it was democratic. (Laughter.) Others believed in the soundness of an institution, because of its conservative character. He had thought time after time, that the proper test was this—always true, and quite independent of party and political changes—Was the institution alive? That was the real test. Was it a living thing which could develop, and was developing? Whether he looked at the venerated Founders still with us, or those who had passed away, or the persons now engaged in the College work, he saw the signs of a life which appeared to adapt itself to changing circumstances—a life which appeared to become more vigorous as time went on. That appeared to him to be the real test as to how the institution stood. (Cheers.) Referring to the honour recently conferred on our friend Sir Charles Lucas, Professor DICEY said : " Sir Charles—I am so glad to call him Sir Charles. I never miss an opportunity. (Cheers.) Firstly, because in this instance we have one of those very rare cases where a man amply deserves what he has got. (Hear, hear) And secondly, because I have some reason to suppose that he does not particularly like to be addressed by that title. (Laughter.) We all intensely rejoice that the honour has been given to him, and he is undoubtedly entitled to it. I have often myself been mis-called Dr. Dicey, when I was only a B.C.L. I was even described in print on a College notice as a D.C.L., when I was not one. But now I am the genuine, undoubted article. (Laughter.) I shall always thank my friend Lord Curzon for putting me into the position of an honest, straightforward doctor." Dr. DICEY then expressed the great satisfaction and pleasure which it had given him to read the work of his friend Trevelyan, on 'Garibaldi." It had brought back to him many recollections and enthusiasms upon Italy. It was really of first-rate excellence, and it was so pleasing to think that it was the work of one of our teachers, who had done so much for us. (Cheers.)

Mr. T. T. S. de Jastrzebski sang " My pretty Jane," and was heartily cheered.

The Right Hon. ALFRED LYTTELTON, K.C., proposed the toast of " The Founders." It is indeed a great honour, he said, to have that toast entrusted to me. It is still more a satisfaction to recognize that out of the Founders of this College there remain to us still five bulwarks against time—Mr. Lowes Dickinson, Mr. Llewelyn Davies, Dr. Furnivall, Professor Westlake, and last, but not least, our friend Mr. Ludlow. (Cheers.) The toast is one we ought to celebrate. The Principal has observed what a marvellous feat it was to have founded this College—to have founded so strong, so vital, so really living and prosperous an institution. I think I can suggest a reason why such vitality and vigorous strength should exist. It is to be found in the words of our great Founder, Mr. Maurice. When considering the foundation of the College, he said we must exclude all "big-wigs." That really is the motto which lies at the foundation of many other good things besides this College; and no one who has lived in the world as long as I have, can be otherwise than profoundly susceptible of its truth. The men who really do great things are those whose contemporaries at the University or school thoroughly believe in. Toynbee and Milner at Oxford, Lightfoot and Henry Sedgwick at Cambridge, were absolutely believed in by their contemporaries when young. Sometimes, no doubt, in after life, those who have started in this manner with the faith of their contemporaries, lapse into the deplorable condition of "big-wigs"; but if they do, and if they keep what is the real truth in them, they recognize that the greater part of the great work which is done in the world is done, not by big-wigs, but by those who inspire them. There are a few big-wigs who are not altogether soured by unjust censures (laughter), or, worse still, puffed up by ignorant praise. But the true function of the big-wig is, when the great fabrics have been erected in this world by younger and far abler men, that they should be allowed, when these fabrics are complete, to dance round them in the somewhat grotesque fashion of the Lord Chancellor in "*Iolanthe*," or with the pompous solemnity of Mr. Rutland Barrington in "*The Mikado.*" (Laughter.) This evening, I confess, makes me very proud. I see around this table, some old friends who were in my Law class twenty years ago. Sitting between Lucas—I am not going to call him "Sir Charles," I would not do anything to offend him— and Sir Frederick Pollock, and flanked by the Principal, it makes me very proud to see that the work of this College is so well fostered by the gentlemen on my left [the Cambridge men], who have done more for it than even I could have expected of the older University. It is but seemly that Macaulay Trevelyan and Goldsworthy Lowes Dickinson, and others I see there, should be carrying on the work started by four out of the five living Founders, all Cambridge men, except Mr. Lowes Dickinson, who did not attend a University, but who is represented so conspicuously here to-night by my friend his son. (Cheers.) Of the two who are going to answer this toast, I cannot make myself juvenile enough to fitly present the praises of Dr. Furnivall. I understand that, not content with sport, he mingles chivalry with it, which, even in my youngest and most vigorous days, I never dared essay. (Laughter.) We also have associated with this toast the honoured name of Professor Westlake. May I say, as one whose avocations have occasionally led me into the same tangled forest of International Law, that, no matter how deep the jungle was, I always found the blazes on the trees of a most admirable and accurate predecessor in Mr. Westlake. (Cheers.) May I also say, before I sit down, and with the utmost depth of affection, that what I said jestingly just now about big-wigs and those who do the real work of the world, is most fitly and admirably illustrated by the acts of Lucas, who sits by me, and who has, during the last thirty years, done without any splash, and with devotion, work as fine as even this College can demand. (Cheers.)

Professor WESTLAKE, in returning thanks, expressed the gratification he derived, year after year, in seeing the progress of the College. It had been fitly described as a living thing. It seemed to him to combine in itself two of the strongest marks of life—two characteristics giving the best promise of the future : the power of assimilation, and the sense of continuity. That the College possessed the power of assimilation we knew from the way in which, ever since its commencement, it had gone on drawing to it whatever most congenial to its aims was to be found in the metropolis. He was led to reflect on the wisdom of Mr. Maurice, when he founded the College, in introducing the sentiment of human fellowship, with as little as possible of rule to bind the future, with the happy result, as events had proved, that the College went on growing, assimilating what was congenial to itself, and therefore living and flourishing. The other note, the sense of continuity, was evidenced by that corporate feeling with the past, which was the best promise of development in the future. It was not a sense of continuity founded on any abstract views, but a sense that we belonged to a living whole, in which past, present, and future were linked together. (Cheers.)

Dr. FURNIVALL, who was greeted with musical honours, returned thanks, and proceeded to remind us of the Children's Treat, fixed for the following Saturday, and to ask for subscriptions, a collection of which, in tumblers, subsequently took place. The Doctor reiterated his old complaint that the College did not do enough for women. He pointed out that for the first time in the history of the world, the Furnivall Sculling Club had put a crew of girls into a racing sculling eight on the Thames. (Cheers and laughter.) He hoped some of us fellows would learn sculling, in order to take the girls out in the summer. Everyone ought to have a sport.. The two things were combined in the College, sport and work, and ought to go together We should strive for a healthy mind and a healthy body. Men ought to learn swimming. He couldn't do it himself. Had been in the water half-a-dozen times, but fortunately having a light boat, could just put his arm round it and hold on ; if it had been a big boat, he would probably have been drowned. However, that didn't matter. He hoped that, following on the work of the Shakespeare Reading Society and Musical Society, we should have more "At Homes" here, Sunday At Homes, for those who had no homes of their own. Some day that sort of thing had got to come, and we should do our share. It was a question with him what to say on an occasion like this. But to his mind, men should learn to trust themselves, not cherish delusions and swallow all the traditions divers people wanted to thrust down their throats. They must use their own brains in politics or religion. He hoped that that independent spirit which had led to greater freedom of thought, would prevail among all men, and bring down all class prejudices. Also, that we might fight against that cursed burden of the House of Lords. (Loud laughter.) One other subject—his friend Mr. Wolmark had volunteered to paint Sir Charles Lucas's portrait and give it to the College. We were deeply indebted to him. (Hear, hear.) Lucas stood as our head man. No doubt others were to come, like Trevelyan. But Lucas stood before the world as representing England with our self-governing Colonies. With his characteristic modesty, he had at first refused to have his picture done, saying he was not fit to be there, and all that sort of stuff and nonsense, but now he had consented. (Cheers.)

Sir FREDERICK POLLOCK proposed the toast of " The Past and Present Teachers and Lecturers." He said all would share his regret that his learned friend Mr. Mure, who should have proposed the toast, was prevented by illness from being present. The names he should couple with the toast, Dr. Oswald, Mr. G. P. Gooch, M.P., and Mr. A. S. Lupton, represented those branches of work in the College which, although outside his own special business of the law, were most interesting to him. Being himself a member of an irresponsible and self-elected oligarchy, and holding it to be an excellent form of government, he shared with Dr. Furnivall the traditional and accepted belief that Shakespeare wrote his own works, and therefore perhaps tended to be somewhat Conservative in matters of literature. (Laughter.) At any rate, he was very glad that the branches of learning to which it fell to him to do honour, covered almost exactly the ground of what, in the older universities, they called "the humanities." English and modern languages were here aggregated with the languages of history. Fifty years ago, however, we were taught Greek and Latin on the one hand, and a smattering of modern languages on the other, without any explanation as to whether they had anything to do with one another. We were not told that Greek never died, that Latin never died; that they were fruitful and had many descendants, and that they lived not only in themselves, but in the foundation of the whole of modern civilization. Dr. Oswald had lived to see the revolution in the teaching of languages. He remembered his name, forty years ago, as an editor of German classics, when himself an elementary learner in that language, having, he need hardly say, neglected it during all his school days. He was glad to hear that the study of languages was flourishing in the College, and very glad that we were not diverted from the humanities in the pursuit of so called "useful" knowledge. His friend Mr. Lyttelton had said quite truly that he (Sir Frederick Pollock) was an Oxford man; but in this College, founded by Maurice and so ably and vigorously supported by Cambridge men, he might be pardoned for saying that he was a Cambridge man before he was an Oxford man, and was a Cambridge man still. (Cheers.) Sir FREDERICK then referred to Mr. Gooch, as representing a younger edition of teachers of History, and as engaged in making history in the House of Commons; and also to Mr. Lupton, as teacher of the classical languages which used falsely to be called "dead." They were in fact living, in this country; and we were fortunately shaking off the old marvellously bad pronunciation of Latin. Even Eton was moving in the right direction in this respect, and when Eton moved, we might be sure the movement was pretty general. (Laughter, and cheers from the Cambridge men.) It moved slowly, like the British intellect, but when once it started, it did not go back; and there was quite as steady a movement at Eton, as there was elsewhere in England of a corresponding kind. (Cheers.)

Dr. OSWALD returned thanks. He had tried, he said, in his time, to lead the study of modern language away from the mere ambition to imitate human speech as accurately as a parrot. People used to think that Latin and Greek were the great keys for opening the stores of past generations, and laying the foundations of knowledge of the great nations that had gone before us; but that French and German were useful for the purpose of addressing a waiter in an hotel—(laughter)—also for travelling purposes. A man once came to him, and said he wanted to learn a little French. "Why a 'little'?" asked Dr. Oswald. He said he only wanted to know a little, to enable him, when he went to France, to ask for things, such as cigars or tobacco. I told him, said the Doctor, that I did not think I would teach him a little of French, but a good deal of French I would try to teach him, if he would stay in the class. The expenditure of time and money would be too great for him only to learn "a little" French; it would be cheaper for him to pay a man to take him about, when he went to France. Continuing, Dr. OSWALD said that few people could afford to spend the

necessary time to learn Latin and Greek. But whatever in the shape of
civilization, or of high-striving aims and doings, could be helped forward by
the study of Latin and Greek, ought to be attempted to be done through
the study of French and German. The aim of students should be to enrich
their minds and deepen their thoughts; to place themselves in a region of
thought above all men, so that nothing that was human could come
strange to them. Cosmopolitanism, which did not and need not contradict
patriotism, was his distinct aim. (Cheers.)

Mr. GOOCH, in responding, said he was not a devotee to public dinners,
but he made an exception in the case of the Working Men's College, for the
dinner of the Old Students' Club had several features which rendered it
quite unique. Firstly, all would agree that it was on this occasion, almost
alone in the course of the year, that we were most conscious—deeply and
inwardly conscious—of the unity and continuity of College life and history.
He had been struck with this and other thoughts, during the speeches we had
heard. At these annual gatherings, in addition to the lightness, gaiety, and
wit, which ran through the speeches, making them so charming and
interesting, there was a deep undercurrent of the ideal running through the
whole thing. We had also a back-ground of glorious and holy memories
and other features of a unique character present to our minds, so that it was
impossible at any other annual dinner to match this one. It could only be
here and at this time, that we were privileged to hear such remarks as fell
from Dr. Furnivall. Mr. Lyttelton had listened to many speeches in the
House of Commons, but even he would agree that Dr. Furnivall was an
exception to the ordinary rule, and that he had struck out a line for himself.
(Laughter.) Instead of the interesting and laborious researches, in which we
knew Dr. Furnivall was daily engaged at the British Museum, anyone would
think that he had been taking part, like Mr. Lyttelton and himself, in the
autumn campaign. One might be sure that the Doctor would be able to
give a very good account of himself as a political orator. Speaking as a
College teacher, Mr. Gooch said the old teachers and students were bound
to one another by a very special link, resting on community of ideas, which
served to hold them to one another in after life and in other parts of the
world. There were two chief reasons why he as an old teacher looked back
with such great satisfaction, pleasure, and veneration to the time he had
spent here. First, there was the strong academic system of the College,
which was altogether excellent. We heard a great deal about the
nationalization of the Universities, especially Oxford. Cambridge, he
supposed, was regarded as perfect, and so it was not discussed. But Oxford
was in urgent need of reform, and to be placed in much closer touch with the
great matters of the nation. He was much interested in Ruskin College at
Oxford—rich in great principles, though not in endowment. But the number
of men who could spare the time to go from their work to study there was
necessarily small. In this College, however, the number of those who could,
whilst engaged in daily tasks and performing their duties to their families,
come to study, was enormously greater. The union between the Universities,
with their culture and ideals, on the one hand, and the great workers of the
head and of the hand in this country, on the other, could not entirely be
carried out at the seat of the Universities themselves; but it could be, and
was being so carried out in this College. So let us always speak up for our
own Working Men's College (cheers), which has been quietly doing this work
for over fifty years. He associated himself with those who had upheld study
as a means of enlarging the intellectual horizon. His own work had been
as a teacher of History, a subject which did not lend itself readily to the
ambitions of the younger men; but those few who crept within the shrine and
sought initiation in the great priesthood, small though their opportunities,
derived full advantage from the least given to them in the study of history.
Secondly, he liked to look back on his association with the College, because
it was a place where friendships were made and kept. He knew no other
place where warmth and fellowship continued and manifested themselves,
or where there was such heartfelt interest in the doings of each and of all.
Sir Charles Lucas got his well-deserved honour; Trevelyan wrote his
"Garibaldi"; and each of us was as much delighted as if the honour had

been earned or the book had been written by a member of his own family. (Hear, hear.) Here we were based upon the great principle of equality—the only possible basis for a really self-respecting and self-maintaining College life. The great characteristic of this place is its absolute toleration. Dr. Furnivall had told us to think for ourselves. That, he thought, we did do in the College. We thought for ourselves and we liked other people to think for themselves—a characteristic by no means to be found everywhere. (Cheers.)

Mr. LUPTON thanked us for the toast, but pointed out that in this College there was no distinction between those who professed to teach and those who came to be taught. Young bloods came from the Universities to teach, but invariably stayed to be taught themselves. It was out of place for him to be classed as a teacher, because he was now no more than an ordinary member of the College. Before he joined, he knew we had had a large number of distinguished teachers here. In the art classes, for instance, Ruskin, Burne Jones, Madox Browne, Lowes Dickinson, Emslie, and many others, had taught. He had a vivid recollection of the people who were here when he first came, as a freshman, into the Common Room, and was taken round the rooms. A newcomer never knew who it might be who was conducting him over the place. It might be one of the most excellent Common Room Committee, or a distinguished scholar of Balliol, like Mr. Moore. It took him a long time to realize that Mr. Jastrzebski was a true-born Yorkshireman. But he had got over his surprise now. Quite recently the question arose, whether we should allow Esperanto to be taught here; and if so, in what section it should be put, under modern language, or literature, or shorthand. The chairman of the Studies Committee asked Jastrzebski, who was director of studies in the modern language section, and who gave it as his opinion that if a man could speak French and German, and particularly Spanish and Portuguese, and also know some Slav and Magyar, there was no need for him to learn Esperanto, so that it would not come within his division. (Laughter.) Many men who had been students stayed on year after year, sacrificing their time and energy for the College —men like Cole, Dale, Reed, Newey, Warren, Emslie, and many others—sometimes for thirty years working and teaching. It was due to the efforts of these, amongst other men, that the great Collegiate spirit, the unique feature which struck every visitor, lived and flourished. (Cheers.)

Mr. F. J. Nield sang " The bait of an average Fisherman."

Sir CHARLES LUCAS, who was greeted with " For he's a jolly good fellow," said he wanted first to return thanks for all the kindness, might he say affection, shown to him during the last few weeks, and now again repeated, in connection with the honour bestowed upon him. Continuing, he said: There is no place like the College, and no friends like College friends. At the Colonial Office I had to deal with the West Indies and thought I knew something about sugar ; but I have come to the conclusion during the last few weeks that I only now know what it means. (Laughter.) I have been taught a good deal in that Office, in connection with sugar, about countervailing duties. All this kindness requires from me a countervailing duty in any little service I can do to the College in the coming time. I want to refer, in the presence of the artist (Mr. Wolmark), to the portrait he is kindly going to do for me. I wanted to explain my reluctance to being painted. I have never yet given the true reason. The real reason was, I did not want a picture, I wanted a wax-work. (Laughter.) I entertained a wild hope that a waxwork figure of myself might appear in a certain Chamber in a certain place, along with the wax-work figures of other eminent men who have had chequered careers (laughter)—all of whom, I have reason to think, were originally members of the Working Men's College. I turn, with relief, from myself, to propose " The Visitors." Some visitors are afraid of staying too long. May I assure our visitors to-night that we shall be glad, if they will become life-long members of the College? (Hear, hear.) Visitors at this time of the year are not always welcome, because they ask for money. Our visitors do not ask for any money ; and what is more curious, we, on this night of the year alone, do not ask them for any, except for Dr. Furnivall's

Children's Treat   But if we don't ask and they don't give us money, we get many other advantages from their presence. I want you to note the representative gathering we have here to-night. The House of Commons is represented by Mr. Lyttelton, Mr. C. P. Trevelyan, and Mr. Gooch ; the London County Council, by Dr. Beaton ; the Civil Service by Mr. Chalmers and Mr. Dodds ; legal and constitutional learning, by Sir Frederick Pollock ; art, by Mr. Caröe and Mr. Wolmark ; literature, by Dr. Sidney Lee, Mr. Whiteing, Mr. Pett Ridge, Mr. Goldsworthy Lowes Dickinson, and Mr. Rogers. I say the collection together of these men in our College is a magnificent advertisement for us. In the best sense of the words, they are "paying guests." (Laughter and cheers.) All the respectable institutions have visitors. The colleges of our old Universities have official visitors, and so do lunatic asylums ; and I want to reassure our visitors to-night by telling them that the inmates of this institution, on this night, are not dangerous, but only melancholy. (Laughter.)   Many of our visitors are returned prodigals. They don't look as if they had lived on husks, but as if they had eaten someone else's fatted calf. First and foremost is my friend, Alfred Lyttelton (cheers), who was law teacher at this College, and what is far more important, president of the Maurice Cricket Club. He afterwards became Secretary of State for the Colonies. I have served under him in both capacities, and my verdict is this : Happy is the land whose ministers carry into public life the spirit of this Working Men's College, and doubly happy, as I testify from delightful experience, are the men who serve such ministers. (Cheers.) I have brought two prodigals of my own to-night, Mr. Dodds and Mr. Rogers. Mr. Dodds comes from the Scottish Office, and all his old friends rejoice in his rise and in his distinction. (Hear, hear.) We hope, with his experience in that office, he will take a class in Scotch. (Laughter.) We note with interest that there is a considerable number of Scotchmen in London who speak English with an accent. Mr. Rogers has just been to Canada, and in Canada was taken for a pirate and shipped home as "undesirable." (Laughter). I think it is monstrous—that our colonials should be flooded with persons of this description. Mr. Rogers will lecture in the coming term on " Pirates and What becomes of Them," with dissolving views. (Laughter.) Another returned prodigal is our old and great friend Mr. Sidney Lee, and it is a delight to us that each time he comes here, he comes with added distinction. (Cheers.) He has come here, I believe, for the express purpose of disputing, as against Dr. Furnivall, that it was not Richard Whiteing who wrote Shakespeare, but Pett Ridge ; and Goldie Dickinson will put into a Modern Symposium the results of the discussion, whilst a tasteful tomb will be designed for them by another distinguished man, Mr. Caröe. Personally, I have a grudge against Mr. Caröe. I was to have proposed his health last year, and spent a long time composing an excellent joke for the occasion, but he never turned up, and the joke never came off. (Laughter.) When I looked back for that joke, to use it to-night, I couldn't find it, so I suppose someone else has used it. Among outsiders, I should like to mention the distinguished name of Mr. Chalmers, of the Board of Inland Revenue. He ought to have spoken to-night, but we will let him off as long as he is Chairman of the Board, if he lets us off paying taxes. (Laughter.) I couple with this toast three names—Mr. C. P. Trevelyan, whom we welcome for his own sake and also because he is the brother of George Trevelyan. We are glad he is here, if only to know how highly we think of that brother, and how greatly we appreciate his brilliant work. The second name is that of Mr. Richard Whiteing, one of our own men, who told us a few years ago so delightfully what he owed to the College for giving him his love of literature. The third name is that of a brilliant writer, Mr. Pett Ridge ; but to the visitors one and all I would say, this Fellowship is the bedrock of our College. We welcome all alike, prodigals and older sinners, returned old friends and new comrades. We ask you to tell of us as you find us, nothing extenuating, for there is nothing for which we owe an apology. Give us a good word ; for, believe me, in doing so you will be giving a good word for one of the soundest and most wholesome communities that ever good men brought into the world. (Cheers.)

Mr. C. P. TREVELYAN said he did not know until just before he entered the hall that he was to speak ; and as everyone naturally expected from an M.P. a longer speech than ten minutes, he mentioned his alarm to his brother, who mistook the occasion of his alarm, and said, "Oh, Charles, you need not fear, there are no women here to-night.   Dr. Furnivall has not yet had his way." (Laughter.) He mentioned that whilst on his way to the College in the Tube, a lady got in, with "Votes for Women" on a brooch on her chest, so he shrank back, fearful lest she should recognize him as one of the four hundred gentlemen who promised to vote for what she wanted ; and he got out two stations before ours, near a police station, where he felt perfectly safe. (Laughter.) Seriously, he had no right to be there, except as the guest of his brother, of whom he was very proud. (Cheers.) He gave two reasons why he was interested in the College—one was its central position in London, and the other its freedom from the test of wealth. It was perhaps the only place where Garibaldi could have had an education, if he had been in England. (Cheers.)

Mr. RICHARD WHITEING likened himself to a sort of Rip van Winkle, having memories of the College, going back beyond the ordinary span of memory. His recollection of the College life dated back—he did not know why he should hesitate to say so—over fifty years   He entered the College in Great Ormond Street, as a callow youth, to know something of this wonderful world of knowledge, which was to him an unknown land ; and feeling rather afraid to cross the threshold, as if there was a something in its very advantages of which he would be unable to avail himself. The College library of that day was a small one, but to his eyes replete with all the knowledge of the world. He felt that in joining the College, as an American put it, he had bitten off rather more than he could chew. He felt he was a stranger in the place. The social changes had not developed as they had since, and so he felt a social barrier. The College was in the making. Socially, he felt himself very much alone. He walked into his class room, did his work, and went home again ; and was rather slow in making friends. The only social advantage offered to him at that time was the privilege of going into the back garden, and having his eye blacked by Tom Hughes. (Laughter.) One of the most precious parts of his memory was that he saw many of the illustrious men who made the College, face to face. He remembered perfectly hearing Maurice himself deliver that address, of which we have heard spoken, on the advantages of liberty in the College, and the form in which he put it. I remember even that he said, "This is Liberty Hall ; every man is to do as he likes, and those who won't do it shall be made." That was the key-note, on which the College was founded, and on which it has since been maintained. There was the minimum of orderly direction, and the maximum of freedom in the direction of the development of one's own individuality. Maurice and those who worked with him laid the foundations broad and deep in every possible way. Their wisdom has been made manifest in the result. The College has developed on the lines laid down then, and in accordance with the wishes and the principles of its Founders. This is a great deal to say. In this, you stand unique. among all the institutions of this kind in London, and for aught I know in the country, as a true democratic institution, forming part of a University in the old beautiful and honourable sense of the term. In conclusion, Mr. Whiteing said that the use he had made of the opportunities he had met with in the College had been of lasting benefit to him throughout the whole of his life. The love of literature for its own sake, though he was fated to have to live by literature, yet held a corner of his heart, as a love pure and unselfish ; and that fact he owed to the teaching he had received here. (Cheers.)

Mr. PETT RIDGE amused us greatly. It seemed to him we were calling too many witnesses in asking three to speak to this toast. Excess of evidence was always a mistake. A little while ago a man brought an action against his employers for injuries to his arm. Counsel for the defendants handled him very gently. "I am sorry, Mr. Jackson, you should have suffered in this way ; I have only one or two questions which I am instructed to ask. Would you mind showing the gentlemen of the jury how high you can lift your arm since the accident? The witness, with every sign of pain and exertion, raised his arm like this (illustrated with appropriate action) about as high as his shoulder, and said "Just about as fur as I can do it, guvnor." "And now will you kindly show the gentlemen of the jury how high you could lift your arm *before* the accident?" Up went the arm straight above his head. (Laughter, in which Dr. Dicey was observed to join with great glee). Mr. Ridge's story of the pickpocket who recounted his smartest coup, stealing four watches, at intervals, from the same old gentleman, at the same spot in the Poultry, as he came outside his office at 5 o'clock, and glanced up at a pretty type-writer girl at a window opposite, likewise occasioned us much merriment, but the reporter cannot introduce here Mr. Pett Ridge's art or skill in narrating it.

Mr. H. C. Dumbrill sang "Biddy Aroo."

Mr. CORNFORD: Fellow students, Your president wrote me, asking me to be present this evening. I replied I should be delighted to come, on one condition, that I remained silent, and under no circumstances would I depart from that resolve. Your president wrote back that as a matter of fact I was regarded here as a sort of gramophone to be turned on at a certain stage, and he wanted me just to say something—I might at least make myself ridiculous for five minutes. I replied with a cool note. A "cool note" is an expression used by Swinburne. Once Emerson wrote a review of one of Swinburne's works. Swinburne said he wrote Emerson a "cool note." Edmund Gosse asked what he wrote; and he said, "I reminded him he was an old and now toothless ape, and that having climbed into fame on the shoulders of Carlyle, he now spits and splutters from," etc. (Laughter.) Well, I wrote Marks a cool note. The venerable scoundrel, with his insidious cunning, only called up an air of innocence, and replied on a post-card that he would be glad of an opportunity of taking my life; but I replied that I would only fight a duel on certain conditions, namely, with carving knives in a dark room. He did not accept the challenge, so I sent the post-card to Scotland Yard, and here I am. Mr. Cornford explained that he was exceedingly disappointed that the arrangements could not be carried out last May for the annual visit to Cambridge, owing to a certain set of microbes, whose disreputable name he neither knew nor cared to know, having got the upper hand of the megacites in his blood, reducing him to a diet of soda water and Trollope's novels. He went on to say that he had a speech in his pocket, all about the academic or the unacademic mind. He was going to deliver it, but would not. He intended saying, but would not do so, that the unacademic mind was educated by life and not by books, whilst the academic mind was educated by books and not by life. He thought that would go down awfully well. Then he was going to point out what is the great product of modern life, and by a delicate transition, lead up to the subject of the evening, and propose the health of the "Old Students' Club." (Laughter.) He proposed that toast, coupling with it the name of the Vice-Principal. (Cheers.)

Mr. JACOB replied, and said his name ought not to have been associated with the toast, but in its place should be that of the late auditor of the Club (laughter), or one of the vice-presidents. One of them, Mr. Grugeon, had lately shown that advancing years could not take away his freshness, by giving a paper to the Field Club on "Shelling peas." It was difficult to think of the College without the Old Students' Club, or to realize what it must have been like before the time of the Supper. It was one of the great and many gifts we owed to our dear old master and teacher, George Tansley. We felt as though he were with us in spirit that night; and we felt that to him we were indebted for one of the best evenings of the year. (Hear, hear.) Mr. Jacob concluded by proposing the health of the Chairman, for whom we all felt great affection and love. (Cheers and musical honours.)

Mr. MARKS, in response, described himself as an "impostor," and returned thanks for the toast, after which "Auld Lang Syne" brought the evening to a happy close.

The list of those present is to be published next month.

COMMON ROOM.

Annual General Meeting.

THE Common Room annual general meeting took place on November 25th, when Mr. SYDNEY BRADGATE presided, as usual, over a goodly number of the members, and the Hon. Secretary presented the Report and balance sheet,* which were adopted by the meeting.

Several questions arose upon the Report, the most important relating to the proposed general rules for College clubs introduced by the Committee in February last, with a view to giving them, amongst other provisions, power to keep a fatherly eye over any Club which might require outside assistance to keep it alive.

Mr. GATES FOWLER moved that the balance sheet be placed upon the Common Room notice board at least seven days before the annual general meeting; and after a short discussion, during which it was pointed out it would be inconvenient to tie the secretary down to any fixed time, the time-limit was winnowed down to "as soon as possible," and the proposal was agreed to.

Mr. H. E. NYE moved that the Common Room Committee be instructed to see that those social events which have no permanent committee to look after them, do not fall through, and that the Committee in future should arrange the dates for such events. He instanced the Joint Clubs' Supper, the Collegians' Dances, and the Children's Treat, and pointed out the advantages of anchoring these floating but important social events under the pilotage of a permanent and responsible committee. A warm discussion followed, one opponent describing it as an insidious attempt to pass some portion of the proposed rules. The motion did of course contain in essence some of their provisions, and it was truly wonderful to listen to the praise which speakers bestowed on the proposition, but which they were unable to extend to the rules. The motion was eventually carried by 23 to 17.

The nominations and heckling were then proceeded with, each having to answer, amongst others, the questions "Are you in favour of the rules?" and "If elected, will you accept office of secretary or custodian." There was a list of thirteen candidates, of whom only two gave a direct affirmative to the first question, whilst to the second an affirmative answer was given by three only. The meeting closed with hearty votes of thanks to the retiring committee, and to Mr. Bradgate for his services as chairman.

The election by ballot took place from Monday, December 2nd, to Monday, December 9th inclusive, and on the last day of the poll, a deal of enthusiasm was caused by the contest between Home Rulers and Non-Rulers, and the result was awaited by some fifty members with unusual interest. At 11.15 p.m., Mr. Murphy, who had kindly acted as returning officer for the past week, announced the following result—Elected: Melzer, 147; Randall, 143; Landells, 112; Hayward, 101; Staal, 98; Offer, 94; Moore, 88. Not elected: Brett, 74; Owen, 73; Gates Fowler, 56; Trott, 46; Liddelow, 45; Hitchcock, 25. Despite the opposition shown to them, all the candidates who had been distinctly in favour of the rules were elected, whilst the non-rulers managed to get their champion in at the top of the poll. The figures were received with thunderous applause.

The poll this year was the heaviest the College has known, 188 members voting in all. This is a sign that the social side is very active and that the Common Room is attracting members. It should, however, draw a good many more, and it is to be hoped that the new committee will work hard to get the "new members" into the social life.

We have to return our best thanks to Mr. Murphy as returning officer, and also to Messrs. Wildey and Perry for their services as scrutineers.

At a meeting of the new Committee held on December 19th, they elected officers as follows—chairman, H. K. Randall; secretary, E. S. Landells; and custodian, M. Staal.

In conclusion, I claim that the much libelled rules have been a direct cause of a great revival of the Common Room social life, and although this may be but faint praise, the result is distinctly good.

H. K. RANDALL, *ex-Hon. Secretary, C.R.C.*

* To be published next month.

COLLEGE NOTES.

The January term begins on the 13th inst., and ends on April 4th, thus lasting twelve weeks. Easter Monday coming late this year, on April 20th, it is not convenient to make the break at Easter.

At the Council Meeting held on November 26th, upon the motion of the Vice-Principal, the Council placed upon record the sense of its pleasure at the honour recently conferred upon Sir Charles Lucas, and at the attainment by Mr. Lowes Dickinson of the age of 88 years. Dr. Furnivall brought before the Council the kind offer of Mr. Wolmark to paint the portrait of Sir Charles Lucas and give it to the College, if Sir Charles would sit for it, and it was resolved to ask him if he would sit accordingly.

The Council was then reconstituted. Under section II., Messrs. R. Hawtrey, E. W. Rowntree, and P. Williamson, not having taught in the past year, retired; and Messrs. R. N. M. Bailey, B. Turner, H. C. Gutteridge, H. G. A. Baker, F. W. Jekyll, E. Cunningham, and A. L. Stephen, come on. Under section III., it was reported that Messrs. H. N. Gill, F. J. Nield, and C. H. Perry (elected members), and Messrs. John Crawley and W. J. Gray (co-opted members), retired; and that Messrs. Nield, Perry, and H. K. Randall had been elected by the students. Messrs. Crawley and Gill were thereupon co-opted. Under section IV., Dr. R. M. Beaton and Mr. A. L. Leon had been re-nominated, and Mr. A. W. Claremont nominated, by the London County Council. Under section V., Messrs. J. A. Forster, T. F. Hobson, and Dr. E. Oswald retired, and were re-elected.

The following officers and representatives were re-elected :— Vice-Principal, Mr. Lionel Jacob; Bursar, Mr. Reginald J. Mure; Auditor, Mr. W. G. Stroud; Executive Committee, Messrs. Sydney Bradgate, J. J. Dent, J. A. Forster, H. N. Gill, T. F. Hobson, W. C. Jones, Sir Charles Lucas, A. S. Lupton, B. P. Moore, Leonard Pocock, E. J. H. Reglar, W. J. Torrington, and E. J. Turner; Librarian, Mr. E. J. Turner; Curator of Museum, Mr. J. F. N. Green; Representatives on National Home Reading Union Council, Mr. R. J. Mure; and on Club and Institute Union, Messrs. J. J. Dent and R. H. Marks.

The Report of the Executive Committee was read and adopted, containing the following interesting information :—
Student and Class Entries.—Despite a demand for term programmes greater than that experienced last year, the number of students who have joined this term is less than in the corresponding term of 1906. For part of this falling off a definite

cause can be assigned, inasmuch as the day classes for Post Office sorters have had to be abandoned, it having been found impossible to hold them in the building whilst it is being used as a London County Council Secondary School for Girls. But, even allowing for these, between 40 and 50 students less have been so far enrolled. Fewer joined during the enrolment week, which was so successful an experiment last year, and from that less favourable start the entries have not as yet recovered. It will be remembered that, after an exceedingly disagreeable summer, the weather in September was remarkably fine; to this is probably due the less favourable condition of our student entries. The decrease has been spread over a large number of classes, so that out of 31 subjects upon which comparison can be made, 11 only show an increase, 19 a decrease, and 1— English Composition—is exactly as it was last year.

The very severe drop in the entries for the Law classes is chiefly due to the loss of Mr. E. J. McGillivray, who had taught in that section for the past two sessions, and had succeeded in attracting a very large number of students. It was with very great regret that the Committee heard that, through pressure of other work, Mr. McGillivray would be unable to teach during the present session. When comparing the two sets of figures, allowance too must be made in French, German, Algebra, and Euclid, for the Post Office sorters who entered for these four subjects alone. Had the conditions remained the same as last year, each of these classes, except Algebra, would have shown an increase. The comparative entries are as follows :—

	1906.	1907.			1906.	1907.
Preparatory Division	49	39	History		5	9
Algebra	45	31	Italian		19	8
Ambulance ...	25	31	Latin		36	30
Arithmetic ...	62	41	Law		74	18
Art	75	45	Botany		8	17
Book-keeping ...	76	52	Building Construction		46	40
Chemistry ...	36	33	Electricity ...		64	36
English Composition	23	23	Geology		8	6
Economics ...	20	13	Geometry... ...		0	16
English Literature	36	27	Sound, Light, and Heat		0	7
Euclid	11	4	Physiology ...		10	5
English for Foreigners	29	27	Portuguese ..		0	1
Esperanto ...	0	9	Singing		45	90
French	174	150	Spanish		35	39
Geography ...	4	6	Shorthand ...		146	161
German	68	49	Violin		16	19
Grammar... ...	38	39	Zoology		6	0
Greek	15	16				
Gymnasium ...	22	32	Class Entries		1326	1169
			Student Entries		929	851

Examination Results.—It is pleasant to report that the number of students who gained certificates again shows the upward tendency noted last year The increase is, however, confined solely to the Higher and Special Divisions, and more especially to the Science and Art Sections of the former. There were, however, many other students who ought to have submitted themselves for examination, but failed to do so. A larger number of students than usual sat for the Senior Student Examination, but only one—A. C. Martin—passed. Martin, having already secured the certificates necessary to claim the Associateship, and having also taught for more than the number of terms requisite to qualify for the Fellowship, has obtained all the three College Honours of Senior Student, Associate, and Fellow in one year. T. M. Balson, who gained the Senior Studentship in 1900, also qualified for and was awarded the Associateship.

The award of the "Tansley" Memorial Scholarship and Prizes was made in almost the same manner as last year. As proposed, however, in the report of November last, the area of inquiry was widened by asking each of the class teachers to suggest the names of students who in their opinion were deserving of this honour. To consider these recommendations and to examine the records, the Studies' Committee appointed a small sub-committee, upon the consideration of whose report a recommendation was submitted to the Executive. Acting upon this recommendation, the Executive unanimously awarded the "Tansley" Scholarship to E. J. H. Reglar, and "Tansley" Prizes of £2 in books to E. J. H. Reglar and J. W. Roberts.

Lectures.—The College has again been very fortunate in securing an attractive list of lecturers both for Thursday and Saturday evenings. The attendances at both have been very good, the Thursday evening series showing a most marked improvement. The return to 8.30 for the hour of commencement has certainly been for the good, and on Thursdays it has given, in many cases, an opportunity of attending the lectures without the necessity of giving up a class. Mr. Rait's series of Thursday lectures upon the "History of London" has proved especially attractive, and has taxed the accommodation of the "Tansley" class room to the uttermost. The College is deeply indebted to Mr. Rait for his lectures, and to its Principal for having secured for it the opportunity of hearing Mr. Rait.

The list of Saturday lectures for the January term is not yet complete, but Professor A. W. Porter, the Rev. A. B. Boyd-Carpenter, Messrs. G. Lowes Dickinson, A. Sutro, E. Radford, and H. Baynes have been kind enough to promise lectures, whilst the Principal, Professor A. W. Kirkaldy, and Mr. T. B. Browning have undertaken to lecture on Thursdays. Of the two series of University Extension lectures arranged here in conjunction with the London County Council and London University Extension Board, that given on Fridays by Dr. Slaughter on "Child Study" has proved quite a success, but the Tuesday series on "Italian Painters" by Mr. Dudley Heath has attracted only a small audience. The London County Council has also allotted to this College a series of lectures on "The Romantic Revival in English Poetry," given until a fortnight ago, by Mr. Guthkelch, and since his breakdown, by Dr. R. G. Watkins. These also have not been a success, a baker's dozen only having taken tickets for them.

Social Functions.—Already reported in the JOURNAL.

Library.—Upon the suggestion of Mr. T. F. Hobson, efforts are being made by the Executive Committee to collect the sum of £100 from certain of the City Companies, for the purpose of supplying the more pressing needs of the Library with regard to books. In response to this appeal, the Skinners' Company has voted twenty guineas, to which Mr. Hobson has been successful in adding donations of ten pounds and five pounds from Mr. Minet and Mr. Smithers respectively. Thanks to the kind offices of Mr. Dent, the Dr. Williams' Trustees have also voted £5 in books, per Mr. Stephen Seaward Tayler. The College has also received a complete set of lenses from Mr. B. J. Rose, and a microscope and slides from Dr. Grubb. Gifts of books to the Library were reported.

The Executive Committee's Report concluded with a reference to the arrangements made with the London County Council, under which the College is being made use of in the day time by one of the Girls' Secondary Day Schools which the Education Committee of that Council is establishing. An agreement has been entered into, in accordance with which the School commenced with about ninety girls on September 16th, and the arrangements made have worked up to the present, and promise to work in the future, with great smoothness and satisfaction to both the bodies concerned. .

The College Accounts for the year ending July 31st, 1907, as audited and printed in the COLLEGE CALENDAR, were then presented, discussed by the Council, and adopted.

At the Shorthand examination held 20th ult.—examiner, Mr. E. H. Carter, H.M.I.—five students sat for the "theory" paper, and one passed, E. J. Burgess ; five entered for speed at 70 words per minute, and two passed, H. O. Driver (excellent) and F. P. Leach ; five took the speed test at 80 words, and three passed, C. H. Thetford (excellent), E. Carter, and H. O. Driver ; and of the two who attempted 90 words per minute, one passed, C. H. Thetford.

Dr. John Forbes, with the assistance of Mr. George Wiltshire, has again scored a very creditable result at the Ambulance examination, conducted last month by Major A. C.

Tunstall. The whole of the sixteen candidates passed, eight for " First Aid," viz., Albert E. Colebourn, Arthur H. Westfield, William H. Chittleburgh, Wilfrid Gilbert, Hector M. Copland, Oscar Maguire, Robert Henderson, and Walter D. W. Peyton; six for vouchers, viz., James Scott, James M. Stears, Henry G. Bennett, Herbert H. Laws, John J. Burford, and William J. Slade; and two for medallions, John E. Willson and Edwin J. Bayliss.

Mr. Julius Jacob examined the Preparatory Division, with the result that the following students passed :—In Arithmetic, F. J. Lake, W. Udall, F. J. C Lawford, and C. L. Marshall, all " excellent "; H. Robinson and F. C. Finney, pass; nine sat. In Dictation, F. J. Lake, " excellent "; F. J. C. Lawford and A. H. Perry, pass; seven sat. In Grammar, H. W. Goff, " excellent "; F. J. C. Lawford and J. Thompson, pass; five sat.

The importance of the occasion and the excellence of the speeches reported must be our excuse for taking up so much space in this month's JOURNAL with the report of the Old Students' Club Supper. But we regret we are obliged to hold over until later, reports of the discussion on Mr. Maurice's paper on Party Government, Miss Spurgeon's lecture on " Ruskin," and other interesting matter.

The seventeenth Joint Clubs' Supper, held in the Coffee Room on December 28, with W. J. Torrington in the chair, lacked nothing of its customary joviality. Between fifty and sixty clubites sat down to table, and the supper was followed by a number of speeches, toasts, and songs, giving opportunity for hearing, amongst others, several of those prominent speakers and singers whose voices are frequently heard in the College.

Randall and Nye are to be congratulated on the great success of the Furnivall Children's Treat, held on December 21st. About 300 poor children partook of the tea, and of these, about 250 who secured tickets had in addition a good romp in the Maurice Hall, where they were also entertained by dissolving views of " Alice in Wonderland," and by the Doctor, in the *rôle* of Father Christmas. On leaving, each child was presented with a toy or some other souvenir, and a bag containing buns, cakes, sweets, oranges, etc.

Professor A. W. Kirkaldy, who has so often lectured in the College, and in other ways shown a great and kindly interest in it, is now Warden of Queen's College, Birmingham. We congratulate him upon this appointment, and wish him every success in his new position. Professor Kirkaldy was unable, through illness, to give his lectures on the "History of Writing" here last term, but has arranged to deliver them in the January term, on Thursdays, January 16 and February 6, at 8.30 p.m.

Mr. J. C. Bailey, well known to us in the College as teacher, examiner, and lecturer, has succeeded Prof. G. W. Prothero as editor of the *Quarterly Review*. Mr. Prothero was in the habit of sending very welcome parcels of magazines, from time to time, to the College, in which, too, we have heard him lecture.

Mrs. Robbie wishes to return thanks, through the medium of the JOURNAL, for the kindness and solicitude shown for her during her incapacity, following upon her accident. She has indeed had a very trying time, not the least part of her troubles being the failure to properly diagnose the nature of the mischief caused by her fall. Her experiences at Portsmouth Hospital, her removal to London, where her injuries were successfully diagnosed at University College Hospital, and the want of proper rest and sleep, have been enough to try the fortitude and patience of anyone; and we can but admire the pluck and resignation with which our cateress has gone through it all, and hope that her present lameness may in course of time be improved.

A few weeks ago, the teacher of our Book-keeping and Commercial Arithmetic classes, Mr. A. J. Bride, informed the Superintendent that he should be absent from his classes for three weeks, and at the end of that time he was back to his classes. In the meantime he had done a scamper to the United States, visiting New York, Boston, and other places, on business. Part of his plan was to endeavour to interview John Roebuck, the first Fellow of the College, who has been in America for over forty years, and who now lives at Winchendon, Massachusetts. Unfortunately Mr. Roebuck was not well enough to travel to Boston to see Mr. Bride; and Mr. Bride had not time enough at his disposal to go to Winchendon, so they were unable to meet. Sometime ago, however, John Roebuck offered to give his portrait to the College, and this he has sent with kindly greetings to his old friends, through Mr. Bride, who safely landed the portrait at the College on his return. The portrait is in oils, and was painted in New York in 1875, by Mr. Alfred Emslie, now a well-known artist, a former teacher of the College Art Classes, and brother of Messrs. J. P. and W. R. Emslie. The portrait has already been hung in the Common Room.

A few of Flint's boxing men and friends have presented him with an "Ideal" Waterman fountain pen—"For our darling Flint." Needless to say, he is their slave for ever.

DEBATING SOCIETY.

IT is pleasing to record that during the past month the interest shown in the Society has considerably increased—a support which has been well merited by the subjects dealt with, and the speakers it has been our good fortune to secure.

The question of Socialism was fully and interestingly dealt with on November 29th, when Mr. Gutteridge, in an able speech, brought forward a motion condemning it, upon the grounds of fettering the commercial activities of our people, vitiating their home life, and being in direct opposition to all that is best in the English character. He was vigorously yet temperately opposed by Councillor Harley, a member of the Independent Labour party, and by the majority of the succeeding speakers. The motion was of course rejected.

December 3rd brought forth a discussion on the Nationalization of Railways; and in suggesting that the adoption of such a policy would be inimical to the best interests of the country, Mr. W. R. J. Hickman adduced a wealth of evidence, and exhibited in a marked degree the keen penetrativeness of the business man who has constantly to deal with hard facts. The opposition, voiced by Mr. Austin Smith, endeavoured to make light of the difficulties suggested, particularly those dealing with the question of finance, and secured the endorsement by nearly all the subsequent speakers of these views—consequently the motion was negatived by a large majority.

The night of the session was undoubtedly December 10th, when Dr. Emil Reich dealt with the question of Germany as a danger to Great Britain. A very large audience closely followed his extremely suggestive utterances, and enjoyed immensely his quaint mannerisms, revealing as they did the possession of a pungent wit. He maintained that Germany does not want any part of the territory of Great Britain, but *did* want to wrest from the British the supremacy of the sea. He believed that war would come between the two nations, about 1912 or 1913, and that the humanitarian argument would not arrest it; that it was bound to come, because the Germans must expand; their own country would not hold them; they were imperialistic, like the British, and must go somewhere, and nothing could prevent it. Conflict—blood and iron—had made both nations what they were, and we could no more stem the Gulf Stream than we could stem the current of history. To avoid this inevitable war, Dr. Reich suggested that the Philippines should be given to the Germans. This would provide the necessary territory to meet the national expansion, and they would then have a place that would take them two centuries to cultivate.

The last meeting of the half session, on December 17th, heard the society in lighter vein, witnessing as it did the humorous attempt of Mr. Moore to pour ridicule on present-day masculine attire, particularly on account of its sombreness. An effective and instructive reply from Mr. Turner, in which the usually disguised trouser was held up as the only remnant of the French Revolution, and as consequently the hall-mark of Democracy, found more favour with the assembly: and the rejection of Mr. Moore's motion left those of us who dress more for comfort than for show, quite relieved to think that we could still slouch about in the old cycling jacket and baggy-kneed trousers affected by every real occupant of the Common Room. The debates will be resumed on Tuesday, January 14th, when Mr. Munro will open on a subject to be announced, and opposed by Mr. Starling. F. E. LIDDELOW, *Hon. Secretary.*

FIELD CLUB WALK.—January 12th, Moor Park, Rickmansworth. Take ticket out to Northwood, back from Chorley Wood, 1s. 10d. Train leaves Baker Street (Met. Ext.) at 9.50.

LONDON: Printed by W. HUDSON & Co., Red Lion Street, High Holborn, and published at THE WORKING MEN'S COLLEGE, Crowndale Road, London, N.W.—January 1st, 1908.

THE WORKING MEN'S · COLLEGE JOURNAL ·

sub:IV

The
Working
Men's
College ·

CROWNDALE
ROAD ·
ST PANCRAS ·
LONDON · N·W ·

FOUNDED
IN 1854
BY THE LATE

Frederick
Denison
Maurice ·

Contents for

FEBRUARY, 1908

Dante
Old Students' Club
Musical Society
College Notes
Joint Clubs' Supper
Childrens' Treat

THE
Working Men's College Journal.

Conducted by Members of the Working Men's College Crowndale Road, London, N.W.

VOL. X.—No. 179.   FEBRUARY, 1908.   PRICE TWOPENCE.

DANTE.*

S we journey through Life, there are three great questions that we can ask ourselves, if we choose.; three great problems that we can try to solve, if we are interested in problems. The first is : How shall I behave to the people I know—to my relatives, friends, and acquaintances? The second is : How shall I behave to the people whom I don't know, but who nevertheless exist and have claims on me—to the government, to society as a whole, to humanity as a whole? And the third question, which some people think of supreme importance, while others neglect it entirely, is this: How shall I behave to the Unknowable? What shall my attitude be towards God, or Fate, or whatever you like to call the invisible power that lies behind the world?

These three questions have existed for all men in all ages. They are inseparable from our humanity. They are no more old-fashioned than they are modern. And it is my intention this evening to call up Dante out of the darkness of six hundred years, and see what answer he gives to them. How did Dante behave to the people he knew? How did he behave to the people he didn't know? And how did he behave to the Unknowable? I think that this is the best way of approaching the great poet. It is hopeless to attempt a detailed account of him. There isn't the time. Let us just put these three questions to him, and so see what he makes of the problems that are bothering us to-day.

But before we begin, I must inflict one or two dates on you —only one or two, for we are not concerned with history ; and I must mention the names of some of the books that Dante wrote.

Dante was born in 1265, when Henry III. was King of England. He was born in Florence, which is to-day part of the Kingdom of Italy, but which was then an independent republic, ruling a territory of about the size of Yorkshire. . We know little about his youth, the two important facts being that when quite a boy, he fell in love with a lady named Beatrice, and that

---

* Paper read to the W.M.C. Literary Society by Mr. E. M. Forster, on November 21st, 1907.

when he was twenty-five years old, Beatrice died.   Like most
Florentines, he entered public life, and in the year 1300
(aged 34) became a member of the government—of the Cabinet,
if I may use the phrase.   He was becoming rather a prominent
person.   And then the blow fell—the blow that ruined him as a
politician, but made him as a poet.   A great fight broke out in
Florence, and Dante's side got the worst of it.   He was exiled.
The remainder of his life he spent wandering about Italy and
Europe, trying to find some champion who would restore him
to the city that he loved so much and had served so faithfully.
He found no one.   He failed absolutely, and died in 1321,
broken-hearted.

So his life falls into two distinct portions—up to 1300, when
he is at Florence and happy ; and after 1300, when he is in exile
and miserable.   And if you agree with most historians, and take
the year 1300 as marking the end of the Middle Ages, it follows
that Dante lived at a most important moment, when the mediæval
world was passing into the modern.

As for his books.   When he was a young man, he wrote a
book called " The New Life," in which he described his love for
Beatrice.   It treats of personal relations.   In it we shall find
some answer to the question, " How shall I behave to the people
whom I know ? "   Then, after he had been exiled, he wrote a
book called " The Empire."   It deals with the world's government and with the destiny of our race on earth.   It is a political
and sociological tract.   It answers the question, " How shall we
behave to the people whom we don't know ? "   And lastly, just
before he died, he wrote the " Divine Comedy," the scene of
which is laid in Hell. in Purgatory, and in Heaven ; and the aim
of which is to answer the question, " How shall I behave to the
Unknowable ? "   He did write other books, but I am only going
to mention these three.

As for " The New Life."   Its " plot " is easily described, and
is I daresay already familiar to you from the pictures of D. G.
Rossetti and A. Holliday.   It opens with an account of Dante's
first meeting with Beatrice, at the somewhat tender age of nine
Nine years later they meet again, and the crisis of his love comes.
Beatrice greets him—gives him her salutation.   Nothing more.
That is the happiest moment that he ever knows on earth.
" And then with her ineffable courtesy, which is now receiving
its reward in Heaven, she gave me her salutation, so that in
one moment I beheld all the bounds of bliss."   His intimacy
with Beatrice goes no further.   We are not even sure whether
she returned his love.   The rest of the book is concerned with
his emotions—how he tried to be near her and fainted in her
presence ; how his love gradually became more manly and more
spiritual.   Then Beatrice dies.   He is overwhelmed with grief.
There is the episode of his infidelity—he is attracted by a lady
who resembles her ; and then he returns to her with remorse, and
determines that some day he will write a poem in her honour.

He fulfilled this promise at the end of his life, by writing the " Divine Comedy," in which Beatrice is the heroine.

Even from this brief sketch, you will have gathered that "The New Life " is rather a queer little book. It is half a diary and half a novel. At one moment Dante describes what actually happened, and at another he is only describing what might have happened, or what he felt. At one moment Beatrice is an ordinary woman who has friends and relatives and goes to dinner parties—an actual woman whom he might marry, as Hamlet might marry Ophelia ; and at another, she seems an inhabitant of heaven, who had strayed by accident into our sordid world. We never know what the poet is up to, and we are apt to close the book with a feeling of irritation. There has been a great deal of talk about Beatrice, but we have not learnt what she was like, nor even whether she loved him. Contrast " The New Life " with the Sonnets of Shakespeare. In the Sonnets, though much is obscure, we do know definitely what the various characters are like. In " The New Life," we only hear that Dante loves Beatrice. Nothing else. He gives us no hint of her personality.

Now, this is a very interesting point, and goes far to answer the question, " How did Dante behave to the people whom he knew?" His answer is, " I regard them as a means to something else "; I regard them as windows in this sordid world, through which I may get a glimpse of heaven. Hamlet loved Ophelia because she was Ophelia. Othello loved Desdemona because she was Desdemona. But Dante loved Beatrice, because she was a means to God ; because the emotions with which she inspired him, took him out of daily life into the life celestial. Here is the great difference between him and Shakespeare, between mediæval and modern thought ; and unless we keep this difference in mind, we shall fail to understand " The New Life," and much else that he wrote. We of to-day naturally ask, " Why didn't Dante marry Beatrice?" But he would have shrunk from marriage as from sacrilege. He would have regarded it as a debasement of his ideal, a concession to the animal element within him. He preferred to worship Beatrice from a distance. And as for marrying—he married someone else. His wife—Gemma Donati was her name—seems to have had no influence on her husband. She was merely his wife, the mother of his children, not a window through which he could see God. Dead, as alive, Beatrice remained the most important person he had ever met ; and so when he came to write the " Divine Comedy," he takes her as his guide through heaven. The little girl he had known from the age of nine, has become a type of celestial wisdom. She meets him on the top of Purgatory, when earthly wisdom, however noble it may be, can help him no more. She takes him into the company of the blessed, to see the saints and the martyrs, the prophets, the Virgin Mary, Christ, the supreme Deity Himself. He had loved her as a woman, and now she shows him the Love that passes all understanding, and moves the universe. " The New Life," which he wrote when he was young, is not complete in itself. It must be considered in connection with the " Divine Comedy," which he wrote just before he died.

But I want to say a little more about this habit of regarding our fellow creatures as windows, through which we may see God—a habit, you must remember, that was not confined to Dante, but was typical of his age. At first sight, there is something sublime in it. It makes a man behave with reverence and courtesy to a woman; he disciplines his body and soul, that he may be worthy of the high thoughts to which she leads him. It inspires him to work : it may inspire a whole life, as it did Dante's, and so give us the " Divine Comedy." But, is it a true compliment to the woman herself? I am not going to answer this question, but I want to suggest it to you. Which seems to pay the truer homage—Dante looking through Beatrice, or Othello looking at Desdemona ; Dante narrating the return of his lady to the angels, or King Lear with Cordelia dead in his arms?

(*To be continued.*)

OLD STUDENTS' CLUB.

PARTY GOVERNMENT AND PROPORTIONAL REPRESENTATION.—(*Continued.*)

THE debate upon Mr. C. E. Maurice's paper on this subject, reported in the December number, was opened by Mr. RIGBY SMITH, who said that Proportional Representation did not seem to him to be an arguable question. Unless representation were proportional, it was not really representation. It had, however, been mathematically discovered that even if all constituencies contained exactly equal numbers of voters, and each constituency returned one member, it might transpire—as the result of an election—that a minority of a little over a quarter of the electors would place into power a government against the views of the majority. For, if each electorate returned a member by a majority of *one*, and if the two parties were so nearly balanced that there was only a Liberal or Conservative majority of *one*, it would follow that the party in power would really only represent about a quarter of the electors—a curious result of mathematics—[Mr. Charles Wright: And imagination]. The great mistake in Hare's proposed system of proportional representation was, that it left the issue partly to chance and partly to officials. The result depended upon the order in which the papers were taken in the counting of the votes ; and the manipulation of the lists of candidates was in the hands of officials.

Mr. CHARLES WRIGHT said the great difficulty about representative government was that, in voting for a candidate, you had to consider many things in priority to his fitness—in fact, the fitness of the candidate was almost the last thing which those who were responsible for bringing him forward could consider. First, they considered whether the candidate had plenty of money. That was a most damaging consideration. In his constituency, his party was in a hopeless minority. If they wanted to run a candidate with any hope of reducing the majority, he must be a man of money, able to see to registration. The fact that a candidate had to do this work at all, seemed to be an abominable scandal. Then we had got into a deplorable habit of looking upon a Member of Parliament, not as a man rendering a service to us, but as a man we were electing as a great favour to him. A constituency actually looked for a man who would reward *them*, for being allowed the privilege of spending laborious days and nights in *their* service. He had very grave doubts whether a system of Proportional Representation would remedy the present condition of things, or whether it would secure a better representation than our present imperfect methods. The machinery devised for the purpose of securing the best man as President of the United States failed in its object—was defeated by elaborate counter-party machinery. Similarly, if an attempt were made here to introduce proportional representation, the two great parties would issue their tickets, and take pains to organize the election in such a way as to neutralize the purpose for which the proportional system was adopted. With regard to the two men Mr. Maurice had mentioned, John Stuart Mill and Leonard Courtney, who found it impossible to keep their seats, there appeared to be, in the Constitution, a device already framed for the very purpose of providing such scholarly men with safe seats—he referred to the membership for the Universities, which returned some of the steadiest party men in the kingdom. Upon the question of party government, it was to be regretted that both sides frequently blackened everything their opponents did, whether they were in agreement with it or not. Especially disastrous was this practice in questions of foreign and colonial policy. Happily, there had been an attempt made to establish continuity in such policy, and a sort of truce had been come to in regard to those matters, which ought to be encouraged. The existence of the House of Lords, as a part of the Constitution, seriously hampered parliamentary government. The fact that that House, with its enormous powers, should be practically an adjunct to the Conservative party; so that that party, whether returned to power by a majority of the electors or not, was always able to control legislation in opposition to the other party, was a very serious obstacle and blot upon our system. (Cheers.)

Mr. BENNY having spoken, Mr. PRESBURG said we ought to do away with plural voting. He thought the people got the government *they deserved.* The evils could only be effectually remedied by educational means, as at this College. The party system was really an ideal system. No great party could prevent the formation of a number of smaller ones, but to attain fundamental reforms, minor differences were sunk, and order arose out of chaos.

Mr. MORSHEAD thought the plan of having two parties, and if possible not more than two parties, was on the whole most suitable for our needs. Whilst the predominance of the House of Lords was admittedly a very serious blot upon the Constitution, yet we had managed to get through somehow without a hopeless entanglement, and he hoped we might again. It was necessary, for the two-party system, that we should not expect too much of it. It was neither possible nor reasonable to expect a Liberal to think of anything but his Liberalism, nor for a Conservative to think of anything but his Conservatism. And we were almost bound to have to put up with the various hitches that had been mentioned. In the memory of his father there exised blots on the electoral system which now seemed incredible. Among the boroughs in Cornwall, all " rotten," there was one which became reduced to having no more than five electors, of whom two—supposed to be one on each side—retired, leaving three voters to decide the election, each of whom held out as long as possible in order to find out how the others were going to vote. When it was said that one of them was offered, the night before the poll, £600 for a single sheep, we might allow that it was purely an imaginary election. With the expansion of the franchise, we had remedied such things as that. The only alteration in present conditions he could suggest was, that it might perhaps be well to reduce the possible life of a Parliament to less than seven years. Holding more frequent elections would inevitably lead to the desire for payment of members, which although unpopular, must come in course of time, and would lead to fresh difficulties. A perfect system of representation was not to be found this side of the seventh heaven. We should have to go on patching and patching, until something nearer to perfection resulted. (Cheers.)

Mr. A. W. MATTHEWS urged the necessity for educating the electorate. He favoured porportional representation, but thought each elector should not vote for more than five candidates. The number of members should be increased from 670 to 1000. [Dissent.]

Mr. S. J. COOMBS said it was wrong to assume that there were only two parties. It was only by conference among the sections that we got something like a party acting together, and it was only by a united party that measures could be carried. We had too much law, and too little business, in Parliament at present. All the elections should be held on the same day. The proportional representation scheme was unworkable. It would throw the issue into the hands of the returning officers.

Mr. TIRRELL thought our members were rather "delegates" than "representatives." A constituency should send to Parliament the best man.

Mr. MAURICE, who was cheered on rising to reply, suggested in answer to the objections raised to the Proportional Representation scheme, that there should be greater publicity in the counting, or ascertaining of the result of the election. He also answered the other points raised by the various speakers, and was accorded a hearty vote of thanks at the conclusion of his reply.

The 207 guests present at the Annual Supper of the Old Students' Club, on 14th December last, were Messrs. R. W. B. Alaway, A. E. Alden, W. V. Aldridge, Rev. B. H. Alford, E. C. Atkinson, Thomas Austin, J. C. Bailey, R. N. M. Bailey, J. T. Baker, T. M. Balson, L. Barnard, W. H. Barnett, Dr. R. M. Beaton, James Benny, W. H. Berry, H. V. Birrell, B. Black, J. Boisson, René Bowden, S. W. Bowen, P. Bradgate, S. Bradgate, E. J. Brennan, H. de Brent, A. J. Bride, G. C. Brignell, John Bromhall, F. E. Brooks, George Buckland, G. T. Butler, D. C. Cambridge, W. D. Caröe, C. G. Cash, Robert Chalmers, C.B., J. R. Chandler, C. S. Colman, A. E. Coombs, A. W. Coombs, S. J. Coombs, F. M. Cornford, John Dale, W. Darker, George Davenport, E W. Davis, W. J. Davis, J. J. Dent, Professor A. V. Dicey, K.C., Principal, G. Lowes Dickinson, J. M. Dodds, C.B., S. Drake, H. O. Driver, E. C. Duchesne, H. C. Dumbrill, Robert Eason, J. Edwards, W. R. Emslie, C. E. Engelhart, H. Eyers, E. J. Field, M. K. Field, R. R. Flint, Douglas Forster, E. M. Forster, J. A. Forster, John Fotheringham, Richard Freeman, Dr. F. J. Furnivall, T. W. Gale, H. Gallagher, J. F. Gay, S. B. W. Gay, G. P. Gooch, M.P., W. J. Gray, J. F. N. Green, Alfred Grugeon, Sydney Grugeon, T. Haigh, B. F. Halford, S. Hamilton, A. Hargreaves, C. E. Harris, E. A. Harrison, Wm. Hart, E. Hayward, R. M. Head, H. G. Henley, A. Hepburn, W. T. Hillier, R. S. Hitchcock, James Holloway, A. E. Homewood, T. Hopkins, George Horne, Wm. Hudson, Charles Iseard, J. F. Iselin, Lionel Jacob, Vice-Principal, Julius Jacob, S. de Jastrzebski, C. T. Jeffery, W. C. Jones, C. P. King, James Kirk, C. H. Kisch, E. J. Lambert, E. S. Landells, Jules Lazare, Dr. Sidney Lee, A. Levett, H. R. Levinsohn, Sir Charles Lucas, C.B., K.C.MG., H. Luetchford, H. H. Luetchford, A. S. Lupton, Right Hon. Alfred Lyttelton, M.P., E. J. Macgillivray, J. D. Macnair, R. H. Marks, C. F. Marshall, A. C. Martin, A. Weight Matthews, J. W. Macauley, J. MacWilliam, C. F. W. Mead, W. G. Medhurst, R. T. Mence, W. R. H. Merriman, H. W. Miles, W. E. Miller, C. T. Millis, Charles Monteath, B. P. Moore, E. D. A. Morshead, J. J. Munro, T. W. Nalder, F. J. Nield, H. Nye, Dr. E. Oswald, A. Owen, S. Walshe Owen, A. U. Penny, J. H. Pert, W. Coope Phelps, T. E. Pickles, Leonard Pocock, E. Pointon, Sir Frederick Pollock, LL.D., D.C.L., Sydney Presburg, H. K. Randall, C. W. Rapley, H. C. Rapley, R. A. Reed, E. J. H. Reglar, W. Pett Ridge, J. Gerald Ritchie, J. W. Roberts, W. A. Robinson, R. Robson, J. D. Rogers, F. C. Roper, B. J. Rose, Alexander Scott, A. B. Shaw, A. H. Singleton, Charles Smith, J. Rigby Smith, —. Souter, M. Staal, Sidney Stagg, M. H. Starling, Adrian Stephen, A. Strohfeldt, H. Sumner, F. G. Sweeting, Mason Tarr, G. A. Taylor, R. E. Taylor, E. Tissier, L. E. Thomas, P. T. Thomas, W. J. Torrington, C. P. Trevelyan, M.P., G. M. Trevelyan, Bernard Turner, E. J. Turner, Juan Victoria, George Wanklin, T. Waterhouse, Professor John Westlake, K.C., W. Whitaker, A. J. White, Richard Whiteing, Herbert Wilcockson, C. E. Wilkinson, Ralph W. Wilkinson, C. R. Williams, J. G. Williams, P. Williamson, Andrew Wilshaw, C. R. Wilson, King Wilson, G. Wiltshire, G. E. Winter, A. Wolmark, Charles Wright, Harold Wright, and G. H. Zeal.

COMMON ROOM ACCOUNTS.

FOR THE YEAR ENDING OCTOBER 31ST, 1907.

Income.	£	s.	d.	*Expenditure.*	£	s.	d.
Balance brought forward	32	18	11	Draught beer	3	14	4
Capitation Grants :—				Bottled beer	6	5	6
February ... 8 10 0				Wine	0	3	9
April ... 6 3 10				Cigars	1	8	2½
September... 4 5 6				Tobacco	3	16	3½
	18	19	4	Cigarettes	4	7	8½
Draught beer	6	12	0	Newspapers and Maga-			
Bottled beer	9	0	0	zines	12	19	8
Wine	0	4	6	Printing and Stationery	2	2	4
Cigars	2	1	8	Donations and Subscrip-			
Tobacco	3	18	0	tions	1	15	6
Cigarettes	5	12	6	Utensils and Repairs ...	24	12	7
Locker rents	1	3	6	Opening night of October			
Newspaper subscriptions				Term, Refreshments ...	0	18	5
and resales	6	2	5½	Postages	0	9	0
Balance from Garden party	0	5	5½	Balance in hand	24	5	0½
	£86	18	4		£86	18	4

Assets.	£	s.	d.	*Liabilities.*	£	s.	d.
Cash in hand	24	5	0½	Contribution towards fur-			
Bottles	0	6	0	nishing Serving Room	3	0	0
Resales of Newspapers				Excess of assets over lia-			
uncollected	0	12	3	bilities	22	3	3½
	£25	3	3½		£25	3	3½

H. K. RANDALL, *Hon. Secretary, C.R.C*

Audited and found correct.—HERBERT N. GILL, November 18th, 1907.

◆·◆·◆

COLLEGIANS' DANCES.

THE 23rd Collegians' Cinderella Dance took place in the Maurice Hall on December 11th last. There was a full attendance of Collegian dancers, with either their wives or sisters or their "lady friends"—a good sprinkling of the latter. A programme of nineteen dances was enjoyably gone through, dancing having started at 7 o'clock. The decorations in the Hall were greatly admired, and the Committee tender their grateful thanks to the Misses Frances and Rose Reglar, who were most unsparing in their kind help in decorating it. The improvement in the floor was a great benefit, and we thank the Executive for so readily coming to our assistance in connection with the planing of it.

The 24th Dance took place on January 4th, when there was again a large attendance, and another long list of dances was successfully negotiated, including the "leap year" dance. The gallantry of the ladies in the attack on the men on this occasion was certainly worthy of admiration, and it is said that everybody was satisfied. Certainly it is hoped that this was the case. Those who were unfortunate enough not to be able to be present on this occasion have a chance on March 28th, when the third and final dance of the season takes place. Tickets will be ready towards the end of February, and can be procured of the committee, consisting of Messrs. Hitchcock, Hogh, Reglar, and West. A. OWEN, *Hon. Secretary.*

W.M.C. MUSICAL SOCIETY.

ON Saturday, January 18th, under the auspices of this Society, a "Ladies'" Concert took place in the Maurice Hall. In point of numbers we think it was the most successful "Ladies" the Society has ever held, the audience numbering between four hundred and fifty and five hundred. Our dear old friend, Dr. Furnivall, was in the chair; and Starling occupied a very prominent and influential position in "the gods." Part one opened with a song, "Out on the Deep," sung by E. W. Davis (Teddy). Miss C. Graefe, in sweet soprano, gave "Unforgotten" and "Once," and as an encore, "Violets." C. R. Oberst, our old Club chum, charmed us with his beautiful tenor voice, which we at the Club all delight to hear, singing "Maire my Girl," and giving as an encore, "The Last Watch." In the name of the College, we wish to thank Oberst for his delightful entertainment, and hope he will come again. Master Tyler, brother of our Tyler, gave us a very fine violin solo, "Scène de Ballet." Through the whole solo the expression and touch was excellent. The audience was especially delighted with Miss Mildred Parr, who, although arriving too late to follow in the order of the programme, was fully forgiven, judging from the way in which her recitations were received and the number of encores she had to give. We trust to have the pleasure of including her name in the programme on many future occasions. Lawrence, my co-secretary, wound up the musical part of the first half of the proceedings by singing that stirring song, "My Old Shako," much to the admiration of "the gods," who were dying to sing a chorus. As an encore, he gave "The Yeoman's Wedding."

One of the oldest, quietest, most staid, least suspected, and best of "College men," in August last, took unto himself a wife. Saturday's concert was chosen as a fitting opportunity to present Jim Holloway—for that is the least suspected one's name—with a very handsome sideboard, as a token of the love and good-fellowship which the College bears towards him. The Doctor, in the name of the College, made the presentation, and in an appropriate speech spoke of the work Holloway had done, and is doing still, in connection with the Field Club and zoology class. The audience sang "For he's a jolly good fellow." and gave

"Three good cheers and one cheer more,
    For Jim and his wife, whom he does adore." .

"The gods," too, insisted upon singing "O Lucky Jim." And then we had just such a suitable and neat reply as we should expect from the hon. secretary of the Lubbock Field Club.

The second half of the programme, arranged by Mr. C. H. Perry, consisted of a collection of Somerset Folk Songs. The Doctor, at our last concert, had brought to the notice of the Musical Society a collection of folk songs, compiled by a friend of his, Mr. Cecil Sharp, of the Hampstead Conservatoire of Music, and he backed this up by presenting us with the book of music. After much time and work, Perry extracted the selection given, and with the very kind and able help of the Misses Frances Reglar and Clara West, Mrs. C. H. Perry, Mrs. Mason Tarr, Messrs. R. E. Tyler, F. C. Hammant, F. Jackson, himself, and Mr. William Cook, as accompanist, he produced the very pleasing result experienced on Saturday. Our old favourite, Hammant, of "Glorious Devon" fame, led the way with Bingo was its name, Sir." The audience struggled manfully with the chorus, but it proved too much for them. Mrs. Mason Tarr sang "Sweet Europe" very sweetly. Mr. R. E. Tyler, the accompanist in the first half, having, we should think, worn out his fingers, offered, like the darling he is, to sacrifice his throat in the interest of the College, in the second half. It wasn't the fault of the audience that he didn't succeed in doing so, judging by the way they insisted upon him singing "John Barleycorn" twice. We may here remark that the edifying chorus, "Sing Ri fol lol the diddle all the dee, right fal leer o dee," came within the mental scope of "the gods," who persisted, so that they might not forget it, I presume, to sing that intricate chorus after every subsequent song. Miss Clara West unfortunately was indisposed, but Mrs. Mason Tarr gallantly came to the rescue by singing "Mowing the Barley" in her stead. We regret the cooing was omitted at the end of each chorus, as it is undoubtedly a very musical ending ; however, the Club girls present supplied the deficit. Mrs. C. H. Perry very daintily sang " As I walked through the Meadows." Miss Frances Reglar sang " A Lover's Task." It was very sweet, and we are going to ask her to sing it again soon ; we fear the lesson did not quite sink into the minds of some College men. Perry, who was so perky, gave, much to the delight of the audience, " A Brisk Young Widow," a song. Whether by accident or by design, he was asked to sing, as an encore, " And now, if you please, I'm ready to try, this breach of promise of marriage."

The Chairman wound up the very pleasant evening by proposing a vote of thanks to the ladies and gentlemen who had so kindly entertained us. " For he's a jolly good fellow," was sung for the Doctor, at the Vice-Principal's suggestion, and the evening ended with " Auld lang syne." G. S. O.

STUDENTS' CALENDAR FOR FEBRUARY.

Sat., 1st.—Lecture, " Dante and his Divine Comedy," Mr. H. Baynes, 8.30.
Sun., 2nd.—Lecture, " The Hebrew Prophets," Rev. B. H. Alford, 6 p.m. Shakespeare Reading, " Midsummer Night's Dream," at the Vice-Principal's house, 7 p.m.
Mon., 3rd.—Lecture, " English Poetry," Dr. R. G. Watkins, 7.30.
Tues., 4th.—Executive Committee, 8 p.m. Lecture, " Italian Painters," Mr. Dudley Heath, 8 p.m. Debating Society meeting, " Home Rule," Mr. Stephen Gwynn, M.P., 9.30.
Thurs., 6th.—Lecture, " The Fundamental Principles of the Law of the Constitution," The Principal, 8.30. Citizens' lunch, 1.30.
Fri., 7th.—Lecture, " Child Study," Dr. J. W. Slaughter, 8 p.m.
Sat., 8th. Chess Match, Wood Green v. Maurice, 8 p.m. Lecture, " Gareth and Lynette," Rev. A. B. Boyd Carpenter, 8.30.
Sun., 9th.—Lecture, " The Hebrew Prophets," Rev. B. H. Alford, 6 p.m. Lubbock Field Club walk on North Downs ; Excursion ticket to Horsley, 2s. ; train. Waterloo (South Station) 10.5.
Mon., 10th.—Lecture, " English Poetry," Dr. Watkins, 7.30.
Tues., 11th.—Executive Committee, 8 p.m. Lecture, " Italian Painters," Mr. Dudley Heath, 8 p.m. Debating Society meeting, 9.30.
Thurs., 13th.—Lecture, " History of Writing," Prof. A. W. Kirkaldy, M.A., B.Litt., 8.30.
Fri., 14th.—Lecture, " Child Study." Dr. Slaughter, 8 p.m.
Sat., 15th. —Old Students' Club meeting, Mr. Richard Whiteing opens on " What is Nietzche's Influence in Politics, Literature, and Art ?" 7.45. Sketching Club Supper, 7 p.m. Lecture, " Colour " (illustrated), Prof. A. W. Porter, 8.30.
Sun., 16th.—Lecture, " The Hebrew Prophets," Rev. B. H. Alford, 6 p.m. Shakespeare Reading, " Two Gentlemen of Verona," 7.30.
Mon., 17th.—Lecture, " English Poetry," Dr. Watkins, 7.30. Chess match, Metropolitan II. v. Maurice, 8 p.m.
Tues., 18th.- Executive Committee, 8 p.m. Lecture, " Italian Painters," Mr. Dudley Heath, 8 p.m. Debating Society meeting, Mr. A. L. Stephen opens, 9.30.
Thurs., 20th.—Lect., " Socialism, its economic basis," Mr. T. B. Browning, 8.30
Fri., 21st.—Lecture, " Child Study," Dr. Slaughter, 8 p.m.
Sat., 22nd.—Lecture, " Some Impressions of Canada," Mr. J. D. Rogers, 8.30.
Sun., 23rd.—Lecture, " The Hebrew Prophets," Rev. B. H. Alford, 6 p.m.
Mon., 24th.—Lecture, " English Poetry," Dr. Watkins, 7.30.
Tues., 25th.—Council Meeting, 8 p.m. Lecture, " Italian Painters," Mr. Dudley Heath, 8 p.m. Debating Society meeting, Mr. C. H. Kisch opens, 9.30.
Wed., 26th.—Chess match, Wheatsheaf v. Maurice, 8 p.m.
Thurs., 27th.—Lecture, " Socialism, its objects and methods," Mr. T. B. Browning, 8.30.
Fri., 28th.—Lecture, " Child Study," Dr. Slaughter, 8 p.m.
Sat., 29th.—Mrs. Tansley's Concert, with Mrs. Julian Marshall's orchestra and choir, 8 p.m.

COLLEGE NOTES.

THE First of February is so far removed from Christmas as to be beyond the influence of the festive season, yet it is not until now that we can survey the social events at the College associated with that time of the year. They filled all the Saturdays during the vacation, as well as one before and one after it. The first in order and in importance, was the Old Students' Supper, on December 14th. On the 21st, came the Furnivall Children's Treat. On the 28th, the Joint Clubs' Supper. On January 4th, the Cinderella Dance. On the 11th, the Chess Match with the Cambridge men and a Smoking Concert. And on the 18th, the Musical Society's Concert (ladies' night). In the organization and carrying out of these six items, a large number of men, and their lady friends too, take willing and cheerful part. It is indeed as great a pleasure to some to prepare for these various annual treats as it is to realize the enjoyment of them, and there are always plenty of volunteers for the work.

At the first meeting of the Executive Committee for 1908, held on January 7th, Messrs. J. F. Hobson, C. H. Perry, and R. H. Marks were co-opted on to that body ; and the Finance, Studies, and Appeal Sub-committees were re-elected.

The next meeting of the Old Students' Club will be held on Saturday, February 15th, when Mr. Richard Whiteing will open on, "What is Nietzche's Influence in Politics, Literature, and Art?" The last meeting of the session will take place on Saturday, March 14th, when the Principal, Prof. Dicey, D.C.L., K.C., will open on "Would the Referendum be suitable and practicable in this country?" Members of the College are invited to join the Club; Subscription, 1s. per annum.

In consequence of the excellence of the work done by Messrs. F. J. Lake and F. J. C. Lawford in the recently held Preparatory Examination, a Scholarship has been awarded to each of these promising students. Attached to this examination there are two Scholarships, the holders of which are entitled to attend any two classes in the Lower Division for one year, free.

On Saturday, January 25th, Mr. E. Radford delivered a Lecture on "Southwell Cathedral." Mr. Radford was well remembered for the delightful series of architectural lectures which he gave at the College previously. In language which could be followed with equal interest by novice or expert, he showed how histories could be deduced from a roof-line, and why and where sculpture was necessary. Above all, he was full of appreciation for the work of the old master masons, who gave such full play to their individualities, and worked for the sake of devotion, not of gain. The lantern slides illustrating the lecture were very beautiful.

Professor A. W. Kirkaldy has kindly sent the College £5, and Miss Estall, £1 1s., for the Maintenance Fund. Doctor Furnivall has most generously given the College twenty-two volumes of "Punch," for the Common Room; he has had them bound in cloth, at a cost of £4 10s.

The College is in want of a recent London Directory, and will be grateful for the gift of one. The one at present in use is four years old, and not a little the worse for wear.

Writing to Mr. A. J. Bride on November 18th last—[Mr. Bride was then in America], Mr. John Roebuck said, "Kindly act as the bearer of my most earnest desire to all who know me, or know of me, to give their best services to the College. Assure all your friends who know me, that my heart warms to them as much as ever. The success of the College seems assured for the future. I only wish I could realize one of the dearest of my desires, namely, that I could find myself within its walls."

Referring to the announcement on the subject in last month's JOURNAL, Miss L. Toulmin Smith writes: "In the *Athenæum* of December 21st, the statement made in the number for December 14th is corrected. 'Dr. Prothero is not retiring from the editorship, and has no intention of doing so. He is merely handing over the control of the *Quarterly Review* for a short time to a deputy, Mr. J. C. Bailey.' The Editor of the *Athenæum* apologizes for the mistake." So do we.

We have received the New Year's address of the teachers of the Vaughan Working Men's College (Leicester) to the students. It exhorts the students to be regular and punctual in their attendances, reminding them that "The members of each class must, with their teachers, have special concern for their class; the various classes—not as isolated units, but as belonging to a living institution—must co-operate with each other for the general good. All make up together one College, and all must work together for the educational and social life." We are glad to note that the Vaughan Working Men's College hopes to be installed in its new home in March next, and that the new building will be a worthy memorial to its Founder, Canon David James Vaughan.

THE "MARKS'" PRIZE.

THIS Prize, to be awarded annually in books to the most successful competitor, is open to all students, and is this year offered to the writer of the best Essay on either of the following subjects :—(a) Discuss Shakespeare's view of Democracy, especially as exemplified by the plays of " Julius Cæsar " and " Coriolanus " ; (b) Criticize the view that the characters of Dickens are caricatures. Essays are to be sent in by April 30th.

JOINT CLUBS' SUPPER.

SWEET seventeen! What a host of dreams the words conjure up! You, gentle readers (courtesy title), with the cares of twice or thrice seventeen winters just thinning out your thatch and with the pressing necessity of gussets in the back of your waistcoat making itself felt, will probably conjure up a delicious vision of some mild-eyed damsel with whom you first practised the gentle art of osculatory reciprocity. Or your thoughts will perchance revert to the time when, unconscious that you were still in the hobble-de-hoy stage of your existence, you invested in an eighteen-penny razor with which to scrape the virgin down from your chin, and, radiant in a captivating necktie covered with pink dogs and yellow horse-shoes, you sallied forth a man! Or when in the hey-day of your youth and ignorance you first entered the College classes, exuberant with the thought that you already knew more than the teacher was ever likely to know, and had kicked open the gates of knowledge, while all the world was at your feet, instead of very much on your shoulders as at present.

But such beatific visions of smooth unruffled chubbiness rise not before me, as I sit toasting my toes, and gazing through the smoke clouds that curl upwards from my pipe. Far other scenes my thoughts recall, for I am looking through the vista of years at the long line of Joint Clubs' Suppers which reached the age of sweet seventeen on December 28th, 1907.

It is quite in the natural order of things (apart from any personal reflection) that the name of this function should start with a "J." Think of the number of nice Christmassy words which start in the same way, such as joviality, jest, jollity, and others. Indeed, the Joint Clubs' Supper may be vulgarly but aptly described as a mixture of joke, jingle, jorums, and jaw. But it will never do to let our Principal see this description, although he does read the *Daily Mail,* so I will merely say, for I like to be perspicuous, that the social function referred to is simply a heterogeneous agglomeration, comprising a mendacious polyglot menu descriptive of commonplace comestibles difficult of deglutition, a toast-list with tangled titutar transformations of tantalizing terminology, productive of periphrastic platitudes, combined with coruscating comicality and pachydermatous polophony as a digestive tabloid. Merely this and nothing more. Still, it's good fun, and the seventeenth supper was no exception, but added another notch to a long tale of happy days.

The attendance was quite the smallest of recent years, as only fifty-three were present; but they made up in quality what they lacked in quantity. To begin with, Torrington was in the chair. Music was represented by Tarr, Haynes, Brodie, and Young; singing by Perry, E. W. Davis, and Lawrence; the Press by Pocock; poetry by Homewood and Nye; literature by Munro; oratory by Cash, Mead, Starling, and Liddelow; earthworms by Holloway; respectability by Marks and Hudson; shipbuilding by Offer; athletics by Barnett; officialdom by Duchesne; paternal pride by Nield and Hopkins; the Colonies by Birrell; and sculling by most of the others. The Coffee Room, where the supper was held, was gay with scraggly holly, artistically arranged by Barnett and Hayward, and mistletoe hung by Melzer; and the good cheer provided by Mignot the caterer vanished like the baseless fabric of a vision. As the knowledge of Esperanto is still confined to a few, the menu was in French, the only item which was understanded by the people, being a free translation of "Fundamental Rule Pudding"—aptly so named, since it was forbidding in aspect, and dire in its effects.

After the eatables had been cleared away by the gallant fifty-three and the uneatables by the caterer, the "Punch à la Jones-Castell" was brought in, disguised in a tea-urn, pipes were lighted, and the company settled itself for a rollicking evening. Haynes gave a pyrotechnic display on the piano by way of introduction, and then the Chairman rose to propose the toast of "The College," which was received with a cheer which made the welkin rattle. Lawrence then interposed with "The Veteran's Song," and asked us in touching accents to wheel his chair to the window, as he wanted to see the king go by. I remember once seeing a jovial gentleman hanging on to a lamppost late one night, and waving onwards an imaginary army, but I never expected that Lawrence would be in the same state. After the audience had got its teeth out of the chorus of Lawrence's song, Mead rose to respond to the toast of "The College," and treated us to chestnuts on toast.

The next stage in this strange eventful history was a speech by Cash, who told us he had come all the way from Stratford-on-Avon in order to be present at the gathering, and who described himself as the "Benjamin of the brethren." Until then I believe nobody knew that he was any relation to the Vice-Principal. I hope he won't start another Druce case! He gave as a toast "The Gas Company" (meaning thereby the Debating Society), the sequence of events reminding one of a penny-in-the-slot meter—cash first, gas after. After Perry had sung, "The Judge's Song," Liddelow, who was accorded musical honours, replied with a neat little speech, and then Hepburn propounded another puzzle, "The Dreadnoughts and Flotilla." It does not need a vast amount of discernment to see that this toast has some connection with the jolly little sculling club which lives and moves and has its being at Hammersmith-on-Mud; but it is not quite so easy to see who are the "Dreadnoughts," and which part of the club forms the flotilla. In these days of rampageous suffragettes it is perhaps wisest to assume that the "Dreadnoughts" are those brave ladies who faced the fire of the *Daily Mirror* camera, and the flotilla the College men who follow in their train, for. if any lady can look upon her face in such a looking glass and still smile, she must be brave indeed. A piccolo solo by A. H. Perry was then announced, on which Starling, of course, must ask, "Will he pick a low note"? Hayward responded for the Furnivalliant scullers, and told us how difficult he found it to speak plainly on so beauteous a subject.

The next item on the programme was the presentation by the Chairman of a set of fish-carvers and fish knives and forks to W. C. Jones, to commemorate his marriage in August last. Many were the nice things said by Torrington; but there is no place for them in this veracious epistle. Jones returned thanks, and enquired if wedding presents were given as a sort of award of merit, or whether they were a consolation prize; after which Haynes sang "Thora." Then Starling was called upon to speak. He was due to propose "The Clubs—Quick and the Dead," and had arranged with Castell to work off a little joke upon the company, by merely proposing the toast and then sitting down without making a speech. But when the toast had been proposed and he went to sit down, he found someone had annexed his chair, so he had to continue speaking. Rising to the occasion, he squared his shoulders, took a term programme from his pocket, and proceeded to read it solemnly to the company. We endured the stodgy mass with exemplary patience; but when the orator drifted off the catalogue of clubs, and proceeded to tell us that "the library is open from, etc., etc." the company went off the deep end with a splash and, rising to its feet, sang, "For he's a jolly good fellow," with one accord, until Starling was reduced to silence. Jones then sang "My Old Shako," after which Castell rose to respond for the Clubs, and thanked the company for coupling his name with the same by "seconding the toast!"

Another presentation then took place, Melzer being called to the front to receive the Cycling Club's attendance prize, which he has won for the second time. The prize took the form of a leather bag, and I hear that the ladies' attendance prize was also a "week-end bag." (Please do not say "Tut! Tut!" gentle reader.) J. J. Munro followed with a toast to "Those at the Gates of Paradise," with which he coupled the name of George Offer. I thought at first that this was an allusion to the fact that Offer has the temerity to go sailing in a home-made boat; but I find on investigation that it is a sly dig at the fellows who are just undergoing the "sweetening" process. Offer replied, and was followed by A. E. Homewood, who dished up two or three little tales told by "The Follies," and proposed the health of the Common Room Committee. Landells returned thanks, and paid a glowing tribute to the work of Randall, who was apparently the fundamental principle of the committee. Being perfectly straight, the new committee has taken him for a ruler, and it is to be hoped they will now know how to draw the line. Jones gave the next toast, which was " The Catches of the Season," but muffed the catch as if the toast were buttered. The proper interpretation of this excuse for a drink should have been " The Ladies," of course ; but he spoke as if the men who had that year joined the ranks of the Benedicts were the toastees, which is absurd, as Mr. Euclid justly remarks. Holloway responded very modestly, and then the Chairman called upon Nye for a song. This elicited a response in the form of a parody on " Love, could I only tell thee," the title of which was " Love, if you'd only told me." Cash also appeared before us in a new guise, that of a *tenore robusto* (with the accent on the " bust "), and sang " Yes, let me like a soldier fall ! " in very good style.

The last toast upon the programme was that of " The Chairman," which was proposed by Pocock and honoured right heartily. The night being yet young, more songs were called for, and Nye appeared before us again with a topical little ditty of his own composition, to the tune of the " Merry Widow " waltz. The words slipped a cog or two now and again, so far as scansion is concerned, and there may have been too much tone-colour for Dumbrill's fastidious taste ; but there is magic in lines such as these :

> Georgie-Porgie, for an orgie, built——a——boat.
> Henry E. Nye, with the keen eye, ver —— ses —— wrote.
> Georgie's boat, they tell me, is pointed as can be,
> But in Henry's verses little point I see.

These are not the exact words, of course, but merely a fraudulent imitation. Other good things followed, including a recitation by Birrell ; but the Coffee Room clock told me my train was getting impatient, so I turned out into the fog and cold just as Castell broke out into song. As I scrambled into my overcoat, the lusty lilt of " The Rio Grande " rang through the air, and the seventeenth Joint Clubs' Supper ended, so far as I am concerned, with

> " So fare thee well, my bonny Castell,
> For I'm off to the Rio Grande."   W. C. J.

MAURICE CHESS CLUB.

THE programme of the Chess Club for the past month was made very interesting from the fact that the home match with Trinity College, Cambridge, figured therein. This event took place on Saturday, January 11th, when our welcome opponents turned up in goodly force. The result was 7½ to 3½, in favour of the Maurice, which was most gratifying to the winning team. A high tea was then taken, presided over by the Vice-Principal, who cordially welcomed our Cambridge friends in the name of the College. Mr. H. A. Webb replied for himself and friends, saying how heartily they appreciated the warm welcome they received. A smoking concert followed (R. H. Marks in the chair), which, thanks to the strenuous efforts of Mr. Nield, proved a great success. The teams were :—

TRINITY.			MAURICE.		
1. H. A. Webb ...	1	—	H. W. Hammant ...	0	
2. B. Goulding Brown	1	—	F. J. Nield ...	0	
3. H. D. Roome ...	1	—	A. E. Thomas ...	0	
4. F. R. Hoare ...	½	—	O. Henke ..	½	
5. A. D. Goodwin ...	0	—	V. Ray ...	1	
6. E. H. Neville ...	0	—	J. F. Halford ...	1	
7. A. W. H. Thompson	0	—	S. R. Briggs ...	1	
8. P. E. Marrack ...	0	—	H. W. Miles ...	1	
9. E. D. Brent ...	0	—	S. Grugeon ...	1	
10. R. M. Wright ...	0	—	J. Foley ...	1	
11. C. K. Hobson ...	0	—	C. H. Marks	1	
	3½			7½	

CORRESPONDENCE.

[Under this heading the Editor will be glad to publish letters of interest to past and present members, but he declines all responsibility for the views therein expressed.]

JANUARY CONCERT CHORUSES.
To the Editor of the WORKING MEN'S COLLEGE JOURNAL.

SIR,—Ralph Rackstraw, in *Pinafore*, sang that he "Knew the value of a kindly chorus," but, as he continued, "Choruses bring little consolation," when used so indiscriminately as they were at the Concert on January 18th. I am referring to the second part only. The first song, "Bingo," had a very good chorus, but this being perhaps unknown, it was not taken up at all. The second song, "John Barleycorn," was obviously well known, the chorus was taken *con animo*—after every succeeding song as well; perhaps with a view to see how much the singers would bear before protesting by refusing to sing. To one singing a sentimental song, the interpolation of a drinking chorus is, I should imagine, the reverse of encouraging. Again, I should think that the tacking on of the conventional hymnal ending to a four-part unaccompanied chorus, is not an exhibition of exact musical knowledge, and that it was disconcerting to the singer. The worst phase was reached when "Mowing the barley," was sung. This, one of the most beautiful songs I know, might have been a common music-hall comic song, if one might judge from the manner in which the interludes were whistled. This manner of appreciation, though eminently satisfactory in the "Mo," was not calculated to encourage the singer (who, by the way, took the song at short notice through the illness of Miss West), or her brother, the pianist. The latter, I may say without any disrespect to the whistlers, was infinitely better able to translate the works of the composer than they were. Insisting on "The Judge's song," as an encore to the "Brisk Young Widow," may show a catholic musical taste, but it is the same taste that moves people to make patch-work quilts, and the world has grown beyond that form of art. This note is written with the pious hope that due attention may in future be paid to the singers at our concerts, it being taken for granted that they have given as much time as any one, if not more, to the study of the songs and the manner in which they should be rendered.—I am, yours faithfully,   C. H. PERRY.

SATURDAY NIGHT LECTURES.
SOUTHWELL CATHEDRAL.

MR. E. RADFORD, LL.M.—to whom we were indebted in 1906 for a course of lectures on "Architecture"—gave an interesting lecture in the Maurice Hall on Jan. 25th, his subject being "Southwell Cathedral," near Nottingham, illustrated by views of its principal architectural features, from a selection of 200 lantern slides placed at his disposal by the photographer, Mr. Evans. The lecturer mentioned that the cathedral was one of the oldest ecclesiastical buildings in England, consisting of a nave with two aisles, two towers at the west end, a transept, a choir with aisles, and a chapter house, the oldest part being pure Saxon work. The towers and other Norman portions, which were built of magnesium limestone similar to that of Bolsover Moor, are throughout in a perfect state of preservation, the mouldings and carved enrichments being as sharp as when first executed. Mr. Radford bestowed encomiums on the ornate details of the free masonry work, skilfully executed in the 13th and 14th centuries, when men put their best artistic feeling into their labour; and asserted that it would be impossible to have such varied work done in our time, under the prevailing competitive conditions of architectural contract and fixed wages for artizans. The ground-plan showed that the length of the cathedral is 306 feet, and the width of the transept from north to south is 121 feet. Reference was made to several whimsical forms, representing the grotesque in architecture, which alone would make the subject of a separate lecture. Canon Jephson, of Southwark, kindly took the chair.   H.

LUBBOCK FIELD CLUB.

TRAMPS IN RAIN AND IN FROST.

On December 8th, the weather was most unpropitious, and consequently the party was small. Heavy rain was descending when we alighted at Leatherhead; and although in the course of the day there were several fine intervals, it was still raining when we started our return journey, and the terrific storm of rain, hail, and wind which we encountered about 2 o'clock, was one we are not likely to forget. Off the hard roads the country was in a fearful state, and we all carried evidence of a heavy day at the finish. After a mile or so along the Bookham Road, we turned across Fetcham Downs and the Common Fields to Polesden Lacy, emerging on Ranmoor Common by Hogden Farm. We then descended White Downs by Park Farm, crossed Deerleap Wood, and encountered the terrific storm above mentioned as we reached the road at Wotton. This necessitated a long halt, and it was 2.30 before we reached our lunch place at Abinger Hatch. We found it difficult to tear ourselves from the cheerful wood fire and face the wind and threatening sky once more. When we emerged, we gave up the idea of reaching the top of Leith Hill, and turned our faces eastward. Passing Wotton House, we reached the road at the Home Farm, and walked as far as the Hatch before realizing the impossibility of catching the 4.28 at Dorking. Accordingly, we altered our plans, and struck through Rectory Wood and up the slippery slopes of White Downs. On reaching the summit we lost the track in the woods, it being by this time quite dark, and had an exciting time before striking the road at Ranmoor. Another change of direction was now decided on, and we followed the straight road back by White Hill and Effingham Village to the Junction, where we caught the 6.5 train. The chief finds were mosses and ferns, but a stoat and a dead ferret were seen and some very large waterfleas bottled. In spite of the stormy weather, the country looked magnificent, especially in the bright intervals and when spanned by a rainbow.

January 12th was a contrast in every way. The day was a brilliant one, and the country in the grip of a sharp frost. Starting from Northwood under Wildey's guidance, we took the path across the railway to Moor Park, and were sliding on a pond just inside the gate when our seventh man joined us, having come by a later train. On leaving the park we crossed Rickmansworth Moor, and followed the canal into Cashiobury Park. The scene seemed almost too arctic for England, especially when a barge broke through the ice and the floes piled up on the gates of the lock. We crossed the park, and took the path through Wippendale Wood, reaching the inn at Chandlers Cross with our appetites in good working order. Our next objective was Sarratt, from whence we struck north over Commonwood and Chipperfield Commons. By this time the mist had began to rise and we turned homeward, Wildey finding us a circuitous but beautiful route. Passing Belsize and avoiding Flaunden, we entered and crossed the valley of the Chess. At the top of the opposite hill, we entered a series of woods, and missing Chenies, reached the Rickmansworth Road some half-mile above Chorley-wood Common. The rough going over the frozen paths made the smooth road a welcome change, and we swung along in grand style until a pond on the Common suggested a last slide. On reaching the station we had a long wait, but even overdue trains arrive at last, and by 5 we were travelling homeward in a comfortable G. C. train. The distance walked could not have been much under twenty miles : and as much sliding and vaulting were also indulged in, it is not surprising that several of the members were the worse for wear during the early part of the following week. Apart from the frost effects, little was noticed of a striking nature, except the mistletoe and curious malformations of the limes in Moor Park.

Next walk, February 9th, on the North Downs. Take excursion ticket to Horsley, 2s. Train leaves Waterloo, South Station, at 10.5. Provide lunch.

J. HOLLOWAY, *Hon. Secretary.*

W.M.C. DEBATING SOCIETY.

THE inaugural meeting of the second half of the session, on January 14th, attracted a goodly number of members, among whom one was pleased to see a large proportion of new students, who, it is hoped, will become regular attendants and frequent interveners in the debates.

The question before the House was that of approving of Female Suffrage, in the support of which Mr. J. J. Munro delivered an excellent speech, containing not only an extremely interesting resumé of the historical aspect of the case, but also a well-reasoned and temperate appeal for an impartial consideration of the matter by the male sex, whose domination on account of superior intellectuality and fitness to make or apply the laws he denied. In opposing, Mr. M. W. Starling made merry over the many feminine traits which he maintained debarred woman from every adequate carrying-out of the duties which would naturally fall to them in the sphere they are attempting to reach. Among the many subsequent speakers, who displayed a remarkable divergency of opinion, extending as it did from the gallantry of Mr. Cash to the cold reasoning of Mr. Dent, whose intimate knowledge of the working woman and her wants is well known, none were more popular than Dr. Furnivall, who favoured us with five minutes' breezy championship of the weaker sex, and who no doubt felt amply satisfied at the carrying of the motion by 18 votes to 15.

On January 21st, Mr. E. Cunningham, M.A., a senior wrangler of Cambridge University, and one of our teaching staff, was good enough to discourse upon the shortcomings of our National Ideals. He laid bare many of the baser aspects of life—sensationalism in our press, commercialism, and the ever-prevailing selfishness which is so characteristic of the age. He pleaded for a larger outlook on life, and dwelt upon the dangers of self-satisfaction in the hours when he contended we were, as a nation, drifting aimlessly along. In opposing, Mr. H. Manton made a very creditable maiden effort, showing that he not only possessed the art of thinking aloud, but could do so with some pretence to oratory, and we shall watch his future career in our Society with interest. He valiantly took up the points raised, and claimed that the College life, and the improvement of the physical and social well-being of the people were typical of our time, and absolved us from the strictures passed by the opener, but the motion was eventually carried.

Among current and coming events may be mentioned :—On Tuesday, January 28th, Mr. R. N. M. Bailey, B.A., moved "That Co-operative Trade is a menace to the public welfare," and was opposed by Mr. W. H. Berry, but lost his motion by the sweeping majority of 18 to 2. On February 4th, Mr. Stephen Gwynn, M.P., will state the case for Home Rule. On February 18th, Mr. A. L. Stephen, B.A., will open. And on February 25th, Mr. C. H. Kisch, B.A., will be the principal speaker.

F. E. LIDDELOW, *Hon. Secretary.*

BOOKS RECEIVED.

"ESSAY on Man," by Rev. William T. Nicholson, B.A., Vicar of Egham. (Sonnenschein, 3s. 6d.)—We must apologise to Mr. Nicholson for our inability to review this work in a proper manner in these limited pages.

"The Christ in Shakespeare," C. Ellis. (May be obtained from Bethnal Green Free Library, post free, 2s. 6d.)

"To-day in Greater Britain," edited by W. Beach Thomas, the first of "The Citizen Books" series. (Alston Rivers, 1s. net.)—Contains much useful information, well arranged.

"First Steps," the Student's Elementary Text-Book of Esperanto, by Leslie P. Beresford, LL.D., M.A. (International Language Publishing Association, 2d.)—A concise and succinct introduction to the new universal language.

DR. FURNIVALL'S CHILDRENS' TREAT.

On Saturday, 21st December last, the walls of the College echoed with the shrill cries of about 300 children, who had been invited, from the neighbourhood, to the annual tea given by the members and friends of the College ; and if volume of sound can be relied upon as a criterion of happiness and enjoyment, the noise given forth by the children was ample evidence that they were having a good time.

The proceedings opened with the usual tea, vast quantities of buns, cake, bread and butter disappearing in double quick time. The children were then taken into the Hall, and entertained themselves with singing, wrestling, and boxing. At 7 o'clock, Mr. W. V. Daniel kindly gave them an hour's interesting magic-lantern entertainment, " Alice in Wonderland " being his subject, concluding with some miscellaneous, zoological, and seafaring pictures, which were much appreciated by our young guests. After the lantern, the Hall was cleared, and a general romp followed ; it was most amusing to see College men and their lady friends returning with enthusiasm to the games of their childhood. The gathering of " nuts and may " and the chopping of oranges and lemons ended in more than one of us emerging from the final struggle with our clothes feeling slightly disarranged. Suddenly there was silence, for " Father Christmas," impersonated by the Doctor, in his snow-covered red robes, appeared in our midst, surrounded by a strong body-guard. The need of this was soon apparent, for the youngsters gave the stalwarts a trying time, until they had safely escorted their charge to the platform. Here the Doctor spoke a few cheery words, hoping that the children, when they grew up, would become members of the College. The little ones were then passed out in batches to receive the usual bag of " goodies," and also a garment where needed, the proceedings closing with a vote of thanks to the Doctor and his supporters.

The Committee wish to extend their heartiest thanks to all the friends and members who so kindly subscribed to the fund, or who sent parcels of clothing and toys, and also to those who so willingly placed their services at their disposal. We have to especially acknowledge the help rendered by Mrs. Bartlett, Misses Francis and Hamilton, Mrs. Martin, Mrs. Pocock, and Miss Toyé; also by Messrs. Hayward, Hogh, Marks, and Staal. Mrs. Robbie and her staff also rendered yeoman service in the preparation of tea, etc. We also gratefully acknowledge parcels from the Misses Coleman, Clements, Chandler, Deane, Dewar, Estall, Fisher, Mrs. Jacob, Misses Jarvis Jones, Hamilton, Mrs. Lamb, Miss Moulden, Mrs. Pocock, Misses Sewell, G. and J. Sutton, D. Smith, and Toyé, Messrs. Hayward, Nye, Rigby Smith, and Tutte. Dr. Furnivall sent a large quantity of books. A welcome surprise gift came from a well-known College man and his friends of one and a half cwt. of toffee, cut up into half-pound packets ; the children's bags were in consequence unusually heavy, but in many instances the extra weight was quickly transferred to their faces and elsewhere. Out of the subscriptions, we supplied twelve girls and twenty-two boys with boots, and thanks are due to Jackman for the kindly help he rendered over this item. Hudson generously supplied the necessary printing free of charge.

A full list of subscribers appears on the Common Room notice board.

H. K. RANDALL, *Hon. Secretary.*

BALANCE SHEET.

	£	s.	d.		£	s.	d.
To various subscriptions				By Provisions	7	9	0
as per list	16	10	6	,, Boots	7	1	4
,, Deficit	0	0	4	,, Toys	1	14	9
				,, Postages and Sundries	0	5	9
	£16	10	10		£16	10	10

Audited and found correct, 25th January, 1908.—A. GOUGH.

Dr. Furnivall subscribed 10s., which was earmarked for and expended in refreshments, and for extra help.

SHAKESPEARE READINGS.

On November 24th, " King John " was read by the Shakespeare Reading Society in the Common Room. It was a ladies' night, and the members had every reason to be proud of their guests, who sustained the women's parts with considerable histrionic ability, Miss Steptoe being especially good in the trying part of Constance. Barnard read King John ; Peck, the Bastard ; Fenton, King Philip, Gates Fowler, Cardinal Pandulph ; and Miss Forsyth, Arthur, to Hayward's Hubert. It was considered by members present the best reading of the year : all were in good voice and at home in their parts, and the play is a good one to read.

On December 8th, " Cymbeline " was the play, and it went slowly, and had to be cut heavily owing to its length.

On Sunday, December 22nd, " Julius Cæsar," was read in the Common Room. H. Eyers sustained the name part ; H. V. Birrell, Cassius ; Sweetman, Brutus ; and W. F. Fenton, Marc Antony. There was a good muster of readers, although some came late.

" Twelfth Night " was read on January 5th, and, on the whole, read well. Miss Steptoe was a dignified Olivia, and Miss L. Walford a sympathetic Viola, a reversal of last year's parts ; while Miss Forsyth was delightfully piquant as Maria, and entered with zest into the fooling of Sir Toby and the Clown. Mead read the Duke's lines, and Fenton's mannerisms fitted Malvolio's character perfectly. Hayward gave Sir Andrew most naturally to the Sir Toby of Gates Fowler. Paterson showed himself to be an ideal Shakespearian Clown, his reading being the best contribution to the merriment of the evening. There was a too general disregard of an old stage aphorism, " Let them have their laugh out," and a good deal of the wit of the dialogue was smothered by the laughter from the previous joke. In spite of this, however, the readings went very well indeed, though we all missed Barnard in Sir Toby's part. Forty-four turned up to read or listen, many late as usual.

The next reading will take place at the Vice-Principal's house, 43, Buckland Crescent, N.W., on February 2nd, at 7 p.m., when " A Midsummer Night's Dream " will be read by Messrs. H. F. Peck, W. F. Fenton, C. F. W. Mead, T. M. Balson, G. Buckland, W. J. Davis, H. Eyers, E. Hayward, H. V. Birrell, W. H. Barnett, Pryor, T. Barnard and T. Paterson, and the Misses Walford, Forsyth, Steele and Steptoe, Mrs. Rolleston, and the Misses Jacob, W. Gates Fowler acting as scene shifter.

W. J. GATES FOWLER.

FURNIVALL SCULLING CLUB.

THESE notes have not appeared for the last few issues of the JOURNAL, but signs are not wanting that our College members are as enthusiastic as ever in sounding the praises of the Club to other College men. At the Joint Clubs' Supper, for instance, Hayward, in responding to the toast of the " Dreadnoughts," paid most delicate compliments to the girls. Castell, too, was very sympathetic, instancing a goodly number of men then present who had enjoyed membership of the old F.S.C., but who had been compulsorily retired by the operation of Rule 20a (copy of Rules, price 3d., supplied to successful candidates for membership).

Winter sculling has been more popular than ever this season ; and on Saturday and Sunday evenings, socials have been as well attended as in previous seasons.

The usual Boxing Day gathering was a great success, though marred by the Doctor's absence. He has, in past years, been unable to tear himself away from the Club in time for the last train, so, unfortunately, on this occasion he successfully resisted the temptation to come to Hammersmith.

The Doctor's Birthday celebration will take place on Sunday, February 9th. H. S. HOWARD, *Hon. Secretary.*

COFFEE ROOM DECORATION FUND.

IN presenting a final report and balance sheet in connection with this Fund, I should like to record a few interesting details connected with it.

The Fund was commenced on the 11th February last, at a Common Room General Meeting, and a Committee was elected for the purpose of collecting £100, that sum being the amount of the architect's provisional estimate.

The amount was collected at the rate of £25 per month, and the fund was declared closed on June 10th. The Committee then met, and a sub-committee was formed for the purpose of considering final estimates, and to see that the decoration was carried out. It was found that we had not sufficient money to carry out the scheme as originally proposed, and the fund was re-opened. The balance was, however, quickly subscribed, and the work commenced and completed in time for the first opening night of last term.

There were in all about 300 subscriptions to the fund, and it is most gratifying to find that so many of our new members supported it.

The collection of this fund is a good sign that the members who came from the old College have not allowed their interest in the welfare of the College to abate, and that they have managed to arouse a similar interest in those who have joined us in our new home. We now have two rooms most artistically decorated, and a small sum spent upon the better furnishing of the Coffee Room will bring both rooms up to a standard of comfort suitable to the most exacting tastes, and it only now remains for the new Common Room Committee to add this finishing touch.

In conclusion, I should like to warmly thank all those members and friends who have so generously subscribed to the fund, and also the members who have given most valuable help in its collection ; and I close this the last chapter with that feeling of satisfaction which follows " something attempted, something done."

BALANCE SHEET.

	£	s.	d.		£	s.	d.
To amount of subscriptions ...	113	6	6	By Postages	1	9	6
„ Interest on Deposit	0	15	3	„ Printing	0	12	1
„ Balance paid by Common Room Committee	2	19	6	„ Stationery	0	4	8
				„ W. D. Caröe, Architect's fees	5	5	0
				„ Tom Crouch, Contract price for decoration of walls and fitments	59	10	0
				„ Bromsgrove Guild of Applied Arts—Contract price for ceiling	50	0	0
	£117	1	3		£117	1	3

H. K. RANDALL, *Hon. Secretary.*

Audited and found correct.—R. H. MARKS, December 6th, 1907.

THE WORKING MEN'S COLLEGE JOURNAL *is supported partly by Annual Subscribers living in different parts of the World, and partly by circulation among the Students and Members. Its success depends upon a regular demand, and to ensure this, the Editor would be glad if as many readers as can will become Subscribers. Subscription 2s. 6d. per annum, post free.*

LONDON : Printed by W. HUDSON & Co., Red Lion Street, High Holborn, and published at THE WORKING MEN'S COLLEGE, Crowndale Road, London, N.W.—February 1st, 1908.

(due P. 145.4

THE WORKING MEN'S · COLLEGE JOURNAL ·

sub: 11

The Woßking Meps College: CROWNDALE ROAD · S? PANCRAS · LONDON · N·W·

FOUNDED IN 1854 BY THE LATE

Frederick Denison Maurice ·

Contents for

MARCH, 1908.

❖❖❖❖❖❖

Dante

Harmony

College Notes

Old Students' Club—
    On Nietzsche

Ruskin

THE

𝔚orking 𝔐en's 𝔠ollege 𝔍ournal.

Conducted by Members of the Working Men's College Crowndale Road, London, N.W.

Vol. X.—No. 180.   MARCH, 1908.   Price Twopence.

DANTE.*
(*Continued.*)

NOTHER point. Hitherto I have been concerned with the people whom Dante liked very much—with the woman, in fact, whom he loved most in the world. But how did he behave to people whom he did not much like, or only knew slightly—to his "bowing acquaintance," if I may use the phrase? Much as we do? No. Much worse. I do not wish to praise our own times over much, but this particular point brings out our strength and Dante's weakness. He was anxious for sublime thoughts; and if his acquaintances did not inspire him, he had no further interest in them, and treated them with discourtesy. He soared higher than we can; but he could sink lower. Here is an episode from the "New Life," which will make clear what I mean.

One day, Dante was staring at Beatrice as she sat in church. Between them sat another lady, who, being in the direct line of the poet's glance, naturally concluded that he was staring at her. Dante determined to profit by her mistake. He was desirous of keeping his love for Beatrice a secret. People knew that he was in love—he had already said so in a poem—but they did not know with whom   "What a good plan," he thought, "if I pretend to be in love with this lady, and so throw gossips on the wrong track. I shall be able to sigh and look pale, and yet no breath of scandal will touch Beatrice." In pursuit of this ingenious plan, he paid a certain amount of attention to the new lady, and wrote her a few poems. All went well, until she had occasion to leave Florence, and so placed the poet in an awkward position. He ought to have been overwhelmed with grief at her departure, but he did not care a straw. The lady was perfectly welcome to leave Florence, and to stop away from it for ever. His spirits remained admirable, but how was he to justify them to her and to her friends? I must again commend his ingenuity. He wrote her another poem, in which he said that his grief at losing her was so tremendous that he showed no outward signs of it at all. So the lady went, in full belief

---

* Paper read to the W.M.C. Literary Society by Mr. E. M. Forster, on November 21st, 1907.

that the young poet loved her; and not long afterwards he found another lady, and began playing the same game with her. He wrote so many poems to this second lady, and sighed to her so much, that he embarrassed the poor creature, and the matter came round to the ears of Beatrice. Beatrice was much annoyed. She seems to have had no idea that Dante loved her, and that these ladies were simply shields to conceal his love. She only saw that here was a young man who was persecuting a girl by undue attentions, and on that ground she withdrew her salutation from him. In modern phraseology she "cut" him, and surely he deserved it.

Now, the earnest student of Dante—who is sometimes rather an alarming person—will accuse me of flippancy on this point. He will say, and truly, that secrecy and subterfuge in love was a literary tradition of the time. True. Yet such a tradition shows a real defect in the minds of the men who adopted it. Let us suppose that Dante did invent the story. The fact remains that he is not the least ashamed of it, and has no notion that he is depicting himself as a "cad." Beatrice is the only woman to whom he owes loyalty—Beatrice, who leads his thoughts heavenwards. He can be false to all others, if he is thus enabled to be true to her. What duties has he to these other ladies? They cannot give him the keys of heaven. What duties has he to people whom he does not passionately love or intimately know? None. And here, I think, is the real defect in his noble character: he cannot be fair to the commonplace.

We of to-day—and I count Shakespeare one of us—try, however unsuccessfully, to look *at* people, not through them. We see our acquaintances as a throng of living creatures, some of whom are tedious, others unpleasing, others positively repugnant, but all of whom are living creatures, not to be injured wantonly. But Dante, in the "New Life," looked through people; and through most of them he saw nothing, and through one of them he saw God. Why should he trouble over the dull majority? Those sublime visions of his, to which none of us can attain, seem to entail these unmanly lapses, to which none of us, I hope, will sink. His answer to the question, "How shall I behave to the people whom I know?" is quite clear, but not, I think, quite satisfactory.

Up to now, we have been examining his personal relations. Now let us examine his relations to humanity, and find out how he behaved to the people whom he did not know. I want to make it clear that I am turning to another aspect of him, for otherwise you will think I am contradicting all that I have just said. In a few minutes I shall be praising his tolerance, his rectitude, his magnanimity—qualities that I have just denied to him. But between a man's behaviour to the people he knows and the people he doesn't know, there is often a wide gulf. Milton was tolerant when he wrote the "Areopagitica," but it did not prevent him bullying his daughters. Carlyle was magnanimous when he wrote the " French Revolution," yet he grumbled to Mrs. Carlyle when the cock crew or the study chimney smoked. And so Dante, though he did not behave well to people who bored him, would have laid down his life for humanity as a whole. He loved humanity as it was never loved again until the eighteenth century. His books are all written to make people better ; his life was one effort to guide the human assemblage into happiness and peace. His was no arm-chair devotion ; he suffered for his ideals, he remained in exile for them ; on their account he died. History has few spectacles more inspiring than Dante's public life. He is to be classed in the little band of men who were absolutely unselfish, and of that band he is by far the most talented member. If a man is unselfish and a genius, he has a very sure claim on immortality. Dante was both, and perhaps his position is unique in the history of the world.

He loved humanity. Then how did he propose to help it ? He tells us in the second of his great books, " The Empire." But before we examine " The Empire," I must make rather a long digression, for if I do not, the book will puzzle us completely. I must point out a second great difference between mediæval and modern thought.

Man consists of body and soul. So the middle ages thought, and so we think to-day. We agree with them. We believe that a material element and a spiritual element go to make us up. All religion, all philosophy, all science, acknowledges the fact. There are within us these two things. But—and here comes the difference—the middle ages thought that between the body and the soul one can draw a distinct line, that it is possible to say which of our actions is material, which spiritual. Body and soul, they thought, are as distinct as the land and the sea, or the earth and the sky, or the night and the day. Matter on this side ; spirit on that, and no connection between them. Each has its own duties, its own functions, its own laws.

Now I need hardly point out to you how different our attitude is to-day. He is a rash man who would assert where the body ends and where the soul begins. Some things are certainly material, just as the sky is certainly dark at midnight. Some things are certainly spiritual, just as the sky is certainly bright at noon. But between the two certainties there intervene the infinite gradations of twilight and dawn. Look at the sky in the evening. Can you be positive whether it is light or dark ? Look at an invalid. Can you be positive whether it is his body or his soul that is diseased ? Most modern thinkers realize that the barrier eludes definition. It is there. but you cannot put your finger on it, be you theologian or biologist. It is there, but it is impalpable ; and the wisest of our age, Goethe for example, and Walt Whitman, have not attempted to find it, but have essayed the more human task of harmonizing the realms that it divides. Not so the men of the middle ages, to whom we will now return.

They desired not to harmonize the body and the soul, but to find out where one stopped and where the other began. Matter on this side: spirit on that, and no connection between them. On the one side, Adam, in whom all die; on the other, Christ, in whom all shall be made alive. Both body and soul are made by God, but he has destined the body for mortality and corruption, and the soul he has destined for immortality. He has linked them together for a little space, to journey through this life in unwilling partnership. But their goals are different.

And having these beliefs, the men of the middle ages naturally turned for help to the greatest event in their past history. Surely Christ, during his ministry on earth, would have told them what to do. In this important question of the division between matter and spirit, surely he would have left them some example, some guide? And surely he had. When the disciples asked him whether they should pay tribute to the Roman tax collector, he had answered, " Render unto Cæsar the things that are Cæsar's, and unto God the things that are God's." Render unto Cæsar the things of the body, and unto God the things of the soul. In other words, Christ had acknowledged the civil power, and Christians must do the same. It is to the government that we must look to guide us in material affairs.

So far, there is nothing fantastic in the mediæval attitude. But they carried their reasoning further, and so plunged into fantasy. They concluded that Christ by the mere mention of Cæsar had given divine approval to the Roman empire, and appointed it as the peculiar guardian of men upon earth. They reflected that Christ had consented in his infancy to be numbered in the census of the Emperor Augustus; that the Apostle St. Paul had boasted he was a Roman citizen, and had appealed from the Jewish law courts to the judgment seat of Nero. The feeling grew that the Roman Empire had a divine mission to govern men's bodies all over the world; and that the Roman Emperor, though he might not know it, was ruling as the agent of God.

This in itself is a strange enough notion. But stranger is to come. When the Roman Empire was destroyed by the barbarians, there sprang up in course of time a *fictitious substitute* called the Holy Roman Empire, which was supposed to carry on its divine mission. As a matter of fact, it did nothing of the sort; you may sum it up as a gigantic fraud. The old Empire really had ruled the world; the Holy Roman Empire only ruled central Europe. The old Empire really had been Roman; the Holy Roman Empire, in spite of its name, was Teutonic. The old Empire may have been pagan, but it brought peace upon earth. The Holy Roman Empire may have been Christian, but it brought little but war. It is a fraud, and yet it is important, because it appealed to that mediæval belief in a sharp division between the body and the soul. Here was the Emperor, God's agent in governing men's bodies. And here was the Pope—for now the Pope comes forward—God's agent in governing men's souls. The Emperor would say to a man " do this," and he would do it. The Pope would say " think this," and a man would think it. Emperor and Pope would together illustrate Christ's precept, " Render unto Cæsar the things that are Cæsar's, and unto God the things that are God's." Here my digression ends. Let me sum it up in tabular form. Mediæval thought divides a man into (i.) the body, which dies, and which while it lives must take its orders from the Emperor; and (ii.) the soul, which is immortal, and which while it remains on earth must take its orders from the Pope. And now let us return to Dante.

Perhaps you will ask, " Why have we ever left him? What have these fantastic ideas to do with the great Florentine poet? My answer is, that though you and I do not believe in the Holy Roman Empire, Dante did; and that it seemed to him the visible channel of God's grace, and the only means of helping humanity on earth. If you said to Dante, " This Holy Roman Empire—it isn't a bit what you say it is. The Emperor's a German princeling; he daren't even come to Italy; he is not even a good man; the whole affair's nothing but a pretence."— if you said this, Dante would reply, " The Holy Roman Empire is ordained by God." If you continued, " But the Emperor and Pope have even quarrelled"; he would reply, " The Emperor and the Pope have both erred, but the institution, the Holy Roman Empire, is ordained by God." Dante was not a Socialist. Far from it. But his attitude can be compared to that of some socialists of to-day. He would not tinker at existing affairs, in the hope of improving them gradually. He must have a theory, and put it into practice at once, no matter how inopportune the moment was. He would save men through the Holy Roman Empire. Some socialists would save them through equality. The Holy Roman Empire was a dream; yet he spoke of it as ordained by God : equality, so far, is a dream, yet socialists speak of it as a natural right. Not for a moment am I blaming these passionate beliefs in a brighter future. But they are beliefs, not facts. They are not justified by history; and the men who hold them occasionally ignore the present and misread the past. So Dante did; so, I sometimes think, do certain socialists now.

Well, grant Dante his Holy Roman Empire. What is he going to do with it? I will quote from his treatise, " The Empire," the force of whose title you will now see. Granting that the Emperor is supreme, how will he lead us into earthly felicity? In the first place, he will give us Peace.

" It is by leisure," he says, " that each man grows sensible and wise ; and as it is for one man, so it is for all men : only by universal peace can humanity advance to its goal. When the shepherds watched their flocks by night, they heard not of riches, nor pleasure, nor honour, nor health, nor strength, nor beauty : but of peace ; for the celestial soldiery proclaimed Glory to God in the highest, and on earth Peace and Goodwill towards men."

There is nothing mediæval or out of date in this. Dante's words are as true to-day as when he wrote them. He never speaks of the beauties of war, like Ruskin or Rudyard Kipling. He has fought in battles himself, he knows what they are like. Peace is the only educational atmosphere for humanity; and peace can only be ensured by an international power, who shall keep the nations from flying at each other's throats. He called this power the Emperor, we call it the Hague Conference; but he, like ourselves, saw the necessity of an arbitrator, to whose decision the Jingo capitalist and the Jingo demagogue must bow, and under whose far-reaching power the myriads of the earth shall dwell together in unity.

And this brings me to his next point. When the Emperor has given us peace, what are we to do with it? We are to dwell together *in unity*; we are to realize the potentialities of the human race *as a whole*. Dante had a firm belief—you can call it right or wrong—that the whole is greater than the sum of its parts; that humanity is greater than the individuals who go to make it up; and that God would receive with a peculiar joy the praise of an united world. The belief verges into mysticism, but you may find it, though in different words, in writers of to-day, such as Tolstoi and Walt Whitman. Just as the city expresses something that the individual cannot express, just as the nation expresses something beyond the scope of the city; so humanity, were it ever united by peace, would express something far beyond the scope of either, and re-enter the terrestrial paradise, which was lost at the primal disunion. The terrestrial paradise is Dante's phrase for the highest earthly bliss, and the Emperor will guide us to it. Of the celestial paradise, in which humanity returns to God and has knowledge of the unknowable, he will speak later.

(*To be concluded.*)

MRS. JULIAN MARSHALL'S LECTURE ON "THE STUDY OF HARMONY."

ON February 6th, Mrs. Julian Marshall, to whom the College is indebted for more than one musical treat, interested a Thursday evening audience —in the Tansley Room—in the subject of Harmony. Previously Mrs. Marshall had held an examination of the class in vocal music conducted by Mr. Mason Tarr, and had considerately borne in mind the benefit to students, on occasion, of a general historical outlook on a main branch of their study. The lecture was of value to all interested in music. A wide view was opened, from the eminence of the lecturer's knowledge of the subject, and all details were made clear in the light of vocal and instrumental illustrations.

Harmony was defined as "notes in *combination* agreeable to the ear," melody being a pleasing *succession* of notes. To reason why the combinations of harmony are pleasing would be to go deep into the science of acoustics; enough, perhaps, to hear that no sound stands alone, that every note carries with it, in mysterious union, its own harmonics—faintly heard, or undistinguished and blended with the fundamental note; and that it is to these natural harmonious intervals that Harmony, joining theory to practice, has gradually felt its way. The prototype of our musical scale or "octave" was the Greek "gamut," which contained the same number of intervals, *i.e.*, five tones and two semi-tones ; but whereas Greek usage and, later, that of the Church had several MODES or *methods* of using the scale (starting on a higher or lower rung, as it were, of the musical ladder), according to which the tones and semi-tones altered their relative positions, modern practice employs two only—the bright and strong Major mode with the interval of a major third at the root of the chord, and the more tender and subdued Minor with the less concordant interval of a minor third as its chief characteristic. Of course "mode" should not be confounded with "key," which is a scale built upon the note from which the key takes its name, each key having its own major and minor modes.

Rudimentary harmony began, when a bass note of one pitch was employed as an accompaniment to a melody. Later, the bass note was made to rise and fall with the melody, attendant upon it as groom upon rider, with the interval of a "fourth" between ; "fourths" being considered the only perfect concords. Then it was found an improvement, if melody and harmony moved with greater freedom, no longer as master and servant, but co-ordinates, each having a tune, but together making harmony. This was counterpoint, *i.e.*, note against note ("point" meaning note), two melodies jointly performed. Subsequently, the conception of "chords" arose, combinations of three and four notes mostly at concordant intervals, but sometimes including intervals which had previously been considered discordant ; the newer view being that discords were not necessarily ugly or incompatible, but that music could not linger or finish on such chords, which required "resolution," *i.e.*, carrying on to some other combination more satisfying and restful. An example was given of the value of these "doubtful" notes. The chord of the "dominant seventh" contains a note, the "seventh," which at first rejected as discordant, has since found a place, to the great enrichment of the effect. While clearly indicating the key to which it belongs, the chord emphatically calls for "resolution," and so forms a means of transition, a stepping-stone in turn through the whole circle of keys.

The lecture was illustrated at various stages by chords on the piano ; and members of the audience were invited to put their knowledge to the test by naming the major and minor varieties, but, like the maidens of the village in the *Sorcerer*, they were "distinctly coy." However the ladies, who were kindly helping Mrs. Marshall, sang specimens of harmony, ancient and modern, and it was easy to imagine that there must be a tendency to perfect harmony in women's voices, inasmuch as—so Mrs. Marshall said—they unconsciously substituted, for some of the specimens of the bare, bald concords which satisfied the old monks, the sweeter and more euphonious harmonies which modern ears demand. Then in four-part harmony, examples of the "dominant seventh" were rendered ; and the audience sang one of Mrs. Marshall's published part-songs, and the lively "Lass of Richmond Hill," also in four parts. For unrehearsed efforts the effect was, we think, not at all unsatisfactory.

In conclusion, we cannot do better than to quote, as correctly as may be, a few of the musical "dicta," some of which, doubtless, each of the audience carried away. "Music is a language, and Harmony is its grammar." "To know Music, we must hear, read, and write it, as we do any other language." "Harmony students should realize the effect in sound of what they see or write on paper, and should write down what they hear." Mrs. Marshall commended Tonic Sol-fa, but thought that to advance far, it was necessary to know also the Old Notation. Almost the last piece of advice was—"Get to know what is your key-note or 'doh,' but learn also to recognise the absolute intervals without reference to the key." G. B. S., in "Cashel Byron's Profession," says—"I am no musician, but I'll just show you how a man that understands one art understands every art."

Perry, from the chair, presented the very hearty thanks of the audience to Mrs. Marshall, who acknowledged them graciously ; and we are fain to think that a pleasant evening was spent on both sides, lecturer and audience mutually interesting each other. C. F. M.

COLLEGE NOTES.

THE sum of £98 0s. 6d. has been collected towards supplying the wants of the Library, for which £150 will, in all, be needed for immediate purposes.   A list of donors is appended.

	£	s.	d.		£	s.	d.
Skinners' Company	21	0	0	F. O. Smithers	5	0	0
Clothworkers' Company	21	0	0	Louisa Marshall	5	0	0
Mercers' Company	20	0	0	Sir Charles Lucas, C.B.,			
Merchant Taylors' Company	10	10	0	K.C.M.G.	5	0	0
W. Minet	10	0	0	Edward Upton	0	10	6
					£98	0	6

The College is much indebted to Mrs. R. B. Litchfield for the gift of several large parcels of books to the Library.

Mrs. Winkworth has kindly presented to the College an oil painting, "The Sons of Toil, a scene near Mount's Bay, Cornwall," well painted by Stanley Barwell, and handsomely framed, and she also sent £1 to defray the cost of having it glazed.

The Executive Committee having sent congratulations to Professor Westlake upon his having attained the age of eighty, he wrote the following letter :—

Dear Mr. Jacob,—I have been greatly surprised by the number of friends from whom I have received kind wishes, but from none have they been more welcome than from the Executive Committee of the Working Men's College. We are united in a common spirit, and can look back on a common achievement, while looking forward to the growth of that achievement in the future as the sure effect of that spirit.   Will you kindly let the Committee know of my gratitude to them for thinking of me, and of my hope that I may yet be able to be among the members of the College for occasions which, whether they are to be few or many, will be prized?   I have had the pleasure of a letter from Professor Dicey, who associates himself with the resolution of the Executive Committee.   Thanking you warmly for your personal kind expressions,—   I am, yours very sincerely,

February 5th, 1908.   J. WESTLAKE.

On the same occasion the University of Oxford conferred upon Professor Westlake the honorary degree of D.C.L. (Feb. 11th).   The *Times* reports the speech of the Regius Professor of Civil Law, Dr. Goudy, made upon the presentation, recounting Professor Westlake's long and distinguished legal career, his succession to Henry Sumner Maine in the chair which he still adorns at Cambridge, his labours in the cause of peace, his distinction as a master of International Law, his being a representative of England at the Hague Conference, and his recent books.

An article by Professor Westlake on the Hague Conference appeared in the January issue of the *Quarterly Review*.

The *Albany* for January contained an allegorical story by Mr. E. M. Forster, entitled "The Celestial Omnibus"; and in its February number appeared an article by Mr. G. P. Gooch, M.P., on the "Prospects of the Session."

The Common Room Committee have arranged a Students and Teachers' Meeting to be held in the Common Room, on Monday, March 2nd, at 9.30 p.m., when Mr. J. P. Emslie will speak of his "Reminiscences of Ruskin." It is proposed to hold a smoking concert during the latter half of the meeting.

The annual general meeting of the W.M.C. Convalescent Home Society will be held in the Coffee Room, on Monday, March 9th, at 9.30 p.m., when Mr. J. J. Dent will take the chair, and all members of the College are cordially invited.

The member of the College at present enjoying the benefits of a stay at the Convalescent Home at Pegwell Bay wrote to some College friends thus :—

Kindly forward me the November and December JOURNALS, so that I may know a little more of how things are going. It is hard to be away from that in which a fellow is interested, though I was never with you so much as I should like to have been ; and when I remember that while being one of the newest students at the College, it is nevertheless through the College that I am now enjoying such immense benefit as my stay at this splendid Convalescent Home affords, I am indeed made to feel deeply grateful, and long to be in two places at once,—here and at Crowndale Road. . . . . Mr. and Mrs. Boyland and the staff generally are very kind to me, and all the residents seem to be thoroughly pleased with the treatment they receive.

The Custodian of the Common Room wishes to draw attention, through the medium of the JOURNAL, to the hat and coat stands in the Common and Coffee Rooms, provided for the use of the members, some of whom appear to prefer to deposit their hats and coats elsewhere than on the pegs. The Custodian would be glad to sell, second-hand, the following periodicals : —*Daily Graphic, Fortnightly, Liberty Review, Model Engineer, Musical Opinion, Positivist Review, Punch, Ueber Land und Meer, University Correspondent, Times.*

There are still a few lockers to be let. Apply to the Custodian, M. Staal, or to E. S. Landells, Hon. Sec., Common Room Committee.

The Leicester (Vaughan) Working Men's College is making a special appeal to their Leicester and other friends for annual subscriptions. It is hoped that when the College is established in its new building, it will be able to work more economically, and will only require about £250 a year in addition to fees and grants.

Listening to Mrs. J. Marshall's lecture on "Harmony," it seemed—writes our reporter—that the art of Music helped us to understand other arts, and more especially, music being *the* language of emotion, the great art of Life. Nor need we fear, with John Stuart Mill, who for a time fell into sadness for this reason, that its possible combinations are exhaustible. While human emotion continues, Music will remain one of its voices, and harmony may be its deepest tone.

OLD STUDENTS' CLUB.

THE INFLUENCE OF NIETZSCHE.

At the third meeting of the club for the present session, held in the Common Room on Saturday, February 15th, Mr. RICHARD WHITEING opened, as the subject for discussion, "What is the influence of Nietzsche in politics, literature, and art?" The chair was taken, as usual, by Mr. R. H. MARKS, president, and there were also present Messrs. T. Austin, J. T. Baker, T. M. Balson, H. V. Birrell, A. A. Bourne, Sydney Bradgate, E. A. Brett, J. C. Castell, C. Castle, A. W. Coombs, S. J. Coombs, John Dale, G. Davenport, W. J. Davis, Robert Eason, W. R. Emslie, Harold Eyers, J. F. Frewer, W. J. Gray, C. Godfrey Gümpel, S. Hamilton, W. P. Harley, E. A. Harrison, E. Hayward, A. Hepburn, S. G. Hersbank, S. J. Hertford, Wm. Hudson, Lionel Jacob, V.-P., W. F. Jennings, E. W. Jones, C. P. King, James Kirk, T. Krauss, A. Levett, J. McWilliam, H. Manton, C. Monteath, E. Murphy, A. H. Perry, Leonard Pocock, E. Pointin, C. W. Rapley, J. Gerald Ritchie, J. W. Roberts, R. Robson, F. C. Roper, W. J. Spray, M. Staal, F. G. Sweeting, H. Trott, G. Wanklin, Herbert Wilcockson, C. R. Williams, and G. E. Winter.

Mr. MARKS introduced Mr. Whiteing as the well-known author of "No. 5, John Street" and other works, whom we were proud to claim as an old student of this College, which he joined about 1857, in which year Mr. Marks also entered as a student in the preparatory classes.

Mr. WHITEING, who was received with cheers, said :—The position of Nietzsche is a sort of all-pervading one just now. It is not so much the position of a man who stands out so that anyone may see him ; his is rather a kind of cryptic influence, that runs pretty well all through some of the best literature of the day. You will find traces of him nearly everywhere. I need not say how much Bernard Shaw is inspired by him. Many of his writings are Nietzsche, straight from the well. We see Nietzsche's influence, too, in some of the great political movements, such as anarchy and nihilism. His admirers claim that he has revolutionized, or is revolutionizing, European thought in all the great subjects of the time, particularly in philosophy and art. That is a great claim. I think at any rate part of it must be allowed. I do not say he is revolutionizing for the better, at this stage, but he is effecting a change. His teaching is something like this. He wants us, he says, to upset, to reverse, all our old sense of values in philosophy and in life ; to give us new ideals—no, I must not use the word "ideals"—he protests against the word,—to change our convictions with regard to pretty nearly everything we have regarded as settled. He comes with a sword to destroy ; his is a work of sheer destruction right through. He starts by destroying morality at once. There is, for him, no such thing, or there ought not to be such a thing, as morality. He says it is a sure sign of a people being in a state of decay, that they have moral notions. With morality, goes religion—Christianity. Christianity, in one of his most startling paradoxes, is nothing but a most ingenious scheme for introducing into the world pity for the weak and suffering. They ought not to be pitied. The only service you can do to them is to destroy them—or let them die out. The great object of life is to produce strong, independent, individualistic persons, who owe no allegiance to any moral or religious idea. Any idea of pity—any idea of any kind that would tend to impair the all-pervading vitality and energy of his system, is to be renounced. The man that Nietzsche has in view as an ideal is an entirely forceful and irresponsible person, who thinks of one thing only.—to develop his own strength, and particularly to develop his own will-power. The Nietzschian conception of life is a modification of the original conception of Schopenhauer—we need not trace it further back than that. As we know, Schopenhauer said that life is simply "will"—the will to live, that is the one thing we are concerned with ; we live not by obedience to any law ; we live simply and solely by the will to live. Nietzsche agreed that that was a very good thing indeed, but he would add something more—the will to power. For what is the good of living simply to live ? The great thing you have to think of, the object and aim in life, is power—power in and for itself ; that is the end of man—to be powerful. According to Nietzsche, that sense of power, that necessity for power, brings with it a morality of its own. His objection to our ordinary morality is that it is supposed to be eternal, immutable, everlasting ; a great truth, discovered once and for ever, from which there is no departure. Nothing of the sort, he says, the real truth is that all the morality you want, all the guiding principle you want, is one that depends on circumstances. In one age those things that are the vices, were the virtues of the past. As you go on, you make a morality for yourself. So, live as you are, strong, and with a necessary contempt and horror of that weakness that stands in the way of strength, and you will be constantly adjusting your morality to the circumstances of the age. In his system the greatest severity, the utmost reprobation, is reserved for the Christian faith ; for it makes the enormous mistake of altogether displacing the point of view, of making the point of view one of compassion, and the preservation of those weak organisms we ought to destroy. He goes on to say that not only was the Christian faith originated by a Jewish people for a definite purpose, but it was one of the most deadly strokes dealt at the Roman Empire. The Jews, passing from one oppression to another, felt they could never meet this great strong world unless they demoralised it ; and so they invented Christianity, and it answered its purpose, for it brought down Rome ; it introduced, instead of the stern virtue of the Roman people, the weakness of compassion, and now, in consequence, the Jews are the masters of the world. That is one of his delicious paradoxes. And he is quite full of those paradoxes, which, however, he gives you with every appearance of the most perfect good-faith. Another thing which he insisted on very strongly was the introduction of what he called the Dionysian spirit in the world. The old Dionysian spirit, including the worship of Bacchus, not merely as the god of wine, but as the vivifying spirit of all nature—the spirit and principle of joy—meant living from the instincts, instead of according to the reason. The key of Nietzsche's system lies in this : we make enormous mistakes in trying to live according to our reason ; he says you cannot live by it, you must live from the instinct of life in you, purely as a child lives ; and if you have lived as a community according to that principle, everything will come to you quite easily and simply. As it is, the poor old world is completely given over to all the weaknesses that come from the loss of the old spirit of instinctive action. The original man, that man who has been made to do duty in so many systems, like Rousseau's savage, lived according to his instincts, and a very fine fellow he was. He lived as the animals lived, and took the consequences. We poor children of this later time are all hide-bound by our moral systems ; we feel the want of all the spring and go that come from instinct. The end and aim of all is the production of a superior person—of that super-man we should all live and strive for. · Our politics, literature, and art—are they tending to produce this superior breed of man ? This man is a sort of ideal of Nietzsche's own. He acts according to his own instincts, divested of all moral restraint, and he represents the next upward move of man. The phase of evolution is this, that man, created by his morals and reason, is played out ; we are now to think only of producing this breed of superior persons, who will destroy the world, or renew it, and have a good time.

Mr. WHITEING proceeded to illustrate the philosophy of Nietzsche, by quoting his words from a "splendid" little book, published by Foulis, "Nietzsche in Outline and Aphorism," by Orage, the editor of *The New Age.* Nietzsche was particularly proud of his literary style. He aimed at redeeming German prose from its heaviness, and to give it the perfect grace of French and the best English prose. As a writer, he had the greatest admiration for Emerson, and he endeavoured to introduce the epigrammatic style into German. He tried to say everything as briefly as possible, aiming at terseness and point, like Emerson. Here are a few of the quotations, beginning with some definitions :—"Sin, the moral interpretation of physiological depression. Redemption, the moral interpretation of physiological recovery." "Mankind *en masse* sacrificed, in order to ensure the growth of a single stronger species of man—that *would* be progress." "Pity—an agreeable emotion of the

instinct of assimilation in its feeblest aspect." "Sin—a Jewish invention."
"Good conscience—sometimes so like a good digestion as to be mistaken
for it." "Look at these superfluous. They steal the works of inventors
and the treasures of wise men ; their theft they call education. Diseased
they are ; they vomit bile, and call it newspaper." "Convictions are more
dangerous enemies to truth than lies." "In all things one thing is impossible,
reasonableness." "No, life has not deceived me. I find it, on the contrary,
year by year more rich, more desirable, and more mysterious—ever since the
day there came to me the great liberator, the thought that life might be an
experiment for the seeker after knowledge ; not a duty, not a fatality, not
a sham and a fraud. 'Life as a means to knowledge,' with this principle in
one's heart, one can not only live bravely, but with joy and laughter." "To
have to combat instincts—that is the formula for decadence : so long as life
ascends, happiness is identical with instinct." "Life is something essentially
immoral." "The secret of a joyful life is to live dangerously." His
contribution to the question of the suffragette : "Man shall be educated for
war, and woman for the recreation of the warrior. Everything else is folly."
(Laughter.) "Thou goest to women ? Remember thy whip." "Not to be
able to take seriously for a long time an enemy, or a misfortune, or even
one's own misdeeds—is the characteristic of strong and full natures." "Not
your sin, your moderation crieth unto heaven." On Art :—"All art," he
says in one place, "is either ascendant or decadent, either leads the will
upwards to increase and power, or downwards to decrease and feebleness."
"All noble art, with all noble religion, breathes gratitude for life ; all
ignoble, decadent, and vacuous art breathes the atmosphere of the chambers
of sleep and death. Great art is a song of praise, an overflowing of life
back to its source, a dithyramb of thanksgiving and gratitude. Decadent
art is, at bottom, a criticism and a complaint ; its root is resentment ; it
turns wearily from life, and would fain lay down the burden of living."
On morality :—"On the day on which with full heart we say : 'Forward
march ! our old morality too is a piece of comedy !'—on that day we shall
have discovered a new complication and possibility for the Dionysian drama
of the 'fate of the soul.'" "There could be no greater, no more fatal
misunderstanding than if the happy, the well-constituted, the mighty in
body and soul were to begin to doubt their own right to happiness." "Life
would be intolerable, but for its moral significance ! But why should not your
life be intolerable ?" "Morals are perpetually being transformed by successful
crimes." "If man would no longer think himself wicked, he would cease
to be so." "Remorse is indecent." "Punishment does not purify, because
crime does not soil." "The means of conserving a superior race are the
means of destroying the inferior race." "The idealist conceals facts from
himself ; the liar from others." "Every triumph of an ideal has been a
retrogressive movement." Of good and evil :—"Aristocratic equation of
values : good = noble = powerful = beautiful = happy = beloved of God.
Plebeian equation : good = wretched = poor = lowly = sufferers = sick = ugly =
beloved of God." "What is good ? All that increases the feeling of power,
will to power, power itself, in man. What is bad ? All that proceeds from
weakness." The Super-man : - "Not 'How is man preserved ?' but 'How
is man surpassed ?'" "He is to come, the redeeming man of the great love
and great contempt, the creative spirit, who, by his thronging power, is ever
again driven away from every corner and other world." "The problem is,
what type of man we are to *cultivate*, we are to *will*, as the more valuable,
the more worthy of life, the more certain of the future." "To women :
Let your hope be called, 'Would that I might give birth to Super-man.'"
Some new commandments :—"Be not virtuous beyond your ability." "It
is better to act wickedly than to think pettily." "If ye have an enemy,
return not good for evil, for that would make him ashamed." "Be sure
to love your neighbour as yourselves, but first of all be such as *love
themselves*." "Higher education and great numbers—that is a contradition
in terms."

Those, continued Mr. WHITEING, are a few of his gems. Perhaps we
ought, in order to understand Nietzsche better, to take the circumstances of

his life. Born in 1844, he was the flower of the German university system—a great student, especially in philology, in which subject he held a very important chair at Basle. He came into close touch with Wagner, who he felt was going to glorify musical art by introducing into it all those conceptions which his disciple had brought into philosophy. He lived for 56 years, and for the last twenty years of his life he was a hopeless invalid, or what is still more serious, a hopeless madman. The greater part of that time he spent in an asylum. The case was not one of hereditary weakness, but his mind went all to pieces. The first of his works gave a clue to his system. The " Birth of Tragedy " was a glorification of the Dionysian spirit—the spirit of joy in the world, absolute joy, absolute want of responsibility, or the sense of responsibility. He said that the Dionysian worship had really been the making of Greece ; and that what ruined Greece was the spirit of the worship of reason, introduced by Socrates, one of the greatest enemies of culture. He brought in reason, and reason killeth everything. Then he wrote much on "values." He urged the reversal of all values. He said, I am going to take all these things you call values, such as morality, and I am going to reverse them, and say they are non-values, and to put true values in their place. In his writings, he puts into the mouth of Zoroaster his own axioms and aphorisms. In one ludicrous fable, he makes Zoroaster go to a fair and see a tight rope, along which an old man is walking gingerly, when an energetic young man with incredible rapidity runs along the rope behind him, and overtaking him, leaps clean over his head, so disconcerting the old man that he falls and is killed. The old man is morality, and all other things of an effete age ; the young one is the spirit of the coming time. In Nietzsche's relations with Wagner, there happened the same thing as in his relations with most people. He always hated or admired in extremes. He adored Wagner, and his praise of him had very much to do with the establishing of Wagner's position in Germany. He went to the first of the great Bayreuth festivals ; but the composer was busy with his festival and did not pay proper attention to Nietzsche. This was enough. He tried to find a better reason for his quarrel with Wagner, when the latter set to work on " The Holy Grail," a Christian myth in music. He declared he had done with Wagner. The same thing happened in his relations, not only with other persons, but with literature itself. His life was strewn with quarrels. To sum up, it seems to me we must come to one of two conclusions about him—it is impossible to take qualified views : either he was the greatest philosopher of all time, or, he was " cracked." I think that an integral part of the study of the man is the fact of his sad ending. His brain was undoubtedly the brain of a genius, but it was a magnificent penny-in-the-slot that would not work ; something was wrong with it. Put an idea in, and it went all over the place, but it did not come out right. Max Nordau very honestly grappled with the problem, when he described him as a "degenerate." He was all sorts of other things, some very great, but he was "wrong." I accept Nordau's estimate, with the addition, that Nietzsche was an *ego*-maniac. The extent to which he was occupied with himself is something almost inconceivable. He was extremely pre-occupied with the fact that he was descended from a Polish nobleman. He went to Poland to establish his claim. Pride and intense personal pre-occupation are characteristics of the insane. Let us look into his ideas, and ask how it was that primitive man created morals ? He must have been extremely dissatisfied with his original instinct, or he would not have started to create. Morality is the only thing we have been trying for, and we are everlastingly getting a little nearer to it. So far from it being true that morals have had their day, the real truth is that they have never yet had their chance at all. We have only yet got to the state that morals, the government of reason, the government that puts a restraint on actions, is just beginning to have a chance. So that he is by himself convicted of a grave inconsistency in the presumption that lies at the root of his own system. Instinct has always been tried ; morals, never. We are trying to give morals their chance to usurp the place of instinct. (Cheers.)

The VICE-PRINCIPAL, after referring to the consummate literary skill with which Mr. Whiteing had put his subject before us in such an interesting and lucid way, said there was a great advantage in having our fundamental beliefs now and again turned inside out. It did not follow that such a man as Nietzsche taught anything of positive utility, but good came from his teaching, because it made us think. We ought not to take too much for granted, as we were rather apt to do. Some of his trenchant sayings had a certain amount of truth. His idea that art was here to make us happy, reminded the speaker of a criticism of Lamb's, "Reading this play makes us happy, and too few of the Elizabethan dramatists thought of that." The greatest art did not make us happy, as did "A Midsummer Night's Dream," —"King Lear," for instance. With regard to morality, some people were too apt to regard it as something that was a restraint always. They spoke of the ten commandments as though they contained the whole of morality, but one did not need to read very much further than them in the Bible alone, to see that they did not cover the whole field ; morality consisted quite as much of positive things which we ought to do, as of mere negations. Living according to instinct was the negative of everything that makes man man, and makes him different from the beasts. The ordinary philosophers, however, who incited Nietzsche to revolt, dwelt on reason as though reason were everything. But reason came late into our lives. We started with instinct. Pascal had told us, "People say you must know before you love— that is the way of the world, but," he said, "the true sense is that you must love before you know." And we all did love before we quite knew—from childhood onwards. If children were to wait till they knew their parents, or parents were to wait till they knew their children, before loving, the whole world would fall to pieces. So, for ordinary philosophers, Nietzsche was of some value. It was most useful and stimulating to us all to have such a challenge thrown down as Nietzsche had given, to old beliefs which we had taken for granted ; and doubly useful was it to have the challenge shown, with such a keen appreciation of the issues at stake on both sides, as had been done by Mr. Whiteing. (Cheers.)

Mr. WILCOCKSON pointed out that the result of merely obeying animal instincts had just been exemplified in the case of the convicted Von Veltheim. There were, too, some Sicilian players now in this country who acted a native drama, in which natural instincts were followed without restraint, leading to a terrific quarrel, in which one of two rival lovers got his throat cut. That was another example.

Mr. KRAUSS, speaking as a fellow-countryman of Nietzsche, said he thought we ought not to take him as a teacher, but rather as a poet—as a stimulator. We should not place his actual phrases under a magnifying glass. He suffered much, under disease and weakness ; hence, perhaps his glorifying of the strong. Whilst not agreeing with all his sayings, he appeared greater if regarded as a stimulator, than if we dissected his aphorisms. (Hear, hear.)

Mr. HARRISON agreed, and also with the Vice-Principal. It was good to be shaken up sometimes. He supposed there was eternal truth—eternal morality—certain broad lines of life which would be valuable for us so long as humanity lasted ; but there was a tendency for us to get quiescent and too much inclined to obey authority without question, to stick to the letter rather than to the spirit of morality. The world was constantly growing, and it was always necessary to re-adapt the principles of life, as we found it in our age and generation. The real question for us to consider was whether the ideas or the forms of morality which we at present worshipped, made for efficiency of life, generally speaking. If not, we must re-adjust them.

Mr. W. R. EMSLIE agreed with the Vice-Principal, particularly because the principles of Nietzsche were so much at variance with those of the Founder of this College, who had endeavoured to put within our reach an education which would enable us to think for ourselves. In that respect the address of Mr. Whiteing was especially valuable. It was refreshing to listen to his exposition of principles so utterly at variance with our own ideas.

Mr. SPRAY, upon Nietzsche's proposal to remove the suffering and the weak, considered it would be most humane to painlessly put an end to the lives of all hopelessly incurable or insane persons.

Mr. HEPBURN was not at all inclined to accept the attitude adopted by the speakers in the debate. He thanked Mr. Whiteing for a subject so ntensely serious and suggestive. It was possible to regard Nietzsche not merely in an apologetic way, nor as one to be laughed at. He could not understand that view of him. He spoke with hesitation in the presence of grave and reverend signiors—until they ceased to be grave. To his mind the Nietzschian philosophy represented what very few men had taken the trouble to make - a carefully reasoned-out scheme. How did a child learn to lie? The first lie was told to avoid punishment. Left to itself, the child would be truthful. So far, morality did not seem to have anything to its credit. The ideas of Nietzsche were not his alone. He would defy any man to find, in William Morris's "News from Nowhere," any action which was not actuated by instinct, and instinct alone. Our founder was our founder because he wanted to be. "All actions," says Krapotkin, "proceed from a man's desire to give himself pleasure." Men act, not according to moral code, but according to their instincts, as governed by their state of intellectual development. [Mr. HARRISON : I hope Mr. Hepburn did not understand me as opposing Nietzsche out and out. I do not suggest he is altogether wrong.] Mr. Hepburn intimated that he took the whole of Nietzsche seriously.

Mr. GERALD RITCHIE said he had been struck with the great similarity between Nietzsche's fundamental pessimism and that of Buddhism. Some of his ideas appeared to have been borrowed from the Indian philosophy. Buddha was a philosopher, utterly discontented with life, who, searching about for a way to solve its enigmas, thought out a philosophy which had been adopted by a large proportion of the human race in the further East. His fundamental basis is, that ignorance is the source of all evil, and that man has it completely within himself to develop his own nature. On looking around him in the time in which he lived, he rejected the whole of the religion of India—rejected the eternal Deity—and laid down the dicta that all existence was bound up with sorrow, that all sorrow comes from desire, and that the only way to extinguish the misery of human life was to put an end to desire. Starting from that point of view, he worked out the very beautiful and well-known moral code of India to-day, which is practically the code of Christianity. Another point that Buddha insisted on was that it was absolutely necessary to get rid of the elusion of self ; till one did that, one was not in a proper state to regard anything properly. Now, Mr. Whiteing had pointed out that the *ego* was the very foundation of Nietzsche's philosophy. Therefore it was interesting to note this extreme contrast between the two thinkers. Setting out upon like errands, from similar causes, it was curious to observe that these two—one in the past ages long ago, and the other in the present stage of advanced Western thought—had arrived at directly opposite conclusions. Both were thinkers of extreme genius. One had succeeded in getting untold millions of people to believe in him ; what Nietzsche would do remained to be seen. (Cheers.)

Mr. GÜMPEL thought Nietzsche's influence had as yet been but small. With regard to his illness, it originated in the Franco-German war, in which he assisted in attending to the wounded, and worked so hard, and with so little regard for himself, that he contracted a kind of influenza. Desiring not to give in to his illness, he dosed himself with medicine so strong that it affected his brain. His principal works were written before that time. He was the personification of egoism ; Buddha was the personification of altruism. Nietzsche's pessimism only began in the later years. Buddha started from the suffering he saw human beings were subject to. Nietzsche was an artist, rather than a philosopher. He was a genius who felt his mental powers cramped. He felt there was something in him, and he brought it out in moments of impulse, in aphorisms, in that spasmodic way we had heard illustrated. He, Mr. Gümpel, hoped Nietzsche's system would never come to pass, for he was himself an altruist to the very core. (Cheers.)

Mr. HARLEY asked for information as to Nietzsche's personal nature—the incidents of his life. He hoped his influence had not affected Bernard Shaw.

Mr. WHITEING replied. As had been said by several, Nietzsche was a great stimulator, and that was the right way to look upon him. He was primarily an artist-poet, and not a dogmatic philosopher with a system. One must take a man of that kind with a sort of allowance ; not look too closely into his every utterance. As to whether he had influenced politics, etc., he (Mr. WHITEING) would say *passim!* all through. Certainly you would find traces of his influence in most of the programmes of the more advanced political thinkers of our day. It was at the root of all philosophic anarchy. It was not necessarily and primarily for blowing things up and destroying them. But it did get away from the concept of a hard and fast law, to a concept of freedom. In that sense it was a very great influence, entering into the ideas and utterances of nearly every advanced thinker. " We are governed too much," said an American humorist. That view was implied in many of the speeches we had just heard. Leave people alone, and their best would come out. As to his influence on Shaw, in the prefaces to the latter's plays, we found the leading ideas were that we must get rid of the obsession of the idea of morals, and elevate instinct to its proper place. In the main, in his philosophy Shaw is Nietzsche, as in his drama he is Ibsen It was amazing that Shaw should have the power he possessed of estimating the truths they taught, and giving those truths an exposition far exceeding in value that of their original authors. As to art, we had seen Nietzsche's influence on Wagner, who found the support he needed in the brilliant advocacy of Nietzsche, and who led the revolution in music. In literature, his influence was extensive, if select, and very much more on the Continent than here. It chimed in with our modern movement ; society, democratic or aristocratic, was impatient of law, impatient of restraint. We could not even get a man comfortably hung, without petitions to save him. There was extreme opposition to anything that weighed hardly upon the individual ; there was discrimination in sentencing criminals, discrimination between first and second offences ; all the growing reaction against the severity of the law was Nietzschian—though in his case not from pity ; it was a reaction of contempt for law. The principle underlying " News from Nowhere " is nothing in the nature of precept or obligation. Nietzsche has done an enormous service in lifting up the too-much-discredited ideas of our too-much-discredited nature. He has restored instinct. But restored instinct is no more a force than our discredited morality is a force. Life is the union and the harmony of great forces, and each one is liable to fail ; as law has often failed, so instinct has failed. Man began with instinct, and his very instinct forced him into the codes. Instinct would again force us back upon codes ; they would be revised codes, but codes after all. (Cheers.)

FURNIVALL CYCLING CLUB.

THE annual general meeting of this club will be held in the Club Room on Saturday, March 7th, at 8 p.m., Dr. Furnivall in the chair. It will be preceded, at 6.30 p.m., by a supper, the inclusive price of tickets for which is 2s. All members proposing to be present at the supper should communicate at once with   W. MELZER, *Hon. Secretary.*

FURNIVALL SCULLING CLUB.

SUNDAY, February 9th, was the day fixed for one of the club's yearly grand functions, the tea to its president, Dr. F. J. Furnivall, in honour of his 84th birthday, Tuesday, February 4th. There was a good muster of members in the morning, and the sculling eight, two sculling fours, and a light double went up gaily against tide to Richmond, while seven members walked across the Park to the New Inn, at Ham Common, where they all dined.—[For fuller notice, see next month's JOURNAL.]

THE STUDENTS' CALENDAR FOR MARCH.

Sun., 1st.—Lecture, "The Hebrew Prophets," Rev. B. H. Alford, 6 p.m. Shakespeare Reading, "Romeo and Juliet," 7.30 p.m., ladies' night.

Mon., 2nd.—Chess Match, Maurice v. St. Martin's (G.P.O.), 8 p.m. Students and Teachers' meeting in Common Room, Mr. J. P. Emslie on "Recollections of John Ruskin in the Working Men's College," 9.30.

Tues., 3rd.—Executive Committee, 8 p.m. Lecture, "Italian Painters," Mr. Dudley Heath, 8 p.m. Debating Society meeting, 9.30.

Thurs., 5th.—Citizens' lunch, 1.30. Lecture, "The Fundamental Principles of the Law of the Constitution," The Principal, 8.30.

Fri., 6th.—Lecture "Child Study," Dr. J. W. Slaughter, 8 p.m.

Sat., 7th.—Lecture, "The English Poor Law System," Mr. A. D. Steel-Maitland, 8.30. Furnivall Cycling Club's supper, 6.30, and annual general meeting, 8 p.m.

Sun., 8th.—Lubbock Field Club walk from Barnet to Hatfield; special tickets, 1s. 5d., of hon. secretary at King's Cross Station (G.N.R.); Train starts 9.11 a.m. ; provide lunch. Lecture, "The Hebrew Prophets," Rev. B. H. Alford, 6 p.m.

Mon., 9th.—Convalescent Home Society's annual general meeting, 9.30.

Tues., 10th.—Executive Committee, 8 p.m. Lecture, "Italian Painters," Mr. Dudley Heath, 8 p.m. Debating Society meeting, 9.30.

Thurs., 12th.—Lecture, "Socialism—its Sociological Aspects," Mr. T. B. Browning, 8.30.

Fri., 13th.—Lecture "Child Study," Dr. J. W. Slaughter, 8 p.m.

Sat., 14th.—Old Students' Club meeting, the Principal opens on "Would the Referendum be suitable and practicable in this country?" 7.45. Chess Match, Finsbury Park v. Maurice, 8 p.m. Lecture, "The Playwright and the Public," Mr. Alfred Sutro, 8.30.

Sun., 15th.—Lecture, "The Hebrew Prophets," Rev. B. H. Alford, 6 p.m. Shakespeare Reading, 7.30.

Tues., 17th.—Executive Committee, 8 p.m. Lecture, "Italian Painters," Mr. Dudley Heath, 8 p.m. Debating Society meeting, 9.30.

Thurs. 19th.—Lecture, "Co-operation—its Methods," Mr. T. B. Browning, 8.30.

Fri., 20th —Lecture, "Child Study," Dr. J. W. Slaughter, 8 p.m.

Sat., 21st.—Lecture, "The Social Ideal," Mr. G. Lowes Dickinson, 8.30.

Sun., 22nd.—Lecture, "Hebrew Prophets," Rev. B. H. Alford, 6 p.m.

Mon., 23rd.—Chess Match, Lud-Eagle v. Maurice, 8 p.m.

Tues., 24th.—Executive Committee, 8 p.m. Lecture, "Italian Painters," Mr. Dudley Heath, 8 p.m. Debating Society meeting. 9.30.

Wed., 25th.—Chess Match, Maurice v. Railway Clearing House, 8 p.m.

Thurs., 26th.—Lecture, "Co-operation—its Results," Mr. T. B. Browning, 8.30.

Fri., 27th.—Lecture, "Child Study," Dr. J. W. Slaughter, 8 p.m.

Sat., 28th.—25th Collegians' Dance, 7 p.m.

Sun., 29th.—Lecture "Hebrew Prophets," Rev. B. H. Alford, 6 p.m.

Tues., 31st.—Executive Committee. 8 p.m. Lecture, "Italian Painters," Mr. Dudley Heath, 8 p.m. Debating Society meeting, 9.30.

Announcements of coming events for insertion in the Students' Calendar should, if possible, be communicated to the Editor by the 20th of the month.

- ◆-◆-◆ -

THE "MARKS" PRIZE.

This Prize, to be awarded annually in books to the most successful competitor, is open to all students, and is this year offered to the writer of the best essay on either of the following subjects :—(a) Discuss Shakespeare's view of Democracy, especially as exemplified by the plays of " Julius Cæsar " and " Cariolanus "; (b) Criticize the view that the characters of Dickens are caricatures. Essays are to be sent in by April 30th.

SATURDAY NIGHT LECTURE.

JOHN RUSKIN.

On November 16th last, Miss Spurgeon gave a most excellent lecture in the Maurice Hall on a subject of great interest to all members of the College —"John Ruskin." The chair was taken by Dr. Furnivall.

Miss Spurgeon expressed the pleasure she felt at being able to speak to us about the man who was, for the first ten years of the life of this College, very closely connected with it. Not only did he for about five years of that time teach Drawing regularly to the students here, but some of the most magnificent and vital writing ever penned by Ruskin formed, as it were, the very basis and starting point of this movement, and was indeed issued as its manifesto. She meant the well-known chapter on "The Nature of Gothic," in the second volume of *The Stones of Venice.* She believed she was right in saying that at the opening lecture of this College, 53 years ago, on October 30th, 1854, Dr. Furnivall distributed to everyone present a reprint of this chapter, which had been written the previous year, and which was an exposition of the conclusion which the study of Art had forced on Ruskin— "the dependence of all human work or edifice for its beauty, on the happy life of the workman." It was this chapter which William Morris came across at Oxford, and which first set fire to his enthusiasms and kindled the beliefs of his whole life. Morris looked upon it as one of the most important things written by Ruskin ; and said of it that in future days it would be regarded as one of the few necessary and inevitable utterances of the nineteenth century. For some fifty years of that century, Ruskin whole-heartedly and devotedly spent himself in every direction, freely giving the best of his marvellous powers of observation, mind, feeling, and expression, for the benefit of the race. He poured forth, voluminously and unreservedly, his views on Life, which were, after all, in the last resort, very simple, and capable of being summed up and expressed in one or two short sentences. For Ruskin was beyond and above all else an ethical teacher ; and amid all his manifold tastes and interests—and no man ever had more—the supremely interesting and vital topic for him, as for Plato, ever was, "What is the best way to live?" In all the eighty odd volumes he had left us, on every conceivable topic : Painting, Sculpture, Architecture, Drawing, Political Economy, Mythology, Education, Geology, Manufactures, Botany, Landscapes, Poetry, Literature, Philosophy, Ethics, Theology, History—in and through all these subjects, which were but different aspects or facets of the one great subject, Life, he was giving his answer to that question, enforcing it, enlarging it, and driving it home with a passion of feeling, a richness of style, a profusion of imagery, and a melody of rhythm and words, which was at times unsurpassed by any writer, ancient or modern. Ruskin himself once said that if he announced a lecture on "Mineralogy," he was pretty certain to come round in it to "Cistertian Architecture" ; while a lecture on "Cistertian Architecture" would most probably open with problems of Minerals! This extraordinary, almost unparalleled, range of subjects was not a proof of Ruskin's lack of concentration, and rambling habit of mind, but rather, in his hands and under his treatment, was it a proof of his unfailing grip on the wider issues of things, of the root problem which gives rise to all other problems—in short, of his instinctive knowledge of the underlying Unity of Life. It did not matter what Ruskin was treating of nominally—Mineralogy, or Cistertian Architecture. He could not speak of any of these things for five minutes, without getting back to what lay at the centre of them all—the purpose of Life, and how man might best act so as to help fulfil that purpose. Ruskin's philosophy of Art, resolved into its simplest terms, was merely this, that all good Art was the expression of good life ; his Political Economy, as summed up in his own words at the end of "Unto this Last," again resolved itself into the same thing : "There is no Wealth but Life—Life, including all its powers of love, of joy, of admiration. That country is the richest, which nourishes the greatest number of noble and happy human beings ; that man is richest who, having perfected the functions of his own life to the utmost, has also the widest helpful influence, both personal and by means of his possessions, on the lives of others." In everything of which he treated, however diverse apparently, he invariably returned to the same point, the sacredness of individual life ; and the supreme importance for all of us—whether as individuals or as a nation—of having, first, as clear a conception as might be of what Life was, and our function in it as individuals ; and secondly, of striving to the uttermost of our powers to fulfil that function, to realize our potentialities, so that we might be to the utmost "available to life," to use his own phrase. Two qualities were eminently needed rightly to understand Ruskin. The first was that sense of humour which carried with it a still more important sense—a sense of proportion. The second was an intellectual quality, the understanding that great truths could only be realized through apparent contradictions ; and that it was indeed an unfailing test of the greatness of a man's thought, of its width as well as its depth, that the nearer it approached to truth, the more paradoxical, the more, in one sense, contradictory, did it become. This was a strange statement, but a true one ; and was merely a recognition of the fact that Truth was a living thing. and that words were but the extremes or poles through which she passed, now from light to shadow, and again from shadow to light. Ruskin was keenly aware of this fact, and often referred to it : " There is not any great principle," he said, " which has not as it were, two natures in it, at least two different colours or sides, according to the things in connection with which it is viewed." Perhaps his most delightful remarks on this point were those in his Cambridge Inaugural Address, where he said :— " Perhaps you have heard that I am rather apt to contradict myself. I hope I am exceedingly apt to do so. I never met with a question yet, of any importance, which did not need, for the right solution of it, at least one positive and one negative answer, like an equation of the second degree. Mostly matters of any consequence are three-sided or four-sided or polygonal, and the trotting round a polygonal is severe work for people anyway stiff in their opinions. For myself, I am never satisfied that I have handled a subject properly till I have contradicted myself at least three times, but twice must do for this evening. I have just said that there is no chance of our getting good Art, unless we delight in it ; next I say, and just as positively, that there is no chance of our getting good Art, unless we resist our delight in it. We must love it first, and restrain our love for it afterwards. This sounds strange, and yet I assure you it is true. In fact, whenever anything does not sound strange, you may generally doubt it being true, for all truth is wonderful. But take an instance in physical matters of this same kind of contradiction. Suppose you were explaining to a young student in Astronomy how the earth was kept steady in its orbit ; you would have to state to him, would you not? that the earth always had a tendency to fall to the sun, and that also it always had a tendency to fly away from the sun. These are two precisely contrary state-ments for him to digest at his leisure, before he can understand how the earth moves."—Equipped with a sense of humour and of proportion, and a realization that only in the reconciliation of apparent contradictions could truth be found, we were in a position to appreciate and not to misunderstand Ruskin. There was but one way thoroughly to understand him, and that was by studying very patiently the growth of his mind as expressed in his books, or in a fair and well chosen selection of them. We must be prepared for difficulties, inconsistencies, obscurities. It would have been very convenient, if Ruskin had prepared a short explanatory text-book of his views—con-venient, but not so profitable for his students. As well might we wish that Plato had left us a handbook of his philosophy, or that Shakespeare had appended notes to Hamlet !

Miss SPURGEON devoted the greater part of her lecture to placing before us some few of Ruskin's leading ideas with regard to education—ideas, she thought, of such perennial value, that it seemed to her they could scarcely be repeated too often. He devoted a great amount of thought, especially in later years, to problems of education. This arose quite naturally out of his work as a social reformer. For what distinguished him from all other social reformers was his repudiation of all merely external methods of reform— institutions, laws, and so on ; and his insistence on individual and social character, as the means and the end. He had written a great deal throughout his books on education, but those books most directly connected with it were "Sesame and Lilies," "A Joy for Ever," "Fors Clavigera," and an admirable chapter in "Time and Tide."

Education, he told us emphatically, did not consist in learning a lot of facts; but in training and developing our own powers of seeing, aspiring, and loving.

Education was learning how to live. In the fifth letter of "Fors," Ruskin says there are three material things, not only useful, but essential to life, pure air, water, and earth. There are also three immaterial things, not only useful, but essential to life, Admiration, Hope, and Love. Admiration, the power of discerning and taking delight in what is beautiful in visible form, and lovely in human character; and necessarily striving to produce what is beautiful in form, and to become what is beautiful in character. Hope, the recognition of the foresight of better things to be reached hereafter; and Love of family and neighbour, faithful and satisfied. Ruskin took this line of Wordsworth's, "We live by Admiration, Hope, and Love," for his literal guide in all education; and the main teaching of all he had written, he said, was contained in it.

The lecturer put before us Ruskin's insistence upon the right use of the eye and the sight, and upon the morality of taste, illustrating her remarks by apt quotations from his works. Finally, she pointed out that his greatest work would be in the nature of stimulus and inspiration, and a general heightening and spiritualizing of standard. The way in which we could best follow Ruskin, and the greatest honour we could do him, was to strive to do and labour as he did; and to do, however humbly, some honest piece of work, into which we might throw our whole soul.

SHAKESPEARE READINGS.

"MEASURE for Measure" was read on January 19th.

On February 2nd, by the kind invitation of Mrs. Jacob, "A Midsummer Night's Dream" was read at her house; Mr. Jacob and the Misses Jacob taking part in the reading. The ladies were in the best form, and the wrangle between Hermia and Helena developed some unexpected capacity for shrewishness in our fair readers. Miss Steele read for the first time in our circle. After the reading, we were hospitably entertained by Mr. and Mrs. Jacob.

On February 16th, "Two Gentlemen of Verona" filled the bill. Changes in the cast at the last moment, due to absentees, militated in some measure against a good reading; but Paterson and Hayward as Speed and Launce delighted us all, and redeemed the evening from dullness. After the meeting, the chairman read a letter from the Executive, granting the prayer of the society to allow our alternate meetings to be ladies' nights. Hence the next reading will be graced by the presence of the fair sex. "Romeo and Juliet" is to be the play.

The society is always ready to welcome new men, and hopes all will remember that the readings are timed to start at 7.30. May I add that Paterson would be glad to receive subscriptions for postages, etc. (1s. per session, voluntary).   W. J. GATES FOWLER.

THE WORKING MEN'S COLLEGE JOURNAL is supported partly by Annual Subscribers living in different parts of the World, and partly by circulation among the Students and Members. Its success depends upon a regular demand, and to ensure this, the Editor would be glad if as many readers as can will become Subscribers. Subscription 2s. 6d. per annum, post free.

LONDON: Printed by W. HUDSON & Co., Red Lion Street, High Holborn, and published at THE WORKING MEN'S COLLEGE, Crowndale Road, London, N.W.—March 1st, 1908.

THE WORKING MEN'S · COLLEGE JOURNAL ·

sub: IV

The Working Men's College

CROWNDALE ROAD · ST PANCRAS · LONDON · N·W·

FOUNDED IN 1854 BY THE LATE

Frederick Denison Maurice ·

Contents for

APRIL, 1908.

Dante
Cycling Club
Field Club
College Notes
Mrs. Tansley's
Concert
Saturday Night
Lecture

THE

Working Men's College Journal.

Conducted by Members of the Working Men's College
Crowndale Road, London, N.W.

Vol. X.—No. 181.   APRIL, 1908.   Price Twopence.

DANTE.*
(*Concluded.*)

AND by the side of this common goal, Dante admits an individual goal. He believes in national and local life; his Emperor is not to introduce a gray cosmopolitanism. Mankind united is not to mean that men are dull. The Emperor is to suppress war, not personality. Our bodies are not to be absorbed into a machine on earth, any more than our souls will be absorbed into a machine in heaven. Even in the next life we shall retain our personality, so why should we lose it in this? It was harmony, not monotony, at which Dante aimed; and I wish I could say the same for the social reformers of to-day. These, excellent as they are, seem to see no path between monotony and war— between the bloodiness of Mr. Rudyard Kipling and the grayness of Mr. Sidney Webb. It is only the poet who points upwards, and offers humanity the example of the stars. Men, like stars, differ from each other in brilliancy. Let them also imitate the stars' harmonious motion.

> Happy, O men, were ye,
> If but your souls were swayed
> By love, as heaven is swayed

—sings the Latin poet, whom Dante quotes. Mankind shall attain salvation through harmony; and the love of humanity, like the love of Beatrice, has led us to the love of God.

It may interest you to know that this is not mere "fine writing." Dante actually suffered for these ideals, unpractical as they may seem to you. Early in his exile, when Florence and all Italy were distracted by war, he thought that the Emperor of his dreams was at hand. Henry of Luxembourg, known to history as the Emperor Henry VII., invaded Italy to restore peace and to establish the Holy Roman Empire, in fact as well as in theory. He was a high-souled monarch, and for a time Dante was hopeful. The Emperor occupied Milan, and advanced southward; and the poet, with increasing excitement, worked in his interests and execrated his enemies. Florence, Dante's own city, beat the Emperor back. The expedition

---

* Paper read to the W.M.C. Literary Society by Mr. E. M. Forster, on November 21st, 1907.

failed, the Emperor died, and things were even worse for Dante
than they had been before. I am not dealing with his life, but
this incident so clearly shows that he practised what he preached,
that it cannot be omitted. In all that Dante writes we have a
feeling of security. It may be tiresome and it may be wrong,
but we may be certain that he really meant it, and would have
died to put it into practice.

We may take it, then, that his book "The Empire" is a
practical offering to humanity, and deals with a question the
interest of which is perennial, namely, the destiny of our race
on earth. Dante believes that as yet we have accomplished
only a fraction of what we could accomplish ; that we have
fallen short of the will of God—to put it in his words ; or, to
put it in modern words, that we are only at the beginning of our
evolution. He believes that for this accomplishment we need
peace and unselfishness ; and that progress begins when a man
turns from the pleasures he must enjoy alone to the pleasures
that he can share with his fellows.

> True love hath this, differing from gold or clay,
> That to divide is not to take away

—wrote Shelley, 500 years afterwards, directly echoing Dante's
words. Repeatedly does Dante warn us against greed, against
setting our desires where companionship is one with loss ; that
is to say, against too great desire for personal possessions.
Don't label him as a socialist. He has a profound respect for
property and rank ; it is harmony, not equality at which he aims ;
and the evils against which he fought are political rather than
economic. But compare him to the socialists in this : he has a
passionate belief that things are not all right as they are, and
that all is *not* for the best in the best of all possible worlds.
The best would come when the divergent types of men
acknowledge some element that makes them one, when national
life is combined with international peace. This state of
material happiness Dante figures by the earthly paradise, where
Adam and Eve dwelt before greed and selfishness had entered ;
and hither, he tells us, we shall be led by the Emperor, appointed
for that purpose by God. Here of course the glorious fabric of
his aspiration falls. There never was such a person as Dante's
Emperor, and there never will be. The Hague Conference,
feeble as it is, has more international power than Henry of
Luxembourg, or the other German potentates for whose coming
the poet so ardently longed. The machinery through which he
would achieve his Utopia is impossible ; but the Utopia remains
as not only one of the most beautiful schemes of the kind, but
also as one of the wisest. It would be hard to find a more just
discrimination between the forces that make men alike and the
forces that make men different—between the centripetal power
that may lead to monotony, and the centrifugal power that may
lead to war. These powers are reconciled in the orbits of the
stars ; and Dante's first and last word to us is that we should
imitate the celestial harmony.

I have spent so much time examining Dante's attitude towards men, that I must be comparatively brief over the question that he deemed all important—his attitude towards God. To him this question is supreme; the things that he knew seemed of little importance, when compared with the Unknowable. Beatrice and the Holy Roman Empire were not ends in themselves, but alike means, by which he could approach the Divine. And thus the "Divine Comedy" is in every sense the greatest book that he wrote—not only because it contains his best poetry, but because it is about the subject that he thought greatest, our behaviour to the Unknowable. The "Divine Comedy," like the "Pilgrim's Progress," takes the form of a journey to God. Dante imagines himself as travelling through the three spiritual kingdoms of Hell, Purgatory, and Heaven, until he actually sees the Love that lies behind the Universe and moves the stars—until he actually knows the Unknowable.

[Mr. Forster here explained, by means of a diagram, the imaginative journey which Dante describes in his book.]

Perhaps the quickest way of getting some idea of the "Divine Comedy" is to realize Dante's conception of the universe, and of that I now propose to give a short account. In his mind, cosmography and theology were closely connected; he believed that one could step out of the material world into the spiritual, as we believe that we can step out of one room into another; hell was really under his feet, heaven was really over his head among the stars. He is perfectly definite; it is even possible to draw a diagram of the universe as he conceived it.

His conception, then, was as follows: In the middle of all things he placed the earth. He believed that the earth was round, but he also believed that it was motionless, and that the sun and the stars revolved round it. He conceived of Hell as a great funnel extending to the earth's centre, and at the centre he placed the Devil. On the opposite side of the earth, *i.e.*, in the Southern Hemisphere, he thought there was a great mountain—Purgatory—where those souls who would ultimately go to Heaven purged away their sins. Heaven consisted of ten circles, the first eight being ruled by the sun, the moon, the five planets, and the fixed stars; the ninth being the *primum mobile*, or moving heaven, which communicated motion to the heavens inside it, and so caused them to revolve round the earth; and the tenth, or Empyrean, being outside time and space altogether, and the abode of reality and of God.

Such was the framework on which he built the "Divine Comedy"—quite definite, and he is equally definite as to time. He imagines himself entering Hell on Good Friday, rising from the dead on Easter Sunday, as did Christ, and entering Purgatory; entering Heaven on Easter Tuesday, and concluding his vision on the Friday after Easter. The action takes a week. As for the date: it is supposed to be the year 1300—the year that modern historians fix as the end of the middle ages. Of course the book itself was written some time after 1300, and thus Dante often refers to events that had actually happened, such as the death of Henry VII., under the guise of prophecy.

As Good Friday approaches then, Dante imagines himself on the surface of the earth, pursued by three wild beasts, who typify the sins of luxury, avarice, and pride. From these beasts he is rescued by the Latin poet, Virgil, who had been sent to his help by a "lady from heaven," *i.e.*, by Beatrice, and who tells him that only by entering the gates of Hell will he get free. The two poets accordingly enter Hell, whose funnel is divided into nine circles, which increase in torment as they decrease in size. This is the most famous part of the poem, and the dramatic episodes of Paolo and Francesca, of Farinata degli Uberti, and of Count Ugolino, are known to thousands who have never followed Dante through the less exciting realms of Purgatory and Heaven. The horror of Hell reaches its climax in the apparition of the devil, a monster with three mouths, in each of which he champs a sinner. The centre mouth holds, as we might expect, Judas Iscariot, but the contents of the other two mouths are somewhat surprising. The sufferers are Brutus and Cassius. We are bewildered until we reflect that Brutus and Cassius murdered Julius Cæsar, the founder of the Empire, just as Judas Iscariot murdered Christ, the founder of the Church ; and that Dante would desire to punish those who did not render unto Cæsar the things that were Cæsar's, quite as severely as those who did not render unto God the things that are God's.

A grotesque episode succeeds. The poets, who have now approached the centre of gravity, take hold of the Devil and begin to climb down his legs; presently they pass the centre of gravity, and find themselves climbing *up* his legs, towards his feet, and after a toilsome ascent, reach the surface of the earth at a point exactly opposite to that at which they went in.

The second part of the poem now commences. Dante and Virgil find themselves standing at the foot of the mountain of Purgatory, which is washed by the waters of the Southern Ocean. It is dark ; then the sun rises, and over the sea a ship approaches, full of redeemed souls who land in the dewy meadows and hasten to their purgation. From the smoke of Hell, Dante has passed to the purity of an earthly morning; and if I had to describe the atmosphere of Purgatory in one word, I think I would say, "cleanliness." Not "rapture," or "knowledge," or "love"; those will be found in Heaven—just the state of cleanliness, through which we must pass before other sensations are possible.

Purgatory consists of seven terraces, on each of which souls undergo an expiation appropriate to their sin. On the summit of the mountain, the highest point on the terrestrial globe, lies the earthly paradise, the goal of our highest earthly effort. You will remember Dante's allusion to it in "The Empire." And here Virgil can go no further. He is not a Christian, and cannot guide his friend to the higher mysteries. In a scene of great pathos, the two poets part, and Virgil goes back to his place in Hell, not to the circles of torment, but to a border region reserved for those gentle heathen who have died without the knowledge of Christ. Now Dante sees a great procession, typifying harmony of the Empire and the Church. In the procession is a shrouded figure who finally unveils herself; it is Beatrice. Thus the whole of Dante's life is, as it were, joining up; the promise he made in "The New Life" is fulfilled; the teachings of "The Empire" is illustrated by the procession; and the Poet, who has no more concern with material affairs, leaves the earth altogether and, with Beatrice as his guide, rises through the encircling belt of fire to Heaven.

We have come to the third part of the poem. Those readers who chiefly admire Dante's dramatic power will find this, the climax of the "Divine Comedy," disappointing; in the realm of bliss we are concerned with sensations rather than with personalities. But those who have followed the poet's spiritual yearnings with due attention and with sympathy will find here a sublime fulfillment, and will perhaps think that the "Heaven" contains the most wonderful words ever written by the hand of man. Dante's account of spiritual happiness and of God has a curious effect on one, which I can only describe as "authoritative"; it seems as if he really did know, as if he has really been outside time and space, and has come back to us with news. To quote his teacher, Aristotle, he has really made "the impossible credible." I have already described the ten heavenly spheres through which he and Beatrice pass, and I will not say more about them now; the poem concludes with a hymn to the Virgin Mary, who in her turn intercedes for him with God. God appears to him as Light; but at the last moment Dante's gaze is strengthened; he sees something even more vivid than light. Three rainbow circles glow against the radiance of Eternity, and in the centre of one of them is the image of a human face.

The vision closes. Dante returns to the earth. He has seen the Love that lies behind the universe and moves the stars.

Here my paper ends. I am afraid that you will find it a little remote, a little hard to follow in parts. There are several reasons for this, one being that it is not a good paper. A second reason, less painful to myself, must also be taken into account, and I will lay it before you, as a conclusion. Briefly put, it is this: Dante tries to look at human affairs with the eyes of God. His standpoint is not in this world. He views us from an immense height, as a man views a plain from a mountain. We, down on the plain, have our own notions of what the plain is like, and at times we reject Dante's description of it as false. We feel that by his very elevation he is not qualified to judge; and that he knows no more about us than we know about the canals in Mars. Here we are wrong. Dante knows a great deal about us. He was himself a soldier, a politician, a scholar, and a lover, and he never forgets his experiences. We are wrong, and yet it is natural that we should find him hard to follow, for his standpoint is not one that we find congenial to-day. Shakespeare stands among us. Though he has walked into Paradise with Queen Katharine, and into Hell with Macbeth, he has also walked with Falstaff into the taverns of Eastcheap. Though Shakespeare is a sublime poet, he is also a jolly good fellow ; and if he walked into this room this evening, we should be very glad to see him. But Dante stands with unwavering feet upon the Empyrean, proclaiming the will of God ; and though his words are full of love and beauty, they gather a certain terror as they pass through the interspaces, and they fall with a certain strangeness upon our ears. We enjoy reading Dante. But if *he* walked into the room this evening, we should make all haste to walk out of it.

FURNIVALL SCULLING CLUB.

To resume our account of the club's doings on February 9th, when Dr. Furnivall's birthday was celebrated : on our way up to Richmond, the double was off first, with Harry Payne stroke, Kate Lock bow. Then came a four, Reglar stroke, Gillies 3, Williams 2, Owen bow, Connie Read cox. Next followed the eight, with Peckham 8, Webb 7, Ethel Allen 6, Mead 5, West 4, Emmie Sewell, 3, Dawson 2, Dr. Furnivall 1, Seamon cox ; and soon after it, catching it in Richmond Lock, came the second four, Hoad 4, Munro 3, Will Allen 2, C. Richardson 1, Jack Sewell cox. To greet the eight on its return, Mr. George H. Radford, M.P. for East Islington, was on the raft with his son ; and soon after arrived Mr. Munday of Putney Hill, with two of his daughters, and a fine birthday cake with Dr. Furnivall's initials, " F. J. F." over its white-sugared surface. The crews joined the large party of over sixty upstairs at tea. Several married couples, old members of the club, turned up, Mr. and Mrs. Jackman, Mr. and Mrs. Colesby, Mr. and Mrs. Bushell, Mr. and Mrs. Hume, Mrs. Manton, etc. After the tea, Jack Munro, in one of his usual happy speeches, proposed the club's congratulations to Dr. Furnivall on starting his 84th year ; and read a pretty dedication to Dr. Furnivall by Dr. Roman Dyboski, of his edition of some early carols and songs in the press for the Early English Text Society. This thanked the Doctor for his sympathy and help ; and these qualities, said the speaker, were shown to everybody who came into contact with Dr. Furnivall, whether learned or not, as all the Club well knew. Needless to say the proposal was adopted by acclamation ; and Dr. Furnivall, in thanking his friends for it, said he little thought, when he first brought some six or eight girls into the room, that the club would have such success and obtain such world-wide fame as it had done through the girls' unique racing sculling eight. The turning point of that success was the joining of a lot of rare good fellows from the Working Men's College, headed by Tom Colesby, who first suggested the buying of an eight. To the Hammersmith men like Will Hume, Corney Clarke, Charley Richardson, and others, the Club was also greatly indebted, while the girls were the real charm of the place. He then spoke of the work of the coming season. After Mr. Radford and Mr. Munday had spoken, the tables were cleared away, and dances, songs, and recitations followed. Songs were given by Messrs. Reglar, Payne, Oberst, McLatter, C. Richardson, Miss Frances Forsyth, and others ; and recitations by Miss Daisy Deane, Tom Barnard, and Mr. Gallagher. Miss Alice Dewar gave a mandolin solo. Mr. Inkersole kindly played for the dances and accompanied the songs.

STUDENTS AND TEACHERS' MEETING.

ON Monday, March 2nd, at 9.30 p.m., a meeting was held in the Common Room to hear Mr. J. P. Emslie give some of his Recollections of Ruskin, in whose drawing classes he was a student in the early days of the College. The meeting was arranged by the Common Room Committee, and was a success in every way. The chair was taken by Mr. A. B. Shaw, M.A., and the Common Room was crowded with students and teachers, the Vice-Principal and several other members of Council being also present. Mr. Emslie is the brother of Mr. W. R. Emslie, our well-known teacher of geography, Euclid, and other subjects, and of Mr. A. E. Emslie, the distinguished portrait painter who formerly conducted the College art classes. These three gentlemen are the sons of Mr. John Emslie, who was one of the earliest and most earnest students and teachers in the College in the days of its foundation. It was a great pleasure to welcome Mr. Emslie in the Common Room, and to hear him read his paper on "John Ruskin"—a paper which proved so full of interest, that at its conclusion the request was made, through Mr. Shaw, that it might be printed in the JOURNAL, and this was kindly acceded to by Mr. Emslie. It is proposed to publish the paper in the succeeding numbers.

At the conclusion of Mr. Emslie's address, a hearty vote of thanks to him was proposed by the chairman, and carried with acclamation.

Then followed songs by Messrs. F. E. Lawrence, E. C. Duchesne, C. F. Marshall, M. K. Field, and others, and recitations by Mr. T. Barnard, forming a pleasant ending to a very interesting evening.

THE COLLEGE MAN'S TOAST.*

HERE's the health of our friends! may their joys increase
    Fair concord around and an inward peace;
With mirth and good-fellowship's moving power,
    May they pass at this Social a genial hour.

In the College man's world there is room for mirth,
    For wisdom is strengthened by pleasure's birth;
And albeit our years may be many or few,
    We may sweeten their flow by a blend that is true.

So good-bye for the nonce to our wonted trend
    Of lectures and classes and tasks without end:
To mild contemplation now bid we adieu,
    As 'tis meet on occasion for e'en sages to do.

To walk in due rhythm with duty and joy,
    Is treasure in pleasure with nought of alloy:
So we'll each bring our quota of greeting or glee,
    Glad speech, elocution, or grand harmony.

                                    G. S.

    * Lines written after reading the JOURNALS containing reports of the Old Students' Club and Joint Clubs' Suppers.

THE "MARKS" PRIZE.

THIS Prize, to be awarded annually in books to the most successful competitor, is open to all students, and is this year offered to the writer of the best essay on either of the following subjects:—(a) Discuss Shakespeare's view of Democracy, especially as exemplified by the plays of "Julius Cæsar" and "Coriolanus"; (b) Criticize the view that the characters of Dickens are caricatures. Essays are to be sent in by April 30th.

FURNIVALL CYCLING CLUB.

THE annual supper and general meeting were held in the Coffee Room on March 7th. The supper, which was due at 6.30, did not begin till 7 p.m., when twenty members sat down to a good feed, provided by Mrs. Robbie. It is about time a College man recognized that a supper or meeting announced for 6.30 is not intended to take place half-an-hour later. This want of punctuality seems to be a habit with College men, very difficult to cure.

At 8 o'clock, Dr. Furnivall, chairman, called upon the hon. secretary to read the report and balance sheet for the past year, the thirteenth of the club's life. The report set forth that out of 28 proposed runs, 26 were carried out, the average attendance being 15, one better than the previous best. The ladies' prize was won by Miss Grace Grinaway, with 86 points. Melzer won the men's prize with 114, the next best scores being those of Wildey, 108; and Young, 102. The club's chief tours and outings were referred to, including the visit to Mr. and Mrs. Denmead's at the Red House, South Mimms, on July 6th, when a very fine tea and a delightful musical evening were much enjoyed. Opportunity was also taken by the Committee to report the marriage of their vice-president, Mr. W. C. Jones, and Miss Minnie Grellier, both of whom had been staunch supporters of the club, and to wish them every happiness and prosperity.

Two proposals were brought before the meeting by Mr. Randall. One, that donations should not be asked for, but that only the ordinary subscription be accepted from the president and vice-president, was lost; but the other, that the Executive Committee be asked to consent to ladies being present at the general meeting and supper, was carried, amidst cheers.

Dr. Furnivall was re-elected president, and Messrs. Julius Jacob and W. C. Jones, vice-presidents. The following were also elected:—Captain, P. Cowling; vice-captain, W. B. Gant; committeeman, A. J. Wildey; and hon. secretary and treasurer, W. Melzer.

The evening concluded with songs by Lawrence, Nye, Balson, Staal, Randall, Howard, Wildey, and Peckham.

The opening run to The Cocoa Tree, Pinner, will be held on Saturday, April 11th; meet at Swiss Cottage or at Shepherd's Bush Empire, at 4.30 p.m. sharp. All College men and friends are invited. Bring music.

At Easter the Club is again going to Brighton; further particulars may be had from the hon. secretary.

Other runs are:—Saturday, April 25th, Ewell; Sunday, May 3rd, Croxley Green; Saturday, May 9th, Harrow Weald.

W. MELZER, *Hon. Secretary.*

BALANCE SHEET, 1907—8.

Receipts.	£	s.	d.	Expenditure.	£	s.	d.
Balance forward	1	12	6	Printing and stationery ...	1	1	8
Donations :—Dr. Furnivall	0	10	0	Club Supper Expenses ...	0	2	6
J. Jacob ...	0	10	0	Maps	0	8	0
Subscriptions : 35 members	1	15	0	Notice board frame ...	0	1	6
do. 18 honorary do.	0	18	0	Cost of 12 badges ...	1	4	0
Sale of 7 badges	0	14	0	Postages	0	8	10
8 badges unsold	0	16	0	Final run expenses ...	0	2	4
				Locker rent	0	2	0
				Surprise run prize ...	0	5	0
				Attendance prizes ...	1	0	0
				Cycling	0	4	0
				In hand { Badges 0 16 0 / Cash 0 19 8	1	15	8
	£6	15	6		£6	15	6

Audited and found correct, W. H. BARNETT.—March 6th, 1908.

LUBBOCK FIELD CLUB.

THE February walk brought out a party of thirteen. The district visited is a favourite one with the club, the starting place being Horsley. On leaving the station, we followed the road due south, until we emerged on Netley Heath. Passing through the woods, and diverging from the Gomshall-track, we reached the open on the summit of Hackhurst Downs, and after a short pause to admire the view below us, descended to the road at Abinger Hammer. Here we found a most convenient inn, and accordingly halted for lunch. That important matter disposed of, we continued in a southeasterly direction by a path which brought us to Sutton. In this part of Surrey, the lanes are, by far, more beautiful than the field paths, and that running down to Felday is one of the best. Passing through the latter village, the guide spent much time considering the possibility of including the top of Leith Hill in the journey, but had reluctantly to abandon the idea. Turning north, we passed through Parkhurst to Abinger, where those new to the neighbourhood were introduced to the stocks. We then crossed the railway at Leasers Barn, and took the direct road to Effingham, having a long wait for the rearguard at the top of the hill. On reaching the "Blucher," we halted for tea, and considering the short notice given, did exceedingly well. Thereafter we had ample time to catch the 6.15 train at Bookham, having covered a round of some eighteen miles.

The day was mild and fair on the whole, although we experienced one shower. On the sand the roads were in their usual good condition, but here and there we found a stretch of heavy going. On Netley Heath the gipsies were offering primroses for sale, but otherwise, with the exception of the Arum and Dog's Mercury, there was little sign of the approaching spring. Of course, in the sandy lanes, mosses and ferns flourished in abundance. Of animal life we saw little. A squirrel detained us awhile on Netley Heath, and certain water bugs were carried into captivity.

Considering the unpromising appearance of the weather, the attendance on the March walk was very good, eleven men meeting at High Barnet at 9.50 a.m. The route followed was a most devious one, and several members hinted a doubt as to whether the country explored was worthy of the time spent over it. Had the footpaths been passable and the original plans adhered to, the verdict would probably have been quite otherwise. We passed through Barnet, and turned off by Hadley Church, taking the road to the north of the Common, Beech Hill, and Trent Park. Shortly after crossing the Ridgway, the guide went astray, owing to building operations rendering his map useless, and led the party through the slums of Chaseside, before recovering the track at Clay Hill. We then crossed White Webbs Park, and followed the road round by Sanders Corner to Goff's Oak, where we lunched. The route then lay across what was once Cheshunt Common, until we reached a private road leading into Derry Wood, which, after some discussion, we resolved to explore. The result was disastrous, as after wading through mud and water for about half-a-mile, we lost our track, and had to retreat again to the solid road. The weather was so threatening and the country so uninviting, that we then decided on making a desperate rush for the 4.40 train at Potters Bar. Accordingly, we climbed the hill to Newgate Street, and then toiled up and down the series of hills that form the road by Northaw Wood, the Ridgway, and Northaw, to the main road at Potters Bar. Nine of us just caught the train, and were not sorry to rest after our long round. The weather was very threatening all day, but we had little actual rain. The roads were walkable, but the less said about the paths the better. Vegetation appeared to have gone backward rather than forward during the month, the one capture of interest being Azolla.

J. HOLLOWAY, *Hon. Secretary.*

BOOKS RECEIVED.—"Building," for January, 1908, published in Sydney, N. S. W.—"The Prevention of Sudden Death from Internal Causes," by C. Godfrey Gümpel, from the author, an old student of the College, published by Watts & Co., price 6d.

COLLEGE NOTES.

The January term ends on Saturday, April 4th, and the third, or April, term begins on Monday, April 6th. The Easter vacation extends from Thursday the 14th, to Wednesday the 22nd inst., inclusive.

At the last meeting of the Old Students' Club for the winter session, held on March 14th, the Principal opened, in his usual lucid and enlightening style, a discussion on the question whether the Referendum is desirable and practicable in this country. There was a goodly muster of members and an instructive debate, of which we hope to give a report next month.

Mrs. Tansley's Concert, on February 29th, was in every way a great success, and it afforded much pleasure to a large and appreciative audience. The College is much indebted to Mrs. Tansley for arranging the Concert, and to Mrs. Julian Marshall and her many helpers in the choir and in the orchestra, for their kindness in providing so well for our musical enjoyment. There were eight or nine rehearsals, the last of which took place at the College on the night before the concert, when Mrs. Tansley was present. We were all very pleased to see her again on the concert night, and to hear her speak on that occasion.

At the Council Meeting held on February 25th, the Vice-Principal, in the chair, announced that the Passmore Edwards Settlement had asked the College to renew the custom of appointing delegates to attend their meetings, and Messrs. G. M. Trevelyan and A. L. Leon had undertaken to represent the College, and had been nominated accordingly. We were very pleased to keep in touch with the Settlement.

It was resolved to send a letter of congratulation to the Rev. J. Llewelyn Davies, one of the founders of the College, upon his attaining the age of 82 years.

The Report of the Executive Committee to the Council, was read, and the following are some extracts therefrom :—

Students and Class Entries.—Attention having been drawn at the November Council meeting to the falling off in the student entries which had been experienced up to that time, and for part of which definite causes could be assigned, the Executive now reported that for the whole of the September term there were seventy-eight students less than in the corresponding term of 1906. Making allowance for the loss of the Post Office sorters and for the great drop in the entries for law, the net falling-off in student entries for that term could not exceed thirty, or almost exactly

3 per cent., a loss which could not be regarded as in any way a serious one. The January term so far had shown an almost exactly similar loss, the number of students being seventy-six less than at the corresponding date of last year. Two subjects alone, Singing and Shorthand, showed a substantial increase. The former, under Messrs. Smith and Tarr's enthusiastic and able teaching, had been accomplishing most excellent and attractive work; whilst the arrangements made by the Directors of the Special Division, Messrs. Pocock and Starling, whereby there was one shorthand class at least on every night in the week, had resulted in the formation of a very strong Shorthand section.

The comparative figures were as follows :—

	1907.	1908.		1907.	1908.
Preparatory Division	36	26	Botany	9	17
Algebra	26	10	Building Construction	51	45
Ambulance ...	9	0	Electricity ...	75	39
Arithmetic ...	36	44	Geology	11	7
Art	86	60	Plane and Practical		
Book-keeping ...	67	47	Solid Geometry	0	16
Composition ...	17	19	Physiology ...	11	6
Economics ...	16	6	Portuguese ...	0	2
English Literature	10	8	Singing	58	85
Euclid	5	7	Spanish	23	23
English for Foreigners	19	12	Shorthand ...	104	146
French ...	170	129	Violin	15	17
Geography ...	6	7	History	7	6
German	67	32	Italian	14	9
Grammar	39	20	Esperanto	0	3
Greek	18	12	Mr. Scott's Class ...	21	19
Latin	26	28	Chemistry ...	45	35
Law	51	17			
			Class Entries	1149	959
			Student Entries	611	535

Classes and Teachers.—With the exception of Mr. Scott's class on "Browning," no new subject had been added to the programme, but an unusual number of teachers had come upon the staff. Mr. Kisch had taken a beginners' class in Greek, so as to enable Greek to be taught in three divisions, like Latin; Mr. E. M. Forster had returned as a Latin teacher; Mr. Nobel had assumed the place of Mr. Jastrzebski as teacher of the advanced German practice class; Mr. Craven had been good enough to take the place of one of our most regular and capable teachers, Mr. J. Jacob, who had been obliged to give up his classes because of indifferent health, but who hoped to resume teaching at no very distant date; Mr. Marrack had undertaken the beginners' Arithmetic; Mr. E. W. Jones, Elementary English Grammar; and Mr. H. R. Lawless, Esperanto. In the Shorthand classes, Messrs. Alaway and Martin had been obliged to retire, and Messrs. Trott and Staal had taken their places. The classes in the Law section taught by Messrs. Freeman and Iselin had been dropped, so that Mr. Gutteridge's class on "Insurance Law" was the only one left in that subject.

Examinations.—Results were reported of the examinations of the Preparatory Division and Shorthand classes. With regard to the latter, the Examiner wrote: "You will see I am keeping a high standard—considerably higher than Pitman's own examinations, as I know from experience."

In Ambulance.—Sixteen sat and all passed, two gaining the Medallion and six securing their second voucher. As a testimony to the zeal and skill with which Dr. Forbes and Mr. Wiltshire had conducted this class, it was pointed out that of the last fifty candidates sent up for examination, only one had failed.

Lectures.—The Saturday lecture list for the session had been a very attractive one, but the attendances had been very uneven, especially since the Christmas vacation. The Thursday series, on the contrary, had shown a distinct improvement in the average of attendance. Hitherto these Thursday lectures had been given exclusively by men, but in the term under notice the College had been favoured by Mrs. Julian Marshall, who gave a lecture on Thursday, January 30th, her subject being "The Study of Harmony."

The two courses of University Extension lectures had remained relatively as noted in the November report. Mr. Dudley Heath's course on "Italian Painters" had not attracted more students, while Dr. Slaughter's audience still kept up its good attendance, and was in his opinion one of the best he had ever lectured to. The course of lectures on "The Revival of Romantic Poetry in England," arranged for and carried on here by the London County Council, was given up a month previously, because of the unsatisfactory attendance of those who had joined.

Library.—As reported in November, upon the suggestion of Mr. Hobson a special effort was being made to raise a fund wherewith to buy some of the books of which the Library stands in need. That fund now amounted to £99 1s. 6d., and the Librarian was engaged in drawing up lists of books from which the Executive might choose those deemed to have the best claim to be purchased. Gifts to the Library since the last report had been received as follows:—

From Dr. Furnivall, "The R. P. A. Annual," C. A. Watts; and "Lessons of the Day," M. D. Conway. From Mr. C. Gatti, "Rise of Christianity," A. Kalthoff; and "Japanese Grammar," H. J. Weintz. From Mr. J. J. Dent, "Venice," A. Berzeuroth; "Montreux," E. Jung; and "Lake of Lucerne," J. C. Heer. From the Authors, "Continuation Schools in England and elsewhere," M. E. Sadler; "The Life and Campaigns of the first Viscount Gough," R. S. Rait; "The Council of Constance to the death of J. Huss," J. H. Wylie; "A Sermon," F. J. Jayne; "The Companies' Act," W. Jordan; and "The Murder of Agriculture," Sir W. E. Cooper. From Mrs. Winkworth, "Rose of the

River," and " The Old Peabody Pew," by K. D. Wiggin. From Rev. J. Ll. Davies, " The National Church," Canon H. Henson. Parcels of books from Rev. J. H. Todd, per Sir Charles Lucas, and from Mrs. R. B. Litchfield, and Mrs. S. H. Butcher. Mrs. Winkworth had also given a picture, "The Sons of Toil," which has been hung in the Club Room.

Social Functions.—The social side of the College continued to flourished with that vigour and enterprise whose growth appeared to have been stimulated so remarkably by the change of air from Great Ormond Street to Camden Town. Continuing, the report dealt with the activities of the Musical Society, the Shakespeare Reading Society, the Maurice Chess Club, and the Collegians' Dance Committee. The thirty-first supper of the Old Students' Club, held on Saturday, December 14th; the seventh Furnivall's Children's treat, on December 21st; the seventeenth Joint Clubs' Supper, on the Saturday following; the visit of the Trinity College chess players on January 11th, and the Musical Society's " Ladies " Concert on January 18th, were all fully noticed.

On Saturday, February 15th,—we still quote from the Executive report—the second supper of the Sketching Club was held in the Club Room, Mr. R. W. Wilkinson in the chair. The supper was followed by a concert, gramaphone performance, and lantern display in the Art Room. Thanks to the admirable arrangements made by Messrs. Wilkinson and Silk, and to the enthusiasm and good-fellowship which characterize this club, a most enjoyable evening was spent.

Mention was made of the meeting of the Old Students' Club, which took place on Saturday, February 15th, when the debate on " Nietzsche's Influence in Politics, Literature, and Art," was opened by Mr. Richard Whiteing, the well-known novelist, in a speech full of interest and suggestion, reported in last month's JOURNAL; and also of the concert which Mrs. Tansley was arranging for February 29th.

The Rev. B. H. Alford gave the last of his lectures on the Old Testament, on Sunday, March 15th. These lectures have extended over the last five years, and those who have attended them have derived much pleasure and benefit from them. Very carefully prepared, and bearing evidence of the great width of knowledge which he brought to bear on his subject, Mr. Alford's discourses have always been full of life and earnestness, and his class has been one of the most excellent the College has had. Mr. Alford is taking a trip to Japan; and although he feels that, owing to his advancing years, he cannot renew his class on his return in the autumn, he by no means wishes to fall out of touch with the College, and so he hopes to come and see us later in the year, and talk to us about the country he is going to visit. We most cordially wish him a pleasant and prosperous voyage.

On May 2nd, at 8 o'clock, a "Ladies'" Concert will be given by the W. M. C. Musical Society in the Maurice Hall.

———

Mrs. R. B. Litchfield has kindly presented to the College a mask of Dante, taken after death, a copy of Cruikshank's Sketch Book, and a large parcel of books.

———

The College is much indebted to Dr. Furnivall for the "Historians' History of the World," published by The Times Book Club, in 25 volumes. He was asked if he would review this work, and agreed to do so on condition that the set of volumes was presented to the Working Men's College. A report of an interview between the publishers' representative and the Doctor, and his letter on the subject of the books, have been widely advertised; and the result is that the College obtains gratis a publication which would cost £9 7s. 6d. to purchase.

———

Mrs. Robbie desires to acknowledge, with many thanks, through the medium of the JOURNAL, a present of a handsome purse, which she has received from the members of the Sketching Club.

———

Writing to Flint, from Quebec, Canada, Mr. Stanley H. Spry, lately a student in the College, says :—

I am sorry I have not written to you before, but I have been travelling about so much that I have not had much opportunity of doing so. I wished also to see a little of the country before expressing an opinion of it. One bit of advice I can give from experience is, not to pay much attention to the information published by the shipping companies or the Government either. Both are apt to mislead ; for instance, I was told by the London agent for Nova Scotia that there was a large demand for men at Amherst, N. S., but on my arrival at Halifax I asked the officials if they advised me to go there, and they said there was no demand at all for men at Amherst. I believe they ask for emigrants at such places in order to cut down the already low rate of wage. Then it states in the Government handbook that there is no demand for clerks in Canada, but I find that a clerk with a knowledge of stenography and typewriting, or book-keeping, stands as good a chance as anyone else.

But I should not advise anyone to go east of Montreal, as the eastern provinces are already well supplied with labour. I was working for two months at Campbelton, N. B., on the railway, and in a timber yard ; but, what with the time lost by rainy weather, and the high price of everything, I did not gain much there.

I next went to Montreal, and worked there for two or three weeks, and then came back to Quebec, where I obtained my present position, as a clerk in the Executive Offices and Stores of the Canadian Militia in Quebec Province. My salary is 11 dollars per week, which is not so bad for this part of Canada, as the hours are short, 9 o'clock to 4.30, and 12 o'clock Saturday. I found my knowledge of stenography and typewriting very useful, in fact it is necessary in my present position. I expect I shall stay here till next spring, and shall then either go south into the States, or west to British Columbia, but that is a long way, and it costs 52 dollars to get there. There are plenty of opportunities in Canada, but it is difficult to find the right place, as the country is so large, and one can only learn by experience. I hope the W. M. C. is having a very successful session, with a greatly increased number of students. Best regards to all.

We deeply regret to have to announce the death, on March 4th, of John Roebuck, of Winchendon, Massachusetts, U.S.A., the first Fellow of the College (1858), in his 78th year. Mrs. Roebuck, and Mr. Roebuck's son and daughter, send their kindest regards to all friends who knew him. Want of space compels us to postpone till next month a more adequate notice of a man so greatly esteemed as was John Roebuck.

On Thursday, February 27th, a deputation of three members of the Leicester Working Men's College, Mr. T. J. Dilworth, Mr. Thomas Brown, and Mr. William Burton, paid a very welcome visit to our College, and went over the building with the Vice-Principal, in order to see whether they could note any points which would be useful to bear in mind in connection with the completion of their new building, which is to be opened next September or October. The institution will then be under one roof, instead of under four, as at present.

Mr. A. Lawrence Lowell, trustee of the Lowell Institute, Boston, Mass., and a cousin of James Russell Lowell, visited this College in October, 1906, since which date the JOURNAL and Term Programmes have been sent him, as issued, and some friendly intercourse has passed between him and our College. In a recent letter to Sir Charles Lucas, he speaks of the value of social gatherings, such as we have here, and expresses the wish that they might have them in the Lowell Institute. He then proceeds to tell of what he has been doing at that Institute, in the following words :—

" There are six kinds of courses, wholly distinct. Doubtless more good would be done in some ways, if they were connected. But then, what I regard as the chief value of the Institute would be lost—that of filling gaps in popular education. For example, one of the latest ventures is the " School for Industrial Foremen." It seemed to me that the community is doing a great deal for the civil engineer at one end of the scale, and for the working man at the other, but little or nothing for the foremen, who might be called the non-commissioned officers of the industrial army. They are however highly important, both economically and socially. So, in co-operation with the Massachusetts Institute of Technology, this school was established. Something of the kind is done at the Manchester Technical School, but not, I think, so systematically. The first year we give the pupils a lot of mechanics, physics, and mathematics (including a little calculus); and the second year, problems, etc., in the laboratories. The school has been going four years and seems to be fulfilling its promise. In order to do for general education what that school does for technical study, I have started this year some courses in co-operation with Harvard. They are more in the line of the work of the Working Men's College, except that they are designed for people who have had a secondary education, that seeming to be the field most neglected here. They are open to both men and women, and are well attended, for the course in general History opened with 150 students admitted, of whom about one-half attend regularly, in spite of the amount of reading required ; and for the course on Literature, I issued as many tickets of admission as the hall would hold (about 300), and was obliged to refuse a couple of hundred more. The courses are conducted as at Harvard, two lectures a week, and a third meeting in small sections. As the courses run, with short breaks, from October 1st to June, it is the most systematic form of University extension, I think, in this country or in England."

MRS. TANSLEY'S CONCERT.

ON Saturday, February 29th, an exceedingly enjoyable Concert, arranged by Mrs. Tansley, took place in the Maurice Hall, Sir Charles Lucas, C.B., K.C.M.G., in the chair. The first part of the entertainment consisted of "The May Queen" (Sterndale Bennett), a pastoral for solo voices, chorus, and orchestra, conducted by Mrs. Julian Marshall, who, with her assistants, had devoted considerable time and trouble to the preparation for the representation. The solo parts were taken by Miss Hettie Stammer, soprano, as The May Queen; Mrs. Herbert Teasdale, contralto, as the Queen; Mr. Stanley Ridout, tenor, as the Lover; and Mr. W. Savage Cooper, bass, as Robin Hood, Captain of the Foresters. Mrs. Eugene Oswald accompanied at the piano. There were about two dozen ladies and gentlemen in the choir, and another two dozen in the orchestra, including a large proportion of violins and other stringed instruments. They all played well together, and did their best that no point should be lost, the result being an extremely admirable performance, which gave the audience a great deal of pleasure.

At the interval, SIR CHARLES LUCAS referred to the absence of the Vice-Principal, which no one regretted more than Mr. Jacob himself and Mrs. Jacob. He then asked us whole-heartedly to show our appreciation of the delightful entertainment we were having. 1908 was good to us, in giving us that additional day for the special purpose of Mrs. Tansley's concert (laughter). But this did not imply that we had that pleasure only once in four years. We looked upon it as an annual treat to the good boys of the Working Men's College. Music had always had a sympathetic home in our College. The older men told us of that good man Mr. Litchfield's singing class; we had a most useful and energetic Musical Society, the president of which was that great composer, Mr. Marks (laughter); and the most thriving class was the Singing Class, under Mr. Smith. The Society, the class, and the College would acknowledge the impetus given to music by these charming annual concerts, and we owed very warm thanks to Mrs. Marshall and her helpers, that night. (Cheers.) SIR CHARLES also referred to Mrs. Marshall's lecture on Harmony, reported in the JOURNAL. Last, but very far from least, he mentioned the name of the lady who first originated these concerts, and to whom we owed their continuance. Mrs. Tansley would be loved at this College for the name that she bore, but we loved her also for herself, and for the affection which she had lavished on the College. Our sympathy went out to her in the severe illness she had undergone, and it was a great delight to see her that evening, when she could behold with her own eyes and hear with her own ears how successful the concert was, and what keen delight it gave to us. (Cheers.)

Mrs. TANSLEY, speaking from the platform, said that anything she had ever done or could do for the Working Men's College gave her extreme delight. Although she initiated the concerts, it was to these kind friends here, and here (indicating the choir and the orchestra), that we owed the real pleasure. They had given us, she ventured to think, a great treat that night. Her friend Mrs. Marshall had spared neither time nor trouble, and she asked us to give her cordial thanks. (Hearty cheers.)

The Duet for violin and viola, with which the second part of the Concert opened, played by Mrs. Ronald Carter and Miss Frances Marshall, was very charmingly rendered, and proved to be a Sonata, in 4 short movements, by Léclair (old French). This was much appreciated by the audience, and would have been heard again with pleasure. The first song in the second part of the programme was to have been Clutsam's "Myrra," sung by Mrs. Herbert Teasdale, the very efficient exponent of "The Queen" in the Cantata; as however the Misses Stuart, who were down to sing a duet later on, were obliged to leave early, Mrs. Teasdale most kindly consented to change places with them, and they sang with much success a duet-version of Böhm's "Still as the Night," giving as an encore Tosti's "Boat-song." Mr. Ridout, always popular, followed with "The Bygone Days," and pleased the audience with an encore. Three English part-songs by Sterndale

Bennett, Walter Macfarren, and J. G. Callcott respectively, were given by the choir in very good style, with taste and finish. Miss Hettie Stammer was the sensation of the evening, and fairly brought down the house with her song, "Three little Birds." She was rapturously encored, and after singing another charming little song, "The Linnet," the audience being still unsatisfied, she sat down to the piano and accompanied herself (with her gloves on, which was real *legerdemain*) in "Market Day." When the applause had subsided, the Orchestra played four charming and tuneful dance movements, described as Egyptian Ballet, by Luigini. These also pleased the audience very much. After this, "The Anchor's Weighed" was sung with much expression by Mr. W. Savage Cooper. Then came Mrs. Teasdale's song, referred to above, and the Concert ended with an inspiriting "Marching Tune," an old Lincolnshire folk-song, arranged and harmonized for Chorus by Mr. Percy Grainger

CORRESPONDENCE.

[*Under this heading the Editor will be glad to publish letters of interest to past and present members, but he declines all responsibility for the views therein expressed.*]

THE MUSICAL SOCIETY IN NEED.

To the Editor of the WORKING MEN'S COLLEGE JOURNAL.

DEAR MR. EDITOR,—New environments create new wants. The Musical Society, in order to live up to the fine hall in which they now give their concerts, are yearning for a piano more worthy of their concerts than the one they bought some ten years ago ; and to that end they desire to ask their friends to help them to raise about £40, in addition to the money they already have in hand. In order to do this, it is proposed to hold 6d. concerts as occasion offers. In view of the fact that the present promising singing classes of the College give signs of the nucleus of a College Choir at no distant date, the need for a good instrument is all the more pressing. The Musical Society would also be grateful for any donations to the Piano Fund, which may be sent to the Secretaries of the Society, or to the President,

R. H. MARKS.

THE STUDENTS' CALENDAR FOR APRIL.

Wed., 1st.—Frederick Denison Maurice died, 1872.
Thurs., 2nd.—Citizens' lunch, 1.30. Shorthand examination, all stages, 7.30.
Sat., 4th.—January term ends.
Mon., 6th.—Third, or April term begins. Smoking Concert, Coffee Room, 9.30.
Tues., 7th.—Executive Committee, 8 p.m. Debating Society meeting, 9.30.
Sat., 11th.—Furnivall Cycling Club's opening run to Pinner, meet at 4.30.
Sun., 12th. — Lubbock Field Club walk. Shakespeare Reading, "The Tempest," 7.30.
Tues., 14th.—Executive Committee, 8 p.m. Debating Society general meeting, 9.30.
Thurs., 16th.—Easter Vacation begins.
Fri., 17th.—Good Friday. Furnivall Cycling Club Easter Tour to Brighton begins.
Mon., 20th.—Easter Monday—College closed.
Wed., 22nd.—Easter Vacation ends.
Sat., 25th.—Furnivall Cycling Club run to Ewell. Collegians' Dance in aid of the Grand Piano Fund, 6.45.
Sun., 26th.—Shakespeare Readers read "The Rivals," 7.30, ladies' night.
Tues., 28th.—Executive Committee, 8 p.m.
Thurs., 30th.—Last day for sending in essays for the "Marks" Prize.

Announcements of coming events for insertion in the Students' Calendar should, if possible, be communicated to the Editor by the 20th of the month.

SATURDAY NIGHT LECTURE.

THE PLAYWRIGHT AND THE PUBLIC.

On March 14th, the lecture by Mr. A. Sutro on "The Playwright and the Public" drew a most appreciative audience.   Mr. Lionel Jacob, Vice-Principal, occupied the chair.   Mr. ALFRED SUTRO said there was a cunning in the selection of this subject, because it not only enabled him to treat of the Drama and its importance to the community, but permitted his fancy to dance behind the curtain and to talk about the manufacturer of plays. Writers were not merely entertainers, but they had to know how to interest the audience without having any audience at all before them.   Opinions differed widely as to the Drama, and while there was the overwhelming enthusiasm of one party, yet there was the cool indifference of the other party tending to the opposite extreme, so that the only safe way was to steer a middle course.   The entertainer gave pleasure within certain limitations of art ; and he wrote not for the individual to read, but for the crowd to listen and to enjoy.   He must give pleasure to secure public patronage.   A writer of plays was in solitude an observer, who noted the trend of human life with its many possibilities of happiness, and with its poignant sorrows. Misery and distress were not predominant in the world, for there was scarcely any human life that had not a ray of hope, or its moments of joy and love.   For successful Drama, it was necessary to keep an eye on the boxes, and to watch the commercial side of art.   Woman alone was the autocrat of the crowd.   Taking one thousand human beings in a theatre, there were not two alike in face or expression, yet all these persons were eager to enjoy, and they behaved as though were dominated absolutely by the same idea, and had the same likes and dislikes.   When the public acted as one homogeneous mass in flocking to the theatre, success was assured.   It was a deadly sin in a writer of plays, when he was weighed in the box office, and found wanting in popularity.   It cost £1000 to produce a play, the expenses amounted to £800 or £900 per week, and there should be at least six thousand people present in the course of a week to see the performance.   These six thousand people were brought together only by the fact of the crowd clamouring to be amused.   They paid for their seats, and did not care a button for the difficulties of a manager or for any one else. Genius had its own laws, and there were men of talent who could not please the public.   When the lighter form of art was preferred, it was the duty of the playwright to write such a play as would give pleasure, though the cause of the enjoyment might not be its superior intellectuality.   Every high-class thoughtful play that succeeded was a distinct good to the community.   While there could be too much high art for Art's sake, the playwright's task was to widen its influence and to raise the ideas of the community.   To end a play happily was more difficult than might sometimes appear.   There were plays of the sexual order, with a mighty purpose in the background, or a deep moral lesson to be enforced, but this problem of life was exceptional ; and there were plays of a questionable character, that excited vulgar buffoonery, or provoked cheap laughter, while indecency smirked and extended across the foot-lights.   Playgoers had their "stars"; the actor was preferred rather than the play.   If the particular actor were left out, the play would be a failure.   This was a serious misfortune for dramatists, and sometimes playwrights found it necessary to write their plays around the star artists in such a manner as would suit their stage powers.   Love was most enthralling in every play, and the playgoer regarded the ecstasy with the greatest esteem.   There were other problems vital in human life that gave rise to strong and real Drama.   The essence of Drama was a conflict of wills so far entangled that all the elements of human nature would be at war.   The audience resented having religion and politics thrust on the stage ; this could be attempted only under the penalty of forfeiting all success.   Entertainers believed in the potentiality of their art, and in the distinct value of the spoken word. The dramatist, with an exalted idea of his mission in life, must be popular, and so the burden rested on the people to see that they applauded. — A hearty vote of thanks was given to Mr. Sutro at the conclusion of his lecture.   W. H.

CONVALESCENT HOME SOCIETY.

AT the general meeting of the W. M. C. Convalescent Home Society, held in the Coffee Room on March 9th, Mr. J. J. Dent in the chair, the following report for the past year was presented :—

It is with great satisfaction that your committee has to report the continuous interest taken by members of the College in this Society. Our membership has increased by nearly 100 per cent., viz., from 106 last year to 210 this year, while the number of donations has increased from 4 to 5. It is encouraging to notice that the spirit of co-operation is making headway, for it is only through a large number paying the small subscription of 1s. per annum, that an institution such as this can succeed.

There were three applications made for admittance to the Home during the year, two of which, however, were withdrawn, and only one member went to the Home, a member of the Economics Class. As a matter of fact, this member stayed at the Home for three months, but the Society only paid for one month of his stay, as our rules do not permit of our charging our funds with more than the expense of four weeks' residence of any one member. As the case in question was a deserving one, however, your Committee was able to arrange for the extension of his stay for another two months at his own expense, at 15s. per week. The actual cost of maintaining each man at the Home is about 23s. per week, so that the Society has been able, although not directly contributing towards his maintenance expenses, at least to benefit him to the extent of 8s. per week for the two months. As will have been seen in the JOURNAL, the member in question speaks very highly of the institution, and it is therefore a great satisfaction to observe that such a goodly proportion of College members are members of the Society. It is certainly not always convenient for any of us, after having gone through a trying period of illness, with its attendant expenditure, to go away to the sea-side for a period of from three to four weeks, and it must be a great comfort to a member to know that, after he has sufficiently recovered, he is able to go away to a comfortable institution like the Home without further straining his resources.

Under the new arrangement with the Home we pay over to them all our funds, and our account is credited with these payments, and is charged at the rate of 15s. per week for every member who uses the Home. We have now a balance in our favour of £14 18s., which at the present moment would enable us to send four members for three weeks each, without creating a debit balance, which I venture to say is a satisfactory state of affairs.

M. STAAL, *Hon. Secretary.*

BALANCE SHEET FOR THE YEAR 1907—8.

Receipts.	£	s.	d.	*Expenditure.*	£	s.	d.
Balance brought forward	6	12	0	Institute Union ...	16	1	0
210 Subscriptions at 1s.	10	10	0	Printing (circulars) ...	1	2	0
3 Donations at 2s. ..	0	6	0	Locker rent	0	2	0
2 do. at 5s. ...	0	10	0	Stamps & receipts books	0	3	0
				Balance in hand ...	0	10	0
	£17	18	0		£17	18	0

Audited and found correct, R. H. MARKS.—March 6th, 1908.

After some discussion the report and balance sheet were adopted ; Mr. Dent was re-elected chairman, and the Superintendent treasurer of the Society ; Mr. A. H. Perry was elected Secretary, and the following members constitute the new Committee :—Messrs. W. R. Emslie, E. Hayward, E. S. Landells, E. Murphy, and H. K. Randall.

It will interest all those who know him to state that Mr. Staal, the late energetic secretary of this Society, intends shortly to return to his native country, Holland.

A PREDECESSOR OF SHAKESPEARE.*

A NOTABLE contribution to Shakespearian literature has been made by Mr. J. J. Munro in his edition of Arthur Brooke's *Romeus and Juliet*, the immediate predecessor of Shakespeare's play of that name, as well as to a lesser degree of his play, *The Two Gentlemen of Verona.* Of Arthur Brooke's life little is known, except that he was a zealous Protestant, and that besides his "tragical history" of the Veronese lovers, he published a work on a Scriptural subject. But Mr. Munro has collected evidence as to the manner of "little" Brooke's death, from which it appears that our poet was drowned in 1563, near Rye, whilst on his way in H.M.S. *Greyhound* to Havre.

In the poem itself there would be little to interest us, were it not for the fact that Shakespeare so largely used Brooke in the construction of his tragedy. The poem is composed in rhyming iambic couplets, the lines being alternately of six and seven feet, a metre that certainly does not err on the side of elegance. Moreover, the subject is one with which a zealous Puritan like Brooke can have been scarcely in sympathy, and indeed in his preface Brooke states that his object in narrating the wrong-doing of the lovers and their deaths is to deliver a warning to the reader, "as the slaves of Lacedemon, oppressed with excess of drink . . . . were to the free-born children, ... to the intent to raise in them an hateful loathing of so filthy beastliness." It may perhaps be partly due to this lack of sympathy with his subject that Brooke's style is, in Mr. Munro's words, "bombastic and grandiloquent"; and the deficiencies in metre and style are not redeemed by any exceptional skill in the construction of the poem. Indeed, as Mr. Munro points out, most of the virtues that can be found in the poem are borrowed from Boaisteau's *Histoires Tragiques*, of which to a large extent the poem is a mere translation.

But whilst Brooke's poem would never have been read for its own merits except by a few antiquarians, the position of Brooke as one of Shakespeare's predecessors makes his work of interest to all who care for English literature, and Mr. Munro, by his scholarly edition, has put all students of Shakespeare under an obligation. In an Introduction of lxii pages, and in the Textual notes, Glossary, and Appendices, the results of much labour and research are embodied; and it would perhaps be ungrateful to cavil at the fact that on the title page the greater poet's name should appear as Shakespeare, whilst in the Introduction the spelling is consistently amended to Shakspere.   A. S. L.

We have received the Ninth Annual Report of the Garden City Association, from which we are pleased to learn that there has been a remarkable acceptance of the principles of the Association during the year 1907. The association held a successful conference at the Guildhall in October last, the proceedings of which have since been published under the title of "Town Planning in Theory and Practice," and this book is having a large sale. Besides Letchworth, Garden Cities have been formed at Port Sunlight, Hampstead, Warrington, and Didsbury.

---

* Brooke's *Romeus and Juliet*, newly edited by J. J. Munro for the Shakespeare Library. Chatto and Windus, 2s. 6d. net.

THE WORKING MEN'S COLLEGE JOURNAL *is supported partly by Annual Subscribers living in different parts of the World, and partly by circulation among the Students and Members. Its success depends upon a regular demand. and to ensure this, the Editor would be glad if as many readers as can will become Subscribers. Subscription 2s. 6d. per annum, post free.*

LONDON: Printed by W. HUDSON & Co., Red Lion Street, High Holborn, and published at THE WORKING MEN'S COLLEGE, Crowndale Road, London, N.W.—April 1st, 1908.

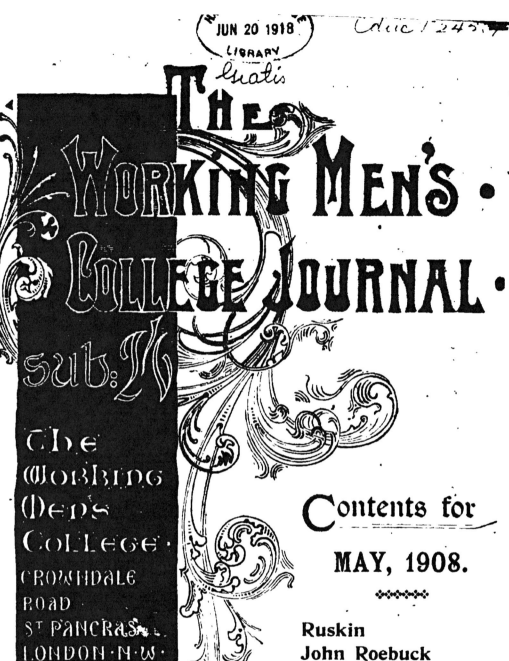

The Working Men's College Journal

The Working Mens College·
CROWNDALE ROAD·
ST PANCRAS·
LONDON·N·W·
FOUNDED IN 1854 BY THE LATE
Frederick Denison Maurice·

sub: 1/1

Contents for

MAY, 1908.

◆◆◆◆◆◆

Ruskin
John Roebuck
Lubbock Field Club
College Notes
Saturday Night
                    Lecture
Debating Society

THE

Working Men's College Journal.

Conducted by Members of the Working Men's College
Crowndale Road, London, N.W.

Vol. X.—No. 182.   MAY, 1908.   PRICE TWOPENCE.

RECOLLECTIONS OF RUSKIN.*

HAVE been asked to say something about Ruskin, and meet with a difficulty at the outset, for his very fame as a learned writer upon Art makes it not easy to speak of him as he was, because we are too apt to regard the critic or philosopher upon artistic matters as an elegant idler—one who lives in an artificial world of his own, concerned only in the contemplation of works of beauty, and regarding them with a consideration which is greater than that with which he regards his fellow-creatures. But with Ruskin, although there probably has never been a keener student of art, or a more philosophical expounder of its principles, yet I do not believe that there has ever been one who was less of a mere *dilettante* than was John Ruskin. "The proper study of mankind is man," says the poet; and with Ruskin, the study of art, his advocacy of its claims, and his personal work in connection with it, were all directed to the consideration of art as an element of humanity. How far did art affect, or how far was it affected by, the times, people, and scenes amidst which it was practised—how far did it express the spirit of an age or a man—how far could it be used as an instrument of good?

When in 1854, the Rev. F. D. Maurice, with the assistance of other equally warm-hearted men as himself, founded the Working Men's College, Ruskin was one of this noble band. A public meeting was held at the no longer existing St. Martin's Hall, and here the scheme of the College was put before the world. At this meeting there was a plentiful distribution of a reprint of that chapter of Ruskin's "Stones of Venice," which is entitled "On the Nature of Gothic Architecture." In this section of the work, he speaks of men engaged in workshops who have to do work that is purely mechanical and devoid of interest, and that in consequence the workman becomes a mere machine, and that his work cannot have any expression of thought or intelligence; of this he writes with regret and with sympathy for the workman.

What wonder, then, that he came forward in this movement for founding a College for Working Men? He threw himself

---

* Paper read by Mr. J. P. Emslie at a Students and Teachers' Meeting in the Common Room, on March 2nd, 1908.

with zeal and energy into the task of teaching drawing. I was one of his pupils, though not from the first. I had been accustomed to draw from my childhood, and had also spent some time in the Government School of Design, so drawing was no new thing to me; but I was astonished at his keenness of perception of any one's capacity, and of his ability in making the most of that capacity. He soon saw that I had had some practice in drawing, and forthwith urged me on to work to the full extent of my knowledge, and then opened out to my view things to which I had not then attained, and showed me how to overcome the difficulties which stood in my way. I am greatly indebted to him for very much that I have learned in the matter of delineation. He had a gift for perceiving a feature, not immediately apparent, in an object, but which, secondary though it was, gave charm or character to the whole. "Don't you see," he said to me one evening, "that lovely swell on the side of the leaf?" "Yes," I said. "Well then," he replied, "you haven't made enough of it in your drawing, and in consequence you've lost a piece of rich form." And thus he would point out to me what I should aim at, and in what Art should exercise itself in its endeavour to depict with effort that which nature of its own spontaneity presented to our view; and he would praise me exceedingly whenever I made any worthy effort. But he was equally severe in blaming me whenever I fell back. I have a vivid recollection of his address to me upon one or two of these occasions. I will not repeat his words, but to use a well-known phrase—"he talked to me like a father."

Most of my fellow-students had not had such advantages of art-training as I had had. Many of them had never endeavoured to draw before they had been in Mr. Ruskin's class. Some of their efforts used to make me look on with wonder—wonder which had a certain amount of pity in it. But Mr. Ruskin was never dismayed by any want of excellence in his pupils' work. Whatsoever his hand found to do, he did with his might. He would sit down before a most unpromising piece of work, and with thorough concentration on the task before him, would set to work to analyze the student's drawing, working on it himself with infinite patience, turning coarseness into delicacy, subduing what was over prominent so as to give greater effect to that which should stand forward. All this time he would be talking to his pupil and explaining why he did certain things, drawing the student out to get understanding to see what was wanted, then pointing out some power, shown in the drawing, but which the student himself had never before known that he possessed; and thus he would repress faults and develop merits to the best advantage of those who had the benefit of his instructions.

Very often if a student, in his endeavour to represent everything, had made too much of a detail, Mr. Ruskin would make a hasty sketch on the margin of the drawing in order to show what was the general form of the object which was being drawn, and how far the drawing had deviated from that general form. I say "hasty sketch," yet the haste of the sketch was not the haste of indecision, but the haste of one who wishes to be as short a time as possible from the main work, and desires his pupil not to lose the thread of the discourse which he is making for that pupil's instruction. These sketches were most masterly, giving the prominent features of an object in exceedingly few, slight, but most expressive touches; not one line too many, not a stroke thrown away, but nothing omitted that could tell in the representation. I am happy in being the possessor of one of these sketches. I was copying Turner's "Mill near the Grande Chartreuse," and Mr. Ruskin pointed out to me that I had made a rock too pointed in form. "Look!" he said, sketching on the margin of my paper as he spoke; "the rock is of that general form, with fissures in its sides, the water flows over its top and rounds that top, then runs down the clefts in its sides and wears away their edges, so that a certain roundness comes into the whole mass."

For a short time I leave off writing to look at this sketch, and I count the lines that compose it: thirty-eight lines, as nearly as I can make them out; they were done in about as many seconds, and the work is a splendid suggestion of a water-worn rock. Below it is a sketch of a tree, slighter and less expressive, but sufficient for the lesson which he gave me. He explained that my tree did not tell its own story sufficiently, and, as he sketched, pointed out that the tree would naturally have grown upright, but being on the side of a steep bank, it declined a little from the perpendicular; as it grew higher, and became heavier from increase of branch and leafage, it declined still farther from the perpendicular, but the lower part of the trunk, being older and stronger than the upper part, was only a little out of the upright; as the branches grew, they naturally shot upward, those on the upper side of the trunk have a free course and grow fairly well, but those on the under side of the trunk fall over with it and droop more and more the nearer they are to the ground; as they near the top, they get a better chance and grow in a more normal fashion, whilst the forms of the masses of leafage on the two sides of the tree differ from each other in consequence of this difference in the growth of the branches. All this history of a life, as shown in the form of a tree, astonished at the same time that it convinced me of its truth, as he spoke and illustrated his meaning by his sketch.

Mr. Ruskin is known to the world as a great writer. I do not know whether justice has been done to him as an artist. I have never seen any work of his that could be called a picture. Of colour he was sensible, but was not happy in rendering it. Whenever any of his pupils wished to work in colour, he would tell them to go to Mr. Rossetti or Mr. Dickinson; for Ruskin said that he knew good colour when he saw it, but would not undertake to teach it. Most of his drawings are little more than elaborate outlines, but they are unequalled of their kind. How wonderfully he has given us the spirit and form of Gothic architecture, the richness, quaintness, and variety of sculpture, and the marvels of curvature and of design in leaves, flowers, rocks, and cliffs,—showing us, in his drawings from nature, those life histories of which I have just given an example in his exposition of the growth of a tree. When, last autumn, I for the first time saw the Alps, I thought of him. I was riding on the railway from Luzerne through Andermatt, St. Gothard, Bellinzona, and Chiasso; all the windows of the train were occupied by the passengers who, as they beheld the scenery, were expressing their wonder and admiration in many European languages, or were silently regarding the marvellous works of nature presented to their view. One gentleman declared that it was the finest scenery he had ever beheld. "I've seen the Rocky Mountains," he said; "they're much larger, but not nearly so beautiful." Nearly all through the journey I was thinking of John Ruskin, of the plates in "Modern Painters," and of his drawings of mountains. I did not think of any landscape painter, however great he might be; but I did think—the thought was forced upon me—of Ruskin's drawings of Alpine scenes. Here, before me, I saw the kind of scenery which Ruskin had depicted, and with so much truth— truth of general aspect and truth of detail, rock form, tree form, tree grouping, glacier, and icy peak. Nothing that I have ever seen conveys to me the sentiment of Alpine scenery so much as Ruskin's drawings. His drawings of old architecture were equally felicitous: his view of the market-place at Abbeville is, I think, a masterpiece; it completely brings before my eyes the whole of that well-composed irregularity.

And the author of these works, who to great natural artistic ability had superadded the advantages of a University education, so that he was able, in his study of the progress and development of art, to study it not only from an æsthetic, but also from an academic and scientific point of view; who, the son of a rich merchant, knew not of the cares of having to struggle for a livelihood—this man, I say, could come to those men less favoured in fortune and education than himself, and offer to them the advantages of instruction in those things in which he was so well favoured by nature and by education. He was a worthy member of that worthy band who founded this College, and whose traditions have been so well continued by their successors; for then as now—though Socialism and similar mystic things had not at that time been heard of—there was antagonism between classes. In illustration of this, I may mention one very little circumstance. The drawing-class room—for the sake of being well lighted for each student—had innumerable gaslights, and in consequence was very hot and dry. One evening the heat became intolerable. On a sudden Mr. Ruskin's very loud voice was heard: "Pray open one of those windows for a few minutes." A window was opened, and after a little time, Mr. Ruskin said, "Thank you, that'll do ; please close that window, or I shall catch a cold "—he then laughed as he continued—" and then I know what'll happen, my friends 'll be saying, ' Oh! you've been to the Working Men's College again,' for that's what they always say whenever I have a cold." With the evidence which this little remark affords, we cannot sufficiently admire the bravery of Mr. Ruskin and his fellow-teachers in their devotion to their self-imposed task ; and whatever skirmishes of outposts may have occasionally taken place between two classes thus newly brought into a somewhat intimate contact with each other, yet all worked well ; and I am sure that any student who is old enough to remember the times of which I speak is grateful for the opportunity then, and till now, afforded him of acquiring a knowledge of things in so many ways beneficial to him.

At the same time that Mr. Ruskin taught the practical part of drawing, he also endeavoured to cultivate taste amongst his pupils. William Miller's engraving of Turner's "Grand Canal, Venice," hung over the fireplace, to give the students an idea of what landscape art should be, though Ruskin has said that no engraver ever did justice to Turner's work, but Miller was the best, while not quite fully understanding his model. There was also an engraving of Canova's statue of Hebe, with Ruskin's comments written in the margin, showing that the lines in the engraving were, with the engraver's desire to show his skill, made so prominent that the figure appeared to be covered with network ; then came a scathing sentence beginning, " The statue is by Canova, and in the worst taste." I cannot remember the remainder of the sentence, but it was one mass of condemnation that I can remember ; and, as I was then a completely devoted believer in every utterance of Ruskin's, I concluded that Canova's fame was utterly undeserved. Consequently when, last autumn, I for the first time saw some of Canova's work, I was greatly astounded at its wonderful power, and had to believe that the Hebe must have been executed in one of those moments when—if we may credit what we are told—genius nods.

There was also in the drawing-class room Albert Dürer's engraving known as the Death's Head Coat-of-Arms. To those who do not know this engraving, I may say that the prominent object in it is a large shield charged with a skull, the skull being represented, not with heraldic flatness, but in full relief, so that the great feature of the work is one of grimness. Above the shield is a helmet, with a grand pair of wings for a crest. A lady stands beside the shield holding a strap, which passes over a staff and, joined to shield and helmet, holds them in their places. Slightly in the rear of the lady is a satyr who, with one hand on the staff, is placing his head near to that of the lady, whose coy smile shows that she is aware that he is manœuvering to get a kiss from her. This grandly

conceived and patiently-executed work was put before us as
an example of thoroughly good art. I once asked Ruskin
what it meant. He replied that it possibly represented the
arms and supporters of some noble Nürnberg family, or it
might pos·ibly be an allegory. Honour, as typified by the arms,
is sustained by the lady ; the satyr, typifying Evil, is endeavouring
to kiss the lady ; if he can succeed, he will, while her attention
is diverted, snatch away the staff over which passes the strap
which the lady holds, and which keeps the shield and helmet
in their places, and then Honour, as symbolized by the arms,
will fall to the ground. I never see this superb work without
thinking of Ruskin's fanciful remarks upon it. It is said that
Turner once, upon reading one of Ruskin's critiques, said :
" Why, he pretends to know more about my works than I do
myself." I do not know whether Dürer would say the same,
but his engraving is altogether as poetic as Ruskin's dissertation
upon it. Often have I looked, with intensest admiration, at
this work as it hung on the wall of the class-room—the first
work I had ever seen of a master of whom I think the more,
the more I study him.

A work by Henry Shaw, F.S.A.—but I forget its title—
Mr. Ruskin had placed in the class-room. The book was full
of chromo-lithographic plates of objects of household and
personal decoration. In the margin of nearly every plate Ruskin
had a comment on the object depicted in that plate. These
comments were in few words, often in one word. One of them
I remember, it was "Execrable"; another, but I forget the
word used, was a term of the highest praise. Most of them
were more or less in tones of deprecation ; he would show
where a design was good in the main, but was spoiled by some
discordant element, or by some straining after an effect beyond
the designer's powers of expression. One of the plates was a
representation of a bellows by Benvenuto Cellini ; the note
upon this was the longest in the book and was one of entire
condemnation, showing how this, that, and the other thing, in
the design was in bad taste. I have a recollection of an ugly
satyr's face and a number of coarse rollicking scrolls floundering
about over the bellows' side, without any leading line, main mass,
or subordinated detail. Every element of the work was scuffling
with its fellow for pre-eminence ; there was an utter want of
quietude in the design, and, with all due deference to Cellini's
great genius, I believe that Ruskin's condemnation of this work
of his was just.

Then, in addition, to these object lessons, Mr. Ruskin
would frequently hold conversations with us on various matters
of taste. On these occasions he was most kind and friendly.
Previously to my joining his class, he had conducted several
sketching excursions into Dulwich Wood, then beyond the
boundary of London ; and at the end of each excursion, he had
invited his pupils to a tea at the " Greyhound " Inn at Dulwich.

One of his pupils spoke, at a College meeting, of what he called
Mr. Ruskin's "brotherly conduct" on these occasions. This
I have also observed in the conversations which he has had
with us, for, though they were given for our instruction, he
always made us feel that he was a friend, not a dictator, so that
no one was afraid to ask any question, and he would freely
impart information from the rich stores of his great knowledge.
These conversations, and the written commentaries of which I
have just been speaking, have laid the foundation of whatever
taste I may happen to possess.

Not only has the taste of his students been benefited by
his directing their attention to beauties of nature and of art
not apparent at first sight, but professional artists, whose
practical knowledge would enable them to fully comprehend
the depth of his knowledge, have spoken of the benefit they
have derived from his society. Mr. Lowes Dickinson, in the
College Jubilee Book, and Sir Edward Burne-Jones, as recorded
in Lady Burne-Jones's life of her husband, have testified to the
great advantage it was to converse with one who had so studied
the principles of art and the influences which affect it. It is
said that Mr. Ruskin suggested the design of, some have said
that be actually designed, the aisle columns of St. Paul's Church,
Herne Hill. Whichever may be the case, it appears from
this that we owe the one undeniably good feature of that
church to Mr. Ruskin. All artists, however, did not agree with
him, even if they were on his side in the art controversies
which then raged; I mean the controversies—then pretty
fierce—respecting Pre-Raphaelitism and Gothic architecture.
The world suffers the latter, but has put down the former,
though I think the world's conscience is not quite easy on the
subject, as one may perceive (thus late) by an occasional
newspaper or magazine article. Mr. Ruskin, in one of his
discourses with his pupils, spoke of something, I forget what it
was, which Holman Hunt ought to do. "But there," said
Mr. Ruskin, "it's no good advising Holman Hunt; he won't
take anybody's advice, he's marked out a course for himself,
and will pursue it."

And yet it was only a few days after this that one of my
fellow-students, who was also a Royal Academy student, and
a portrait painter, told me that he had been speaking to
Mr. Ruskin about some art matter, telling what difficulties he
was striving to overcome, and of advice which friends had
given him; whereupon Mr. Ruskin had said, "There, if you
go following people's advice, you'll never do anything at all."
"What," asked my friend, "could I say to him? Was I to
say to him, Am I then to reject the advice you are now giving
me? And why do you blame Holman Hunt for doing what
you suggest to me that I ought to do?" Perhaps Mr. Ruskin
could foresee to what heights Hunt's determination would
ultimately lead him. Hunt had, at that time, about 1857, done

much splendid work; he had (as he tells us in his "Pre-Raphaelitism: a Fight for Art") set himself a task and, in pursuance of it, had rejected advice which, if followed, would probably have caused him to become a common fashionable painter. He, in consequence, had had to lead a very hard life, and of his struggle we have reaped the benefit in the pleasure which we derive from the contemplation of his masterly paintings, in which he goes from strength to strength till finally, in "The Lady of Shalott," he seems to have excelled himself. When I first saw this splendid piece of colour, I could not, for a few moments, believe that it had been painted by an Englishman; it seemed to me as if it must have been the work of some old Venetian.

(*To be continued.*)

JOHN ROEBUCK.

In our last issue space only permitted us to announce the death of John Roebuck in America, in March last, with an intimation that a fuller notice would appear in our next number. John Roebuck, wood turner by trade, like Alfred Grugeon, made his mark alike in the College, of which he was one of the earliest Fellows, and in the Nineteenth Middlesex Volunteer Corps, of the second company of which he became captain. As a result of attending the Inaugural Meeting in St. Martin's Hall, he was one of the "First Nighters," *i.e.*, one of those who joined the College on its opening night, October 26th, 1854. Roebuck was then in his twenty-third year. Shortly after the College was founded, the Council started an Adult School in the Hall of Association, 34, Castle Street, Oxford Street, which was afterwards held in the basement of No. 45, Great Ormond Street; and of this school, Roebuck, in succession to William Rossiter, was for some years the appointed teacher. In 1859, on the formation of the Nineteenth Middlesex, which originated in the College, and of which Tom Hughes was Colonel, Roebuck was the first sergeant, and ultimately became Captain, when his Colonel presented him with his regimental sword and equipments. He was known in the corps as a hard worker, a most efficient officer, and a crack shot. In 1864, he left England for America, where he remained up to the time of his death. On taking leave of the College an address signed by the Principal, the Rev. F. D. Maurice, on behalf of all, was presented to him which said:—

We look back upon the past and remember how you have been a part of the College from its foundation. In 1854, you came; in 1855, you assisted in the work of teaching; in 1856, you won a certificate in Algebra and Euclid; in 1858, you became a Fellow and Member of Council; you also served long on the Executive and Finance Committee; you have for three years been captain of a College company in the 19th, and as such notably successful. Those are your College honours, your College roll, to us very memorable. Manfully have you, a working man, trod what we call the royal road to learning—diligence; and in our little Society, in which you have moved so continually, you have always been to us an upright, faithful, and most helpful friend, sustaining by marked example the best purposes of the College; emphatically, one of us; heartily giving of your best to us; heartily accepting what we in turn had to bestow. For this we are most especially grateful; for without you, and men like you, the Working Men's College—in so many respects, and above all in its social aims, an experiment—must have been a short-lived enterprise. Though we must part now, we believe—were the Atlantic twice as broad—we shall be fellow-workers still, fellow-workers in the good cause in which you have striven here. That the poor man, and in a sense all men, may win the privilege that wait on knowledge; that the clear voice of truth may be better heard; that class may be united to class, not by necessity only, but by generous duties and common sympathies; that the humblest labour shall be accounted honourable, and the daily life of the worker be felt to be, as it is, a sacred trust to himself and his fellow men; herein is our task and yours, our hope and your hope, for

"Unto him who works, and knows he works,
That same grand year is ever at the door."

On the occasion of Mr. Bride's visit to America in November last, Roebuck sent the College the portrait which Mr. A. E. Emslie painted of him in 1875; and he was greatly pleased to know that it had been hung in the Common Room in company with those of many men whom he delighted to honour, especially George Tansley, referred to by him as "my dearest friend and fellow-worker of them all." The College, although so far removed, was always a living thing to him, and his interest in it and his friends there was an abiding one, and never flagged. His greatest wish in later years was to be able to see it once more.

LUBBOCK FIELD CLUB.

IN spite of the unpromising condition of the weather on April 11th, no fewer than fifteen men turned out for a ramble on some Surrey Commons. It was dull and heavy in London, misty at Epsom, and matters got worse until a heavy shower at Oxshott cleared the air at mid-day. Under foot the country was in very bad condition, the mud being a revelation to the novices, and consequently the distance covered, some nineteen miles, was a very respectable walk. Starting from Epsom, we crossed the railway, and followed it on to the common. The swampy state of the ground made progress difficult, but in due course we got round "The Wells," and reached Ashtead Common. Here we missed two of our men, and although a search party was sent out, up to the time of writing nothing has been heard as to their fate. Crossing the Kingston Road, we entered Stoke Wood by Steer Lane and emerged on Oxshott Heath, encountering a tremendous downpour en route, as mentioned above. We lunched at Oxshott and then made our way, partly by road, and partly by path, to Cobham, where two more of the party left us. We then followed a path by the Mole to "Pointers" and an equally picturesque road to Wisley Common. After a long halt by Ockham Mere, we turned south and made our way to Effingham Station. From here a particularly muddy track connects the three commons known as Effingham, Bank's, and Bookham, and into this, after some hesitation, we plunged. We reached Bookham Station in good time for the 6.15 train. Vegetation was decidedly backward, although some good shows of primroses were seen. Moschetal, Periwinkle, Cowslips, Wood Anemones, Celandine, and Gorse were in flower, and large quantities of Butcher's Broom were noticed. Great numbers of dead toads were on view in Ockham Pond, where also some curious Infusoria, forming masses of jelly a couple of inches in diameter, were found. The secretary reported another pond simply alive with big waterfleas.

The next outing will take place on May 10th, to Fawkham, Mr. J. Fotheringham having for the fourth time invited the club to visit him at his delightful Kentish home. As arrangements have to be made with the railway, it will be necessary for all members wishing to take part in this, the pleasantest outing of the year, to send in their names before April 30th, to

J. HOLLOWAY, *Hon. Secretary.*

COLLEGE NOTES.

THE Senior Student Examination, which will be held, according to the term programme, at the end of June or the beginning of July, in Arithmetic, Grammar, and History, is a stepping-stone to the Associateship and Fellowship of the College. It is now some years since there was a "boom" in Senior Students. 1894 was a record year, yielding no fewer than eleven of these stalwarts, of whom four were Senior Student Scholars. The grade of Senior Student may also be obtained, apart from this examination, by any member taking three first stage certificates, one in each subject, if gained within three years, or by taking two advanced stage certificates, one of them being for arithmetic. But the examination we have referred to affords an opportunity, which should not be lost sight of, for a capable student to qualify for the highest College honours.

Attention is drawn to the course of lectures on Tuesday evenings, at 8 o'clock, by Mr. Bernard Turner, B.A., on the "Life, Works, and Speeches of Edmund Burke."

Mr. E. H. Carter, B.A., of the Board of Education, examined the Shorthand classes on April 2nd, and granted certificates to the following :—In the Theory, E. J. Burgess, A. Gude, and Leonard C. Pike. For Speed, at 80 words, W. A. Ball, H. H. Hughes, F. P. Leach, and S. J. Watson ; and, at 100 words, C. H. Thetford. Thirteen students sat, of whom two attempted higher rates of speed in addition to the tests for which they obtained certificates.

On Monday, April 13th, a meeting of Students and Teachers, arranged by the Common Room Committee, was held in the Common Room. Mr. A. Hepburn took the chair, and Mr. A. S. Lupton gave a spirited and masterly address on "College Ideals," characteristic of the speaker. In dealing with the College traditions, he passed in review the work of the various founders and of those who had followed them. He emphasized the ideal of good-fellowship and the absence of class distinction in the College, dwelt upon the necessity for wider and classical reading—a favorite topic of his—and ended his remarks with an appeal to students, new and old, to maintain the old tradition of the College so well exemplified by the work of the men he had mentioned, and particularly by that of George Tansley.

The annual general meeting of the Debating Society was held in the Common Room on Tuesday, April 14th, when Mr. A. E. Homewood took the chair for the last time this season. It was gathered from the secretary's report that the society was in a most flourishing condition, having had a very varied series of highly interesting and educational discussions, and altogether a most successful year, although the number of new speakers had been few. A motion was introduced and discussed, calling for a larger number of literary debates in future seasons and for the alteration of the title of the society to the "Literary and Debating Society"; and it was also suggested that the society should devote certain of its meetings to holding a Parliament. Both motions were postponed. In place of the retiring officers, Mr. Sidney Stagg was elected president; Mr. Liddelow, vice-president; and Mr. Alexander Hepburn, secretary—all exceedingly popular appointments, and ones which should ensure the success of the society's meetings next term.

Mr. J. Kuylman, of Amsterdam, who was a member of this College ten years ago, and is now a professor of English in Holland, paid our College a visit last month, and was delighted with the new building. He says the Dutch have a Working Men's College in Amsterdam, which they call "Ons Huis" (Our Home), and which is devoted to evening class teaching, the principal studies being the French, German, and English languages. Mr. Kuylman taught there for a time. They have common and coffee rooms, as we have; also singing classes and social meetings, but the social life is not so much developed as it is with us.

The Harriers.—The idea that the studious inclinations of the ordinary College man leave him no time or disposition to engage in the more vigorous sports, has recently received a decided set-back in the formation in the College of what may prove to be the nucleus of a strong harriers' club. The suggestion of a periodical run out was thought to be a good one, and a notice was put up inviting the names of any who felt disposed to take part in a short canter of a few miles around the circle of Regent's Park. A large number of probable starters subscribed their names to the list, and the first meet took place on Wednesday, April 8th, at 9.30 p.m., and was entirely successful, fully justifying the decision to continue the runs. There is no subscription levied, and any members interested in this extremely healthful and convenient form of exercise should talk to C. F. W. Mead, who is arranging the meetings.

The last Collegians' Dance of the Season took place in the Maurice Hall on Saturday, April 25th, and was generally agreed to be the most successful of the four which have been held. The Committee had decided to devote the proceeds to swelling the Grand Pianoforte Fund, which will be enriched by several pounds as the result of this subscription. The band gave excellent support to a delightful programme, and there was not that over-crowding which had marked the previous dances. Mr. A. Owen and his committee are to be congratulated on the well organized and most enjoyable gatherings which have resulted from their efforts.

The Musical Society's Concert, arranged for May 2nd, at 7.30 p.m., in aid of the Piano Fund, promises to be a big success. According to the posters, Tom Barnard and Miss Forsyth will appear in a dramatic duologue, by the kind permission of the author, Mr. Alfred Sutro; Davis, Fenton, Barnett, and McWilliam will interpret the rôles in one of the funniest of all farces; Green will give us two of Chevalier's most entertaining monologues; Miss Olive Cooke, Miss E. Graife, and Mrs. Perry will sing, as also will Hammant, Lawrence, Paterson, and Perry, whilst Nield will inform us, incidentally, what Melzer, Munro, Dr. Furnivall, the Sketching Club, and the Common Room Committee have been saying and doing. With R. H. Marks in the chair, Tarr at the piano, Nye as scene shifter, Lawrence as call-boy, and Offer as stage carpenter and lime-light man, all should go well.

Sheridan's comedy, "The Rivals," will be read by the Shakespeare readers at the final meeting of the season, on May 3rd, at 7.30—a ladies' night.

The Common Room Committee have purchased and placed in the Coffee Room two large upholstered arm-chairs of special design for comfort, made to their order at a cost of five guineas, and they have also provided some more wooden arm-chairs for that room.

Mr. John Fotheringham, of Fawkham, has repeated his kind invitation to the Lubbock Field Club to pay him a visit on May 10th, and the hon. secretary will be glad to hear from those members wishing to avail themselves of the same, in order that the necessary arrangements may be made.

The Annual College Sports are arranged to be held on Saturday, July 11th, at Wembley Park.

Mrs. Roebuck, writing on April 6th, from Winchendon, Mass., says: "We are very much pleased with the kind, sympathetic letters I have received from my husband's old College friends. He appreciated so highly anything from the College, or any one connected with it. I think he kept every scrap of anything about the College. His son Arthur has his father's prizes—a silver cup, teapot, medals, gun and sword; and books by F. D. Maurice, Tom Hughes, and Dr. Furnivall, all of which he will prize."

The Common Room Committee are arranging a number of Saturday afternoon outings, the first of which will take place on Saturday, May 9th, when, through the kindness of Mr. D. C. Cambridge, twenty-five members will be shown over Barclay and Perkins's Brewery. Full particulars will be found on the notice board in the Common Room.

Mr. Dent has presented to the Common Room the Co-operative Wholesale Societies' Annual for 1908.

Some of the members of the Rev. B. H. Alford's class have secured a large photograph (18 by 20) of Orchardson's portrait of Mr. Alford, which has been suitably framed and hung in the Common Room.

SHAKESPEARE READINGS.

On March 1st, "Romeo and Juliet" was read, the audience was the largest of the season, and the reading was generally good. As usual, Miss Steptoe, who took the part of Juliet, gave the lines as Shakespeare must have meant them to be spoken. Special reference, too, should be made to Miss Steele's brilliant rendering of the nurse's part, which partook more of the nature of acting than of mere reading. Romeo's impersonation was entrusted to Barnard, who executed it with much feeling, whilst Peck was an able exponent of Tybalt. Harley read Mercutio with the necessary vigour, and Gates Fowler was the gentle confessor. The visitors expressed great pleasure at the reading.

Henry IV., part I., was read on March 15th, when the striking features were Mead's Prince Hal and Harley's Hotspur, both of which were excellent. Hayward was responsible for Falstaff.

It is suggested that the society shall hold a summer reading in Epping Forest. Those ladies and gentlemen who desire to assist will kindly notify Paterson as soon as possible, so that the matter may be arranged betimes.

GATES FOWLER.

THE STUDENTS' CALENDAR FOR MAY.

Sat., 2nd.—Musical Society's Concert, 7.30 p.m. Geometry examination, 6 to 10 p.m. Art examinations begin.

Sun., 3rd.—Furnivall Cycling Club's run to Croxley Green. Shakespeare Readers read "The Rivals," 7.30.

Mon., 4th.—Maurice Chess Club annual general meeting, 9 p.m.

Tues., 5th.—Executive Committee, 8 p.m. Mr. B. Turner's lecture on Burke, 8 p.m. Physiology examination, 7 to 10 p.m.

Thurs., 7th.—Citizens' lunch, 1.30. Geology examination, 7 to 10 p.m.

Sat., 9th.—Cycling Club's run to Harrow Weald. Building Construction examination, 6 to 10 p.m. C. R. C. outing to Barclay and Perkins's Brewery.

Sun., 10th.—Lubbock Field Club visit Mr. Fotheringham at Fawkham.

Tues., 12th.—Executive Committee, 8 p.m. Mr. B. Turner's lecture on Burke, 8 p.m.

Thurs., 14th.—Electricity examination, 7 to 10 p.m.

Fri., 15th. Sound, Light, and Heat examination, 7 to 10 p.m.

Sat., 16th.—Machine Construction examination, 6 to 10 p.m.

Sun., 17th.—Cycling Club's run to Virginia Water.

Mon., 18th.—Theoretical Inorganic Chemistry examination, 7 to 10 p.m.

Tues., 19th.—Executive Committee, 8 p.m. Mr. B. Turner's lecture on Burke, 8 p.m.

Fri., 22nd.—Botany examination, 7 to 10 p.m.

Sat., 23rd.—Cycling Club's run to Ruislip. Practical Inorganic Chemistry examination, stage 2, 5.15 to 10.30. Cornford Cambridge Excursion.

Mon., 25th.—Practical Inorganic Chemistry examination, stage 1, 7.15 to 9.30.

Tues., 26th.—Executive Committee, 8 p.m. Mr. B. Turner's lecture on Burke, 8 p.m.

Sun., 31st.—Cycling Club's run to Chipperfield.

Announcements of coming events for insertion in the Students' Calendar should, if possible, be sent in by the 20th of the month.

SATURDAY NIGHT LECTURE.

THE SOCIAL IDEAL.

On Saturday, March 21st, Mr. Goldsworthy Lowes Dickinson, of King's College, Cambridge, son of Mr. Lowes Dickinson, one of our founders, gave a thought-compelling lecture at the College under the above title. Mr. Lionel Jacob, Vice-Principal, took the chair.

Mr. DICKINSON referred, at the outset, to two books recently published, one by Mr. Mallock, and the other by Mr. H. G. Wells, as representing the attitudes between which people seemed to be oscillating on Social questions. Mr. Mallock, he said, is nothing if not hard-headed. All Englishmen like hard-headed people. The only objection to them is that you cannot get anything into their heads except what is there already. Mr. Wells is a genial man. He makes Socialism so delightful that it is like the lion in "A Midsummer Night's Dream"—it roars like any sucking dove. He puts Socialism to us in a way in which I think it ought to be put, especially to a British audience. I do not think the German version will do. The rigid theory, scientifically based, of the war of the classes, rarely appeals very strongly to any great number of Englishmen. I think we are more inclined to agree to some general direction in the way of progress, than to formulate cut and dried schemes. I do not anticipate that we can produce a millenium by legislation, or any other method. One awkward factor, not created by our institutions, is "nature." Nature has put all sorts of extremely disagreeable conditions into life, one of which is the original curse of labour. I do not imagine that the Anarchists have solved the problem, when they say, everyone shall do more or less what he is inclined to do—that everyone will be inclined to do some of the work necessary at the moment, and that all work will be turned into play. I do not think that Socialistic idealism implies that kind of Utopia. I do not think it can possibly imply that we are to have no more earthquakes, volcanoes, or shipwrecks; although one hopes it may imply that there need not be famines, because those are things that can be provided against. I do not think it can possibly guarantee to every individual a perfectly happy life, for there is a certain truth in Goldsmith's couplet,

> "How small of all that human hearts endure,
>   That part which laws or kings can cause or cure."

The fact remains, however, that quite a new spirit came into the world somewhere about the eighteenth century, and it has hardly yet begun to work out its consequences. I mean the belief that human institutions are not matters of fate, like earthquakes and volcanoes, but matters of human will; that what is called human nature is not an ultimate, final, unalterable fact, always to be connected with such things as the existence of classes, wealth, poverty, etc., but that a great deal can and will be modified. I regard a great deal of the quarrel on these questions as a quarrel, not as to the means of doing what you want, but as to what you want; and if you like, at bottom, as a question of what religious people call "faith." I don't think faith is the antithesis to—still less incompatible with - science and knowledge. I think all knowledge becomes valuable, according as it is accompanied by a change in will—that is to say, a certain belief in a determination to do certain things. If you look through history, I think it is clear that almost always in the West, and still more in the East, men have hitherto accepted their social institutions, just as they have accepted the facts of nature, as so much fate. Not until the eighteenth century did the doctrine of a belief in progress enter into the consciousness of the West; and it is that, at bottom, that underlies the movement which is sometimes summed up broadly as Socialism, but for which I would rather find another word, because Socialism is generally used as a synonym for everything that is monstrous and absurd and extreme. Wells calls the two parties "men of good-will," and "men who are not of good-will." Men of good-will, whatever they may think about the immediate possible direction for advance, do want, sooner or later, to make profound modifications in our social institutions; and they come to believe a great many things are possible, or may become possible, which have not in the past been considered possible at all. Their discontent with what exists is not simply passive ; it is an active quest to find what is wrong, and to find what you want to substitute for the wrong, and how you are going to do it. Now, I think that the quarrel that men have with the existing state of things is certainly not because they hold that society in the West is worse than it has been. It is a reasonable doctrine, that society is better than it has ever been before, in many important respects, and that there is reality in the belief in progress ; but people think they can make it better still. Criticism of what exists turns upon the conceptions of Justice and Liberty. There is nothing about which men quarrel more fundamentally, nothing about which they care more, than what is signified by those two abstract words, justice and liberty. Men of many schools—probably Mr. Mallock among them—hold that much in our society is unjust ; and I may remind you that I think we are beginning to have a rather new conception of justice. I don't know if you have read the Republic of Plato. It is certainly the greatest of all the Utopias, but it represents a conception of justice which I do not believe we or our successors are going to adopt. It assumes as a fundamental fact that Society is divided, and ought to be divided, into fixed classes, and especially into a governing class and a class of governed. And Plato, carrying out the conception to its logical extreme, assumes that these classes are fixed and hereditary, and that each of them is bred for its proper function ; and he holds mainly, that what you want to do is to produce a class of proper rulers, and then all the problems of society will solve themselves. The paradox was that the rulers or governors ought to be philosophers. But Plato did not mean by a philosopher, what I am sure you mean—a person who sat in a corner making metaphysical theories that were not true. He meant a person of the highest possible aptitude and training, physically, morally, and intellectually ; and trained by a perfect discipline, as well as by an intellectual theory. His thesis was that if you established his Republic, you would have perfect harmony between the classes, and therefore you would have perfect justice. Now, I think that sort of conception of justice has ordinarily been before men's minds throughout history. Society has been arranged in classes, or castes. Legislators, moralists, reformers, have always tried to make each class do its duty. I do not wish to throw contempt on that view. But I do not think it is the notion of the future. I do not think it is what people think of now, when they think of justice. A great deal has happened since the French Revolution. The conception of justice which men are coming to have generally, is a democratic conception ; and I suggest to you that it is a very much too narrow view of Democracy to suppose it means merely throwing the franchise open to all men, or even to all women. Democracy means something which cuts much deeper than that. It means really that everyone is to count alike. I do not mean to be alike. I think it is a travesty upon democracy to say that it wants everyone to be alike. But it does mean that there are not to be classes, in the sense that there are now in most countries, and that there have been throughout history so far. It means the abolition of privilege ; and that again means a great deal more than would appear at first sight. The French Revolution, and all that followed it, cut away a great deal of privilege, and amongst other things, the idea that there should be classes of people set apart by law for certain functions, or exempt by law from certain obligations. But we see now that the distinctions of class depend on something more subtle than that ; they depend on economic factors, and on the institution of property. There can be no doubt that the socialistic analysis of modern society is sound on that point ; and that the modern privilege depends on the fact that private persons own the means of production and distribution, and on the fact that all wealth is handed on by private persons to their children. That means, that you have always, on the one hand, rent and interest and profit receivers, and on the other hand, wage-earners. This economic class-system exists in the old countries, and progressively in the new. It is possible for a man to rise from the bottom of the ladder to the top, but it is a very rare and difficult thing. The rule is, to rise a little, or sink a little. On the whole the classes are fairly stereotyped. That view does not conflict with the generalization that every private soldier carries in his knapsack the *batón* of the field marshal. But the real question is—How many have the chance of using it? These are the facts on which, more and more, people begin to indict Society on the score of justice. It is a negative proposition. They say, it does not seem just that a man's position should depend on the position of his parents. The fact that it does so, is due to particular institutions, and, amongst other things, to the law allowing the inheritance of property. I could, of course, engage in a long and harrowing picture of what poverty means, and what wealth means, but I need not do so. I will presume that all that is in your minds ; and the problem that there is what the earlier advocates of Democracy feared or hoped, is true—that political democracy means, quite inevitably, some attempt to modify the fundamental institution of property, in the interests of the same ideal which produced political democracy.

Then, in the second place, there is the question of "liberty." The main attack on Socialism used to be based on the ground that it was going to take away everyone's liberty. Seeley, in his "Essay on Liberty," tries to distinguish the various senses in which the word is used. Shelley, he points out, once used it in the sense of meaning something to eat. There is something in that view. I maintain that one kind of liberty does mean something to eat. That is an economic liberty, as distinct from administrative liberty. Can a system be introduced, of governmental legislation which, though it might make us less free, would not make us less happy than we are? What is freedom? Poverty makes a man more un-free than anything else possibly can. Nature has imposed the chief slavery— the slavery of work ; it is no use kicking against that. That applies to all except the fortunate few. For the rest, it depends on the amount of time they have for leisure, the amount they have laid by for sickness, for the rainy day ; upon that depends the essence of liberty. It is preposterous to say that the mass of the people in any modern state are free, in the sense that a certain minority are free. The working classes were less free before the factory laws than they have been since. Regulations or governmental rules do not necessarily decrease freedom ; they may increase it. I personally think rules a great nuisance. But I should think it rather preposterous to say, then we will not have any, because I can get on without them. And it confuses all the issues to say, that government means coercion. As government becomes more popular, it means the rules people lay down for themselves, in order to co-operate harmoniously ; and they make them, because they will have a more harmonious and freer life, under rules, than without them. A good deal of the attack on socialistic legislation depends on the confusion of two things —(i.) coercion ; and (ii.) regulation, on which the mass of the people voluntarily agree, in order to live life in a more harmonious, free, and satisfactory way. I am sure that people of the Anglo-Saxon race, whether socialistic or not, want liberty, and do not want to diminish it, just as they want justice. They are united at all events in this—that they do not desire the tying-up of their activities, out of a sheer love of red tape. To my mind, the way we ought to look at the thing called Socialism is opposite to the way in which the press are looking at it ; opposite to the way in which a certain number of Socialists are looking at it, and in which an immense number of people who read the press are looking at it. Before you can do anything reasonable with the latter, you have got to get out of their heads the notion that what is called "property"—which means the present rules for holding and disposing of property—is something ultimate, fundamental, and final, on which the well-being of society depends ; and the notion that there are no means of altering it, without the destruction of Empire, the family, and all other things, of which Lord Rosebery is so much afraid. Any fundamental change in the rules governing property must necessarily affect a great many people. It would affect Lord Rosebery's descendants a great deal. But that is not the only, nor the right, way to look at the matter. You ought to look at it, and see if you cannot discover a more reasonable method of distributing property, so as not to upset the things we really value. This is a perfectly reasonable suggestion; and it is a most extraordinary thing to me that you cannot mention the word "property," without a kind of awful tremor running through the company, or without every kind of bad motive being imputed to you. As if we were all in love with property! People say the same things about Collectivism, or collective management. I wish I had the kind of mind that makes political economists. I have not. If I had, I would re-write Economics with a new bias. For everyone, including the man of science, has his bias. Political economists have a bias of extraordinary admiration for a system of free trade everywhere, for open competition, for buying in the cheapest market and selling in the dearest, etc. But a modern economist of the intelligence of Adam Smith, or Ricardo, might with advantage set himself to weigh the other side of their arguments; and to point out the degree to which open competition does *not* produce the kind of utilities you want, as and where you want them. I commend to your attention a recent book, "Social Conditions in West Ham," containing a perfectly dry statistical account of the development of that district. Houses for working-men have been put up there on a system which works out so that the worst article, and the one least possibly suitable for its purpose, is being supplied by people whose only object is to make money out of it. Then again, you cannot get decent food for the poor, without an army of inspectors to prevent it being poisoned and adulterated, who see to their business most inefficiently. The deterioration and adulteration of the necessities of life is necessarily a heavy indictment of our competitive system.

German collectivists have a creed and formula which they apply to the existing condition of affairs. They say, it is working itself out so that there are going to be fewer and fewer rich people, who will own the means of production; and there are going to be more and more wage-earners, and ultimately, by the State assuming the control of property, the community will hold all the capital and will employ all the people. But this, like every other generalization, is too simple for the facts. The idea of the community running everything is in itself preposterous to many people. Mr. Winston Churchill, for instance, says that the notion of Government offices, as big as Hyde Park, running all the trade and commerce in the country, is not only absurd, but is unthinkable. Perhaps it is. At the same time, you must remember that you have a certain amount of successful public-conducted business done already. If the State is to do communal trading or business, it will not run it with the present kind of civil servant. You will have to recreate the political machinery. There are some business men, more or less predatory, who run enormous businesses and have the necessary brains to do it. The whole of the oil business of the world, I believe, is controlled by two great syndicates—one American, and the other Russian. Certain kinds of business can be run in a centralized way. The collectivist would say that the kind of men who run them now would run them under Collectivism, only for the community, instead of for private ends. Of course, you would need to have a totally different method of appointing people. But a system of communal trading, properly controlled and managed, will, I think, be a solution which may be found to be in many cases satisfactory. Another ingenious idea has been put forward, that we should retain our present method of private and competitive business; but that the State should be the rent receiver and debenture-holder, and own the capital and the land, and let it out. Possibly that idea might be applicable in some directions. If ever the State became the owner of the land, it could simply take the rent, as the landlords do now, and let the land be handled by private persons. Or it could hold, and lease out to companies, the railways and steamers, and take the rent. However, I do not think it is very useful for us, or for anyone, to say that this or that is the way things are to be done in the future. Yet, it is important that people should turn over in their minds the various suggested methods, and that experiments should be made. I hold no brief for municipal trading, as we stand at present, but it is of great importance that experiments be made and the results recorded. When one puts what I may call the case for socialistic changes in this vague way, people of positive minds get very impatient. They want one to give them a cut and dried scheme in writing—so that they may knock it over. But, even if they succeed in doing so, that is not conclusive. Two processes will have to go on together, one a process of conversion, and the other a process of experiment. It is my own private belief, that the conversion has got to include, not only the men of the working class – who, I expect, have but the vaguest notion of what Socialism means—but also the employers and owners of property. I have the honour to possess some friends in the city, with whom I always quarrel consistently, and who give me the most dismal impression of the intellectual attitude of the City man on social ideals. He is very unintelligent outside his business; as nervous as a child, so much so that he shudders with horror when a Liberal government comes into power, even before it has begun to do anything at all. Although to a certain extent his heart is in the right place, for he is generally a good husband and a good father, yet socially his heart is not in the right place. He regards his particular income as though he had made it all himself, and as though it were not contributed to by the whole organization of which he forms a part. Although he has got so much of it, and other people have got so little, he has a hard and fast idea of "my property, which I have got, and for which I am going to fight at the hustings." You will not get on much further while that attitude exists in any class, especially while it exists amongst the ablest business men we have. I suggest to you that the Social Ideal means a change of heart, a change of will, and a change of intelligence. There is a tremendous amount of conversion to be done. And then again, everyone knows that it is a most extraordinarily difficult thing to touch a thing like modern society, without doing something or other that you did not expect to do at all. There is a licensing measure before Parliament. I have no particular dislike for publicans or brewers, but the attitude of the trade is not the attitude of a body of men anxious to do the best they can for society; and the methods adopted are not hopeful for that section of society who are trying to help on society. Then, there is the eight hours' day for miners; as soon as a bill is introduced with this object, the owners say the prices of coal must be raised; but why should it be necessarily the consumer, and not the person who draws the dividends, who has got to suffer? What I am driving at is this: Behind the economic laws, which I do not dispute, as long as they are true, lies the presumption of a certain state of mind or will—the will to get all you can, and give up nothing. Now, it is no use trying to build up a better community on that basis. What is wanted is an intellectual change. It is extraordinarily difficult to change oneself in these things, and much more difficult to convert anyone else; but if you want to make a transition to a socialistic state, classes and individuals will have to be prepared to make sacrifices of that nature which is now called confiscation. However gently you are let down in the process, you can do nothing except on the hypothesis that some one is going to be let down, and I see no reason why that should be called confiscation. Suppose we all agree that the economic rent of land should belong to the community, and not to private persons, and it is arranged that this shall be accomplished at the end of a time limit of fifty years, there need not be any great hardship to anyone. Present owners would get an annuity for fifty years, after which so much property would be taken away; but who would feel it? If you wish to re-organize a thing like property, you must, in equity, make that transition as easy as you can. It is possible to conceive of a progressive restriction upon inheritance, by a graduated increase of death duties, which would effect the vesting of property in the community, without causing hardship. Such words as "confiscation" and "robbery" ought not to be flung about indiscriminately; but people ought to regard property as a thing guaranteed by the law for the public good, and which should be from time to time modified, as gradually as possible, so as to prevent harm to the community, but which cannot be tied up for ever by an iniquitous system. There is only one way of making people look at these questions properly, and that is to arouse in them the passion for an ideal. This is not impractical. It is really the most practical thing in the world. Mr. H. G. Wells, in his book, "New Worlds for Old," talks to us in a perfectly genial, kindly, unsensational, and sensible manner. He does not set down cut and dried theories, but he does introduce the attitude of good-will. Given good-will, you can approach your economic difficulties with some hope that you may find some useful way out of them. Mr. Mallock's book, with all the sound sense it displays, is the exact opposite to the kind of book you want to help you in this matter, because it is bad-will and not good-will that it pre-supposes. This is not really a matter of science or theory, but of "will"—what are you going to choose human nature to be and make it be, first, in yourself, and secondly in others, and most important of all, in your own children? (Cheers.)

Mr. JACOB proposed a cordial vote of thanks to the lecturer, which was given in the usual way.

W.M.C. DEBATING SOCIETY.

THE placid but interesting course which the Society has marked out for itself this session has been very steadily pursued since the previous notes were written; and the result is certainly satisfying to those of us who seek rather the deliberate opinion of our fellow-member quietly expressed than the declamation of the superficial student.

Among the more important of the subjects discussed may be mentioned Co-operative Trading (Tuesday, January 28th), in connection with which Mr. R. N. M. Bailey, B.A., opposed Mr. W. H. Berry, Secretary of the Club and Institute Union, producing a debate which showed how very deeply this policy has a hold on the average College man.

No one regretted more than Mr. Stephen Gwynn, M.P., his inability, owing to the pressure of parliamentary business, to open the discussion on Home Rule, on Tuesday, February 4th, a regret which he personally expressed on a subsequent occasion when he was able to be present. The thanks of the Society are due however to the Hon. Hugh O'Neill, who, visiting us as an opposer, undertook to open the debate, and in so doing revealed not only an intimate acquaintance with the Irish question as presented on the other side of the Channel, but the natural gift of oratory which seems to be every Irishman's birthright. On this occasion also Mr. Cash treated us to one of his eloquent perorations, and altogether this may be regarded as one of the most successful evenings of this year.

In directing attention to the question of self-government in Egypt and India (Tuesday, February 11th), Mr. Merriman, B.A., distinctly raised the level of the topics ordinarily dealt with, besides presenting an object-lesson to the average man of the responsibilities of Empire, which, though so lightly regarded, are none the less real and urgent problems in every-day politics. Mr. A. H. Perry, who kindly consented to oppose at a moment's notice, gave us one of those interesting speeches which reveal the width of his view and the extent of his knowledge.

The failure of the Jury system has also been forcibly expounded by Mr. A. L. Stephen, B.A. (Tuesday, February 18th), although we were not on that occasion in any mood to dispose of our ancient privilege.

The views which Mr. C. H. Kisch, B.A., set forth against the creation of Wages Boards, on Tuesday, February 25th, revealed in a marked degree the great difficulties under which the social reformer is working, even when dealing with so obvious an evil as sweating; and the informing speech of the Secretary of the Anti-Sweating League, Mr. Mallon, who was the opposer, gave us an opportunity of getting to closer quarters with one of the greatest curses of modern civilization.

Mr. John Scott, B.A., whose extensive experience as a schoolmaster enabled him to draw very largely upon the practical results of inquiry into the subject, would not countenance for a moment any steps for the compulsory feeding of school-children ; and after learning from him the many aspects of this question, it certainly behoves one to pause before launching so large and costly a scheme as that contained in the Government's bill of 1906. It was extremely interesting that on this evening, Tuesday, March 3rd, Mr. Randall made his *debût* as an opposer, and the vigorous onslaught he made on his opponent's case, on the grounds of expediency and humanity, was very much to the taste of a good many members.

Probably in presenting the subject of Municipal Trading, on Tuesday, March 10th, Mr. Williamson, a prominent member of the Crouch End Parliament, was to some extent ploughing too well known a field ; but his aptness of speech, combined with a thorough knowledge of the case, certainly made one very willing to undergo a restatement of the position, and Mr. E. F. Wise, though valiant to a degree, must have found his task of opposing none too light.

The payment of Members of Parliament, a subject recurring somewhat frequently in these days, was Mr. Duncan Todd's theme on Tuesday, March 17th, and he certainly dealt with it in a most interesting and comprehensive manner. Although Mr. A. H. Perry was able to bring forth some strong arguments to the contrary, the victory was overwhelmingly with the opener.

However slack members may have been in their attendance during the session, a large number were present on Tuesday, April 14th, when the annual meeting of the Society took place.   F. E. LIDDELOW, *Hon. Secretary.*

W. M. C. MUSICAL SOCIETY.

THE Musical Society spent a merry hour and a half at their smoking concert in the Coffee Room, on March 15th, Mr. R. H. Marks, the president, being in the chair. The students turned up in good numbers, there being standing room only. Lawrence opened the programme with "A Soldier's Song," followed by C. F. Marshall with "A Hunting we will go," the choruses of both songs being sung by the students. Hitchcock, a new member, then recited in very good style, a scene from "A Tale of Two Cities," and another member, with like excellence, recited "My Lord Tom Noddy." More fresh talent was welcomed in J. F. Winter, who sang "Drake's Drum." Duchesne then gave us a new ditty, entitled "The Animals' Band"; this seemed to put the fellows in a very happy vein, and as an encore he had to give them "The Poacher." "Queen of my Heart" was next on the list, and was very tenderly sung by Ainge. Birrell met with a very warm reception, his recitation being Kipling's "Mandalay." Offer came next with "Beer, Beer," in song only, approval being shown by the way the chorus was taken up. Priest sang the now familiar "My Old Shako." Our old favourite Barnard then recited in his own charming way, "Jemini and Gurgo," which of course was very warmly appreciated. "The Village Blacksmith" was well sung by Davis, and the programme concluded by Winter, who simply delighted the fellows with "Solomon Levi," and an encore, "McPherson." Our old friend Tarr was at the piano the greater part of the evening, Tyler acting during the remainder.   F. E. L.

THE WORKING MEN'S COLLEGE JOURNAL *is supported partly by Annual Subscribers living in different parts of the World, and partly by circulation among the Students and Members. Its success depends upon a regular demand, and to ensure this, the Editor would be glad if as many readers as can will become Subscribers. Subscription 2s. 6d. per annum, post free.*

LONDON: Printed by W. HUDSON & Co., Red Lion Street, High Holborn, and published at THE WORKING MEN'S COLLEGE, Crowndale Road, London, N.W.—May 1st, 1908.

THE WORKING MEN'S COLLEGE JOURNAL

sub: M

The Working Men's College.
CROWNDALE ROAD
ST PANCRAS
LONDON N.W.

FOUNDED IN 1854 BY THE LATE

Frederick Denison Maurice.

Contents for

JUNE, 1908.

Ruskin

College Ideals

Mrs. Tansley

College Notes

Debating Society

Lubbock Field Club

Working Men's College Journal.

Conducted by Members of the Working Men's College
Crowndale Road, London, N.W.

VOL. X.—No. 183.   JUNE, 1908.   PRICE TWOPENCE.

RECOLLECTIONS OF RUSKIN.*
(*Concluded.*)

 LAST saw Mr. Holman Hunt, a few years ago, in the Church of St. Paul, Herne Hill. In this church, Mr. Ruskin had often worshipped ; and after his death, it was thought by the vicar and parishioners, that a tablet to his memory should be placed in it. This tablet, when erected, was unveiled by Mr. Holman Hunt, who spoke of the long years of friendship which he had enjoyed with Mr. Ruskin, and of the sympathy of view, in art matters, which the two friends had. He told us of meeting Ruskin in Italy, when Ruskin said that he had just been seeing some pictures by Tintoret which he had not seen for twenty years, and that he had then formed the same opinion of them which he had formed when he first saw them ; and concluded therefrom that his first study of them had not been hasty or ill-advised, and that his further studies of twenty years had confirmed him in a belief in the soundness of the principles on which he had formed his method of Art study.

Not far from the Church of St. Paul, at No. 28, Herne Hill, is the house in which Mr. Ruskin spent his childhood and youth. It was, until lately, occupied by his niece, Mrs. Severn, and her husband, the well-known water-colour painter. About a year ago I was permitted to view this house, with its interesting art treasures and Ruskin memories. The principal, amongst the latter, was the garret wherein I saw the bed in which he had slept when young, and, above it, the shelf on which his books had been kept. I was shewn also some of his school-books, and the little caps and frocks which he wore in his childhood. Relics always provoke the spirit of doubt : the hat, for instance, at Madame Tussaud's, of the Duke of Wellington. If one cannot bring one's self to believe that it really has been on the mighty head of the Great Duke, one despises it as a common ugly chimney-pot hat. But these Ruskin relics leave us no room for doubt as to their genuineness. What greatly charmed me in this little room was the view from its window ; through it I looked over fields, dotted with many a tree or group of trees,

* Paper read by Mr. J. P. Emslie at a Students and Teachers' Meeting in the Common Room, on March 2nd, 1908.

to the softly-outlined hill of Norwood: a very beautiful view, and still beautiful in spite of the destruction of the park-like domain on the opposite side of the road, and the running through that domain of a brand-new road with brand-new formal red-brick houses. So exquisite is the view, how much more so must it have been many years ago; and what influence may the sight of it every morning when he woke, have had upon the mind of the child Ruskin? How may his love of nature and of hill-form have been nourished in his earliest years, by this charming scene so constantly before him?

Mr. Ruskin, while insisting upon minuteness and completeness of execution in the representation of objects, also called his pupils' attention to the higher work of art as shown in composition. His object in teaching Drawing was, as he frequently told us, not to make artists, but to train the eye and taste so that the ordinary man should have an appreciation of some of the difficulties of art-work, and an enjoyment, not hitherto possessed by him, of the beauties of painting and sculpture; if, beyond this, any of his pupils had naturally a gift for art, this would soon show itself; but his (Mr. Ruskin's) only concern was to teach them, with a view to enabling them to see and to judge for themselves. And so, amongst other things, he gave us some addresses on the subject of composition; and we heard of principal groups, and secondary groups, and what he called the Law of Repetition, which was his description of the effect produced by repeating, on a small scale, the form of the principal mass in the picture—as, for instance, when the form of a huge mountain in the distance is imitated by a crag in the foreground, and a sense of harmony is thereby diffused over the whole work. After he had spoken, he would perhaps say: " There, now you can go and compose pictures; that is, if you have the gift. I haven't it, but know its laws and can teach them to you, leaving you to apply them, if nature has endowed you with the ability to do so." And one evening, looking at the work of a student who was copying a group of bottles, baskets, and other objects of still life, he said: " That's exceedingly well grouped; did you arrange that?" " No," was the reply, " Mr. Dickinson grouped them." Whereupon Mr. Ruskin remarked: " Ah! I thought it was the work of a master. Can't you see how well those objects contrast and balance each other? That's a thing that I couldn't in the least do myself, but I know directly I see it, when it's well done."

Of one of Mr. Dickinson's pictures, the portrait of the Rev. F. D. Maurice, which was exhibited at the Royal Academy in 1859, Mr. Ruskin wrote, in his Notes on the Exhibition of that year: " Like, and good; an entirely well-meant and well-wrought portrait," and then went on to speak of the artist's " endeavour to paint all the expression of an expressive face "— a very happy tribute both to Mr. Dickinson's genius and to the face which that genius has so faithfully depicted. Mr. Maurice's was, indeed, an expressive face, full of an earnestness which would have been hardness, had it not been considerably softened by the affection and human sympathy which lit it up. I can well remember the kind smile of encouragement with which he greeted me when—an awkward youth in my 'teens—I first, and with diffidence, ventured to ask him a question in a class which he conducted for the study of the Bible. How his knowledge of his subject impressed me! I have since heard it said of Savonarola, and of Luther, that each of them knew the Bible by heart. I thought that this must have been the case with Mr. Maurice; for I have many times, in answer to a question as to some obscure text, heard him say where he believed it was, and turning over the leaves of his Bible, almost immediately find it, and in the place which he had mentioned.

At that time it was the custom to hold a general meeting of Teachers and Students at the beginning of each term. The meeting began with a tea, and was followed by an address from the Principal, and speeches from various teachers on the subjects they taught or were about to teach—as shown on the printed programme given to each student present. Here one might behold the expressiveness of Mr. Maurice's face, as he spoke of the high aims which he set before the students, and earnestly described the difficulties which beset him in his endeavour to understand those whom he wished to benefit, and offered sympathy at the same time that he asked for it. Here also Mr. Ruskin would make some eloquent speech upon the Art of the day, or some special need of his class. Other teachers would discourse upon Mathematics, Science, or other subjects. Mr. Ruskin's speech always occupied a prominent place upon these occasions. He also gave several lectures; one of them was on the subject of Normandy, at the request of some students of the College who were about to make an excursion into that province of France. In addressing them, he said that he could only tell them of some of the notable things of Normandy, not give them practical instructions for travelling, nor tell them what to take, as each man knew best what it was that he liked to travel with—"So," he said, "each one of you will take what he pleases in his knapsack; but there's one thing which I hope that every one of you will put into his knapsack, and that is, plenty of Patriotism. I wish you to understand me in this matter: by patriotism I mean, not only that you should love your country, as you ought to do that; but you should also love other people's country. So many people go abroad only for the purpose of vaunting England to the disparagement of other nations, and they cause a great deal of ill-feeling in consequence. This ought not to be. You ought to love your country, just as you love your father and mother; but you must remember that other people love their country, and their father and mother; and to be always praising your country and speaking ill of other countries is as if you were to say, Oh! my father and mother are very good people, but

your father and mother are very bad people." This was uttered
in the time of good feeling which came after the Crimean War,
and before the Dr. Bernard trial—which trial gave so very severe
a shock to that *entente cordiale* which had been brought into
existence by the Franco-English Alliance of the Crimean War.

It was in 1857, and while teaching at the College, that Mr.
Ruskin brought out his "Elements of Drawing," a book full of
valuable instruction of a practical nature ; and equally valuable
in its advice with regard to the things to be studied, as an
assistance to the formation of the mind of him whose hand is
practically engaged in Art. He directs the students as to the
authors whose works should be read, and the painters whose
pictures should be studied as good, or avoided as bad, examples ;
or how far certain painters' works may be studied advantageously,
or passed over in certain parts of their work which are bad. He
says, "You may look, with trust in their being always right, at
Titian, Veronese, Tintoret, Giorgione, John Bellini, and
Velasquez ; the authenticity of the picture being of course
established for you by proper authority." Alas ! alas ! what is
proper authority ? A picture which is in the National Gallery
was, when first placed there in 1860 or 1861, entitled "Portrait
of Ariosto, by Titian." After a while somebody discovered that
the portrait did not resemble a certain authentic portrait of
Ariosto. The title of the National Gallery picture was then
changed to "Portrait by Titian." Time went on until it was
thought that the portrait was not by Titian, but by Palma
Vecchio, and the picture was re-named accordingly. Then
again, doubt entered the minds of the authorities, and the
picture was next entitled, "Portrait, Venetian School." So its
name remained for some years, when it was brought back to the
old "Portrait by Titian" ; and so, for the present, its name
remains, though Mr. Herbert Cook, in his "Life of Giorgione,"
claims for Giorgione the authorship of this work and of four
others in the gallery, all of which are attributed to other painters,
whilst Miss Logan says, that a "Head of a Shepherd" at
Hampton Court is the only work of Giorgione's in this country—
a work which Mr. Herbert Cook declares to be not by Giorgione,
but by Torbido. Great numbers of pictures by famous painters
have documentary evidence of their authenticity ; but too often
we meet with such a history as the one I have just been telling,
a history which may make us ask, Who shall decide, when doctors
disagree ?

In the closing part of the preface to his "Elements of
Drawing," Mr. Ruskin says : "Lastly, if any of the directions
given subsequently to the student should be found obscure by
him, or if at any stage of the recommended practice he find
himself in difficulties which I have not enough provided against,
he may apply by letter to Mr. Ward, who is my under drawing-
master at the Working Men's College, and who will give him
any required assistance, on the lowest terms that can remunerate

him for the occupation of his time. I have not leisure myself in general to answer letters of inquiry, however much I may desire to do so; but Mr. Ward has always the power of referring any question to me, when he thinks it necessary."

In these words, Mr. Ruskin was doing great service to one of his pupils. Mr. Ward was, at the time of publication of the " Elements of Drawing," engaged in some office. He had long been a student in the Drawing class, and had gained Mr. Ruskin's esteem by his diligence and ability, and had been promoted to the post of assistant-teacher. Here he had proved his ability as a teacher, and had earned the commendation which Ruskin had written of him—commendation which enabled him to start on a career for which he had a desire. He was very successful as a teacher of drawing, and in the branch of painting which he followed, he was exceedingly able.

To two other of his College pupils, Mr. Ruskin was equally friendly. Of George Allen it is perhaps hardly necessary to speak, so well is his history known to the world; how, originally a carpenter, he became an engraver, then, when Ruskin disagreed with the ordinary ways of publishing, he was engaged by Ruskin to publish for him, which publishing he did in a house at Orpington, far from the noise of London, to which city he had ultimately to return, there to carry on the business of publisher as others did.

Another pupil of Ruskin's, and one who ultimately attained to some fame, was J. W. Bunney. The son of a merchant captain, he had, when very young, made several voyages round the world. At an early age, he took to drawing, but the death of his father compelled him to abandon art and apply himself to less attractive work. When I first joined the Drawing class, he was engaged at a bookseller's, and was a hard-working fellow-student whose work was greatly admired by Ruskin. After a while he saw that tide in his affairs which he took at the flood; for a time his work was hard, but, in 1858, he made a number of drawings in Derbyshire which so charmed Mr. Ruskin that he gave Bunney commissions, which occupied two summers, to make drawings in Italy and in Switzerland. After this, Bunney's reputation rose high, and he ultimately became famous as a painter of Venetian scenes.

I have frequently heard Ruskin say that he had no wish that his pupils should become dissatisfied with their work, and strive to become artists; he had no wish to make them artists, but to teach them by means of the practice of Drawing to see beauties in nature and in art which would add to their enjoyment. It will be seen, however, from what I have just said, that when he perceived ability, he would give it the most friendly encouragement. When to that ability was joined perseverance, Ruskin would extend that help which would enable endeavour to succeed in its aim. Nor, if I may believe what I have heard, was he less backward in giving whatever aid he could to others. His advocacy of the Pre-Raphaelites is well known. How much did they owe to the support to their cause which was given by his powerful pen? Personally he was the friend of these then young and unknown men; personally he was the friend of artists who had won their fame; and he was also the friend of his pupils, most of whom were men who had to work for their daily bread. He loved art and he loved beauty, but only for the sake of his fellow-men, and as far as art and beauty could minister to the happiness of his fellow-men.

When, last November, I was at Venice, I went to the north bank of the Canale della Guidecca to see the Pension Calcina, within whose hall is written up, in large letters, "John Ruskin lived and worked here." On the front of the building is a marble tablet with an inscription, which I read with great difficulty, having the very slightest knowledge of the Italian language. But the inscription appeared to me to be to the effect, that the Municipality of Venice. had placed this tablet to the memory of John Ruskin, who was a deep admirer of works of art in painting, sculpture, architecture, ironwork, wood-carving, and embroidery, and who loved the workman as well as his work. I may not have correctly rendered the sense of this inscription; I do, however, hope that I have, for I would fain believe that the warm-hearted Venetians, no less than so many of his own countrymen, are well able to testify not only to his taste as an expounder of principles of Art, but also to his sympathetic regard for his fellow-men.

STUDENTS AND TEACHERS' MEETING.

COLLEGE IDEALS.

On Monday, April 13th, a very successful meeting of students and teachers was held in the Common Room, Mr. A. S. Lupton addressing us upon "College Ideals." Mr. A. Hepburn occupied the chair, and after a brief and witty opening, called upon Mr. Lupton, who was received with loud applause.

Mr. Lupton said:—I feel that I am here under entirely false pretences; they never told me Dr. Furnivall was going to be here to-night. In himself he embodies the best tradition of the College, and is one of the unfortunately few members left who knew from personal knowledge what the ideals were. But it is the custom of the College at the beginning of each term to ask the new members to come, and to try to make them feel at home in the College; that is one of the best and first reasons for this gathering of students and teachers. The Common Room life is, and certainly ought to be, one of the central features; and in it we ought to help each other a great deal towards finding out what our work in life is. Only to-night Dent was reading one of the many "rags" which adorn this room, and suddenly put the poser, "What do you think you are put on earth for?" He quoted the answer from the same "rag"—"To make love to a woman." That seems to be an utterly inadequate conception. I should have said, that we ourselves are linked between the past and the future; and that our duty is to sift out the good points from our ancestors, if we have any (laughter), and try and hand them on to the future. I think that this College is one of the best institutions to help towards that ideal. When we come here, we inherit—what is always delightful—the spirit and tradition of the best institution which I know. When we come here, we are at once introduced to a circle of ideas that has been gathered together by the men who have founded and kept on this College. In a certain sense, we have them with us still—[indicating their portraits on the walls]. Maurice, Hughes, Dickinson, Kingsley—are here, and George Tansley is over the mantel piece. New comers have only the portrait to rely upon. I remember the great impression George Tansley made on me, when I came here after my delightful time at Cambridge. He was a man who had deserted business, as I understood, to devote his time to the College. He preferred to come here, and with an enthusiasm and an inspiration that were extraordinarily infectious, he devoted his whole time and energy to organizing the classes, and to binding together the students and teachers of the College in various ways ; and I think the spirit of George Tansley is still in a very large measure amongst us (applause). Then by the side of him is Lowes Dickinson, who still occasionally comes amongst us, and who has left us these wonderful productions of his art, so that the College shall for ever have these ideal portraits of our great men. Then there are Charles Kingsley, Forster to whom we owe the decoration of this room, and Westlake, Roebuck, and Litchfield. These last are only names to the new comers, but those who have read the College History will know what a large part they had in the formation of the tradition of this College.

When we come here we are at once born into a new circle of ideas, and I think those ideas pre-eminently good. One of the qualities of this College which, I think, strikes everyone, partly our heritage from these great men, is the way in which everybody mixes together ; that is essentially the College spirit, and to my mind it marks out this College from any place I know. Any man—if he contributes of what he knows, and of what he does not know—is welcome here. Of course, to a certain extent, one gets that spirit at Oxford and Cambridge, but not quite to the same extent. There one gets an artificial distinction between the Dons and the Under-graduates, and possibly, the type of person such as that late Master of Trinity, who, when he was out on a country walk one day, and it came on to rain, was accosted by one of his own pupils, who came up and said, " Master, will you have a share of my umbrella ? " Whereupon he replied, " All communica-tion must be made through the Senior Tutor." (Laughter.) I do not think that spirit is so strong now ; but still, you do not meet on level terms with your tutors and your dons, and that prevents at once a free and level interchange of thought between the different scholars of the College, and it at once pre-vents the College from being a College in the proper sense—that is, a body of men joined together with common objects and for common purposes.

In this place, the new-comer does not know who he is talking to ; and I think that is a splendid idea. A young man once took a peep in and was going away, when Flint got him by the collar and dragged him up to me. I went through the various notices with him, and finally he made up his mind that he was going to join the Spanish class. I asked him why, and got the peculiar answer that " He didn't know anything, and wanted to learn more." On investigation, I found that what he really wanted to join was the class for mechanical drawing. Within thirty seconds he had entered for the Mechanical Drawing class ; and then he turned to me and said, " What class have you taken a ticket for ? " I must say that that showed a most splendid spirit, and I only wish that we did not know anything of anyone's past history, and could always meet each other in this way.

If a man holds an opinion, he has to defend it according to the amount of sense that is in it. I frankly confess that on many points I do not think the least alike with any of the people with whom I discuss them ; but while they may think my views absolutely insensate and pig-headed, they do not say they are, simply because they hold the opposite view. They are quite pre-pared to discuss it from the point of view of—What sense is there in it ? Presumably the other person's view is not quite right, and I am prepared to admit that mine is not ; but by discussing them on terms of equality, we may each of us get a step forward to the absolutely correct view. Then there is an enormous amount in the different points of view from which the great difficulties and problems of life can be studied. I know that up at Cambridge one gathers an enormous amount of fresh light upon the problems of the day, from the fact that one of the men will be a man of science, discussing it from his point of view, another will be an historian, and then a mathematician, and then a student of economics or a theological student, while I am a mere classic. And I think the endeavour to get these different points of view for the great topics of the day, is an essential part of the work of a real College. The problems are at once of enormous difficulty. You have got the industrial problem, and I hope that in the generations to come the conditions of industry will be entirely revolutionized (cheers); but I am by no means sure that the tendency at present is in the right direction, and I think that one of the faults underlying the study of the problem is that it is made the question of rival political organizations. Of course, there is improvement in the form of the government, the form of organization, and the social structure; but to my mind, all these points are of secondary importance. The great thing is to educate both the employer and the employed, largely in questions of intellect and technical skill, and still more in the direction of feeling that, whatever their position in the scheme of industry, they all ought to be working for a common object. That is the great point that is lost sight of in foreign countries, and unfortunately by the majority in our own country. It is in its basis a war between the different classes—a question of "downing" one and "up with" the other. That I do not believe is sane. The object of industry will be to the common good of all; and I hope that the College does something to make that belief, and that in the future it will take practical form. In the early days, I think, problems of this kind were more closely before our fathers than they are before us to-day, because the College in its conception was largely a Co-operative movement. Co-operative societies are growing more and more prosperous every day; and I hope the College in future will draw nearer to its original state.

The College, in another way, offers great opportunities for the development of its students. You know, all of you, how prejudiced I am against journalism. As an entire mental diet, I do not think the daily newspapers are to be recommended. If you have been brought up on this type of literature at the first start, solid books that require continued effort are hopelessly dull and unintelligible. The question is largely one of acquired taste; and I believe that if you can only get that taste, it adds considerable happiness to life. Personally I enjoy reading the classics, though I would not for one moment suggest that everyone should study Latin and Greek; but wherever a man's tastes lie, he should develop them to something better. Natural Science will bring enormously new thoughts, and add new light and interest to all the common objects that make up so much of our daily life, and the same applies to other subjects. History seems to be absolutely neglected, yet I do not believe that you can get a real grip of any of our social problems, unless you have a sound acquaintance with the history, largely and mainly, of this country. And if you trace it back to the other countries from which our own civilization was made, and get to know more of the peculiarities of the men and institutions that make up our past, the firmer will be the grip you will have on the present, and the more you will be able to get, so far as we have the power to get, a view from the present into the future.

Then, we have all those societies that give a man social company and true friendship—the Field Club, the Musical Society, the Debating Society, etc. And in them, we can find men of our own calibre, and can have real society and friendliness in a way which I doubt could be obtained in any other place. We have here a body of men and a body of teachers who regard learning for its own sake; and who are zealous to study the great thoughts of the great men of the present and the past, and to do something to hand on the lamp of intellect, learning, and scholarship to our descendants in the future. (Hearty cheers.)

When Mr. Lupton sat down, the chairman called upon Dr. FURNIVALL to move a vote of thanks, and the Doctor in a characteristic breezy speech managed to tell us about his Sculling Club and many other of his pet subjects.

We were then entertained with an exceptionally good musical programme. The Glee Club, after many years of silence at our concerts, gave us two items, a glee, "In absence," and a trio, "Ye shepherds, tell me." We should be pleased to hear them more often, for it is a pity such talent should be smothered in some top back room of the College. Immediately after the Doctor's speech, Marshall commenced with an appropriate song, "The Boys of the Old Brigade." Mr. Sydney Davis sang "Thora," and "Bid me to Love" as an encore. Addison sang the "Old Cavalier," and was so rapturously received that he too had to furnish an encore, "Lighterman Tom." Birrell recited "Gunga Din," and Luetchford gave us two of his humorous songs, "Side Slips" and "It does go," Castell finishing up with "Rio Grande." The evening was a most entertaining one, and we trust all new students will join us in the Common Room at the next meeting, which will be duly announced on the notice boards.

MUSICAL SOCIETY'S PIANOFORTE FUND.

THE amount of this fund, for which at least £40 is required, now stands at £24 1s., made up of the following sums :—

	£	s.	d.		£	s.	d.
Concert (May 2nd) ...	14	3	6	W. A. Crapp	0	2	6
Dance (on account) ...	4	0	0	W. C. Cutts	0	2	6
R. H. Marks ...	2	0	0	C. Godfrey Gümpel ..	0	2	6
R. W. R. Stokes	1	1	0	B. J. Rose	0	2	0
Charles Wright ...	1	0	0	E. A. Harrison ...	0	1	0
W. R. Emslie	0	10	0	J. Kirk	0	1	0
H. Wilcockson ...	0	10	0				
H. J. Hartley	0	5	0		£24	1	0

The committee have to offer their sincere thanks to Mr. Jack Owen and his colleagues for their work and organization in carrying through the dance of April 25th. This proved the most enjoyable of the series, although not so well attended as the previous dances. A sum of £4 on account has been handed over to our secretary. The whole-hearted and enthusiastic manner in which the members gave their assistance towards the furtherance of the concert on May 2nd, assured that function a financial success. Some two dozen members took in hand the distribution of the tickets, and the manner of their canvassing was the means of disposing of some 553. It is worthy of mention in this connection that Messrs. Flint and Staal were responsible for over two-fifths of the total sales. Without the aid of George Offer, we should have found it difficult to stage the farce, the scenery being a capital example of raising "something from nothing," having for its foundation various portions of furniture found in different parts of the College. Messrs. Beach, Guillard, and Mogg were responsible for the lighting effects, and midst a chaos of wire and fittings, made it possible for us to dispense with a drop curtain. We also have to acknowledge the cordial assistance given us by members of the Art class, not only for the loan of some of their furnishings, but also in the preparation of sundry stage fitments. Again Tarr gave us his ever-ready help at the piano, whilst Lawrence, Staal, and other College men were to be found busy doing whatever came into their heads or hands. We also owe a deep debt of gratitude to Mr. R. H. Marks, for the indefatigable manner in which he has been working to obtain donations for us, and also for his occupying the chair on the evening. The position of the chairman at a students' concert cannot in any sense of the term be called a sinecure. Those College men and ladies who provided the entertainment gave us of their best, and the committee desire to thank them one and all for their kindly assistance. The audited account, which appears in the Common Room, shows that the receipts were £13 16s. 6d. for tickets and £1 19s. for programmes, whilst the expenses for printing were £1 12s., leaving the sum mentioned above. Thanks to the kind co-operation of the Executive Committee, we were enabled to use the hall free of charge. A report of the concert will appear next month. H. NYE.

COLLEGE NOTES.

THE College has sustained a sad loss in the death of Mrs. Amelia Tansley, who passed away on the 14th May, at the age of 67. She had been an invalid for about twelve months, and she bore her illness with much fortitude. Those who came into contact with her in the early part of this year, in connection with the concert which she gave at the College on February 29th, know how bravely and with what determination she fought against her weakness, and persevered in carrying out what she had set her mind and her heart upon, in spite of her sadly decreased bodily strength. She died calmly and with resignation. The qualities she showed at the close of her life were those which might be expected from one of such strength, sweetness, and nobility of character as was Mrs. Tansley. Members of our Council, life-long friends of her and her late husband, our dear friend George Tansley, have told us what a fitting help-mate she was to him; and our knowledge of them both helps us to understand how it was possible for him to devote the best and ripest part of his life and energies to the service of the College, and to do for it more than any other man has done or could do. Mrs. Tansley has always been a good and true friend of the College, and a good and true friend of College men, old and young, from the early days of its history to the present time. She was endowed with the gift of appreciation of good music and good poetry, and it gave her great delight to hear these and to see others enjoying them. In the arrangement and carrying out of social gatherings of College members and their friends, at her own house as well as at the College, she was always extremely successful, and on those occasions her guests or audiences have been privileged to hear and take part in singing or reading music and poetry of the very best that composer or author has ever written. In many ways Mrs. Tansley has been a great help and a great power in the work of the College, and now that she has gone, we shall miss her sadly.

The funeral took place on Tuesday, May 19th. There was a service at St. Paul's Church, St. John's Wood, and interment afterwards at the Hampstead Cemetery, the chief mourners being Miss Tansley and Mr. and Mrs. Arthur Tansley. A number of College friends were also present; the Principal, Professor A. V. Dicey, K.C., came up from Oxford for the purpose of attending; the Vice-Principal and Mrs. Jacob, Sir Charles Lucas, C.B., K.C.M.G., Mr. and Mrs. C. Edmund Maurice, Miss Janet Lowes Dickinson, Mr. Reginald J. Mure, Dr. and Mrs. Eugene Oswald, Mr. and Mrs. J. A. Forster, Mr. and Mrs. William Lawrence, Mr. Alfred Grugeon, Mr. John Fotheringham, Mr. R. H. Marks, Mr. Edward Lawrence, Mr. and Mrs. J. Rigby Smith, Miss A. Smith, Mrs. Peck, Mr. and Mrs.

C. F. Marshall, Mr. and Mrs. Leonard Pocock, Mr. and Mrs. Perry, Mrs. and Miss Jackson, Mrs. Lambert, Miss Mercy Murray, Mrs. Julian Marshall, Miss Hutchings, Mrs. Mason Tarr, Miss Hamilton, and Messrs. J. T. Baker, Wm. Hudson, E. C. Duchesne, H. R. Levinsohn, Wm. Tarr, W. H. Phelan, F. J. Nield, John Payton, and Robert Cummings, were amongst those there. In the course of the service at the Church, the hymn "O God, our help in ages past," and at the grave, the hymn "Now the labourer's task is o'er," were sung with much tenderness and impressiveness.

Before the commencement of formal business at the Council meeting held at the College the same evening, the Vice-Principal, addressing the members of Council present, spoke of Mrs. Tansley's long and valuable friendship with the College and its members, of the way in which she had helped and supplemented the work of her late husband, George Tansley, and of the great good she had done in fostering the social life by means of gatherings of College men and their lady friends. He referred to the concert arranged by Mrs. Tansley in February last, and to her devotion and care in carrying it out; and also to the gift, recently made by her to the College, of her husband's study chair. Within a week of her death, she had been talking to him about the inscription that was to be placed upon it. Throughout her life and up to the very last, she had shown the keenest interest in the College and its work, and we felt deep sorrow upon her death. Dr. Oswald and Mr. R. H. Marks— the friendship of both of whom with Mr. and Mrs. Tansley dates back to more than forty years ago—also addressed the meeting and testified to the very high esteem in which Mrs. Tansley was held, and the sense of great personal loss sustained by all her many friends in the College.

In the report of the Executive Committee presented to the Council, feeling reference was made to the recent decease of Mr. John Roebuck, an old friend of Mr. and Mrs. Tansley, who joined the College on its opening night, October 26th, 1854. The report contained the customary references to current doings in the College, and the following paragraphs are taken from it :—

Student and Class Entries.—The falling off in student entries, which occurred in the September and January terms of this session, has naturally affected the returns for the present term. Thus far, however, the decrease has not been quite so marked as in the former terms, and is again partly due to the cessation of the Post Office Sorters' classes. Making allowance for the loss of those classes, the net decrease up to date is certainly not greater than forty. It must be noted, too, that the Council meet this year a week earlier than last year, and that last year's class entries for this term were exceptionally good.

The comparative figures are as follows :—

	1907.	1908.		1907.	1908.
Preparatory Division	12	11	Law	10	4
Algebra	17	8	Botany	10	9
Ambulance	14	11	Building Construction	33	21
Arithmetic	37	26	Electricity	75	33
Art	86	58	Geology	12	9
Book-keeping	33	24	Machine Construction		
Economics	12	5	and Drawing	26	27
English Composition	8	18	Practical Plane and		
English Literature	14	26	Solid Geometry	0	18
Euclid	4	6	Physiology	12	5
English for Foreigners	7	8	Sound, Light and Heat	0	8
French	114	90	Singing	54	40
Geography	4	1	Spanish	15	23
German	41	33	Esperanto	8	3
Grammar	15	20	Shorthand	80	86
Greek	13	8	Violin	14	10
History	5	5	Chemistry	45	29
Italian	16	11	Portuguese	0	1
Latin	22	21			
			Class Entries	868	624
			Student Entries	407	341

Classes and Teachers.—There have been but few changes this term either in the classes or in the teaching staff. The Rev. B. H. Alford's Sunday class ceased as usual before Easter ; and Mr. John Scott has not been able to continue his course on Browning's Poems throughout this term. Mr. Bernard Turner, a former teacher of Grammar, however, offered to take a class in English Literature to fill Mr. Scott's place, selecting as the subject " The Life, Works, and Speeches of Edmund Burke." This class has attracted seventeen students—a number which is large considering the late period of the session, and the fact that Mr. Turner is unable to take the class on the same evening as Mr. Scott had done. Owing to pressure of other work, Mr. Stephen has been compelled to give up his History class, for which the College seemed fortunate enough to have secured Mr. W. G. G. Leveson-Gower as teacher. Unluckily, after having given one lesson, Mr. Leveson-Gower has found it impossible to continue, owing to his duties unexpectedly embracing evening work. Mr. Brignell, who was absent last term through illness, has been able to return ; but your Committee regret that Mr. Butler is still unable to resume his class in Practical Mathematics, and that Mr. W. R. Emslie, another tried and faithful teacher, has been prevented by serious illness from continuing his classes in Geography and in the Preparatory Division. The Geography class has been given up, but Mr. Reglar has been good enough to take over Mr. Emslie's work in the Preparatory Division. There has been one change in the Shorthand Division, Mr. Sweetman having taken Mr. Staal's place. The College is indebted to Dr. Forbes and Mr. G. Wiltshire for their kindness in taking up the Ambulance class again this term.

Examinations.—The results of the Algebra and Shorthand examinations were announced. Those of the examinations conducted by the Board of Education, the Society of Arts, and the London Chamber of Commerce, held during the last few weeks, and for different subjects in which College students entered, will not be known for some months. The London County Council appointed the College this year as a centre for one of the Board of Education Examinations, and has also used it recently for other examinations conducted both by themselves and by the Board of Education.

Library.—The following books have been given to the Library since the last report: By G. E. Defer—"Hendricks," W. Kingston; P. Newman—"Mad Humanity," Forbes Winslow; Dr. Furnivall—"Romeo and Juliet," Brooke; J. L. Paton—"St. Martin," Guillard; The Librarian—A Classified Dictionary, Sonnenschein; E. Upton—History of Co-operation (2 vols.), Holyoake; A. S. Lupton, twenty-four books in modern editions of Greek and Roman Classics; Rev. J. H. Todd, per Sir Charles Lucas, a parcel of books; The Times Book Club, per Dr. Furnivall —"The Historians' History"; Miss J. Bonham-Carter, 64 numbers of the "Economic Journal," vols. I. to XVI.

Other gifts to the College have been :—From Mrs. Tansley, the study chair of the late George Tansley; Mr. John Scott, busts of James Watt and Robert Browning; and from Mrs. Litchfield, a mask of Dante.

Various social functions were reported, and then two items were mentioned which do not fall under any of the usual headings. In the year 1895, an application for pecuniary assistance was made to, and favourably considered by, the Technical Education Board of the London County Council. One of the usual conditions attached to such grants was, that the Board should be represented in some way on the Governing Body of the Institution thus benefited. Accordingly the Council passed a new rule, enabling members or nominees of other Educational Bodies to be appointed by our Council as members thereof. One of the four members of the Technical Education Board thereupon appointed a member of this Council was Mr. A. L. Leon, who has ever since used ungrudgingly his wide experience and influence for the good of the College. Owing to circumstances not entirely within his control, Mr. Leon has had lately a little more spare time, and of this he has been good enough to devote some to the College by allowing himself to be co-opted on to the Executive Committee.

Following the good example of our Cambridge friends, Mr. R. N. M. Bailey, cordially supported by our Oxford teachers and members of Council, has organized a week-end excursion to

Oxford, upon the same lines as those pursued by Mr. Cornford at Cambridge. May 30th has been chosen as the date of this excursion, for which the Rev. R. G. Parsons, of University College, has most kindly undertaken to act as host. Fifteen members have been invited for this initial visit, which it is hoped may prove so attractive to both hosts and guests that a bond with Oxford may be formed, similar to that now connecting our College with Cambridge.

Mr. Percy Thompson conducted the Algebra examination, and C. E. Horsman obtained an " excellent," with 86 per cent. of maximum marks.

Tom Martin, a well-known and popular student of the College, and the grandson of Tommy Martin, one of the earliest of the old students, sailed for Canada on April 16th, and has already found a billet in a Railway Company's office in Toronto, at a good salary. His many friends here will be glad to hear of this success, and wish his progress may continue in the New World.

· There is not time for us to fully report, in this number, the experiences of the lucky forty members who took part in the Cambridge trip on May 23rd, 24th, and 25th. Those of them whom we have met, however, tell us that they had a most glorious time, which we can well believe from past experiences ; that everything went off well, and that all their fifty hosts were most kind and hospitable. The gratitude of the whole party to Mr. Cornford for so kindly organizing the excursion, and to his many friends for helping to make it the great success it was, is real and hearty.

The Oxford excursion has not yet taken place, as we go to press, but before the month of May is out, we have no doubt the party fortunate enough to be selected for it will be having a very good time at that University.

We are glad to hear that there have been six essays sent in for the Marks Prize. This is very good for the first year. Mr. Cornford is most kindly judging the essays.

As already announced, the College Annual Garden Party and Field Sports will take place on Saturday, July 11th, at the " Ship," Eastcote, near Pinner—instead of Wembley as previously stated. A full programme of events for both ladies and gentlemen is being arranged, and prizes will be awarded. Tickets may be obtained from Flint, or from any of the club secretaries or Common Room Committee-men.

Mr. Melzer has been appointed Custodian of the Common Room, *vice* Mr. Staal, resigned, the latter being on the eve of removing to Holland.

On Saturday, June 13th, Mr. H. R. Levinsohn will conduct a party of College men over the National Portrait Gallery, St. Martin's Place, Trafalgar Square, W.C. Meet outside at 3.30. Will those who intend to go kindly put their names on the list on the Common Room board?

As announced by the Tonic Sol-fa Association (in union with the Tonic Sol-fa College), thirty-two choirs will participate in the 51st Choral Festival at the Crystal Palace, on June 27th, at 6 p.m. The Working Men's College choir will be present.

Mr. Robert Blackford Mansfield, whose death at the age 84 has recently been announced, was the brother of Mr. Charles B. Mansfield, one of the founders of, and first teachers in, this College, and one of the most devoted of the young men who in 1854 gathered round Frederick Denison Maurice. It was Charles Mansfield who introduced Mr. Lowes Dickinson to Maurice, and so got him to help in the work—(see College History, page 28). Mr. R. B. Mansfield wrote several books and also edited some of his brother's works, and through him, was brought into close contact with the Christian Socialist movement in its early stages. He contributed to the College Building Fund, and subscribed annually to our funds.

We regret to have to record the death, at his home in Hampstead, on May 12th, of Mr. George William Fox, at the age of 54, after a lingering illness, extending over three or four years. Mr. Fox joined the College in 1875, and was a prominent member of the French class with his friend Upperton, who recently died in South Africa. During the time that Tansley was Director of the Preparatory Classes, Fox and Sir Charles Lucas were teachers in that division, and he always retained the most affectionate regard for his director and his fellow-teacher. Up to the time of his illness, he was of a most cheery disposition, and much interested in the College, his connection with which he maintained to the last as a member of the Old Students' Club and a subscriber to the JOURNAL. Mr. Fox leaves a widow and two daughters.

MRS. TANSLEY.

I WISH to add some words to those of the Editor about the dear friend whom we have just lost. They shall be few; for Mrs. Tansley did not expect or wish much to be said of her services to the College, of which she was a life-long friend. She took it as a matter of course that you should do as much as you possibly can for your friends. It was through the College that she came to know George Tansley, to whom she was married in

1863. In those days he was giving to the College in his own strenuous way all the time that he could spare—and much more than any one else would have spared—from active business ; but the soul of the College was Mr. Litchfield, just as in later days it was George Tansley. Mr. Litchfield—Mrs. Tansley would say—first taught her what good music was. She was in his Singing class, and joined his College walks ; and always spoke of him in terms of affection and respect. She understood exactly the limits of woman's work in an institution like ours. The education and the daily social life belong to the men alone. For the education of women she laboured elsewhere, taking an active part in the College in Queen Square, as long as it was restricted to women, and afterwards helping to found the College for Working Women in Fitzroy Street, Fitzroy Square. In our College she soon found her rightful place. Mr. and Mrs. Tansley in the earlier years of their married life lived near Great Ormond Street, and kept open house for members of the College, who were their most intimate friends. Mrs. Tansley, while keeping these old friends, made newer ones among successive College generations ; for she retained even in mature years something of the fresh heart and the frank enthusiasm of a girl. I have heard her talk in words of very real friendship of many College men, from Jack Bromhall to Perry, Tarr, and Barnard. She would make the social gathering centre round some enjoyment in common, either of poetry— above all of Shakespeare—or of the best music. She cared only for the best that art could give, and would pass by all that was common and inferior. In her own rendering of poetry or music, there was a rare mixture of feeling and understanding. So that in her one realized that good taste was more than a grace ; it was an outward sign of a finely touched spirit that had its fine issues.

The words that Mrs. Tansley inscribed on her husband's tomb might fitly stand on her own too : "Blessed are the pure in heart, for they shall see God." She had a clearness and rightness of judgment that would brook no compromise with what was unworthy, mean, or common. In all that she said or did, there was proof of a well-balanced nature ; and blended with the womanliness that won our hearts was the strength that never spared herself. In her growing weakness during the last year, she did not falter nor cease to plan kindnesses. It was a wonderful triumph of the spirit over the body ; no one who saw it but could be the stronger and better for it. When I saw her only six days before her end, she settled the inscription on her last gift to the College—her husband's study-chair ; the College was ever in her thoughts. She has well earned her rest. Beside her grave, the members of the College who used to meet at her house for music led the hymn in which we all joined : " Now the labourer's task is o'er." The touching words and the music, as they died away amid the fresh green of spring and under the blue sky, were our farewell to one who laboured bravely and had loved all beautiful things.   Lionel Jacob.

COMMON ROOM CATERING.

THE catering of the Common Room has recently been the subject of an inquiry by a joint sub-committee, consisting of Messrs. J. J. Dent and W. C. Jones, representing the Executive Committee, and Messrs. E. Hayward and H. K. Randall representing the Common Room Committee, with Mr. S. Bradgate as chairman.

A searching inquiry was made into the whole subject of the method of catering, and a full report thereon was subsequently submitted to and adopted by the Executive Committee.

The report, among other things, recommended that the Common Room Committee should form a sub-committee to look after the catering and revise the tariff where necessary. This sub-committee has been duly formed, and the tariff revised. The sub-committee, Messrs. Hayward and Randall, with E. S. Landells, hon. secretary, Common Room Committee, meet from time to time to consider any business or points arising upon the catering; and members are asked to co-operate with them, by at once advising them of any suggestions or complaints they wish to make in regard to the refreshments.

The revised tariff shows the following reductions in prices — Coffee, from $1\frac{1}{2}$d. to 1d. per cup; cafe-au-lait, from 2d. to $1\frac{1}{2}$d. per cup; cocoa (Van Houten's and Rowntree's), from $1\frac{1}{2}$d. to 1d. per cup; pot of tea, roll and butter, from $3\frac{1}{2}$d. to 3d.; round of toast, from 2d. to $1\frac{1}{2}$d.; small plate of ham or cold meat, 2d.; large plate of ham or cold meat 3d.; Welsh rarebit, from $2\frac{1}{2}$d. to 2d.; pickles, $\frac{1}{2}$d. and 1d. An arrangement has been made with a large poultry farmer in Suffolk, for a supply of new laid eggs throughout the year.

An endeavour has been made to generally improve the quality of refreshments sold in the College. When the numbers are again at full strength in September next, it is hoped that a greater and more varied selection will be possible, but the success of this experiment entirely depends upon the support given by the members.

FURNIVALL CYCLING CLUB.

THE Club started the season on Saturday, April 11th, with the usual run to the "Cocoa Tree," Pinner, where forty-two members sat down to tea. The party went for a walk in the lanes, and the rest of the evening was spent in dances and songs. We left Pinner at 10.30 p.m., and had a pleasant ride back. The thanks of the club are due to the Misses F. and R. Reglar, N. Moulden, and Dockery, Mr. and Mrs. Mason Tarr, and Messrs. Nield, E. W. Davis, and others who helped to make the evening most enjoyable.

About twenty members participated in the Easter tour to Brighton, which was again as successful as ever, except, however, that the accommodation at Devonshire Place was on a par with the state of the weather.

Unfortunately, the Saturday run to Ewell had to be abandoned, partly owing to the College Dance being on the same day. The Croxley Green run on Sunday, May 3rd, was spoiled by the inclement weather in the morning, only the captain and his aide-de-camp turning out. On Saturday, May 9th, fifteen members cycled to the "City," Harrow Weald, and after a good tea at "The Case is altered," went for a walk round the Common. The popular run to Virginia Water, on Sunday, May 17th was again well attended, twenty-two members being present. After lunch, the party went into the park, some to the ruins and waterfall, whilst others preferred to sit in the shade of the massive chestnut trees. After tea at the "Red Lion," Sunningdale, we discovered that the stableman had apparently been playing darts on our tyres; this delayed us so considerably that we did not leave until 8 o'clock.

At Whitsun, the club will probably go somewhere near the Chilterns in Buckinghamshire. The other fixtures for the month are :—Sunday, 14th, Bookham ; Sunday, 21st, Hedgerley ; Sunday, 28th, Ranmore Common.

W. MELZER, *Hon. Secretary.*

W.M.C. DEBATING SOCIETY.

In concluding the survey of the Debating Society's activities during the past session, it is pleasing to be able to record that the final meetings were marked by increased and enthusiastic attendances, interest and broadness of subject, and well-sustained and informing speeches, all which augurs well for the continuance and expansion of one of the best means within the College walls of learning to know one's fellow-members, and the real trend of thought by which they are animated, besides extending one's own knowledge of the political, social, financial, and literary aspects of the day.

To some this may seem to smack of egotism, but the statement is really the outcome of a regretful remembrance of a past inner knowledge of the real working of this society; for by a salutary rule providing for a new executive each year, by which it must be admitted freshness and vigour is imparted to its doings, a secretary's life is all too short either to accomplish his own small ideas or to continue and cement the many new companionships which became his by right of office.

Since the last notice was penned, we have enjoyed, on Tuesday, March 24th, a caustic critical analysis of the Licensing Bill by Hepburn, combated by the quiet yet none the less penetrating thoughts of Reglar on the subject. The manner in which the College men crowded the Common Room on this occasion, and helped by their speeches and oral punctuation, either of assent or dissent, to make the meeting so huge a success, is exceedingly pleasing, whether from the point of view of a society meeting, or as an expression of the comradeship which binds us together.

For reasoned wit, expressed in the manner typical of an accomplished speaker, it would be very difficult to beat the opening of Mr. Bernard Turner on the question of abolishing Newspapers, on Tuesday, March 31st, when Offer, whose courage deserves recognition, ventured to do battle on behalf of the daily "rags," as the lofty would term them.

Finally, we were fortunate enough to secure an opening by Mr. E. M. Forster, B.A., on Literature as a stimulator rather than as a soother, which led to our discovering Mr. J. F. Winter, B.A., who in opposing revealed a cultured and forceful style of oratory, all too rare in these enlightened days. Future secretaries will do well to stalk this gentleman, when arranging their syllabuses.

And then we came to the annual meeting, which always provides so much sport for the prowlers after excitement. Fortunately the secretary had decided to orally account for his stewardship, as best befits a society whose principal duty is the cultivation of the art of speaking, instead of committing it to cold and unresponsive paper, as of yore. What an opportunity for the stickler for precedents! Led by Randall, who constituted himself head of the insurgents, they deployed in fine style, and for upwards of an hour there was sniping, affairs of outposts, engagements of pickets, rushes, and finally the outflanking of the defenders, who had to capitulate by 15 votes to 11, despite the masterly handling of the meeting by Homewood. From thence we passed to consideration of means of extending our usefulness. Acting on behalf of Munro, Mead ventured to suggest the amalgamation of the Literary Society, a proposal which was deserving of more generous treatment than it secured. That certain evenings should be devoted to the holding of a mock parliament, was another brilliant suggestion. That openers and opposers should be rigidly confined to their scheduled time, was a demand also put forward; but it is hoped members will not unduly press this point, as the complexity and interest of a subject frequently demands some greater amplification. The desirability of the opposer being allowed the right of reply was mooted. And finally, that the annual report should always be written, as the sticklers had discovered that the rules were eloquently silent on this point. These were merely suggestions submitted for mature consideration, as the constitution of the society demands written notice of any proposed alteration, signed by twelve members, to be read at the meeting preceding its discussion.

The good humour of the meeting having exhausted itself in this direction, recourse was had to the more serious business of electing a new executive, and the final choice of Stagg as president, and Hepburn as secretary, is as satisfactory as it is delightful to do honour to such bulwarks of our society, and with them at the helm we can confidently rely upon an exceedingly good time in 1908-9. The new committee consists of Messrs. Kisch, Landells, Randall, Mead, C. H. Perry, and A. H. Perry.

Any attempt on my part to estimate the work accomplished during the past session would savour of presumption; but it may be of interest, as showing our diversity and range of thought, to give a list of the subjects discussed. Among the political will be found the House of Lords, the Colonial aspect of Tariff Reform, Home Rule, and Socialism. Turning to the social side, there appears on the list Old Age Pensions, Sweated Labour, Co-operative Trading, Feeding of School Children, Nationalization of Railways, Municipal Trading, and Licensing Reform, all pressing questions of the hour, vitally affecting us who are part of the great, and when it realizes its strength, powerful and effective democracy. And then Imperialism, Literature, and some of the lighter aspects of life.

And what of the men who have so freely given of their time and thought in an attempt to elucidate the cardinal principles underlying these subjects? To the teaching staff in particular are our best thanks due, for there is hardly a man in the term programmes who has not been impressed, and willingly impressed, into our service, and come through the ordeal with an excellence almost amazing. If the aim of the College is really the intermingling of teachers and taught, then the Debating Society has this session fully maintained its constant endeavour to bring about such a condition, and we believe that the teachers have been fully repaid by the larger aspect of our life revealed to them by its agency. F. E. LIDDELOW, *Hon. Secretary.*

MAURICE CHESS CLUB.

THE Maurice Chess Club held its annual general meeting on May 4th, Mr. C. Godfrey Gümpel presiding. The report and accounts for the past season were received and passed. The accounts showed a small credit balance, which, in view of the club's difficulties, during the past two seasons, in making ends meet, was considered very satisfactory. Many thanks are due to J. F. Halford, the late hon. secretary, who has so ably managed the club's affairs during such a trying time, for the healthy condition in which he has left them; and to Mr. Gümpel for a splendid match set and board, presented by him to the Club.

The following were elected officers of the club for the coming season:— President, H. R. Levinsohn, B.A.; vice-presidents, Sir C. P. Lucas C.B., K.C.M.G., R. H. Marks, L. Jacob, B.A, L. Pocock, S. Bradgate, E. R. Cole, E. T. Colesby, A. S. Lupton, B.A., B. P. Moore, B.A., Wm. Hudson, S. de Jastrzebski, J. Jacob, B.A., and C. Godfrey Gümpel; hon. secretary and treasurer, J. Foley; match captain, A. E. Thomas; committee, F. J. Nield, J. Crawley, V. Ray, J. F. Halford, and W. Fulton.

Last season's championship tournament is not yet completed, the delay being caused by the severe illness of F. W. Chambers, one of the club's most prominent players, and who, so far, has acquitted himself remarkably well in the tournament. In the handicap tournament, V. Ray, J. F. Halford, and A. Levitt finished 1st, 2nd, and 3rd, respectively; and S. R. Briggs and O. Henke, respectively, won the 1st and 2nd match average prizes in last season's match.

The club decided to enter once again the C Division of the City of London Chess League in the ensuing season, and trust to be more successful than in former years.

We shall again have the pleasure, in October or November, of visiting Cambridge, and playing a team at Trinity College; and in the early part of next year, of entertaining them at home, and hope to repeat last season's successes, but we are not over sanguine. We also have hopes of meeting a team from one of the Oxford Colleges.

J. FOLEY, *Hon. Secretary and Treasurer.*

LUBBOCK FIELD CLUB.

THE May excursion was in many ways a memorable one. Favoured by magnificent weather, after a most unpromising previous week, the club saw one of the prettiest parts of the garden of England under the best possible conditions. The late spring had merely served to save up the best of the spring flowers for our benefit, and the woods were gay with primroses, wood anemones, wood sorrel, wood spurge, violets, bluebells, early purple orchis, and cuckoopints. The numerous orchards, however, with their great masses of bloom, outshone even the best show of wild flowers; and one cherry orchard in particular, near Kingsdown, made a picture that will not readily be forgotten by those who saw it.

Another fact that made the day a red-letter one in our annals was that we were the guests of Mr. J. Fotheringham, at his beautiful home at Barnshatch, nestled among the hills in a district round which the railways circle, without intruding unpleasantly near. This is the fourth time the club has partaken of Mr. Fotheringham's hospitality, previous visits having been made in summer, autumn, and almost winter.

The party numbered fourteen, and travelling by a late train, reached Farningham Road at 11.45, where our host was waiting. Under his guidance, we followed a series of paths across the Darent to Horton Kirkby and thence to Barnshatch, halting from time to time to explore woods, hunt for eoliths, or discuss the theory of dewponds. On reaching "Ivybank," we were welcomed by Mrs. Fotheringham and her daughters, and were soon enjoying such a repast as seldom falls to the lot of a L. F. C.-ite on his wanderings. Having done justice to the same, we walked through the woods to Kingsdown Church, where we saw the reredos carved by Miss Fotheringham and the altar rails turned by our president, Mr. Grugeon. We also spent some time admiring the grand old yews in the churchyard. Continuing south across the main road, we visited the gravel-pit near Oaklands, in order to renew our acquaintance with the great chalk boulder deposited there ages ago by some wandering iceberg. Future visitors will see little of this boulder, as it has almost all been removed. Some of us hurried on to some meadows which should have been gay with cowslips, but were not. We were, however, compensated by a glorious view along the Darent Valley, extending right across the Thames into Essex. We then made our way back to "Ivybank," where after tea had been disposed of, some of us smoked and lounged, while others explored the orchard, and were instructed in the mysteries of grafting. All too soon the time arrived to take our leave, Pocock thanking our kind host and hostesses for the enjoyable day we had had. We followed a series of paths leading us north-east across the Farningham Road to Eynsford. As the daylight faded, we were obliged to halt from time to time in order to enjoy the better the song of the nightingales. We returned by the 9.3 train from Eynsford.

The next walk will take place on June 14th, when it is proposed to walk along the chalk hills from Caterham to Westerham. Take pedestrian tour ticket No. 10, but reverse direction, *out* to Caterham, *back* from Westerham, 2s. 6d. Train leaves Charing Cross (S. E. R.) 9.15, London Bridge, 9.20, but does not call at Cannon Street. Provide lunch As Miss Jacob has kindly offered to provide tea for the party, the secretary will be glad to hear from those intending to turn out.   J. HOLLOWAY, *Hon. Secretary.*

THE WORKING MEN'S COLLEGE JOURNAL *is supported partly by Annual Subscribers living in different parts of the World, and partly by circulation among the Students and Members. Its success depends upon a regular demand, and to ensure this, the Editor would be glad if as many readers as can will become Subscribers. Subscription 2s. 6d. per annum, post free.*

LONDON: Printed by W. HUDSON & Co., Red Lion Street, High Holborn, and published at THE WORKING MEN'S COLLEGE, Crowndale Road, London, N.W.—June 1st, 1908.

The Working Men's College Journal

sub: M

The Working Men's College,
CROWNDALE
ROAD·
St. PANCRAS·
LONDON·N·W·
FOUNDED
IN 1854
BY THE LATE
Frederick
Denison
Maurice·

Contents for

JULY, 1908.

Visits to Oxford
    and Cambridge
Lubbock Field Club
College Notes
Musical Society's
        Concert

THE

Working Men's College Journal.

Conducted by Members of the Working Men's College
Crowndale Road, London, N.W.

| VOL. X.—No. 184. | JULY, 1908. | PRICE TWOPENCE. |

VISIT TO CAMBRIDGE.

"IT has been said that in human life there are moments worth ages. In a more subdued tone of sympathy may we affirm that there are days which are worth whole months—I might say—even years." WORDSWORTH'S *Guide to the Lakes.*

THOUGH referring to climate and aspects of Nature in the Lake district, these lines of a graduate of Cambridge University and a Poet laureate may perhaps be not inaptly used to record impressions received at Cambridge. Impressions received not only from the beauty of a favoured day of spring, when soft air was breathing over newborn blossoms and verdure, nor gathered solely from the antique grace of College Hall and Chapel, pilastered front or stately avenue ; but chiefly gained from the greeting extended to us, warm and genial as the spring sunshine, and from the kindness we experienced, which began with the welcome to the first comers and ended only with the speeding of the last parting guest.

It was about two o'clock on Saturday afternoon, May 23rd, when the early arrivals met at the gateway of Trinity College, an ancient and venerable tower which, like many things at Cambridge, has been smoothed and mellowed by the hand of time. Under its wide arch opens the smaller entrance of the porter's lodge, and into this sanctum we dived, to deposit our week-end bags, like swallows carrying their pellets of clay to a nest under the eaves. In the front of the gateway there is a statue of the founder or some benefactor of the College in ancient dress, looking out over the forecourt where bicycles by the dozen lean idly against the walls. I think it is related in Darwin's "Voyage of the Beagle," that the Guachos of the Pampas disdain to *walk*—to go even a hundred yards, they spring into the saddle of a waiting horse ! Somewhat similarly, in Cambridge we seemed everywhere to see the bridle thrown over the neck of the patient "bike." However, two of us, having a couple of hours to spend before the general assembly at Mr. Cornford's rooms, started on a perambulation of the town, the results of which I will try to describe.

As at Oxford, the railway station does not occupy a very picturesque position; still, though remote from the Colleges, on the one hand, it is also removed from some rather drab suburbs, on the other. From the outskirts of the town and the Gog-magog Hills beyond, two roads converge northwards upon the Market Place, near which they combine, cross the river Cam, and reach out to the country. If a letter "A" be imagined, the right-hand limb representing the Hills Road, the left-hand Trumpington Street, the Market Place just within the apex, and in place of the single bar, several, representing cross streets and lanes, a rough idea will be gained of the lines on which, though chiefly on the left-hand thoroughfare, most of the colleges are situated.

Following, from the railway station, the right-hand road, we soon came to "Emmanuel" and "Christ's," their sober architecture contrasting with the intervening buildings of the ordinary residential and business character; but a glimpse at a street-turning, of a broad, grassy, park-like space, "Parker's Piece," and an upward glance at the fine tower and spire of the Roman Catholic Church, added other views to a succession sufficiently attractive.

Arrived at the Post Office, a short street, the "Petty Cury,' one of the busiest in Cambridge, led us to the Market Square; a wide area covered, at the time of our visit, with mushroom-like booths, overflowing with flowers and the usual country provisions. The bustle going on and the spread of canvas under the shadow of Great St. Mary's, the University and Parish Church, lent a somewhat continental appearance to the scene, which might have been one in France or the Netherlands. On the exterior of the chancel of St. Mary's we found a fine memorial tablet to the Eastern-county soldiers of the Boer war, for whom, as for Bunyan's "Valiant," the trumpets had sounded on the other side. Pursuing our course to Bridge Street, we passed Sidney Sussex College, where in 1616 Oliver Cromwell was a member, and by Jesus Lane, which leads to Jesus College, outlying among open meadows. Then we paid a short visit to the Church of the Holy Sepulchre, one of the four *round* churches in England, where the transition from bright sunlight to the dark interior, with its circle of massive Norman columns and tiers of arches above, was very impressive.

Returning by the front of St. Mary's Church and King's Parade, our attention was arrested by the ivy-draped stone arcading which, like a chancel screen, separates the busy street from the quiet space beyond. Above these arches rise turrets and pinnacles, stained-glass windows gleam between ranks of buttresses, and the Tudor Rose blooms, in stone, on the panelled walls of the famous Chapel of "King's." This, the finest building in Cambridge, and a splendid specimen of the Perpendicular style of Gothic architecture, may well be looked upon by the visitor as the central and culminating point. Adjoining, on the right hand, is Trinity College, and further on, "John's," with its massive tower; to the left lie the ancient red brick Courts of "Queens'," and in the hinterland "Clare." These and other colleges, though fronting towards the street, reach out in the opposite direction, by their gardens and grounds, to the river and beyond, forming a practically continuous pleasaunce, the famous "Backs," in beautifying which Art and Nature seem to have vied. Here are flowers, trees isolated and in avenues, a river flowing by sloping lawns and under graceful bridges, paths shaded by immemorial elms, classic stone fronts and red brick gables, and views of distant towers and spires. Here, indeed, one could quote Meredith's words and say, "I raise my head to aspects fair," and forget that there are foul ones, from which we turn away.

But fair as the prospect was, and bright though its colours are, even in recollection, its smile held no greeting special to *us.* Nature goes a long way, but the supreme want is Human nature, and we now turned our steps to the rooms in "Trinity," where the friendly-looking name of "Cornford" on the door seemed in itself a welcome, where the owner's handshake made the stranger "at home," and where even the carpet had the feel of one's native heath.

At tea there was a pleasant party, and everyone did well, though in view of the numbers of our main body who had now arrived, the amplest private resources might have been strained, but the early comers at the festive board, their thirst assuaged, hastened to wait upon their less fortunate brethren. Introductions to Mr. Cornford having been made by our adjutant, Duchesne, we began to feel, under these cheering influences, as pleased as if we had received honorary "degrees," and the impression deepened when our august host handed us documents which, if not title-deeds to fame, coupled our names with many who doubtless will become famous. On perusing the papers, we found our "quarters," and with whom of our own men we were linked, and last and not least, the names of those friends of Mr. Cornford, friends of the W. M. C., and now in some degree we would like to think *our* friends, who had been requisitioned to show us hospitality. As to what that hospitality was like, one can only say—after reading pages of "Visit to Cambridge" in the JOURNAL, which have all one tale to tell, and hearing personal reminiscences now among the cherished traditions of the College—"the half has not been told."

Our party now being grouped into threes and fours, and having made the acquaintance at Mr. Cornford's of some of our hosts to whom we were bound for the evening and the morrow, we wended our different ways until we met again late in the evening at the same place for the final reunion and "good night." From this point, therefore, each group had its own experiences, and though in the course of our voyages we spoke other convoys of the W. M. C., steering different courses, and occasionally put into port together, there was more than enough of interest to keep everyone's attention so fully engaged that it was to the voyage's end that most of us deferred of his cargo of recollections to undo the " corded bales."

On Saturday evening, Mr. C. K. Hobson, of Trinity, entertained us, Staal, Mason Tarr and myself, to dinner at the "Union," the University Club, which is open to members of the sister University also. Its splendidly furnished apartments can give points even to the Common Room of the Working Men's College. We found the evening pass all too quickly in the company of our gentle and genial host, who returned with us at last through the now quiet streets to the Courts of Trinity, and we felt that this beginning of our University experience was pleasant indeed. At Mr. Cornford's rooms were assembled most of our own men and some of our new friends. The circle, seen through drifts of tobacco-smoke, appeared to own Cornford as a presiding genius who had raised it with his magic wand, the whole scene, and the day's experience, seeming almost too strange and good to be true. It was soon time for that rest which even undiluted enjoyment demands. We parted. I walked across the lawn with a certain "Fellow of Trinity," who showed me my room and bade me a hearty "good night," and in a few minutes, so it appeared, there was a knocking at the door, and the pleasant voice of the College bed-maker was heard announcing Sunday morning.

When I rose, sunbeams were streaming through the openings of the battlemented parapet, and with half-an-eye it was easy to see another fine day was before us. Upon meeting Tarr he poured into my ear the complaints with which the nightingales outside the College window had filled his, and Staal related that his sleep had been haunted by the sound of bells, but, as we said, it is such things as these that help to make the charm. Conducted by Duchesne, we had a short stroll in the fresh morning air to the rooms of the Hon. H. Lubbock of Trinity, where we were due to breakfast. Mr. Lubbock is the son of our former Principal, Sir John Lubbock, after whom the College Field Club is named. It is pleasant to think that though Sir John Lubbock is lost to the College, as Lord Avebury he still retains his interest in it. Proof of this is not needed—if it were, the Field Club could supply it—but it was gratifying to hear these sentiments from the lips of Lord Avebury himself, who, in his son's rooms, honoured us Collegians with his distinguished company. After breakfast, we enjoyed cigarettes with our host until it was time to meet at Mr. Cornford's, whence a visit to the Library of Trinity had been planned.

Trinity Library, the work of Sir Christopher Wren, forms one side of Neville Court; it has a similar colonnade, and harmonizes perfectly with the older portions. Within, the chequered marble flooring of its long gallery leads the eye to the statue with which " Trinity " honours her poet and man of action, Byron, while the treasured manuscript of " In Memoriam " speaks of another great poet who has helped to make Trinity College famous. All round lie close packed volumes in cases of unvarnished oak, plain as the old bindings, except where at intervals screens, enclosing perhaps priceless manuscripts, break out into carved design, and in heartwood of oak we find the delicacy of leaves and branches. We followed Mr. Cornford, who is, we suppose, as a Fellow, in some sense one of the proprietors of this splendid collection, as he pointed out to us the objects of greatest interest.

After this there was just time for an independent stroll through the " Backs " before partaking of lunch at the kind invitation of Mr. T. Hickman, of " King's," at his apartments in King's Parade. Here we saw how College men are accommodated outside the College precincts, though not beyond the reach of College authority. Mr. Hickman, a rowing man, gave us an interesting account of the peculiar " bumping " method of racing, on the Cam, and after talking of the river, we ourselves spent a couple of hours in a Canadian canoe, floating past Clare Bridge and the " Bridge of Sighs," or moored from time to time, our attention divided between the scenes on the river and on its banks.

For tea we were due at Mr. F. Keeling's in the great Court of Trinity. Mr. Keeling lives at the top of one of the towers which mark the angles and sides of this Court. We climbed the circular staircase to the turret, and were soon ensconced in his easiest chairs, or with our backs propped against the ancient roof-timbers which slant down and form a kind of " settle " by his fireside. From his windows we had a splendid view of the whole Court, the finest in Cambridge, then ripening in the rosy tints of the afternoon sun, but destined to hold the grey shades of evening ere we parted from our host. Keeling—if he will forgive the omission of the prefix—is a Socialist, a Fabian, and a debater at the " Union," and I for one was well content to listen long to the exposition of views which seemed the acme of sweet reasonableness, and with which one's own seemed (naturally) quite in accord. After this we saw, but were not tempted to climb to, the aerie on the top of a dormer window which is his sleeping apartment, roofed by the sky. We were pressed to stay, and did, until we found another College party, who were to be Mr. Keeling's supper guests, coming up the winding stair, when we made room by getting out of the window. Soon, Mr. Keeling was entertaining one party inside his rooms and another on the parapet, and however this may appear in cold print, in reality it was delightful.

Our host finally conducted us from his own to another hospitable table, that of Mr. Shove of the neighbouring College of " King's," on the ground floor this time. We sat round, and supper and talk went on together. Mr. Shove showed us great kindness and so did his friends, several of whom " dropped in."

I think we understood there that some had been "gated," but if it was the case that they might not pass the College gates after 8 p.m., it may have been a loss to them, but decidedly the gain was ours.

At last the great day came to an end. I have not, from my own point of view, said half enough, but I will not attempt to say more except to express personal thanks to Mr. Cornford, who probably will never know the full extent of the pleasure he was the means of giving. We met again that evening at his rooms, that is, those who had not returned, and again next morning at breakfast before the early train.

It was altogether a grand occasion in every possible way, and one always to be remembered. Every true Collegian who participated must feel deeply grateful to our own College, to Duchesne our conductor, and above all to Cornford of Trinity, "our" Cornford, and his Cambridge friends.

C. F. MARSHALL.

The several Colleges at Cambridge have so many points of lasting interest, that, in presenting a short narrative of the visit of the Working Men's College party on May 23rd, much has to be omitted from notes taken on the spot. To visit a great seat of learning, where various degrees are granted and conferred by the University, affords unbounded pleasure to those men who would really aspire to be thus honoured, but whose working position in life has been in other directions, rendering such distinction impossible. Here the gates of knowledge are opened wide, and at one college or another we met with a master, a president, or a provost, who were the "heads of the colleges," together with the public orator, the proctors, and several tutors, deans, fellows, moderators, examiners, and graduates—many of whom are in themselves veritable storehouses of the learning of all the ages, and whose minds have been so disciplined by study as to cause them to be regarded as the great thinkers and scholars of our time. The boards of studies regulating the curriculum were classified as Mathematical, Classical, Moral Science, Natural Science, Theological, Medical, Oriental, Legal, Historical, Musical, Modern and Mediæval Languages, with a long array of professors and lecturers. There were Divinity, Law, and Physics Schools, the keeping of all the Acts being entirely at the discretion of the respective professors. While undergraduates might appear to have an easy time, in reality much hard work was done at colleges where a high standard was maintained, in order to make the most of the intellectual as well as the social life of Cambridge.

Sundays and certain other days are known as "surplice-days," which form one of the "sights" peculiar to a University. On the Sunday when we were there (May 24th), the Bishop of Winchester came in procession at 2.15 from the Senate House to Great St. Mary's Church, known as the University Church, where there was a large gathering of members of Cambridge University, clad in their gowns and hoods. The day being England's "Empire Day," the sermon preached by the Bishop dwelt on the expansion of the empire, and its Colonial strength and commercial development in remote parts of the world; on the strides made in the scientific and mechanical advancement of our time; on the growth and progress of thought in all directions; and indicated the duties and larger responsibilities in connection therewith that devolved on the nation in its world-wide heritage. A peculiarity of the service was the attitude of standing at the "Bidding" Prayer, instead of kneeling, as customary at churches and chapels since the time of Archbishop Laud.

At Emmanuel College, the Rev. F. W. Head was untiring in his efforts to give our two men the best of welcomes. For once we were treated as Fellow-Commoners, being permitted at 7.30 p.m. on Saturday to dine in Hall with the tutors, and afterwards to adjourn to the Fellows' room. We spent the remainder of the evening at Mr. Head's house, where a life-like portrait of Frederick Denison Maurice, hanging in the study, formed an interesting link with our own College in London, reminding one of the time when Maurice was a Cambridge professor. On Sunday morning we were able to attend 8 o'clock service in Chapel, followed by celebration of the communion. At 9 o'clock we had breakfast with Mr. and Mrs. Head, in company with the Dean of Emmanuel, who is University Proctor. Then we went for a pleasant saunter by the banks of the Cam, and at 11.30 we joined Mr. Cornford, who took a party to see the Library at Trinity. At 1.15 p.m. we were due to enjoy the friendship and hospitality of Mr. H. H. Sills, at King's; and this was followed by our being present at the afternoon choral service, at 3.30, at the famous King's College Chapel, where we had seats within the screen.

After the conclusion of the service at King's, we pursued our way to Newnham College, where a small party had been invited to see Miss Jane Harrison, and to take tea at 5.15 p.m. We were then taken over the college by a few lady students who were giving the usual three years' study and residence at Newnham, required to qualify them to enter for the respective triposes. There were separate dining halls attached to the several buildings, which had been erected at different times during the past fifty years, owing to the steady but continuous increase in the number of candidates since the foundation of the college. The Library, with its three-sided recesses and overhead daylight, having a separate table and seats to each, and books classified around, appeared to be a delightful place for quiet reading and work. We made the discovery of a large volume on "Thucydides," with the name of F. M. Cornford on the title-page; but the author had kept this unknown to us—perhaps, as a little secret of his own! Miss Harrison has always been devoted in her efforts for the higher education of women; and when in London many years ago, she was connected with and taught in the College for Working Women, at that time in Queen Square, but now located at 7, Fitzroy Street. After a most cordial reception and an hour's conversation in Miss Harrison's room, we made our way back to Cornford's rooms at Trinity, to gather some tidings as to the remainder of our party and their perambulations. At 7.30, we both —Crawford and I—returned to Emmanuel, to spend the evening with Mr. and Mrs. Head, to whom we were ready to unfold some episodes of what had occurred since the morning—altogether a day well occupied, but leaving so many colleges unseen.

The opportunity afforded by Mr. F. M. Cornford—and formerly by Mr. G. M. Trevelyan—to students of the Working Men's College to go to Cambridge, and to be the guests of University graduates and undergraduates, is a privilege that is gratefully esteemed by everyone of the men who have been selected from year to year. There one is brought into personal contact with the ways and methods of those who have the advantage of superior training and high intellectual culture. The friendly greetings, the social intercourse, and a participation in the congenial surroundings of Cambridge college life are realized phenomena to be remembered with the greatest pleasure in after years.   WILLIAM HUDSON.

⸻

As one of the band of College men who recently invaded Cambridge, I would ask a little space in your crowded columns to say how thoroughly I enjoyed the trip. It would, I feel, be putting things mildly to describe our reception as a kind and generous one. Indeed it seemed to me as though our hosts had reserved their whole energies for our visit, and found the utmost joy in using them in our entertainment. In any case they were always ready and delighted to take any trouble, if by doing so they could add to our enjoyment. Mr. Cornford in particular, was unsparing in his efforts, and the delightful ingenuity with which he sought to diminish the nature or amount of his own kindness, constituted a charm which no one could fail to appreciate. I am afraid it would be rather beyond my powers to express the thoughts and feelings to which my imagination was moved by all that I saw at the University. I was naturally much impressed by the size and grandeur of the colleges, and I can only say that I experienced a real delight as well as a deep, though not disagreeable, sense of awe, as I wandered through their ancient courts or climbed their quaint old stairs. I am sure everyone will agree that visits to such great and venerable institutions as Cambridge University give considerable instruction as well as pleasure, and I think that very hearty thanks are due to those who spend such a lot of time and trouble in making our annual trip a success. For my part, I spent a most delightful time, and I shall always have pleasant recollections of my two days' residence at Trinity College.   J. MCWILLIAM.

⸻

Our forty-nine hosts at Cambridge were—at *Trinity College*, Mr. F. M. Cornford, Rev. J. C. How, and Messrs. C. K. Hobson, C. G. Darwin, J. R. M. Butler, L. C. Garrett, E. Ph. Goldschmidt, A. P. Kirkpatrick, D. S. Robertson, Hon. H. Lubbock, H. S. J. Philby, W. N. Ewer, H. A. Webb, J. B Hales, R. W. Howard, H. G. Easterling, G. Saunders, F. Keeling, F. C. Thompson, H. A. Hollond, and A. S. Towsey; at *St. John's*, Rev. H. F. Stewart, and Messrs. H. F. Russell Smith, R. Meldrum, E. A. Benians, A. Y. Campbell, V. W. J. Hobbs, W. G. Constable, V. K. Haslam, N. S. Subbarao, and G. I. C. Marchant; at *Caius*, Messrs. F. J. M. Stratton and A. Ramsay; at *Queens'*, Rev. C. T. Wood; at *Emmanuel*, Rev. F. W. Head and G. G. Hooper; at *Jesus College*, Rev. F. I. Foakes Jackson; at *St. Catherine's*, Messrs. Clifford Gudgeon and R. F. Sheppey-Greene; at *King's*, Messrs. A. D. Schloss, H. H. Sills, R. W. Coit, T. Hickman, H. Y. Oldham, R. C. Brooke, and G. Shove; at *Trinity Hall*, Mr. T. Thornely; at *Christ's*, Mr. A. E. Shipley; and at *Newnham College*, Miss Jane Harrison.

The following are the names of the forty members of our College who, with Mr. Duchesne, participated in the visit to Cambridge:—H. V. Birrell, H. Crawford, H. J. Davey, W. J. Davis, C. W. Deuchar, C. F. Endersby, R. W. Everard, H. Eyers, P. A. Fielding, A. Gude, A. Hallett, E. Hayward, A. Haynes, J. Hagerty, R. Hagerty, R. S. Hitchcock, Wm. Hudson, H. H. Hughes, F. S. Lakeman, F. E. Liddelow, W. Lloyd, J. McWilliam, C. F. Marshall, C. Morley, E. Nobel, G. J. Offer, A. Owen, A. U. Penny, H. Pert, F. J. Reeve, R. L. Robinson, C. W. Smart, C. E. Smethers, M. Staal, A. H. B. Stock, R. W. Stokes, Mason Tarr, A. Towles, J. G. Williams, and W. Windley.

LUBBOCK FIELD CLUB.

ON June 14th the Club had a most enjoyable walk on the borders of Kent and Surrey. Starting from Caterham, we began by climbing the hill to the east of the town, and on reaching Tillingdown Farm, found a path leading into Marden Park. After following the Drive past the house, we ascended the opposite hill and followed the fence until we emerged from the Park at the Rifle Range. Just across the road a path led down the steep hill towards Gadstone, and we followed this some distance in order that half the party might enjoy the view, while the other and more energetic section, employed itself orchid-hunting. This division of labour was considered so satisfactory that the same programme was repeated whenever a stretch of open downs was encountered, and as our walk was along the crest of the Downs, opportunities arose fairly frequently. Consequently in a day of about 9½ hours the distance walked by the party was barely 12 miles, although it is only fair to mention that the rotameter is useless for tracing the devious wanderings of the orchid-hunters. On reaching the hill above Oxted chalk-pit, the question of lunch was to the fore, and after some discussion the small minority that craved for an inn was outvoted, and we raided a cottage near Flint House Farm. We fared very well, scattered in two picturesque groups on the banks of the adjoining lane. After a short examination of the neighbouring wood, we pursued our course by the very picturesque road to Botley Hill, our highest point (875 feet). We scattered through the woods that border the road, and as a result lost Cambridge, who it seems was gloating over a Fly Orchis he had found. After a long wait, the rest of the party wandered on through Tatsfield, and after some difficulty found its way to "The Wym," where the Misses Jacob and some friends were waiting us, and where we found our missing man. We were soon discussing a glorious tea and other matters, seated in the gardens. After tea, all too quickly it became necessary to look after our line of communications, and guided by our hostess and Mr. Julius Jacob, we wended our way Westerhamwards. On arriving within touch of the road, we were left to our own devices, and in due course returned by the 7.35 train.

Although an early morning shower and a falling barometer had induced those of little faith to air their macintoshes, we were favoured with grand weather, and saw the fine succession of views to the best advantage. The chief captures of interest were among the orchids, of which eight kinds were seen in flower.

The best thanks of the Club are due to our kind hostesses for the hospitable manner in which we were entertained at the "Wym."

The next walk will take place on July 12th, in the Lea Valley. Take excursion tickets to Broxbourne, 1s. 9d. Train leaves Liverpool Street at 9.56.   J. HOLLOWAY, *Hon. Secretary.*

W.M.C. DEBATING SOCIETY.

The following is the Balance Sheet of the Debating Society :—

SESSION, 1907-8.

Receipts.	£	s.	d.	Payments.	£	s.	d.
Balance forward ...	1	2	6	Tobacco and Pipes .	0	3	3
22 Subscriptions ...	1	2	0	Receipt Book	0	0	6
Sale of Surplus Tobacco	0	1	1	Postage	0	5	6
				Locker Rent	0	2	0
				Printing	0	14	6
				Balance	0	19	10
	£2	5	7		£2	5	7

Audited and found correct.—B. S. HITCHCOCK.

F. E. LIDDELOW, *Hon. Secretary.*

COLLEGE NOTES.

LAST year, owing to the illness of our good friend Mr. Cornford of Trinity College, Cambridge, we were, as a College, debarred from the pleasure of our annual visit to the University. This year, our members have been fortunate enough to participate in two visits, one to the University of Cambridge, on May 23rd, 24th and 25th, and the other to the University of Oxford, on May 30th and 31st and June 1st. Both visits were eminently and equally successful, and the forty men who went to Cambridge, and the fourteen others who went to Oxford, are unanimous in declaring that they never spent better week-ends. Mr. Duchesne went, as befits our Superintendent, to both, and played his part right well. Mr. Cornford organized, arranged for, and carried out the visit to Cambridge, as usual, with the assistance of some fifty friends there, with consummate skill and delightful modesty. It was a happy and entirely praiseworthy inspiration which led Mr. R. N. M. Bailey, one of our teachers, who is an Oxford man, to arrange, in conjunction with the Rev. R. G. Parsons, of University College, Oxford, for the first of what we hope will be a very long series of Oxford visits. Modelled on the good old "Trevelyan-Cornford" plan, this excursion went off excellently and without a hitch, some of Mr. Parsons's friends helping to make it the success it was. Accounts of both trips appear in this number, with the addition, in the case of Oxford, of the visitors' "billets" (page 378).

Of the six essays sent in for the "Marks" prize, Mr. Cornford has adjudged the best to be that of Mr. J. G. Newlove, who selected for his theme the first of the two subjects open to him, namely, "Discuss Shakespeare's view of Democracy, especially as exemplified by the plays of *Julius Cæsar* and *Coriolanus*." In the course of his exhaustive and extremely useful report upon the essays submitted, Mr. Cornford said :—

Of the six essays sent in, three,—Mr. Newlove's, Mr. Liddiatt's, and Mr. Penny's—were of distinct merit in their various ways. The other three were less substantial productions, on which less thought and trouble seemed to have been spent.

The prize is awarded to Mr. Newlove. His essay is superior to the others in point of form—well arranged, and clearly written in a straightforward and correct style. It shows evidence of considerable reading. A good, honest piece of work, on which I congratulate him.

A word of praise is due to Mr. Liddiatt and Mr. Penny.

Mr. John Godfrey Newlove, the first "Marks" prizeman, joined the College in October, 1907, taking up the study of English History, Composition, and Grammar. He received his early education at the "Stanley Council School," Medburn Street, N.W., a fact which should give his present success a local interest. He entered the Civil Service, obtaining a post in the Central Telegraph Department, and is, therefore, a colleague of

Munro, Rennie, and Austin. Always of a studious turn of mind, he found in "Sociology" sufficient scope for his peculiar abilities and tastes, and it was through the reading and study of the writings of social reformers that he became an ardent Socialist. Joining the Social Democratic Party followed as a natural consequence, and he entered enthusiastically into the movement. He has attended many courses of lectures on Economics and Industrial History, and is the holder of an Oxford Delegacy Certificate, and of one issued by the Co-operative Union. Mr. Newlove's hobbies are reading and walking.

As briefly announced in the June number, the College Annual Garden Party and Field Sports will take place on Saturday, July 11th, in the grounds of "The Ship" Inn, Eastcote, near Pinner. "The Ship" is situated about a mile from Pinner Station, and is approached through beautiful wooded country and field paths. All College men are cordially invited to join the party and enter for the various events on the programme, which will contain several especially attractive items for our lady friends. Entries will be taken on the ground, no charge being made for them, and prizes will be given, at the close of the Sports, to the winners of each event. The Sports will be started promptly at 3.30 p.m., tea will be served at 5 o'clock, and a concert will be held in the pavilion at 8. Tickets, including a fruit tea and return railway journey from Baker Street, may be obtained from College club secretaries, R. R. Flint in the office, and from the Common Room Committee, at the price of 2s. 6d. each.

The Sports and Garden Party offer an opportunity for young and old members of the College to meet in the open air, amid beautiful surroundings, and under the most pleasing conditions. It is, we think, due to the Common Room Committee and others who have interested themselves in promoting this event, that all members, past and present, should make a point of reserving the half-day on July 11th, and go down to Eastcote to join in or see the Sports. We hope that all readers of the JOURNAL who can possibly do so, will take advantage of the occasion, and it will be a real pleasure for us to meet them on the ground. The Editor will be only too delighted to forward tickets in exchange for half-crowns, to all those who may require them ; and as a heavy outlay has already been made for railway tickets, and considerable liability incurred in connection with the necessary catering, we hope there will be a quick and steady demand.

Mr. Sonnenschein has kindly presented to the College a cabinet of geological specimens and a large cabinet of physics apparatus.

Mr. John MacDonald, Editor and Proprietor of the *Western School Journal*, Topeka, Kansas, U.S.A., and old student of the College, writes with two years' subscription to the JOURNAL, and says :—

The JOURNAL is a welcome visitor, and I find it interesting from beginning to end. The "Recollections of Ruskin" I have enjoyed very much. How well I remember that chapter "On the Nature of Gothic Architecture," from "Stones of Venice!" We used it in Dr. Furnivall's classes. I have my copy yet, and it will stay with me until the end.

I did not know Mr. Roebuck, but I have a somewhat dim remembrance that I called on him in New York City in 1866 or '67. Our meeting was very brief. Some years ago I wrote you that I had found another student of the College, Rev. W. S. Crouch, of Maple Hill, Kansas, living about twenty-five miles from here. He is both prosperous and popular, and one who listens to his sermons finds plenty of food for thought and reflection.

An evening or two ago, I again took down my copy of *The Working Men's College*, 1854—1904, and began a second or third reading of it. Of course the Great Ormond Street part interests me more than any other, but all of it is good reading. How well I remember the Common Room! Mr. Vernon Lushington, then in the prime and strength of his manhood, Mr. Litchfield, and others are plainly visible to me through the dimness, chatting to groups of students, and out in the office I can see Mr. Shorter, bending low over his books. I have a number of his receipts now. I still can clearly hear Mr. Litchfield in the arithmetic class—Barnard Smith's book —"Now examine your answer, and ask yourself if that is a reasonable answer from the conditions ;" and Mr. Vernon Lushington's voice in the geometry class is yet audible to me as he commended the student who emphasized the "must" in the statement that therefore the point A *must* coincide with the point B. Dr. Furnivall's laugh, too, in the grammar class, when some student blundered in an unconsciously humourous way, still comes to me across the years, with its mirthful, sympathetic tone.

My last look at the College was in September, 1894. I was at the opening meeting for that year. It is possible, or even probable, I may see the College in its new home next September. I hope you will pardon the length of this letter. One who is old takes to reminiscences as a duck takes to water.

One of those who "assisted" at the Furnivall Children's Treat last Christmas was Mr. Sidney S. Rumble, of Capetown, a friend of a member of the College. He has returned to the Cape, whence he has written as follows :—

When I was in England last winter, I visited the W.M.C. on several occasions, through the instrumentality of one of your members, and I think it only my duty to write and express my appreciation of the very kind and cordial welcome I received. I had the pleasure of assisting at the entertainment for children last Christmas, and I must confess that, although I had lived in London for the greater part of my life previously to coming to this country, this particular scene was one which left a deep impression on me ; an impression which I doubt if I shall ever forget. But what I was particularly struck with was the true democratic spirit which prevailed, and the thorough absence of chilly aloofness which we people coming from the colonies find so very trying in English life. If I am right –and I feel sure I am—in believing this to be one of the main principles upon which the W.M.C. is founded, I can only say that it is fully upheld by the members with whom I came into contact.

Under date Kyoto, Japan, May 17th, 1908, the Rev. B. H. Alford writes to the Secretary of the Old Students' Club, "This is to tell you of our safe arrival in the sacred city of Old Japan, full of Shinto and Buddhist temples, where formerly the Mikado lived in complete seclusion. We had a pleasant voyage, but hot in the tropics; here it is quite cool again. Best remembrances to all."

Mrs. Julian Marshall, our examiner in Music, who has so often assisted at entertainments in the College, conducted the twenty-second annual concert of the South Hampstead Orchestra, at the Queen's Hall, Langham Place, on June 4th, when Mischa Elman played several violin solos, and about twenty of our members and friends were in the audience. Mrs. Marshall had to conduct with her left hand on this occasion, having broken a small bone in her right hand some days previously.

Mr. McCarthy, a popular exponent in the College of the arts of gymnastics and calisthenics, has been re-engaged, after a short absence, as instructor for the October term. An addition is to be made to the existing apparatus in the Gymnasium, in the shape of a new punching ball.

Mr. James Warren, sub-curator of the College Museum, is forming a Geological Field Club, and a map and other articles required for the purposes of the members are about to be purchased.

A smoking concert, with short speeches, will open the October term, on September 19th. Mr. Sidney Lee will distribute certificates and give an address, on October 31st. Mr. W. Pett Ridge, Sir F. Swettenham, Mr. Arthur Tansley, and Mr. Rose are amongst the lecturers for the term, during which Miss Spurgeon will take a class on " Ruskin," on Fridays.

HODGSON PRATT MEMORIAL.

A COMMITTEE has now been formed for the purpose of establishing some suitable memorial of the life work of Mr. Hodgson Pratt, and it is suggested that the chief part of the memorial should take the form of travelling scholarships enabling workers of either sex to become acquainted with technical and social development in foreign countries or the colonies, or in the endowment of a scholarship at one of the universities, with the establishment of a prize essay ; all these to bear Mr. Pratt's name.

J. C. Gray, Co-operative Union ; J. Frederick Green, International Arbitration and Peace Association ; and B. T. Hall, Working Men's Club and Institute Union, Club Union Buildings, Clerkenwell Road, E.C., are the joint secretaries of the committee, which includes several well-known members and friends of this College, amongst them being Lord Avebury, treasurer, Sir George Trevelyan, Sir C. P. Lucas, C.B., K.C.M.G., Dr. Eugene Oswald, Mr. T. F. Hobson, Mr. L. Jacob, Mr. J. J. Dent, Mr. C. E. Maurice, Mr. J. M. Ludlow, and Mr. L. Pocock. Cheques and postal orders should be made payable to the Hodgson Pratt Memorial Fund, and crossed " Robarts Lubbock & Co."

THE OXFORD VISIT.

MAY 30th—31st, 1908.

THE Oxford visit, the first for a number of years, but let us hope the precursor of many others, was a round of unblemished enjoyment from beginning to end. Our first experiences were common to the whole party. Mr. Parsons met us at the station and showed us our sleeping quarters.   Then we went to University College, where we had tea and saw the beautiful Common Room and Hall. Afterwards we were taken over the Bodleian, the Radcliffe, the Divinity School, etc., and, after a stroll in Christchurch Meadows, dispersed in couples to our various hosts for supper.   Our host—Nye's and mine—was Mr. Conybeare of New College, with whom we spent a most pleasant evening, strolling about the lovely college gardens and discussing all manner of things with that philosophic calm that comes of a well-lined inner man.   Next morning we went to St. John's College, where Mr. A. G. Edwards gave us breakfast in Hall.   Later, during a most idyllic morning, spent chiefly on the Isis and Cherwell, he showed us what wonders can be done with a punt pole.   After lunch, which took the form of a pleasant river picnic with Mr. G. E. Fawcus, of New College, we also tried punting, and did not get very wet—considering.   Our whole party met again at "The Orchard," where in Professor Dicey's beautiful garden we had a warm welcome. Mrs. Dicey was unfortunately not well enough to be present, but some lady friends of the Professor, including Mrs. and Miss Toynbee, entertained us, and the whole experience was delightful.   Nye and I had supper with Mr. P. J. Patrick at Corpus Christi, and most of us met again at the concert at Balliol.   Here German music was discoursed, after the manner of those who perform "ops.":

> They played him a sonata—let me see !
> " *Medulla oblongata* "—key of G.
>   Then they began to sing
>   That extremely lovely thing,
> " *Scherzando ! ma non troppo, p.p.p.*"

And so home, next morning.

This is a bald and bare account of our doings.   Words do not convey an idea of the beauty of the Colleges, with their grey walls, their windows gay with flowers, quiet gardens and velvety lawns ; of the rivers, overarched with trees of fresh spring green or of brilliant blossom all aglow in the magnificent weather.

Nor would they describe the hospitality of our hosts, nor the atmosphere of College life.   The latter is an indefinable air of culture and refinement, unaffected even by the occasional ebullience of youthful undergraduates.   I have noticed it before at Cambridge ; indeed, it appears peculiar to universities, and makes one wish for more, and makes everyday life seem sordid and unworthy for some time to come.

The visit was admirably organized, and Mr. Parsons and Mr. Bailey deserve congratulation, as well as thanks, for its success.   A. E. HOMEWOOD.

To say that the excursion to Oxford was an enjoyable one, is to say in an awkward and flat way, a great deal less than one feels on the matter. Indeed it is impossible for me to put into language half of the pleasure I got out of the visit. From beginning to end there was not a dull or idle moment. Everything it was possible to see or learn in so short a time we saw and learned.

With my usual muddleheadedness I set off from King's Cross, and what with the yelling of the porters and the frantic haste of intending passengers, I endeavoured to "hurry up" in accordance with instructions bawled into my ears at every turn, and, as I generally do, hurried into the wrong train. After passing several stations, I asked a fellow passenger if London trains usually took about an hour to travel from King's Cross to Paddington. The answer was, "Great Scott, you are miles from Paddington." The result of that remark was that I got out of the train at the first stopping place, and worried every uniformed official I could see, as to when and from what platform the next train for Paddington would start. One pompous-looking individual I asked three times. Now whether this man thought I was having some fun at his expense, or whether he was bad-tempered I am unable to say, but at any rate the third query got no audible reply, but some very expressive looks were showered upon me. However, I kept on smoking, and as I jumped into the train said, "This is right for Paddington, isn't it?" He simply replied "hurry up," without the aspirate. On arriving at Paddington I got into another train, and a man came up and asked me where I was going. This time I was determined to stick, and informed him that I was going to Timbuctoo if that train was going there. He muttered something about fools, and I sat down in a corner seat.

I got to Oxford at last, and set off to find the rooms set apart for the use of Pettit and me. I did not find them, but Pettit found me, and hauled me off to George Street, where, after being introduced to the landlady, and washing, we set off for University College and met Mr. Parsons and several of ours, among them being Mr. Duchesne and the Editor. After seeing the Shelley Memorial and Mr. Parson's rooms, we were taken across the meadows and shown the barges. After the walk we returned to the colleges, and were divided into parties and sent off to different hosts. Pettit and I went to Queen's and were introduced to Mr. Wakeman, who gave us a first-class welcome, and a good time, first at dinner, and then at the theatre. At about 11.30 p.m. we retired to our rooms and to bed, where in spite of the industry of a church clock which advertised its existence every fifteen minutes, we slept soundly. Early on Sunday morning we started for New College, Pettit stopping every now and then to compare some extraordinary picture postcards with the actual scenes. Possibly we were extra hungry that morning, for we got to New College just a bit too soon. However, we enjoyed the view from Mr. Tyndale's window, and when he was ready we sat down to breakfast and conversation. After breakfast Mr. Tyndale suggested Chapel, and as I am not a chapel or church-going man, I confess I was a little alarmed at the thought. Why I should have been so, I do not know; but Mr. Tyndale may congratulate himself on giving me, at any rate, an experience that was not simply delightful, but glorious. I can hear that organ yet, and can remember distinctly everything that passed. It is not possible for me to thank Mr. Tyndale sufficiently for his suggestion.

After chapel, our host took us round the colleges and showed us their gardens, pointing out many beautiful and interesting things. Indeed we saw so much that it would be out of the question for me to describe them all, nor do I think my descriptions would be sufficiently interesting to the readers of the JOURNAL ; but I can assure you that for real and thorough enjoyment, nothing could have been better.

At one o'clock Mr. Tyndale left us in Mr. Watkin's rooms, where we remained in possession for a few minutes. Soon, however, Mr. Watkin came in and we were at home at once. A few minutes later with a shout and rush Mr. Reynolds, a friend of Mr. Watkin's arrived, and after some handshaking and talking set the rest of us to work laying the table-cloth. We succeeded after some struggles and sat down feeling quite heroic, but a man who brought up some victuals, without a word, and with a twinkle in his eye, immediately set about altering things. I'm sure we did it beautifully, but there, it is impossible to please some people.

What a time we had to be sure ! We ate and talked, and talked and ate, until at last we had to stop and make for the river for punting exercise ; but alas ! the punt had disappeared ; some mis-guided individual had with malice aforethought collared it. Now I believe the audacious individual was a member of the W. M. C., and I would suggest to him that if ever he meets Mr. Reynolds, he should apologize quickly or run. Never mind, we spent a splendid afternoon chatting in Mr. Reynolds's rooms, and at four o'clock when our hosts left us at Professor Dicey's gate, their apologies for the loss of the punt were quite unnecessary.

At Professor Dicey's the clans gathered, and we had tea in the garden, and I must say if everybody enjoyed themselves half as much as I did, they were fortunate indeed. In a very short time I found myself taking tea with and talking to a lady, without the least shyness, and as confidently as if I owned the place. I was amazed when Pettit said, "It's time we were going." That's the worst of these good things, they are gone so quickly. We rushed off to Corpus Christi, where we dined with Mr. Haigh, who talked rowing and other things, and showed us his oar. Here again we had to tear ourselves away, and scurry off to the station to catch the train for Paddington. I was more than sorry to leave Oxford. If I may trespass further on your space, I would like to mention two things that struck me forcibly. The first was the hearty good-fellowship shown us by the men at Oxford. They never spared themselves in the least ; they showed us everything that was beautiful or interesting ; they worked for our pleasure as if their lives depended on our enjoyment, and did it all without hurry or bustle. The second thing was the way the men spoke of their colleges. Each man seemed to think his college the best, and did not hesitate to say so, if necessary. This I think, Sir, is a most important and admirable thing, although I am bound to admit that I believe them to be curiously mistaken, for after all ours is the best.

CHARLES E. HORSMAN.

———

We—Sweeting and I—arrived at Oxford at 5.15, were met by Mr. Bailey, and after tea at the station, started rambling over Oxford. After seeing Worcester and St. John's Colleges, the gardens of which are very pretty, we were introduced to our first host, Mr.

Parker of St. John's. We had supper in hall, an amusing feature of the meal being the rapidity with which it was served and eaten ; you were hardly ·conscious that you had finished your soup, when the plate was swept from sight by an eagle-eyed scout, and the beef was before you awaiting its fate. After supper we adjourned to Mr. Parker's rooms and spent a most pleasant evening with him and two friends of his. We talked for some time about the College, and then the conversation became general, ranging from the sublimity of Bernard Shaw to the depths of demonology. On Sunday morning early we went for a walk in St. John's Gardens, and then to New College to breakfast with Mr. Bewley. After breakfast, sight seeing, which included New College chapel and tower, Christ Church with a " quad " much like Trinity College, Cambridge, and Magdalen occupied us till one o'clock. We went to Balliol College to lunch with Mr. S. K. Rae, and afterwards paddled in a punt, in rather unconventional style, on the river, and arrived back late, so that we had to hurry somewhat towards the College Mecca, Professor Dicey's house in the Banbury Road. Of the delightful tea-party on the lawn, let the future College historian tell ; suffice it here to say that a more pleasant afternoon or a more pleasant scene would be difficult to imagine. We had supper at Keble College with Mr. Perry Okeden, a most delightful host, and had the good fortune to drink from a "sconce" which some hapless wight down the table had had to provide. After a short chat with Mr. Okeden in his rooms, with cake, biscuits, coffee, cigarettes, and tobacco at our service, we left for the station, as our train left at 8.20. We should like to remark how cordial was the welcome given us wherever we went ; there was the same " good fellowship " about our several hosts that was so pleasant a feature at Cambridge, and our heartiest wish on leaving Oxford was that we should see those who had so kindly entertained us at Crowndale Road.   J. W. ROBERTS.

FURNIVALL SCULLING CLUB.

THE Annual Regatta was fixed for Saturday, May 30th. Starting in the afternoon of that day and by dint of keeping the competitors well up to the "scratch," or their respective handicaps, all the events were decided by the following Friday evening—this being well inside our previous time records. Brown won the rum-tums, and Hoad the gigs, the men's fours being won by Hoad (stroke), Williams, Brown, and Gillies. A four made up by the Misses E. Sewell (stroke), Mills, A. Dewar, and J. Fisher, was victorious in the girl's fours, and the Barker Cup (mixed doubles) fell to Miss E. Allen and H. S. Webb, who met the holders of the cup (Miss E. Sewell and F. S. Sammons) in the final.

Mr. G. H. Radford, M.P., one of our vice-presidents, entertained the club at his house at Surbiton on Sunday, June 14th. A goodly number of members foregathered in his charming garden, and after partaking of tea and fruit salad, listened to the old club glees and Mr. T. Barnard's inimitable recitations. Mr. J. H. Munday, of Cedar Lodge, 21, St. John's Road, Putney Hill, has very kindly invited the club to his house on Sunday, July 5th.

The annual fours race with the Polytechnic R. C. takes place on Saturday, July 4th. The Polytechnic are sculling their four this year, instead of rowing as in previous years. A good fight is expected.

H. S. HOWARD, *Hon. Secretary.*

VISIT OF W. M. C. MEN TO OXFORD UNIVERSITY.

SATURDAY, MAY 30TH, AND SUNDAY, MAY 31ST, 1908.

Below are given the names of the visitors, and those of their hosts, with the respective Colleges of the latter. The time between meals was spent in sight-seeing, or on the River Cherwell, in punts, under the thoughtful care and guidance of the host of the preceding meal, who made it his duty, in each case, to deliver up his guests to the next entertainer on the list.

Breakfast, Monday, at our respective rooms.

Visitor.	Tea	Dinner.	Breakfast.	Lunch.	Tea	Supper.
Jas. Holloway, R. M. Emslie		Mr. M. Heseltine, New College.	Mr. I. S. Hood, Magdalen.	Mr. F. H. Senneck, New College.		Mr. R. B. Winser, Corpus Christi.
H. Nye, A. E. Homewood		Mr. J. J. Conybeare, New College.	Mr. A. G. Edwards, St. John's.	Mr. G. E. Faalcus, New College.		Mr. P. J. Patrick, Corpus Christi.
E. S. Landells, H. K. Randall		Mr. Villiers, Magdalen.	Mr. G. C. Robson, New College,	Mr. Boxsey, University College.		Mr. L. Lefroy, Balliol College.
F. J. Nield, C. H. Perry	With Rev. R. G. Parsons in University College Common Room.	Mr. Wills, Magdalen.	Mr. E. R. Morgan, New College.	Mr. F. J. Romanes, St. John's.	At Professor A. V. Dicey's, "The Orchard."	Mr. A. G. Heath, New College.
L. Pocock, E. J. H Reglar		Rev. R. G. Parsons, University College, Mr. H. F. Houlder, St. John's.	Mr. E. N. Blandy, Balliol College	Mr. H. T. Wade-Gery, New College.		Mr. R. B. Turbutt, Christ Church, at Eastgate Hotel.
C. E. Horsman, J. C. Pettit		Mr. O. Wakeman, Christ Church.	Mr. H. G. E. Tyndale, New College.	Mr. E. J. Walker, New College.		Mr. C. R. Haigh, Corpus Christi.
J. W. Roberts, F. G. Sweeting		Mr. C. L. Parker, St. John's.	Mr. C. H. Bewley, New College.	Mr. H. K. Rae, Balliol College.		Mr. Perry Okeden, Keble College.
E. C. Duchesne		Entertained by Rev. R. G. Parsons and Mr. R. N. M. Bailey.				

W. M. C. MUSICAL SOCIETY.
"GRAND PIANO" CONCERT.

QUITE superfluous would it be for us to announce that on May 2nd a Ladies' Concert was held in the Maurice Hall under the auspices of the above Society, as there is an individual in the College who left no room on any notice board or door in the building for any other announcement but that of this Concert, and moreover, there is another person, Staal by name, who persisted in selling tickets to everyone who entered the College during the two months preceding the date of the Concert, whether they required them or not. Yet will we chronicle the fact that on this date a sixpenny Concert, very ably arranged, took place to help the Musical Society in its endeavours to provide a grand in the place of the cottage piano now used at our concerts in the Hall.

The Concert opened with "Zampa," a pianoforte solo, by G. H. Langford. Like all openings, the effect was spoiled by the many late arrivals among the audience, but as early birds, we can truly say that this solo was very excellently performed. We hope to have the pleasure of hearing Langford again under better circumstances. F. E. Lawrence gave us, with his usual gusto and good taste, "Three for Jack," chorus very weak, as "the gods" were without a leader. Our friend Miss C. Graefe of "Violets" fame, sang very sweetly "The Lavender Girl." Unhappily a wretched motor horn outside tried an accompaniment. In a mysterious manner, Paterson flew, glided, or floated on to the stage, singing, "If the Man in the Moon were a Coon, Coon, Coon, what would you do"? The chorusers awoke, and demanded an encore. Paterson walked in this time, and sang "Charlie Macniel." The Scotch overcame the chorus. Perry the comedian (some distinction is necessary) next sang that highly philosophical song, "Ah! don't the days seem lank and long." Our old favourite Green, very kindly spared us an evening of his busy life and recited "A Fallen Star," with musical accompaniment. The College folk will have their sixpen'orth, and Green had to sing "Mafficking Night." He certainly should earn the reputation of a quick change artist; two minutes in which to change in appearance from a broken-down actor to a coster on the spree is sharp work. With some persuasion, the audience were pacified with the assurance that they would hear him again in the second half.

If we were in the habit of being gallant, we should certainly say,—and we will be for once,—that never was "Queen of Angels" sung by a lady more suitable than Miss Graefe. More of the same kind was demanded, and very sweetly Miss Graefe rendered "The Lover and the Bird." Our old chum, Tom Barnard, to introduce whom is needless, and Miss Forsythe entertained us, through the kindness of the author, Mr. Alfred Sutro, with a splendid dualogue, entitled "A Game of Chess." If we did not know that Tom Barnard was such a splendid actor, we should marvel why he wasn't mated long ago. Christopher! I wonder, does he always make love like that? And Miss Forsythe,—well, she managed it in three moves.

Our chairman, "Bobby" Marks, next reminded us that the object of the concert was to raise money for the Grand Piano Fund. "Many of us," he said, "might think that the piano we now have is good enough for our purpose, but that is not the view of our musical experts, who consider that until we have a piano that will do them justice we cannot ask many of our most able friends either to sing or to play for us, and thus enable us to ensure the continued success of our concerts. Lack of a suitable instrument, precludes us from asking a brilliant pianist to give us a selection. Our friend Perry, who is an authority, declares it is absolutely necessary that we should have a piano suitable to the capacity of the hall, which demands a larger volume of sound than can be obtained from the piano we have. If we hire a piano, as we have recently had to do, the cost is a guinea each time. Moreover the possession of a grand piano will help us to let the hall to better advantage. We ask your valuable help and support to enable us to maintain these concerts up to the level they have reached, and this you can all do by becoming members of the Musical Society, the subscription to which is a shilling a

year, entitling members to a copy of each programme in advance. We do
not wish to unduly push the Fund, but we are firmly resolved not to refuse
any offers of help, and not a few of them we have already had. Time was
for many years when the College had no concerts, no piano, and no staff
talented artistes. When the College had a function, or wanted an annual
concert, it was obliged to import outside talent, and to hire a piano. The
advent of the Musical Society some twelve years ago, engineered mainly by
Perry and Dumbrill, changed all that. The Musical Society in those days
went energetically to work, bought a piano at a cost of about £30, and raised
that amount by means of concerts and subscriptions. Since its foundation it
has given frequent smoking concerts in the Coffee Room, and some 118 other
concerts. It has been an active agent in promoting good fellowship among
our students, in fostering the social life in the College by making us known
to the women folk of our members, and in bringing out and encouraging
that talent which, without such an opportunity, might have lain dormant.
In doing these things the Musical Society claims to have justified its existence,
and to have done useful work for the College, hence its hope that the present
appeal may not be in vain." (Cheers.)

Twenty minutes was spent in struggling for coffee, and then with
trying to find the ladies to consume it. Duchesne is "Fond o' his pipe and
the Ladies,"—some eventually found their missing ones in his room. The
second half of the programme was opened with "No. 1, Round the Corner,"
farce in one act. Actors, W. J. Davis, W. Fenton, W. H. Barnett, and
J. McWilliam. It went off without a hitch, and everyone thoroughly enjoyed
it. Special thanks are due to the actors; they spent a great deal of time in
rehearsals, in fact, every time we saw McWilliam, he had the copy of the farce
in his hand, and was distinctly heard to say "Herrre's a letter fur ye, sir,"
Davis, whose rendering of the principal part was simply splendid, was
seen practicing quite a fortnight beforehand, shutting the tails of fellow
coats in various doors. After the cheers at the end of the farce had subsided
F. C. Hammant, of "Glorious Devon" fame, sang us that grand old Jacob
song, "In the Heather, my Lads." As an encore he gave "Glorious Devon."
There was a rowdy person in the front who suggested singing the chorus.
It *was* sung. Perry and his charming wife gave us a little Gilbert and
Sullivan—a duet, "The Duke and the Duchess." Our old friend "John,
pint of beer" (Nield) sang us that old classic "Any Rags," the author's
name on the programme appearing as "With Trimmings," a deep joke on
somebody's part, we suspect. The singer yelled "Any rags?" and then
waited a six-bar pause before the next yell, and yet there was but one
person in that whole audience of five hundred souls who had the wit (and
he borrowed that) to fill in the gap with, "We've an old piano" Miss Olive
Cooke very kindly came to the College and sang us very sweetly "May
Morning." A Musical Monologue, "'E can't take a roise out of Oi," was
ably rendered by Green. The audience clamoured for more, so he gave us
an encore, "What fur du 'e luv oi." Both these were given in character, and
both were fully appreciated, as Green's recitations always are. Miss
Olive Cooke very prettily sang to us "Heigho." We echo, "Heigho," and
hope to have the pleasure of hearing her again. The concert was wound up
by "Auld lang syne."   G. S. O.

THE WORKING MEN'S COLLEGE JOURNAL *is supported partly by
Annual Subscribers living in different parts of the World, and
partly by circulation among the Students and Members. Its success
depends upon a regular demand, and to ensure this, the Editor
would be glad if as many readers as can will become Subscribers.
Subscription* 2s. 6d. *per annum, post free.*

LONDON: Printed by W. HUDSON & Co., Red Lion Street, High Holborn, and published
at THE WORKING MEN'S COLLEGE, Crowndale Road, London, N.W.—July 1st, 1906.

The Working Men's College Journal

Gratis

sub: 2d

The Working Mens College.
CROWNDALE ROAD
ST PANCRAS
LONDON·N·W·
FOUNDED IN 1854
BY THE LATE

Frederick Denison Maurice·

Contents for

AUG.-SEP., 1908.

College Sports
Cambridge Visit
Library
College Notes
Mr. Louis Dyer
Old Students' Club
Saturday Outing

THE

Working Men's College Journal.

Conducted by Members of the Working Men's College
Crowndale Road, London, N.W.

Vol. X.—No. 185.   AUG.-SEPT., 1908.   PRICE TWOPENCE.

GARDEN PARTY AND FIELD SPORTS.

FORTUNATELY, on Saturday, July 11th, there was a break in the wet and forbidding weather that prevailed during the first half of the month, otherwise the College Garden Party and Field Sports might easily have been spoiled by rain.   As it was, the weather was kind to us, and all those concerned in promoting the event having worked with right good will, one of the most successful and enjoyable of "Sports" days was the result.   The spot chosen by the Common Room Committee, or by Randall and Landells, their chairman and secretary, for the holding of the Sports, turned out to be a very prettily-situated field close to "The Ship" Inn, Eastcote, supposed to be distant about a mile from Pinner Station, on the Metropolitan Railway.   This mile, however, doubled itself before the field was reached, but no one objected, because the way to it lay across fields, and over stiles, and amid charmingly rural scenery.   Randall, Landells, Staal, and Nye were foremost in the necessary preparation work, and they pressed into the service Mr. A. S. Lupton, to whose fertile brain, it is understood, several novelties on the programme were due.   There were three events of a humourous, mirth-provoking description, which had not figured in the list in previous years— a Pig-sticking Competition, a Blindfold Driving Race, and a Catching-the-Train race.   For the first of these, a truly artistic and finely developed pig was painted upon the grass in whitewash by that *doyen* of the Art Classes, Ebenezer Silk, who, by-the-bye, was snap-shotted in the act, pail and whitewash brush in hand, by Denton, in the midst of an admiring circle of ladies and gentlemen.   A large square of spectators having been formed around the pig thus delineated, the competitors for the event— ladies only—were blindfolded, provided with skewers or hairpins stuck through their visiting cards (postcards bearing their names), turned round twice, and then started from each side of the square, to march towards the centre and stick their carded skewers as near to the pig's eye as their errant footsteps would allow.   Some laughable scenes were the result—one lady stuck her particular card far outside the square itself, let alone the pig.

In the Blindfold Driving Race, each pair of competitors consisted of a lady driving a blindfolded gentlemen, by means of reins tied to the arms, along a twisting and tortuous path, marked out with the whitewash brush aforesaid, between bottles; the horse and driver covering the course in the shortest time, and upsetting the fewest bottles, winning the prizes. This was a cleverly arranged and amusing event. But the one which provoked the most laughter was the Catching-the-Train Race. Divested of jacket, collar, tie, and boots, and provided with newspapers, the thirty competitors were supposed to be engaged in reading the latter, when the bell rang, and they had to fold up their papers, dress, *first finding their boots*—which had been carefully mixed,—and then commence to walk, and at the final signal, to run for the train—the winning post.

It was good to see Randall, who had done so much to make the Sports a success, come in first in the 80 yards Sprint Race. And it is scarcely necessary to say that Duchesne and McWilliam won first prizes in the Three-legged Race, with great agility and apparent ease. Much enthusiasm was shown over the Tugs of War, and when it was found that the victory in these trials of strength and endurance, both in the men's and in the ladies' tugs, lay with the Furnivall Sculling Club members, the winners were cheered in a way that showed they were popular, and that the spectators regarded the result with satisfaction.

There was another novelty this year worthy of note. Mr. Lupton had composed a Limerick, which was printed on each copy of the programme, and each purchaser was entitled to try for the prize by filling in the last line—one programme, one try. This helped to sell the programmes. The last lines were collected at tea-time, and judged by Mr. Lupton, the prize falling to Miss Dora Jenkins, the daughter of an old College and Maurice Rowing Club member, Mr. J. W. Jenkins. The tea, like all the other items, went well. It was well served and there was plenty of it—plenty, that is to say, of bread and butter, strawberries, lettuce, cake of different kinds, preserves, and tea. Everyone of the 231 merry souls who sat down to it was satisfied, and without a doubt, all enjoyed the tea. Although teachers and members of the Executive Committee were, with a few exceptions, mostly conspicuous by their absence, the Vice-Principal and Mr. Lupton took an active part in the Sports in their capacity of judges, and at the conclusion of them the Vice-Principal distributed the prizes, consisting of well-chosen books, to the winners, in the pavilion, where the rest of the evening was spent in singing and dancing.

The following are the results of the various events :—

SPRINT RACE, 80 yards, men only. Two prizes. 19 entries, taken by W. Melzer.—First heat, R. Hagerty (1), F. Goodwin (2), E. Hagerty (3). Second heat, H. K. Randall (1), Lawrence and Bartlett, tie (2). Final, H. K. Randall (1), J. W. Bartlett (2), F. Goodwin (3).

THROWING THE CRICKET BALL. Ladies only. Two prizes. 19 entries taken by H. E. Nye.—Miss M. Ellis (1), Mrs. Defer (2).

THREE-LEGGED RACE. Four prizes. T. M. Balson took entries from 16 pairs of competitors.—First heat, E. C. Duchesne and J. McWilliam (1), E. and J. Hagerty (2). Second heat, W. H. Barnett and C. T. Young (1), Crockford and Best (2). Final, Duchesne and McWilliam (1), E. and J. Hagerty (2).

VICTORIA CROSS RACE. M. Staal took entries from 12 pairs of competitors.—L. R. B. Pearce and A. H. B. Stock (1), E. J. H. Reglar and J. C. Castell (2).

NEEDLE AND THREAD RACE, for ladies and gentlemen. E. Hayward took entries from 33 pairs of competitors.—First heat, J. McWilliam and Miss Louie Haynes (1), T. Hopkins and Miss Letitia Hunter (2). Second heat, C. F. W. Mead and Miss R. Miles (1), L. Barnard and Mrs. Pocock (2). Third heat, R. J. Gillies and Miss G. Jarvis (1), H. Howard and Miss D. Smith (2). Final, R. J. Gillies and Miss G. Jarvis (1), T. Hopkins and Miss L. Hunter (2).

PIG-STICKING COMPETITION, ladies only. Entries taken by T. M. Balson — Miss M. E. Coulter (1), Miss Hamilton (2).

BLINDFOLD DRIVING RACE. Entries taken by M. Staal. First heat, C. T. Young and Miss Dockery. Second heat, Mr. and Mrs. F. J. Nield. Third heat, J. C. Castell and Miss D. Klemm. Fourth heat, L. Pearce and Miss A. B. Hellier. Fifth heat, G. F. Drake and Miss C. Hagerty. Semi-finals, first heat, C. T. Young and Miss Dockery ; second heat, L. Pearce and Miss Hellier. Final, L. Pearce and Miss Hellier (1), C. T. Young and Miss Dockery (2).

SLOW BICYCLE RACE, for ladies. One prize, won by Miss A. B. Hellier.

CATCHING THE TRAIN RACE. Two prizes.—J. W. Roberts (1), J. C. Castell (2).

SLOW BICYCLE RACE, for men. Two prizes offered. First heat, C. W. Deuchar (1), H. E. Nye (2). Second heat, L. R. B. Pearce (1), Gould (2). Final, L. R. B. Pearce (1), C. W. Deuchar (2). As Pearce had already won two first prizes, Deuchar alone took a prize in this event.

CIGARETTE RACE, for ladies and gentlemen. Four prizes. C. T. Young and Miss Dockery (1), Mr. and Mrs. Hopkins (2), W. H. Barnett and Miss Barnett (3), A. Owen and Miss Jarvis (4).

TUG OF WAR. College Clubs (four a side). Entries taken by H. E. Nye. Four prizes. First rounds : Furnivall Sculling Club beat Musical Society, Debating Society beat Cycling Club, Swimming Club beat Gymnastic Society, Art Class beat Common Room Committee. Semi-finals, Sculling Club beat Debating Society, Art Class beat Common Room Committee. Final, Sculling beat Art. Winning team, Howard, Gillies, Owen, and Siemen.

TUG OF WAR. Ladies only (four a side). Entries taken by H. E Nye. Four prizes.—First rounds : Miss Hagerty's team won against Mrs. Curry's and afterwards against Mrs. Nield's. Scullers beat Cyclists. Final, Scullers beat Miss Hagerty's team. Winning team, the Misses C. Clements, V. Deane, A. Dewar, and R. Miles.

LIMERICK COMPETITION.—Winner Miss F. D. Jenkins. Last line, filled in by her, is shown in italics, below.

> A lady went in for a race,
> But the others excelled her in pace.
> She summoned her wits,
> And gave them all fits,
> By *fainting—that settled the case.*

PRIZE-WINNERS AND PRIZES.

FIRST PRIZES.

H. K. Randall, Sprint, " Rhoda Fleming " (Meredith). Miss M. Ellis, Throwing the Cricket Ball, " Adventures of Harry Richmond " (Meredith). E. C. Duchesne and J. McWilliam, Three-legged Race, " Seven Lamps of Architecture " Ruskin), and Keats' Poetical Works, respectively. L. R. B. Pearce, Victoria Cross, and Blindfold Driving Races, " Pride and Prejudice," and " Sense and Sensibility " (Jane Austen), " Shirley," and " Villette " (Charlotte Brontë). A. H. B. Stock, Victoria Cross Race, " Three London cycling maps." R. J. Gillies and Miss G. Jarvis, Needle and Thread Race,

"Tess of the d'Urbevilles" (Hardy), and "Pickwick," and "Nicholas Nickleby" (Dickens), respectively. Miss M. E. Coulter, Pig-sticking, "Pendennis," and "Vanity Fair" (Thackeray). Miss A. B. Hellier, Slow Bicycle and Blindfold Driving Races, "Far from the Madding Crowd," and "Under the Greenwood Tree" (Hardy). J. W. Roberts, Catching the Train Race, Mediæval Town Series—Oxford, Cambridge, Rouen, Bruges. C. W. Deuchar, Slow Bicycle Race, "Ivanhoe," and "Kenilworth" (Scott). C. T. Young and Miss S. Dockery, Cigarette Race, "A Wanderer in London" (E. V. Lucas), and "East Lynne" (Mrs. H. Wood), respectively. H. S. Howard, R. J. Gillies, A. Owen, and J. H. Siemen, Men's Tug, "Diana" (Meredith), "Flowers" (J. E. Taylor). "Slingsby Castle" (St. Clair Brooke), and Cycling Maps for North and West London, respectively. Misses C. Clements, V. Deane, A. Dewar, and R. Miles, Ladies' Tug, "Skirts of a Great City" (Mrs. Arthur Bell), "The Baxter Family" (Alice and Claude Askew), "Alton Locke" (Kingsley), and Elizabeth Barrett Browning's Poetical Works, respectively. Miss F. Dora Jenkins, for the Limerick, Wordsworth's Poetical Works.

SECOND PRIZES.
J. W. B. Bartlett, Sprint, Boswell's "Life of Johnson" (2 vols.). Mrs. Defer, Cricket Ball, "Marriage of William Ashe" (Mrs. Humphry Ward). E. and J. Hagerty, Three-legged Race, "To Arms!" (Andrew Balfour), and "Peter the Whaler" (Kingston). E. J. H. Reglar and J. C. Castell, Victoria Cross Race. "Dr. Jekyll and Mr. Hyde" (R. L. Stevenson), and Alfred de Musset's "Comedies"—translation, respectively. Thomas Hopkins and Miss Lettie Hunter, Needle and Thread Race, "Wuthering Heights" (Sisters Brontë), and "David Copperfield" (Dickens), respectively. Miss Hamilton, Pig-sticking, "In Memoriam" (Tennyson). C. T. Young and Miss S. Dockery, Blindfold Driving, "Tale of Two Cities" (Dickens), and "Old Curiosity Shop" (Dickens), respectively. J. C. Castell, Catching the Train, Robert Browning's Poems. Mr. and Mrs. Thomas Hopkins, Cigarette Race, "Romany Rye" (Borrow), and "Redgauntlet" (Scott).

◆•◉•◆

VAUGHAN WORKING MEN'S COLLEGE, LEICESTER.

THE Report of this College for the session ending Easter, 1908, was presented to the members in the large hall of the new building, which is now finished, and the fittings, it is expected, will soon be complete. The report states that the students have at length a home worthy of its founder, in which to carry on the educational and social work he had so much at heart. The building provides commodious class rooms, a fine lecture hall, a Common Room for Men and a Common Room for Women. As a result of this addition to the accommodation, a considerable development in the social side is expected. In the local examinations, 39 first-class certificates, 25 second. and 13 third were gained; 15 gained First Aid certificates, 14 Nursing certificates, and 5 gained medallions. The examiners' award for drawing had not come to hand. The governing body of the College consists of the Mayor of Leicester, the Vicar of St. Martin's, the Chairman of the Local Educational Committee (ex officio members), 4 representative members elected by the Town Council, and 8 co-optative members, elected for five years, the first co-optative members, who were elected for life, being mainly old friends of the College. The numbers attending during the past session were, men, 915; women, 680; total, 1595, and the quality of the work done in the past year is reported to be in every way satisfactory.

The building and site will, it is expected, be found to have cost nearly £9000, and there remains about £1500 yet to be raised. The Committee believe this money will be forthcoming when the full state of affairs is brought before the numerous friends of the College. The students themselves have started an auxiliary maintenance fund.

THE CAMBRIDGE VISIT.

A Belated Fragment.

A supreme combination of delightful spring and summer weather throughout, together with unbounded hospitality, leaves acutely pleasurable memories behind of this year's "College" outing to Cambridge.

Owing to the same aggressive, in point of size, heraldic supporters being used, there is a bewildering similarity between some of the college gateways. This, however, does not apply to that of Trinity, perhaps the most imposing of all, King's not being lost sight of. One cannot but be impressed by the former's huge court and stately Jacobean fountain; nor with the smaller, three-cloistered court beyond. Here, on reaching Mr. Cornford's loft-like "den," one almost expected, because of this characteristic, to find it hung with bunches of marjoram and other culinary adjuncts. However, where the preponderating books allowed of any furnishings, these were acceptable, and quickly dissipated any prematurely formed impressions of the above nature—the whole making a very enticing sanctuary, of which we were not slow to avail ourselves.

At nightfall the ascent of a darksome turret was preliminary to four of us being initiated into undergraduate life, and it may be truly said that we not only observed well but proved ourselves appreciative auditors, drinking in all that we could. Sunday morning brought a renewal of sight-seeing, including the exclusive Fellows' garden, with its charming seclusion and well-blended wild and cultivated nature. The "Backs" are indescribably beautiful, with their apparently always animated river, glorious turf, and magnificent trees, each the complement of the other.

Trinity library with its priceless M.SS., etc., is full of interest, but belies its architectural exterior. The first sight is amazing of the stupendous lines of that grotesque monster, King's College Chapel, which, although redeemed, with some exceptions, by its details, is, as a whole, impossible. May it be said that further acquaintance with college life excited one's sense of humour, not through any lack of hospitality which, on the contrary, was generosity itself, but at the picnic-like mode of living which seems to prevail? This added to the delights of the experience, and the only momentary embarrassments to which we found ourselves subjected were those when occasion demanded the increasingly feeble attempts at thanks.   C. Morley.

LUBBOCK FIELD CLUB.

A party of nine spent Sunday, July 12th, in exploring a part of the valley of the Lea. Starting from Broxbourne station, the view from which has been spoilt beyond recognition by a tremendous bridge, we followed the towing path as far as King's Weir. We then crossed the river and took a long path across the meadows and up the hill, until the Nazing road was reached. A short distance along this, we found a track leading to Galley Hill Wood, and spent much time in thoroughly examining a pond at the edge of it. From here an old bridle road leads to Nazing Gate, and very rough going we found it. We halted for lunch at the King Harold's Head, where the party indulged in much innocent merriment over a misunderstanding that arose between Britt and the hostess. Our road then lay for a mile or so over the exposed and uninteresting Nazing Common, and thence by an even less interesting road by Tyler's Cross to Roydon. Here the rain, that had long been threatening, started to descend in earnest, so we sought the shelter of a convenient inn and had tea. Although we lingered a considerable time over the meal, there was no improvement in the weather, so we decided to leave those who had made no provision against rain, to wait some two hours for the next train. The rest of us pushed on through the village, past the "Stocks" and the "Cage," probably the best preserved examples in the country, until we reached the old Mill on the river Stort. As the weather cleared up, the walk by the little used towing path down to the junction with the Lea at Dob's Weir was most enjoyable. The rest of the journey back to Broxbourne was along the banks of the Lea Navigation, and suffered somewhat in comparison.

There were few captures of interest made, but among the plants of the waterside, the giant musk and the flowering rush claim mention. Several water rats were observed at close quarters, while the dragonflies were, as always, things of beauty.

The next walk is arranged for August 9th, when Crawley will conduct the party through some of the prettiest parts of Kent. Take pedestrian tour ticket No. 3, reverse direction, that is *out* to Orpington, *back* from Eynsford, 2s. 3d. Train leaves Charing Cross, 9.20; Cannon Street, 7, and London Bridge, 12, minutes later. Provide lunch.

J. HOLLOWAY, *Hon. Secretary.*

FURNIVALL CYCLING CLUB.

THE runs for this season have again been well attended, and it is a great satisfaction to report that several new members are joining us on our trips in the country, and that a few more ladies have been introduced.

At Whitsun, 13 members had a very enjoyable outing at Princes Risboro'. We stayed at the Cross Keys Hotel, where we were very well accommodated. Nobody complained of being starved, as on our last tour, at Easter.

On Sunday, June 14th, 16 members spent the afternoon at Bookham, and the Hedgerley and Ranmore Common runs were attended by 15 and 17 members respectively. Owing to the dull weather, the Saturday run on July 4th, was only attended by 6 members, and they had a very wet ride home. On Sunday, July 12th, we had our Surprise run. After the Captain had taken us as far as Totteridge, the members gave in their guesses. The venue was Batchworth Heath, near Northwood, and the prize will, I think, be awarded to Miss Gant, who guessed Northwood. This run again proved very popular, 15 members attending it. On Sunday, July 26th, we cycled to Esher Common in the morning, and found many punctures on our way. In the afternoon, we were entertained to tea by Dr. Furnivall on Canbury Island. The thanks of the Club are due to Dr. Furnivall and his friends for the kind way he entertained 17 of our members, and we hope to be able to visit him annually for many years to come.

Future runs :—Sunday, August 9th, East Horsley; Saturday, August 15th, Elstree; Sunday, August 23rd, Chenies; Saturday, August 29th, Stag Hill; Sunday, September 6th, Chobham Common; Saturday, September 12th, Hadley Woods; Sunday, September 20th, Burnham Beeches; Sunday, Sept. 27th, Welwyn; and the Final run to Pinner, Saturday, October 3rd.

W. MELZER, *Hon. Secretary.*

THE LIBRARY.

THE College Library has been enriched this year by gifts of books which already exceed in numbers three times as many as those given during the whole of 1907. Some of these have already been announced in reports to the Council and in the JOURNAL, but they have not all been chronicled in these pages. Noteworthy are the following :—

From the Clothworkers' Company—46 volumes, principally scientific text-books and works.

Merchant Taylors' Company—23 volumes, economics, scientific, and literary works.

Skinners' Company 6 books by Tolstoy, Maeterlinck, and other authors.

Dr. Williams's Trust—23 books by various authors.

Mrs. J. G. Butcher—54 volumes of ancient and modern classics.

Mrs. R. B. Litchfield—53 volumes, literary, scientific, classical, and general.

Sir Charles Prestwood Lucas, C.B., K.C.M.G.—39 volumes, classics, economics, and scientific works.

A. S. Lupton—24 volumes of the ancient Greek and Roman classics.

T. F. Hobson—Electricity and Magnetism, Harvard Lectures on Greek Subjects, " Return to Protection " (Smart).

The Librarian—" Ancient Britain and Julius Cæsar's Invasions " (Holmes).

F. O. Smithers—" Mediæval England" (Bateson), Radio-activity (Rutherford), Social England (6 vols.).

Carlo Gatti—" In the name of the law " (Bebro). " A shorter working day " (Hatfield and Gibbins).

R. N. M. Bailey—" Annals of Tacitus " (Ramsay).

Miss Bonham Carter—" The Economic Journal " (Vols. 1 to 17).

H. Bergen—" Troy Book, 1412—20 " (Lydgate).

Charles A. Brown—" Law of Landlord and Tenant " (Woodfall), 9th edition.

The Canadian Government—Atlas of Canada.

Anonymously —3 of Lamartine's works and two other books.

About £100 has been received towards the fund recently opened for the purchase of additional books for the Library, for which purpose about £150 will, in all, be required. There are many gaps which need filling, especially in up-to-date books upon subjects taught in the College classes or dealt with in courses of lectures. Both money and gifts of books are very welcome.

FURNIVALL SCULLING CLUB.

ON Saturday, July 4th, the Polytechnic Rowing Club revenged our victory of last year by handsomely beating our four. This annual event was sculled for the first time on equal conditions, the Polytechnic men sculling in one of our boats. We had put forward men of our best—Hoad (stroke), Munro, Williams, Richardson, Ingram (cox)—all of whom had won their club " blues." Experienced judges had pronounced them to be as fast a crew as the club had yet put out, but—the Polytechnic men put four lengths of daylight between the boats at the finish. We must train more next time.

Our third outing for the benefit of the local poor children took place on Saturday, the 18th. Of six boat-loads, only four braved the rain's fury and reached Kew, the children's Sunday frocks looking sadly bedraggled on arrival. However, a walk through the gardens, followed by tea and dancing at the club-house, soon filled their cup of happiness.

H. S. HOWARD, *Hon. Secretary.*

COLLEGE NOTES.

AT the Meeting of Council held on 14th July, the Vice-Principal, from the chair, expressed the pleasure they felt at seeing Mr. W. R. Emslie again amongst them, after his absence through illness. A letter was read from Mr. A. G. Tansley thanking the Council for their condolence upon the death of his mother, Mrs. George Tansley.

The Report of the Executive Committee, written by the Superintendent, was read by him. Reference was made therein to the recent deaths of Mr. R. B. Mansfield and Mr. G. W. Fox, already noticed in these pages. The results of the examinations, so far as known, were reported to the meeting, as also were the arrangements already made for lectures to be given in the October term, the award of the first "Marks" prize to Mr. J. G. Newlove, and the recent gifts to the Library. Those important social events, the excursions to Oxford and Cambridge and the College Garden Party and Field Sports, received a large share of attention in the report, which after discussion was adopted.

The first term of the fifty-fifth College year commences on Monday, September 21st. The week preceding that date will be devoted to the enrolment of new members, and we venture to repeat the request that each reader of the JOURNAL will kindly make an effort to introduce at least *one* new student to the College at the beginning of the new term.

The Opening Meeting will take place on Saturday, September 19th, at 8 o'clock, in the Common and Coffee Rooms. Addresses will be given by Sir Charles Lucas, C.B., K.C.M.G., and the Vice-Principal, and a smoking concert will be arranged. All new students, as well as old, will be specially welcome on this occasion.

Amongst the new classes arranged for the coming term are these :—"Shakespeare—Twelfth Night and Julius Cæsar," G. M. Trevelyan, M.A., Tuesdays, 8—9.30 ; "Ruskin," Miss C. Spurgeon, Fridays, 7.30—9 ; "History of our own Times," F. A. Simpson, B.A., Fridays, 8—9.15 ; "Law—Patents for Invention," K. R. Swan, B.A., Mondays, 8—9 ; "Workmen's Compensation Act," H. G. Robertson, B.A., Wednesdays, 8—9.30 ; "Elementary Economics," C. H. Kisch, B.A., Tuesdays, 8—9 ; "Greek for Beginners," J. A. Barlow, M.A., Tuesdays, 8—9.15 ; "Swedish," Carlo Gatti, Thursdays, 8.15—9.15 ; Mr. Gatti also takes three classes in Italian and two in Portuguese. A "Life" class, Wednesdays, 8—10, is added to Mr. R. W. Wilkinson's list of Art classes.

Mr. B. P. Moore, B.A., examined the students in English Composition on June 26th, and in the Advanced stage, for which four sat, H. O. Driver and L. R. B. Pearce passed, whilst in the Elementary, seven sat, and three passed, J. W. Howat, J. G. Cole, and W. Windley.

Mr. E. J. MacGillivray, B.A., LL.B., examined two students in the Law of Insurance, on July 6th, and passed R. W. Everard.

In Latin, Advanced stage, four sat for examination by Mr. J. F. Winter, B.A., and two passed, J. McWilliam and T. H. Newman.

French claims the largest number of successes. Mr. B. Domville, M.A., examined in the three stages. For the Advanced, two sat and both passed, T. E. Pickles and A. Hepburn. Five sat and all passed in the Intermediate stage, namely, I. J. Bush (exc.), D. W. Seath (exc.), C. H. Ricks, W. H. Walker, and A. H. B. Stock. Six sat for the First stage, and four passed, C. Morley (exc.), H. Eyers (exc.), A. Leakey (exc.), and J. Hugo.

Mr. T. T. S. de Jastrzebski examined in German, on June 25th, when three sat for the Advanced, and one passed, Robert D. Paul (exc.). In the First stage, four sat and three passed, John Crawley (exc.), Désiré Bardin, and Joseph Hale.

The following Science and Art examination results are to hand:—Geology, three sat, and all passed, Arthur H. Casey and John W. Bagshaw taking 2nd stage, 2nd class, certificates, and William E. White, a 1st stage, 1st class. In the three subjects, "Sound," "Light," and "Heat," separately, Arthur C. G. Beach, sat and passed, 2nd stage, 2nd class in each. In "Sound, Light, and Heat," four sat, and three took 1st class, 1st stage, certificates, René Bowden, William J. Carvosso, and William E. White. Mathematics (Division I.) William D. Mogg, 1st stage, 2nd class. Machine Construction and Drawing, nine sat, and four passed, all in the 1st stage, Brian C. Elliott and Alec. H. Yeoman, 1st class, and Henry Pateman and Reginald J. James, 2nd class. Practical Plane and Solid Geometry, 1st stage, five sat, and three passed, W. J. Bowman and Charles Deuchar, 1st class, and Charles J. Hall, 2nd class. Freehand Drawing, George D. Drake sat and passed, 2nd class. Model Drawing, four sat, and all passed in the 2nd class, William A. Ball, Harry A. Thirlwall, William G. Copland, and Alfred T. Hurt. Drawing from the Antique, Edward Weatherhead sat and passed, 2nd class. Perspective, Richard E. Tyler took a 2nd class certificate.

In the Society of Arts Examinations, Stage II., four students gained certificates, Emil Alter in English, 2nd class; Harry Cornelius Hunter in French, 2nd class; Henry Samuel Parr in Spanish, 2nd class; and Albert Urry in Spanish, 1st class.

Euclid, Book I.—Mr. Percy Thompson, B.A., examined on June 25th, three sat, and one passed, P. A. Fielding.

Three of Mr. Mason Tarr's class in Music sat for and passed the examination in that subject, namely, W. E. Tuttle and S. J. King, both "excellent," and Miss R. E. Edbury. Ten of Mr. Mellish's class were examined in the Violin, and five passed, Miss Burrell (exc.), Miss Stowe (exc.), Master Roe (extra College), A. C. Weber, and George Wilkins.

In the examination arranged by the University Extension Board for the students who attended Mr. Dudley Heath's course of lectures on "Italian Painters," Charles W. Smart obtained a certificate.

For Arithmetic, 1st stage, nine sat, on June 29th, and four passed, C. E. Horsman (exc.), W. J. Bowman (exc.), W. F. Jennings, and H. W. Stagg. In the Advanced Stage, six sat on July 6th, and three passed, C. E. Horsman (exc.), A. H. B. Stock, and W. J. Bowman.

Mr. H. R. Levinsohn, B.A., examined in English Grammar, for which sixteen students sat, and eight passed, C. E. Horsman, F. G. Justice, S. J. King, C. F. Marshall, J. C. Pettit, J. W. Roberts, A. H. B. Stock, and W. Windley.

Mr. Levinsohn also examined in English for Foreigners, and F. W. Eichborn passed.

Two students sat for the Senior Student examination, conducted by Messrs. H. R. Levinsohn, Sydney Bradgate, and A. S. Lupton, on July 7th and 8th, but neither satisfied the examiner in the History section, although one of them, A. H. B. Stock, got through in English Grammar and Arithmetic.

The Preparatory Division was examined by Mr. Julius Jacob, B.A., during the last week in June, but as no man took more than one subject, he was unable to make a recommendation for the scholarship. S. J. Noakes passed in Arithmetic. In Grammar, for which five sat, L. Favier, W. Martin, F. W. Eichborn, and A. B. Swinyard all obtained over 75 per cent. of marks, whilst Popilli passed.

At the Shorthand Examination held on June 25th, Mr. E. H. Carter examined, and E. J. Burgess passed in the theory, for which four sat, and F. P. Leach obtained a certificate in speed, at 100 words per minute.

Mr. A. E. Turberville, F.C.A., examined the Advanced Class in Book-keeping. Two sat, but one had to give up, through indisposition; the other, L. L. Trapp, gained an "excellent."

In "First Aid," eight members of the Ambulance class sat for examination, and again the whole of the examinees passed. The examiner, Surgeon Lieut.-Col. Lees Hall (retired) congratulated the men on their work, remarking it was one of the best classes he had examined. We like to congratulate Dr. Forbes and Mr. Wiltshire, the instructors, also, on the continued good result of their effective teaching and pains-taking trouble. The following are the names of those who passed :— For the "First Aid" certificates, Walter Henry Pratt, Alfred Owen, Jasper Charles Bray, Edwin Arthur Doun, and Walter Frederick Richards ; for vouchers, Herbert Edward Winkworth and Edward Harold Chappell ; and for medallion, Arthur Harry Casey.

Mr. Charles Smith, the teacher of the Chemistry classes, in the course of a lengthy and valuable report on the work of the session, 1907—1908, speaks of the effect of the new College rule, in the science classes, that students *must* enter for examinations. This had the effect of weeding out slack members as the session drew near its close, whilst the effort of the keen student became tauter under the pressure of the impending examination. The work and attendance of the Advanced class were consistently excellent. This class was formed at short notice, and its successful launching was largely due to the help kindly given by Mr. Luetchford. Altogether seven students sat for the examinations, an increase of two over the number who sat last year.

The Geological Field Club has been formed, with Mr. G. Ansell as honorary secretary, to whom inquiries should be addressed. The club holds excursions to places of geological interest and discussions in the Museum.

The Tansley Swimming Club meets on Thursday evenings at 7.30, at the Baths in Prince of Wales Road. Tickets for the first class Swimming Bath may be obtained by members of the hon. secretary, W. H. Barnett, at the College, for 4d. each.

"The Outlook" says—"A further volume about Canada, in Sir C. P. Lucas's 'Historical Geography of the British Colonies,' will be published shortly bv the Oxford University Press. The author, Professor H. E. Egerton, confines himself to history, starting with British rule to the Quebec Act, and ending with the Dominion of to day. The volume contains several appendices, ten maps, and an index. Mr. J. D. Rogers, who wrote 'Australasia' for the same series, will deal with the geography of Canada, in another part to be issued shortly."

MR. LOUIS DYER.

To those men who went to represent the College at the Oxford Commemoration of 1907, when the Principal, with many other distinguished men, received his D.C.L., the news of the death of Mr. Louis Dyer, reported in the *Times* of the 21st July, must have come as a shock. On that occasion Mr. Dyer waited at Balliol's gate until he found our men, entertained them to luncheon in Mr. Urquhart's rooms in the College, together with Mr. Urquhart and an American professor, and afterwards, with pride and evident pleasure, conducted them over the College he loved so well. Mr. Dyer then seemed in the prime of life, cheery and alert, and he made our men realize what an amiable and delightful a man he was, and how his kindly spirit harmonized with the dignified and reposeful air of Oxford. He died in London on July 20th, at St. Thomas's Home, from the effects of a very severe operation.

"Mr. Louis Dyer," says the *Times*, "was born in Chicago in 1851; he entered Balliol in 1875, and was with a distinguished set, including Lord Milner, Lord Midleton, Sir Thomas Raleigh, the late Sir Clinton Dawkins, Sir C. P. Lucas, the master of Magdalene, and others, with whom he remained on terms of friendship to the end of his life. He was a ripe and wide-minded scholar, with keen and varied intellectual interests, which made him a welcome companion in academic as in other circles; but what was most remarkable about him was his single-hearted humanity and sweetness of disposition, which drew friends to him wherever he went. He was so kindly, so ready to give time and trouble to the service of his friends, that few could resist his charm. It is not only in the Common Room of his own beloved Balliol that Louis Dyer will be missed, but to many others, both old and young, Oxford and the world will seem a poorer place without his genial presence."

In 1889, Mr. Louis Dyer married Margaret Macmillan, sister of his friend, the late Malcolm Macmillan, and daughter of Alexander Macmillan, a staunch friend of our College, of our founder, Frederick Denison Maurice, and of Lowes Dickinson and Tom Hughes. It is pleasant now to call to mind that Mr. Dyer was present as the guest of Sir Charles Lucas at the Old Students' Supper of 1904. As a friend of the Principal and of Sir Charles, Mr. Dyer could not but be a friend of the College, and when showing our men over Balliol he expressed his readiness to do anything in his power to help the College. Thanks to the efforts of the Principal and Sir Charles we are now storing up pleasant memories of Oxford and Balliol; to the men gathered together in Mr. Urquhart's rooms after the 1907 Commemoration the most abiding memory will be the kindly presence and courteous services so cheerfully rendered to them on that day by Mr. Louis Dyer.

OLD STUDENTS' CLUB.

THE REFERENDUM.

AT the last meeting of the Club, held in the Common Room on Saturday, March 14th, R. H. Marks in the chair, the Principal, Professor A. V. DICEY, K.C., opened the discussion on the subject : " Is the Referendum desirable and practicable in this country ? " There were sixty-five members present, Messrs. J. T. Baker, T. M. Balson, Leopold Barnard, George Beavis, Sydney Bradgate, John Bromhall, C. G. Cash, J. C. Castell, Charles Castle, S. J. Coombs, W. C. Cutts, John Dale, W. J. Davis, J. J. Dent, Professor A. V. Dicey, William Duke, S. Ettershank, W. R. Emslie, H. Eyers, R. Freeman, T. W. Gale, H. Gallagher, C. Godfrey Gümpel, W. P. Harley, A. Hepburn, S. J. Hertford, William Hudson, J. F. Iselin, Lionel Jacob, C. T. Jeffery, W. F. Jennings, K. Johnson, J. R. Jones, C. P. King, James Kirk, G. Ledwith, A. Levett, H. R. Levinsohn, J. D. Macnair, J. McWilliam, R. H. Marks, A. W. Matthews, C. Edmund Maurice, E. D. A. Morshead, J. J. Munro, G. J. Offer, G. S. Offer, G. C. Peckham, H. A. Perry, T. E. Pickles, Leonard Pocock, E. Pointin, C. W. Rapley, R. A. Reed, J. Gerald Ritchie, F. C. Roper, E. W. Silk, W. J. Spray, M. Staal, Sidney Stagg, M. W. Starling, W. Tirrell, George Wanklin, L. A. Waterfield, and G. E. Winter.

The PRINCIPAL said he proposed to answer three questions. What is the Referendum ? Why do I recommend its introduction to a certain extent in this country ? What are the objections, and the answers to them ? The Referendum is a democratic institution, and also a conservative institution in the widest sense of the term. It was created in Switzerland, where it exists both in a simple form, and also with a great number of complexities which would not concern us here The Referendum, as it exists in Switzerland, so far as it need concern us, is this : When any part of the Swiss constitution is changed, the measure is first passed by both Houses of Parliament, and then, before it can pass into law, it has to be submitted to, and passed by, a majority of the electors. There is this additional requirement—at least ten out of the nineteen cantons must be in favour of the measure. Besides laws affecting the constitution, any federal law passed by the Federal Parliament may be submitted to the people, if 30,000 electors petition for this to be done. If we wished to apply the system to laws affecting our constitution, the course to be adopted would be to pass an Act of Parliament enacting that any law which referred to certain definite topics, to be mentioned in the schedule such as the succession to the crown, the modification of the House of Lords, or the Act of Union – should be submitted for approval to the vote of the electors. There would be the advantage of the full discussion of the bill in both houses in the first instance, and such a Referendum would restore the veto, which has become more or less obsolete, and would place it in the hands, not of the Crown, but of the people. The Referendum exists now, under different names, in other countries besides Switzerland. Practically speaking, no change in the constitution of any American state takes place, without a reference to the votes of the citizens. Something of the kind has also been introduced into the Australian Commonwealth. There, on some constitutional matters, if the two houses disagree, a measure may be referred to the people for approval or disapproval. I think something in the nature of a Referendum is wanted in this country, to meet certain defects in our system. We need to keep and consider any question of serious importance, apart from other questions which have nothing to do with it. If such questions were decisively dealt with according to the wishes of the majority of the electors, the Government would be more free to proceed with the business of the country. If such a question as Home Rule were decided in this way, every man would say, That point is settled ; we can now occupy our minds with other matters. I cannot conceive that the question of women's votes can be properly decided by a mere balance of parties in the House of Commons. It would be better to refer a question which concerns us all so nearly, to the votes of the people themselves. Members, under our present system, do not really consider only whether the Licensing Bill is good or bad ; they have to think how it will affect the Government on questions having nothing to do with it, such as Unionism or Free Trade. It is highly desirable that no great change should be made in any direction unless the people have made up their mind on the subject. The objections alleged against the Referendum are that it would diminish the power of the House of Commons, and that it would keep back reform. To a certain extent it would cut down the power of the Commons, but it would leave them the power to prepare and approve a measure, and submit it to the will of the people. Occasionally, delay would result, but there would be a great advantage in getting large reforms—measures upon great matters—passed with the assent of the people as a whole.

Mr. C. E. MAURICE urged that the success of the Referendum in Switzerland was no reason for its introduction here. The Swiss had nothing like the number of complicated topics that arose in England, nor had they any foreign or colonial policy. He did not think we should get a straight-forward answer from the people on a Referendum on such subjects as the House of Lords, or the union of England and Ireland, or female suffrage. However the question might be put, half the people would want to answer something else. It is not a good thing that the making of a law should be left to the people; that is not the idea of representative government. If a particular law were referred to the people and passed, too much good would be expected of it; no law could produce more than a limited amount of good.

Mr. ISELIN supported the opener. He had studied the effect of the Referendum in Switzerland and thought it could be applied here. It would not, in his opinion, increase the influence of the "party" game upon legislation, but quite the contrary. Now-a-days the initiative in legislation was passing out of the hands of the House of Commons into the hands of the Cabinet. That he thought a serious and a dangerous feature. In view of the decadence of the initiative of the private member, he should like to see introduced, as a necessary corollary, a referendum to the people. If a certain number of electors required a question discussed, the Government should thereupon prepare a bill and have the matter discussed in parliament.

Mr. CASH thought it impossible for us to apply the Referendum principle as the British constitution existed at the present time. The very basis of the constitution would need altering. With reference to private members, we should be reduced to chaos if every one were invested with the power of initiating legislative projects. We had a kind of Referendum now, when Parliament was *adjourned* with a view to an autumn session, as distinct from being *prorogued*; any great question under discussion at the time received consideration up and down the country with some approximation to the Referendum principle. Although the Referendum itself might be applicable in a little republic like Switzerland, it was unfitted for so mighty and complex a structure as the British Empire. It was, he thought, foreign to the genius of our constitution.

Mr. COOMBS favoured a three years' Parliament, rather than a Referendum.

Mr. RITCHIE said the question divided itself into two parts, the Referendum on constitutional points, and the facultative Referendum, as it existed in Switzerland. Suppose we took four great constitutional questions, the veto of the House of Lords, adult suffrage, women's suffrage, and Home Rule; and suppose a bill dealing with any of them had passed through both the House of Commons and the House of Lords, it would, he thought, be quite unnecessary to refer it to a Referendum. After the enormous amount of discussion and the party changes that would be brought about before the question had reached the final stage, there would be no need to fight it out again in the country. Then, as regards the facultative Referendum, our legislation was of such a complicated character, the questions arising were so great and far-reaching, that he could not see the advantage in their being thrashed out again after they had passed both Houses. We are not given to legislating in a hurry as it is. Even with an unprecedented majority it was difficult to pass measures like the Education and Licensing Bills, and the existing veto was sufficient, without a further reference to the people and a possibility of all the work being undone.

Messrs. Levinsohn, Morshead, Bradgate, Hepburn, and G. J. Offer, also contributed to a capital and well-sustained debate, and Professor Dicey replied.

SATURDAY AFTERNOON CONDUCTED OUTINGS.

THE NATIONAL PORTRAIT GALLERY.

THE second outing of the season took place on Saturday, June 13th, when the National Portrait Gallery, at St. Martin's Place, was visited by a party of College men, under the direction of Mr. H. R. Levinsohn, who was the Librarian for a period of ten years at the old College in Great Ormond Street, and who organized in 1905 the work of having all the books rearranged at the present commodious Library at Crowndale Road.

On a previous visit to the National Portrait Gallery (conducted by the late Sir Joshua Fitch), the party was taken especially to see the principal Paintings, but on this occasion our guide led us at the outset straightaway into the Sculpture Gallery, on the left-hand side of the main entrance. Among the busts, statuettes, effigies, masks, and medallions placed around the gallery, our attention was directed to those of the men of light and leading of the nineteenth century, who were contemporary with the founders and the supporters of our College, notably those of Whewell, Tait, Dean Stanley, Lecky; Macaulay, Thackeray, Leech, Cruickshank, Carlyle, Tennyson; Buckland, Hooper, Faraday, Darwin, Huxley; Canning, Palmerston, Brougham, Beaconsfield, Bright, Samuel Morley, and several others. The medallion of Robert Owen, 1858 (by Leverotti), was referred to by our guide as representing the man who was a forerunner of Maurice, in his endeavours for an improved state of Society, aiming at a pure social ideal, though he was not connected with the work of our College.

In a piece of true sculpture, the subject can be seen and studied to advantage, and a resemblance to the real outward form of the person may be secured and in after years exhibited, almost to a perfect identification. This was noticed by a careful observation of Boehm's full-length recumbent figure of Arthur Penrhyn Stanley, 1881. The finely-modelled features were brought out by the artist with an expression of such life-like reality as to be at once recognized by anyone who had known Stanley in actual life, either when he was seen conducting the service at Westminster Abbey, or when he was present and gave an address at an opening meeting in the Oval Room of our old College, in Great Ormond Street: the very man seemed to be there, permanently fixed in contour for the generations yet to come. He was one of the closest personal friends of Maurice.

Near to this figure of Dean Stanley was placed in a glass-case Woolner's Mask of "Frederick Denison Maurice, 1805—1872, Divine, Professor of Literature and Philosophy, and Philanthropist. Death-mask presented, March, 1905, by Lowes Dickinson." Here we stood for a few moments and pondered over this memorial gift to the gallery, as a mark of loving respect and esteem from the donor. Mr. Lowes Dickinson—the painter of Maurice's portrait in our College—is still among us as one of our surviving Founders; and we felt that in this presentation was to be seen the reverential act of a devoted disciple still living, in memory of his great leader, who had fought the good fight until 1872, and then passed away. In the early days at the Working Men's College, Frederick Denison Maurice was known chiefly by his previous earnest endeavours in London and in different parts of England to improve the conditions of the working classes, one of his lectures delivered at the Town Hall, Southampton, and published in 1851, being entitled: "The Reformation of Society, and how all Classes may contribute to it." Associated with him at public meetings and lectures, during the years 1850—1853, were Tom Hughes, Charles Kingsley, J. M. Ludlow, F. J. Furnivall, E. Vansittart Neale, T. Shorter, and many other zealous workers. In October, 1854, the Working Men's College in London was founded, when friends from the Universities interested in Education voluntarily joined Maurice, in this important social movement for the common welfare. Among those friends were Ruskin, Rossetti, Burne Jones, Woolner, Dickinson, Mansfield, McLennan, Davies, Westlake, and Litchfield. Within seven years afterwards, fourteen other Working Men's Colleges were inaugurated in the provinces to adopt the methods of Maurice.

After looking at the mask of Maurice, and then turning to see the busts of Alfred Tennyson, we recalled the time when these two friends

were on the most affectionate terms, as evidenced by the fact that in
January, 1854, Tennyson wrote a poem, "To the Rev. F. D. Maurice,"
commencing with the lines:—

> "Come, when no graver cares employ,
> Godfather, come and see your boy."

At the present time, the nation reveres the memory of both, for the
distinctive parts enacted by them in the social and the literary progress of
England—the one as an educational Reformer and Co-operator, and the
other as a great Victorian Poet.

In Mr. Levinsohn we had a conductor who was able to keep our party
fully interested by relating a number of reminiscences incidental to the
various objects seen. He told many anecdotes, choice and pithy, that clung
to the memory and recurred to one's mind for several days afterwards.
After spending over an hour in the Sculpture Gallery on the ground floor,
Mr. Levinsohn took the party into Room I. on the top floor of the building.
This room is devoted to a valuable collection of Early Portraits, in which
the arrangement in chronological order was commenced. On the same
floor, the historical sequence was continued through eleven other rooms,
and covered a period of 275 years (from 1485 to 1760), extending from the
Tudors to the time of George II. The historical critics in our party entered into a free discussion with our guide as to the relative merits of some of
the courtly characters depicted, a few of whom were known to have been
depraved in their thoughts, tastes, and desires, and were far from being exemplary. But in history or biography, the sorry tale is told ; and instead of
adding to the lustre of our country's glory, such notorious individuals have
become in our time merely the objects of opprobrium and condemnation.

We were afterwards conducted to see the Paintings on the first floor,
where we recognized many faces of well-known men and women. There
were two portraits of Maurice—one taken in early life, and the other taken
at the later period when we knew him at Great Ormond Street. We saw
the separate portraits of Cobden, Lyell, and Tait, each painted by Lowes
Dickinson, of which the full-length one of Cobden was presented, in
1870, to the National Portrait Gallery, by 474 members of the Reform
Club. Many great and heroic personages are there, the inspiring sight of
whom may well quicken humbler mortals to noble deeds of valour. We
noted the various classes in the arrangement of the paintings in the rooms on
this floor as comprising Divines, Philosophers, Judges, Statesmen, Politicians,
Actors, Dramatists, Artists, Engravers, Architects, Men of Science, Naval
and Military Men, Explorers, Literary Men and Women, and Royal
Persons of the XVIII. and XIX. centuries. Among the several Collected
Portraits specially hung for separate view, our party was entranced by Sir George
Hayter's large picture of "The Interior of the House of Commons at the
meeting of the First Reformed Parliament, 5th February, 1833," which
measured 118¼ inches by 199 inches, and exhibited an assemblage of 375
portraits on the one canvas. The complete gallery has been formed during
the last half-century. In 1856, the British Historical Portrait Gallery
was founded, and while in 1869 there were only 288 portraits, as many as
982 were acquired by the year 1896, when the new National Portrait Gallery
was opened to the public. The total number in 1907 was 1646, including
the photographs and the engraved portraits accumulated and to be seen
in other parts of the building.   WILLIAM HUDSON.

THE WORKING MEN'S COLLEGE JOURNAL *is supported partly by
Annual Subscribers living in different parts of the World, and
partly by circulation among the Students and Members. Its success
depends upon a regular demand, and to ensure this, the Editor
would be glad if as many readers as can will become Subscribers.
Subscription* 2s. 6d. *per annum, post free.*

LONDON: Printed by W. HUDSON & Co., Red Lion Street, High Holborn, and published
at THE WORKING MEN'S COLLEGE, Crowndale Road, London, N.W.—August 12th, 1908.

Gratis. Educ P245.4

The Working Men's College Journal ·

sub: h

The Working Men's College · CROWNDALE ROAD · ST PANCRAS · LONDON · N·W·

FOUNDED IN 1854 BY THE LATE

Frederick Denison Maurice ·

Contents for

OCTOBER, 1908.

Opening Meeting
Lubbock Field Club
College Notes
Club News
Professor Dicey on
      the Constitution
Student's Calendar

Working Men's College Journal.

Conducted by Members of the Working Men's College Crowndale Road, London, N.W.

VOL. X.—No. 186.　　　OCTOBER, 1908.　　　PRICE TWOPENCE.

THE OPENING MEETING.

T the Opening Meeting of the College for the session, 1908—1909, held in the Common and Coffee Rooms on Saturday, September 19th, Mr. Lionel Jacob, B.A., Vice-Principal of the College, took the Chair, and a striking address was delivered to the students and teachers present by Sir Charles Lucas, C.B., K.C.M.G., formerly Vice-Principal, on the subject of "Patriotism." Dr. Furnivall and Mr. J. A. Forster also spoke, and after the talking and some coffee and cake, we smoked our pipes, and enjoyed one of the best smoking concerts that we have had in the College.

The VICE-PRINCIPAL, addressing his hearers at the outset as "friends, students, and teachers," welcomed them all, old and new, with hearty words. To those *new* students and teachers who came for the first time, he said we were going to make them, as soon as possible, "old." We seem, he continued—referring to the fine weather—to have started at the beginning of summer. In the spring, says the poet, a young man's fancy lightly turns to thoughts of love. In the autumn, we hope it turns to study—I fear rather more heavily, and less willingly. This College is primarily a place for study— not so much a place for teaching, as for learning. There are establishments known as "crammers," where learning is put into small pills and made digestible, assimilated for awhile, and then forgotten　Not so here. We want men to come here to learn, with the help of those who are called "teachers," but who are really "helpers." All students have, as much as the teachers, to make an effort for themselves ; all have to understand that if they do not make themselves learn, they will not learn. You will have to take an active part in the work ; to ask and answer questions ; to study at home ; to submit yourselves to tests, and see what is lacking, and the more you recognize what is lacking, the better for you. Yes, first, this is a College for study. A college, it has been said, is a place where you get a great deal of useless knowledge. I hope you will get a certain amount of useless knowledge here—useless in the sense that it will not pay you in pounds, shillings, and pence. Many of the men who come here come because they find that the subject they want to learn will help them in their daily work—a very good reason for coming, for a man ought to try and improve his position; and morever, if he acquires knowledge useful to himself, and becomes more efficient at his work, that is a good thing for the community—if all worked efficiently, we should be saved a huge amount of trouble. At the same time, however, you should try to learn something for yourself, apart from what will make you more efficient in your work. If you are studying arithmetic, for instance, it is not enough merely to learn dodges for shortening work; it is best to understand the principles of it, and so be able to apply it whenever you want it. If you are learning French, which again may be useful in your work, you ought not to stop there, but should learn to talk with French people, read the works of the great French writers, and widen your knowledge, so that you may be citizens, not only of your island country, but of the great world. Studies that do not actually help you in your work yet help you as men, give you a wider interest in things, and take you out of the small life that is so apt to hamper us and make us of little account. If you go to Mr. Trevelyan's Shakspere course, or to learn from Miss Spurgeon about Ruskin, whom we are proud to think of as one of the first teachers here, you will learn somewhat how to read great authors—a possession that will remain to you for life. Science and art also, each in its way, will help to enrich your life. That is our object, and you as students should aim at that in this College. Another feature of the College is this: It is not merely a bundle of classes; it forms a whole system, trying to cover as much as possible of the field of knowledge. Its parts are not isolated; each forms part of one system of knowledge. Boys at school look upon their masters as natural enemies. When boys grow into men, they find these natural enemies are human beings, although they are not treated as such, and they begin to comprehend them better. In a college like this, there is not the boyish feeling any longer, and if the college is worth anything to the student, he has gone to the opposite pole, knowing that if he is to make the most of his teacher, that teacher is to be his friend. Those who have taught here are glad to think of their old students as real and faithful friends. Besides that bond between teacher and taught, there ought to be something of the same bond of friendship between those who are in the same class together, doing the same work, and doing it as with friends, in good fellowship. With this bond, they will get more from their work, than if they study alone. So that, although this is a place, in the first instance, for study, yet it is also a place for friendship and good fellowship, of which these rooms are a symbol, for they are the gift and work of old and present students. Here you can meet and talk over your studies and other subjects, and can enjoy one of the great charms of friendship and fellowship, the opportunity of discussing all things—everything and anything. So I would say, come often to these rooms—the oftener you come, the oftener you will wish to come. One more remark : the College lasts, while the members of it pass away; some are taken away to other parts of the world, others pass to other employments—the whirl of life takes them away, some die ; the College remains, and with it remains the unceasing tradition of good work and good fellowship, a tradition initiated by Maurice, our Founder, there [indicating his portrait on the wall] and represented to-day in one of our founders now present, Dr. Furnivall (cheers), ever young and ever fresh in activity in the College—a tradition, also, embodied in George Tansley, whose portrait hangs there, who did as much as anyone in the College in his lifetime, and whose name is never mentioned here without respect and love. Carry on that tradition, and try and get as much as you can in a right way, out of the College, taking and giving; taking in the first instance when you come here, and giving when you grow older. I hope this will be a very fruitful session to the members of the Working Men's College. (Cheers.)

Dr. FURNIVALL, who was received with cheers, said he hoped the new men would turn out to be as good as the old ones. The object of the College was to make men, and to make a man a better man. He urged members to take part in the social life, and get at the spirit lying at the bottom of it. The spirit of the College, at bottom. was mutual help ; and if men got help here, then they should give help afterwards. (Cheers.)

SIR CHARLES LUCAS's ADDRESS ON "PATRIOTISM."

Sir CHARLES LUCAS said :—This year has been a great year for gatherings and conferences, and to me the most interesting was the gathering at Quebec, in Canada, where men and · women of different races met to commemorate the founding of Canada, three hundred years ago, by Samuel Champlain. a man of patience, endurance, and foresight, who, like the founders of our College, built for the coming time. They met there also to commemorate the twin deaths of Wolfe and Montcalm. I should like to talk to you about how Wolfe trained himself for future greatness. Men have a habit of thinking that greatness comes all at once, but it is not so. Montcalm upheld a doomed cause with wonderful courage and chivalry. Each one gave his life for his country. Cotemporaneous with the Quebec celebrations, we have the Franco-British Exhibition, in which two great countries show the world, in friendly co-operation and kindly rivalry, what their respective mother lands and their colonies can bring forth. The object lesson of Quebec and the Franco-British Exhibition is "patriotism"—true patriotism—strong, intense love for and pride in your country, without being aggressively hostile to other lands and other peoples. It is a right, a manly, and a wholesome spirit—a spirit which made St. Paul say he was "a citizen of no mean city." Patriotism is the soul of the Working Men's College. It was founded to make good citizens, and therefore I would try and say a word or two to you about patriotism to-night. Some of you may know the story, the old Greek story, of Solon, the wise man of Greece, and Crœsus, the rich king of Lydia. Crœsus asked Solon, Who was the happiest of men?—and he thought Solon would mention himself, because of his riches. The wise man answered: A certain man he knew, who died for his country. Crœsus asked, Who was the second happiest? and Solon said: There were two young men living with their mother, and there was a gathering for a festival at some distance which she much desired to attend, and the cattle were not at hand to draw her, and the young men drew the cart themselves, that their mother might not lose the festival. And that night the young men slept in the temple, and in the morning they were dead, for "those whom the gods love die young." The wise man of Greece put as the happiest man, the man who loved his country; and as the second happiest, the men who loved their parents. Those two loves are closely akin, for patriotism is the love of the fatherland. You cannot have a fatherland without a past, you cannot have a father without somebody who is older; and I want to drive in this point, that the true patriot is conscious of the past of his country; he is reverent to it, he clings to the traditions and memories of the past of which he is a product. It is characteristic of the young—and I was once young myself—to think that the world only began when they came into it, and certainly to think that all went wrong until they came into it. This is true, not only of young men and women, but also of young conditions in a state. The young democracy always thinks the past was rottenness, and that the true thing is the present and the future. But this is an untrue and a mean conception. "The old order changeth and giveth place to new, and God fulfils Himself in many ways." Carlyle says, "The English land here and now is the summary of what was grand and wise and noble and accordant with God's truth in all the generations of Englishmen." The patriot never forgets the past, nor that what he has and is is the result of those who have gone before. He has a standard up to which he tries to live, and principles which he endeavours to maintain. It is men's duty to try and leave the world better than they found it; this is a debt that they owe to those who made it what it is. Homer wrote, "We boast to be better than our fathers"—meaning, "It is our calling to be better than our fathers." They gave us so much; we have advantages they never had, and in our turn we must leave the world better than it was when our fathers handed it on to us. To the young men coming here to-night for the first time, I say that the most precious possession of this College is its past. Cut away its traditions, and it would be but a barren foundation. We work as in the presence of our founders, trustees of what they have left to us; and it is our bounden duty to leave it not less, but more, to those who come hereafter. The patriot always remembers the past. The patriot remembers also that no class and no party and no interest in the state is the whole state. All men in this state and country are, or ought to be, citizens; all have rights and duties; no class and no party has a monopoly of the whole duty of man. Our College was founded as a protest against class feeling and prejudice; it was founded to increase the feeling of brotherhood among men, and to help men of all parties and of all classes, so far as possible, to all and equal benefits and chances. In the past—in the time when this College was founded—monopolies of the upper classes were most in view; it may well be that in the coming time we shall have to fight and protest against monopolies and class interests lower down in the social system. We hear much talk of the Labour Party. Labour or work is the great blessing of *all* men, and I hold that you take away from its nobility when you associate it with a *party*. The man who learns what this College was founded to teach will never confound a party or a class with the State as a whole, and will condemn strong class feeling as dismembering the country he loves. . Once more, a patriot has σωφροσύνη, sane-mindedness. His wares are not always in the shop window. He has no love for posters and headlines in half-penny newspapers. He remembers, as Carlyle tells us, " Deeds are greater than words," and " Insincere speech is the material of insincere action." He realizes that one little bit of good work is worth all the smart speeches in the world. Carlyle says of England, " Thy Epic, unsung in words, is written in huge characters on the face of this planet— sea master, cotton trader, railways, fleets and cities, Indian Empires, Americas, New Hollands—legible throughout the solar system." He is preaching there that the English are doers rather than talkers. The Greeks said, and I think it one of their wisest sayings, the soundest states were those in which the *middle* element was large. The soundest men, the wisest and justest citizens, are those who are not carried into extremes, who shun advertisement, and prefer doing the smallest bit of real good work to making exaggerated speeches about themselves or smart criticism of other people. A patriot is a man who, loving his country, is ready to make some sacrifice for his land and his fellow citizens. Carlyle, when speaking of " Wages for Work," points out that after all, no man can sell his life or his work, and says, " My brother the brave man has to give his life away." This lesson was taught by the men who founded this College, and by the men who have followed in their footsteps. Carlyle, again, tells us " Life was never a May game for men." No, it is not ; but it is rich in blessings for those who love and work for their land and their fellow-men, for those who are—as the young men who are here to-night will, I hope, be—patriots to England and true sons of the Working Men's College. (Hearty cheering.)

Mr. J. A. FORSTER then spoke of the College as a place full of dear memories to him. As to the life he led in it, and its doings in the early days, it was much the same as we might read in some recent numbers of the COLLEGE JOURNAL. There were the same country walks, trips to the Universities, and fun and frolic through the summer. He spoke also of the spirit of comradeship which our Founder, Frederick Denison Maurice, put into the College,—of the strength and permanency of his work, and the duty we owed him of preserving and handing on the College, unimpaired and strengthened, to those who come after us. He was pleased to see that the Library contained many of Maurice's works, and that the book of his life, written by his son, bore evidence of good and frequent use. He suggested that we should have a class in the College for the study of Maurice's works and life. It should be attractive, and would be of immense benefit educationally, owing to Maurice's enormous range of thought. (Cheers.)

In the smoking concert which followed the speeches, there was plenty of evidence that the College possesses, amongst its members, many excellent vocalists. The songs were well sung, and enlivened by them, the rest of the evening sped heartily and pleasantly. The following items were rendered : Piano, R. E. Tyler and Haynes ; F. E Lawrence, " The Soldier's Song " ; Jackson, " The Ballad Singer " ; F. J. Nield, " When your pants begin to wear " ; Brignell, " The Village Blacksmith " ; W. Hagerty, " The Old Shako " ; R. Hagerty, " The Yeomen of England " ; C. H. Perry, " A Policeman's lot is not a happy one," and encore, " The Judge's song " ; R. E. Tyler, " The Wolf " ; T. A. Paterson, " The Spanish Guitar " ; H. K. Randall, " Good Company " ; C. H. Perry, " Blue Blood " ; E. C. Duchesne, " The Animals' German Band," and encore, " Jack's Yarn " ; M. W. Starling, " The First Lord's Song " ; Jackson, " Alice, where art thou ? " and R. Hagerty, " The Veteran's Song " ; " Auld Lang Syne."

LUBBOCK FIELD CLUB.

On Saturday, August 9th, a small party of four, with John Crawley as guide, spent a very pleasant day in the valley of the Darenth and neighbourhood. The weather was all that could be desired, the heat of the sun, though great, being tempered by light airs, and making the contrast of shady woods and lanes more welcome. Starting from Orpington, we made our way to Chelsfield Church, and passing through the churchyard, pursued field paths to Halstead, where we disposed of lunch at an inn. Then we climbed to Knockholt Pound, and followed more paths till we reached the well-hidden, but strong and commanding fort on the top of Polhill, known as Halstead Fort, close to which a long and refreshing rest was indulged in, on the hill-top, in the shady and cool centre of a beautiful and peaceful beech wood, where we were much struck by the various pleasing effects of light and colour; smooth, clean, and lofty tree trunk and light green foliage; brown leaf carpet and green undergrowth; and vistas here and there of surrounding hill slopes seen through the trees. The descent from this haven of rest proved very steep and sudden, into the valley, which we followed to Shoreham, where we had a very good tea at an inn known to Crawley. After this came the most enjoyable part of the day, so far as walking was concerned, the temperature being lower, and the scenery along the valley and by the stream to Eynsford being very pretty and pleasing. During the day we passed by and through numerous fruit fields, orchards, and hop gardens, as well as some of the finest fields of wheat and barley in full ear, that we remembered to have seen. The most striking natural phenomenon observed was the number and tameness of the brown-breasted robins. At one resting place early in the day, while Crawley was amusing us with an account of an Elephant and Castle Theatre drama, a young robin introduced himself, and perching on a twig near the writer, engaged in a sweet and low twittering conversation, after which he came again and again to observe us, and to partake of a crumb or two from the lunch bundle.   L. P.

September 5th will be a memorable date in the annals of the Field Club, as on that day nineteen members availed themselves of Lord Avebury's kind invitation to visit him at his beautiful home at High Elms. The invitation originated, like so many other good things, at Cambridge, where in May last a party of our men, including Mr. Duchesne, met Lord Avebury at the rooms of his son, the Hon. H. Lubbock, of Trinity College. The party included Mr. Alfred Grugeon, our veteran president, and Mr. John Fotheringham, both of whom were officials of the Field Club of the seventies. The weather record for some time past had consisted of a series of wet days, relieved only by a few storms of exceptional severity, so that the Club was particularly fortunate in selecting a fine day for the trip.

Reaching Orpington at 3 o'clock we walked through Farnborough, and on arrival at High Elms were welcomed by Lord and Lady Avebury in the hall. We then had a stroll through the park, where, in spite of damage caused by the recent storms, the trees and shrubs were at their best. From time to time our host stopped to discuss a botanical point with Mr. Grugeon, or to direct attention to some particularly interesting plant, as for example the bamboos that had flowered this year, and in consequence died, an Australian acacia in which leaves are simulated by leaf stalks, although at times the characteristic acacia leaves appear, and the purple loosestrife with its three types of flowers. On arrival at the pond with its varied water lilies, we halted to see the great trout and golden orfe fed, and disturbed a water hen. Nesting boxes had been fixed to many of the trees, but we were informed that they had not been taken advantage of to any extent. We returned to the house and partook of tea in the dining room, after which Lord Avebury conducted us to the hall, and showed us many of his treasures, with explanations and comments which were, if possible, even more interesting. The wall cases were full of flint implements, showing every gradation from the rude eolith to the highly-finished neolithic implement. A small case contained a series of inscribed cylinders from Babylon, dating from the reign of Nebuchadnezzar. One buried beneath a foundation stone, gave an account of the building to be erected above, others were promissory notes and I.O.U.'s, particularly interesting to Lord Avebury as a financial expert. Another small case contained an interesting set of coins, Greek and Roman, valuable as works of art, and interesting from their association with such great names as Alexander, Cæsar, and Marcus Aurelius. Another case was devoted to British coins dating from pre-Roman to our own times. Lord Avebury pointed out how the beautiful design of the Macedonian States was adopted by the Ancient Britons, and in the hands of their coiners degenerated into a meaningless series of lines. The work of the early Saxons was even worse, and the gradual improvement was illustrated by many specimens, some, like the "Rose Noble," strikingly beautiful. The gun money of James II., labelled 30 times its proper value, came in for appropriate comment, coins of Philip and Mary recalled memories of Hudibras, while the origin of the figure of Britannia on our copper coins was demonstrated by a comparison with the Roman original. The disappearance of the ship and lighthouse was referred to with regret. Turning to another small case, Lord Avebury showed us how the Chinese "cash" originated from "knife" money, and how the thumbmark of an Empress on the original wax model has been perpetuated. In another room, Lord Avebury's youngest son's museum, we were shown fragments of a mammoth disinterred from a neighbouring gravel pit, together with remains of rhinoceros and musk ox. The last room visited was the library, in which Lord Avebury's famous observations on "Ants, Bees, and Wasps" were made. Here a fine geological relief map of the south-east of England gave occasion for an interesting sketch of the structure of the Weald, and the explanation of the directions taken by Kentish rivers. Close by was an address, illustrated with copies of prehistoric drawings, which compelled attention.

As time was getting on, the secretary thanked Lord Avebury for his kind reception of the club, and for the trouble he had taken to explain the many interesting objects we had been privileged to see, and after a few words from our host we took our departure. We escorted Mr. Grugeon to Orpington Station, and as it was still light, walked as far as Chelsfield with Mr. Fotheringham and Pocock before starting on our homeward journey.

Sunday, September 13th, was devoted to a walk from end to end of Epping Forest. A start was made from Forest Gate at 10.20, and the route followed was across Wanstead Flats and Park to the Whipps Cross Road. This part of the journey was hurried over in order to meet the Gospel Oak contingent, which arrived at Wood Street at 11.15. The united party, fourteen in number, entered the Forest opposite the "Rising Sun," crossing the Woodford Road just above the Waterworks. The next road encountered was at Hale End, where we crossed into Higham Park by the "Sale." Keeping east of the lake, we followed the Ching brook across Chingford Hatch Plain until we reached Chingford Plain and Connaught Water. Turning off by the red path we made our way to Fairmead and halted at the "Owl" for lunch. We then crossed the High Beach and Epping Roads and after a rest on top of Warren Hill, entered the Green Ride at the Earl's path. From this point we followed its devious course north-eastward through Loughton Earthworths and Monk Wood, across the furze ground by Jack's Hill and alongside Ambresbury Banks to Epping. There was just time for a cup of tea before turning off to the station for the 5.14 train home. The weather was heavy, but remained fine all day, and consequently we were able to see the forest at its best, still in the glory of full summer foliage. Little was noticed of special interest botanically, but that little was chiefly in the ponds near Wathamstow. In that part of the forest blackberry hunters were much in evidence, and the abundance of tramcars did not please us. In fact the general opinion was that it would have been wiser to have started at Chingford or Loughton.

The next trip will take place on October 11th, when it is proposed to visit the country south of Clandon. Take excursion ticket to Clandon, 2s. 3d. Train leaves Waterloo (South Station) at 10.5. Provide lunch.

J. HOLLOWAY, *Hon. Secretary.*

COLLEGE NOTES.

DURING the current term, we are to have several important and interesting courses of lectures on Thursday evenings. The Principal will lecture on " The French Republic " on Thursdays, November 5th and December 3rd. Mr. T. Morison, M.A., formerly Principal of the Mohammedan College at Aligarh, will deliver a course on "India," on the four Thursdays in October. Mr. R. Rait, M.A., whose disquisitions on London have already proved so popular, will give three lectures on Thursdays, November 12th, 19th and 26th, on "The Place of London in English History." And on December 10th and 17th, Prof. A. W. Kirkaldy, M.A., B.Litt., is to visit us again, and tell us about "The History and Principles of Taxation." All these, like the Saturday night lectures, begin at 8.30 p.m., except Mr. Rait's, which commence at 8.15.

Of much interest, especially to the older generation of College members and friends, is an announcement which has recently appeared in the Parish Magazine of Kirkby Lonsdale, Westmoreland, by the Rev. J. Llewelyn Davies, the vicar of that parish, and one of the founders of this College—to the effect that, after nearly twenty years' service there, he is resigning the vicarage of Kirkby Lonsdale, and intends to remove with his daughter to some house in London or its suburbs about the end of the year. There is a prospect that his parishioners' loss may be our gain, for Mr. Davies may again be able to come amongst us more frequently than has been the case for many years, in the College which he helped so well to establish, and to which he is so much attached.

Twelve students were successful in passing the Spanish examination, namely, in the Advanced, H. S. Parr and A. Urry ; Intermediate, G. E. Lewis, Henry Mortieau, J. Macaine, and H. W. Windsor ; Elementary, S. W. Burns, John Boisson, A. Corrodi, J. Parsons, J. Pert, and E. J. Price. Mr. A. Urry also passed with distinction the Chamber of Commerce senior Examination in this subject.

Board of Education examinations.—Botany, nine sat, six passed ; 1st stage, 2nd class, William E. White, George E. Buckland, Edward H. Chappell ; 2nd stage, 1st class, Chas. T. Buckhurst, Henry T. Wilkin ; 2nd class, Thomas D. Morgan. Theoretical Inorganic Chemistry, eight sat, seven passed ; 1st stage, Herbert E. Hunter and Samuel H. Searle took 1st class, and William D. Mogg and Charles E. Scuffle, 2nd class certificates. 2nd stage, Henry S. Yates and Charles H. R. St. John took 1st class, and Hubert Luetchford a 2nd class certificate. Practical Inorganic Chemistry, for 1st stage, five sat and four passed, William D. Mogg, Charles E. Scuffle, and Herbert E. Hunter taking 1st class, and Thomas Shine, a 2nd class certificate. For 2nd stage, three sat and all passed, Henry S. Yates, Hubert Luetchford, and Charles H. R. St. John, all 1st class. The last-named very pluckily stuck to his work in the class, in spite of a serious injury to his left hand, which was ultimately condemned to be amputated, after occasioning some months of suffering. The operation has since been successfully performed.

Physiology, two sat, and passed, Edward H. Chappell and Claudius M. Denis, both 1st stage, 2nd class. Magnetism and Electricity, nine sat and one passed, William H. Chittleburgh, 1st stage, 2nd class. Mineralogy, one sat and passed, Arthur H. Casey, 1st stage, 1st class. Eleven sat and five passed in Building Construction and Drawing. In 1st stage, Walter Mann took a 1st class, and Brian C. Elliott and Harold G. Atkins, 2nd class certificates. In 2nd stage, Harry C. Hunter obtained a 1st and Charles W. Deuchar a 2nd class.

Board of Education Art examinations :—Design, 1st stage, Jesse James took a 2nd class. Memory drawing of plant form, Richard E. Tyler, 2nd class. Drawing in light and shade from a cast, eleven sat, and four passed, 2nd class, Arthur Major, William J. Beaver, William A. Ball, and Alfred T. Hurt.

Mr. Newlove, the writer of the first "Marks" Prize Essay, has selected for his prize the undermentioned set of books, which he has chosen with the view of studying for his B.Sc. (Econ.)—

"Economic Interpretation of History," E. R. A. Seligman ; "Introduction to Political Science," J. R. Seeley ; "State in Relation to Labour," S. Jevons ; "Central Government," Traill ; "Political Economy in England," L. L. Price ; "Industrial History of England," H. de B. Gibbins ; "Economic History, Part I.," W. J. Ashley ; "Landmarks in England" and "Industrial History," Townsent Warner ; "English Constitution," Bagehot ; "Elementary Politics," Raleigh ; and the following Lecture Syllabuses :—"The English Citizen," "The Industrial Revolution," J. A. Marriott ; "Industrial History," J. Owen ; "Three Centuries of Working Class History," W. A. S. Hewins ; "Making of Wealth" and "Sharing of Wealth," J. A. Hobson.

With the view of making the College more widely known amongst the inhabitants of St. Pancras, the Advertising Committee, Messrs. Randall, Nye, and Reglar, have had printed a neat little eight page pamphlet, containing illustrations of the College front, the Maurice Hall, the Library, the Common Room, the Coffee Room, the Chemical Laboratory, and the Art Room, with some descriptive letter-press and a map showing our location, and several thousands of these were addressed and posted to residents in the district, just before term began. As a result, the numbers of student entries are satisfactory.

Mr. Randall, whose energies on the Common Room Committee have so often been manifest, has taken in hand the preservation and mounting of the very fine collection of weapons, rhinoceros horns, and other spoils of the chase, presented to the College some few years ago by Mr. Virgil Allen, who brought them home from Africa, having secured some of them at the risk of his own life, and after enduring much hardship and trouble in getting them.   With the assistance of Mr. Guilland, Mr. Randall has had some of these trophies cleaned, polished, and mounted, and hung in the Coffee Room.   Mr. Allen has now sailed for Manaos, in South America, and Mr. H. V. Birrell has also departed hence, for Brazil.

The visit to the Franco-British exhibition of twenty College members at the expense of Sir Charles Lucas, C.B., K.C.M.G., was postponed from the 12th to the 19th September, when, we understand, they had a very pleasant time.   It was fortunate for them that the date was altered, as the 12th was, it is said, the most crowded day at the Exhibition, many would-be visitors being unable to obtain admission, owing to the crush at the gates.   We hope to receive an account of this event.

On the 19th also, we are told, Mr. E. J. H. Reglar organized a party of some sixty members and friends to see the Exhibition. Those who went on that day were debarred from taking part in the opening meeting at the College.

We in the College are all very pleased to hear of the marriage of Tom Barnard and Miss Frances Forsythe, which took place on September 13th.   Barnard is a great favourite.   He has won our hearts by his *bon camaraderie*, his cheerfulness, and his intense desire to please and help.   We all like to hear his excellent recitations, which have done so much to make our concerts and social gatherings successful and enjoyable, and we all like Barnard himself.   Fresh in the memory is his dialogue with Miss Forsythe, in "A Game of Chess," at the Concert of 2nd May last, when he was well mated by her on the platform of the Maurice Hall.   Now that she has mated him in a wider and a deeper sense, we join in wishing them prosperity and all happiness.

Another College man, and old student, Mr. Frank Collins, better known some few years ago, when he was one of the habitués of the Common Room, was married on August 17th, to Miss Amy Elizabeth Budge, at the Parish Church, Addiscombe, where he lives.   Cheery, jocund, and light-hearted as he is, we can picture him going happily and easily through life in his new condition, even without our blessing, which however we most cordially vouchsafe, upon his "making his last bow to us as a bachelor."

Mr. J. J. Dent, member of our Council and Executive Committee, whose interest in all Co-operative movements is so deep and well known, has been unanimously re-elected President of the Council of the Southern Co-operative Education Association.

———

We regret to see the annonncement of the death of Mr. Charles Algernon Whitmore, for many years subsequent to 1886, Conservative M.P. for Chelsea, in succession to Sir Charles Dilke. Prior to his election to Parliament, Mr. Whitmore took great interest in the College, and was for a long time a prominent teacher and member of Council. Mr. Whitmore and Sir Robert Mowbray, both Fellows of All Souls' at that time, did much to entertain a College party on a visit to Oxford University, and invited it to tea at All Souls'. Mr. Whitmore, who was very popular in his day, was chairman of the first Common Room Committee, the institution of which, and the name of Common Room, as used in the College, were both due to him, and he was usually present at the College Supper. Mr. Louis Henry Player, a member of the Old Students' Club, who was in his Consitutional History Class, says, " I remember him for his extreme courteousness, kindness, and amiability. His class seldom consisted of more than four or five. This was more than thirty years ago, and I can only remember the names of Bogue and Macdonald. The subject of these lectures did not appeal to many, whose existence, like mine, was passed in the daily routine of the workshop. No reception or social function prevented him from meeting his class ; he was always there to greet us with as much cordiality as if we had paid him half-a-guinea a lesson ; at all times he seemed to take a real interest in the personal welfare and prospects of his students, and was ever ready with sympathy and advice." After his election to Parliament in 1886, Mr. Whitmore practically severed his active connection with the College, with the exception of occasionally attending meetings to promote the Building and Maintenance Fund, but he remained one of our trustees to the end. Mr. Whitmore was a Balliol man, and he rendered the College a signal service in introducing Sir Charles Lucas to it.

———

Prof. J. Churton Collins, the noted lecturer and professor of English Literature who died last month, was a good friend of the College, in which he has appeared on several occasions as a Saturday Night lecturer.

———

References to the College have appeared in several papers lately. One of the best was in the *Weekly Times and Echo* of September 20th, from the pen of our fellow-member, John Crawley. The *Daily Mail* had previously published a more highly coloured, if less accurate, notice.

The College is again indebted to its Musical Society for a very good concert, held on Saturday, September 26th, when lady friends of students formed the larger proportion of the audience and a delightful programme was prepared and gone through.

The *Spectator* of August 29th contains a critical notice of the official "History of the War in South Africa," the compilation of which was entrusted by the Government to Major-General Sir Frederick Maurice, K.C.M.G., son of our Founder. The third volume of this work has now been issued by the publishers, Messrs. Hurst and Blackett, London.   Price 21s. per vol.

The Misses Buckie, the sisters of the late College teacher and friend of that name, have returned to their old address at No. 16, Upper Rock Gardens, Brighton, where the Cycling Club and other members of the College have so often stayed with them, and they will be very pleased again to cater for the requirements of any students, teachers, or friends desirous of visiting that popular sea-side resort.

MAURICE CHESS CLUB.

At the time of writing no fixtures have been arranged, but it is expected that before October all matches will be fixed up. The club having entered the C Division of the City of London Chess League, the programme will be rather heavier than it was last season, but with the assistance of the new chess-playing members of the College, who are cordially invited to join us, we hope to go through the season successfully. Special arrangements are being made as to matches and tournaments, for which support is asked.

The formation of a beginners' class, for the teaching of the game to beginners, and of a coaching class for the more advanced players, has been suggested, and if sufficient members are forthcoming, these will be started soon. The club's most prominent players have kindly promised to assist in this work. Those, therefore, who are keen on acquiring a knowledge of the game, are advised to take advantage of this opportunity.

The committee desire to point out to members of the College who take an active interest in the game, but who have not yet participated in any of the club's matches, that there is plenty of room for more members playing in the matches, and that good average players may count on being selected on half of them, if they wish it, and can afford the time. Notices will from time to time be posted on the club's board, in the corridor.

J. FOLEY, *Hon. Secretary and Treasurer.*

FURNIVALL SCULLING CLUB.

THE half-yearly general meeting will be held on Sunday, October 4th, at 7 p.m. It will be necessary, in view of the pending registration of the club, for members to approve all the existing rules. Opportunity will be taken to amend them where experience has found this to be expedient, and all the club orators are expected to be in battle array on this occasion.

H. S. HOWARD, *Hon. Secretary.*

CORRESPONDENCE.

[Under this heading the Editor will be glad to publish letters of interest to past and present members, but he declines all responsibility for the views therein expressed.]

To the Editor of the WORKING MEN'S COLLEGE JOURNAL.

DEAR MR. EDITOR,—Sometime ago I read in the JOURNAL a report of a discussion in which Mr. Charles Wright held that a man should not be at liberty to bequeath his real and personal estates as he wished, but that they should revert to the State, as is effected at present in a mild form by the operation of the death duties. Would Mr. Wright give me the names of some works of reference from which some data might be taken for a debate on the subject ?—Faithfully yours, CHAS. H. HOLDEN.

92, Spencer Place, Leeds, 15th September, 1908.

VISIT TO MISS FORSTER'S.

AN invitation to tea, for Sunday, August 20th, from Miss Forster of Abinger Hammer, was received through Mr. E. M. Forster, who has been teaching Latin at the College, by some half-dozen of our members. The acceptance of this kind invitation gave the party at the same time an opportunity for a walk in the neighbourhood of Dorking. They accordingly took train to Dorking Station and proceeded by way of The Denbies, Wotton, and Friday Street, and in the afternoon arrived at Abinger Hatch, where they made a short halt and inspected the old stocks and whipping post, and where, according to arrangement, they were met by Mr. Forster, who conducted them towards Abinger Hammer. The weather, though generally fine and bright, was inclined to be unsettled all day, and when almost in sight of their destination a storm came on which compelled them to take refuge under an oak. The tree soon ceased to afford much shelter from the rain, and two of the members got rather damp. However, the party duly arrived at Abinger Hammer, and it was not long before they were sitting down to some inviting refreshments, and in the general conversation which ensued one of our members took the opportunity of expounding to one of our charming entertainers his scheme for the kidnapping of the children of poor and vicious parents. In due course the party made a short tour in the immediate vicinity of their hostess's residence, and Mr. Forster interested them by pointing out where ran the old Pilgrims' Way from Winchester to Canterbury, and also the route which tradition says the French will take in their march on London—*when* they invade us ! After a smoke and a talk in the garden, the party took leave of their entertainers and were again conducted by Mr. Forster for some two miles on their way towards Dorking through some woods, one of which, by reason of the twilight and the grandeur of the trees, was particularly impressive. Dorking Station was duly reached, and on the homeward journey the party passed a unanimous vote that they had, thanks to Miss Forster and Mr. E. M. Forster, spent a day worthy of remembrance.

THE W.M.C. GEOLOGICAL CLUB.

THE members of this club assembled at the College on Tuesday, September 1st, when Mr. J. F. N. Green, B.A., gave an interesting and instructive lecture on "The Ancient Rocks at St. David's," finely illustrated by lantern slides and specimens. Mr. Green has done some valuable work in this district, and his remarks were much appreciated by those present.

Since the formation of the club, some interesting papers have been given, by Mr. W. Herron, "Fossil Mammals" ; Mr. J. Warren, "Geology of Hampstead" ; and Mr. R. Bowden, "Some Factors in the determining of Climate." Outdoor work has been done by visits to pits and sections at Charlton, Erith, Crayford, "Kenwood Farm," Hampstead, and Golder's Green. All members of the College interested in Geology are invited to join the club. GEORGE ANSELL, *Hon. Secretary.*

PROF. DICEY AT THE CONSTITUTION CONGRESS.

AT the International Congress on Political Constitutions, opened on August 7th in the Congress Hall of the Franco-British Exhibition, our Principal, Professor Dicey, K.C., D.C.L., read a paper entitled "What are the Guarantees against Oppression which are provided by the Constitution?" A report of the paper appeared in the *Times* of August 8th, from which we extract the following :—

Dealing first with the question of the kind of oppression that we had reason to fear, Professor Dicey said we certainly need not fear the tyranny of the King ; no one, again, dreaded the "influence" of the Crown, nor feared the tyranny of the House of Lords. All the dangers, in short, guarded against by the Magna Charta, by the Bill of Rights, and other august constitutional instruments, were obsolete. The particular perils of royal or aristocratic tyranny with which our ancestors struggled had passed away ; and if we were to speak the language of common sense, he must be allowed to add that the venerable documents, such as the Magna Charta, which were supposed to guard our liberties, were interesting records of most important conflicts, but were now for all practical purposes of little importance. What was it then that we did fear? We dreaded the passing of laws, and still more the administration of the law, in accordance not with the deliberate and real will of the majority of the nation, but in accordance with the immediate wishes of a class, namely, the class— to use an inoffensive term— of wage-earners We feared class legislation, nor could any one say that the fear was unreasonable. He asked them to consider for a moment the Trade Disputes Act. Parliament had seen fit to confer upon trade unions, whether of men or of masters, an immunity from legal liabilities which was not possessed by any other person or body of persons throughout the United Kingdom. The Old-Age Pensions Act was a piece of legislation which may be wise or unwise. All he asserted was, that the Act introduced a tremendous change—as many persons thought, a calamitous revolution—of our whole social system ; that it was passed in a hurry ; that the Government and the Houses of Parliament passed the Act all but unanimously, and passed it without even waiting a few months in order to receive the report of a Royal Commission, appointed to inquire into the expediency or the inexpediency of the policy which the Old Age Pensions Act embodies. The mode in which those two statutes were passed was, indeed, more alarming than their contents. Look wherever they would, they saw statutes which limited the freedom of men or of women to enter into otherwise lawful contracts, and to sell their own labour on such terms as they themselves saw fit to accept. He looked with suspicion on the legislative benevolence of workmen whose philanthropy must surely recognize the fact, that if barmaids be excluded from their accustomed work, barmen would be paid for performing it. Nor was it only in legislation that a Government in search of popularity might practically trench upon the freedom of individuals. Any Government which proclaimed that it would not make use of powers conferred upon it by Act of Parliament for the suppression of boycotting, must be held responsible for the crime which it did not suppress. Such an Executive exercised, in a new and particularly odious form, that suspensing power which had been formally denied to the Crown. This authority to suspend the action of the law had not yet, they would be told, been exercised in Great Britain. Whether the assertion was absolutely true, in spirit at least, he was not certain ; but a precedent set in one part of the United Kingdom admitted, if sanctioned by popular feeling, of easy extension. Turn the matter which way they would, they could not deny that men, who wished to be ruled in accordance with fixed laws, sanctioned by the deliberate will of the majority of the nation, had reason to fear what he might briefly call legislative oppression.

Many of our so-called guarantees against the kind of oppression which we had reason to fear were obsolete or unreal. We have relied, for instance, on our Parliamentary Constitution; but we now knew that Parliament itself and a Government appointed by the House of Commons might come to represent the opinion, not of the nation, but of a class, and turn into an instrument of oppression. The veto of the King for all practical purposes was obsolete, though it might some day become again of importance. The power of the House of Lords to resist the clearly-expressed will of the House of Commons could very rarely be exercised. Many placed reliance on our system of Party government; but the experience of the last twenty-five years proved that no part of the Constitution whatever was safe against the sudden attack of any party which had obtained a momentary majority in the House of Commons. If many of the old guarantees against class legislation were broken down, what were the securities on which we could still rely? They were to be found chiefly in the good sense and in the spirit of fairness which on the whole prevailed throughout the country. Our main protection was, after all, a sound condition of public opinion. If, however, we looked for something more definite than a state of feeling, which was liable to change, we must fix our eyes upon several institutions, which modified the working of government in England, to an extent which hardly obtained sufficient recognition. The House of Lords, for instance, still possessed an element of authority of which it had not as yet learnt to make true use. It might still exert immense power, if it came to understand that its true function at the present day was not to oppose the will of the nation, by which he meant the deliberate and permanent resolve of the majority of the electorate, but to protect the rights of the nation, by preventing any Party, by whatever name it might be called, from carrying through important and far-reaching legislation to which the electors had not given their assent. The House of Lords should, and he was convinced could, if properly led, exercise a suspensive veto.

The non-payment of the members of Parliament was an arrangement which, sooner or later, was certain to be attacked in the name of the democracy. It excluded from politics the professional politician. This was quite enough to satisfy any man of common sense, that it was an arrangement which ought at all costs to be maintained. Then there were two other features of the Government of England which were absolutely essential to its good working. The one was the independence of the Judges, the other the independence, and, therefore, the exclusion from political life, of the whole body of the Civil Service. There were signs of a popular idea which might any day obtain dangerous strength—that the magistrates of a given county ought in some way to represent the political parties into which the country was divided; and that notion, if once accepted, was logically quite as applicable to the Judges of the High Court as to a bench of magistrates. It was to the credit of the Lord Chancellor that he had openly resisted a calamitous demand, and they might hope that his example might be a precedent that would be followed by all his successors. In the matter of the Civil Service, too, they might notice signals of danger. In an unfortunate hour the field of politics was again opened to Civil servants, at any rate in their capacity of electors; and occasions had recently arisen in which it seemed to have been forgotten, that the immunity of a Civil servant from criticism depended upon his being the servant, and not the colleague, of the Minister to whom he privately gave aid which must often take the form of advice.

Discussing the question whether it was possible to obtain further guarantees against legislative oppression, he suggested that in the first place they should resist at all costs any attempt to weaken the existing guarantees, such as they were, against the attempts of partisans to govern in the interests of a class, rather than in accordance with the lasting interest of the nation. In the second place, everything should be done that could be done to diminish the area of party government. Much was done in that direction when admission to the Civil Service was made dependent upon examination. In the last place, let them carefully consider whether the time had not come when, in one form or another, we might introduce into the public life of our country that final appeal to the voice of the nation which was known as the referendum. That institution had several obvious recommendations. It was at once strictly conservative and strictly democratic   It enabled the electors to pronounce a definite verdict upon a definite issue, without being called upon as they were at a general election to decide at once a number of questions, which politicians had purposely muddled up together, and none of which had with any clearness been set before the electorate.   It reminded the House of Commons of the disagreeable fact, which members of the House were apt to forget, that even with the best intentions they might utterly misjudge and misrepresent the wishes of the electors whom they desired to please.   The referendum lay at the very basis of Swiss constitutionalism ; it had been introduced into the Constitution of the Australian dominion, and in reality, though not in name, it existed in every State of the American Union. The moment had come when this conservative and democratic institution had arrested the attention of a leading statesman.   "If," said Lord Rosebery in his protest against the Old Age Pensions Bill, "I had moved the amendment which would have most recommended itself to my mind, I should have moved that this Bill be made the subject of a Referendum to the country at large; because we know from the express announcement of the Prime Minister, that it was no part of the programme on which the Government consulted the country at the last election.   I think, therefore, that such a proposal would have been justified, and that the country was entitled to have been consulted before so grave an operation was entered upon."   These words spoke for themselves.   They had a very wide application.   (Cheers)

THE STUDENTS' CALENDAR FOR OCTOBER.

Fri., 2nd.—"England and Modern Europe," F. A. Simpson, B.A., 8.15.

Sat., 3rd.—Lecture, "Sir Stamford Raffles, Founder of Singapore," Sir Frank Swettenham, K.C.M.G., 8.30.   Furnivall Cycling Club's final run to Pinner.

Sun., 4th.—Shakespeare Reading, "The Taming of the Shrew," 7.30 (ladies' night).   Furnivall Sculling Club general meeting, 7 p.m.

Tues., 6th.—Debating Society Meeting, 9.30, Councillor J. H. Harley, I.L.P., on State labour-providing

Thurs., 8th.—Lecture. "India," T. Morison, M.A., formerly Principal of the Mohammedan College at Aligarh, 8.30.   W.M.C. Musical Society meeting at 8.30, to form an Orchestral Society.

Fri., 9th.—Miss C. Spurgeon's course of classes on "Ruskin" begins, 7.30.

Sat., 10th.—Lecture, "London in Sunshine," W. Pett Ridge, 8.30.

Sun., 11th.—Lubbock Field Club walk and blackberry foray.   Train leaves Waterloo (South Station) at 10.5, for Clandon.

Mon., 12th.—Students and Teachers Meeting, 9.30, E. C. Duchesne opens on "What is an educated man ?"

Tues., 13th.—Debating Society meeting, 9.30.

Wed., 14th.—Annual General Meeting of the Musical Society, 9.45.

Thurs., 15th.—Lecture, "India," T. Morison, M.A., 8.30.

Sat., 17th.—Lecture, "The Man, Samuel Johnson," J. C. Bailey, M.A., 8.30.

Tues., 20th.—Debating Society Meeting, 9.30.

Wed., 21st.—Course on "Workmen's Compensation Act," H. G. Robertson, B.A., begins, 8 p.m.

Thurs., 22nd.—Lecture, "India," T. Morison, M.A., 8.30.

Sat., 24th.—Old Students' Club Meeting, Mr. C. E. Maurice opens on "Is the difference between Socialism and Individualism one of principle or of degree ?" at 7.45.   Lecture, "The Problem of the Painter," (The divergence between mediæval and modern aims), Hawes Turner, B.A., 8.30.

Mon., 26th.—Course on "Patents for Invention," K. R. Swan, B.A., begins at 8.

Tues., 27th.—Debating Society Meeting, 9.30.

Thurs., 29th.—Lecture, "India," T. Morison, M.A., 8.30.

Sat., 31st. -Distribution of Certificates and Address by Sidney Lee, D.Litt., 8.30.

LONDON: Printed by W. HUDSON & Co., Red Lion Street, High Holborn. and published at THE WORKING MEN's COLLEGE, Crowndale Road, London, N.W.—October 1st, 1908.

The Working Men's College Journal

The
Working
Men's
College
Crowndale
Road
St. Pancras
London·N.W.
Founded
1854
by the late
Frederick
Denison
Maurice.

Contents for

NOVEMBER, 1908

An Educated Man
Marks Prize Essay
College Notes
Musical Society
Leicester College
Shakespeare Readers
Club News

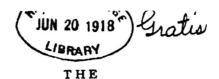

THE

𝔚orking 𝔐en's 𝔆ollege 𝔍ournal.

Conducted by Members of the Working Men's College
Crowndale Road, London, N.W.

| VOL. X.—No. 187. | NOVEMBER, 1908. | PRICE TWOPENCE. |

STUDENTS AND TEACHERS' MEETING.

WHAT IS AN EDUCATED MAN?

RRANGED by the Common Room Committee, with
Martin Starling in the chair, a meeting of students
and teachers was held in the Common and Coffee
Rooms on Monday, October 12th, when our
Superintendent, Mr. E. C. Duchesne, read a paper
upon the above question.

Education, he said, in its nature, aims, and effects, is a topic
around which as a whole, and more especially around certain
aspects of it, rage controversies with which most of us are
acquainted and some familiar, but into these I do not propose
to enter to-night. It is apparent, however, that our view of what
education really is, and in what its functions consist, must
necessarily determine in a large degree what we consider should
be the nature of its product. It will clear the ground, therefore,
if we very briefly attempt to define what we understand by
education. Although warned by the *Westminster Gazette* no
later than Friday last that definitions are perilous things, I will
have the hardihood to define Education as "that process which
draws out or represses, develops or endeavours to stunt, the
latent powers of man." This, you will say, is a very general
definition—true, but what I want to emphasize is that education
ought not to be concerned with what an individual does not
possess, but with the powers, however small, which are inherent
in him. Practical people will certainly say that this is an impossible ideal; that it involves for the educator the task of
ascertaining the individual powers of each of his pupils. With
that I should cordially agree, *not* as an objection, but as an
object at whose attainment every teacher should earnestly aim.
There are far too many who in practice, if not in theory, regard
education as a process analogous to that inflicted upon fowls in
poultry yards. In these, the unfortunate animals are compelled
by mechanical means to swallow daily a certain amount of food
which they are left to digest as best they may. In precisely
similar style many think the work of education accomplished,

if only a certain number of facts are rammed into students' heads, without considering that mental dyspepsia is almost certain to result from such treatment. Now, man is a complex animal, and if my definition be true, education must concern itself with the three sides of his nature, physical, mental, and spiritual. This indeed should be the case, and it is encouraging to observe that even the present London County Council is beginning to recognize, albeit in a timid and moderate degree only, that bodily fitness is an indispensable condition for mental activity, and that the latter is diminished as the former declines. Napoleon, I believe, once said that an army marches on its stomach; substitute "brain" for "army," and the statement would be equally true. However, I am going to-night to leave the physical and spiritual, the lowest and highest of man's triple attributes, to take care of themselves, not from any lack of appreciation of their importance, but simply from lack of time, as I intend to confine myself to the mental point of view only.

Now, what are the latent powers of the mind upon which education should be brought to bear, and to what purpose should those powers be trained? It would be impossible as well as inadvisable to-night to go into too minute sub-divisions; moreover I hope that discussion and criticism will follow this paper and fill up many of its obvious defects, so I will lay it down that every man possesses, in greater or less degree, three mental powers—*observation, memory, deduction*—with a fourth which is not, I think, a purely mental attribute, but is nevertheless a highly important factor in mental education—*imagination*. This last, I may observe, in some men appears to be completely absent; whereas in others it blossoms forth in a rank, luxurious growth, to which a not altogether complimentary name is usually given. In this form, I need hardly say, repression and extinction are the true functions of education.

It is not my intention to discuss the relative importance of these four powers, but it may be useful to point out that—

(i.) Observation supplies us with facts.

(ii.) Memory stores these facts for use.

(iii) Deduction enables us to assign them their value, and to arrange them as links in some train of thought or argument.

(iv.) Imagination supplies the wants of the aesthetic side of our minds, and gives vividness to our impressions.

If, therefore, I am right, it is easy to deduce that an educated man is one whose observation, memory, deduction, and imagination have been properly developed and trained.

I assume that each of us here has the ambition to be an educated man, and would like to know by what steps that ambition may be attained. Before discussing the latter, however, I should like to ask what purpose should furnish the ground of such ambition?—at what goal should we aim? In his essay, "Of Wisdom for Man's Self," Francis Bacon observes, "Divide with reason between Self-love and Society: and be so true to thyself as thou be not false to others, especially to thy king and country. It is a poor centre of a man's actions, *himself.*" There, I venture to assert, is the true principle of education. The principle, that education should not be considered chiefly as a means whereby a man should benefit himself, but that on the contrary its principal value should consist in the amount of benefit which the man can confer upon his country and his kind. No one ought to regard education as a method of securing his own material good and advancement solely. There is, of course, a sense in which individual success and prosperity involves the prosperity of the community as a whole, but that altruistic view, is, I fear, the one most often lost sight of. We here are all members of a college whose foundation we owe to a man who, in season and out of season, urged this view of education. In this respect as in others, Maurice was, in the forties and early fifties of the nineteeeth century, the voice of one crying in the wilderness. As Mr. Litchfield has recorded—"One leading feature of the College was that it wholly rejected the idea that the value of Education turns upon its usefulness in regard to a man's trade or profession, or in other words upon its helping him to get on. The plea addressed to working people by speakers and writers urging the importance of education was *then* most commonly of this kind. They would say, in effect, though wrapping it up in finer phrases, ' Education will put you in the way of improving your position. If you are a clerk, knowing French may make a difference of ten shillings or more a week in the salary you can earn. Or if you are an engineer, think of Stephenson and Arkwright. By becoming ingenious mechanists, they made great fortunes; they rose out of their class. Study mechanics, and you may do the same.' Of this plausible doctrine, Maurice would have none. He always insisted that if knowledge and culture, science and literature,'are any good, the good is something apart from trade utility. He denounced too the pitiful fraud of dangling before the working man the prospects of 'rising out of his class,' when one knew that that ambition, whether worthy or unworthy, can succeed in only one out of ten thousand cases."—Speaking as it were in the presence of our Founder, I would urge the present race of College men to make Maurice's ideal of education their own more than many of them apparently are inclined to do. Fitness for exercising the rights and duties of citizenship, Maurice preached as the goal of every man's education. And if that was important then, it is infinitely more so now. For consider for one minute what has happened since this College was founded. Political power has gradually shifted from the classes to the masses. As Mr. J. A. R. Marriott has put it, " Democracy has been admitted not merely to a full; but to a preponderating share, in political control. The British people have deliberately decided to try an experiment which is without precedent and without parallel in the history of the world ; they have determined to attempt to rule, not merely a great kingdom, but a world-wide empire, by means of a democratic machinery. It is an experiment which, viewed with detachment, is of supreme and unique interest to the student of political science; but to us success or failure is a matter of political life or death, and insistent anxiety must necessarily overpower the sense of political curiosity." Upon what, in the ultimate resort, does the success or failure of this stupendous experiment depend? In my opinion, solely upon the attitude of our working classes towards education. If the democracy does not insist upon educating itself up to its responsibilities, I see nothing but failure, complete and irretrievable, for the empire to which we belong. Fourteen years ago, Sir Richard Jebb averred that "our elementary education, unless crowned by something higher, is not only barren, but may even be dangerous. It is not well to teach our democracy to read, unless we also teach it to think." In the same address he asserted, and backed up his assertion with ample proof, that technical and scientific instruction is wholly inadequate as the be-all and end-all of real education. There are problems already insistent, and others looming in the distance, all pregnant with good or evil to the commonwealth, which will require and should receive, not the often unreasoning zeal of the political partizan, but the sober and reasoned consideration of every man who, by his vote and influence, will have a direct responsibility in the decisions which are bound to be taken. Consider, for instance, the present Licensing Bill. A great trade considers, like the craftsmen of Ephesus, that their craft is endangered. Forthwith the rush and roar of special trains are heard, crowds are induced or compelled to attend, and London streets are rendered hideous one Sunday by the blare of bands and by hilarious shouting, until the whole assembly is gathered to Hyde Park to shout "Confiscation and robbery" and "Great is bung of the British," whilst crocodile tears are dropped over the piteous fate awaiting the widow and the orphan, if these obnoxious provisions are enacted. I express no opinion of this Licensing Bill. My point is that the brewers would not have gone to all that trouble and expense, if they had perforce to realize that they had to deal with an intelligent and educated electorate; they would then have spent their money in different and quieter ways. I read some time ago an article in which the writer urged that no one should be allowed to vote until or unless he or she had passed a qualifying examination. The idea is good, it appears quixotic; but if it could be carried out, if reason—even imperfect reason—could be appealed to, instead of political prejudice and passion, no reform effected hitherto would, I believe, have accomplished one-tenth of the good which such an arrangement would produce. My first point, then, is to urge you to take no narrow or selfish view of education; recall to mind constantly that you are members of no mean empire, and resolve that, as far as in you lies, you will make yourselves worthy of your privileges and of your responsibilities alike.

(*To be concluded.*)

THE MARKS PRIZE ESSAY, 1908.

PRINTED below is the winning essay, written by Mr. John G. Newlove, and awarded the prize by the examiner, Mr. F. M. Cornford, Fellow of Trinity College, Cambridge. The numbered footnotes contain Mr. Cornford's remarks and Mr. Newlove's replies to them.

SHAKESPEARE'S VIEWS ON DEMOCRACY,

WITH SPECIAL REFERENCE TO THE PLAYS OF "JULIUS CÆSAR" AND "CORIOLANUS."

" DEMOCRACY is that form of government in which the sovereign power is in the hands of the people collectively, and is exercised by them either directly or indirectly through elected representatives or delegates."—(Encyclopædic Dictionary.)

INTRODUCTION.

Of the great English Renaissance—which was not only a revival of Letters, but of Art, of Philosophy, of Science, of Commerce—the Shakespearean Drama was the most permanent expression. Few can deny the genius of Shakespeare, or fail to recognize his attainments in almost every department of knowledge, without which it would have been impossible to create such a number of characters so completely distinct from one another. Carlyle's eulogy of him in "The Hero as Poet" is about as complete as one could desire. He tells us that "Shakespeare is the chief of all Poets hitherto, the greatest intellect who, in our recorded world, has left record of himself in the way of Literature. On the whole, I know not such a power of vision, faculty of thought, if we take all the characters of it, in any other man." These remarkable powers, however, must not blind us to his attitude towards the questions which agitate the minds of men, upon some of whom his opinion might make a deep impression. Of such questions, that of democracy must be accorded a foremost place in the political thought of these islands at the present time. It is opportune as well as interesting, therefore, to learn what "the thousand-souled Shakespeare" has to impart regarding the sovereignty of the people.

We feel bound to conclude, after a careful study of his plays, that Shakespeare was not enamoured with the democratic sympathies possessed by many of his contemporaries. On the contrary, he seldom misses an opportunity to exhibit his contempt for the people of lowly birth. Whether in comedy, history, or tragedy, his principal characters always represent those of high rank.[1] It has been urged in defence of this policy that, by so doing, Shakespeare only followed the custom of the time. If such were the case, it is a weak defence of a genius who, we imagine, should lead, even if the example did not receive popular favour immediately. Upon closer examination, this excuse is found to be still weaker. Amongst the men of genius and high literary repute who immediately preceded, or were con-

---

[1] I don't feel that this is a defect from the *artistic* point of view, from which alone an artist must be judged.—F. M. C.

The exclusive use of aristocrats as principal characters does not necessarily impart artistic qualities, while it may afford an example of bias.—J. G. N.

temporaneous with Shakespeare, we observe the names of Sir Thomas More and Sir Philip Sydney. With such creative power as the great dramatist possessed, it would not have been difficult for him to have given us at least one play based upon "Utopia" or "Arcadia."[2]   Again, if Robert Greene could give us as hero a mere pound-keeper, in the "Pinner of Wakefield," Shakespeare might have bequeathed one English historical play to mark the growth of democracy.[3]   The whole of them, from *King John* to *Henry VIII.,* entirely ignore the subject, except for occasional deprecation of popular risings.

The lack of democratic sympathy in Shakespeare is partially due to the environment of the dramatist himself.   There is little doubt that he very soon became a favourite with Elizabeth, some writers going so far as to assert that the *Merry Wives of Windsor* was written at the special request of the Queen.   At her death we find Chettle, in "Englande's Mourning Garment," writing with regard to the patronage she bestowed upon Shakespeare :—

> Nor does the silver-tongèd Melicert
> Drop from his honied muse one sable teare
> To mourne her death *that graced his desert,*
> *And to his laies opened her royall eare.*

"Coriolanus" and "Julius Cæsar."

In the plays with which we are immediately concerned, two distinct views of democracy are brought out in bold relief.   "Julius Cæsar" affords several examples of the easiness with which the populace can be turned from one opinion to another, while in "Coriolanus," every patrician character is made to extol the omnipotence of aristocratic institutions, and to despise "the fusty plebeians," "the beast with many heads."   The derisive scorn of Caius Marcius is not so likely to find favour with the mob, reduced to desperation by hopeless destitution,[4] as is the suave conduct of a Menenius, but both exhibit an equal contemptuousness for those whom they hope to keep in subjection.

Passing to an analysis of the plays, the two main views stated above are presented in a variety of ways.   Taking them in historical sequence, we may say that in

"Coriolanus"

the aristocratic bias shows itself in three different aspects :—

I. The one-sided delineation of the character of Coriolanus.
II. The idea that only the classes should exercise the function of government.
III. The representatives of the democracy are merely demagogues, who, through grudging envy, incite the people to animosity.

---

[2] I must say I am glad he didn't.   And is "Arcadia" *democratic?*—F. M. C.

[3] Was this a question of much interest at the time, and was it a fit subject for Shakespearean drama?—F. M. C.

Democratic ideas did not disappear entirely under the Tudors, although they were temporarily overshadowed by other considerations.   If it was not a fit subject for Shakespearean drama, he should have abstained from noticing democracy altogether.—J. G. N.

[4] These rhyming words produce an ugly effect of sound.—F. M. C.

I. THE CHARACTER OF CORIOLANUS.—Were we not aware that the materials for this play were taken from Sir Thomas North's translation of " Plutarch's Lives," it would be difficult to reconcile the account given by the celebrated Greek philosopher and historian with the Coriolanus depicted by Shakespeare. Plutarch records that Coriolanus was " so choleric and impatient that he would yield to no living creature, which made him churlish, uncivil, and altogether unfit for man's conversation ; yet men, marvelling much at his constancy, that he was never overcome with pleasure nor money, and how he would endure easily all manner of pain and travels ; thereupon they well liked and commended his stoutness and temperancy." Again, his " imperious temper and that savage manner which was too haughty for a republic." Further on we read that he indulged his " irascible passions on a supposition that they had something great and exalted in them." He lacked that " due mixture of gravity and mildness, which are the chief political virtues and the fruits of reason and education. . . . . . . He never dreamed that such obstinacy is rather the effect of the weakness and effeminacy of a distempered mind, which breaks out in violent passions like so many tumours." According to Shakespeare, however, the hero of the play did not always exhibit this pride and arrogance. He restricted such displays to the lower orders, and through Menenius we are told that

His nature is too noble for the world. *

II. THE RIGHT OF THE ARISTOCRACY TO GOVERN.—Quite early in the play the omnipotence of aristocratic government is manifested. Chancing to meet a body of citizens whose intention it is to storm the senate, Menenius is made to exclaim,

You may as well
Strike at the heaven with your staves as lift them
Against the Roman state, whose course will on
The way it takes, cracking ten thousand curbs
Of more strong link asunder than can ever
Appear in your impediment.   (Act 1, Scene 1).

Again, in the same scene the idea of the dependent position of the common people is brought out :

You shall find
No public benefit which you receive,
But it proceeds or comes from them to you,
And no way from yourselves.

Such belief finds more emphatic utterance in Caius Marcius when he says :

Five tribunes to defend their vulgar wisdoms,
Of their own choice : one's Junius Brutus,
Sicinius Velutus, and I know not—'Sdeath !
The rabble should have first unroof'd the city,
Ere so prevail'd with me ; it will in time
Win upon power, and throw forth greater themes
For insurrection's arguing.

Menenius.   This is strange.
Marcius.   Go ; get you home, you fragments !

* I don't think this is a strong point. Shakespeare might choose for his dramatic purposes to represent an aristocrat, without thereby showing any *prejudice.* He was never *bound* by his authorities in his conception of a character.—F. M. C.

I agree that Shakespeare was not bound by his authorities, otherwise he would have given us the *true* Coriolanus, not a man who could revile the plebeians and yet have a nature "too noble for the world."—J. G. N.

For his defeat of the Volsces before Corioli, Caius Marcius is sur-
named Coriolanus, and upon the return of the Roman army he is
proposed as consul.   The tribunes of the people are perturbed at this,
and very soon come into conflict with Coriolanus.   In Act 3, Scene 1,
we are given several examples of aristocratic presumption.   Thus :—

Coriolanus.   It is a purpos'd thing, and grows by plot,
    To curb the will of the nobility :
    Suffer 't, and live with such as cannot rule
    Nor ever will be rul'd.

Again,

                This double worship,
    Where one part does disdain with cause, the other
    Insult without all reason ; where gentry, title, wisdom,
    Cannot conclude but by the yea and no
    Of general ignorance,—it must omit
    Real necessities, and give way the while
    To unstable slightness : purpose so barr'd, it follows
    Nothing is done to purpose.   Therefore, beseech you,—
    You that will be less fearful than discreet,
    That love the fundamental part of the state
    More than you doubt the change on 't, that prefer
    A noble life before a long, and wish
    To jump a body with a dangerous physic
    That's sure of death without it, at once pluck out
    The multitudinous tongue ; let them not lick
    The sweet which is their poison.

The same year (470 B.C.) that Coriolanus was elected consul, witnessed a severe famine in Rome, and he strongly opposed the free
distribution of the contents of the Sicilian corn-ships.   During an
altercation with the tribunes he takes occasion to refer to the incident, and in two pointed outbursts we have the opinion expressed
that the distribution of food to the people, as well as their participation in government, would mean ruin to the state.[6]

Coriolanns.   Tell me of corn !
    This was my speech, and I will speak 't again,—
Menenius.   Not now, not now.
1st Senator.   Not in this heat, sir, now.
Coriolanus.   Now, as I live, I will.   My nobler friends,
    I crave their pardons :
    For the mutable, rank-scented many, let them
    Regard me as I do not flatter, and
    Therein behold themselves :   I say again,
    In soothing them, we nourish 'gainst our senate
    The cockle of rebellion, insolence, sedition,
    Which we ourselves have plough'd for, sow'd and scatter'd,
    By mingling them with us, the honour'd number ;
    Who lack not virtue, no, nor power, but that
    Which they have given to beggars.

---

[6] In actual history, this custom of distributing corn gratis (*not* at times
of special famine, it is true) *had* a disastrous result.   It attracted the rural
population into Rome, where all the most worthless and idle lived by these
doles, and the rural districts tended to be depopulated of *free* labour, and to
become large estates worked by *slaves* under very bad conditions.—F. M. C.

A man who would oppose the distribution of food in time of special
famine can hardly be considered a friend of the people.   The conditions of
the rural population could not have been satisfactory, otherwise Rome would
not have attracted them.—J. G. N.

A little further on he says :—

> Whoever gave that counsel, to give forth
> The corn o' the store-house gratis, as 'twas us'd
> Sometime in Greece,—

Menenius.   Well, well ; no more of that.

Coriolanus. Though there the people had more absolute power,
> I say, they nourish'd disobedience, fed
> The ruin of the state.

All of which reminds us of the speech delivered by Lord Ravensworth in the House of Lords, during the discussion on the second reading of the Reform Bill of 1867. "Democracy," he said, "embodied the spirit of encroachment, and was never satisfied with what it obtained ; no doubt when this Bill was passed, there would be demanded a still further extension of those liberties which would be so widely extended by this measure. It was to be hoped that such demands would not be complied with."* Such utterance, we think, is a fair paraphrase of Shakespeare's opinion on the right of democracy to a voice in government.'

An attempt by the enraged citizens to seize Coriolanus leads to a *mêlée,* in which they are driven off. In the interim before a second assault, Cominius persuades Coriolanus to proceed to his house and leave Menenius to appease the mob. For he says :—

> Now 'tis odds beyond arithmetic ;
> And manhood is call'd foolery when it stands
> Against a falling fabric. Will you hence,
> Before the tag return? whose rage doth rend
> Like interrupted waters, and o'erbear
> What they are us'd to bear.

Menenius.   Pray you, be gone ;
> I'll try whether my old wit be in request
> With those that have but little : this must be patch'd
> With cloth of any colour.

He tells us immediately afterwards, however, that he would the citizens—

> Were in Tyber ! What, the vengeance !
> Could he not speak 'em fair?

When Coriolanus censures his mother because of her apparent disapproval of his hasty conduct, she replies :—

> I would have had you put your power well on
> Before you had worn it out.

Coriolanus.   Let go.

Volumnia. You might have been enough the man you are
> With striving less to be so ; lesser had been
> The thwartings of your dispositions if
> You had not show'd them how you were dispos'd.
>
>   (Act 3, Scene 2).

Again, when one of the senators despairs of the mob being reconciled, Volumnia says :—

> Pray be counsell'd.
> I have a heart as little apt as yours,
> But yet a brain that leads my use of anger
> To better vantage.

---

* Parliamentary Debates, 1866—7.

' You have not shown that it is more than Coriolanus's opinion—a very different thing.—F. M. C.

But Coriolanus scorns the idea of repentance, and Volumnia is obliged to suppress her own nature to reason with him. Thus :—

> If it be honour in your wars to seem
> The same as you are not,—which, for your best ends,
> You adopt your policy,—how is it less, or worse,
> That it shall hold companionship in peace
> With honour, as in war, since that to both
> It stands in like request ?

After much reasoning, assisted by Menenius and Cominius, the consul is prevailed upon to face the people, with the assurance that all will be well if he will but "answer mildly." Coriolanus wrestles with himself in an attempt to do so, but ultimately the accumulated passion busts forth, and when the citizens decide upon his banishment, he exclaims with bitter warning :—

> You common cry of curs ! whose breath I hate
> As reek o' the rotten fens, whose loves I prize
> As the dead carcases of unburied men
> That do corrupt my air, I banish you ;
> And here remain with your uncertainty !
> Let every feeble rumour shake your hearts !
> Your enemies, with nodding of their plumes,
> Fan you into despair ! Have the power still
> To banish your defenders ; till at length
> Your ignorance,—which finds not, till it feels,—
> Making but reservation of yourselves,—
> Still your own foes,—deliver you, as most
> Abated captives, to some nation
> That won you without blows ! Despising,
> For you, the city, thus I turn my back :
> There is a world elsewhere. [8]

(To be concluded.)

- - - ◆·◉·◆ - - -

CORRESPONDENCE.

CLASS LIBRARIES.
To the Editor of the WORKING MEN'S COLLEGE JOURNAL.

DEAR SIR,—We are anxious to form class libraries in connection with the advanced classes in modern languages, to supplement the works in the College library, and to stimulate the study of the literature of the country whose language is being learned.

May I through your columns appeal to all members who possess works in French, German, Spanish, and Italian, more particularly by modern authors, which they can spare, to send them to me for this purpose ?

I shall, with your permission, be glad to acknowledge all donations through the columns of the JOURNAL.—Yours faithfully,

S. DE JASTRZEBSKI,
Director of Modern Languages Section.

October 1st, 1908.

---

[8] Most of these quotations do not seem to me to prove more than that Shakespeare has represented in his play aristocrats, speaking as such—not that he *endorses* their sentiments. Whether he does so, or not (and I agree with you that he does to some extent), is a very difficult question of criticism, and needs careful discussion. It can hardly be *proved*, one way or the other, but depends on the general impression left by the whole play on one's mind, rather than on any isolated passage.—F. M. C.

[7] and [8] It was after studying the whole play that I formed the opinion as to the moral.—J. G. N.

THE CHILDREN'S TREAT.

To the Editor of the WORKING MEN'S COLLEGE JOURNAL.

DEAR MR. EDITOR,—I shall feel obliged if you can find room in the JOURNAL for my gentle reminder, that the Children's Treat will take place after Christmas this year, on January 9th, 1909. I feel sure that the generous support we have hitherto received will not be lacking for the coming event. The money received is always spent up to the last penny, so that there is never too much, but always a feeling at the distribution that we could have managed with a few pounds more. If any of our friends are in a position to supply us with a magic lantern, cinematographic, or other suitable entertainment for the children, to last about one hour, I shall feel obliged if they will put themselves in communication with the joint-secretaries. All sums of money, clothing, toys, etc., should be forwarded to the College, and will be gratefully acknowledged by either Offer or Nye. —Yours sincerely, F. J. FURNIVALL.

THE STUDENTS' CALENDAR FOR NOVEMBER.

Sun., 1st.—Shakespeare Reading, "As you like it," 7.30 (ladies' night).
Tues., 3rd.—Debating Society Meeting, J. Seymour Lloyd (London Municipal Society) opens, "That the undue extension of trading enterprises on the part of Municipal Authorities is contrary to the public interest," 9.30.
Thurs., 5th.—Lecture, "The French Republic," Prof. A. V. Dicey, M.A., D.C.L., LL.D., K.C., Principal, 8.30. Maurice Chess Club v. Fulham Chess Club, home (League Match), 8 p.m.
Sat., 7th.—Lecture, "Parliament at Work," (illustrated), Henry Rose, 8.30.
Sun., 8th.—Lubbock Field Club's outing; take pedestrian tour ticket *out* to Beaconsfield, back from Slough, 1s. 11d. ; train leaves Paddington, 9.23 a.m.
Mon., 9th.—Latest day for nomination of student members of the Council. Common Room General Meeting and Election, 9.30.
Tues., 10th.—Maurice Chess Club v. London Rifle Brigade, match at 130, Bunhill Row, E.C., 8 p.m. Debating Society Meeting, G. M. Trevelyan, M.A., opens, 9.30.
Thurs., 12th.—Lecture, "The Place of London in English History," R. Rait, M.A., 8.15.
Sat., 14th.—Lecture, "The Awakening of Turkey," G. P. Gooch, M.A., M.P., 8.30. Maurice Chess Club v. Trinity College, at Cambridge, 4.30.
Sun., 15th.—Shakespeare Reading, "Richard II.," 7.30.
Mon., 16th.—Election of three student members of Council begins. Declaration of poll, Common Room Committee, 10.30.
Tues., 17th.—Maurice Chess Club v. Athenæum II., home, 8 p.m. Debating Society Meeting, 9.30.
Wed., 18th.—A Chamber Concert by the Musical Society in the Maurice Hall, 9 p.m.
Thurs., 19th.—Lecture, "The Place of London in English History," R. Rait, M.A., 8.15.
Sat., 21st.—Old Students' Club meeting, E. D. A. Morshead, M.A., opens on "Have we gained or lost, politically, by freely admitting aliens into England?" 7.45. Lecture, "Liquefaction of Gases" (with experiments), J. F. Spencer, D.Sc., Ph.D., 8.30.
Mon., 23rd.—Declaration of poll, student members of Council.
Tues., 24th.—Council Meeting, 8 p.m. Debating Society Meeting, 9.30.
Wed., 25th.—Musical Society's Smoking Concert in Coffee Room, 9.30.
Thurs., 26th.—Maurice Chess Club v. Toynbee Hall, league match at 306, High Holborn, W.C., 8 p.m. Lecture, "The Place of London in English History," R. Rait, M.A., 8.15.
Sat., 28th.—27th Collegians' Dance, 6.45.
Sun., 29th.—Shakespeare Reading, "King Lear," 7.30 (ladies' night).

COLLEGE NOTES.

THE College gallery of portraits of men who have helped to make its history has been enriched by the addition of two oil paintings by Mr. A. Wolmark, one of Dr. F. J. Furnivall, and the other of Sir Charles Lucas. We shall all value these pictures very highly, and we are under a deep debt of gratitude to Mr. Wolmark for transferring to canvas in the admirable way he has done these representations of two of our leading spirits, and for so generously giving them to the College.

Mr. A. H. Hawkins (Anthony Hope) has very kindly presented the Library with 24 bound volumes of *The Bookman*, a valuable literary journal published in the United States.

The election of student members to the Council takes place during the week beginning November 16th. Three are to be polled for, selected by and from the fellows, student teachers, associates, senior students, and those students who are at least of one year's standing. Candidates must be nominated on or before the 9th inst.

The retiring student members, elected and co-opted, are A. E. Homewood, Leonard Pocock, W. J. Torrington, E. R. Cole, and A. Weight Matthews, all of whom are eligible for re-election.

The Common Room Committee election and general meeting also take place this month. On November 9th, at 9.30 p.m., the outgoing Committee will place before the members present their report and accounts for the past year; questions and criticism will be invited, and the candidates for election on the new Committee will be nominated, seconded, and heckled. They will not know whether they are elected until seven days later, for the poll is taken during the week following the election. Any member of the College of six months' standing is eligible for election and may exercise the suffrage.

René Bowden, who is gazetted Tansley Prizeman and Scholar for this year, appears to have first joined the College in the year 1895. He seems from the first to have had a great liking for Applied Science, and we find that he gained a certificate for Geometrical Drawing after he had been a member of the College one year. In 1897, no fewer than four successes stand to his credit, Machine Construction, 1st stage, 1st class; Practical Geometry, 1st stage; Freehand Drawing, 1st stage, 1st class; and Model Drawing, 1st stage, 2nd class. Two certificates fell to his efforts in the following year, one for Machine Construction, 2nd stage, 2nd class, and one for Electricity, 1st stage, 2nd class. Another year's work was crowned by a 2nd class in

Advanced Electricity. This was followed in 1900 by a 2nd class in Mechanics, and in 1902, by a 1st class in Geology. He turned his attention to German in 1902, and as a result gained a certificate in the following year. There came a gap in Mr. Bowden's record at this time—a gap of five years, but that he had been industrious is shown by a 1st class, Sound, Light, and Heat, in 1908, when it is also recorded that he was awarded a College certificate marked "excellent" for proficiency in Geology.

The other two Tansley Prizes have been awarded to Sydney William Burns, and A. Harold B. Stock. Mr. Burns, who is one of the most capable of our practice class teachers, in both French and German, joined the College in October, 1892. Although he is best known for his interest in foreign languages, his long list of examination successes is not by any means confined to them, as will be seen from his record, which shows that he has taken the following certificates and College honours :—

1893, Grammar, 1st stage—1894, Grammar, advanced, "excellent"; Tonic Sol-fa, elementary stage; Staff Notation, first stage—1895, Arithmetic, first stage, "excellent"—1896, Arithmetic, advanced, "excellent"; Senior Student Scholar—1897, Book-keeping—1898, French, 1st stage—1901, German, 1st stage, "excellent"—1902, German, advanced, "excellent"; French, advanced—1903, French, Chamber of Commerce, senior, dist. in written; French, Society of Arts, grade 2, class 2—1904, Commercial Law (College), pass; Commercial Law, Chamber of Commerce, with distinction; Associate Scholar, and Fellow of the College—1908, Spanish, elementary.

Mr. Stock joined the College more recently, in October, 1906, but his record since then has been a very promising one. His education, as Mr. Duchesne will no doubt have noted with appreciation, has concerned itself with the physical, as well as with the mental side of our nature, for he is an ardent cyclist and a good gymnast. At College examinations, he has gained the following certificates :—

In 1907, French, elementary stage, "excellent"; Arithmetic, 1st stage, "excellent"; Shorthand, 120 words per minute; and Economics—and in 1908, French, intermediate stage; Grammar, 1st stage; and Arithmetic, 2nd stage.

Mr. L. R. B. Pearce, whose name appears on the current Honours List as having passed in advanced English Composition, was one of the candidates for Matriculation in the examination held in September last, and the pass list contains his name. Mr. Pearce is a bright, intelligent, young fellow, whose only regret is that his studies preclude his taking a prominent part in the social life of the College. Like Mr. Stock, however, he found time to attend this year's sports, and he was successful in several of the events of the day. Mr. Pearce is prevented from joining the College this term, but he has sent along his brother, with the sound advice, "Go thou and do likewise."

Writing to the hon. secretary of the Old Students' Club from Dresden, on August 17th, Mr. Karl Brückner says :—

Lieber Freund,—Endlich sollen Sie aus dem Elblande etwas wieder hören. Es ist am Strande der Elbe zu schön, als dass ich in die Sommerfrische, man könnte auch sagen, Sommerkälte, ginge, denn hier haben wir gute Luft und schöne Natur in Hülle und Fülle. In Dresden sind jetzt Tausende von Fremden, besonders von Ihren Landsleuten, die sich nicht fürchten, von den Deutschen aufgefressen zu sein. Was sagen Sie denn zu dieser fortwährenden Schreiberei von Invasion Deutschlands in England und umgekehrt? Ist es nicht rein lächerlich, nur daran zu denken? Was hätten denn die Deutschen von einem Kriege mit England und umgekehrt? Würden sich nicht beide Nationen den grössten Schaden selbst zufügen? Es ist eine elende Aufhetzerei des Volkes, und die Zeitungsschreiber verdienen den Galgen, die fortwährend nur Hetzartikel bringen. In Deutschland denkt kein Kind an einen Einfall in England, aber die immerwährenden Press-artikel von den bezahlten Redakteuren über Deutschland sind nie beruhigend und klug, denn über kurz oder lang wird es trotz Ententen zu einem Kriege, aber mit Frankreich, kommen, denn die Franzosen denken sich sicher und gedeckt durch die Verträge mit anderen gegen Deutschland. Es wird immer geschrieben Deutschland wäre nerveur darüber. Ich kann nur sagen, ich merke hier nichts davon, wir sind für alle Fälle so gerüstet, dass wir auch alleinstehend Niemanden fürchten. Russland ist völlig ohnmächtig, und Oesterreich ist auch nur angewiesen. Ein grosser Fehler der englischen Politik steht darin, dass die gelbe Rasse durch Japan an der Spitze der Macht gelangt ist. Für ganz Europa, besonders aber für England, wird sich das bitter rächen, denn sie haben sich einen grossen Nebenbuhler auf wirtschaftlichen und auf politischen Gebiete geschaffen, und die Geister, die sie riefen, werden sie nicht wieder los werden.

Und nun noch etwas von Flottenbau. Lieber Himmel, diese einfältige Angst vor unsern paar Schiffen! Wir werden doch nie so viel Schiffe bauen, dass wir etwa England gleich kommen wollen. Wir wollen unsern Handel schützen, und über kurz oder lang werden diese Schiffsbauten durch Luftkreuzer auch überflüssig werden. Wer wird denn England anfallen? Niemand. Kein Kind denkt in Deutschland, nur die alberne Journalistik und überspannte Politiker denken und schreiben davon. Auch wollen wir ja mit Frankreich anbinden, aber alle Zeichen deuten darauf ein, dass der Deutschen Geduldsfaden bald immer einmal reissen wird, und dann wird Frankreich die Zeche bezahlen müssen.

Alle Völker sind zu Grunde gegangen durch Völlerei und Sittenlosigkeit. Wir Europaer sind auf dem schönsten Wege dazu und unsere westlichen Nachbarn geben dazu ein zu schlechter Vorbild. Die Sittenlosigkeit ist leider bei uns vortreten, denn sonst könnten solche Eulenburgische Schmützdinge nicht vorkommen. Uns ekelt diese Geschichte an, denn Edelleute sollten von solchem sittlichen Schmutz fern bleiben, aber dieser Schmutz wird durch lüsterne Zeitungen breit getreten, denn wir haben ja leider Pressfreiheit, oder vielmehr, Pressfrechheit, alles ist erlaubt, auch der Schlechteste. Wird einmal der gesunde Sinn der Völker siegen, oder wird's so weiter gehen? Hoffen wir, dass es einmal besser werde mit der Menschheit. Die heutigen Zustände, mit Lug und Trug überall, sind mir zuwider, und das heissen christliche Völker! Die Missionare sollten nicht hinausgehen in alle Welt, sondern die alte Welt christianisiren und bessern.

———

From the Board of Education two belated examination results have come in, viz., in Geometrical Drawing, Richard E. Tyler, 1st class; and Work accepted for Art Class Teacher's Certificate, Harry Thirlwall.

Through our old friend, teacher, and examiner, Dr. Eugene Oswald, the College has a bond of sympathy with the English Goethe Society, of which he is secretary and has been a member since its foundation in 1886. The society was founded for the purpose of promoting the study of Goethe's work and thought, and in 1891 its scope was extended, so that, while always keeping Goethe as the central figure, attention might also be directed to other fields of German literature, art, and science. At its meeting on October 28th, Mr. Oscar Browning, M.A., was the lecturer, his subject being Goethe's " Wahlverwandtschaften."

We heartily congratulate Dr. Oswald upon his having attained the age of 82 years, or, as Dr. Furnivall would put it, his 83rd birthday. In the *Hampstead and St. John's Wood Advertiser* appears the following :—

"MANY HAPPY RETURNS OF THE DAY" to Dr. Eugene Oswald, of 129, Adelaide Road, who was born October 16th, 1826; at Heidelberg, but has lived in England since 1852, and is a naturalized Englishman. For more than 25 years, Dr. Oswald was Instructor at the Royal Naval College, Greenwich, and he has been actively interested in the Working Men's College, now of Crowndale Road, ever since 1860. His contributions to literature have been very numerous and varied, while his political letters to a leading Portuguese paper have made him so well known in Portugal, that the late King on the occasion of his 80th birthday made him a Knight Commander of the Ancient and Noble Order of Christ. His home has at all times been the meeting-place of men and women of the brightest intellect, and he has always been to the fore in any movements for the advance and progress of his fellow-men. He was for many years President of the Carlyle Society, and is the active Secretary of the English Goethe Society. Among some of his distinguished pupils are Prince Edward and Prince Albert of Wales.

From the *St. Pancras Gazette* of August 21st, we take the following cutting :—

In the presence of a great gathering of friends, the wedding of Councillor Dr. John Forbes, 1, Hurdwick Place, and Miss Beatrice Nellie Renders, took place yesterday at Regent Square Presbyterian Church. The bridegroom is one of the best liked of the younger medical men of St. Pancras, is a member of the Borough Council, and the highly-esteemed teacher of the ambulance class at the Working Men's College, Crowndale Road. The bride is the elder daughter of Mr. Albert Renders, 28, Harrington Square, the well-known manager of the Holborn Restaurant, and a young lady in every way qualified to make a charming matrimonial partner for the popular young medico.

Dr. Forbes had kept this quiet, or we might sooner have been able to add our congratulations, which we now most heartily tender to him and his wife.

Mr. J. C. Bailey being unable to attend at the College on Saturday, October 17th, to give his lecture on " The Man, Samuel Johnson," (which is postponed), Mr. Herbert Baynes very kindly lectured in his stead, on that evening, on " The Oldest Book of our Aryan Race—the Rig-Vêda." The Rev. Alfred Butcher, pastor at the Wesleyan Mission, Camden Street, took the chair.

Mr. John MacDonald, the editor and proprietor of the *Western Schools Journal,* of Topeka, Kansas, who was a student in the College in the early days of its existence and a member of Dr. Furnivall's class at that time, paid a visit to London, and to the College, on September 28th, with a friend, Mr. Donald Rose, and was glad to see, in its fine new building and well-appointed class rooms, library, lecture hall, and social rooms, such striking evidence of its material welfare and progress

Mr. V. Hereck called in at the office the other day to say "good-bye," he having obtained a good appointment at Baden, in South Germany. He would on no account, he said, sever his connection with the College, and enrolled himself as an Old Student. His leaving England has given him the opportunity to express his appreciation of the help he has received from students and teachers alike, during the two years he has been a member. "I have experienced," he says, "nothing but kindness at the hands of everybody here, and shall look back upon the past two years as the pleasantest and most useful years of my life." Mr. Hereck had as a fellow-passenger, Mr. W. P. Barrett, who was a member of Mr. E. J. Turner's Composition class, and whose destination was Düsseldorf, where he is taking up an appointment.

A book which all College men should get and read is "Shakespeare's Life and Work," by F. J. Furnivall, M.A., Ph.D., D.Litt., one of our Founders, and John Munro, student of this College, recently published by Cassell and Co., Ltd., at 9d. net, in cloth. Its chapters tell the tale of Shakspere's parents, boyhood, education, marriage, and departure from Stratford; of Shakspere's London; of the development of his Works and their succession, and their four periods; of the Doctor's experience in Shakspere work; Shakspere revealed in his works; continuation of his biography; his will, tomb, and descendants; and of English drama before Shakspere. Some of the chapters are written by Dr. Furnivall, others by Munro, and others again by them jointly. In the appendix is Munro's synopsis of Shakspere's Life, metrical tables, and index of bibliography. The book forms a very valuable and interesting guide to the student of Shakspere.

Mr. A. E. Shipley, M.A., F.R.S., Fellow of Christ's College, who has so often and so kindly entertained parties of College men on the occasions of the annual visits to Cambridge, is the author of "Pearls and Parasites, a series of essays on Scientific Subjects," recently published in demy octavo, with illustrations, at 7s. 6d. net.

On October 13th, Mr. W. J. Read, of the National Union of Clerks, opened a discussion in room 24 at the College, on "Should clerks be trade unionists?"

W. M. C. MUSICAL SOCIETY.

OCTOBER 8th, 1908, will live in our memory—a red-letter day. In addition to forming an Orchestral Society, we had delivered to us our new grand piano, by Pleyel. This is *history*.

In 1899, through the goodness of Mr. R. H. Marks, we bought our Broadwood pianette, which put us in a position of independence. Until then we were under a pleasant obligation, first to Miss Hutchings, and then to Mr. Cole's nephew, for the loan of a piano ; and on great occasions—*i.e.,* ladies' nights—our old accounts show that we were forced to hire one. When the debt on the Broadwood had been repaid, we commenced to form a depreciation fund, which, in the 1907 accounts, had risen to £21. This spring we made a determined effort to materially augment that. A sixpenny concert was given in its aid, the dance committee organized a special "foot shuffle," and a series of generous donations raised the princely sum of £57 8s. We were now in the market, and the point discussed was whether we should cut our coat according to our cloth, or mortgage our future, borrow some more cloth, and so get "a thing of beauty and a joy for ever." After much deliberation, we chose the bolder course. Heroically we resisted the blandishments of low-priced second-hand grands, borrowed £30 from the Executive Committee, and purchased a 120 guinea "Pleyel" short Grand. We have promised to repay this loan in three years, so we rely on the loyalty of our members to enable us to do so. It is almost certain that when Tarr or Victor Homewood coax forth the dulcet tones of the treble and the sonorous sounds from the bass, the heart of the stoniest will melt, and unloosing his purse-strings, he will pour into our depleted coffers the thank-offerings of a contented soul. We owe £30; we have in hand about £7 10s., which will be required to launch the Orchestral Society.   C. H. PERRY.

The piano now in the Coffee Room is for sale. Offers should be made to any member of the Musical Society committee, or to their secretaries, Victor Homewood and F. E. Lawrence.

The following further subscriptions to the Piano Fund have been received :—

	£	s.	d.		£	s.	d.
R. H. Marks	1	0	0	M. Staal	0	1	0
J. F. Frewer	0	1	0	W. J. Hill	0	2	6
The Dance Committee ...	0	4	0	Leonard Pocock	1	1	0

F. E. LAWRENCE.

ORCHESTRAL SOCIETY.
(BRANCH OF THE W.M.C. MUSICAL SOCIETY.)

ON Thursday, October 8th, at a well-attended meeting, it was resolved to form an Orchestra. Mr. S. de Jastrzebski, in his introductory speech, pointed out that our College should possess an orchestra, and it was his deep regret that though his early musical training had been wide, it had not included an orchestral instrument. He said quite truly that a jew's harp, a zither, and a "family piano," have no place in a well-regulated and self-respecting band ; and till a revolution in his family prevented his playing the first four bars of the "Carnival of Venice" for the 2000th time—the air painfully picked out without any accompaniment—this had formed his instrumental experience, but he had much pleasure in doing all he could to form an orchestra. Resolutions were passed calling one into being, and deciding that the subscription should be 2s. 6d. per session for men, to include membership of the Musical Society, and 1s. 6d. for ladies, the latter being subject to the permission of the Executive. Mr. L. Read was elected as secretary, and Messrs. Watson, Dundas, Mason Tarr, William Tarr, and C. H. Perry were elected as the committee. The committee at this first meeting appointed Messrs. Mason and William Tarr to act as joint conductors ; and it is hoped that by the time this appears in print we shall have had our first rehearsal, fixed for October 29th, with William Tarr, conductor. Our ideal is Beethoven's C Minor Symphony, but we shall first play other music.   C. H. PERRY.

MUSICAL SOCIETY'S CONCERT.

UNDER the chairmanship of our old College friend Pocock, the 125th concert was held on September 26th, in the Maurice Hall. Whether it was owing to the lengthened summer weather, or to the habit our audience have of coming behind time, the fact remains that the start had to be delayed some twenty minutes. Then our old friend Tyler, now secretary and conductor of the Glee Club, started the evening with a pianoforte solo from "Poet and Peasant," which was very ably rendered. By singing "Nita Gitana," Mr. W. Hagerty made his debût to an audience in the Hall. To the College men his was a familiar figure ; the "smokers" have known him long. Miss Margaret Warren, daughter of that very old College friend of geological fame, next very sweetly sang "The better land." This was her first appearance at our concerts ; we trust she will come again. Our Lawrence's brother, Mr. Gerald Lawrence, spared us an evening out of his many engagements, and sang to us in very sweet tenor, "For Remembrance," and as an encore "'Tis the Day." A young lady friend of ours, but very old friend of the College, Miss Bromhall, who has delighted us so often in the past, charmed us again with a very laughable monologue, "Her Wedding Day." More was demanded, and "Shopping, or the gentle art of making up one's mind," stirred the audience once more. The long and loud applause was sufficient sign that Miss Bromhall had recaptured the hearts of her audience. Gounod's grand "Lend me your aid," was very feelingly rendered by Tyler. Our old favourite, Miss Phœbe Craib, came once more to us, and sang very, very sweetly "The Fairy's Lullaby." One song from Miss Craib was quite insufficient, so we were treated to another—one that we have so often heard, and yet that is just as new to us as ever, "My curly-headed Babby." Our old friend Oberst very kindly came at very short notice, and sang to us "The Lute Player." We always look forward to his performance with anticipation of pleasure, and on this occasion we were not disappointed. It's not to be wondered at that "Riggles" insisted on leaving his song on the programme as "selected," for he had the audacity to dig up "Longshoreman Billy." This was much appreciated, however, and the gallery wanted more, but Riggles declined.

The CHAIRMAN : This is the 125th concert of the Working Men's College Musical Society, one of the largest and most important—some say, *the* largest and most important—society or club in the College. We of the Musical Society, however, know that all branches of the College work are of equal importance ; we know that all branches of that noble tree bear their fruit in due season, and we know how we depend upon and derive our sustenance from the unity of the branches in the parent stem, and from the depth and strength of the roots of our foundation. Hence the members of the Musical Society, like the leaves upon the branches, move in unison, as though swayed in rhythmic cadence to the strains of music, to play their part in the maintenance of the College welfare.

The Chairman gave a kindly message from the absent president, R. H. Marks, who would be thinking of us all. He also referred to a recent happy event, the marriage of our dear friend Tom Barnard and Miss Forsythe, both of whom took part in the last concert. We valued Barnard, he said, for his kind help, always so willingly and unselfishly given, in reciting so admirably at these concerts, but we in the College valued him still more for himself, as a good comrade, as a man it was always pleasant to meet, to grasp by the hand, and talk to. We wished Mr. and Mrs. Barnard all happiness. Announcements followed, *re* formation of Orchestral Society—rally round Tyler, and buck up the Glee Club—clothing for the children's treat—piano fund still open—invite new members—hearty thanks to all helpers, especially the ladies—ten minutes interval.

William Hagerty opened the second half of the programme with a song "The Charmed Cup," and gave as an encore, "Farewell." We trust he doesn't mean it. Miss Warren charmed us with "If I built a world for you." "Love, could I only tell thee" was very pleasingly rendered by Mr. Gerald Lawrence. Miss Bromhall gave us a very touching little story, "Harry, a story of the Soudan War." As an encore, she dried our tears with "The Matinée Hat." "Tommy Lad" was very grandly sung by Tyler. Like the singing of the birds in spring, came the "Violet Girl," by Miss Craib, and as an encore "Vanity Fair." Oberst brought down the house with his splendid rendering of "Myrra," and further delighted us by singing "Margery Green." Another dig-up, "My Cosy Corner Girl"—"Riggles" had well estimated our taste—we thoroughly enjoyed it.

It is our very sorrowful duty to record the fact that for the first time in the history of the College, the concert was not wound up by singing "Auld lang syne." G. S. O.

SHAKESPEARE READINGS.

THE Shakespeare Readers inaugurated their season in the Common Room on Sunday, October 4th, 1908, when Ye Pleasantlie Conceited Comedie yclept "The Taming of a Shrew" was read. Fifty ladies and gentlemen came to entertain and be entertained, and it was decidedly encouraging to the committee to note that an early start could have been made, but for the lateness of one gentleman who was important to the play. Miss Steptoe sustained the rôle of Katharine, and was charming in her mimic rage, while Peck outstormed her as Petruchio. The rest were scarcely up to our usual standard, but somehow all were pleased. There was an air of festivity over the whole meeting, for we were honoured by the presence of Barnard's bride, and a small presentation was made by the regular readers to Mr. and Mrs. Barnard. For this a cheerful picture was chosen, "Poppyland," by A. M. R. King. Barnard responded on behalf of both, and humourously remarked that for once she let him do the talking. He cast about in his inimitable way for the reason or reasons for the presentation; having come to the conclusion, by way of many excursions into various backwaters appertaining to the river of love and courtship, that the real reason was that he had married Miss Forsythe, he paid her a stately Shakespearian compliment in blank verse. Of course having got so far, he was stopped by a torrent of applause. He said he was not sorry, as his throat was sore. Altogether it was a very merry evening, and we all congratulate the man whom everybody likes on marrying the woman who is liked by us all. Happy be their lot throughout their journey. May they lose none of their old friends and gain all the new ones they want to make!

In "A Winter's Tale," on October 18th, Barnard took the part of Leontes, and made a splendid reading. Prior was great as the rogue Autolycus, "littered under Mercury and picker-up of unconsidered trifles," and moreover a chanter of rhyme. Eyres was a good Camillo, Mead read well Paulina's lines, and Balson was delightful as Hermione, the much abused queen.

After the reading, the annual business meeting was held. Wallace Davis was unanimously elected to the chair, which Paterson readily vacated. He was accorded a hearty vote of thanks for his past service, which he gracefully acknowledged. Eyres, Barnard, Paterson, and Gates Fowler were chosen as committee.

The matter of cuts was discussed, and it was decided to cut as before, for reasons of time and dramatic continuity only. The lateness of the start was also brought up, and a prompt start at 7.30 was agreed to. The plays are to be chosen by the committee, and the list up to and including the Christmas reading will be published in the JOURNAL for the information of those interested. It was agreed that voluntary donations of 1s. per member, to cover the necessary outgoings for postages and occasional copies of the plays, should be accepted. Wallace Davis will be glad to receive these.

The Committee will be pleased to have new names of would-be readers down on the notice, which is always promptly posted in the corridor, and will welcome members of the College to the readings, which are held at 7.30 sharp, alternate Sundays. Alternate readings, ladies' nights. New lady readers will meet with a cordial welcome also. GATES FOWLER.

LEICESTER VAUGHAN WORKING MEN'S COLLEGE.

AN event of much interest to all our members took place on Monday, 12th October, when the new building of the Vaughan Working Men's College at Leicester was opened. The history of this college may be read in a handsome booklet printed for the occasion. It owes its origin to the same movement as our own, its founder being Canon Vaughan, a follower of Maurice. It dates from 1862, and has steadily grown in importance, the number of students of both sexes—for it admits women as well as men—being last session nearly 1600. The building just opened cost £8,500, and is both handsome and spacious, in style somewhat resembling our own. Its arrangements show great care and forethought on the part of the Committee, and especially of the Vice-Chairman, the Rev. E. Atkins, upon whose shoulders the chief burden—he would certainly not term it a burden—has fallen since Canon Vaughan's death. The opening meetings were two: one in the afternoon for friends and supporters, held in the fine lecture room at the College; the other in the evening for students, held at a large outside hall. Both were fully attended and most enthusiastic. Sir Oliver Lodge, Principal of Birmingham University, formally opened the College, and delivered a very suggestive address to the students. Among the other speakers were the Bishop of Peterborough and the Mayor of Leicester; and, as representatives of our College, the Principal, the Vice-Principal, and the Rev. J. Llewelyn Davies, D.D., a life-long friend of Canon Vaughan. There were also very cheering speeches from old students who had taken active part in the College work for many years; one of them had been Mayor of Leicester. It was made abundantly clear that what we term with pride the College spirit, lives and thrives equally among our friends of the Vaughan Working Men's College. We wish it continued success and a long course of happy usefulness on the lines that it has made its own.

L. J.

FORMAL REPORT.

The handsome new building of the Leicester Working Men's College, which was founded by the Rev. Canon Vaughan in 1862, was opened by Sir Oliver Lodge, Principal of the Birmingham University, on October 12th. Among those present, besides many influential local friends, were the Mayor and Mayoress of Leicester, the Bishop of Peterborough, Lady Mary Glyn, General Sir Luther Vaughan, G.C.B., and Lady Vaughan; Professor A. V. Dicey, Principal, Working Men's College, Mr. Lionel Jacob, Vice-Principal, Working Men's College; Mrs. Margaret Vaughan, and the Rev. E. Atkins. Mr. A. W. Faire, J.P., presided. Sir Oliver Lodge, in the course of his address, suggested that perhaps the governing body of the College might ultimately be able to separate the youthful element from the adult element, by leaving the former to the Education Committee, so that the College would be more for working men and women of mature age. The object of the institution was of the highest kind—to give every man his chance in life. Those who founded institutions like these, dreamt dreams and saw visions, and now we realized to some extent their ideals. David James Vaughan was one of those men who saw far in advance of his time, his motto being "Sirs, ye are Brethren." The Rev. J. Llewelyn Davies said, the late Canon Vaughan was for over sixty years his loved and honoured friend. The Leicester College was a worthy daughter of the London Working Men's College, in the foundation of which he had the honour of bearing a humble part. Professor A. V Dicey spoke of the value of such institutions, in awakening a sort of *esprit de corps* comparable to that which was attained at the Universities.

At the evening meeting held in the Association Hall, the Mayor in the chair, Sir Oliver Lodge gave an address to the Students, Teachers, and Friends of the College; and at the conclusion of it, Professor Dicey moved a hearty vote of thanks to Sir Oliver Lodge, which was seconded by the Rev. J. D. Carnegie (who referred appreciatively to the work done by Mr. Atkins for the College), and was carried with applause. Mr. Lionel Jacob proposed the following resolution, which was seconded by Mr. A. W. Faire, J.P., and carried by acclamation:—"That this meeting of students, teachers, and friends of the Vaughan Working Men's College, on the occasion of the formal opening of the new building, recognizes with reverent gratitude the great work inaugurated by the late David James Vaughan, D.D., and presided over by him until his death in 1905; and further, in commending the work to be carried on in the new College to the working men and women of Leicester, earnestly hopes that the traditions he so ardently cherished may be maintained."

The cost of the new building and site was about £8,500, of which £1,600 has yet to be raised. The main entrance is in Great Central Street.

LUBBOCK FIELD CLUB.

A WEEK of brilliant summerlike weather, combined with the promise of blackberries, brought out a record party on October 11th, no fewer than twenty-three men putting in an appearance. Clandon was the starting point, and we followed the road south as far as the New Park, where we turned off to East Clandon across the fields. On reaching the road, a long wait was necessary to collect the crowd before crossing the Downs, owing to the blackberries occurring too early in the day. On reaching the training ground on Clandon Downs, we diverged to the west and followed the edge of Netherlands Wood, to the top of the hill above Sherborne Farm. After a halt to admire the view, we descended to the road and walked into Shere, where we stopped at the "White Horse" for lunch. Keeping south of the Tillingbourne, we then skirted Albury Park to Albury Heath, and turning north, returned to the Silent Pool, where we spent some time in the cool before climbing the 350 feet to the top of the Downs again. Once on top, we slowly made our way through the brambles towards Newlands Corner, where we had a long halt to collect our scattered forces and allow the glorious prospect to soak into us. The arrival of autumn had made little impression on the aspect of the country, but the heavy mists that collected in the valleys as the sun sank impressed on us the fact that the summer was over. Still, whatever the season, one can never tire of the view from Newlands Corner, extending from Leith Hill to Hindhead, with the picturesque chapel of St. Martha perched just below. Reluctantly we turned north along the road, and in due course found ourselves in the 5.55 train, homeward bound. The distance walked was about twelve miles, and nothing of special note was encountered, even the much advertised blackberries being scarcely worth the trouble of collecting.

The November walk will take place on the 8th, when it is hoped and expected that the autumn tints will be in all their beauty. Burnham Beeches and Clieveden will be the objectives, and Beaconsfield the starting point. Take pedestrian tour ticket No. 1, out to Beaconsfield and back from Slough, 1s. 11d. Train leaves Paddington at 9.23; provide lunch.

J. HOLLOWAY, *Hon. Secretary.*

W.M.C. DEBATING SOCIETY.

THE Debating Society has started on its old course with renewed vigour ; Stagg as president has not made a speech to mar his perfect impartiality, while even the inexorable bell seems to have acquired a politer tone. Of the old stagers none are missing, although with the exception of Lupton, Scoffham, Hayward, Randall, and "Bill" Perry, most of the talking has been left to the newcomers. The new blood is the feature of the session so far. Of the twenty-five who have joined, quite half are militant, and the names of Topping, Peyton, Newlove, Foy, and Marten, will be household words ere long. And there is Ewer, who says "hear, hear," when he is contradicted, and argues the point even unto the eleventh hour, and Barlow whose only fault is that he has failed to follow up his first success. The subjects have been as follows :—

September 29th.—"That our national safety requires the assumption that Germany is preparing for war with England." A S. Lupton, M.A., opener ; J. A. Barlow, M.A., opposer. Carried.

October 6th. —"That it is the duty of the community to so organise industry as to provide work for every man and woman competent and willing." Councillor J. H. Harley (I.L.P., St. Pancras), opener ; W. H. Scoffham. opposer. Carried, 54 to 16. Eight new members joined.

October 13th.—"That the Government can and should establish a minimum living wage and a maximum working day in all industries." W. Topping, opener ; W. H. Foy, opposer. Carried, 33 to 10. Three new members joined.

October 20th.—"That Mr. Haldane's Territorial Scheme has failed of its object." Theodore Morison, M.A., opener ; Captain Abell, opposer. Carried 21 votes to 19.

October 27th.—"That this House deplores the attitude of the British people towards the political aspirations of their Asiatic fellow-subjects." Opener, Mr. W. N. Ewer, B.A.

FURNIVALL SCULLING CLUB.

THE winter sculling season started on Sunday, 4th October. The summer-like weather, and the fact that the tide served us badly, were no doubt responsible for the poor turn-out, only the Doctor, Miss K. Harris, and Owen, West, Allen, Brown, and Howard essaying the pull to Richmond. The half-yearly general meeting was held in the evening. Dr. Furnivall opened with a retrospect of the season's doings, soundly rating members for not braving adverse tides to join him at Kingston on the summer Sundays, though he recognized the advantages that the girls claimed for the well-shaded Eel Pie Island at Twickenham. The hon. secretary and the hon. caterer then presented their cash statements, both showing a balance on the right side. The club now keeps up an average membership of 100, the men slightly preponderating. College men and, of course, their lady friends, are reminded that the club can easily accommodate fifty more members. Then came a batch of resignations—Miss Moulden from the captaincy, Richardson from the commissariat department, and Howard from the secretaryship. After the meeting had recorded its thanks to these officers for their past services, the following members were appointed in their places— Miss C. Clements, captain, H. Manton, caterer ; and that much-occupied man, W. Melzer, hon. secretary. Should a Collegian complain that the Common Room is not all it should be, will he please remember that Custodian Melzer is worrying the Furnivall Sculling Club for arrears of subscriptions. Should a member of the Cycling Club find his last puncture unrecorded by Melzer in the JOURNAL, let him not forget that his secretary has probably been distraining on the Furnivall Sculling Club's (men's section) "shorts" and "sweaters," for unpaid locker rents. The greater part of the general meeting's time was taken up in formulating new club rules consonant with the requirements of the club registrar, for the club had decided to register at its previous general meeting. Before many months are over, members will have become shareholders, and the committee the directorate, of the Furnivall Sculling Club, Limited.   H. S. HOWARD, *late Hon. Secretary.*

THE COLLEGE AT THE FRANCO-BRITISH.

THE College excursion, at Sir Charles Lucas's invitation, to the Franco-British Exhibition, took place on Saturday, September 19th.

The party met Mr. Duchesne in the Science Section at 3.30, and proceeded to the Western Australian Court, where they were met by Mr. A. Gibb Maitland, a government geologist from Western Australia, who conducted them over the Court. They were first supplied with catalogues, etc., and then Mr. Maitland proceeded to explain the mineral section to them. Gold, he said, was well represented, both by nuggets and by ores of various kinds. A remarkable set of nuggets are the three known as the Commonwealth, which is the shape of Australia; the map of England nugget and the map of France nugget, also shaped as implied by their names. Remarkable nuggets, specimens of kaolin containing gold, jasper, tin and copper ores, and asbestos, were examined, also some interesting photographs of a native red-ochre mine, known as the "Welgi mia" (War paint) Mine, in the Weld Range, Murchison. The red ochre, a pure hœmatite, an iron ore, was mined by the natives with sharp-pointed sticks, and they used it to ornament their bodies. Mr. Maitland showed us, with the aid of a map, the principal geological features of the country, the Kalgoorlie water supply, and the one coal-field, at Collie, in the south west. Many other objects of interest were inspected, before we thanked Mr. Maitland for his kindness, and dispersed in search of tea and to view the other wonders of the Exhibition. Some of us went with Mr. J. F. N. Green to the Science Section, where he explained the more interesting exhibits.

W. A. HERRON.

MAURICE CHESS CLUB.

THE season's matches are arranged: twenty-seven to be played in all—nineteen friendlies, and eight "C" Division City of London League matches.

Of the league matches, two are down for decision at home, Fulham C. C. and Harlesden C. C., kindly consenting to play at the College. Hitherto no League matches have taken place at the College, so even with only two matches we may consider the result of our venture very satisfactory. Nine friendlies also are to be played at home.

Two home-and-home matches have been arranged with Trinity College, Cambridge, the one at Cambridge to take place on November 14th. Negotiations failed to bring about home-and-home matches with University College, Gower Street, the fixtures clashing.

The course of the friendly matches up to the present has been very "unfriendly" to us, we having lost to Claremont C. C., 6 to 4, and to Highbury C. C., 4½ to 3½; but we hope to regain the ground.

The result of our first league match against Hampstead, to whom we lost 8 to nil—all defaults, last time, is very favourable: the following is the score:—

Hampstead.			Maurice.		
1. E. Wiltshire	...	½	—	A. E. Thomas ...	½
2. P. H. Williams	...	0	—	J. W. Hammant ...	1
*3. E. Haselden	...	0	—	O. Henke ...	0
4. A. A. Richards	..	½	—	V. Ray ...	½
5. H. G. Dash	...	0	—	J. F. Halford ...	1
6. J. A. Shaw	...	0	—	O. Ray ...	1
7. J. E. Baxter	...	1	—	W. Fulton ...	0
8. A. C. E. Hughes	...	1	—	R. Levitt ...	0
		3			4

*Board 3 to be adjudicated.   J. FOLEY, *Hon. Secretary and Treasurer.*

SATURDAY NIGHT LECTURES.

SIR STAMFORD RAFFLES, FOUNDER OF SINGAPORE.

THE first Saturday evening lecture of the term was delivered by Sir Frank Swettenham, K.C.M.G., on October 3rd, when the chair was taken by Mr. C. A. Harris, C.B., and the audience, though somewhat small, was appreciative and much interested. The following report of the lecture appeared in the *Times* :—

SIR F. SWETTENHAM expressed the opinion that "Raffles was one of the greatest Englishmen who ever lived, and said that although people in this country appeared to know little of him, his name was a household word in Singapore, and was held in the highest respect by the Malays, whom he dearly loved. The son of a captain in the West India trade, he was born at sea off Jamaica on July 5th, 1781. A visit which he paid to Calcutta in 1810 was the turning-point in his career. Acting on his advice, and with his active co-operation, Lord Minto fitted out an expedition with the object of capturing Java from the Dutch. The enterprise, singularly well planned and brilliantly executed, resulted in the conquest of an empire and its addition to British territory. Appointed Lieutenant-Governor, Raffles ably conducted his administration for $4\frac{1}{2}$ years, abolishing slavery and conciliating the native princes. On the restoration of Java to the Dutch in 1816, Raffles was relieved from his post, and left Java for England, to the regret of all classes. In England he was knighted, a reward so singularly inadequate to the services rendered, that the Prince Regent himself remarked upon the fact. Afterwards he was given charge of the East India Company's station in Bencoolen, on the Sumatra Coast, with the title of Lieutenant-Governor. Proceeding thence to Calcutta, he unfolded a plan to Lord Hastings for forming a settlement in the island of Singapore ; and, notwithstanding much opposition in various quarters, succeeded in laying firmly the foundation of good government there. He visited the island three times. When he finally left it in June, 1823, its success was assured, and Raffles had achieved the great object of his life, and had done something to counterbalance the loss of Java. Between the foundation of Singapore and Raffles's final departure from the Far East, this man of many parts and framer of great schemes suffered many trials. In 1824 illness drove him back to England. On the voyage the vessel took fire, and Raffles thus lost a valuable scientific collection and most of his other effects. In England he founded and became first president of the Zoological Society, London, for the collection of living specimens, in Regent's Park. In 1826 the East India Company called upon him to refund a sum of over £22,000, salaries and interest thereon for ten years ; and almost at the same moment he heard of the failure of a great Indian house of business, by which he lost £16,000. These misfortunes and demands were more than he could bear, and he died suddenly on July 5th, 1826, at the early age of 46. It was to this ardent patriot, who had conceived a great dislike for Dutch forms of administration, that the British Empire owed its possession of Singapore, the emporium of Southern Asia and the Indian Archipelago."

THE WORKING MEN'S COLLEGE JOURNAL *is supported partly by Annual Subscribers living in different parts of the World, and partly by circulation among the Students and Members. Its success depends upon a regular demand, and to ensure this, the Editor would be glad if as many readers as can will become Subscribers. Subscription* 2s. 6d. *per annum, post free.*

LONDON: Printed by W. HUDSON & Co., Red Lion Street, High Holborn, and published at THE WORKING MEN'S COLLEGE, Crowndale Road, London, N.W.—November 1st, 1908.

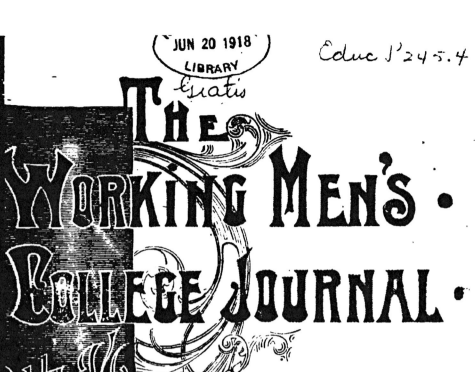

THE WORKING MEN'S · COLLEGE JOURNAL ·

Pub: N

The Working Men's College
Crowndale Road.
St Pancras
London·N·W·
Founded
in 1854
By the late
Frederick
Denison
Maurice·

Contents for

DECEMBER, 1908

An Educated Man
Marks Prize Essay
College Notes
Common Room
Old Students' Club
Saturday Night
         Lectures

THE

𝔚orking 𝔐en's 𝔆ollege 𝔍ournal.

Conducted by Members of the Working Men's College
Crowndale Road, London, N.W.

Vol. X.—No. 188.   DECEMBER, 1908.   Price Twopence.

STUDENTS AND TEACHERS' MEETING.

WHAT IS AN EDUCATED MAN?
(Concluded.)

MY second point is to indicate how this may be accomplished. Professor Michael Sadler, in an address given to a Co-operative Congress here some months ago, defined education as "the Science of Social Service," and pointed out that the object of all true social service was to ensure that progress was made in all the conditions under which we live and move and have our being. Now, we are very apt, I fear, to look upon human progress as something automatic, mechanical, or even inevitable; whereas in truth it is an uncertain procedure, liable to stop or even to retrograde, dependent entirely upon the intelligent co-operation of men with the powers and forces all around them. The extraordinary material developments of recent years have given us this idea of the inevitableness of progress; discovery follows upon discovery, invention upon invention, until we get so bewildered and impressed by the increase of material prosperity and facilities, that we lose sight of the fact that there are factors in real progress other than those appertaining to physical and mechanical science, and we need the reminder that if we neglect these, we do so at our peril. Material prosperity is by itself no guarantee either of real progress or stability, as the fates of Rome and of Spain are sufficient to convince us. Now, for any man to attempt to co-operate with or to control these forces by which he is surrounded, without having first learnt something about them is, I aver, simply to court disaster. We British have long been noted for our belief in the policy of "muddling through"; we have often—too often—trusted in our luck, but we may do so once too often, and then it will be useless to repine. Disaster— I do not mean in war only—may overtake us, so complete as to be irreparable; and unless we do our best to put our house in order, the only thing posterity will be able to say is, "Serve them right." Now, in this matter of education, I want you first of all to draw a distinction between an educated man and a scholar. Many of us have neither the time nor the ability to become the latter, but for our comfort let it be known firstly that given the determination, almost everyone nowadays may be truly educated, and secondly that a scholar is not necessarily a really educated man. You have met, and so have I, men who upon some subjects were profoundly learned, whilst upon others, vitally important in everyday life, they have exhibited a child's ignorance, without the child's curiosity. A scholar is often merely a specialist, with all a specialist's defects and limitations. So do not let the idea of the impossibility of your ever becoming a scholar depress you, or prevent you from trying to become an educated man. It would, I think, be a bad day for us all, if everyone could claim to be a scholar. I will now assume that at any rate you have each so trained, or will so train your powers of observation and memory, that you will grasp and retain those facts which come under your notice, either in the world around you or in the books you read. A distinguished German teacher has asserted that the powers of observation and memory in average boys and girls can so be trained that, as far as ordinary school work is concerned, books are a luxury in which it is needless to indulge, and that oral teaching is all that is required. I mention this, not because I wish to urge you to rely only upon the oral teaching in this College, but merely to illustrate what seem to be the potential capabilities of the human mind in this respect, if properly trained.

What subjects, then, do I think requisite to educate a man? Well, in the very fore-front I put a subject which is not, I am sorry to say, very popular in this College—History, and after it —Science. If it be admitted that the part we play in life is controlled partly by the men who have lived before us and those who are living with us, and partly by great natural forces, some of which we can control by obeying the laws which govern them, others of which however seem at present entirely beyond that control—it follows that history, as the knowledge of how man individually and collectively has become what he is, and science, as the knowledge of nature and its processes, are indispensable in any scheme of real education. By history, I do not mean English history only—it is not enough to realize how we have become a nation, how our present state of government and society has been slowly and painfully formed; we must also learn how other nations have grown, why some of those who have held positions very similar to our own have lost most of what they had, and some have wholly disappeared. History thus studied will teach us what mistakes others have committed, and also how we may avoid errors of the same kind. In our own history, you will learn how many things, which we now regard as intolerable abuses, have grown up and into our social fabric; you will realize from that, how hard and slow a business it must be to remove these things, and also you will see that patience, as well as zeal, is more necessary than perhaps you have been inclined hitherto to allow. In the words of one of the students of Ruskin College, you ought then to say : "Already the training we have received here seems to have broadened our views. As a main result there has been a revelation of the things we do not know. It has come somewhat in the nature of a shock to most of us, that there are two sides to every question—even to the fiscal controversy." Such a student has at any rate taken the first step in the path of knowledge. Then, as to science : here I do not urge that an ordinary man could or should attempt completely to master even one of the divisions of that vast realm of knowledge we call science, but what I do assert is that every man should attain some clear conception of what science has accomplished and is accomplishing, that he should strive to grasp what the scientific method is, and that he should take up the serious study of some one science. What a wonderful world will then be revealed to him ; what a different appearance will be worn by many of those things which we are apt to regard even with indifference ! Consider for one minute the triumphs of electricity, and imagine, if you can, how a knowledge of the principles and methods of this science will cause you to appreciate at their true value the manifold uses to which electricity is now put. Or take chemistry—where in the realm of fiction is there anything more fascinating than in the discoveries and predictions of this science? Do you not remember how a Russian chemist predicted, not long ago, as the result of his investigations into the atomic composition of matter, that certain substances, whose very existence had not then been ascertained, would be eventually discovered? How, moreover, he prepared a table assigning these unknown bodies their proper place in what we used to call the elements of which the material globe is composed? How some of those then unknown bodies have since been discovered, and found to correspond with his prediction? Further, he asserted that all forms of matter were in essence one, differing only in the arrangement of their constituent atoms, and that in his judgment methods would be found whereby one substance could be transmuted into another; this prediction Sir W. Ramsay a few weeks ago justified, by announcing that he had succeeded in turning silver into copper. I say a man who has realized these things, and the methods by which they are attained, must have a wider outlook upon the world in general, a saner appreciation of the realm of nature, and a vastly increased capacity for gauging the direction in which human progress is likely to proceed.

Finally, an educated man should have some real knowledge and understanding of those things which, lying outside the province of history and science, have stirred the imagination and emotions of the world. Music, poetry, art, and literature, one at least of these should be taken up by an educated man. "The man that hath not music, That is not stirred with concord of sweet sound, Is fit for treasons, stratagems and spoils—Let no such man be trusted." That perhaps is going rather far, for I have known most excellent persons upon whom neither the most fearsome discord, nor the most lovely harmony has any effect whatever; but the root idea is sound, for the man whose imagination can be stirred by neither music, poetry, art, nor literature is a cold-blooded individual, capable of any villainy.

You may think the programme I have sketched a wide one, almost an impossible one for those whose time is so largely occupied in what is quaintly called "making a living." It is not so large as it seems. It is not necessary to read and study a large number of books; what is imperative is that those books should be of the best. Two things I would urge as practical advice: first, be content with nothing less than the best, to lay the foundations of your education firm and broad; secondly, remember that education is, like all other good things, a thing that should end only with your life; and when you have laid your foundations, see that you continue to build a superstructure worthy of that foundation, and worthy of that citizenship to which you as Englishmen have been and are being called.

To sum up, I will repeat: An educated man need not be a scholar—he must have a sound knowledge (1) of the history of mankind and its progress; (2) of the methods and aims of science as a whole, and of some one branch of science in particular; (3) of one at least of those products of human genius which stir the imagination and influence the emotions. To accomplish this, he need not read much, but he must read the best; he must set himself a high ideal; he must recognize that this is no task to be entered upon in a careless and light-hearted manner, but one that needs all the determination and grit of which he is capable.

Cato began to learn Greek when he was 80; and Lord Brassey stated the other day that when he was 73, he had commenced to learn German. If these two distinguished men did not consider their education completed at these late periods of their lives, I see no reason why we should not feel equally dissatisfied, and determine to remedy our defects.

Finally, let me commend to you Bacon's dictum—"*Reading* maketh a full man; *writing*, an exact man; *speaking*, a ready man."

I am only too conscious that I have said nothing new, it has all been very trite and commonplace; my only comfort is that the statement of even the trite and commonplace is not always entirely without value.

The hearty cheering that arose, when Mr. Duchesne finished his paper, showed how keenly it was appreciated. In response to the chairman's invitation for remarks upon the subject, Munro pointed out the disabilities under which the working-man of to-day laboured in the pursuit of knowledge.

Starling announced that the meeting purposed giving itself up to the pursuit of Orpheus, and an excellent smoking concert followed. Haynes began it, at the piano. Then came S. A. Sweetman, with "Father O'Flynn"; McLatter, "Out of the night"; M. K. Field, "The Admiral's Broom"; Tom Barnard, "Evans's Dog Hospital" (Charles Pond), encore, "Nina, Ninette, Ninon"; Hammant, "Ho! Jolly Jenkin"; Wolsey, "Drinking"; W. Hagerty, "Thora"; J. Perry, "My First Smoke," recitation; E. C. Duchesne, "The Animal's Band"; "Auld Lang Syne."

THE MARKS PRIZE ESSAY, 1908.

SHAKESPEARE'S VIEWS ON DEMOCRACY.
(*Concluded.*)

THE most important moral of the play is, we think, contained in Act 3, which indicates very plainly Shakespeare's views concerning government. Coriolanus reiterates the opinion that the aristocracy is created to govern, while the utterances of Menenius and Cominius, in Scenes 1 and 3, and Volumnia in Scene 2, suggest the means by which the power should be exercised. Briefly stated, the dramatist is of opinion that it is safer to temper aristocratic power with kind words, even if they contain an empty meaning. Such a policy will strengthen the governing class, and democracy is not so likely to revolt.

III. CHARACTER OF DEMOCRATIC LEADERS.—The manner in which Shakespeare delineates the characters of the tribunes furnishes another example of his attitude. Throughout the play Sicinius Velutus and Junius Brutus are continually depicted as vulgar demagogues, whose envious and malignant nature merely excites the people against the upper classes.* They spread false and exaggerated reports simply to stir popular sentiment, and enrich themselves at the people's cost.† One passionate disciple of Shakespeare writes them down as "mean in motive and deficient in capacity, yet *astute enough* to undermine the popularity of Coriolanus!"‡ On the other hand, a writer of some repute, in attempting to defend the dramatist as sympathetic to democracy, insists that the tribunes are presented as straightforward and clearheaded.§ Let their methods and utterances decide which of these opinions is most in harmony with the views of Shakespeare.

During an effort to restrain the mutinous citizens (Act 1, Scene 1), Menenius draws a comparison between the plebeian complaint against the senate and the "rebellion of *all* the body's members against the belly." He attempts to show that just as the stomach performs a service to the human body, although its activity may not be apparent, so the patricians discharge an equally important function in the body politic. Revolt against the belly or the patricians will be equally disastrous. The analogy would be more correct, had Menenius proceeded to show that, when the stomach does not

* "Shakespeare—Characters." By C. C. Clarke.
† "What is Shakespeare?" By L. A. Sherman.
‡ "William Shakespeare: his Life, his Works, his Teaching." By G. W. Rusden.
§ "Ten plays of Shakespeare." By S. A. Brooke.

function properly, some inducement has to be applied   By withholding the distribution of food, as provided by law, the patricians were not performing their proper function.   Shakespeare ignores this aspect of the case,[9] and instead, makes Menenius rebuke the leader of the mutineers :—

> *Menenius.*   What do you think,
> You, the great toe of this assembly ?
> *First Cit.*   I the great toe !   Why the great toe ?
> *Menenius.*   For that, being one o' the lowest, basest, poorest,
> Of this most wise rebellion, thou go'st foremost :
> Thou rascal, that art worst in blood to run,
> Lead'st first to win some vantage !

We are first introduced to the tribunes Sicinius and Brutus in Act 2, when Menenius is discussing with them the fortunes of the Roman Army against the Volsces.   Menenius admits the people do not like Marcius.   The tribunes concur, and when pressed give their reasons.   In the ensuing dialogue is given the first intimation of their characters.

> *Menenius.*   You blame Marcius for being proud ?
> *Brutus.*   We do it not alone, sir.
> *Menenius.*   I know you can do very little alone ; for your helps are many, or else your actions would grow wondrous single : your abilities are too infant-like, for doing much alone.   You talk of pride : Oh ! that you could turn your eyes towards the napes of your necks, and make but an interior survey of your good selves !   Oh ! that you could !
> *Brutus.*   What then, sir ?
> *Menenius.*   Why, then you should discover a brace of unmeriting, proud, violent, testy magistrates—alias fools—as any in Rome.

The tribunes, knowing that he is by repute a "humorous patrician," control their irritation, although Menenius punctuates his humour with the assurance that—

> What I think, I utter ; and
> Spend my malice in my breath.

As soon as Sicinius and Brutus hear that the senate desires to appoint Coriolanus consul, they decide to employ his contempt for the plebeians in order to kindle their antagonism against him.   This done, they will select an opportunity,

> When his soaring insolence
> Shall reach the people—which time shall not want,
> If he be put upon 't ; and that's as easy
> As to set dogs on sheep—will be his fire
> To kindle their dry stubble ; and their blaze
> Shall darken him for ever.   (Act 2, Scene 1).

The character of the tribunes is again exhibited, when they meet the citizens after Coriolanus has been accepted as consul.   Their advice to the people to remind the consul of his attitude towards the lower ranks had not been observed, although he received them mockingly. The reproach of the tribunes for their "childish friendliness" causes the citizens to regret their action.   Sicinius and Brutus play upon

---

[9] Is it not rather *Menenius* who ignores it ?   Of course, *he* would.— F. M. C.

My point was that Shakespeare recognized that the story of the "rebellious members" breaks down when pursued to its logical conclusion. The dramatist only recognized that aspect which makes the patricians omnipotent.   To have held an even balance, one of the plebeians should have spoken the other view.—J. G. N.

this, and persuade them to revoke their consent. In order to shield themselves from the suspicion of instigating this action, the tribunes add dishonesty to their other qualities of intrigue. They tell the people to declare that they only supported Coriolanus, because the tribunes advised them to do so. On his way to the market place to complete the ceremonies of election, Coriolanus is met by the tribunes, who inform him of the changed attitude of the people. When he accuses them of being responsible for it, Brutus attempts to evade the charge by pleading surprise. They goad him to wrath, in order that he may more quickly displease the people. Their plans succeed, and in Act 3, Scene 1, we are given a description of the conflict. The language of the tribunes is certainly not what we should expect from responsible leaders of men, more especially from those whose supposed purpose it is to excite the anger of another. Scene 3 of the same act opens with the tribunes pursuing their policy of playing upon the temper of Coriolanus. Thus—

> *Brutus.* Put him to the choler straight. He hath been us'd
> Ever to conquer, and to have his worth
> Of contradiction : being once chaf'd, he cannot
> Be rein'd again to temperance ; then he speaks
> What's in his heart ; and that is there which looks
> With us to break his neck.

Coriolanus is quickly roused ; the citizens are easily fired ; and despite the intercession of Menenius and Cominius, they decide to banish the man whom but a short time ago they had chosen consul.

Yet another side to the character of the tribunes is depicted after the expulsion of Coriolanus :—

> *Brutus.* Now we have shown our power,
> Let us seem humbler after it is done
> Than when it was a-doing. (Act 4, Scene 2).

This would suggest that the welfare of the people was only used as a means for them to exhibit their own importance.

Having been driven from Rome, Coriolanus leagues with his enemies, the Volsces, to destroy his country. The people become reconciled, and confident in their security, until word is brought that the Volsces, with Coriolanus at their head, are advancing against the city. In such times, responsible leaders are expected to maintain self-control, in order to gain a thorough knowledge of approaching danger. Not so Brutus and Sicinius. The former rushes into a frenzy, and orders the bearer of such tidings to be whipped, while the latter refuses to believe the report. Neither attempts to discover whether it is authentic. Menenius supplies the words of wisdom when he suggests

> Reason with the fellow,
> Before you punish him, where he heard this ;
> Lest you shall chance to whip your information,
> And beat the messenger who bids beware
> Of what is to be dreaded. (Act 4, Scene 6).

When the report becomes known, it is suggested that Coriolanus shall be asked for mercy. Who is to ask it? Cominius tells us—

> The tribunes cannot do 't for shame ; the people
> Deserve such pity of him as the wolf
> Does of the shepherds.

The tribunes are foremost in their pleading that Menenius should intercede. Finally, Coriolanus succumbs to the pleading of Volumnia, and Rome is saved.

Almost every character in the play—even down to the conspirators in the final scene—is made to expose the fickleness of the crowd.

But, with capable leaders, with leaders who are straightforward and fearless, such a shortcoming could be converted into a virtue. Such men must be different from Brutus and Sicinius.

While not prepared to accept in its entirety the sweeping conclusions of Hazlitt,[*] we certainly think the play justifies the verdict, that "there never was embodied a more perfect representation of the abstract principle of aristocratic assumption than we find delineated in the play of *Coriolanus.*"[†]

" JULIUS CÆSAR."

Although democracy is not so severely criticised in *Julius Cæsar* as in the play we have been considering, additional evidence is forthcoming in support of the view that Shakespeare was not very kindly disposed towards " the many."

The strong hand of Cæsar had made him all-powerful in Rome, and he had crushed every attempt at resistance on the part of the Pompeians. The Republic had ceased to exist except in name, and now some of his friends wished to bestow on him the title of King.

The play opens by introducing us to " a rabble of citizens," who are making holiday for the purpose of applauding Cæsar as he passes to the capitol. They are rebuked by the tribunes Flavius and Marullus, whose utterances convey a two-fold opinion of the people. Through the latter, Shakespeare brings out the fickleness of the " mob," while the admonition of Flavius illustrates how easily a few soft phrases can subdue and deceive the people. The worship of Cæsar incites the hostility of such Republicans as Marcus Brutus and Cassius, neither of whom attends the ceremony, but they obtain an account of the proceedings from Casca. Here again, the instability of democracy is illustrated. Casca recounts how Antonius thrice offered the crown to Cæsar, who was less inclined to refuse it at each offering. Commenting upon the behaviour of the people, he says :—

> If the tag-rag people did not clap him and hiss him, according as he pleased and displeased them, as they us'd to do the players in the theatre, I am no true man.   (Act 1, Scene 2).

We are not concerned here with the details and murder of Cæsar, and it is not until Act 3, Scene 2, that democracy is again noticed. It is in this scene that the famous oration of Mark Antony beginning,

> Friends, Romans, countrymen, lend me your ears ;
> I come to bury Cæsar, not to praise him—

is delivered. The conspirators have given him permission to speak to the people, after Brutus has explained the reason for the murder of Cæsar. After hearing Brutus, the citizens are unanimous in their commendation of the murder, but the eloquence and tactics of Antony completely reverse that opinion. He recalls the brave deeds of Cæsar which had made Rome great, and how he thrice refused the crown—acts which deserve some consideration now he is dead. The appeal succeeds, and one by one the citizens defend the dead Cæsar, whom a little time before they were proclaiming a tyrant. Their menacing attitude towards Antony is changed to one of reverence. He takes advantage of this to excite their imagination as to the provisions of Cæsar's will, and tests their allegiance to the conspirators, thus—

> I fear I wrong the honourable men
> Whose daggers have stabb'd Cæsar ; I do fear it.

[*] "Characters of Shakespeare's Plays." By W. Hazlitt.
[†] "Shakespeare—Characters." By C. C. Clarke.

Fourth Cit. They were traitors : honourable men !

Second Cit. They were villains, murderers. The will ! read the will.

The citizens form a ring, and Antony makes another speech over the mantle of Cæsar which enrages them :—

    First Cit. O piteous spectacle !

    Second Cit. O noble Cæsar !

    Third Cit. O woeful day !

    Fourth Cit. O traitors ! villains !

    First Cit. O most bloody sight !

    Second Cit. We will be revenged.

    All. Revenge !— About !— Seek ! - Burn !— Fire !— Kill !— Slay ! Let not a traitor live.

Then, under the plea of not wishing to incite them to mutiny, Antony fans the flames of their sentiments until they are ready to do anything to avenge the murder of Cæsar. Having succeeded in his object, Antony exclaims :—

    Now let it work ! Mischief, thou art afoot,

    Take thou what course thou wilt !

Scene 3, although short, is sufficient to illustrate another view of the popular character. The citizens lose control of themselves entirely, and commit excesses upon innocent persons. From this we infer that democracy can be encouraged to acts of a most irrational character by astute statesmen. While feeling bound to confess that such opinion is not without some foundation, we think the fault is not so much with democracy as with those men who abuse the trust it puts in them. We cannot have a new democracy, but it is not impossible to produce leaders of men who will be content to guide, instead of to deceive.

THE OTHER PLAYS provide further illustrations of Shakespeare's views of democracy. Whenever he has occasion to refer to the aristocracy, it is in terms of exaltation. The Roman patricians or English nobles are equally "pillars of the state." The Roman plebeians or the populace of England are invariably mentioned with scorn. They are presented as frivolous, incapable of considering questions affecting the interests of the state. The fact that both peer and peasant are made of the same material does not appear to concern Shakespeare very much. We get a good example of this in the second part of *Henry VI.* In Act 4, Scene 2, the rebel leader, Jack Cade, holds forth as follows :—

    .There shall be in England, seven half-penny loaves sold for a penny ; the three-hooped pot shall have ten hoops ; and I will make it felony to drink small beer. All the realm shall be in common, and in Cheapside shall my palfrey go to grass. And when I am king,—as king I will be,—

    All. God save your majesty !

    Cade. I thank you, good people : there shall be no money ; all shall eat and drink on my score ; and I will apparel them all in one livery, that they may agree like brothers, and worship me their lord.

    Dick. The first thing we do, let's kill all the lawyers.

    Cade. Nay, that I mean to do.

The murder of the clerk of Chatham because he can write, is quite a minor affair to what "the rebellious hinds, the filth and scum of Kent," intend to do with the nobility. In every scene until Cade is killed, the rebels are made to behave in a most irresponsible, one might almost say, uncivilized manner. The presentation of the Kentish rebellion is typical of Shakespeare's view of popular risings. Another example is afforded by the dialogue between the Earl of Westmoreland and the Archbishop of York, in the second part of *Henry IV.* (Act 4, Scene 1).

Another link in our chain of evidence is the manner in which the dramatist utilized his profound knowledge of English Law.* One eminent writer, after much reflection, is of opinion that his ideas of equity did not favour the cause of democracy. Nowhere in any of his writings is there a "hint of sympathy with personal rights against the sovereign, nor with parliament, then first assuming a protective attitude towards the English people."† At the time Shakespeare was writing *Henry IV.*, a severe struggle for supremacy was being fought between the Chancery Court, the favourite of the court party, and the Common Law, "with its trial by jury, the bulwark of popular rights." Through Sir John Falstaff, Shakespeare boastfully alludes to the progress of the former over the latter.

CONCLUSION.

Sufficient evidence has been adduced, we think, to support the view that Shakespeare had little sympathy with the masses, their interests, or their rights. He saw their weaknesses, but instead of suggesting means for conquering them,[10] chose to scorn and ridicule. We close our volume of Shakespeare with a feeling of disappointment that such genius was not spent in furthering the progress of the people, and open Shelley with a new hope for democracy, and all that word implies.[11]   JOHN G. NEWLOVE.

THE "MARKS" PRIZE.

THIS prize is offered, this College year, for the best essay written by a student on any one of the following subjects :—(a) Compare the state of England and of the British Empire at the beginning of the Nineteenth, and at the beginning of the Twentieth Century. (b) The Policy of Oliver Cromwell and its results. (c) The Influence of the French Revolution on English Politics. Essays are to be sent in to the Superintendent by 30th April next.

---

* "Falstaff and Equity." By C. E. Phelps.   † Ibid.

[10] This was not his business as a dramatist, surely.—F. M. C.

Shakespeare saw the weaknesses and enlarged upon them ; a friend of the people, while pointing out their shortcomings, would embody in the plays suggestions for overcoming them. - J. G. N.

[11] I think this is a good essay—clearly arranged and well written ; and showing that a good deal of trouble has been taken over it.

The subject is a very difficult one. Several points need discussion :—

(i.) The opinions put into the mouths of dramatic characters must never be attributed to the author, unless it is obvious that some character is a mere puppet through whom the author himself chooses to speak. The better the dramatist, the less he will do this, the more he will let his characters speak for themselves.

(ii.) The position and aims of democracy in Shakespeare's time were very different from what they are now. You have mentioned this at the end. I think I should have *begun* with it—a brief sketch of what "democracy" meant to Shakespeare's contemporaries.

(iii.) How far is his picture of "democracy" in *Roman* times (which again was historically a very different thing) meant to apply to Elizabethan democracy? To a large extent, I think ; but this topic ought to be briefly discussed, before inferences are drawn. Might not Brutus, the Republican, be regarded as standing for some of the things "democracy" means? I agree with your general estimate of Shakespeare's attitude ; but, as I have indicated, much of your proof seems to me irrelevant, as neglecting (i.) above.

But nothing is harder to get at than Shakespeare's own opinions on any subject—just because he is an excellent dramatist. After all, the strongest advocate of democracy might very well aim at making aristocrats seem odious, by representing them as proud and scornful ; and, further, there are at all times unscrupulous and ignorant demagogues, who deserve scorn.— F. C.

SHAKESPEARE READINGS.

SUNDAY, November 1st, was a ladies' night. A comedy was read—" As you like it," the reading being a highly successful one from every point of view. All seemed to read up to one another, and to appreciate the necessity of promptness in taking up the cue, which is the first point of a good comedy reading. Furthermore, all seemed happy in their parts, though the leading man was heard to whisper to the leading lady that he felt awkward. There was nothing, however, to show this, for Mead and Miss Steptoe made love to each other quite naturally, and Rosalind's bantering pretence with Orlando in the forest was just delicious. Barnard, as Jacques, was excellent as usual, and so " the seven ages "—those classic lines so often quoted—were well delivered, and the character of the man who pursued Melancholy as a mistress was properly brought out. For the rest, what shall we say, save that all were good, all were pleased ! Mrs. Barnard as Celia, Miss Reglar as Audrey, to the life, and her sister at the piano. To old members Paterson's Touchstone is a familiar joy, and to new ones a revelation. Hayward put a good deal of character into the small part of William, and was much appreciated. Over eighty ladies and gentlemen were present—a record for the Society.

Since writing the above, the society has had a great loss in the person of its president for the year. Mr. Wallace Davis has passed into the shadows. Suddenly in his sleep, during the night of November 4—5, the dread summons came to him. To add anything in the way of eulogy is superfluous to those who have known him, and impertinence to those who lacked the privilege. He was buried at East Finchley on November 10th. A small cross of lichen, lilies, and Parma violets was offered by the Readers, as their last tribute to their president. May he rest in peace, and light perpetual shine on him !

On November 15th, " Richard II." was the play. Barnard read the lines of the ill-starred king ; Fenton, Bolingbroke ; Mead, Aumerle ; Pryor, Northumberland ; Paterson, York. Munro read the parts of several men who had not turned up. Owing to the absence of readers, the parts were shockingly duplicated, and lack of time led to the last act being severely cut. At the conclusion of the meeting, the members present deputed Mr. Gates Fowler to express their condolence with the sisters of the late chairman. Mr. Gates Fowler was afterwards elected chairman. The readings start at 7.30 p.m., and ladies and gentlemen will doubtless make every effort to be in their places in time to start. W. J. GATES FOWLER.

HE is gone
Who lately was our Chief. Bereft
His kindly presence, patient courtesy,
The quiet welcome of his honest smile,
We feel a loss that words can ill express.
    Whether in Concert, Reading, or in talk,
In WALLACE DAVIS found we ever one
Whose genial soul and willing help did cheer'
This Common Room, wherein we nightly meet.
    From England's greatest writers had he drawn
Full store of humour and of pathos true,
With which were mixt in him a charming grace,
Offspring of sympathy and self repressed.
    Hush'd tho' his voice, still'd now his active brain,
His spirit here abides, and long by us
His loving friends, his mem'ry shall be kept.
His influence upon us is not spent ;
It lingers in our minds, as fragrance does
In after recollection of sweet flow'rs.
    At home, in office, and within these walls
Will he alike be mourned ; his remembrance
Held by all in honour and respect.

COLLEGE NOTES.

On Saturday, October 31st, Dr. Sidney Lee distributed the certificates and prizes gained by the students in the past year, and gave an exceedingly interesting address on "The Impersonality of Shakespeare's Art," in the Maurice Hall. The "Tansley" and "Marks" prizemen were loudly cheered, as also was Mr. L. R. B. Pearce, amongst others, he having matriculated last September.

When Mr. Hawes Turner kindly came on October 24th and gave us his excellent lecture on "The Problem of the Painter," he was shown over the College, and he was good enough to give us some valuable expert advice on two matters, one of which we all regard as highly important. Mr. Turner is the keeper and secretary of the National Gallery, and speaking with the knowledge and authority which this position carries, he told Mr. Lupton he thought we ought now to have Mr. Lowes Dickinson's portrait of Frederick Denison Maurice examined by a competent man, with the view to ensuring its permanent preservation in a proper state. Steps are being taken to have this done. The other matter on which Mr. Turner gave us the benefit of his experience was as to the floor of the Library. This is at present out of harmony with the room; it looks dirty and shows every mark and stain, and should be rubbed over with some preparation, the name of which Mr. Turner has furnished, to give it a proper surface and polish, so that it may more easily be cleaned and may harmonize with its surroundings. It is gratifying to know that Mr. Hawes Turner was once a member of the College.

On Saturday, November 14th, just before Mr. Gooch's lecture on "The Awakening of Turkey," the portraits of Dr. Furnivall and Sir Charles Lucas were unveiled by the Vice-Principal in the Maurice Hall. We hope shortly to be able to present a report of the proceedings on this interesting occasion.

The Rev. W. Burnett has kindly presented the College with a framed photograph (nearly life size) of the Hon. James Russell Lowell, late American Ambassador to this country, who visited the old College on more than one occasion, being once a guest at the Old Students' Club Supper.

In the January term, on Thursday evenings, a new class will be started in Elocution, conducted by Tom Barnard, our popular reciter, who needs no introduction to those who have heard him at our concerts. Mr. Barnard has conducted classes in the subject for two years at the Battersea Polytechnic. The fee will be 5s. a term.

At a Committee meeting of the Tansley Swimming Club held on October 23rd, it was resolved that, owing to the difficulty in fixing a night suitable for the club to meet with any degree of success for practice, the club be wound up, and it was decided that the balance in hand of £2 11s. 4d. be handed over to the Musical Society as a donation to the Piano Fund.

The thirty-second Supper of the Old Students' Club, or College Supper, will take place in the Maurice Hall on Saturday, December 19th, at 7 p.m., but it is advisable to assemble punctually at 6.30, to avoid delays and have a word or two with old friends beforehand. This Supper is the chief social event of the College year, and tickets for it, price three shillings each, may be obtained in the office or of the hon. secretary of the Club. The following teachers, students, and friends of the College are expected to be present :—the Principal, Professor A. V. Dicey ; the Vice-Principal, Mr. Lionel Jacob ; Professor Westlake, Dr. Furnivall, Dr. Oswald, R. N. M. Bailey, T. M. Balson, S. Bradgate. A. J. Bride, J. Bromhall, F. M. Cornford, J. J. Dent, J. A. Forster, E. M. Forster, G. P. Gooch, M.P., T. F. Hobson, A. E. Homewood, J. Jacob, S. de Jastrzebski, A. S. Lupton, Jules Lazare, H. R. Levinsohn, B. P. Moore, T. Morison, C. H. Perry, L. Pocock, H. K. Randall, E. J. H. Reglar, B. J. Rose, A. B. Shaw, G. M. Trevelyan, W. J. Torrington, E. J. Turner, Juan Victoria, and R. W. Wilkinson.

The eighteenth Joint Clubs' Supper will be held on Saturday, January 2nd, when W. C. Jones will take the chair. Tickets, price 2s. 6d. each, may be obtained in the office.

Mr. J. H. Trott, College student and teacher of shorthand, left England for Brisbane on October 31st, in the North German Liner "Roon," having determined to try his fortune in life in the Australian Commonwealth. He carried with him the good wishes of his many friends in the College, with which he intends to keep up his connection.

We much regret to record that on November 5th the members lost, by sudden death, one of their number, Mr. Wallace J. Davis, who was greatly liked and respected by his confrères. Mr. Davis, who was 53 years of age, was introduced to the College by the late Samuel Standring the younger, some thirty-three years ago, but he was away from the College for several years until he rejoined about five or six years ago. In 1882 he was a member of the old Maurice Rowing Club. He was a very good reader and reciter, and had for a long time taken part in dramatic entertainments, recitals, and readings in the neighbourhood where he lived, whilst his excellent recitations at the College will long be remembered here, especially his "Owl Critic" and "Uncle Podger." He was also the principal performer in the farce, "No. 1, Round the Corner," acted at the College concert of 2nd May last, when he afforded the audience considerable gratification by his well-sustained drollery. At the last general meeting of the Shakespeare Readers he was elected their president, and his last act appears to have been the writing of a letter, on the eve of his death, with regard to the arrangements for the next play. He was at the College on the evenings of the 1st, 2nd, and 3rd of November. The cause of his sudden end was syncope following pneumonia. The funeral took place on November 10th, the service at Holy Trinity Church, Stroud Green, and the interment in East Finchley Cemetery. There were present at the church or cemetery, besides the deceased's brother, two sisters, and other friends, several members of the College, namely Messrs. E. C. Duchesne, E. S. Landells, M. W. Starling, William Hudson, Leonard Pocock, W. H. Barnett, T. A. Paterson, G. E. Buckland, H. Gallagher, and R. H. Marks. The funeral was also attended by the following members of the firm and staff of Messrs. Murray, Hutchins, and Stirling, by whom Mr. Davis was employed :—Mr. W. C. Murray, Mr. Frederick Stirling, Mr. Richard Stirling, and Messrs. Harrison, Pringle, Sturt, Waller, Dutton, Conway, and Bragington.

With this number of the JOURNAL ends its tenth volume, comprising the years 1907 and 1908. The bound volume, with contents and title-page, and two years' calendars, may be obtained from the Editor, price 5s. Those readers who wish to have their own numbers bound, should send them, with Calendars, to the College, addressed to the Editor, who will supply the contents and title-page, and have the volume bound for 1s. 6d.

May we also remind our subscribers that their subscriptions are renewable on January 1st? It will save some little trouble if these are kindly sent without any further reminder being necessary. And if those readers who are not already annual subscribers will be good enough to become so, this will help to form a guarantee fund for the publication of the JOURNAL, and reduce financial risk.

From Crowndale Road the JOURNAL bears the news across the seas,
Of College work and College play, our comrades old to please ;
To Scotland, France and Germany, Jamaica and the Cape,
To China, Turkey, and the States, its varied courses shape ;
The Indies and Australia its monthly pages greet,
Wherein with names of College chums our distant members meet.
Tho' they abroad a life may lead of trouble hard to bear,
Serene at home in Common Room our common weal we share ;
Debate and Shakespeare Reading, a pipe, a game of chess,
The paper or the magazine, the talk that all things bless—
Thus passes by, from term to term, the social life we lead,
Whilst in our classes earnest men of learning sow the seed.
Of all that's done, indoor and out, the JOURNAL tells the tale ;
So send along a half-a-crown to guarantee its sale.

Mr. Richard Whiteing, the well known author of "No. 5, ohn Street" and other works, who was a student in this College many years ago, has been elected an honorary member of the College. We hope he will make as much use of the privileges of membership as time and circumstances will permit.

W.M.C. GEOLOGICAL CLUB.

On September 22nd, Mr. C. Barclay gave an interesting paper on "The possibilities of Coal in the Home Counties," a subject which he will deal with again later. On September 29th, G. Ansell read a short paper on "Diamonds, and some of the localities where they are obtained." On October 6th, Mr. J. Warren delivered a short lecture on "Flints," etc. And on October 13th, Mr. W. E. Miller gave a most instructive paper on "Minerals used in Medicine," finely illustrated by specimens of minerals in the native state, as well as specimens prepared for use in medicine.

GEORGE ANSELL, *Hon. Secretary.*

MAURICE CHESS CLUB.

Our doings during the past month have been great. Two more League matches were played, *versus* Lud Eagle II. and Fulham, whom we beat by the comfortable margins of 7 to 1, and 6½ to 1½, respectively. The game upon which the result of the Hampstead league match depended was adjudicated a draw, enabling Maurice to win by 4½ to 3½. Played three and won three in the League is not at all bad; but the stiffest hurdle has yet to be jumped. I refer to Toynbee Hall, whom we play next.

In the friendly match with Maida Vale, we lost by 6½ to 1½; but against London Rifle Brigade we put up a score of 7½ to 2½, and against Athenæum 9 to 1.

Our annual visit to Trinity College, Cambridge, took place on November 14th. The match, which was most exciting, ended in a draw of 4½ to 4½. A full report of our doings is promised by "Our Special Correspondent." I do not wish to resort to scandal, but if the gentleman in question—to whose lot, I might add, fell the sleeping on Mr. Webb's sofa—is, at the time of writing his report, imbued with the "spirits," which veracious Levitt assures us were the next morning departed from their glass tombs, he will probably commit himself. He complained badly of cold feet, when he awoke on Sunday morning; conclusive proof that the spirits did not come in contact with the lower parts of his anatomy.

The return match with Trinity College will probably be played on Saturday, December 12th, at home; and it is hoped that all College members will give them a jolly good welcome. The match will commence at five o'clock; concert at eight.

The following is the score of the Trinity match :—

Trinity College.			Maurice.		
1. H. A. Webb	... 1	—	F. W. Chambers	...	0
2. B. Goulding Brown	... ½	—	V. Ray	...	½
3. L. Illingworth	... 1	—	J. F. Halford	..	0
4. F. R. Hoare	... 1	—	O. Ray	...	0
5. H. E. Foster	... 0	—	H. W. Miles	...	1
6. J. W. Nicholson	... 0	—	J. Foley	...	1
7. D. Lever	... 0	—	W. Melzer	...	1
8. H. W. Turnbull	... 1	—	S. Grugeon	...	0
9. H. T. Mayo	... 0	—	A. Levitt	...	1
	4½				4½

J. FOLEY, *Hon. Secretary and Treasurer.*

OLD STUDENTS' CLUB.

INDIVIDUALISM AND SOCIALISM.

AT the first meeting of the Club for the present session, held on Saturday, October 24th, R. H. Marks, president, in the chair, the balance sheet was approved, and officers re-elected ; the chairman announced the approaching departure of two members, J. H. Trott and L. A. Waterfield, for Brisbane, and the Club wished them "Good Luck"; after which Mr. C. EDMUND MAURICE, son of our Founder, opened for discussion the question, "Is not the difference between Individualism and Socialism one of degree and not of principle?" The following were present :—Thomas Austin, J. T. Baker, L. Barnard, George Beavis, Benjamin Black, P. J. Brett, S. J. Coombs, A. W. Coombs, Charles Castle, W. C. Cutts, J. J. Dale, Harold Eyers, E. J. Field, E. M. Forster, R. Freeman, T. W. Gale, H. Gallagher, Sydney Grugeon, C. Godfrey Gümpel, S. Hamilton, Alexander Hepburn, W. Hudson, Julius Jacob, C. T. Jeffery, E. W. Jones, C. P. King, C. H. Kisch, E. J. Lambert, E. S. Landells, H. Manton, R. H. Marks, A. W. Matthews, C. E. Maurice, C. F. W. Mead, H. W. Miles, C. Monteath, E. D. A. Morshead, G. S. Offer, Alfred Pegram, Louis Perdrian, Leonard Pocock, E. Pointon, A. H. Perry, V. Ramage, H. K. Randall, C. W. Rapley, F. C. Roper, W. J. Spray, Sidney Stagg, M. W. Starling, E. Tissier, George Wanklin, L. A. Waterfield, C. R. Williams, A. Wilshaw, G. Wiltshire, G. E. Winter, and Charles Wright—58 in all.

Mr. Maurice's paper proved to be a short historical summary of the developments of both Socialism and Individualism from very early times. We give below some extracts from his address :—

Socialism, he said, considered as the desire to put all private concerns under a central power, is much older than Individualism. Originally it was a pagan idea. Indeed, it might almost be said that the deepest religious conviction of the Greek and Roman was the devotion to the State ; the rights of the individual as against the State were hardly recognized. Christian teaching introduced the idea of a private responsibility of each individual man and woman to an unseen power, and thereby came into conflict with the idea that the law of the State was the sole supreme authority. But, as our Christian Church drew into contact with a nominally reformed State, there did arise for a time a complete form of Christian Socialism, sanctioned and enforced by law. The Guilds of the middle ages, which gradually secured rule in the towns, did undertake to interfere in all concerns of life, to regulate the prices of food and dress, and to punish severely certain offences which are now left generally to special arrangement, or at strongest to general principles of law. But the Guilds were often in the hands of a wealthy and exclusive body of merchants ; and the continual attempts to break down their exclusiveness only partially succeeded. When, in the fourteenth century, Wyclif appealed again to the old Christian principle of the responsibility of each man to God, he attacked not only the rules of monks and friars, but also those of the Guilds, which, like the monastic rules, claimed to rest on religious sanction. His protest against Socialistic interference with the individual was no doubt the more welcome to the poorer classes of Englishmen, because, just at that time, Parliament was claiming to fix the wages of workmen in the interest of their employers. From the time of Wat Tyler to that of Jack Cade, one of the chief grievances of the poor was the prohibition by law of any attempt to raise wages. Individualism was then the assertion of the rights of the poor against the rich. But in the sixteenth century, though English Protestantism remained in many ways an individualistic principle, the noblest and wisest leaders of the movement were forced to develop a socialism of their own. The reckless plunder of the monasteries, and the rise on their ruins of a heartless class of landlords, who enclosed commons and raised rents, produced protests from More and Latimer which point in the direction of a more democratic Socialism ; and the savage legislation against vagrants and mendicants, which followed the abolition of the monasteries, naturally led to a reaction in favour of more humane treatment, and thus produced the Poor Law of Elizabeth, which was at once the triumph of a semi-religious

State Socialism, and the origin of all the modern controversy between Socialism and Individualism. In the latter part of the seventeenth and the beginning of the eighteenth century, two great socialistic ideas were embodied in legislation: the idea that the State was responsible for the conveyance of the correspondence of its citizens, and the idea that the citizens might find greater security for their income by investing in the funds of the State. From the middle of the eighteenth century to the middle of the nineteenth century, however, there is a general movement for throwing off legislative restraints and undoing unwise interference with life. The movements for the abolition of slavery, for the removal of laws against Roman Catholics and Dissenters, for the freedom of publishing debates, for freedom of press and meeting, and finally for freedom of trade, all mark the individualistic feeling. But two movements were gathering force during this period, which though not Socialistic in themselves, prepared the way for new Socialistic developments. One was the discovery of the new machines for promoting various forms of industry. This, by increasing the amount of work done, led to the larger forms of industrial organizations. At first, the factory system, by freeing the workmen from the immediate paternal control of the smaller tradesman and by weakening the bonds of apprenticeship, seemed to tell in favour of individual freedom. It was soon evident, however, that the workmen had been placed by the new changes even more in the power of the employer than before ; and the growth of the desire for larger fortunes and the employment of men in numbers too large to allow of personal intercourse with employers, tended to aggravate the distinction of classes and to promote a cry for regulation, which till then might have been settled between master and apprentice in an amicable way. The other movement of which I spoke was the movement for parliamentary reforms. In securing to the poorer classes a greater influence in the State, it naturally suggested to them the use of State power for rectifying their relations with their employers. Out of these different causes, there arose a bitter conflict between the principles of Individualism and Socialism in the middle of the nineteenth century. On the one hand, the employers saw in the principles of free trade a justification of a complete policy of *laissez faire* in home affairs ; and on the other hand, the workmen and their champions began to disbelieve in middle-class remedies, and to advocate more and more the interference of the State in the settlement of their grievances. This conflict, lasting roughly speaking from 1830 to 1870, produced that bitter antagonism which finds its echo in the present attempt to pit Individualism against Socialism. But an echo is always a rather unreal thing. And when, on the one hand, the fiercest screamers against Socialism accept without any serious struggle such ultra-socialistic measures as old-age pensions and free meals for children ; and, on the other hand, many who are certainly friendly to Socialism approve so ultra-individualistic a movement as the so-called passive resistance to the payment of rates decreed and levied by the State, surely the battle-cries of Individualist and Socialist alike are become almost farcical. A gallant army of inspectors has crushed out the traditions of *laissez faire* at home ; abroad the principle of international arbitration is gaining an equally decisive victory over the old doctrine of non-intervention. Indeed, if rightly considered, each of these nominally opposed principles can often be stated in the language of its opponents. It was to save a number of obscure individuals from being crushed by a huge industrial machine, that the Factory Acts were introduced ; while the champions of such individualism as is still possible can plead, that they are trying to secure more efficiency to the State by preventing it from being crushed by overwork. I heard only the other day a striking instance of the way in which Socialistic and Individualistic principles are both necessary to the same movement. I was present at a meeting for promoting the development of small holdings in country districts. One of the speakers, a zealous champion of the cause, complained that the Board of Agriculture was not doing its full duty in this matter, partly because it did not bring sufficient pressure on County Councils, and partly because it did not use the power, given to it by the Act, of starting model small holdings as an encouragement to others to do the same. "No," replied another equally zealous worker in the

movement ; " if the Board of Agriculture brought too much pressure on the
County Councils, those Councils which were favourably disposed to work
the Act would feel that their liberty was being interfered with, and would
show less initiative and less zeal in the matter ; and as to the model holdings,
any action of that kind would discourage those people [he mentioned names]
who were now taking the lead in granting small holdings on their own
estates." I confess that, like our Principal in a discussion of last session,
I agreed with both sides ; and I felt that both feelings were necessary to the
effective working of the movement.   The feeling for individual liberty is
cherished as strongly, even as aggressively, by many Socialists as by the
extremest Individualist ; and on the other hand, no practical politician now
believes that we can limit the State to the functions of a policeman.   Let
me say, in conclusion, that the importance of recognizing this common bond
between Socialist and Individualist is due, not only to the necessity for a
mutual understanding between those who are working for a common end,
but also to the consideration that there are clear moral issues which are now
dividing and which must divide certain political thinkers, and these issues
are apt to be obscured and lost sight of, when people are blinded by false
war cries and unreal struggles.   (Cheers.)

    Mr. CHARLES WRIGHT :—Everything that emanates from Mr. Maurice
is always fresh to us, because he brings to bear upon the problems presented,
the mind of the historian, as well as his own great historical knowledge.
But, very much as I was interested in his paper, I must say that I felt a great
sense of disappointment when he sat down, because I could not help feeling
he had stopped short of the vital problems of to-day.   It is impossible for
us to discuss a more serious and living subject than that which he has
introduced ; and although I am speaking unpremeditatedly, the subject of
Socialism and Individualism is constantly in my mind.   Now, I am inclined
rather to agree with the proposition which Mr. Maurice has submitted—with
the addition of the words, " for the practical purposes of life."   I add these
words, because it does seem to me that the two principles are opposed, but
that at our present stage of development, no practical man can possibly
attempt or hope to establish Individualism, pure and simple.   We have
advanced so much along the line of socialistic experiment, that nothing can
prevent our advancing still further.   (Hear, hear.)   I feel very strongly that,
while one shrinks from the application of extreme socialistic principles to
our present complex society, it is impossible for a man with any sense of
humanity—perhaps that is too strong an expression—for a man who is alive
to the sufferings of those about him, to acquiesce in the present state of
society.   (Hear, hear.)   That is the fault I constantly find with the *Spectator.*
During the present week we have had the question of unemployment
brought prominently before the House of Commons, and we have had the
Prime Minister and the Cabinet facing the question to the best of their
ability, and making certain proposals to deal with it.   What has the
Spectator to say?   The utmost it can say in the way of praise is that the
Government proposals might have been worse, and after explaining at
considerable length how bad they are, it concludes by saying : " But we
shall be asked : What is our own remedy ? "   And their answer is—Leave
it all to the Poor Law.   But let us suppose that the able editor of the
Spectator, instead of having to write an article in his library, had to stand
up in the House of Commons and propound that policy as a minister.   We
know perfectly well he would immediately be voted out of office.   So that
here we have the *Spectator*, representative of a great and intellectual body
of opinion, proposing what is absolutely useless and impracticable.   I think
the Chancellor of the Exchequer is thoroughly alive to present-day conditions.
He sees that things cannot go on on the old basis ; that the problem of the
starving man on the one side and the millionaire on the other is quite
incompatible with the views of to-day.   So he is evidently turning his mind
towards rectifying this state of things, so far as possible, by taxation.   It
seems to me that what statesmen have to do, at the present day, is to try
and alleviate distressing inequalities in such a way as will not be entirely
unacceptable to any great section of the nation.   In a real and practical

sense I think, after all, the difference between Individualism and Socialism is only a question of degree. We have now a vast number of undertakings and commercial projects conducted by the community, and I do not think anybody would seriously wish to go back on them. The question is whether they should be further extended, or not. It is objected to them that they create a great army of officials, who become a power in the state, and use that power for their own ends; also that as municipalities are not bound to make profits, laxity of management results. I think there is immense force in these objections. It is urged, however, and I think rightly, on the other hand, that where you have great undertakings which are essential to the community, you must have a large amount of laxity of management. They become in the nature of monopolies. The experiment of the late Sir George Livesey in the South Metropolitan Gas Company was only possible because that company had a monopoly. It would not be possible in an ordinary competitive commercial undertaking. Taking the case of great companies controlling gas, water, etc., I think the Socialist may fairly argue that those companies are just as open to the charge of laxity, and corruption in management, as state monopolies would be. I do not think the hope for the future lies in Individualism—in going back from state enterprise; but that it lies in increasing and promoting in every possible way the sense in each citizen of corporate responsibility, of not living to himself, but for the benefit of the community. Only in so far as we are successful in doing that, can the State be healthy. Undoubtedly, if we are to have a great extension of Socialism, it is of the highest importance that our community should be composed of citizens who prefer the welfare of the community to the welfare of the individual. But, is it hopeless to try and convince all classes of the truth in this matter? I don't think the wealthy need convincing very much more than the poor. Supposing, however, that we cannot for some time, at any rate, do anything complete in the way of rectifying the gross inequalities that exist, by the extension of State action, the question is—Can it be done to a considerable extent by the readjustment of taxation? After a long experience in business life, I believe that the accumulation of wealth is more a matter of luck than of merit; and that there can be nothing radically wrong in readjusting taxation, so that a man of inordinate wealth has to disburse a reasonable proportion of it for the benefit of the community at large. Progression on these lines should be slow and tentative. No very drastic change ought to be made at once. We shall have to watch the effect of each experiment, but we cannot submit to the doctrine of *laissez faire*. (Cheers.)

The chairman having read cards from Mr. Richard Whiteing and Mr. Gerald Ritchie regretting their absence—

Mr. GÜMPEL defined Individualism as "every man for himself, and, as a solatium, God for us all"; but with the addition, "the devil take the hindermost." Socialism was not so easy to define. Like the chameleon, it presented a different colour if looked at from different sides. We might describe it as a form of society in which the freely elected executive held and controlled for the benefit of the community all land and capital, and determined and regulated the production and distribution of wealth, on the principle that the worker should enjoy the full fruits of his labour and should not be exploited by his fellow-man. This was distinctly opposed to Individualism. To his mind the difference between Individualism and Socialism was *not* one of degree only, but of strict principle.

Mr. S. J. COOMBS deplored the depreciation of the initiative and inventive spirit in this country. He thought a more or less collective system would be best, if everyone was inspired to do his duty. He wanted to see this bad individualistic spirit razed.

Mr. JULIUS JACOB pointed out that the opener and speakers had not dealt with the question on the agenda, but only with the merits of the two systems. The reason was that the question was not debateable, because Socialism and Individualism were absolutely opposed. No doubt the tendency of the last fifty years had been in the direction of Socialism. But people might go back on that, and it might be found that the whole tendency of present-day legislation was to create an unemployable class. By caring, out of humanity, for men out of work, we might be injuring the community, in the long run, and that might make us retrace our steps towards extreme Individualism. By a preferential treatment of the unfit, you created an ever larger unfit class. Although the two principles mentioned in the motion were absolutely opposite, there might be a combination of them in the very distant future in the form of the anarchism advocated by Kropotkin—everyone working for the good of the community, not because it was the law of the State, but because it was left to individual free will for everyone to work in his own way for the common good.

Mr. POINTON was followed by Mr. MORSHEAD, who was almost entirely, not perhaps quite, in warm agreement with the sentiments expressed by Mr. Maurice. Like him, he had not such terror about changes as was electrifying a considerable part of society. Many of us failed to recognize how socialistic we were. Afraid of other people's Socialism, our own seemed to them to be as bad as their's seemed to us. The real principle was *noli timere*—don't get in an awful funk. Fear was really dangerous, and so far as he knew, nothing else was.

Mr. SPRAY was anxious to know how the two opposite principles could be assimilated. There was a fundamental difference between them.

Mr. STARLING pointed out that most people did not support a proposal, unless they thought it would benefit them in the long run. Again, it was not till a man was tolerably well settled in life that he began to think of benefiting others. He was not quite so sure about its being the socialistic lines that led us to agree to recent reforms ; he thought it was more or less a sense of justice that produced measures like the Old Age Pensions and Workmen's Compensation Acts.

Mr. HEPBURN'S definition of an Individualist was—" A man who does things because he wants to." It did not follow that an Individualist should be inimical to the State. There were benevolent despots. It was also conceivable that a man, without regard to principle, by dint of education, should really want to do good—and should promote Socialistic reforms. And when a man with a high-souled desire to benefit the community does things for no other reason than because he wants to, you reach the joining of the two extremes, in the assertion that an Individualist, as we understand him, may be educated to the point of becoming a Socialistic Individualist.

Mr. MAURICE summed up and replied. He pointed out that Individualism did not secure liberty ; nor Socialism, happiness and equality. Each question, as it arose, must be considered on its merits ; and we should not be distracted from the real issue by these two names, nor by the bad characteristics imputed to either of them.

Mr. MAURICE writes that he would like his paper to be considered as introductory to a series of discussions on the reform of the conditions of society. He felt that some of his audience were disappointed with what they considered the inconclusiveness of his paper, and he is not sorry that they had that impression. Its object was much more to clear the ground of certain fallacies than to assert a definite principle. But the more important point is with regard to future discussions, and he asks, Could not a series be arranged ?

BALANCE SHEET, 1907—8.

Receipts.	£	s.	d.	*Expenditure.*	£	s.	d.
Balance forward ...	3	2	9	Printing, postage, etc. ...	5	19	0
266 Subscriptions ...	13	6	0	Rent of locker ...	0	2	6
From College, for Supper				Mrs. Robbie & assistants	0	10	0
printing	0	11	6	Piano Fund—donation	2	0	0
				Maintenance Fund do....	5	0	9
				Children's Treat do....	0	10	0
				Balance forward ...	2	18	0
	£17	0	3		£17	0	3

R. H. MARKS, *President and Hon. Secretary.*

COMMON ROOM GENERAL MEETING.

On Monday, November 9th, the annual general meeting was held in the Common Room, to receive the report and accounts of the Common Room Committee for the past year, and proceed with the election of the next year's committee. Mr. Sydney Bradgate took the chair, and at the outset referred to the loss the College had sustained in the recent death of our fellow-member, Mr. Wallace J. Davis, and moved a vote of condolence with his relatives, which was carried unanimously. The Report and Balance Sheet were read by the hon. secretary, Mr. H. K. Randall, and after discussion, were carried *nem. con.*, on the motion of Mr. C. H. Perry, seconded by Mr. R. H. Marks, both of whom referred to the Report as the "best we have ever had." A vote of thanks to the outgoing secretary and committee was proposed by Mr. Bradgate, seconded by Mr. Marks, and carried with acclamation ; after which a special vote to Randall for the splendid work he had done as hon. secretary was proposed by Mr. B. P. Moore, seconded by Mr. Gates Fowler, and also carried with acclamation.

Nominations for the new committee were received, and the various candidates were subjected to the usual heckling, in which the taste of beer, and the old proposed new rules figured most prominently. Messrs. R. H. Marks and J. C. Castell were elected as tellers, and it was announced that the election would take place from November 16th to 23rd inclusive.

STATEMENT OF COMMON ROOM COMMITTEE ACCOUNTS,
for the year ending October 31st, 1908.

Expenditure.	£	s.	d.	Income.	£	s.	d.
Draught beer	8	16	2	Balance brought forward	24	5	0½
Bottled beer	7	14	11	Capitation grants : —			
Wine	0	8	6	February .. 7 16 8			
Tobacco	4	6	8½	April ... 5 7 0			
Cigars	1	19	5	September... 3 12 10			
Cigarettes	5	7	2½		16	16	6
Newspapers and Magazines	14	5	8	Draught beer	8	14	0
Printing and stationery	2	17	6½	Bottled beer	11	5	0
Donations and subscrip-				Wine and ullages ...	0	6	0
tions	1	16	0	Tobacco	5	2	0
Utensils and repairs ...	4	2	3	Cigars	2	18	4
Furniture	19	15	8	Cigarettes	6	17	6
Postages	0	18	3	Locker rents	1	10	0
Miscellaneous	1	2	11	Newspaper subscriptions			
Deficit on Sports account	3	9	4½	and sales	3	9	11½
Balance in hand	4	8	9				
	£81	4	4		£81	4	4

Liabilities.	£	s.	d.	Assets.	£	s.	d.
Benskins, for draught beer	1	1	0	Cash in hand	4	8	9
Balance of assets over				Bottles	0	6	0
liabilities	3	16	9	Resales Newspapers un-			
				collected	0	3	0
	£4	17	9		£4	17	9

November 4th, 1908. Audited and found correct.—HERBERT N. GILL.

H. K. RANDALL, *Hon. Secretary, C. R. C.*

Matter held over till next month :—Common Room Report, Dr. Sidney Lee's Address, Reception of Portraits of Dr. Furnivall and Sir C. P. Lucas, Presentation to Dr. Forbes, Maurice Chess Club v. Trinity College, Lubbock Field Club. and Furnivall Sculling Club.

SATURDAY NIGHT LECTURES.

LONDON IN SUNSHINE.

THERE was a crowded audience on October 10th, to hear Mr. W. Pett Ridge tells us, in his inimitable way, some of his stories—in which comedy and tragedy are so closely intermingled—about the life lived in London by the poorer classes, a phase of existence which he has studied narrowly. Mr. Lionel Jacob, Vice-Principal, took the chair.

Mr. PETT RIDGE, though he wanted to be a sun-dial, asked us first to stroll with him in the shadow. He remembered once being in the shade, at a bull-fight in Spain. During a not very attractive part of the entertainment, when the poor horses were being dragged, much against their will, into the arena, he overheard an American lady remark to her friend—"This is the most repulsive, objectionable, and distressing sight I have ever witnessed in the whole course of my existence ; lend me your opera glasses." (Laughter.) Mr. Pett Ridge proceeded to narrate the history of the Clank family, of Somers Town, N.W., of whom the parents just escaped the Act of 1870, who lived within a stone's throw of the College, and whose general custom it was to do harm by stealth and blush to find it fame. Mrs. Clank made the beds every evening at ten and did the washing on Saturdays, but the appearance of the articles was so little changed by the process that it seemed to be more a form of ritual on her part than anything else, and their value may be guessed from the fact that although they were very openly displayed within reach of every passer-by, not one garment was ever lost. Mr. Clank and the rest of the family were described in detail in similar fashion, and several anecdotes were introduced to still further lighten the story. A London magistrate, recognizing a friend in court, invited him to take a chair beside him on the bench ; and the friend, indicating a certain section of the occupants of the place, remarked, "You seem to have a pretty tough and difficult lot to deal with this morning." "Hush," said the magistrate, "those are the solicitors." (Laughter.) He (Mr. Pett Ridge) always cultivated friendliness with the magistrates and police of London. He believed in being on the right side, like the old lady in church who crossed herself not only at the proper places, but also when the name of Satan was mentioned. "Civility costs nothing," he went on, "and you never know what may happen." (Laughter.) Those who went to the lecture will remember the story of the son, James Clank, at the police court ; of the second son, "Maizy Pop." so called because he always wore a straw hat, summer and winter ; of the youngest, Cyril, and the good influence upon him of the County Council school in school hours, and of Mr. Pett Ridge's boxing class later. Like the youngest son, the youngest daughter was the best. Undersized and aged 14½, she was general servant at a lodging house at £8 a year, "service in London being paid for at so much per yard" The coming of the milkman in the morning was rather a pleasant interlude for her. It was convention that made him say, what an attraction she was to him ! Convention it was that she should answer that, so long as her eyesight remained good, she should never be attracted by the milkman. Convention required the milkman to thereupon threaten to put an end to his life in the Regent's Canal. And by convention, Daisy would glance into the milk-pail and observe that he appeared to have been there already. (Laughter.)

The sunshine in Mr. Pett Ridge's lecture consisted principally of the progress of another family, the Wessons, in their rise from a lower to a middle class position. Flashes of humour and anecdotes were abundant ; the audience were much delighted, and hearty rounds of applause testified to their enjoyment of a very entertaining, as well as instructive, narrative.

THE AWAKENING OF TURKEY.

Mr. G. P. GOOCH, M.P., lectured on this subject on November 14th, when the Vice-Principal again took the chair. The following report of Mr. Gooch's address appeared in the *Daily News* :—Turkey, under the old régime, he said, was based on avarice, corruption, bribery, and espionage. The first and greatest of the evils was the insecurity of life ; another evil was the uncertainty of the honour of women ; a third, the absence of justice. Justice was non-existent. Macedonia, continued Mr. Gooch, had been a hell upon earth for years. Only as they realized what had been the lot of the peasant in that country did they fully realize what a beneficent change had taken place. English policy towards Macedonia had for the last few years been entirely unselfish. That had been recognized by Turkey and by Europe. But England's earnest efforts and the intense sympathy she had shown towards Turkey by her disinterested foreign policy, had not been of any purpose in bringing about any reform, owing to the position of the three Great Powers, Russia, Germany, and Austria. Europe had tried and had failed, and when one began almost to despair, unsuspected and unexpected a well of courage, heroism, and statesmanship showed itself in the ranks of the Turks themselves. If the work that had now begun was to continue and to be a permanent success, the vast bulk of the Turkish citizens throughout the Empire would have to do three things—first, they must recognize for the first time the equality of the Christian with the Musselman ; secondly, the equality of women and men ; and thirdly, they must create a law which should stand on its own feet and be based on utility and reason, and not on tradition, however sacred.

STUDENTS' CALENDAR FOR DECEMBER.

Tues., 1st.—Debating Society Meeting, 9.30.
Thurs., 3rd.—Lecture, "The French Republic," Prof. A. V. Dicey, D.C.L., K.C., Principal, 8.30. Maurice Chess Club v. Maida Vale, league match at 306, High Holborn, 8 p m.
Sat., 5th.—Lecture, "Shakespeare and a National Theatre," W. Poel, 8.30.
Tues., 8th.—Debating Society Meeting, 9.30.
Wed., 9th.—Workers' Education Association Meeting—"The formation of a North London branch," at 8 p.m. Chamber concert in Maurice Hall, at 9. Members may bring lady friends.
Thurs., 10th.—Lecture, "The History and Principles of Taxation," Prof. A. W. Kirkaldy, B.Litt., 8.30. Maurice Chess Club v. Chess Bohemians, match at 69, Gracechurch Street, 8 p.m.
Sat., 12th.—Lecture, "The Vegetation of the Alps," Arthur G. Tansley, M.A., 8.30. Maurice Chess Club v. Trinity College, Cambridge, here, at 5 p.m.; concert after, at 8 p.m.
Sun., 13th.—Lubbock Field Club walk, take excursion to Epsom, 1s. 6d., from Waterloo, South, 10.5. Shakespeare Reading, "Julius Cæsar," 7.30.
Tues., 15th.—Maurice Chess Club v. Railway Clearing House, match at College, 8 p.m. Debating Society Meeting, 9.30.
Thurs., 17th.—Lecture, "The History and Principles of Taxation," Prof. A. W. Kirkaldy, 8.30.
Sat., 19th.—32nd Annual Supper of the Old Students' Club, assemble at 6.30.
Wed., 30th.—Musical Society's Concert, 8 p.m., ladies' night.

Sat., 2nd Jan.—18th Joint Clubs' Supper, assemble at 6.30.
Sun., 3rd.—Shakespeare Reading, "Twelfth Night," 7.30 (ladies' night).
Sat., 19th.—Furnivall Children's Treat.

W. M. C. MUSICAL SOCIETY.

THE piano in the Coffee Room is still for sale. Offers will be gladly received by any member of the Committee, or the secretaries, Victor Homewood and F. E. Lawrence. The following further subscriptions to the Piano Fund have been received :—

	£	s.	d.			£	s.	d.
Old Students' Club ...	2	0	0	F. O. Smithers		2	0	0
Balance of Swimming				Miss Hamilton		0	5	0
Club funds	2	4	4	Alexander Naughty ...		0	10	6

F. E. LAWRENCE.

THE LIBRARY.

THE disposition of the fund which has been and is being raised for the Library is proceeding, and the Librarian will be glad to receive suggestions from students and teachers as to the books which, in their opinion, ought to be upon the shelves. Since our last announcement the undermentioned additions have been made. Those following the name of the Skinners' Company have been purchased out of their donation to the fund of £21. The others have very kindly been presented to the Library by the persons named as donors.

The Skinners' Company. — English-Italian Dictionary (Millhouse), Government of England, 2 vols. (A. L. Lowell), Thirty Years War (Gardiner), Taxation of Liquor Trade (Rowntree and Sherwell), Dictionnaire des Sciences, des lettres, et des arts (Bouillet), Poverty, a study of town life (B. S. Rowntree), Walks in London, 2 vols. (J. C. Hare), Theory of International Trade (C. Bastabe), Life and Labour in London, 12 vols. (C. Booth), Philosophy of Common Sense, and The Creed of a Layman (F. Harrison), Principles of Political Economy (Sidgwick).

From Dr. F. J. Furnivall.— Life and Letters of G. J. Holyoake (J. McCabe).

From J. Munro.—The Century Shakespeare.

From Mr. Penny.—Drink (Hall Caine).

From the Commonwealth of Australia.—Official Year Book.

From Prof. A. V. Dicey, Principal.—Law of Torts (M. Bigelow), Conflict of Laws (Dicey), Law of the Constitution (Dicey).

From Mrs. Winkworth.—The House of Commons, its Place in National History (J. B. Masterman), 2 copies, Letters of Queen Victoria, 3 vols.

From the Librarian.—Plain Tales from the Hills (Kipling), Tales of Mean Streets (Morison), Memories and Portraits and the Art of Writing (R. L. Stevenson), Dr. Jekyll and Mr. Hyde.

Anonymous.—National Temperance (Gourloy), Grammatica della Lingua Italiana (P. Petròchi), When good fellows get together (Bennett).

FURNIVALL CYCLING CLUB.

IN spite of the beautiful summerlike weather on Saturday, October 3rd, it was with a sincere feeling of regret that I pedalled towards Shepherd's Bush, to meet the party bound for "Ye Cocoa Tree," Pinner, our usual final rendezvous. It made me think of the good times I had had, not only during the past year, but also during the past five years, with the past and present members of the Club. We arrived at Pinner at 6 o'clock, and soon afterwards the captain appeared with the Swiss Cottage contingent. Altogether 23 ladies and 24 men sat down to tea, and after a walk through the lanes, returned for a social evening which was extremely successful. The thanks of the Club are due to the Misses Reglar, Moulden, Craib, and Dockery, and Messrs. Nield, Nye, W. Hagerty, and R. Hagerty, for entertaining us with songs, etc. We started our return journey about 10.30, in a very thick mist, and dispersed at Willesden.   W. MELZER, *Hon. Sec.*

THE WORKING MEN'S COLLEGE JOURNAL *is supported partly by Annual Subscribers living in different parts of the World, and partly by circulation among the Students and Members. Its success depends upon a regular demand. and to ensure this, the Editor would be glad if as many readers as can will become Subscribers. Subscription 2s. 6d. per annum, post free.*

LONDON: Printed by W. HUDSON & Co., Red Lion Street, High Holborn, and published at THE WORKING MEN'S COLLEGE, Crowndale Road, London, N.W.—December 1st, 1908.

WORKING MEN'S
COLLEGE.

Crowndale Road, N.W.

Founded in 1854 by Frederick Denison Maurice.

PROVIDES instruction at the smallest possible cost (the teaching being for the most part unpaid) in the subjects with which it most concerns English Citizens to be acquainted, and thus tries to place a liberal education within the reach of Working Men.

CLASSES

IN

ARITHMETIC	GREEK	FRENCH	MATHEMATICS
BOTANY	LATIN	GERMAN	ECONOMICS
PHYSIOLOGY	LAW	SPANISH	ELECTRICITY
GEOLOGY	ART	HISTORY	GEOGRAPHY

SHORTHAND, BOOK-KEEPING, &c.

FEES from HALF-A-CROWN.

The 32nd ANNUAL SUPPER of the OLD STUDENTS' CLUB (the College Supper) will take place on SATURDAY, DECEMBER 19th, at 7 p.m. Assemble at 6.30.